AMERICAN MUSEUM OF NATURAL HISTORY

BIRDS

OF NORTH AMERICA

AMERICAN MUSEUM ᴼⱯ NATURAL HISTORY

BIRDS
OF NORTH AMERICA

DORLING KINDERSLEY

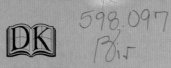

598.097
B15

LONDON, NEW YORK, MUNICH, MELBOURNE, AND DELHI

DORLING KINDERSLEY

Senior Art Editors
Caroline Hill, Ina Stradins

Senior Editor
Angeles Gavira Guerrero

US Senior Editor
Jill Hamilton

Project Editor
Nathan Joyce

Designers
Sonia Barbate, Helen McTeer

Editors
Jamie Ambrose, Lori Baird, Tamlyn Calitz, Marcus Hardy, Patrick Newman, Siobhan O'Connor, David Summers, Miezan van Zyl, Rebecca Warren

Design Assistant
Becky Tennant

Editorial Assistants
Elizabeth Munsey, Jaime Tenreiro

Creative Technical Support
John Goldsmid

Production Editor
Maria Elia

Production Controller
Rita Sinha

Jacket Designer
Mark Cavanagh

Illustratrors
John Cox, Andrew Mackay

Picture Editor
Neil Fletcher

Picture Researchers
Laura Barwick, Will Jones

Managing Art Editor
Phil Ormerod

Managing Editor
Sarah Larter

Publishing Manager
Liz Wheeler

Art Director
Bryn Walls

Publisher
Jonathan Metcalf

DK INDIA

Design Manager
Romi Chakraborty

Editorial Manager
Glenda Fernandes

Project Designer
Malavika Talukder

Designers
Pallavi Narain, Mahua Mandal, Govind Mittal

Editors
Aakriti Singhal, Alicia Ingty, Pankhoori Sinha, Kingshuk Ghoshal

DTP Co-ordinator
Balwant Singh

DTP Designers
Harish Aggarwal, Dheeraj Arora, Jagtar Singh, Preetam Singh

Art Director
Shefali Upadhyay

Head of Publishing
Aparna Sharma

AMERICAN MUSEUM OF NATURAL HISTORY

Editor-in-chief
François Vuilleumier

Project Coordinators
Caitlin Roxby, Molly Leff

DEDICATION

We dedicate this book to the memory of John Bull, John Farrand, and Stuart Keith, top birders, field guide authors, AMNH colleagues, first-rate ornithologists, and friends

First American Edition, 2009

Published in the United States by
DK Publishing
375 Hudson Street
New York, New York 10014

09 10 11   10 9 8 7 6 5 4 3 2 1

ND089—March 2009

Copyright © 2009 Dorling Kindersley Limited
All rights reserved

A catalog record for this book is available from the Library of Congress.

ISBN 978-0-7566-4272-3

DK books are available at special discounts when purchased in bulk for sales promotions, premiums, fund-raising, or educational use. For details, contact: DK Publishing Special Markets, 375 Hudson Street, New York, New York 10014 or SpecialSales@dk.com.

Printed and bound in China by Toppan, China

Discover more at
www.dk.com

CONTRIBUTORS

David Bird
Nicholas L. Block
Peter Capainolo
Matthew Cormons
Malcolm Coulter
Joseph DiCostanzo,
Shawneen Finnegan
Neil Fletcher
Ted Floyd
Jeff Groth

Paul Hess
Brian Hiller
Rob Hume
Thomas Brodie Johnson,
Kevin T. Karlson
Stephen Kress
William Moskoff
Bill Pranty,
Michael L. P. Retter
Noah Strycker

Paul Sweet
Rodger Titman
Elissa Wolfson

Map Editor
Paul Lehman

Project Coordinator
Joseph DiCostanzo

CONTENTS

HOW THIS BOOK WORKS

This guide covers just under 900 North American bird species. The species are organized into three sections: the first profiles common North American species, with each given full-page treatment; the second covers rarer birds in quarter-page entries; the third section consists of a list of rare visitors.

▽ COMMON SPECIES
The main section of the book features the 654 most commonly seen bird species in the North American region. Each entry is clear and detailed, following the same easy-to-access structure.

▽ INTRODUCTION
The species are organized conventionally by order, family, and genus. This means that related birds appear together, preceded by a group introduction. The book follows the most up-to-date avian classification system, based on the latest scientific research.

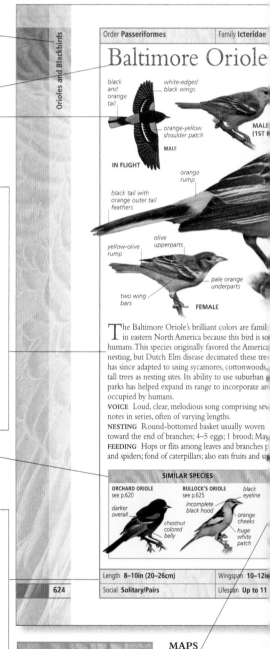

Order **Passeriformes**　　　　Family **Icteridae**

Baltimore Oriole

black and orange tail

white-edged black wings

orange-yellow shoulder patch

MALE

MALE (1ST

IN FLIGHT

orange rump

black tail with orange outer tail feathers

olive upperparts

yellow-olive rump

two wing bars

pale orange underparts

FEMALE

The Baltimore Oriole's brilliant colors are famil[...] in eastern North America because this bird is so[...] humans. This species originally favored the America[...] nesting, but Dutch Elm disease decimated these tre[...] has since adapted to using sycamores, cottonwoods,[...] tall trees as nesting sites. Its ability to use suburba[...] parks has helped expand its range to incorporate ar[...] occupied by humans.
VOICE Loud, clear, melodious song comprising sev[...] notes in series, often of varying lengths.
NESTING Round-bottomed basket usually woven [...] toward the end of branches; 4–5 eggs; 1 brood; May[...]
FEEDING Hops or flits among leaves and branches p[...] and spiders; fond of caterpillars; also eats fruits and si[...]

SIMILAR SPECIES		
ORCHARD ORIOLE see p.620	**BULLOCK'S ORIOLE** see p.625	*black eyeline*
darker overall	*incomplete black hood*	*orange cheeks*
chestnut colored belly		*huge white patch*

Length 8–10in (20–26cm)	Wingspan 10–12i[...]
Social **Solitary/Pairs**	Lifespan Up to 11

624

GROUP NAME
The common name of the group the species belong to is at the top of each page.

COMMON NAME

IN FLIGHT
Illustrations show the bird in flight, from above and/or below —differences of season, age, or sex are not always visible.

DESCRIPTION
Conveys the main features and essential character of the species including:

VOICE
A description of the species' calls and songs, given phonetically where possible.

NESTING
The type of nest and its usual location; the number of eggs in a clutch; the number of broods in a year; the breeding season.

FEEDING
How, where, and what the species feeds on.

SIMILAR SPECIES
Similar-looking species are identified and key differences pointed out.

LENGHT, WINGSPAN, AND WEIGHT
Length is tip of tail to tip of bill; measurements are averages or ranges.

SOCIAL
The social unit the species is usually found in.

LIFESPAN
The average or maximum life expectancy.

STATUS
The conservation status of the species; the symbol (p) means the data available can only suggest a provisional status.

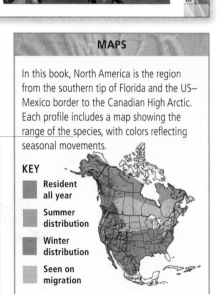

MAPS

In this book, North America is the region from the southern tip of Florida and the US–Mexico border to the Canadian High Arctic. Each profile includes a map showing the range of the species, with colors reflecting seasonal movements.

KEY

- **Resident all year**
- **Summer distribution**
- **Winter distribution**
- **Seen on migration**

SYMBOLS

♂ Male	♣ Spring
♀ Female	☼ Summer
☾ Juvenile	❦ Autumn
☾ Immature	❄ Winter

MAPS
See panel, left. The occurrence caption describes the bird's preferred habitats and range within the North American region.

CLASSIFICATION
The top band of each entry provides the scientific order, family, and species names (see glossary, pp. 728–30 for full definitions of these terms).

Species *Icterus galbula*

black head

straight blue-gray bill

black upper breast

orange underparts

MALE

IGHT: strong with rapid wing beats; full nstrokes during flight provide great power.

RFECT FOR FORAGING
e Baltimore Oriole forages alone in dense age of trees and bushes or on the ground.

OCCURRENCE
Forest edges and tall, open mixed hardwoods, especially close to rivers; regularly uses forested parks, suburban and urban areas with abundant tall trees. Small numbers winter in southeastern US and Florida, but most birds move to Mexico, Colombia, and Venezuela.

Weight 1¹⁄₁₆–1¼oz (30–35g)

Status **Secure**

HABITAT/BEHAVIOR
Additional photographs reveal the species in its typical habitat or show the bird exhibiting typical behavior.

COLOR BAND
The information bands at the top and bottom of each entry are color-coded for each family.

PHOTOGRAPHS
These illustrate the species in different views and plumage variations. Significant differences relating to age, sex, and season (breeding/nonbreeding) are shown and the images labelled accordingly; if there is no variation, the images have no label. Unless stated otherwise, the bird shown is an adult.

FLIGHT PATTERNS
This feature illustrates and briefly describes the way the species flies. See panel below.

VAGRANTS ▷
Very rare visitors and peripheral bird species are listed at the back of the book with a brief description, including where the species is from.

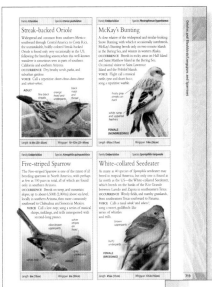

◁ RARE SPECIES
Over 60 less common birds are presented on pp. 702–719. Arranged in the same group order used in the main section, these entries consist of one clear photograph of the species accompanied by a description of the bird.

VAGRANTS

T͟HE LIST THAT FOLLOWS CONSISTS OF species that occur only very rarely in North America (defined as Canada and the continental US). Vagrants to North America arrive from both the Northern and Southern Hemispheres—Europe, Russia, and Siberia, and eastern Asia as well as South America, Africa, and Oceania. The US and Canada are well placed to receive birds that are blown off course from eastern Asia and Siberia, crossing the Pacific, and from Europe, crossing the Atlantic. Western Alaska has a particularly high concentration of vagrants because the western tip forms a series of islands, the Aleutians, that reach almost all the way across the Bering Sea to Russia.

The occurrence of these species is classified by the American Birding Association as rare, casual, or accidental depending on how often they have been seen, and this terminology is used in the comment section on each species. Rare birds are seen every year, but in low numbers. Casual visitors have been seen in North America at least half a dozen times, including three times in the last 30 years. Accidental species have been recorded in Canada or the US no more than three times.

COMMON NAME	SCIENTIFIC NAME	FAMILY/SCIENTIFIC NAME	DESCRIPTION
Waterfowl			
Bean Goose	Anser fabalis	Waterfowl/Anatidae	Rare visitor from N Europe and Asia to SW Alaska
Pink-footed Goose	Anser brachyrhynchus	Waterfowl/Anatidae	Casual from Greenland, Iceland, and Europe to East coast
Lesser White-fronted Goose	Anser erythropus	Waterfowl/Anatidae	Accidental from Eurasia to Atlantic coast of Canada and US
Barnacle Goose	Branta leucopsis	Waterfowl/Anatidae	Accidental from Greenland and N Europe to the Maritime Provinces, Canada
Common Pochard	Aythya ferina	Waterfowl/Anatidae	Rare visitor from Europe and central Asia to W Alaska
Falcated Duck	Anas falcata	Waterfowl/Anatidae	Casual from Asia to western Alaska
Baikal Teal	Anas formosa	Waterfowl/Anatidae	Asian duck; casual in W Alaska and in western provinces and states
White-cheeked Pintail	Anas bahamensis	Waterfowl/Anatidae	Accidental from the Caribbean and N South America to Florida and the Gulf coast
Spot-billed Duck	Anas poecilorhyncha	Waterfowl/Anatidae	Accidental from Asia to SW Alaska
Albatrosses, Petrels, and Shearwaters			
Wandering Albatross	Diomedea exulans	Albatrosses/Diomedeidae	Accidental from oceans of Southern Hemisphere
Yellow-nosed Albatross	Thalassarche chlororhynchos	Albatrosses/Diomedeidae	Casual from Indian and S Atlantic Oceans to Atlantic and Gulf coasts

720

FLIGHT PATTERNS

Simple line diagrams are used to illustrate eight basic flight patterns.

wingbeats

Woodpecker-like: bursts of wingbeats between deeply undulating glides.

Finch-like: light, bouncy action with flurries of wingbeats between deep, undulating glides.

Grouse-like: bursts of wing beats between short, straight glides.

Sparrowhawk-like: straight, with several quick, deep beats between short, flat glides.

Gull-like: continually flapping, with slow, steady wingbeats.

Duck-like: continually flapping, with fast wingbeats.

Kite-like: deep, slow wingbeats between soaring glides.

Swallow-like: swooping, with bursts of wingbeats between glides.

EVOLUTION

Ornithologists agree that birds evolved from dinosaurs about 150 million years ago, but there is still debate about the dinosaur group from which they descended. Around 10,000 species of birds exist today, living in many different kinds of habitat across the world, from desert to Arctic tundra.

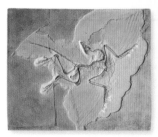

MISSING LINK?
Archaeopteryx, shown here as a 145-million-year-old fossil, had dinosaur-like teeth and a long tail, but birdlike feathers.

SPECIATION

What are species and how do they evolve? Species are biological entities. When two species of a genus overlap they rarely interbreed and produce hybrids. The North American Flicker has an eastern (yellow-shafted) and a western (red-shafted) form; after the discovery that these two forms interbreed in the Great Plains, the flickers, which were formerly "split" into two species, are now considered one. In other cases, a previously single species, such as the Sage Grouse, has been divided. Such examples illustrate how species evolve, first by geographic separation, followed in time by overlap. This process can take millions of years.

BIRD GENEALOGY

The diagram below is called a phylogeny, and shows how selected groups of birds are related to each other. The timescale at the top of the diagram is derived from both fossil and DNA evidence, which allows ornithologists to estimate when different lineages of birds diverged. The names of groups shown in bold are those living in North America.

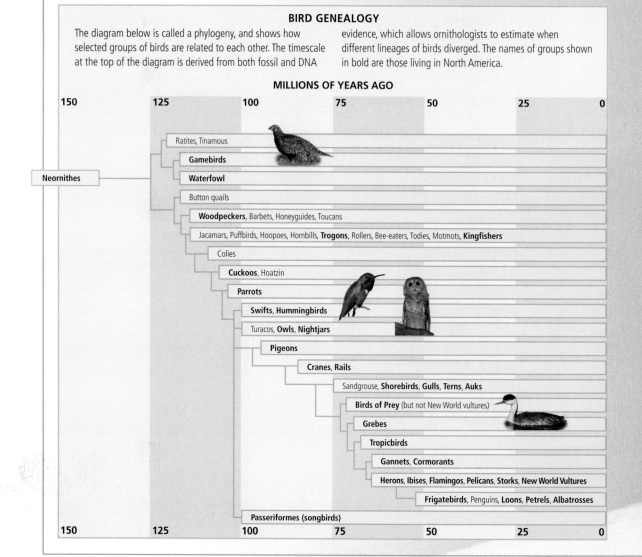

MILLIONS OF YEARS AGO

150   125   100   75   50   25   0

Neornithes

- Ratites, Tinamous
- **Gamebirds**
- **Waterfowl**
- Button quails
- **Woodpeckers**, Barbets, Honeyguides, Toucans
- Jacamars, Puffbirds, Hoopoes, Hornbills, **Trogons**, Rollers, Bee-eaters, Todies, Motmots, **Kingfishers**
- Colies
- **Cuckoos**, Hoatzin
- **Parrots**
- **Swifts, Hummingbirds**
- Turacos, **Owls, Nightjars**
- **Pigeons**
- **Cranes, Rails**
- Sandgrouse, **Shorebirds, Gulls, Terns, Auks**
- **Birds of Prey** (but not New World vultures)
- **Grebes**
- Tropicbirds
- **Gannets, Cormorants**
- **Herons, Ibises, Flamingos, Pelicans, Storks, New World Vultures**
- **Frigatebirds**, Penguins, **Loons, Petrels, Albatrosses**
- Passeriformes (songbirds)

150   125   100   75   50   25   0

BLENDING IN
This magnificent species is diurnal, unlike most other owls, which are nocturnal. The Snowy Owl breeds in the Arctic tundra and if the ground is covered with snow, it blends in perfectly.

CONVERGENCE

The evolutionary process during which birds of two distantly related groups develop similarities is called convergence. Carrion-eating birds of prey are one example. Old World vultures belong to the hawk family (Accipitridae), while New World vultures are more closely related to storks. However, both groups are characterized by hooked bills, bare heads, and weak talons.

PARALLEL EVOLUTION
The African longclaws (family Motacillidae) and North American meadowlarks (family Icteridae) show remarkable convergence in plumage color.

CAPE LONGCLAW

WESTERN MEADOWLARK

EXTINCTION

During the last 150 years, North America has lost the Passenger Pigeon, the Great Auk, the Carolina Parakeet, the Labrador Duck, and the Eskimo Curlew. Humans either hunted them out of existence or destroyed their habitat. Some species that seemed doomed have had a reprieve. Thanks to a breeding and release program, the majestic California Condor soars once again over the Grand Canyon.

OVERHUNTING
The Passenger Pigeon was eradicated as a result of relentless hunting.

CLASSIFYING BIRDS

All past and present animal life is named and categorized into groups. Classifications reflect the genealogical relationships among groups, based on traits such as color, bones, or DNA. Birds make up the class "Aves," which includes "orders;" each "order" is made up of one or more "families." "Genus" is a subdivision of "family," which contains one or more "species." A species is a unique group of similar organisms that interbreed and produce fertile offspring. Some species have distinct populations, which are known as subspecies.

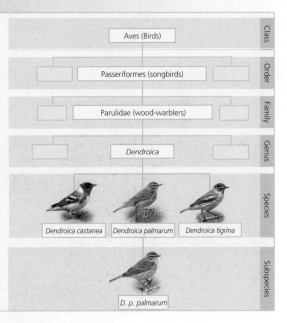

Aves (Birds)	Class
Passeriformes (songbirds)	Order
Parulidae (wood-warblers)	Family
Dendroica	Genus
Dendroica castanea Dendroica palmarum Dendroica tigrina	Species
D. p. palmarum	Subspecies

ANATOMY AND FLIGHT

IN SPITE OF THEIR EXTERNAL DIVERSITY, birds are remarkably similar internally. To allow flight, birds require a skeleton that is both rigid and light. Rigidity is achieved by the fusion of some bones, especially the lower vertebrae, while lightness is maintained by having hollow limb bones. These are connected to air sacs, which, in turn, are connected to the bird's lungs.

"hand"

"forearm"

neck vertebrae

bill

furcula

keeled sternum

fused tail vertebrae

secondaries

uppertail coverts

tail feathers

rump

tertials

scapulars

primaries

axillaries

breast

bill

undertail coverts

belly

toes

SKELETON
Avian skeletal features include the furcula (wishbone), the keeled sternum (breastbone), and the fused tail vertebrae.

FLIGHT ADAPTATIONS

For birds to be able to fly, they need light and rigid bones, a lightweight skull, and hollow wing and leg bones. In addition, pouch-like air sacs are connected to hollow bones, which reduce a bird's weight. The air sacs also function as a cooling system, which birds need because they have a high metabolic rate. The breast muscles, which are crucial for flight, attach to the keeled sternum (breastbone).

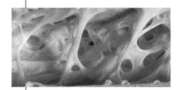

BIRD BONE STRUCTURE
Most bird bones, except those of penguins and other flightless birds, are hollow, which reduces their weight. A honeycomb of internal struts makes the bones incredibly strong.

LEGS, FEET, AND TOES

When you look at a bird's leg, you do not see its thigh, which is inside the body cavity, but the leg from the knee down. When we talk about a bird's feet we really mean its toes. The shin is a fused tibia and fibula. This fused bone plus the heel are known as the "tarso–metatarsus."

enables grip on ground

WALKING
Ground-foraging birds usually have a long hind claw.

enables strong grip on branches

CLIMBING
Most climbers have two toes forward and two backward.

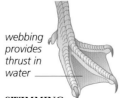

webbing provides thrust in water

SWIMMING
Water-loving birds have webbing between their toes.

used to grasp prey

HUNTING
Birds of prey have powerful toes and strong, pointed claws.

UNDERPARTS
Underwing coverts have a regular pattern of overlapping rows. Short feathers cover the head, breast, belly, and flanks. In most birds, the toes are unfeathered.

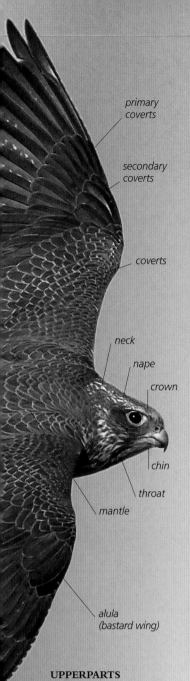

primary
coverts

secondary
coverts

coverts

neck

nape

crown

chin

throat

mantle

alula
(bastard wing)

FEATHERS

All birds, by definition, have feathers. These remarkable structures, which are modified scales, serve two main functions: insulation and flight. Special muscles allow birds to raise their feathers or to flatten them against the body. In cold weather, fluffed-out feathers keep an insulating layer of air between the skin and the outside. This insulating capacity is why humans often find wearing "down" jackets so effective against the cold. The first feathers that chicks have after hatching are down feathers. The rigidity of the flight feathers helps to create a supporting surface that birds use to generate thrust and lift.

TYPES OF FEATHERS

Birds have three main kinds of feathers: down, contour, and flight feathers. The rigid axis of all feathers is called the "rachis."

DOWN FEATHER **CONTOUR FEATHER** **FLIGHT FEATHER**

WING FUNCTIONS

Flapping, soaring, gliding, and hovering are among the ways birds can use their wings. They also exhibit colors or patterns as part of territorial and courtship displays. Several birds, such as herons, open their wings like an umbrella when foraging in water for fish. An important aspect of wings is their relationship to a bird's weight. The ratio of a bird's wing area to weight is called wing loading, but this may also be affected by wing shape. An eagle has a large wing area to weight ratio, which means it has lower wing loading, whereas a swallow has a small wing area to weight ratio, and therefore high wing loading. This means that the slow, soaring eagle is capable of much more energy-efficient flight than the fast, agile swallow.

LONG AND BROAD
The broad, long, rectangular wings of an eagle allow it to soar. The outstretched alulae (bastard wings) give it extra lift.

POINTED
Broad at their base and tapering toward a point, and bent at the wrist, a swallow's wings enable fast flight and sharp turns.

SHORT AND ROUND
Short, broad, and round wings enable warblers to move between perches and to migrate long distances.

UPPERPARTS

The wing feathers from the "hand" of the bird are the primaries and those on the "forearm" are the secondaries. Each set has its accompanying row of coverts. The tertials are adjacent to the secondaries.

WING AERODYNAMICS

The supporting surface of a bird's wing enables it to takeoff and stay aloft. Propulsion and lift are linked in birds—which use their wings for both—unlike in airplanes in which these two functions are separate. Large and heavy birds, like swans, flap their wings energetically to create propulsion, and need a long, watery runway before they can fly off. The California Condor can takeoff from a cliff with little or no wing flapping, but the Black and Turkey Vultures hop up from carrion then flap vigorously and finally use air flowing across their wings to soar. This diagram shows how air flow affects lift.

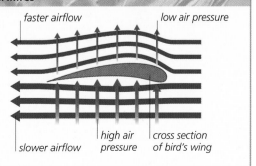

faster airflow

low air pressure

slower airflow

high air pressure

cross section of bird's wing

MIGRATION

UNTIL RECENTLY, THE MECHANICS, or the "how" of migration was poorly understood. Today, however, ornithologists know that birds use a variety of cues including visual and magnetic, whether they migrate by day or by night. Birds do not leave northern breeding areas because of the winter cold, but because day-length is getting shorter.

NIGHT MIGRANTS
During migration, ornithologists can point a telescope on the moon and count the birds that cross its surface.

REFUELING
Red Knots make a stop on their long journey to probe for mollusks and crustaceans.

INSTINCTIVE MOVE

Even though many birds use visual cues and landmarks during their migration, for example birds of prey flying along the Appalachians, "instinctive" behavior must control much of how and where they move. Instinct is a loose term that is hard to define, but ornithologists generally understand it as a genetically programmed activity. They assume that natural selection has molded a behavior as complex as migration by acting on birds' DNA; this hypothesis is reasonable but hard to prove. Nevertheless, it would seem to be the only explanation why many juvenile shorebirds leave their breeding grounds after their parents and yet find their way to their final destination.

NAVIGATION

One of the most puzzling aspects of migration is understanding how birds make their way from their breeding grounds to their destination. Ornithologists have devised experiments to determine how the different components of a navigation system work. For example, if visual landmarks are hidden by fog, a faint sun can give birds a directional clue; if heavy clouds hide the sun, then the birds' magnetic compass may be used to ascertain their direction.

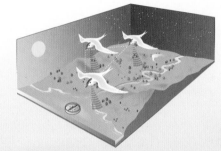

FINDING THE WAY
These birds coordinate information their brains receive from the sun, moon, stars, landmarks, and tiny pieces of magnetite, and use it as a compass.

OVERLAND FLIERS
Sandhill Cranes migrate over hills and mountains from their Arctic tundra breeding grounds to the marshes of the Platte River in the midwestern US.

GLOBETROTTERS

Some bird species in North America are year-round residents, although a few individuals of these species move away from where they hatched at some time in the year. However, a large number of North American species are migratory. A few species breed in Alaska, but winter on remote southwest Pacific islands. Others breed in the Canadian Arctic Archipelago, fly over land and the Pacific Ocean, and spend the winter at sea off the coast of Peru. Many songbirds fly from the Gulf Coast to northern South America. The most amazing globetrotters, such as the Red Knot, fly all the way to Tierra del Fuego, making only a few stops along the way after their short breeding season in the Arctic tundra. The return journeys of some of these travelers are not over the same route—instead, their entire trip is elliptical in shape.

EPIC JOURNEY
The Arctic Tern is a notorious long-distance migrant, breeding in northern regions and wintering in the pack ice of Antarctica after flying a round-trip distance of about 25,000 miles (40,000km).

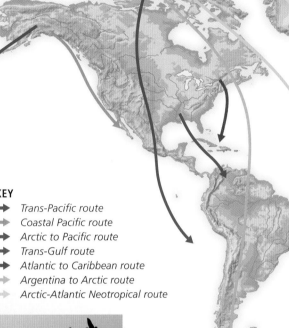

KEY

➤ Trans-Pacific route
➤ Coastal Pacific route
➤ Arctic to Pacific route
➤ Trans-Gulf route
➤ Atlantic to Caribbean route
➤ Argentina to Arctic route
➤ Arctic-Atlantic Neotropical route

NEOTROPICAL MIGRANT
Many wood-warblers, such as this Blackpoll Warbler breed in boreal forests, before migrating to their wintering grounds in the Caribbean, or Central or South America.

MIGRATION ROUTES
The map above shows the range of migration routes that some North American species take to and from their breeding grounds.

V-FORMATION
Geese and other large waterfowl fly in a v-formation. The leader falls back and is replaced by another individual, saving energy for all the birds.

PARTIAL MIGRANT

The American Robin is a good example of a partial migrant, a species in which the birds of some populations are resident whereas others migrate out of their breeding range. Most Canadian populations of the American Robin fly south, US populations are largely resident, and quite a few from either population spend the winter in the Southwest, Florida, or Mexico.

KEY
■ Breeding distribution
■ Resident all year
■ Nonbreeding distribution

COURTSHIP AND MATING

Whether monogamous or not, males and females need to mate for their species to perpetuate itself. With most species, the male plays the dominant role of advertising a territory to potential mates using vocal or visual displays. Females then select a male and if the two respond positively to each other, a period of courtship follows ending in mating. The next step is nest building, egg laying and rearing the young.

DANCING CRANES
During courtship, Sandhill Cranes perform spectacular dances, the two birds of a pair leaping into the air with wings opened and legs splayed.

DISPLAYS

Mutual attraction between the sexes starts with some sort of display, usually performed by the male. These displays can take a number of forms, from flashing dazzling breeding plumage, conducting elaborate dancing rituals, performing complex songs, offering food or nesting material, or actually building a nest. Some birds, such as grebes have fascinatingly intricate ceremonies, in which both male and female simultaneously perform the same movements.

WELCOME HOME
Northern Gannets greet their mates throughout the breeding season by rubbing bills together and opening their wings.

LADIES' CHOICE
On a lek (communal display area) male Sage-Grouse inflate chest pouches while females flock around them and select a mate.

COURTSHIP FEEDING

In some species, males offer food to their mate to maintain the pair-bond. The Male Common Tern routinely brings small fish to a mate in a nesting colony, spreading his wings and tail until she accepts the fish.

MAINTAINING RELATIONS
A male Northern Cardinal offers food to the female, which is a way of reinforcing their pair bond.

BREEDING

After mating, a nest is made, often by the female, where she lays from one to a dozen eggs. Not all birds make nests. Nightjars, for example lay their eggs directly on the ground. In many species incubation doesn't start until the female has laid all the eggs. Incubation, again usually done by the female, varies from about twelve days to about 45 days. Songbirds ranging from the temperate zone to the Arctic show a range in clutch size with more eggs produced in the North than in the South. The breeding process can fail at any stage, for example a predator can eat the eggs or the chicks. Some birds will nest again but others give up breeding for the season.

POLYGAMY
This Winter Wren collects nesting material for one of the several nests he will build.

MONOGAMOUS BONDS
Some birds, such as Snow Geese, remain paired for life after establishing a bond.

MATING TERNS
Mating is usually brief, and typically takes place on a perch or on the ground, but some species mate in the air. This male Black Tern balances himself by opening his wings.

MUTUAL PREENING
Many species of albatross, like these Black-footed Albatrosses from the Pacific, preen each other, with one bird softly nibbling the feathers on the other's head.

SINGLE FATHER

A male Red-necked Phalarope incubates eggs in the Arctic tundra. Phalaropes are well known for their reversal of breeding roles. The female, who is the larger and more colorful of the two sexes, aggressively competes for males, and after mating with several of them, plays no role in nest building, incubation, or caring for chicks, but tends to her territory instead. Although the chicks can feed by themselves immediately after hatching, they remain with a male before growing feathers and living on their own.

NESTS AND EGGS

Mᴏsᴛ ʙɪʀᴅ sᴘᴇᴄɪᴇs ʙᴜɪʟᴅ ᴛʜᴇɪʀ ᴏᴡɴ ɴᴇsᴛ, which is a necessary container for their eggs. Exceptions include cowbirds, which lay their eggs in other species' nests. Nest-building is often done by the female alone, but in some species the male may help or even build it himself. Eggs are incubated either by females alone, or by males or females, depending on the species. Egg shells are hard enough to sustain the weight of incubating parents, yet soft enough for a chick to break its way out. Eggs, consisting of 60 percent water, contain a fatty yolk for nourishment of the embryo as well as sugars and proteins.

NEST TYPES

In addition to the four types shown below, nests range from a simple scrape in the ground with a few added pebbles to an elaborate woven basket-like structure. Plant matter forms basic nest material. This includes twigs, grass stems, bark, lichens, mosses, plant down, and rootlets. Some birds add mud to their nest for strength. Others incorporate animal hair or feathers to improve its softness and insulation. Female eider ducks pluck down feathers from their belly. Some birds include bits of plastic or threads in their nests. Many birds make their nest or lay their eggs deep inside the empty burrows of other animals. Burrowing Owls nest in prairie dog burrows, where they coexist with the rodents.

UNTIDY NEST

Huge stick nests, built on top of dead trees, are the hallmark of Ospreys. They also use custom-made nesting platforms erected by humans specifically for them.

EGG CUP

A clutch of three blue robin's eggs rest in a cup nest made of grass stems. Robins build their nests either in shrubs or trees.

NATURAL CAVITY

This Northern Saw-whet Owl is nesting at the bottom of a cavity in a tree that has probably been excavated by a woodpecker.

NEST BOX

Cavity-nesting bluebirds have been affected by habitat loss, and compete with other birds for nest sites, which may include human-made structures.

COMPLEX WEAVE

New World orioles weave intricate nests from dried grass stems and other plant material, and hang them from the tip of branches, often high up in trees.

EGG SHAPES

There are six basic egg shapes among birds, as illustrated to the right. The most common egg shapes are longitudinal or elliptical. Murres lay pear-shaped eggs, an adaptation for nesting on the narrow ledges of sea cliffs; if an egg rolls, it does so in a tight circle and remains on the ledge. Spherical eggs with irregular red blotches are characteristic of birds of prey. Pigeons and doves lay white oval eggs, usually two per clutch. The eggs of many songbirds, including sparrows and buntings, are conical and have a variety of dark markings on a pale background.

COLOR AND SHAPE
Birds' eggs vary widely in terms of shape, colors, and markings. The American Robin's egg on the left is a beautiful blue.

PEAR SHAPED   **LONGITUDINAL**   **ELLIPTICAL**

NEAT ARRANGEMENT
Many shorebirds, such as plovers and sandpipers, lay four conical eggs with the narrow ends pointed in toward each other.

CONICAL

OVAL

SPHERICAL

HATCHING CONDITION

After a period of incubation, which varies from species to species, chicks break the eggshell, some of them using an egg tooth, a special bill feature that falls off after hatching. After a long and exhausting struggle, the chick eventually tumbles out of the shell fragments. The transition from the watery medium inside the egg to the air outside is a tremendous physiological switch. Once free of their shell, the hatchlings recover from the exertion and either beg food from their parents or feed on their own.

FOOD DELIVERY
Tern chicks, although able to move around, cannot catch the fish they need to survive and must rely on their parents to provide food until they can fly.

PARENTAL GUIDANCE
Birds of prey, such as these Snowy Owl owlets, need their parents to care for them longer than some other bird species, and do not leave the nest until their feathers are sufficiently developed for their first flight.

BROOD PARASITISM

Neither cowbirds in the New World nor cuckoos in the Old World make a nest. Female cowbirds deposit up to 20 eggs in the nests of several other species. If the foster parents accept the foreign egg, they will feed the chick of the parasite until it fledges. In the picture below, a tiny wood-warbler feeds its adopted chick, a huge cowbird hatchling that has overgrown the nest.

FAST FEEDER
Coots, gallinules, and rails hatch with a complete covering of down and can feed themselves immediately after birth.

IDENTIFICATION

S OME SPECIES ARE EASY TO IDENTIFY, but in many cases, species identification is tricky. In North America, a notoriously difficult group in terms of identification is the wood-warblers, especially in the fall, when most species have similar greenish or yellowish plumage.

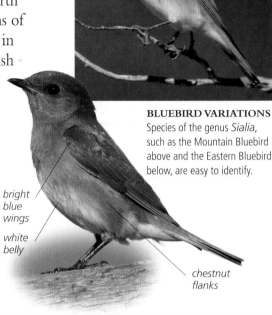

BLUEBIRD VARIATIONS
Species of the genus *Sialia*, such as the Mountain Bluebird above and the Eastern Bluebird below, are easy to identify.

GEOGRAPHIC RANGE

Each species of bird in North America lives in a particular area that is called its geographic range. Some species have a restricted range; for example, Kirtland's Warbler occurs only in Michigan. Other species, such as the Red-tailed Hawk, range from coast to coast and from northern Canada to Mexico. Species with a broad range usually breed in a variety of vegetation types, while species with narrow ranges often have a specialized habitat; Kirtland's Warblers' is jack pine woodland.

bright blue wings

white belly

chestnut flanks

SIZE AND WEIGHT

From hummingbird to Tundra Swan and from extra-light to heavy, such is the range of sizes and weights found among the bird species of North America. Size can be measured in several ways, for example the length of a bird from bill-tip to tail-tip, or its wingspan. Size can also be estimated for a given bird in relationship with another that is familiar. For example, the less familiar Bicknells' Thrush can be compared with the well-known American Robin.

SIZE MATTERS
Smaller shorebirds, with shorter legs and bills, forage in shallow water, but larger ones have longer legs and bills and can feed in deeper water.

SEMIPALMATED SANDPIPER **LESSER YELLOWLEGS** **HUDSONIAN GODWIT** **LONG-BILLED CURLEW**

GENERAL SHAPE

Just as birds come in all sizes, their body shapes vary, but size and shape are not necessarily correlated. In the dense reed beds in which it lives, the American Bittern's long and thin body blends in with stems. The round-bodied Sedge Wren hops in shrubby vegetation or near the ground where slimness is not an advantage. In dense forest canopy, the slender and long-tailed Yellow-billed Cuckoo can maneuver easily. Mourning Doves inhabit rather open habitats and their plumpness is irrelevant when it comes to their living space.

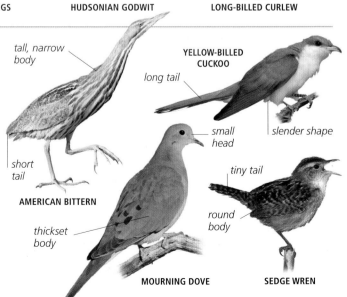

tall, narrow body

YELLOW-BILLED CUCKOO

long tail

short tail

small head

slender shape

AMERICAN BITTERN

tiny tail

round body

thickset body

MOURNING DOVE **SEDGE WREN**

BILL SHAPE

These images show a range of bill shapes and sizes relative to the bird's head size. In general, bill form, including length or thickness, corresponds to the kinds of food a birds consumes. With its pointed bill, the Mountain Chickadee picks tiny insects from crevices in tree bark. At another extreme, dowitchers probe mud with their long thin bills, feeling for worms. The avocet swishes its bill back and forth in briny water in search of shrimp.

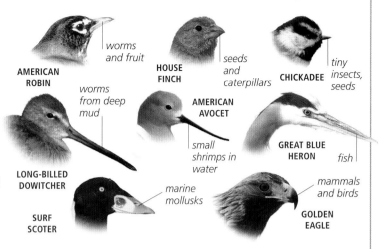

AMERICAN ROBIN — *worms and fruit*
HOUSE FINCH — *seeds and caterpillars*
CHICKADEE — *tiny insects, seeds*
LONG-BILLED DOWITCHER — *worms from deep mud*
AMERICAN AVOCET — *small shrimps in water*
GREAT BLUE HERON — *fish*
SURF SCOTER — *marine mollusks*
GOLDEN EAGLE — *mammals and birds*

WING SHAPE

Birds' wing shapes are correlated with their flight style. The long, round-tipped wings of the Red-tailed Hawk are perfect for soaring, while the tiny wings of hummingbirds are exactly what is needed to hover in front of flowers and then to back away after a meal of nectar. When flushed, quails flutter with their round wings and quickly drop down.

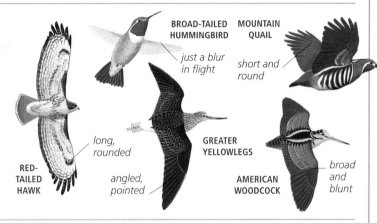

BROAD-TAILED HUMMINGBIRD — *just a blur in flight*
MOUNTAIN QUAIL — *short and round*
RED-TAILED HAWK — *long, rounded*
GREATER YELLOWLEGS — *angled, pointed*
AMERICAN WOODCOCK — *broad and blunt*

TAIL SHAPE

It is not clear why some songbirds, like the American Goldfinch, have a notched tail while other similar sized birds do not. Tail shapes vary as much as wing shapes, but are not so easily linked to a function. Irrespective of shape, tails are needed for balance. In some birds, tail shape, color, and pattern are used in courtship displays or in defensive displays when threatened.

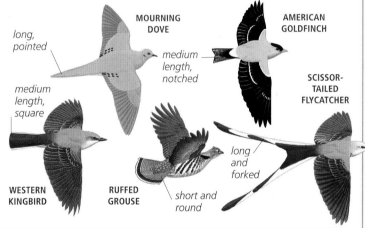

MOURNING DOVE — *long, pointed*
AMERICAN GOLDFINCH — *medium length, notched*
WESTERN KINGBIRD — *medium length, square*
RUFFED GROUSE — *short and round*
SCISSOR-TAILED FLYCATCHER — *long and forked*

COLORS AND MARKINGS

Melanin and carotenoid pigments determine color. Gray and brown birds have melanin (under hormonal influence), yellow and red ones carotenoid (derived from food). Flamingos are pink because they eat carotenoid-rich crustaceans. Diversity in color and markings also results from scattering of white light by feathers (producing blue colors) and optical interference (iridescence) due to the structural properties of some feathers.

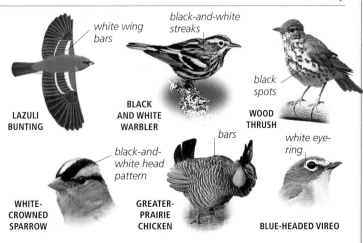

LAZULI BUNTING — *white wing bars*
BLACK AND WHITE WARBLER — *black-and-white streaks*
WOOD THRUSH — *black spots*
WHITE-CROWNED SPARROW — *black-and-white head pattern*
GREATER-PRAIRIE CHICKEN — *bars*
BLUE-HEADED VIREO — *white eye-ring*

SPECIES GUIDE

Families **Phasianidae**, **Odontophoridae**

GAMEBIRDS

THIS DIVERSE AND ADAPTABLE group of birds thrives in habitats ranging from hot desert to frozen tundra. Gamebirds spend most of the time on the ground, springing loudly into the air when alarmed.

QUAILS

Among the most terrestrial of all gamebirds, quails are also renowned for their great sociability, often forming large family groups, or "coveys," of up to 100 birds. The five species found in western North America each live in a specific habitat or at a particular elevation, but the single species found in the East, the Northern Bobwhite, ranges over a variety of habitats.

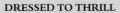

DRESSED TO THRILL
With its striking plumage, Gambel's Quail is one of the best-known desert birds in southwest North America.

GROUSE

The most numerous and widespread of gamebirds, the 12 different species of grouse can be divided into three groups based on their preferred habitats. Forest grouse include the Ruffed Grouse in the East, the Spruce Grouse in the North, and the Sooty Grouse and Dusky Grouse in the West.

Prairie grouse, including the Sharp-tailed Grouse, are found throughout the middle of the continent. All three tundra and mountaintop grouse or Ptarmigan are found in the extreme North and the Rockies. Grouse often possess patterns that match their surroundings, providing camouflage from enemies both animal and human.

GRASSLAND GROUSE
The aptly named Sharp-tailed Grouse is a common sight on summer prairies, strutting in search of grasshoppers.

PHEASANTS & PARTRIDGES

These Eurasian gamebirds were introduced into North America in the 19th and 20th centuries to provide additional targets for recreational hunters. While some introductions failed, species such as the colorful Ring-necked Pheasant adapted well and now thrive in established populations.

SNOW BIRD
The Rock Ptarmigan's white winter plumage camouflages it against the snow, helping to hide it from predators.

| Order **Galliformes** | Family **Cracidae** | Species ***Ortalis vetula*** |

Plain Chachalaca

round wings

longish neck

ADULT

IN FLIGHT

large, dark eyes

curved, chicken-like bill

brown upperparts with green sheen

ADULT

long, fanned-out, white-tipped tail

chocolate-brown outer wing feathers

FLIGHT: slow, labored wing beats to move for short distances between shrubs.

A large, dull-brown to olive-green bird found only in the US in the lower Rio Grande Valley, the Plain Chachalaca deftly moves through trees and shrubs while foraging, almost running along and hopping among the branches. The males develop a distinct reddish to pink, naked-skin facial patch and throat during the breeding season. South Texas is the northernmost edge of this species's range. About a dozen other chachalaca species are found from Mexico and Central America to Argentina.

VOICE Boisterous, three-syllable *cha-ca-lak* common in the early morning and late evening hours; especially loud when pairs or groups call in unison.

NESTING Loose accumulation of twigs, leaves, and moss in shrubs and small trees along watercourses; 2–3 eggs; 1 brood; April–July.

FEEDING Eats a wide variety of plant matter, such as leaves, tendrils, or buds; also berries.

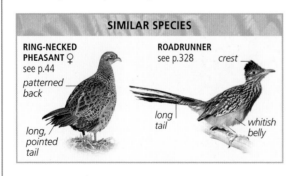

SIMILAR SPECIES

RING-NECKED PHEASANT ♀
see p.44

patterned back

long, pointed tail

ROADRUNNER
see p.328

crest

long tail

whitish belly

THE *CHA-CA-LAK* BIRD
Neck outstretched, a male gives its raucous call, showing the red, bare skin on its throat.

OCCURRENCE
In North America, occurs only along Texas's lower Rio Grande River valley, where it lives in shrubby and woody areas, and edges of brushy thickets along river bottoms. Otherwise, it is a tropical Mexican and Central American species.

| Length **20–23in (51–58cm)** | Wingspan **24–27in (61–68cm)** | Weight **19–20oz (550–575g)** |
| Social **Flocks** | Lifespan **Up to 8 years** | Status **Secure** |

Order **Galliformes**	Family **Odontophoridae**	Species **Oreortyx pictus**

Mountain Quail

ADULT
dark, round wings
budding crest feathers
chicken-like bill
long, head plumes
white stripe
chestnut chin and throat
dark, brownish gray upperparts
IN FLIGHT
"zebra-striped" underparts
JUVENILE
bluish gray breast
reddish orange undertail feathers
ADULT

FLIGHT: runs rather than flies; initial flight is rapid and startling, but bird quickly descends.

The most diagnostic field marks of the Mountain Quail are its deep-gray body offset by a chestnut-colored throat and "zebra-striped" flanks edged in black and buff, and its thin, usually vertical head plumes. Although common in its territory, this secretive species has not been well studied. A resident of thick scrub and shrub forests throughout higher elevations of western coastal mountain ranges, it is also the largest quail found in the US. The Mountain Quail is an adept runner, even uphill, and often prefers running to flying.

VOICE Males emit crowing *qu-ook* to attract mates; scattered coveys reunite using whistled *kow, kow, kow*, often repeated more than a dozen times in succession.

NESTING Shallow scrape lined with plant matter, often on steep inclines under overhead cover; 9–10 eggs; 1 brood; March–June.

FEEDING Mostly eats fruit, seeds, and subterranean bulbs; also eats insects and mollusks; females and young birds consume more insects than males.

COURTING CALLS
A territorial male Mountain Quail advertises its presence with loud crowing.

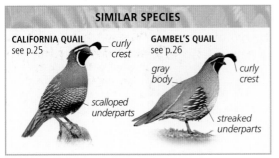

SIMILAR SPECIES

CALIFORNIA QUAIL see p.25 — curly crest, scalloped underparts

GAMBEL'S QUAIL see p.26 — gray body, curly crest, streaked underparts

OCCURRENCE
Year-round resident in Washington, Oregon, California, Idaho, and Nevada; also northern Baja California, in mixed evergreen and oak forests at mid- to high elevations, especially those with substantial understory. Ranges along coastal and inland mountains.

Length **9–11in (23–28cm)**	Wingspan **14–16in (35–41cm)**	Weight **8–9oz (225–250g)**
Social **Flocks**	Lifespan **Up to 3 years**	Status **Localized (p)**

Order **Galliformes**	Family **Odontophoridae**	Species **Callipepla squamata**

Scaled Quail

rounded wings

MALE

IN FLIGHT

generally duller than male

gray feathers on tail

FEMALE

short tail

white-tipped, brown crest

short, stubby bill

brownish face

largely unmarked, brown upperparts

conspicuous scaled pattern on underparts

MALE

FLIGHT: capable of explosive take-off and short bursts of speed over short distances.

The Scaled Quail was named for the scale-like appearance of its chest, neck, and belly feathers. It is also called the "Blue Quail," because of its bluish sheen in some lights, or "Cottontop," because of the fluffy white tip to its crest. This species of quail is well known for its preference, and ability, to run quickly instead of flying, to avoid danger. The population in the US periodically endures a "boom and bust" cycle that may be tied to rainfall and subsequent food shortages or abundance, but is also influenced by grazing practices. The Scaled Quail is regularly hunted throughout its range.

VOICE Flushed or separated covey (flock) uses two-syllable *CHE-kar* call to reunite; males shriek and squeal to attract a mate.

NESTING Shallow bowl on the ground, lined with grasses; 10–12 eggs; 1 brood; April–September.

FEEDING Usually consumes a variety of plant seeds, but also eats leaves, insects, and grain when available; a seasonal opportunist.

SIMILAR SPECIES

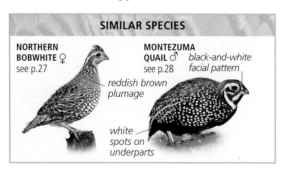

NORTHERN BOBWHITE ♀
see p.27

reddish brown plumage

white spots on underparts

MONTEZUMA QUAIL ♂
see p.28

black-and-white facial pattern

SOMETIMES BLUE
The bluish sheen that earned this species its nickname is visible here around the neck.

OCCURRENCE
A common species in arid rangeland and semidesert of western Texas, New Mexico, and eastern Arizona, preferring less dense vegetation than other quails. Thrives in varied grass habitat with mixture of scrub and shrub for overhead cover.

Length **10–12in (25–30cm)**	Wingspan **13–15in (33–38cm)**	Weight **6–8oz (175–200g)**
Social **Flocks**	Lifespan **Up to 3 years**	Status **Secure**

| Order **Galliformes** | Family **Odontophoridae** | Species ***Callipepla californica*** |

California Quail

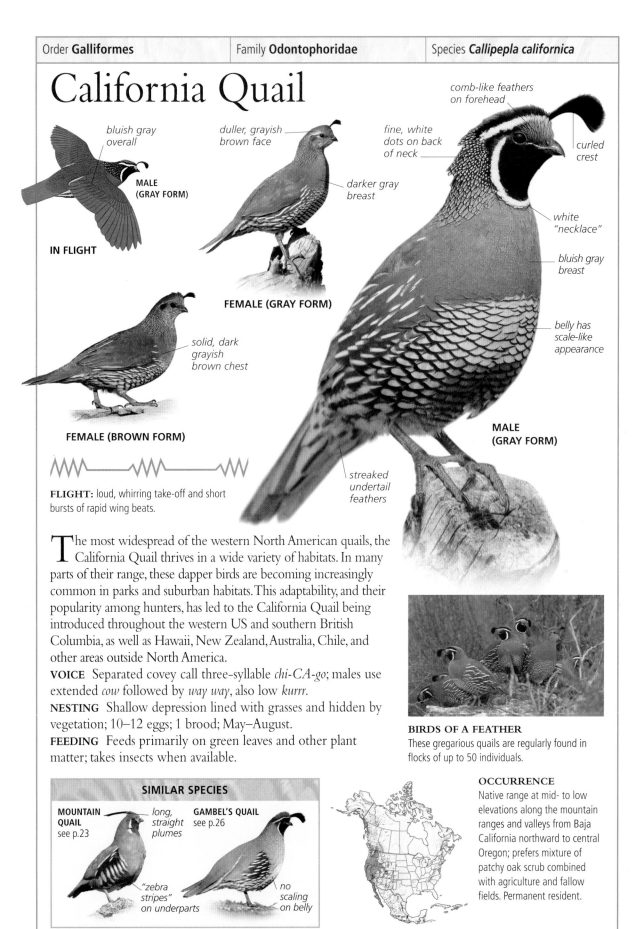

bluish gray overall

MALE (GRAY FORM)

IN FLIGHT

duller, grayish brown face

darker gray breast

FEMALE (GRAY FORM)

comb-like feathers on forehead

fine, white dots on back of neck

curled crest

white "necklace"

bluish gray breast

belly has scale-like appearance

solid, dark grayish brown chest

FEMALE (BROWN FORM)

FLIGHT: loud, whirring take-off and short bursts of rapid wing beats.

streaked undertail feathers

MALE (GRAY FORM)

The most widespread of the western North American quails, the California Quail thrives in a wide variety of habitats. In many parts of their range, these dapper birds are becoming increasingly common in parks and suburban habitats. This adaptability, and their popularity among hunters, has led to the California Quail being introduced throughout the western US and southern British Columbia, as well as Hawaii, New Zealand, Australia, Chile, and other areas outside North America.

VOICE Separated covey call three-syllable *chi-CA-go*; males use extended *cow* followed by *way way*, also low *kurrr*.

NESTING Shallow depression lined with grasses and hidden by vegetation; 10–12 eggs; 1 brood; May–August.

FEEDING Feeds primarily on green leaves and other plant matter; takes insects when available.

BIRDS OF A FEATHER
These gregarious quails are regularly found in flocks of up to 50 individuals.

SIMILAR SPECIES

MOUNTAIN QUAIL
see p.23

long, straight plumes

GAMBEL'S QUAIL
see p.26

"zebra stripes" on underparts

no scaling on belly

OCCURRENCE
Native range at mid- to low elevations along the mountain ranges and valleys from Baja California northward to central Oregon; prefers mixture of patchy oak scrub combined with agriculture and fallow fields. Permanent resident.

| Length **9–11in (24–28cm)** | Wingspan **12–14in (30–35cm)** | Weight **6–7oz (175–200g)** |
| Social **Flocks** | Lifespan **Up to 6 years** | Status **Secure (p)** |

Order **Galliformes**	Family **Odontophoridae**	Species ***Callipepla gambelii***

Gambel's Quail

short, broad wings

MALE

finely marked neck

rust-colored crown

black, drooping plume

black face

grayish back

IN FLIGHT

brown and white streaks

plain, grayish head

grayish brown face

pale belly

FEMALE

pale undertail

black spot on belly

MALE

G ambel's Quail is a highly social bird of the low–elevation deserts and valley floors of the Southwest, particularly Arizona and northern Mexico, where it it often known as the Desert or Arizona Quail. While tolerant of hot, dry conditions, its breeding success depends entirely on local rainfall, which produces the green plants that make up most of its diet. Gambel's Quail is a popular game bird throughout its range, readily identified by its drooping black "topknot," or plume, in addition to its distinctive calls.

VOICE Most common call: *chi-CA-go-go*; males attract mates with *kaa* or *kaaow;* alarmed birds utter *chip-chip-chip.*

NESTING Small depression defined by twigs and lined with grass and leaves, usually within cover; 10–12 eggs; 1 brood; March–June.

FEEDING Feeds mainly on seeds, green leaves, and grasses, also berries, cactus fruit; insects eaten by young and breeding birds.

FLIGHT: prefers running; makes short, explosive flight of rapid wing beats followed by glide.

SHOWING OFF ITS CHEST
This Gambel's Quail shows its distinctive blue, white, and blackish underparts.

OCCURRENCE
Strongly associated with scrub/shrub river edge or gulley vegetation, including mesquite, various grasses, and a variety of cactus species, especially where these species border agricultural properties.

SIMILAR SPECIES

MOUNTAIN QUAIL
see p.23
long, thin, straight plume

chestnut-brown face

broadly striped flanks

CALIFORNIA QUAIL ♂
see p.25
buff forehead

scaly lower belly; no black spot

Length **9½–11in (24–28cm)**	Wingspan **12½–14in (32–35cm)**	Weight **6oz (175g)**
Social **Flocks**	Lifespan **Up to 4 years**	Status **Secure**

| Order **Galliformes** | Family **Odontophoridae** | Species *Colinus virginianus* |

Northern Bobwhite

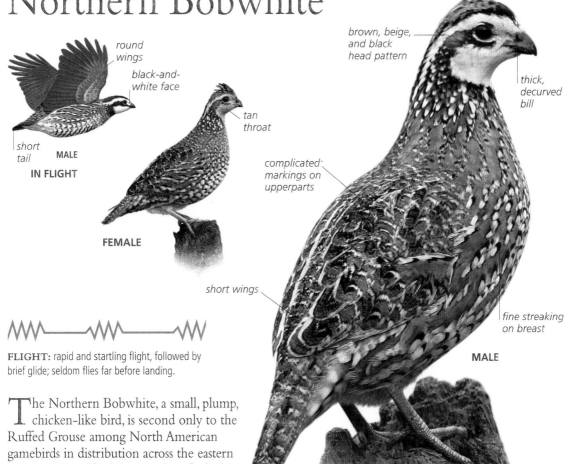

round wings

black-and-white face

short tail

MALE
IN FLIGHT

tan throat

FEMALE

short wings

brown, beige, and black head pattern

thick, decurved bill

complicated markings on upperparts

fine streaking on breast

MALE

FLIGHT: rapid and startling flight, followed by brief glide; seldom flies far before landing.

The Northern Bobwhite, a small, plump, chicken-like bird, is second only to the Ruffed Grouse among North American gamebirds in distribution across the eastern US states. Loved by hunters, when flushed it erupts in "coveys" of 10 to 20 individuals, bursting from groundcover and dispersing in many directions. Large numbers are raised in captivity and released to supplement wild populations for hunting.

VOICE Characteristic *bob-WHITE* or *bob-bob-WHITE* whistled by males in breeding season; call to reunite flock includes *hoi-lee* and *hoi* following dispersal.

NESTING Shallow depression lined with plant matter, located on ground within sight of an opening; 10–15 eggs; sometimes multiple broods per season; January–March.

FEEDING Forages for wide variety of plant matter (seeds, buds, leaves), and insects, snails, and spiders, depending on the season.

COVEY LIFE
Male, female, and immature Northern Bobwhites live together in tight flocks called coveys.

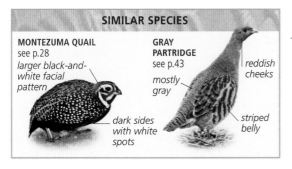

SIMILAR SPECIES

MONTEZUMA QUAIL
see p.28
larger black-and-white facial pattern

dark sides with white spots

GRAY PARTRIDGE
see p.43
mostly gray

reddish cheeks

striped belly

OCCURRENCE
Widely distributed but only locally common in much of the eastern US, and in Mexico, southward to Guatemala. Most often associated with agricultural fields, it thrives in a patchwork of mixed young forests, fields, and brushy hedges. A permanent resident.

| Length **8–10in (20–25cm)** | Wingspan **11–14in (28–35cm)** | Weight **6oz (175g)** |
| Social **Small flocks** | Lifespan **Up to 6 years** | Status **Declining** |

Order **Galliformes**	Family **Odontophoridae**	Species *Cyrtonyx montezumae*

Montezuma Quail

"clown-like," black-and-white head

streaked back

short, tan crest

thick bill

dark throat

MALE

mottled inner wing feathers

conspicuous white spots on black background

short tail

MALE

IN FLIGHT

short crest

cinnamon to light tan belly

FEMALE

FLIGHT: leaps into flight using rapid wing beats, usually landing nearby; prefers to run.

The male Montezuma Quail is unmistakable with its "clown-like" black-and-white face and white-spotted underparts, but its secretive nature makes this species difficult to study. It differs from other quail species in its woven dome nests and its restricted social behavior. When threatened, it prefers to crouch, walk, and then run from danger, but it may also crouch and freeze in place, then suddenly burst into flight.

VOICE Males produce a loud, descending buzzy whistle *wheeerrr*, sometimes compared to the sound of a bomb falling; female emits low descending hoots.

NESTING Woven grass or leaf dome with a single entrance; 10–12 eggs; 1 brood; June–August.

FEEDING Eats fallen acorns and bulbs; scratches ground for tubers with specialized claw on each foot; insects when available.

REMARKABLE PATTERN
This species is also known as "Harlequin's Quail" due to its extraordinary facial pattern.

SIMILAR SPECIES

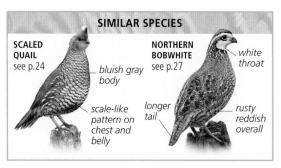

SCALED QUAIL
see p.24

bluish gray body

scale-like pattern on chest and belly

NORTHERN BOBWHITE
see p.27

white throat

longer tail

rusty reddish overall

OCCURRENCE
Habitat is a mixture of grassy and open pine-oak woodlands at 4,000–6,000ft (1,200–1,800m); also found in arid scrubland. Predominantly a Mexican species, whose range extends northward into southern New Mexico, Arizona, and parts of southern Texas.

Length **8½–9in (21–23cm)**	Wingspan **11–12in (28–30cm)**	Weight **6–7oz (175–200g)**
Social **Family groups**	Lifespan **Up to 7 years**	Status **Localized**

| Order **Galliformes** | Family **Phasianidae** | Species ***Meleagris gallopavo*** |

Wild Turkey

MALE (EAST)

IN FLIGHT

tail fanned in display

humped back

no feathers on head

long legs

MALE (EAST)

rusty tail with black band

black-and-white barred wings

unfeathered blue-and-red head

large red wattles

hair-like "beard" on breast

dark overall

iridescent bronze-and-purplish body

FEMALE

dark body, with bronze iridescence

MALE (WEST)

Once proposed by Benjamin Franklin as the national emblem of the US, the Wild Turkey—the largest gamebird in North America—was eliminated from most of its original range by the early 1900s due to over-hunting and habitat destruction. Since then, habitat restoration and the subsequent reintroduction of Wild Turkeys has been very successful.

VOICE Well-known gobble, given by males especially during courtship; female makes various yelps, clucks, and purrs, based on mood and threat level.

NESTING Scrape on ground lined with grass; placed against or under protective cover; 10–15 eggs; 1 brood; March–June.

FEEDING Omnivorous, it scratches in leaf litter on forest floor for acorns and other food, mostly vegetation; also takes plants and insects from agricultural fields.

FLIGHT: after running, leaps into the air with loud, rapid wing beats, then glides.

COLLECTIVE DISPLAY
Once the population expands into new areas, numerous males will be seen displaying together.

SIMILAR SPECIES

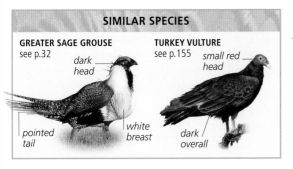

GREATER SAGE GROUSE see p.32

dark head

pointed tail

white breast

TURKEY VULTURE see p.155

small red head

dark overall

OCCURRENCE
Found in mixed mature woodlands, fields with agricultural crops; also in various grasslands, close to swamps, but adaptable and increasingly common in suburban and urban habitats. Quite widespread, but patchily distributed across North America.

| Length **2¾–4ft (0.9–1.2m)** | Wingspan **4–5ft (1.2–1.5m)** | Weight **10–24lb (4.5–11kg)** |
| Social **Flocks** | Lifespan **Up to 9 years** | Status **Secure** |

| Order **Galliformes** | Family **Phasianidae** | Species *Bonasa umbellus* |

Ruffed Grouse

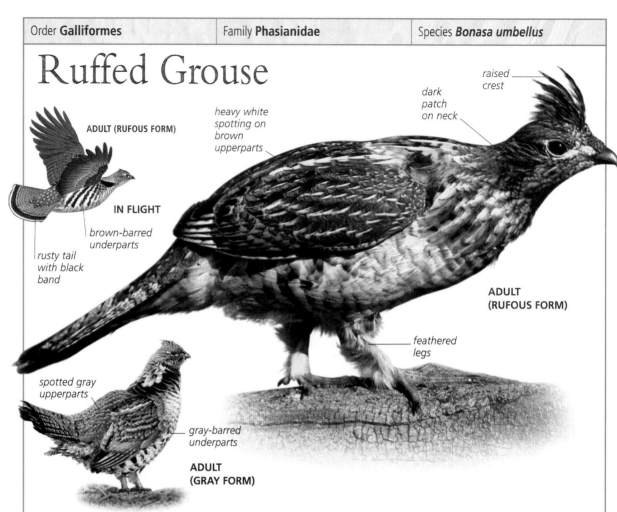

ADULT (RUFOUS FORM)

heavy white spotting on brown upperparts

raised crest

dark patch on neck

IN FLIGHT

brown-barred underparts

rusty tail with black band

ADULT (RUFOUS FORM)

feathered legs

spotted gray upperparts

gray-barred underparts

ADULT (GRAY FORM)

The Ruffed Grouse is perhaps the most widespread gamebird in North America. There are two color forms, rufous and gray, both allowing the birds to remain camouflaged and undetected on the forest floor, until they eventually burst into the air in an explosion of whirring wings. The male is well known for his extraordinary wing beating or "drumming" display, which he performs year-round, but most frequently in the spring.

VOICE Hissing notes, and soft *purrt, purrt, purrt* when alarmed, by both sexes; males "drumming" display when heard from distance resembles small engine starting, *thump…thump…thump...thump… thump…thuthuthuth.*

NESTING Shallow, leaf-lined bowl set against a tree trunk, rock or fallen log in forest; 6–14 eggs; 1 brood; March–June.

FEEDING Forages on ground for leaves, buds, and fruit; occasionally insects.

FLIGHT: an explosive take-off, usually at close range, glides for a short distance before landing.

OCCURRENCE
Found in young, mixed habitat forests throughout northern US and Canada. Southern edge of range extends along higher elevations of the Appalachians and middle levels of the Rocky Mountains, if suitable habitat is available.

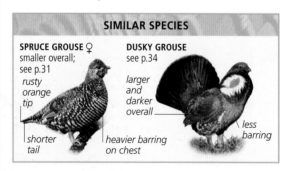

SIMILAR SPECIES

SPRUCE GROUSE ♀
smaller overall;
see p.31

rusty orange tip

shorter tail

DUSKY GROUSE
see p.34

larger and darker overall

less barring

heavier barring on chest

WARM RED
The rufous form of the Ruffed Grouse is more common in hotter parts of the continent.

| Length **17–20in (43–51cm)** | Wingspan **20–23in (51–58cm)** | Weight **20–22oz (575–625g)** |
| Social **Solitary/Small flocks** | Lifespan **Up to 10 years** | Status **Secure** |

Order **Galliformes**	Family **Phasainidae**	Species *Falcipennis canadensis*

Spruce Grouse

MALE (FRANKLIN'S)

IN FLIGHT

white spots on black tail

paler overall

FEMALE (TAIGA)

heavy barring on underparts

mottled gray-brown upperparts

bright red comb above eye

black throat

black breast

white spots on underparts

gray upperparts

heavily barred underparts

FEMALE
F. c. franklinii
(FRANKLIN'S)

mostly blackish tail

MALE
F. c. canadensis
(TAIGA)

Perhaps because of the remoteness of their habitat and lack of human contact, Spruce Grouse are not afraid of humans. This lack of wariness when approached has earned them the name "fool hens." Their specialized diet of pine needles causes the intestinal tract to expand in order to accommodate a larger volume of food to compensate for its low nutritional value. There are two different subspecies of Spruce Grouse (*F. c. canadensis* and *F. c. franklinii*), both of which have red and gray forms.

VOICE Mostly silent; males clap their wings during courtship display; females often utter long cackle at dawn and dusk.
NESTING Lined with moss, leaves, feathers; often at base of tree; naturally low area in forest floor 4–6 eggs; 1 brood; May–July.
FEEDING Feeds mostly on pine but also spruce needles; will eat insects, leaves, fruits, and seeds when available.

FLIGHT: generally avoids flying; when disturbed, bursts into flight on whirring wings.

RUFOUS BAND
The male "Taiga" subspecies displays the thin rufous band on the tip of his tail.

OCCURRENCE
Present year-round in forests dominated by conifers, including Jack, Lodgepole, Spruce, Red Spruce, Black Spruce, Balsam Fir, Subalpine Fir, Hemlock, and Cedar. Found from western Alaska to the Atlantic Coast.

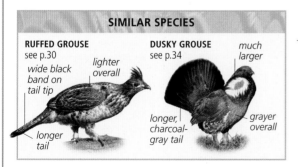

SIMILAR SPECIES

RUFFED GROUSE
see p.30

wide black band on tail tip

lighter overall

longer tail

DUSKY GROUSE
see p.34

much larger

longer, charcoal-gray tail

grayer overall

Length **14–17in (36–43cm)**	Wingspan **21–23in (53–58cm)**	Weight **16oz (450g)**
Social **Solitary**	Lifespan **Up to 10 years**	Status **Secure**

| Order **Galliformes** | Family **Phasianidae** | Species *Centrocercus urophasianus* |

Greater Sage Grouse

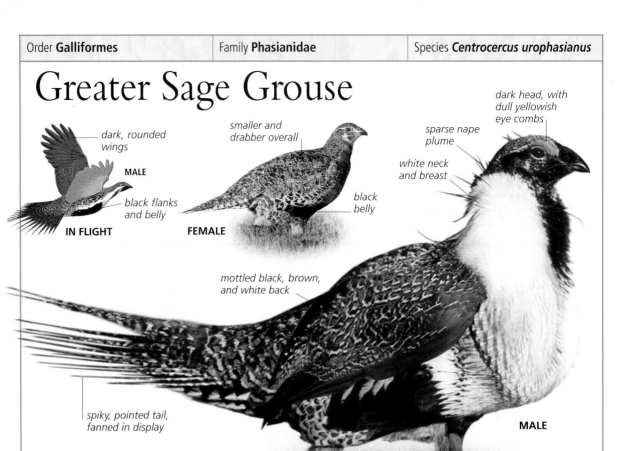

dark, rounded wings

MALE

black flanks and belly

IN FLIGHT

smaller and drabber overall

FEMALE

black belly

dark head, with dull yellowish eye combs

sparse nape plume

white neck and breast

mottled black, brown, and white back

spiky, pointed tail, fanned in display

MALE

FLIGHT: fast, strong; rapid initial wing beats at take-off, followed by a glide-and-flap sequence.

The Greater Sage Grouse is by far the largest native North American grouse. Each spring, the males gather on communal sites, known as leks, where they compete for females with spectacular courtship displays. As many as 40 males may gather at a lek for these events. Once widespread, Greater Sage Grouse populations have declined, as human encroachment on sagebrush habitats has increased.

VOICE Clucks repeatedly when flushed; male makes odd popping sounds with throat sacs when displaying.

NESTING Depression scraped into soil next to protective cover of grass or sagebrush branches; 6–10 eggs; 1 brood; March–May.

FEEDING Eats mainly on sagebrush leaves; also eats insects, fruit, flowers, and succulent green plants when available.

IMPRESSIVE SHOW
The male's courtship display is remarkable—he inflates his air sacs, fans his tail and struts around.

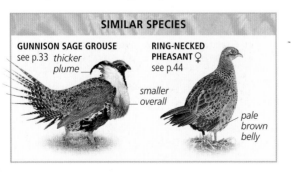

SIMILAR SPECIES

GUNNISON SAGE GROUSE see p.33 *thicker plume*

RING-NECKED PHEASANT ♀ see p.44

smaller overall

pale brown belly

OCCURRENCE
In North America its present distribution is a fraction of its formerly large range in the vast sagebrush plains of the West. Breeds in a variety of habitats, the ideal being composed of several sagebrush species of varying heights.

| Length **19½–30in (50–76cm)** | Wingspan **32–39in (81–99cm)** | Weight **2½–6½lb (1–3kg)** |
| Social **Flocks** | Lifespan **Up to 6 years** | Status **Vulnerable** |

Order **Galliformes**	Family **Phasianidae**	Species ***Centrocercus minimus***

Gunnison Sage Grouse

long, spiky, pointed tail, fanned in display

thick, black nape plume

dark head, with dull yellow eye combs

mottled brown, black, and white back

white breast and neck

MALE

MALE

black belly and flanks

IN FLIGHT

smaller and drabber overall

FEMALE

FLIGHT: flushes on loud wing beats, followed by flap-glide-flap sequence for a brief flight.

In the 1990s, ornithologists discovered differences between the populations of the Gunnison Basin, Colorado, and other Sage Grouse populations. This lead to the description of a new species, *minimus*, in 2001. There are fewer than 10 breeding populations within this restricted area, and further loss of its habitat due to cultivation and development puts this species at risk of extinction.

VOICE Clucks repeatedly when flushed; male makes about 9 booming sounds in succession when displaying.

NESTING Scrape in areas with abundant grass beneath overhead sagebrush; 7–9 eggs; 1 brood; March–May.

FEEDING Primarily eats sagebrush leaves; also other green plant matter, and insects.

COURTSHIP DISPLAY
The male's thick nape plume is a prominent feature of his courtship display.

SIMILAR SPECIES

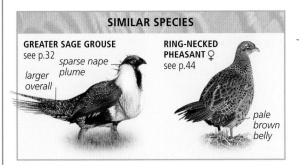

GREATER SAGE GROUSE
see p.32

sparse nape plume

larger overall

RING-NECKED PHEASANT ♀
see p.44

pale brown belly

OCCURRENCE
Found only in the Gunnison Basin, Colorado, this species prefers areas of mixed, tall sagebrush with significant overhead cover and ground-based succulent plant foliage, especially in areas along river corridors. Also found where there is deciduous scrub and fruit-bearing trees.

Length **21–23in (53–58cm)**	Wingspan **33–36in (83–91cm)**	Weight **2½–5¼lb (1–2.4kg)**
Social **Flocks**	Lifespan **Up to 6 years**	Status **Vulnerable**

Order **Galliformes**	Family **Phasianidae**	Species ***Dendragapus obscurus***

Dusky Grouse

MALE

pale underwing

IN FLIGHT

broad, rounded black tail

barred crown and neck

mottled brown back

small bill

short, plain brown wings

gray belly

FEMALE

MALE (DISPLAY)

red wattle over eye

bare red or purple air sacs

gray underparts

white scales on flanks

Once considered a Blue Grouse subspecies, the Dusky Grouse was recently reclassified as a species in its own right, separate from the Sooty Grouse. Male Dusky Grouse can be identified by their courtship displays, which are primarily ground-based and quieter than those of the Dusky Grouse, and by their reddish purple air sacs. The Dusky Grouse also has a plainer tail, lacking the grayer tip of the Sooty, and its chicks are more gray than brown.

VOICE A series of five soft hoots; also a hiss, growl, and cluck; females emit a whinnying cry.

NESTING Shallow scrape, usually lined with dead grass, leaves, or other plants, located under shrubs, against rocks or logs; 7–10 eggs; 1 brood; March–May.

FEEDING Feeds on leaves, flowers, fruit, also some insects; evergreen needles, buds, and cones in season.

FLIGHT: loud, short-distance flight with rapid wing beats before gliding to the ground.

FREEZING FOR SAFETY
This female Dusky Grouse stands still as a statue, relying on camouflage, not flight, for protection.

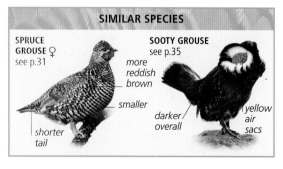

SIMILAR SPECIES

SPRUCE GROUSE ♀
see p.31

more reddish brown

smaller

shorter tail

SOOTY GROUSE
see p.35

darker overall

yellow air sacs

OCCURRENCE
Found in the northern, central Rocky Mountains in Canada and US in high or mid-altitude open forests and shrublands. Typically uses older, denser, mixed or evergreen forests at higher elevations in winter, more open-country, lighter forests at lower elevations in summer.

Length **16–20in (41–51cm)**	Wingspan **25–28in (64–71cm)**	Weight **2½–2¾lb (1.1–1.3kg)**
Social **Solitary/Winter flocks**	Lifespan **Up to 14 years**	Status **Localized**

Order **Galliformes**	Family **Phasianidae**	Species **Dendragapus fuliginosus**

Sooty Grouse

MALE

IN FLIGHT

gray band at tip of tail

barred tail with gray tip

heavily mottled

FEMALE

dark cheek patch above pale throat

yellow air sacs on side of neck

deep-red wattle

dark upperparts

MALE (WINTER; NON-DISPLAYING)

short, stiffly curved wings

dark underparts

MALE

FLIGHT: rapid take-off when pursued; short initial burst followed by flap-and-glide sequence.

The Sooty Grouse, like the Dusky Grouse, was recently reclassified as a separate species. Although primarily distinguished by its restriction to coastal mountain ranges, plumage and behaviorial displays help differentiate the male Sooty Grouse from the Dusky Grouse. During courtship displays, which are most often performed in trees, the male Sooty Grouse shows rough, yellow air sacs. Females and chicks have a browner overall appearance to their plumage than those of the Dusky Grouse.

VOICE Loud six-syllable hooting; also growl, hiss, cluck, *purrr*.
NESTING Shallow depression lined with dead vegetation, usually under small pine trees; 5–8 eggs; 1 brood; March–May.
FEEDING Feeds primarily on evergreen needles, especially Douglas Fir; will take leaves, grasses, fruit, and insects when seasonally available.

CAUTIOUS PEEK
Female Sooty Grouse disturbed on the ground peer up through grasses to check for danger.

SIMILAR SPECIES

SPRUCE GROUSE ♀
see p.31

reddish brown

smaller

shorter tail

DUSKY GROUSE
see p.34

dull-red wattle

dark-red air sacs during display

browner overall

OCCURRENCE
Found west of the Rocky Mountains in Canada and the US, from sea level to the timberline. Breeds at lower elevations in open areas with grassland, forest clearings, and shrubs, and moves up into thicker evergreen forests at higher elevations in winter.

Length **16–20in (41–51cm)**	Wingspan **25–28in (64–71cm)**	Weight **2½–2¾lb (1.1–1.3g)**
Social **Solitary/Winter flocks**	Lifespan **Up to 14 years**	Status **Secure**

| Order **Galliformes** | Family **Phasianidae** | Species *Tympanuchus phasianellus* |

Sharp-tailed Grouse

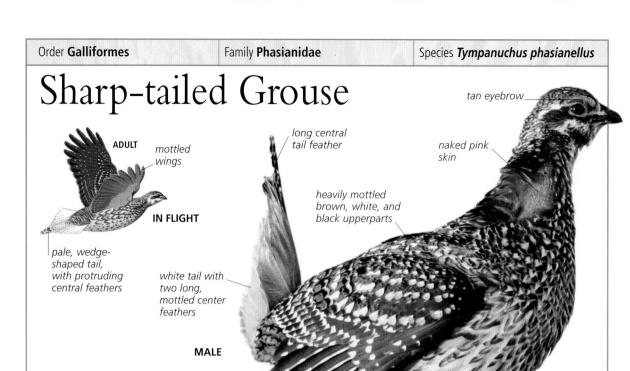

tan eyebrow

naked pink skin

ADULT

mottled wings

IN FLIGHT

long central tail feather

heavily mottled brown, white, and black upperparts

pale, wedge-shaped tail, with protruding central feathers

white tail with two long, mottled center feathers

MALE

brown wings with white dots

white underside, with dark brown arrowheads along flanks

FLIGHT: flushes from hiding on rapid wing beats to flight speed, then onto glide-flap-glide sequence.

The most widespread species of its genus, the Sharp-tailed Grouse is able to adapt to the greatest variety of habitats. It is not migratory, but undertakes seasonal movements between grassland summer habitats and woodland winter habitats. These birds are popular with hunters and are legal quarry in most of their range. Elements of this grouse's spectacular courtship display have been incorporated into the culture and dance of Native American people, including foot stomping and tail feather rattling.
VOICE Male calls a variety of unusual clucks, cooing, barks, and gobbles during courtship; females cluck with different intonations.
NESTING Shallow depression lined with plant matter close at hand as well as some feathers from female, usually near overhead cover; 10–12 eggs; 1 brood; March–May.
FEEDING Forages primarily for seeds, leaves, buds, and fruit; also takes insects and flowers when available.

PRAIRIE DANCER
The courtship dance of the Sharp-tailed Grouse heralds the arrival of spring to the grasslands.

SIMILAR SPECIES

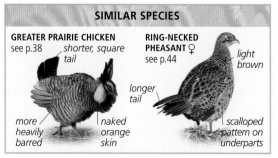

GREATER PRAIRIE CHICKEN
see p.38
shorter, square tail
more heavily barred
naked orange skin

RING-NECKED PHEASANT ♀
see p.44
light brown
longer tail
scalloped pattern on underparts

OCCURRENCE
Has a northern and western distribution in North America, from Alaska (isolated population) southward to northern prairie states. Prefers a mixture of fallow and active agricultural fields combined with brushy forest edges and woodlots along river beds.

| Length **15–19in (38–48cm)** | Wingspan **23–26in (58–66cm)** | Weight **26–34oz (750–950g)** |
| Social **Flocks** | Lifespan **Up to 7 years** | Status **Declining (p)** |

Order **Galliformes**	Family **Phasianidae**	Species *Tympanuchus pallidicinictus*

Lesser Prairie Chicken

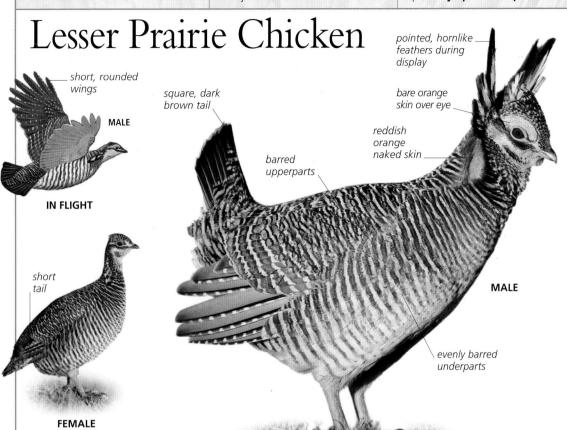

MALE

short, rounded wings

IN FLIGHT

square, dark brown tail

barred upperparts

pointed, hornlike feathers during display

bare orange skin over eye

reddish orange naked skin

MALE

evenly barred underparts

short tail

FEMALE

Destruction of its native shortgrass prairie and oak scrub habitat has drastically reduced the range and numbers of the Lesser Prairie Chicken. The species is sensitive to fences, buildings, and power line towers, and females do not nest near such structures, further reducing its already restricted habitat. Recently, the appeal of the courtship display, in which the male leans forward, while raising its tail and head feathers, has earned attention, leading to increased awareness of the species and efforts to reverse its decline.

VOICE Male "booms" or gobbles series of high, hooting notes during courtship display; females occasionally "boom" on lek; both sexes cackle when flushed.

NESTING Shallow scrape lined with available plant matter and feathers under brush or scrub; 10–12 eggs; 1 brood; April–July.

FEEDING Feeds on leaves, buds, and insects, especially grasshoppers, during summer; grains and seeds in colder months.

FLIGHT: explosive takeoff followed by glide-flap-glide sequence when threatened.

DAILY FLIGHT
More than other grouse species, this species uses flight to move between locations.

OCCURRENCE
Primarily native shortgrass prairie mixed with shrub woodlands; fallow fields; occasional agricultural properties, restricted to parts of Colorado, Kansas, Oklahoma, New Mexico, and Texas.

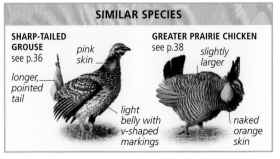

SIMILAR SPECIES

SHARP-TAILED GROUSE see p.36

pink skin

longer, pointed tail

light belly with v-shaped markings

GREATER PRAIRIE CHICKEN see p.38

slightly larger

naked orange skin

Length **15–17in (38–43cm)**	Wingspan **23–26in (58–66cm)**	Weight **27–34oz (775–975g)**
Social **Flocks**	Lifespan **Up to 5 years**	Status **Vulnerable (p)**

Order **Galliformes**	Family **Phasianidae**	Species *Tympanuchus cupido*

Greater Prairie Chicken

rounded wings

MALE

IN FLIGHT

display feathers against neck

barred overall

MALE

square tail

no display feathers

FEMALE

two sets of feathers raised during display

orange skin over eye

MALE (DISPLAYING)

beard-like feathers

bright orange skin of "air sac"

FLIGHT: bursts from cover with loud, rapid wing beats when approached.

Once common in prairie and woodland areas across central North America, populations of the Greater Prairie Chicken have been greatly reduced as their habitats have given way to agriculture. During the breeding season, males aggressively defend territories called "leks" and perform dramatic displays. They proclaim their vigor and entice females by stamping their feet, inflating the prominent air sacks on their necks, and "booming."

VOICE During courtship, males emit "booming" sounds like a three-part low hoot; also cackling calls.

NESTING Depression in soil lined with vegetation and feathers, in thick grass or other cover; 10–12 eggs; 1 brood; April–July.

FEEDING Eats berries, leaves, seeds, and grain; also insects.

BOOMING MALES
At a "lek" in the early morning, a male sends out a booming call and displays to attract a female.

SIMILAR SPECIES

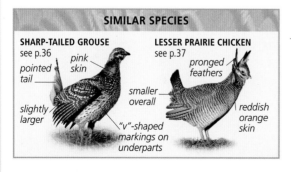

SHARP-TAILED GROUSE
see p.36

pink skin

pointed tail

slightly larger

LESSER PRAIRIE CHICKEN
see p.37

pronged feathers

smaller overall

reddish orange skin

"v"-shaped markings on underparts

OCCURRENCE
Separate populations occur in the Dakotas, Minnesota, Colorado, Nebraska, Kansas, Illinois, Oklahoma, and Missouri. Breeds in openings mixed with oak-forested river corridors, especially where these interact with areas of native tallgrass prairie; resident year-round.

Length **15½–17½in (40–45cm)**	Wingspan **26–29in (66–74cm)**	Weight **30–36oz (850–1,000g)**
Social **Flocks**	Lifespan **Up to 4 years**	Status **Vulnerable**

Order **Galliformes**	Family **Phasainidae**	Species *Lagopus leucurus*

White-tailed Ptarmigan

all-white overall

ADULT (WINTER)

IN FLIGHT

red naked skin over eye

lichen-like coloration and patterning

FEMALE (SUMMER)

small, black bill

ADULT (WINTER)

varied breeding plumage is turning white with molting feathers

MALE (LATE SUMMER)

The smallest and most southerly of the three North American ptarmigans, the White-tailed Ptarmigan's native range is still largely intact. In the winter, its almost completely white plumage—unique among the gamebird species—blends it in perfectly to its icy mountainous home. Its plumage is one of several adaptations to the inhospitable environment it inhabits. The feathers on its feet increase the surface area in contact with the ground, and so help to prevent the bird from sinking into the snow.

VOICE Males emit various cackling clucks, *cuk-cuk-cuuuk* during display; females cluck, purr, and growl softly.

NESTING Scrape in ground lined with plants and feathers; 4–8 eggs; 1 brood; May–June.

FEEDING Feeds heavily on willows, eating mostly leaves, buds, and twigs; insects when nesting.

FLIGHT: rarely flies unless pursued; flush on explosive wing beats, then flap-and-glide sequence.

WHITE ON WHITE
Immobile on white snow, the male blends in superbly with the wintry surroundings.

SIMILAR SPECIES

ROCK PTARMIGAN ☼
see p.40
grayer summer plumage
larger overall

WILLOW PTARMIGAN ☼
see p.41
reddish brown summer plumage
red comb
larger overall
white underparts

OCCURRENCE
Has a more restricted distribution than Rock and Willow Ptarmigans, occurring from Alaska south to Idaho and Montana; small isolated populations exist in Colorado and New Hampshire. Strongly associated with willow stands above tree-line; also meadows and evergreen stand mixtures.

Length **12in (30–31cm)**	Wingspan **20–22in (51–56cm)**	Weight **12–16oz (350–450g)**
Social **Large flocks**	Lifespan **Up to 15 years**	Status **Secure**

| Order **Galliformes** | Family **Phasianidae** | Species *Lagopus mutus* |

Rock Ptarmigan

mostly gray upperparts

black tail

MALE (WINTER)

all-white wings

gray wing patch

IN FLIGHT

MALE (SUMMER)

brown-and-black barring

white wings

small bill

small, round head

red comb

mottled belly

FEMALE (SUMMER)

"salt-and-pepper" barring on gray upperparts

small, delicate bill

black line between eye and bill

white plumage

FEMALE (WINTER)

MALE (WINTER)

white belly

feathered feet

MALE (SUMMER)

FLIGHT: bursts into flight with rapid wing beats, followed by gliding and shallow flapping.

The Rock Ptarmigan is the most northerly of the three ptarmigan species found in North America. Although some birds make a short migration to more southern wintering grounds, many remain on their breeding grounds year-round. This species is well known for its distinctive seasonal variation in plumage, which helps to camouflage it against its surroundings. Ptarmigans are a common food of the Inuit, who inhabit the same Arctic habitat.

VOICE Quiet; male call a raspy *krrrh*, also growls and clucks.
NESTING Small scrape or natural depression, lined with plant matter, often away from cover; 8–10 eggs; 1 brood; April–June.
FEEDING Feeds on buds, seeds, flowers, and leaves, especially birch and willow; eats insects in summer.

IN BETWEEN PLUMAGE
Various transitional plumage patterns can be seen on the Rock Ptarmigan in spring and fall.

OCCURRENCE
Prefers dry, rocky tundra and shrubby ridge tops; will use edges of open meadows and dense evergreen stands along fairly high-elevation rivers and streams during winter. Occurs throughout the Northern Hemisphere in Arctic tundra from Iceland to Kamchatka in far east Russia.

SIMILAR SPECIES

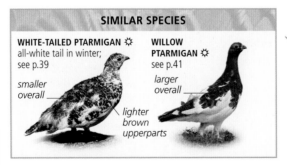

WHITE-TAILED PTARMIGAN ☼
all-white tail in winter; see p.39

smaller overall

lighter brown upperparts

WILLOW PTARMIGAN ☼
see p.41

larger overall

| Length **12½–15½in (32–40cm)** | Wingspan **19½–23½in (50–60cm)** | Weight **16–23oz (450–650g)** |
| Social **Winter flocks** | Lifespan **Up to 8 years** | Status **Secure** |

| Order **Galliformes** | Family **Phasianidae** | Species *Lagopus lagopus* |

Willow Ptarmigan

red comb

black bill

black bill

rich reddish brown body

reddish brown body

black tail

white between eye and black bill

all-white body

ADULT (WINTER)

IN FLIGHT

MALE (SUMMER)

ADULT (WINTER)

lacks red comb

yellow-brown body

dark, scaly bars

white belly

FEMALE (SUMMER)

feathered feet

MALE (SUMMER)

FLIGHT: strong, rapid wing beats before gliding; prefers to walk.

The most common of the three ptarmigan species, the Willow Ptarmigan also undertakes the longest migration of the group. The Willow Ptarmigan is an unusual gamebird species, as male and female remain bonded throughout the chick-rearing process, in which the male is an active participant. The "Red Grouse" of British moors is a subspecies (*L. l scotians*) of the Willow Ptarmigan.

VOICE Variety of purrs, clucks, hissing, meowing noises; *Kow-Kow-Kow* call given before flushing, possibly alerting others.

NESTING Shallow bowl scraped in soil, lined with plant matter, protected by overhead cover; 8–10 eggs; 1 brood; March–May.

FEEDING Mostly eats buds, stems, and seeds, but also flowers, insects, and leaves when available.

PERFECT BLEND-IN
Its reddish brown upperparts camouflage this summer ptarmigan in the shrubby areas it inhabits.

OCCURRENCE
Prefers tundra, in Arctic, sub-Arctic and subalpine regions. Thrives in willow thickets along low, moist river corridors; also in the low woodlands of the sub-Arctic tundra.

SIMILAR SPECIES

WHITE-TAILED PTARMIGAN ☼
see p.39

browner plumage

smaller overall

ROCK PTARMIGAN ☼
see p.40

grayer plumage

darker

| Length **14–17½in (35–44cm)** | Wingspan **22–24in (56–61cm)** | Weight **15–28oz (425–800g)** |
| Social **Winter flocks** | Lifespan **Up to 9 years** | Status **Secure** |

Order **Galliformes**	Family **Phasianidae**	Species *Alectoris chukar*

Chukar

short, round wings

white face

MALE

IN FLIGHT

gray crown

pink bill

pale pinkish gray back

white face with thick black border

short, gray tail with red outer feathers

striking flank stripes

ADULT

whitish underbelly

pink-red legs

A native of Eurasia, from eastern Europe to China, the Chukar was brought to North America in the early 1890s. In the mid-20th century, nearly a million birds were released in more than 40 US states and six Canadian provinces, after the Chukar became popular as a game bird. While most introductions failed, the species did succeed in some areas, especially on steep mountain slopes in the West. Chukars form large communal groups, or crèches, of up to 100 young birds, with 10–12 adults overseeing them.

VOICE When flushed, a thin whistled *peee*, then a series of squeals *pittoo-pittoo-pittoo*; *chukka-chuka-chuka-chuka* reunites flushed or dispersed covey.

NESTING Shallow scrape lined with nearby dead vegetation, well-concealed among shrubs and rocks on hillside; 7–12 eggs; 1 brood; March–May.

FEEDING Eats mainly seeds from various grasses and green succulent plants; berries; also eats insects.

FLIGHT: explosive takeoff from cover, usually heading downslope when flushed.

SIMILAR SPECIES

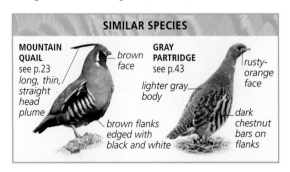

MOUNTAIN QUAIL
see p.23
long, thin, straight head plume

brown face

brown flanks edged with black and white

GRAY PARTRIDGE
see p.43

lighter gray body

rusty-orange face

dark chestnut bars on flanks

MAKING AN EFFORT
Perched on a rock, this Chukar calls loudly, stretching its neck to increase vocal capacity.

OCCURRENCE
Introduced to the West, released for shooting in the East; found on wide open areas and steep slopes at high elevation, up to 2,500m (8,200ft), with a mix of deep, brushy canyons and hillsides of loose rocks and boulders, sparse bush, low woody shrubs, grasses and aromatic herbs.

Length **13½–15in (34–38cm)**	Wingspan **19–22in (48–56cm)**	Weight **18–23oz (500–650g)**
Social **Family groups**	Lifespan **Up to 3 years**	Status **Secure**

Order **Galliformes**	Family **Phasianidae**	Species *Perdix perdix*

Gray Partridge

ADULT

brown, rounded wings

dark cinnamon tail

IN FLIGHT

rusty head

underparts gray overall

horseshoe-shaped belly patch

ADULT

cinnamon face

gray neck and chest with fine black barring

gray back with fine barring

ADULT

chestnut barred gray flanks

FLIGHT: erupts from cover on loud, rapid wing beats; levels off, flaps and glides; flies low.

A member of the pheasant family, the Gray Partridge is native to Eurasia. Introduced to North America in the late 18th century, it became a resident after repeated re-introductions. Hunters call it the Hungarian Partridge or "Huns" for short. This species has benefited from the mixture of agricultural and fallow fields, that resulted from long-term conservation programs, and its population is stable or expanding in the west. The isolated eastern populations, however, are declining due to changes in land use. This species is popular with hunters in both North America and Europe.

VOICE Short *kuk-kuk-kuk*, quickly and in a series when alarmed; *prruk-prruk* between adults and young when threatened.
NESTING Shallow depression in soil lined with vegetation, usually in hedgerows; 14–18 eggs; 1 brood; March–May.
FEEDING Eats mostly seeds and row crops such as corn and wheat; succulent green leaves in spring; insects when breeding.

NOISY TAKEOFF
When the Gray Partridge takes flight its wings make a loud, whirring sound.

OCCURRENCE
Primarily agricultural fields of crops including corn, wheat, and oats, as well as associated hedgerows and fallow grasslands. Most birds are nonmigratory, but there is some movement by eastern birds after breeding.

SIMILAR SPECIES

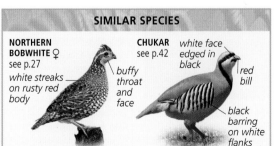

NORTHERN BOBWHITE ♀
see p.27
white streaks on rusty red body

CHUKAR
see p.42
white face edged in black
buffy throat and face
red bill
black barring on white flanks

Length **11–13in (28–33cm)**	Wingspan **17–20in (43–51cm)**	Weight **12–18oz (350–500g)**
Social **Family groups**	Lifespan **Up to 4 years**	Status **Secure**

| Order **Galliformes** | Family **Phasianidae** | Species *Phasianus colchicus* |

Ring-necked Pheasant

long tail

pale rump

short, round wings

MALE

pointed tail

FEMALE

IN FLIGHT

long, pointed tail

green-black head

orange-copper flanks

MALE (DARK FORM)

pale brown body

bold black markings

red face wattles

FEMALE

iridescent ear tufts

white neck ring

iridescent bronze sheen

barred underparts

MALE

FLIGHT: bursts vertically from cover on loud rapid wing beats; levels off, flaps, then glides.

A native of Asia, the variable-looking Ring-necked Pheasant was originally introduced in North America for recreational hunting purposes, and is now widely distributed across North America. Birds released after being bred in captivity are used to supplement natural reproduction for hunting purposes. In the wild, several females may lay eggs in the same nest—a phenomenon called "egg-dumping." There is a less common dark form, which can be distinguished principally because it lacks the distinctive white band around the neck.

VOICE Male emits a loud, raucous, explosive double note, *Karrk-KORK*, followed by loud wing-flapping; both sexes cackle when flushed.

NESTING Shallow bowl composed of grasses, usually on ground in tall grass or among low shrubs; 7–15 eggs; 1 brood; March–June.

FEEDING Feeds on corn and other grain, seeds, fruit, row crops, grass, leaves and shoots; eats insects when available.

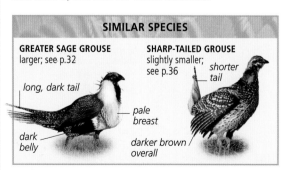

SIMILAR SPECIES

GREATER SAGE GROUSE larger; see p.32

long, dark tail

dark belly

pale breast

SHARP-TAILED GROUSE slightly smaller; see p.36

shorter tail

darker brown overall

FLUSHED OUT
The Ring-necked Pheasant is a powerful flier when alarmed or flushed out of its cover.

OCCURRENCE
Widespread across southern Canada and the US; prefers mixture of active agricultural crops (especially corn fields), fallow fields, and hedgerows; also cattail marshes and wooded river bottoms. The Ring-necked Pheasant is native to Asia from the Caucasus east to China.

| Length **19½–28in (50–70cm)** | Wingspan **30–34in (76–86cm)** | Weight **1¼–6½lb (0.5–3kg)** |
| Social **Solitary/Flocks** | Lifespan **Up to 4 years** | Status **Secure** |

Family **Anatidae**

WATERFOWL

Recent scientific studies indicate that waterfowl are closely related to gamebirds. Most species molt all their flight feathers at once after breeding, making them flightless for several weeks until they grow new ones.

GEESE

Ornithologists group geese and swans together into the subfamily Anserinae. Intermediate in body size and neck length between swans and ducks, geese are more terrestrial than either, often being seen grazing on dry land. Like swans, geese pair for life. They are also highly social, and most species are migratory, flying south for the winter in large flocks.

SWANS

Swans are are essentially large, long-necked geese. Their heavier weight makes them ungainly on land, and they tend to be more aquatic than their smaller relatives. On water, however, they are extremely graceful. When feeding, a swan stretches its long neck to reach water plants at the bottom, submerging up to half its body as it does so. The Trumpeter Swan is North America's largest native waterfowl, growing up to to 5ft (1.5m) long, and weighing up to 25lb (12kg).

DUCKS

Classified in their own subfamily, called the Anatinae, ducks are more varied than swans or geese, with many more species. They are loosely grouped by their feeding habits. Dabblers, or puddle ducks, such as the Mallard, teals, and wigeons, eat plants and other edible matter like snails. They feed by upending on the surface of shallow water. By contrast, diving ducks, a group that includes scaups, scoters, eiders, mergansers, and the Ruddy Duck, dive for their food deep underwater.

INSTANT TAKEOFF
Puddle ducks like the Mallard can shoot out of the water and into the air.

GAGGLING GEESE
Gregarious Snow Geese form large, noisy flocks during migration and on winter feeding grounds.

Order **Anseriformes**	Family **Anatidae**	Species ***Dendrocygna autumnalis***

Black-bellied Whistling-Duck

white wing bar

all-black underwing

ADULT

IN FLIGHT

pink feet extend beyond tail

wings dark underneath

gray face and upper neck

pale eye-ring

pinkish red bill

ADULT

chestnut upperparts

chestnut neck and breast

pale patch on wing

ADULT

black belly

short, black tail

long, pink, rubbery-looking legs

FLIGHT: flies with slow wing beats, with legs extending beyond body and neck drooping.

The Black-bellied Whistling-Duck is one of only two North American species of whistling-duck. Unlike most other waterfowl, they have long legs and an upright posture when standing. Whistling-ducks used to be known as "tree-ducks" because they perch on trees while they roost and nest. With its distinctive red bill and long, pink legs, the Black-bellied Whistling-Duck is spectacular and unmistakable.

VOICE Soft wheezy series of 5–6 notes *pit pit weee do dew*; flight calls include a *chit-chit-chit*, often heard at night.

NESTING Tree holes, occasionally on ground, sometimes uses nest boxes; 9–18 eggs; 1–2 broods; April–October.

FEEDING Feeds on seeds in agricultural fields or submerged vegetation in shallow water; also eats insects and mollusks; largely nocturnal feeder.

UPRIGHT STANCE
Long necks and an upright posture help these ducks to keep a sharp eye out for predators.

SIMILAR SPECIES

FULVOUS WHISTLING-DUCK
dark legs; see p.47

tawny head and belly

UNDERCARRIAGE
Whistling-ducks drop their legs down and stretch their necks forward when landing.

OCCURRENCE
Prefers shallow, freshwater habitats; rice fields are a common foraging habitat; also occurs along shorelines and mud bars. Casual west to southeastern California and occasionally east as far as Florida. Northernmost populations move south for the winter, but generally resident.

Length **18½–20in (47–51cm)**	Wingspan **34–36in (86–91cm)**	Weight **23–35oz (650–1025g)**
Social **Flocks**	Lifespan **Up to 8 years**	Status **Localized**

Order **Anseriformes**	Family **Anatidae**	Species *Dendrocygna bicolor*

Fulvous Whistling-Duck

ADULT

dark wings

white rump

gray feet extend beyond tail

IN FLIGHT

tawny head and underparts

tawny buff head and neck

faint crest

gray bill

ADULT

white flank plumes

barred back

tawny buff underparts

Although often thought of as dabbling ducks, whistling-ducks act more like swans, as they form long-term pairs, but without an elaborate courtship display, and the male helps to raise the brood. The Fulvous Whistling-Duck is a widespread species in tropical regions, but in the US it is closely associated with rice fields, where numbers of these noisy birds have steadily recovered from the use of pesticides in the 1960s.

VOICE High-pitched squeaky *pi-teeeew*; often calls in flight.

NESTING Simple bowl-shaped nest made of plant matter; among dense floating plants, or on ground; 6–20 eggs; 1 brood; April–September.

FEEDING Filter feeds on rice, seeds of water plants, insects, worms, snails, and clams by swimming, wading, or dabbling along or below the surface.

FLIGHT: fairly shallow wing beats; legs extend beyond tail.

BOTTOMS UP!
When feeding in water, the bird often up-ends to feed on snails and submerged rice seeds.

SHORT NECKED
The Fulvous Whistling-Duck is shorter-necked than its black-bellied cousin, and can be confused with other ducks when its long legs are hidden.

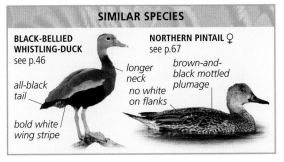

SIMILAR SPECIES

BLACK-BELLIED WHISTLING-DUCK see p.46

all-black tail

bold white wing stripe

NORTHERN PINTAIL ♀ see p.67

longer neck

no white on flanks

brown-and-black mottled plumage

OCCURRENCE
Permanent resident in southern Texas and Florida; range expands in summer to coastal Texas and Louisiana. In the US, often found in rice fields, together with the Black-bellied Whistling-Duck. Casual vagrant as far north as British Columbia and Nova Scotia.

Length **16½–20in (42–51cm)**	Wingspan **33–37in (85–93cm)**	Weight **19–34oz (550–975g)**
Social **Flocks**	Lifespan **Up to 7 years**	Status **Localized**

| Order **Anseriformes** | Family **Anatidae** | Species *Anser albifrons* |

Greater White-fronted Goose

gray wing feathers

ADULT

white rump band

IN FLIGHT

white tip to tail

white flank streak

pink bill with white base

brownish gray head

darker chocolate-brown upperparts

larger body

longer legs, bill, and neck

bright orange legs

MALE
A. a. frontalis **(TUNDRA)**

A. a gambeli (TULE)

brown underparts with black bands

dull yellowish orange bill

no belly barring

JUVENILE

The Greater White-fronted Goose is the most widespread goose in the Northern Hemisphere. It is easily distinguished by its black-barred belly and the patch of white at the base of its bill. There are five subspecies, two of which are most commonly seen in North America. The "Tundra" (*A. a. frontalis*), makes up the largest population, breeding across northwestern Canada and western Alaska. The "Tule" (*A. a. gambeli*), while the largest in stature, occurs in the fewest numbers, and is restricted in range to northwest Canada.

VOICE Laugh-like *klow-yo* or *klew-yo-yo;* very musical in a flock.
NESTING Bowl-shaped nest made of plant material, lined with down, constructed near water; 3–7 eggs; 1 brood; May–August.
FEEDING Eats sedges, grasses, berries, and plants on both land and water in summer; feeds on grasses, seeds, and grains in winter.

FLIGHT: strong, direct flight; flies alone, in multiple lines, or in a V-formation.

FLIGHT FORMATIONS
This heavy-bodied, powerful flier can often be seen in tightly packed flocks.

SIMILAR SPECIES

CANADA GOOSE
see p.52

black head, neck, and bill

white chin strap

HEAVY GRAZER
Grass is the major component of this goose's diet.

OCCURRENCE
Different habitats are utilized, both for breeding and wintering. Nesting areas include tundra ponds and lakes, dry rocky fields, and grassy slopes in Alaska and northern Canada. In winter, coastal marshes, inland wetlands, agricultural fields, and refuges are used along Pacific Coast, southern US, and Mexico.

| Length **25–32in (64–81cm)** | Wingspan **4¼–5¼ft (1.3–1.6m)** | Weight **4–6½lb (1.8–3kg)** |
| Social **Flocks** | Lifespan **Up to 22 years** | Status **Secure** |

Order **Anseriformes**	Family **Anatidae**	Species ***Chen canagica***

Emperor Goose

ADULT

all gray underwing

short neck

dark underparts

white tail

IN FLIGHT

white head and nape

small pink bill

silver-gray plumage with thin black-and-white edges

black throat

MALE

scalloped appearance

orange legs

dusky head

yellow legs

JUVENILE

In North America, this small, elegant goose is restricted to coastal Alaska. With its white head, black throat, and patterned silvery-gray body and wings, the Emperor Goose is a distinctive bird. During migration, they congregate to feed in large estuaries along the Alaskan Peninsula. The Alaskan population of these birds declined drastically during the 1960s–80s, but has remained stable since then.

VOICE Calls rapid high-pitched *kla-ha kla-ha kla-ha*, deep ringing *u-lugh u-lugh* when alarmed; on ground, also grunts.

NESTING Scrape-type nest usually lined with grasses in elevated areas along rivers, marshes, in permafrost, and dead vegetation; 3–6 eggs; 1 brood; May–August.

FEEDING Eats mostly roots, shoots, and bulbs during nesting; in winter, feeds mostly on clams, mussels, and plants.

FLIGHT: direct with comparatively rapid wing beats for a goose; migrates in large flocks.

LONG-TERM RELATIONSHIP
The Emperor Goose is a monogamous species, with pairs forming life-long bonds.

SIMILAR SPECIES

SNOW GOOSE (BLUE FORM); see p.50
bigger bill with black patch
blacker back
pale wing feathers

ROSS'S GOOSE (BLUE FORM); see p.51
orange bill
different neck pattern
white wing feathers and belly

OCCURRENCE
Breeds in Arctic and subarctic coastal salt marsh habitats in Alaska and eastern Russia. A large proportion of the population nests within 9 miles (15km) of the coast at Yukon-Kuskokwim Delta. Majority winter on the Alaska Peninsula and on ice-free beaches in the Aleutian Islands.

Length **26in (66cm)**	Wingspan **4ft (1.2m)**	Weight **3½–6¼lb (1.6–2.8kg)**
Social **Flocks**	Lifespan **Up to 22 years**	Status **Vulnerable**

| Order **Anseriformes** | Family **Anatidae** | Species **Chen caerulescens** |

Snow Goose

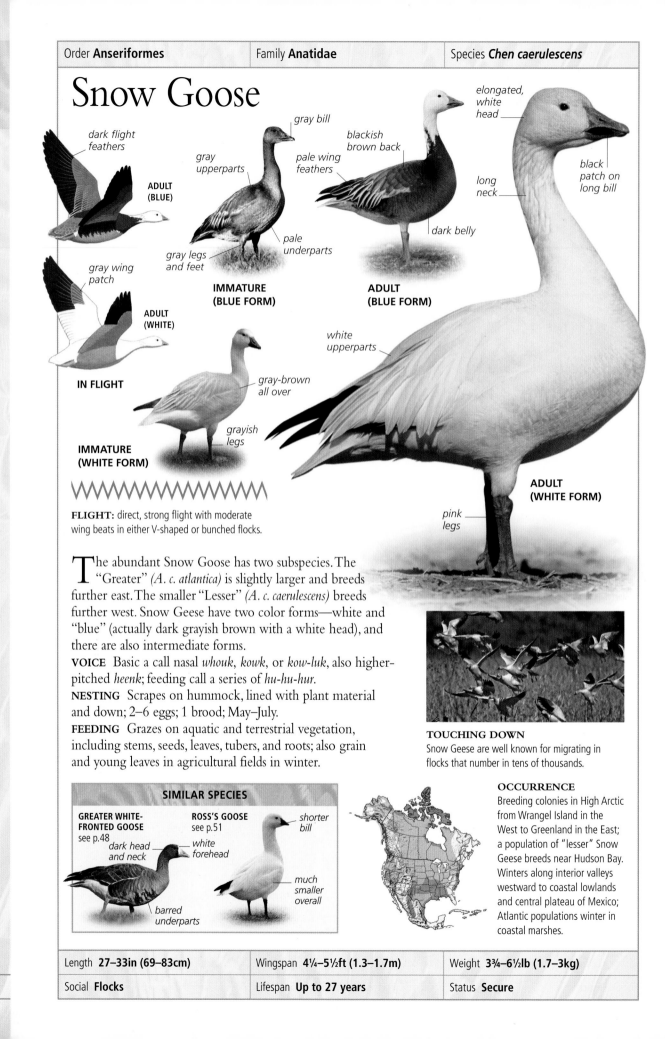

dark flight feathers

ADULT (BLUE)

gray bill

gray upperparts

pale wing feathers

blackish brown back

elongated, white head

black patch on long bill

long neck

dark belly

pale underparts

gray legs and feet

IMMATURE (BLUE FORM)

ADULT (BLUE FORM)

white upperparts

gray wing patch

ADULT (WHITE)

IN FLIGHT

gray-brown all over

grayish legs

IMMATURE (WHITE FORM)

ADULT (WHITE FORM)

pink legs

FLIGHT: direct, strong flight with moderate wing beats in either V-shaped or bunched flocks.

The abundant Snow Goose has two subspecies. The "Greater" (*A. c. atlantica*) is slightly larger and breeds further east. The smaller "Lesser" (*A. c. caerulescens*) breeds further west. Snow Geese have two color forms—white and "blue" (actually dark grayish brown with a white head), and there are also intermediate forms.

VOICE Basic a call nasal *whouk*, *kowk*, or *kow-luk*, also higher-pitched *heenk*; feeding call a series of *hu-hu-hur*.

NESTING Scrapes on hummock, lined with plant material and down; 2–6 eggs; 1 brood; May–July.

FEEDING Grazes on aquatic and terrestrial vegetation, including stems, seeds, leaves, tubers, and roots; also grain and young leaves in agricultural fields in winter.

TOUCHING DOWN
Snow Geese are well known for migrating in flocks that number in tens of thousands.

OCCURRENCE
Breeding colonies in High Arctic from Wrangel Island in the West to Greenland in the East; a population of "lesser" Snow Geese breeds near Hudson Bay. Winters along interior valleys westward to coastal lowlands and central plateau of Mexico; Atlantic populations winter in coastal marshes.

SIMILAR SPECIES		

GREATER WHITE-FRONTED GOOSE
see p.48

ROSS'S GOOSE
see p.51

shorter bill

dark head and neck

white forehead

much smaller overall

barred underparts

see p.48 ... see p.51

| Length **27–33in (69–83cm)** | Wingspan **4¼–5½ft (1.3–1.7m)** | Weight **3¾–6½lb (1.7–3kg)** |
| Social **Flocks** | Lifespan **Up to 27 years** | Status **Secure** |

Order **Anseriformes**	Family **Anatidae**	Species *Chen rossii*

Ross's Goose

ADULT (WHITE)
black wing tips

IN FLIGHT

light gray crown
gray wash on upperparts
dusky line through eye

IMMATURE (WHITE FORM)

round head
short, triangular bill
short, deeply furrowed neck

clean white upperparts

mostly dark brown upperparts
white rump and tail

ADULT (BLUE FORM)

reddish pink legs

ADULT (WHITE FORM)

FLIGHT: strong and direct, with rapid wing beats.

This diminutive white goose is not much bigger than a Mallard, and half the weight of a Snow Goose; like its larger relative, it also has a rare "blue" form. About 95 percent of Ross's Geese nest at a single sanctuary in Arctic Canada, the rest breed along Hudson Bay and at several island locations. Hunting reduced the population to just 6,000 in the early 1950s, but the species has rebounded substantially, becoming more common along the East Coast as numbers improve.
VOICE Call a *keek keek keeek*, higher-pitched than Snow Goose; also a harsh, low *kork* or *kowk*; quiet when feeding.
NESTING Plant materials placed on ground, usually in colonies with Lesser Snow Geese; 3–5 eggs; 1 brood; June–August.
FEEDING Grazes on grasses, sedges, and small grains.

TRAVELING IN FAMILIES
Family groups migrate thousands of miles together, usually from northern Canada to central California.

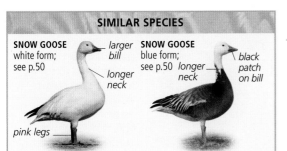

SIMILAR SPECIES

SNOW GOOSE
white form;
see p.50
larger bill
longer neck
pink legs

SNOW GOOSE
blue form;
see p.50
longer neck
black patch on bill

OCCURRENCE
Breeding grounds are amidst tundra in a number of scattered, High Arctic locations. Main wintering areas in California. On the wintering grounds, it feeds in agricultural fields, and also grasslands. Roosts overnight in several types of wetlands.

Length **22½–25in (57–64cm)**	Wingspan **3¼ft (1.1m)**	Weight **1¾–4½lb (0.85–2kg)**
Social **Flocks**	Lifespan **Up to 21 years**	Status **Localized**

Order **Anseriformes**	Family **Anatidae**	Species **Branta canadensis**

Canada Goose

plain grayish brown wings with darker flight feathers

ADULT

IN FLIGHT

white u-shaped patch on rump

very long neck

black head

grayish brown upperparts and sides

broad white chin strap

paler upper breast

white undertail feathers

ADULT

smaller, white chin strap

ADULT

dark brown overall

The Canada Goose is the most common, widespread, and familiar goose in North America. Given its colossal range, it is not surprising that the Canada Goose has much geographic variation, and 12 subspecies have been recognized. With the exception of the Cackling Goose, from which it has recently been separated, it is difficult to confuse it, with its distinctive white chin strap, black head and neck, and grayish brown body, with any other species of goose. It is a monogamous species, and once pairs are formed, they stay together for life.

VOICE Male call *honk* or *bark*; females have higher pitched *hrink*.
NESTING Scrape lined with available plant matter and down, near water; 1–2 broods; 2–12 eggs; May–August.
FEEDING Grazes on grasses, sedges, leaves, seeds, agricultural crops and berries; also insects.

FLIGHT: strong and direct with fairly slow, deep wing beats; often flies in V-formation.

TRICK OF THE LIGHT
A low sun can play tricks—these birds are actually pale grayish underneath.

SIMILAR SPECIES

GREATER WHITE-FRONTED GOOSE
see p.48

white on base of pink bill

bright orange legs

CACKLING GOOSE
see p.53

steep forehead

smaller overall

OCCURRENCE
Variety of inland breeding habitats near water, including grassy urban areas, marshes, prairie, parkland, coastal temperate forest, northern coniferous forest, and Arctic tundra. Winters in agricultural fields, mudflats, saltwater marshes, lakes, and rivers.

Length **2¼–3½ft (0.7–1.1m)**	Wingspan **4¼–5½ft (1.3–1.7m)**	Weight **6½–9¾lb (3–4.4kg)**
Social **Flocks**	Lifespan **Up to 25 years**	Status **Secure**

| Order **Anseriformes** | Family **Anatidae** | Species *Branta hutchinsii* |

Cackling Goose

plain grayish brown wings

ADULT

small, black head

white u-shaped patch on rump

IN FLIGHT

broad, white neck ring

black line separates white chin strap

darker breast

ADULT
B. h. leucopareia

dark brown breast

ADULT
B. h. minima

small stubby bill

white chin strap

no black under chin

pale breast

black tail

ADULT
B. h. hutchinsii

The Cackling Goose has recently been split from the Canada Goose; it can be distinguished from the latter by its short stubby bill, steep forehead, and short neck. There are four subspecies of Cackling Goose, which vary in breast color, ranging from dark on *C. h. minima,* fairly dark on *C. h. leucopareia,* and pale on *C. h. hutchinsii.* The Cackling Goose is much smaller than all subspecies of Canada Goose, except the "Lesser" Canada Goose, which has a longer neck and a less sloped forehead.

VOICE Male call a *honk* or *bark;* females have higher pitched *hrink;* also high-pitched yelps.

NESTING Scrape lined with available plant matter and down; 2–8 eggs; 1 brood; May–August.

FEEDING Consumes plants in summer; in winter, grazes on grass livestock and dairy pastures; also in agricultural fields.

FLIGHT: strong with rapid wing beats; flies in bunched V–formations.

LITTLE GEESE
Cackling Geese are tiny when seen together with the larger Canada Goose.

OCCURRENCE
At the northernmost fringe of the Canada Goose's range, in the tundra, it breeds on rocky tundra slopes from the Aleutians east to Baffin Island and Hudson Bay. Winters from British Columbia to California, also central US, Texas, and New Mexico in pastures and agricultural fields.

SIMILAR SPECIES

CANADA GOOSE see p.52
more sloped forehead
larger overall (except one subspecies)

BRANT see p.54
all black head
thin white neck ring

| Length **21½–30in (55–75cm)** | Wingspan **4¼–5ft (1.3–1.5m)** | Weight **2–6½lb (0.9–3kg)** |
| Social **Flocks** | Lifespan **Unknown** | Status **Secure** |

| Order **Anseriformes** | Family **Anatidae** | Species *Branta bernicla* |

Brant

pale bars across wings

ADULT (WESTERN)

ADULT (EASTERN)

white rump

black neck and head

IN FLIGHT

grayish white flank patch

broad white necklace crosses throat

dark gray-brown upperparts

black chest

bold, white rump

small, white "necklace" not crossing throat

barred flanks with pale belly

black neck stops abruptly at breast

bold, barred flanks

very dark belly

ADULT
B. b. nigracans (WESTERN)

B. b. hrota (EASTERN)

A small-billed, dark, stocky sea goose, the Brant winters on both the east and west coasts of North America. There are two subspecies in the US (three overall)—the pale-bellied "Atlantic" Brant (*B. b. hrota*), found in the east, and the darker "Black" Brant (*B. b. nigricans*), found in the west. In addition, there is an intermediate gray-bellied form that winters in the Puget Sound region on the Washington State coast. Unlike other North American geese, the Brant feeds mainly on eelgrass in winter.

VOICE Nasal *cruk*, harsh-sounding in tone; rolling series of *cut cut cut cronk*, with an upward inflection at end.

NESTING Scrape lined with grass, plant matter, and down on islands or gravel spits; 3–5 eggs; 1 brood; May–July.

FEEDING Eats grass and sedges when nesting; eelgrass in winter; also green algae, salt marsh plants, and mollusks.

FLIGHT: rapid and strong; low, irregular flight formations.

GRASSY MEAL
In winter, Brants forage almost exclusively on eel grass between the high and low tide marks.

OCCURRENCE
Breeds in colonies in northern Canada and Alaska, and winters along both Pacific and Atlantic coasts. The western breeding population of the Brant ("Black") winters from the Aleutian Islands to northern Mexico, while the pale-bellied form ("Atlantic") is restricted in range to the East Coast.

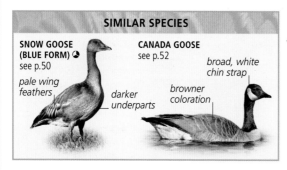

SIMILAR SPECIES

SNOW GOOSE (BLUE FORM) ⚥
see p.50

pale wing feathers

darker underparts

CANADA GOOSE
see p.52

broad, white chin strap

browner coloration

| Length **22–26in (56–66cm)** | Wingspan **3½–4ft (1.1–1.2m)** | Weight **2½–4lb (1–1.8kg)** |
| Social **Flocks** | Lifespan **Up to 25 years** | Status **Secure** |

| Order **Anseriformes** | Family **Anatidae** | Species **Cygnus olor** |

Mute Swan

ADULT

extended neck

IN FLIGHT

long, pointed tail extends past toes

black-based dusky bill

blotchy brown body

JUVENILE

small knob on bill

FEMALE

swollen knob during breeding

MALE

conspicuous black knob at base of orange bill

white overall

often arches wings over back

large, heavy body

long, "S" shaped neck

ADULT

One of the heaviest birds in North America, the Mute Swan was introduced from Europe due to its graceful appearance on water, if not on land, and easy domestication. However, this is an extremely territorial and aggressive bird. When threatened, it points its bill downwards, arches its wings, hisses, and then attacks. Displacement of native waterfowl species and overgrazing by this species have led to efforts to reduce its numbers in North America.

VOICE Not mute; hisses, grunts, snorts, and snores; during courtship, trumpets, although more quietly than other swans.

NESTING Platform nest of plant materials, built on ground near water; 4–8 eggs; 1–2 broods; March–October.

FEEDING Dabbles, dips, and upends, mainly for underwater plants, but occasionally for small creatures too.

FLIGHT: strong, steady wing beats; creating a distinctive whirring and throbbing sound.

FORMATION FLYING
Groups of Mute Swans will sometimes fly in a line, and at other times, as here, they will arrange themselves in a "V" formation.

SIMILAR SPECIES

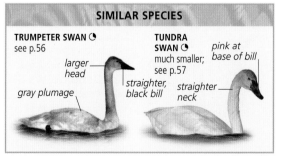

TRUMPETER SWAN ☾
see p.56

larger head

gray plumage

TUNDRA SWAN ☾
much smaller; see p.57

straighter, black bill

pink at base of bill

straighter neck

OCCURRENCE
Bulk of population is found along the Atlantic Coast from Maine to North Carolina; smaller populations around the Great Lakes and southern British Columbia. Breeds and lives year-round on sluggish rivers, ponds, or lakes, preferring still water with emergent vegetation.

| Length **4–5ft (1.2–1.5m)** | Wingspan **6½–7½ft (2–2.3m)** | Weight **12–32lb (5.5–14.5kg)** |
| Social **Pairs/Family groups** | Lifespan **Up to 21 years** | Status **Localized** |

| Order **Anseriformes** | Family **Anatidae** | Species *Cygnus buccinator* |

Trumpeter Swan

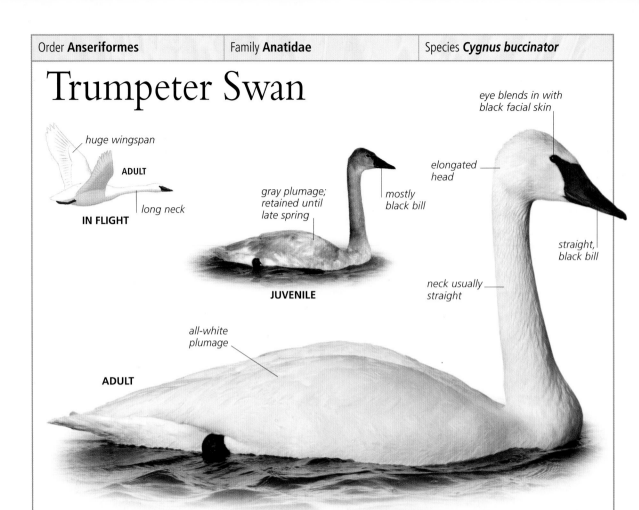

huge wingspan

ADULT

long neck

IN FLIGHT

eye blends in with black facial skin

elongated head

gray plumage; retained until late spring

mostly black bill

straight, black bill

neck usually straight

JUVENILE

all-white plumage

ADULT

North America's quintessential swan and heaviest waterfowl, the Trumpeter Swan is a magnificent sight to behold. This species has made a remarkable comeback after numbers were severely reduced by hunting in the 1600-1800s; by the mid-1930s, fewer than a hundred were known to exist. Active reintroduction efforts were made in the upper Midwest and Ontario to re-establish the species to its former breeding range. The Trumpeter Swan's characteristic far-reaching call is usually the best way to identify it.

VOICE Call nasal, resonant *oh-OH* reminiscent of French horn.
NESTING Large mound made of plant matter on raised areas near or in freshwater; 3–6 eggs; 1 brood; April–September.
FEEDING Eats algae and aquatic plants, including moss, at or below the surface; feeds on grain in pastures and fields.

FLIGHT: slow, heavy, ponderous wing beats; "runs" on water's surface when taking off.

RUSTY STAINING
Trumpeter Swans often have rufous-stained heads and necks due to probing in iron-rich mud.

OCCURRENCE
Alaskan and northern Canadian breeders go south to winter; others remain year round at local places such as Yellowstone National Park. Found on freshwater lakes and marshes with plenty of vegetation on which to feed. Also found on estuaries in winter.

SIMILAR SPECIES

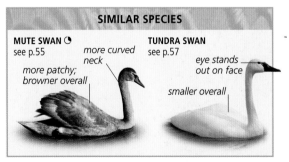

MUTE SWAN ◐
see p.55

more curved neck

more patchy; browner overall

TUNDRA SWAN
see p.57

eye stands out on face

smaller overall

| Length **4¼–5ft (1.3–1.5m)** | Wingspan **6½ft (2m)** | Weight **17–28lb (7.5–12.5kg)** |
| Social **Flocks** | Lifespan **Up to 24 years** | Status **Secure** |

Order **Anseriformes**	Family **Anatidae**	Species *Cygnus columbianus*

Tundra Swan

ADULT

small head and bill

fairly thick neck

dark legs

IN FLIGHT

dull grayish body

dirty pink bill

JUVENILE

eye stands out from face at close range

yellow facial skin next to eye

large yellow bill patch

BEWICK'S SWAN

all-white plumage

ADULT

Nesting in the Arctic tundra, this well-named species is North America's most widespread and smallest swan. Two populations exist, with one wintering in the West, and the other along the East Coast. The Tundra Swan can be confused with the Trumpeter Swan, but their different calls immediately distinguish the two species. When they are silent, weight and bill structure are the best way to tell them apart. In Eurasia, this species is known as Bewick's Swan and possesses a larger yellow patch at the base of its bill.

VOICE Clear, high-pitched yodelling *whoo-hooo* calls mixed with garbles, yelping, and barking sounds.

NESTING Mound-shaped nest made of plant matter near water; 3–6 eggs; 1 brood; May–September.

FEEDING Eats aquatic vegetation, insects, mollusks; also grain.

FLIGHT: flight pattern like that of other swans but with slightly faster wing beats.

LARGE WINTER FLOCKS
Its size, white plumage, and flocking habits make the Tundra Swan a conspicuous species.

SIMILAR SPECIES

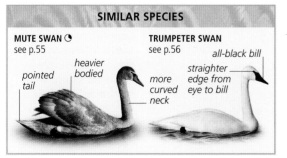

MUTE SWAN ☾
see p.55

pointed tail

heavier bodied

TRUMPETER SWAN
see p.56

more curved neck

straighter edge from eye to bill

all-black bill

OCCURRENCE
Nests around lakes and pools in northern tundra from the Aleutians to the Yukon, and east to northwest Quebec. Winters in southern British Columbia, western US, and mid-Atlantic states, mostly New Jersey to south Carolina. Winter habitat includes shallow coastal bays, ponds, and lakes.

Length **4–5ft (1.2–1.5m)**	Wingspan **6¼–7¼ft (1.9–2.2m)**	Weight **12–18lb (5.5–8kg)**
Social **Flocks**	Lifespan **Up to 21 years**	Status **Secure**

Order **Anseriformes**	Family **Anatidae**	Species *Aix sponsa*

Wood Duck

blue wing patch

long wings

MALE

IN FLIGHT

head held high

bold, tear-shaped eye-ring

smaller crest

brownish breast

white-edged feathers

FEMALE

subdued facial pattern

brown eye

grayish bill

IMMATURE

burgundy flanks

long, dark tail

MALE

red eye

complex, white facial markings

helmet-like head profile

black tip of bill

white-flecked maroon breast appears black at a distance

white, vertical breast stripe

The male Wood Duck is perhaps the most striking of all North American ducks. With its bright plumage, red eye and bill, and its long sleek crest that gives its head a helmet-shaped profile, the male is unmistakable. It is related to the Mandarin Duck of Asia. The Wood Duck is very dependent on mature swampy forestland, and is typically found on swamps, shallow lakes, ponds, and park settings that are surrounded by trees. Although it adapts to human activity, it is quite shy. When swimming, the Wood Duck can be seen jerking its head front to back. Of all waterfowl, this is the only species that regularly raises two broods each season.

VOICE Male gives a wheezy upslurred whistle *zweeet*; female's call a double-note, rising *oh-eek oh-eek*.

NESTING Nests in natural tree cavities or nest boxes in close proximity to water; 10–13 eggs; 2 broods; April–August.

FEEDING Forages for seeds, tree fruits, and small acorns; also spiders, insects, and crustaceans.

FLIGHT: rapid flight with deep wing beats; flies with head up; leaps straight off the water.

PLAIN BELLY
Wings raised, a male reveals one of the only plain areas of its plumage—its pale belly and undertail.

OCCURRENCE
Usually found throughout the year, along rivers, streams, and creeks, in swamps, and marshy areas. Has a preference for permanent bodies of water. If good aquatic feeding areas are unavailable, the Wood Duck feeds in open areas, including agricultural fields.

SIMILAR SPECIES

BUFFLEHEAD ♀
see p.83

white on cheek

shorter neck

shorter tail

HOODED MERGANSER ♀
narrower wings; see p.86

no eye-ring

long, tan crest

Length **18½–21½in (47–54cm)**	Wingspan **26–29in (66–73cm)**	Weight **16–30oz (450–850g)**
Social **Small flocks**	Lifespan **Up to 18 years**	Status **Secure**

Order **Anseriformes**	Family **Anatidae**	Species *Anas strepera*

Gadwall

conspicuous white patch

mostly white underwings

MALE (WINTER)

white belly **IN FLIGHT**

silvery gray area

rusty sides

MALE (ECLIPSE)

brown, scalloped back

dark eyestripe

white wing patch

FEMALE

dark grayish overall

brown, rounded head

black bill

black uppertail

MALE (WINTER)

orange-yellow legs

finely patterned gray flanks and breast

Although the Gadwall's appearance is somewhat somber, many birders consider this duck one of North America's most elegant species because of the subtlety of its plumage. Despite being common and widespread, Gadwalls are often overlooked because of their retiring behavior and relatively quiet vocalizations. This dabbling duck is slightly smaller and more delicate than the Mallard, yet female Gadwalls are often mistaken for female Mallards. Gadwalls associate with other species, especially in winter.

VOICE Low, raspy *meep* or *reb* given in quick succession; female *quack* similar to that of female Mallard, but higher-pitched and more nasal; high-pitched *peep*, or *pe-peep*; both sexes give *tickety-tickety-tickety* chatter while feeding.

NESTING Bowl nest made of plant material in a scrape; 8–12 eggs; 1 brood; April–August.

FEEDING Dabbles on the surface or below for seeds, aquatic vegetation, and invertebrates, including mollusks and insects.

FLIGHT: direct flight with fast wing beats; leaps straight off the water.

BROOD ON THE MOVE
Females lead their ducklings from their nest to a brood-rearing habitat that provides cover and ample food for the ducklings to forage.

SIMILAR SPECIES

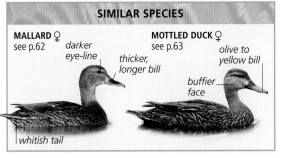

MALLARD ♀
see p.62

darker eye-line

thicker, longer bill

whitish tail

MOTTLED DUCK ♀
see p.63

olive to yellow bill

buffier face

OCCURRENCE
From the western prairie pothole country of Canada and the northern US, the Gadwall's range has expanded as it has adapted to man-made bodies of water, such as reservoirs and ponds. In winter, mostly found on lakes, marshes, and along rivers.

Length **18–22½in (46–57cm)**	Wingspan **33in (84cm)**	Weight **18–45oz (500–1,250g)**
Social **Winter flocks**	Lifespan **Up to 19 years**	Status **Secure**

| Order **Anseriformes** | Family **Anatidae** | Species *Anas americana* |

American Wigeon

MALE (BREEDING)

white underwing patch

rufous-edged wing feathers

dark smudge around eye

gray head

narrow, black line along bill

IN FLIGHT

gray head contrasts with pinkish brown breast and flanks

long, pointed tail

warm brown breast and flanks

FEMALE

cream forehead and crown

green band from eye to nape

MALE (BREEDING)

black-tipped bill

black rump

pinkish brown flanks

Often found in mixed flocks with other ducks, the American Wigeon is a common and widespread, medium-sized dabbling duck. This bird is an opportunist that loiters around other diving ducks and coots, feeding on the vegetation they dislodge. It is more social during migration and in the nonbreeding season than when breeding.

VOICE Slow and fast whistles; male's most common call a slow, high-pitched, wheezy, three-syllable *whew-whew-whew*, with middle note loudest; also, a faster *whee* whistle.

NESTING Depression lined with plant material and down, usually in tall grass away from water; 5–10 eggs; 1 brood; May–August.

FEEDING Grazes on grass, clover, algae, and, in agricultural fields; feeds on many seeds, insects, mollusks, and crustaceans during the breeding season.

FLIGHT: rapid, fairly deep wing beats; leaps almost vertically off the water.

COMING IN FOR LANDING
This male's cream-colored forehead is clearly visible, as is the sharp contrast between the white belly, and the pinkish breast and flanks.

FLAPPING WINGS
This bird has a white patch on its underwing, while the Eurasian Wigeon has a gray patch.

OCCURRENCE
The northernmost breeder of the dabbling ducks, occurs from Alaska to the Maritimes. Prefers pothole and grassland habitats; found almost anywhere near water in winter. Winters south to northern South America and the Caribbean, in freshwater and coastal bay habitats.

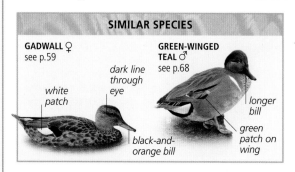

SIMILAR SPECIES

GADWALL ♀
see p.59

white patch

dark line through eye

GREEN-WINGED TEAL ♂
see p.68

longer bill

green patch on wing

black-and-orange bill

| Length **17½–23in (45–58cm)** | Wingspan **33in (84cm)** | Weight **1⅛–3lb (0.5–1.3kg)** |
| Social **Flocks** | Lifespan **Up to 21 years** | Status **Secure** |

Order **Anseriformes**	Family **Anatidae**	Species *Anas rubripes*

American Black Duck

rich violet patch

white underwing

dark tail

MALE **IN FLIGHT**

heavily streaked head and neck

olive bill

FEMALE

cinnamon-edged flank feathers

pale head

dark cap

narrow, dark eye-line

greenish yellow bill

dark body

MALE

The American Black Duck, a large dabbling duck, is closely related to the Mallard. In the past, the two species were separated by different habitat preferences—the American Black Duck preferring forested locations, and the Mallard favoring more open habitats. Over the years, these habitats became less distinct as the East was deforested and trees were planted in the Midwest. As a result, there are now many hybrids between the two species. It has also been argued that the introduction of Mallards to various areas in the East has further increased interbreeding. The American Black Duck breeds throughout a wide area in the northern part of its range. When breeding, males can be seen chasing away other males to maintain their territories.

VOICE Male's call a reedy *raeb*, given once or twice; female *quack* sounds very similar to Mallard.

NESTING Scrape lined with plant material and down, usually on ground or close to water; 4–10 eggs; 1 brood; March–September.

FEEDING An omnivore, the American Black Duck eats plant leaves and stems, roots, seeds, grains, fruit, aquatic plants, fish, and amphibians.

FLIGHT: fast, shallow, and regular; often flies in groups.

DARK PLUMAGE
This species is the darkest of all the Mallard-type ducks that occur in North America.

OCCURRENCE
Nests in eastern Canada and adjacent areas of the US in a variety of habitats including northerly and mixed hardwood forest, wooded uplands, bogs, salt- and freshwater marshes, and on islands. Resident in the central part of its range, but large numbers winter in saltwater marshes.

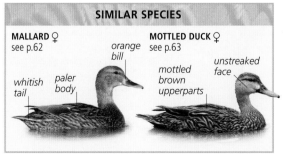

SIMILAR SPECIES

MALLARD ♀
see p.62

orange bill

whitish tail

paler body

MOTTLED DUCK ♀
see p.63

mottled brown upperparts

unstreaked face

Length **21½–23in (54–59cm)**	Wingspan **35–37in (88–95cm)**	Weight **1½–3½lb (0.7–1.6kg)**
Social **Flocks**	Lifespan **Up to 26 years**	Status **Secure**

| Order **Anseriformes** | Family **Anatidae** | Species *Anas platyrhynchos* |

Mallard

broad-based wings

short, round, pale tail

MALE (WINTER)

heavy body

short, round, pale tail

FEMALE

dark eye-line and cap

yellowish brown back

orange bill with blackish patch

FEMALE

mottled brown belly

metallic green head

grayer head

olive-yellow bill

MALE (SUMMER)

rusty underparts

IN FLIGHT

brown underparts

whitish outer tail feathers

short, black curls above white tail

blue wing patch

warm gray body

bright yellow bill

narrow, white neck collar

chestnut-brown breast

MALE (WINTER)

The Mallard is perhaps the most familiar of all ducks, and occurs in the wild all across the Northern Hemisphere. It is the ancestor of most domestic ducks, and hybrids between the wild and domestic forms are frequently seen in city lakes and ponds, often with patches of white on the breast. Mating is generally a violent affair, but outside the breeding season the wild species is strongly migratory and gregarious, sometimes forming large flocks that may join with other species.
VOICE Male's call a quiet raspy *raab*; during courtship a high-pitched whistle; female call a *quack* or repeated in series.
NESTING Scrape lined with plant matter, usually near water, often on floating vegetation; 6–15 eggs; 1 brood; February–September.
FEEDING Feeds omnivorously on insects, crustaceans, mollusks, and earthworms when breeding; otherwise largely vegetarian; takes seeds, acorns, agricultural crops, aquatic vegetation, and bread.

FLIGHT: fast, shallow, and regular; often flies in groups.

STICKING TOGETHER
The mother leads her ducklings to water soon after they hatch. She looks after them until they can fend for themselves.

OCCURRENCE
Occurs throughout the region, choosing shallow water in natural wetlands, such as marshes, prairie potholes, ponds, and ditches; can also be found in man-made habitats such as city parks and reservoirs, preferring more open habitats in winter.

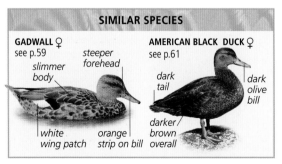

SIMILAR SPECIES

GADWALL ♀ see p.59

slimmer body

steeper forehead

white wing patch

orange strip on bill

AMERICAN BLACK DUCK ♀ see p.61

dark tail

dark olive bill

darker brown overall

| Length **19½–26in (50–65cm)** | Wingspan **32–37in (82–95cm)** | Weight **1⅞–3lb (0.9–1.4kg)** |
| Social **Flocks** | Lifespan **Up to 29 years** | Status **Secure** |

| Order **Anseriformes** | Family **Anatidae** | Species *Anas fulvigula* |

Mottled Duck

iridescent blue-green wing patch

bright white underwing

MALE

IN FLIGHT

dark eye-line

dull green to orange-yellow bill

paler breast than male

duller orange legs than male

FEMALE

unstreaked face and throat

paler edges to dark body feathers

dark body

pale buffy head and neck

no white on tail

olive-yellow bill

MALE

orange legs

A long with the American Black Duck, the Mottled Duck belongs to the so-called "Mallard complex," in which all three species are closely related and interbreed easily, especially with introduced Mallards. There is concern that the fertile hybrid ducks produced may dilute the purity of the Mottled Duck population, and so eventually displace it. The Mottled Duck is always a little smaller and darker than the similar female Mallard, and lacks a white edge to the blue wing patch.
VOICE Males give a variety of raspy *raab* calls; females *quack*.
NESTING Bowl-shaped depression constructed in dense grass; 8–12 eggs; 1 brood; January–September.
FEEDING Dabbles for aquatic vegetation, crustaceans, mollusks, insects, rice, seeds, and some small fish.

FLIGHT: direct with regular wing beats; flies at relatively low levels.

COLOR CONTRAST
The male Mottled Duck has a yellower bill than the smaller, orange-billed female.

STANDING MALE
This male has a cleaner, buffier face and brighter orange legs than the female Mottled Duck.

OCCURRENCE
Prefers shallow freshwater wetlands, breeding on coastal marshes. This nonmigratory species has distinct populations in the Gulf of Mexico between Alabama and Tamaulipas, and in central and southern Florida, though both populations may stray slightly outside this range in winter.

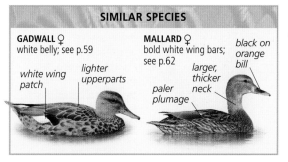

SIMILAR SPECIES

GADWALL ♀
white belly; see p.59

MALLARD ♀
bold white wing bars; see p.62

black on orange bill

white wing patch

lighter upperparts

larger, thicker neck

paler plumage

| Length **17½–24in (44–61cm)** | Wingspan **33–34in (83–87cm)** | Weight **21–46oz (0.6–1.4kg)** |
| Social **Flocks** | Lifespan **Up to 13 years** | Status **Declining** |

Order **Anseriformes**	Family **Anatidae**	Species *Anas discors*

Blue-winged Teal

powdery blue forewing with green patch

MALE (BREEDING)

white facial crescent

IN FLIGHT

white underwing stripe

broken, contrasting, white eye-ring

pale eyebrow, dark cape, and eye-line

grayish brown overall

FEMALE

pale spot at base of bill

white facial crescent

dark grayish head

black bill

MALE (FALL)

black spots on rich, buff-brown breast and flanks

white facial crescent

long, blackish bill

rich tan flanks

warmer brown overall

MALE (BREEDING)

conspicuous white patch

This small dabbling duck is a common and widespread North American breeding species. With a bold white crescent between bill and eye on its otherwise slate-gray head and neck, the male Blue-winged Teal is quite distinctive. The Blue-winged and Cinnamon Teals, along with the Northern Shoveler, constitute the three "blue-winged" ducks; this is a feature that is conspicuous when the birds are flying. The Cinnamon and the Blue-winged Teals are almost identical genetically and interbreed to form hybrids. The Blue-winged Teal winters mostly south of the US and migrates north in spring.
VOICE Male a high-pitched, raspy *peew* or low-pitched *paay* during courtship; female a loud single *quack*.
NESTING Bowl-shaped depression lined with grasses, close to water's edge, in meadows; 6–14 eggs; 1 brood; April–September.
FEEDING Eats seeds of a variety of plants; feeds heavily on insect larvae, crustaceans, and snails, when breeding.

FLIGHT: fast, twisting flight; flies in compact, small groups.

OUTSTRETCHED MALE
Wing stretch behavior shows the white feathers between the blue forewing and green rearwing.

OCCURRENCE
Nests across North America, with highest numbers in the prairie and parkland regions of the midcontinent. Prefers shallow ponds or marshes during nesting; freshwater to brackish water and (less so) saltwater marshes during migration. In winter, prefers saline environments, including mangroves.

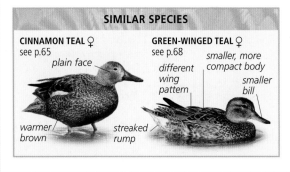

SIMILAR SPECIES

CINNAMON TEAL ♀
see p.65

plain face

warmer brown

GREEN-WINGED TEAL ♀
see p.68

smaller, more compact body

different wing pattern

smaller bill

streaked rump

Length **14½–16in (37–41cm)**	Wingspan **23½–25in (60–64cm)**	Weight **11–18oz (300–500g)**
Social **Flocks**	Lifespan **Up to 17 years**	Status **Secure**

| Order **Anseriformes** | Family **Anatidae** | Species ***Anas cyanoptera*** |

Cinnamon Teal

powdery blue forewing

MALE

IN FLIGHT

white underwing stripe

warm brown, upperparts with rust tinge

plain face pattern

shoveler-like bill

FEMALE

dull yellow legs

solid cinnamon color

conspicuous orange to red eye

long, spoon-shaped, black bill

MALE

True to his name, the male Cinnamon Teal is unmistakable in its overall rusty brown color and blazing red eyes. A fairly small duck, the Cinnamon Teal is the only North American dabbling duck species that does not breed in the Great Plains and prairies of the midcontinent. Most of its population winters in the coastal marshes and interior wetlands of Mexico. The Cinnamon Teal is common in the West, and even seen in tiny roadside pools. Closely related to both the Northern Shoveler and Blue-winged Teal, the Cinnamon Teal's wing pattern is indistinguishable from that of the latter.

VOICE Male a snuffled *chuk chuk chuk*; female a loud single *quack* and soft *gack gack gack ga*.

NESTING Shallow depression lined with grass near water; 4–16 eggs; 1 brood; March–September.

FEEDING Feeds on seeds of many plant species; adds aquatic insects, crustaceans, and snails, when breeding; omnivorous.

FLIGHT: rapid wing beats; very agile, making sharp turns.

FLOCKING TOGETHER
The cinnamon-colored males and tan females are often found in flocks.

SIMILAR SPECIES

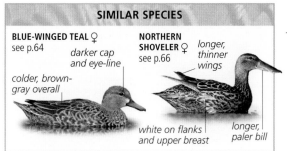

BLUE-WINGED TEAL ♀
see p.64

darker cap and eye-line

colder, brown-gray overall

NORTHERN SHOVELER ♀
see p.66

longer, thinner wings

white on flanks and upper breast

longer, paler bill

OCCURRENCE
Found in freshwater and brackish habitats of various sizes, such as marshes, reservoirs, flooded fields, ponds, ditches, and stock ponds. In the southern part of its wintering range, can also be found in tidal estuaries, salt marshes, and mangrove forests. Widespread in Central and South America.

| Length **14–17in (36–43cm)** | Wingspan **22in (56cm)** | Weight **10–17oz (275–475g)** |
| Social **Winter flocks** | Lifespan **Up to 12 years** | Status **Secure** |

Order **Anseriformes**	Family **Anatidae**	Species *Anas clypeata*

Northern Shoveler

IN FLIGHT

grayish blue wing patch

whitish tail

long bill

FEMALE

pale blue wing patch

heavy fronted

MALE

dark, narrow eye-line

brown overall

dusky olive-gray to orange bill

pale-edged, brown flank feathers

FEMALE

yellow eye

large, dark spatula-shaped bill

dark green head

MALE

white breast

chestnut belly and flanks

black-and-white rump

The Northern Shoveler is a common, medium-sized, dabbling duck found in North America and Eurasia. It is monogamous—pairs remain together longer than any other dabbler species. Its distinctive long bill is highly specialized; it is wider at the tip and contains thin, comb-like structures (called "lamellae") along the sides, used to filter food items from the water. Shovelers often form tight feeding groups, swimming close together as they sieve the water for prey.

VOICE Male call a nasal, muffled *thuk thuk…thuk thuk*; also a loud, nasal *paaaay*; female call a variety of *quacks*, singly or in a series of 4–5 descending notes.

NESTING Scrape lined with plant matter and down, in short plants, near water; 6–19 eggs; 1 brood; May–August.

FEEDING Forages for seeds; filters small crustaceans and mollusks out of the water.

FLIGHT: strong direct flight; male's wings make a rattling noise when taking off.

UPSIDE DOWN FEEDER
This male upends to feed below the water's surface, revealing his orange legs.

FILTER FEEDING
Their bills open, these ducks sieve small invertebrates from the water.

OCCURRENCE
Widespread across North America, south of the tundra. Breeds in a variety of wetlands, in edges of shallow pools with nearby tall and short grasslands. Occurs in fresh- and saltmarshes, ponds, and other shallow bodies of water in winter; does not feed on land.

SIMILAR SPECIES

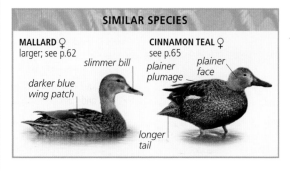

MALLARD ♀
larger; see p.62

darker blue wing patch

slimmer bill

CINNAMON TEAL ♀
see p.65

plainer plumage

plainer face

longer tail

Length **17½–20in (44–51cm)**	Wingspan **27–33in (69–84cm)**	Weight **14–29oz (400–825g)**
Social **Flocks**	Lifespan **Up to 18 years**	Status **Secure**

| Order **Anseriformes** | Family **Anatidae** | Species ***Anas acuta*** |

Northern Pintail

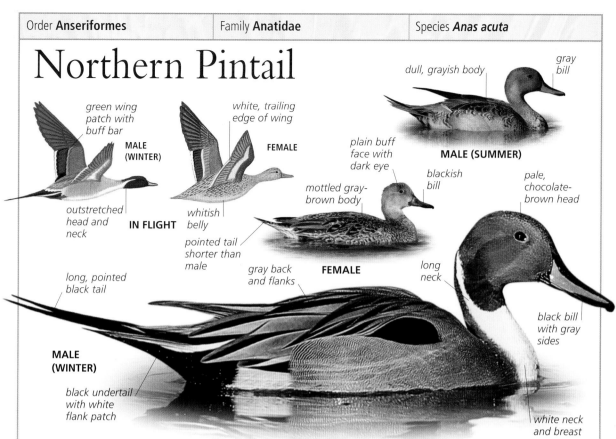

green wing patch with buff bar

MALE (WINTER)

outstretched head and neck

IN FLIGHT

white, trailing edge of wing

FEMALE

whitish belly

pointed tail shorter than male

dull, grayish body

gray bill

MALE (SUMMER)

plain buff face with dark eye

blackish bill

mottled gray-brown body

FEMALE

gray back and flanks

pale, chocolate-brown head

long neck

black bill with gray sides

long, pointed black tail

MALE (WINTER)

black undertail with white flank patch

white neck and breast

An elegant, long-necked dabbler, the Northern Pintail has extremely distinctive marking and a very long tail—in fact, the longest tail to be found on any freshwater duck. One of the earliest breeders in the year, these ducks begin nesting soon after the ice thaws. Northern Pintails were once one of the most abundant prairie breeding ducks. However, in recent decades, droughts, combined with the reduction of habitat on both their wintering and breeding grounds, have resulted in a significant decline in their population.

VOICE Male call a high-pitched rolling *prrreep prrreep;* lower-pitched wheezy *wheeeee*, which gets louder then drops off; female call a quiet, harsh *quack* or *kuk* singularly or as short series; also a loud *gaak*, often repeated.

NESTING Scrape lined with plant materials and down, usually in short grass, brush, or even in the open; 3–12 eggs; 1 brood; April–August.

FEEDING Feeds on grains, rice, seeds, aquatic weeds, insect larvae, crustaceans, and snails.

FLIGHT: fast, direct flight; can be very acrobatic in the air.

FEEDING TIME
Even when tipping up to feed, these pintails can be identified by their long, black, pointed tails.

SIMILAR SPECIES

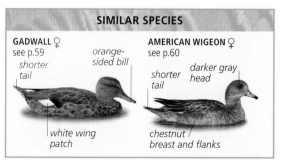

GADWALL ♀
see p.59

shorter tail

orange-sided bill

white wing patch

AMERICAN WIGEON ♀
see p.60

shorter tail

darker gray head

chestnut breast and flanks

OCCURRENCE
Widely distributed in North America; breeding in open country in shallow wetlands or meadows in mountainous forest regions. Found in tidal wetlands and saltwater habitats in migration and winter; dry harvested and flooded agricultural fields in autumn and winter.

| Length **20–30in (51–76cm)** | Wingspan **35in (89cm)** | Weight **18–44oz (500–1250g)** |
| Social **Flocks** | Lifespan **Up to 21 years** | Status **Declining** |

Order **Anseriformes**	Family **Anatidae**	Species *Anas crecca*

Green-winged Teal

MALE
green-and-black patch on hindwing

short neck

IN FLIGHT

gray flanks

rufous head

dark green ear patch

small, narrow, black bill

black-spotted breast

white vertical bar

finely detailed pattern

yellowish buff undertail feathers

MALE

horizontal, white line on sides

lacks white wing bar

A. c. crecca (EURASIAN)

darker face

steeper forehead

FEMALE

shoulder feathers with narrow pale edges

weaker face pattern

JUVENILE

The Green-winged Teal, the smallest North American dabbling duck, is slightly smaller than the Blue-winged and Cinnamon Teals, and lacks their blue wing patch. Its population is increasing, apparently because it breeds in more pristine habitats, and further north, than the prairie ducks. The species has three subspecies, *A. c. crecca* (Eurasia), *A. c. carolinensus* (North America), and *A. c. nimia* (Aleutian Islands). *Carolinensus* males have a conspicuous vertical white bar, whereas Eurasian *crecca* males do not.

VOICE Male call a high-pitched, slightly rolling *crick crick*, similar to cricket; female a call quiet *quack*.

NESTING Shallow scrape on ground lined with nearby vegetation, often placed in dense vegetation near water; 6–9 eggs; 1 brood; April–September.

FEEDING Eats seeds, aquatic insects, crustaceans, and mollusks year-round; also feeds in grain fields in winter.

FLIGHT: fast flight; often flying in twisting, tight groups reminiscent of shorebird flocks.

SINGLE PARENT
The female duck is deserted by her partner during incubation, so she must provide all parental care.

OCCURRENCE
Breeds north of the tree line in Alaska and Canada—around ponds in forest and deciduous woodlands. Prefers shallow wetlands with vegetation. In winter and migration, inland marshes, sloughs, agricultural fields, and coastal marshes. Winters south of the Caribbean and in southern Mexico.

SIMILAR SPECIES

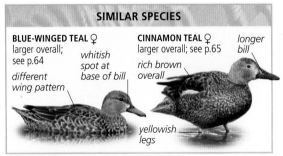

BLUE-WINGED TEAL ♀
larger overall; see p.64

whitish spot at base of bill

different wing pattern

CINNAMON TEAL ♀
larger overall; see p.65

rich brown overall

longer bill

yellowish legs

Length **12–15½in (31–39cm)**	Wingspan **20½–23in (52–59cm)**	Weight **7–16oz (200–450g)**
Social **Flocks**	Lifespan **Up to 20 years**	Status **Secure**

Order **Anseriformes**	Family **Anatidae**	Species **Aythya valisineria**

Canvasback

light gray forewing

black rump and tail

belly appears white

MALE

long neck, held horizontally in flight

IN FLIGHT

dark with mottled gray patches

distinct white eye-ring

dingy brown underparts

IMMATURE

dingy brownish gray upperparts and sides

extended tear drop

FEMALE

brown breast

high, peaked black crown

bright red eye

rich chestnut head and neck

black breast

white to pale gray back and flanks

black at both ends

MALE

A large, elegant, long-billed diving duck, the Canvasback is a bird of prairie pothole country. Its specialized diet of aquatic plants has resulted in a smaller population than other ducks. With legs set toward the rear, it is an accomplished swimmer and diver, and is rarely seen on land. Weather conditions and brood parasitism by Redheads determine how successful the Canvasback's nesting is from year to year.

VOICE Mostly silent except during courtship when males make soft *cooing* noises; females emit a grating *krrrrr krrrrrr krrrrr*; females give loud *quack* when taking off; during winter, both sexes make soft wheezing series of *rrrr rrrr rrrr* sounds.

NESTING Platform over water built of woven vegetation; occasionally on shore; 8–11 eggs; 1 brood; April–September.

FEEDING Mainly eats aquatic tubers, buds, root stalks, and shoots, particularly those of wild celery; also eats snails when preferred plants are unavailable.

FLIGHT: direct strong flight; one of the fastest ducks; forms V-shaped flocks.

DEEP WATER
Canvasbacks prefer deeper-bodied waters that support the aquatic vegetation they eat.

OCCURRENCE
Found in potholes, marshes, and ponds in prairie parkland, tundra; northerly forests preferred where their favorite foods grow. Winters in large numbers in large bays and lakes, and deltas, with smaller numbers scattered across North America and Mexico.

SIMILAR SPECIES		

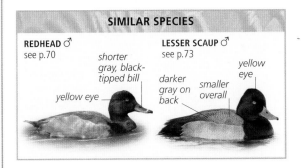

REDHEAD ♂
see p.70

shorter gray, black-tipped bill

yellow eye

LESSER SCAUP ♂
see p.73

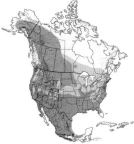

darker gray on back

smaller overall

yellow eye

Length **19–22in (48–56cm)**	Wingspan **31–35in (79–89cm)**	Weight **1¾–3½lb (0.8–1.6kg)**
Social **Flocks**	Lifespan **Up to 22 years**	Status **Secure**

| Order **Anseriformes** | Family **Anatidae** | Species **Aythya americana** |

Redhead

MALE
- dark-gray forewing
- brick-red head
- black breast

IN FLIGHT

FEMALE
- dark crown
- tawny brown overall
- gray bill with black tip

MALE (ECLIPSE)
- yellow eye
- white band

MALE
- medium-gray mantle and sides
- black rump
- brick-red upper neck and head
- yellow eye
- long blue bill with black tip
- black lower neck

The Redhead, a medium-sized diving duck belonging to the Pochard group, is native only to North America. Only when seen up close is it apparent that the male's seemingly gray upperparts and flanks are actually white, with dense, black, wavy markings. The Redhead often feeds at night and forages mostly around dusk and dawn, drifting during the day. It parasitizes other duck nests more than any other duck species, particularly those of the Canvasback and even other Redheads.

VOICE Male courtship call a wheezy rising then falling *whee ough*, also *meow*; female call a low, raspy *kurr kurr kurr*.

NESTING Weaves solid nest over water in dense vegetation such as cattails, lined with down; 7–14 eggs; 1 brood; May–September.

FEEDING Omniverous; feeds on aquatic plants, seeds, tubers, algae, insects, spiders, fish eggs, snails, and insect larvae; diet is variable depending on location.

FLIGHT: direct flight; runs on water prior to takeoff.

MALE DISPLAY
This male is performing a spectacular courtship display called a head throw, while remaining otherwise completely still on the water.

EASY IDENTIFICATION
The long blue bill with a whitish band and black tip is clearly visible in males.

OCCURRENCE
Breeds in shallow wetlands across the Great Basin and Prairie Pothole region, very densely in certain marsh habitats. The bulk of the population winters in coastal lagoons along the Atlantic Coast and the Gulf of Mexico.

SIMILAR SPECIES

CANVASBACK ♀
see p.69
- wedge-shaped black bill
- grayish back

RING-NECKED DUCK ♀
see p.71
- peaked head shape
- dark-brown back

| Length **17–21in (43–53cm)** | Wingspan **30–31in (75–79cm)** | Weight **1⅜–3¼lbs (0.6–1.5kg)** |
| Social **Flocks** | Lifespan **Up to 21 years** | Status **Secure** |

| Order **Anseriformes** | Family **Anatidae** | Species *Aythya collaris* |

Ring-necked Duck

dark forewing

MALE

bold white underwing

IN FLIGHT

dark brown back

bold white eye-ring

white band on bill

FEMALE

tall, peaked head

gray bill with white band at base

yellow eye

thin chestnut ring

black neck and breast

rounded gray sides

MALE

A resident of freshwater ponds and lakes, the Ring-necked Duck is a fairly common medium-sized diving duck. A more descriptive and suitable name might have been Ring-billed Duck as the bold white band on the bill tip is easy to see whereas the thin chestnut ring around the neck can be very difficult to observe. The tall, pointed head is quite distinctive, peaking at the rear of the crown. When it sits on the water, this bird typically holds its head high.

VOICE Male normally silent; female makes low *kerp kerp* call.

NESTING Floating nest built in dense aquatic vegetation, often in marshes; 6–14 eggs; 1 brood; May–August.

FEEDING Feeds in water at all times, either by diving, tipping up, or dabbling for aquatic plant tubers and seeds; also eats aquatic invertebrates such as clams and snails.

FLIGHT: strong flier with deep, rapid wing beats; flight somewhat erratic.

UNIQUE BILL
A white outline around the base of the bill and the white band on the bill are unique markings.

FLAPPING WINGS
Bold white wing linings are apparent when the Ring-necked Duck flaps its wings.

SIMILAR SPECIES

LESSER SCAUP ♂
see p.73

rounded head

wavy-patterned gray mantle

TUFTED DUCK ♂
see p.704

crested tufts

white sides

OCCURRENCE
Breeds across Canada, south of the Arctic zone, in shallow freshwater marshes and bogs; sporadically in the western US. Winters in freshwater and brackish habitats such as swamps, lakes, estuaries, reservoirs, and flooded fields. Migrants are found in the Midwest near stands of wild rice.

| Length **15–18in (38–46cm)** | Wingspan **24–25in (62–63cm)** | Weight **1⅛–2lbs (500–900g)** |
| Social **Flocks** | Lifespan **Up to 20 years** | Status **Secure** |

Order **Anseriformes**	Family **Anatidae**	Species *Aythya marila*

Greater Scaup

gray forewing

broad, white wing stripe

MALE (NONBREEDING)

IN FLIGHT

little or no white around bill

medium to dark brown overall

gray-brown sides **JUVENILE**

bold white patches at base of bill

FEMALE (NONBREEDING)

smooth, round, black head with purple-green gloss

blue-gray bill, wider at tip

gray-frosted shoulder feathers and sides

reduced white around bill

wavy-patterned gray back

FEMALE (BREEDING)

dark brown overall

MALE (BREEDING)

almost all white sides

blackish brown head

gray-and-brown back

MALE (ECLIPSE)

A great swimmer and diver, the Greater Scaup is the only diving duck (genus *Aythya*) that breeds both in North America and Eurasia. Due to its more restricted coastal breeding and wintering habitat preference, it is far less numerous in North America than its close relative, the Lesser Scaup. The Greater Scaup forms large, often sexually segregated flocks outside the breeding season. If both scaup species are present together, they will also segregate within the flocks according to species. Correct identification is difficult.

VOICE During courtship, male call a soft, fast, wheezy *week week wheew*; female gives a series of growled monotone *arrrr* notes.

NESTING Simple depression lined with grasses and down, nest sites need to have dense cover of vegetation from previous year; 6–10 eggs; 1 brood; May–September.

FEEDING Dives for aquatic plants, seeds, insects, crustaceans, snails, shrimp, and bivalves.

FLIGHT: strong, fast, and agile; flocks shift and twist during prolonged flight.

FOND OF FLOCKING
Male Greater Scaups, with distinct black and white markings, flock together on the water.

SIMILAR SPECIES

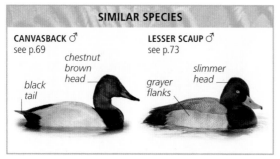

CANVASBACK ♂
see p.69

chestnut brown head

black tail

LESSER SCAUP ♂
see p.73

slimmer head

grayer flanks

OCCURRENCE
Majority breed in western coastal Alaska on tundra wetlands; also in lower densities in northwest and eastern Canada. Almost all birds winter offshore, along the Atlantic and Pacific coasts, or on the Great Lakes due to increased food availability. Small groups found inland and midcontinent, on unfrozen water bodies.

Length **15–22in (38–56cm)**	Wingspan **28–31in (72–79cm)**	Weight **1¼–3lb (0.6–1.4kg)**
Social **Flocks**	Lifespan **Up to 22 years**	Status **Declining**

| Order **Anseriformes** | Family **Anatidae** | Species *Aythya affinis* |

Lesser Scaup

MALE

IN FLIGHT

whitish underwings

black head

whitish belly

brown back

rich brown head and neck

white patch around base of gray bill

brown flank feathers with gray fringes

FEMALE

pale brown flanks

brown rear end

MALE (1ST WINTER)

narrow head with bump at the rear

purple-green gloss on head

narrow, thin, blue-gray bill

dark wavy pattern on upperparts

black rear end

MALE

pale flanks

black breast and neck

The Lesser Scaup, far more numerous than its somewhat larger relative (their size and weight ranges overlap), is also the most abundant diving duck in North America. The two species are very similar in appearance and are best identified by shape. Identification must be done cautiously as head shape changes with position. For example, the crown feathers are flattened just before diving in both species; thus, scaups are best identified when they are not moving.
VOICE Males mostly silent except during courtship when they make a wheezy *wheeow wheeow wheeow* sound; females give repetitive series of grating *garrrf garrrf garrrf* notes.
NESTING Nest built in tall vegetation or under shrubs, sometimes far from water, also on islands and mats of floating vegetation; 8–11 eggs; 1 brood; May–September.
FEEDING Feeds mainly on leeches, crustaceans, mollusks, aquatic insects, and aquatic plants and seeds.

FLIGHT: rapid, direct flight; can jump off water more easily than other diving ducks.

PREENING SCAUP
Ducks are meticulous preeners, and the Lesser Scaup is no exception.

SIMILAR SPECIES

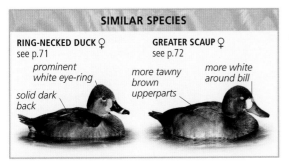

RING-NECKED DUCK ♀
see p.71

prominent white eye-ring

solid dark back

GREATER SCAUP ♀
see p.72

more tawny brown upperparts

more white around bill

OCCURRENCE
Breeds inland from Alaska to eastern Canada in open northern forests and forest tundra, most farther north. Winters in the Caribbean, southern US, and south to northern South America. Majority winter along coasts; others winter inland on lakes and reservoirs.

| Length **15½–17½in (39–45cm)** | Wingspan **27–31in (68–78cm)** | Weight **1–2¾lb (0.45–1.2kg)** |
| Social **Flocks** | Lifespan **Up to 18 years** | Status **Secure** |

| Order **Anseriformes** | Family **Anatidae** | Species *Polysticta stelleri* |

Steller's Eider

blue band of feathers

MALE

black collar

IN FLIGHT

blue patch

dark brown overall

gray bill

FEMALE

flat crown

head mostly white

moss-green patch

paler than female

JUVENILE

pointed tail

curved feathers

MALE

black spot on side

pale rufous-cream belly and breast

The smallest of the four species of eiders, Steller's Eider differs from the others in appearance and behavior. With its steeper forehead, flatter crown, and the way that it floats higher on the water, it resembles a dabbling duck. Steller's are the synchronized swimmers of the duck clan. In late winter, large groups dive in unison to feed, creating a spray as they disappear and then surface together. Only part of the Pacific population breeds in Alaska, with Point Barrow being the center of their breeding range. Both the Arctic and Pacific populations have recently declined in numbers, and are now classified as vulnerable.

VOICE Female a rapid, harsh growling call; also loud *qua-haaa* or *cooay;* males growl but are rarely heard.
NESTING Mound made of grasses, moss, and down on ground near freshwater tundra ponds; 5–10 eggs; 1 brood; June–August.
FEEDING Dives for marine invertebrates including, worms, snails, crustaceans, and small fish; eats mostly insect larvae on breeding grounds.

FLIGHT: twists and turns in flight; rises easily when taking off from water.

STRENGTH IN NUMBERS
Outside the breeding season, Steller's Eiders are very social and congregate in large flocks, sometimes in tens of thousands.

OCCURRENCE
Pacific population breeds mainly in Russia's far northeast; small numbers breed in Alaska. About half the Russian population molts and winters in large groups along estuaries and lagoons on the Alaska Peninsula and Aleutian Islands; the other half winters along the Kamchatka Peninsula and in north Norway.

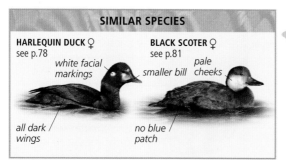

SIMILAR SPECIES

HARLEQUIN DUCK ♀
see p.78

white facial markings

all dark wings

BLACK SCOTER ♀
see p.81

smaller bill

pale cheeks

no blue patch

| Length **17–18in (43–46cm)** | Wingspan **28–30in (70–76cm)** | Weight **27–34oz (775–975g)** |
| Social **Flocks** | Lifespan **Up to 12 years** | Status **Vulnerable** |

Order **Anseriformes**	Family **Anatidae**	Species **Somateria fischeri**

Spectacled Eider

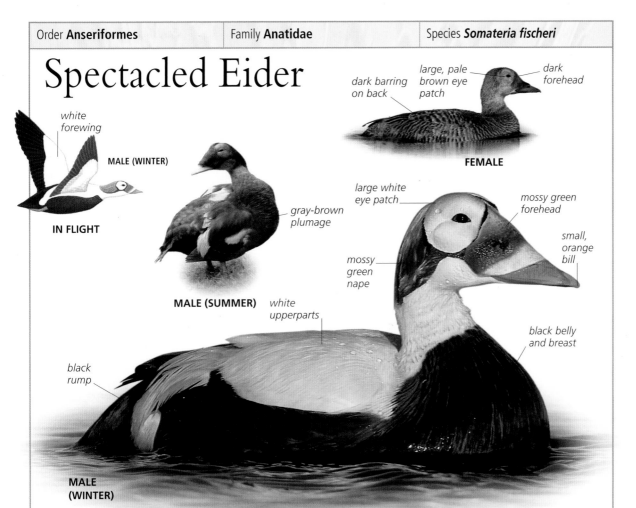

white forewing

MALE (WINTER)

IN FLIGHT

large, pale brown eye patch

dark barring on back

dark forehead

FEMALE

gray-brown plumage

MALE (SUMMER)

large white eye patch

mossy green forehead

small, orange bill

mossy green nape

white upperparts

black belly and breast

black rump

MALE (WINTER)

S eeing the striking Spectacled Eider requires traveling to remote tundra in the far north of Alaska. Their numbers are few and much of their life is spent offshore, with males spending up to 11 months of the year at sea. Larger than the Steller's Eider, in flight, the male Spectacled Eider reveals more black extending up the breast than the other eiders, and the females have gray, rather than white, underwings.

VOICE Males a faint *ho HOOO* during display, otherwise silent; females a rapid clucking call *buckbuck buckbuck* with emphasis on second syllable; also guttural rolled *gow gow gow.*

NESTING Shallow depression filled with grasses and down, on ground along shorelines; 2–6 eggs; 1 brood; May–September.

FEEDING Eats mainly mollusks; when breeding, diet is more varied and includes crustaceans, insects, and vegetable matter.

FLIGHT: rapid wing beats; flies in lines; no gliding or soaring.

DISTINCTIVE HEAD
It gets its name from the round patch of whitish feathers around its eye, which look like spectacles.

OCCURRENCE
Arctic coastal breeding sites are separated and remote; most breed in northern Russia, few in Alaska. Almost all winter in dense flocks on small ice-free areas south of St. Lawrence Island, in the Bering Sea, diving as deep as 230ft (70m) to feed on mollusks on the seafloor.

SIMILAR SPECIES

KING EIDER ♀
see p.76

larger bill

thicker neck

v-shaped pattern on flanks and sides

COMMON EIDER ♂
see p.77

longer, orange bill

dark cap

white breast

Length **20½–22½in (52–57cm)**	Wingspan **33in (83cm)**	Weight **2–4lb (0.9–1.8kg)**
Social **Large flocks/Colonies**	Lifespan **Up to 15 years**	Status **Vulnerable**

| Order **Anseriformes** | Family **Anatidae** | Species *Somateria spectabilis* |

King Eider

MALE (BREEDING)

white underwing

IN FLIGHT

short neck

long-billed profile

brown-black upperparts

scalloped breast

"v"-shaped markings on sides

FEMALE

white patch on face

MALE MOLTING (2ND WINTER)

white breast

orange to reddish frontal shield, outlined in black

pale blue crown and nape

green cheek

reddish orange bill

long feathers form triangular "sails"

rose blush on breast

MALE (BREEDING)

white flank patch

black underparts

The scientific name of the King Eider, *spectabilis*, means "worth seeing," and its gaudy marking and coloring around the head and bill make it hard to mistake. Females resemble the somewhat larger and paler Common Eider. The female King Eider has a more rounded head, more compact body, and a longer bill than the male. King Eiders may dive down to 180ft (55m) when foraging.

VOICE Courting males give a repeated series of low, rolled dove-like *arrrrooooo* calls, each rising, then falling, followed by softer *cooos*; females give grunts and croaks.

NESTING Slight depression in tundra lined with nearby vegetation and down; 4–7 eggs; 1 brood; June–September.

FEEDING Dives for mollusks; other food items include crustaceans, starfish, and when breeding, insects and plants.

FLIGHT: direct and rapid flight; migrates in long lines, abreast in a broad front, or in clusters.

GROUP FLIGHT
Migratory King Eiders move in large groups to their northern breeding habitats.

SIMILAR SPECIES

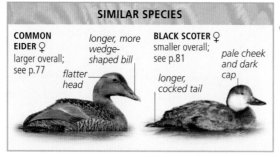

COMMON EIDER ♀
larger overall; see p.77

longer, more wedge-shaped bill

flatter head

BLACK SCOTER ♀
smaller overall; see p.81

pale cheek and dark cap

longer, cocked tail

OCCURRENCE
Nests along coasts and farther inland than Spectacled or Steller's Eiders in the high Arctic, on a variety of habitats; around low marshes, lakes, and islands; prefers well-drained areas. During winter, found mostly along the southern edge of the ice pack, in coastal waters up to 66ft (20m) deep.

| Length **18½–25in (47–64cm)** | Wingspan **37in (94cm)** | Weight **2¾–4¾lb (1.2–2.1kg)** |
| Social **Flocks** | Lifespan **Up to 15 years** | Status **Secure** |

Order **Anseriformes**	Family **Anatidae**	Species **Somateria mollissima**

Common Eider

black cap

olive-green wash on nape

greenish olive bill

FEMALE

brown overall

MALE (WINTER)

IN FLIGHT

whitish underwing

black rump and tail

dark brown overall

MALE (SUMMER)

white flecking

MALE (2ND WINTER)

white breast, with rose tinge

long, sloping forehead

mottled, black-and-brown upperparts

FEMALE

MALE (WINTER)

The largest duck in North America, the Common Eider, is also the most numerous, widespread, and variable of the eiders. Four of its seven subspecies occur in North America, and vary in the markings and color of their heads and bills. Male Common Eiders also have considerable seasonal plumage changes, and do not aquire their adult plumage until the third year.

VOICE Repeated hoarse, grating notes *korr-korr-korr;* male's owl-like *ah-WOO-ooo;* female's low, gutteral notes *krrrr-krrrr-krrrr.*

NESTING Depression on ground lined with down and plant matter, often near water; 2–7 eggs; 1 brood; June–September.

FEEDING Forages in open water and areas of shallow water; dives in synchronized flocks for mollusks and crustaceans, but consumes its larger prey above the surface.

FLIGHT: strong flight with relatively slow wing beats; flies in undulating lines, low over the water.

BROODING FEMALE
Females line their nests with down plucked from their bellies, and cover the eggs with their bodies.

SIMILAR SPECIES

KING EIDER ♀
smaller overall;
see p.76

flatter crown

thicker neck

shorter, more concave bill

SURF SCOTER ♀
see p.79

dark brown overall

shorter, wedge-shaped bill

OCCURRENCE
Arctic breeder on coastal islands, peninsulas, seldom along freshwater lakes and deltas near coast. One population is sedentary in the Hudson and James Bays region. Other populations winter in the Bering Sea, Hudson Bay, north British Columbia, Gulf of St. Lawrence, and along the Atlantic Coast.

Length **19½–28in (50–71cm)**	Wingspan **31–42in (80–108cm)**	Weight **2¾–5¾lb (1.2–2.6kg)**
Social **Flocks/Colonies**	Lifespan **Up to 21 years**	Status **Secure**

Order **Anseriformes**	Family **Anatidae**	Species *Histrionicus histrionicus*

Harlequin Duck

MALE

dark wings above and below

short neck

pointed tail   **IN FLIGHT**

dark sooty brown overall

broad face with whitish patches

scaly, pale brown lower breast and belly

FEMALE

white bands down either side of back

slate-blue with bright rusty sides

two white bands perpendicular to breast and neck

two white facial spots

rust crown stripes

very round head

steep forehead

small dark bill

white crescent

MALE

This small, hardy duck is a superbly skillful swimmer, diving to forage on the bottom of turbulent streams for its favorite insect prey. Despite the male's unmistakable plumage at close range, it looks very dark from a distance. With head and long tail held high, it can be found among crashing waves, alongside larger and bigger-billed Surf and White-winged Scoters, who feed in the same habitat.

VOICE Male a high-pitched squeak earning it the nickname "sea mice"; female's call a raspy *ekekekekekek*.

NESTING Nests near water under vegetation or base of tree; also tree cavities; 3–9 eggs; 1 brood; April–September.

FEEDING Dives for insects and their larvae, and fish roe when breeding; in winter, eats mollusks, crustaceans, crabs, snails, fish roe, and barnacles.

FLIGHT: rapid and regular wing beats; usually flies low over water, in pairs or small groups.

MALE GROUPS
After the breeding season, many males may gather and forage together.

PAIR IN FLIGHT
Note the crisp white markings on the slate-blue male in flight.

OCCURRENCE
Breeds near rushing coastal, mountain, or subalpine streams. During winter, found in small groups or mixed in with other sea ducks close to the shore, particularly along shallow rocky shorelines, jetties, rocky beaches, and headlands.

SIMILAR SPECIES

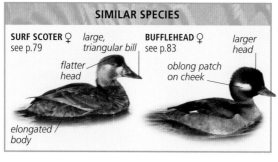

SURF SCOTER ♀ see p.79

large, triangular bill

flatter head

elongated body

BUFFLEHEAD ♀ see p.83

larger head

oblong patch on cheek

Length **13–21½in (33–54cm)**	Wingspan **22–26in (56–66cm)**	Weight **18–26oz (500–750g)**
Social **Small flocks**	Lifespan **Unknown**	Status **Secure**

Order **Anseriformes**	Family **Anatidae**	Species *Melanitta perspillata*

Surf Scoter

MALE

black wings overall

compact body

IN FLIGHT

whitish facial patches

dark brown overall

all-dark bill

FEMALE

black forehead

small, white patch on nape

IMMATURE MALE (2ND WINTER)

white eye

white forehead

large, black spot on bill

white nape

velvety black feathers

long tail feathers

swollen, orange bill with white base

MALE

Surf Scoters, one of three species of scoters living in North America, migrate up and down both coasts, often with the other species. They take their name from the way they dive for mollusks on the sea floor, in shallow coastal waters, through heavy surf. Groups often dive and resurface in unison. Black and Surf Scoters can be difficult to tell apart as both have all-black wings. The underside of the Surf Scoter's wings are uniform black, wheras the Black Scoter has gray flight feathers, which contrast with the black underwing feathers.

VOICE Normally silent; courting male's variety of calls includes liquid gurgled *puk-puk*, bubbled whistles, and low croaks; female call a harsh *crahh*, reminiscent of a crow.

NESTING Ground nest lined with down and vegetation on brushy tundra, often under low branches of a conifer tree; 5–10 eggs; 1 brood; May–September.

FEEDING Dives for mollusks and other aquatic invertebrates.

FLIGHT: strong wing beats; flies in bunched up groups; male's wings hum or whistle in flight.

DISTINGUISHING FEATURES
The white forehead and bright orange bill, in addition to its red-orange legs and feet, identify male Surf Scoters.

SIMILAR SPECIES

GREATER SCAUP ♀
see p.72

no white patches on cheek

thinner bill

WHITE-WINGED SCOTER ♀
see p.80

long, sloping forehead

longer bill

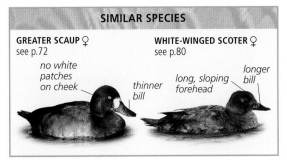

OCCURRENCE
Nests on lake islands in forested regions of interior Alaska and northern Canada. Nonbreeders in summer and adults in winter are strictly coastal, with numbers decreasing from north to south along the Pacific coast. In the East, most overwinter in the mid-Atlantic coast region.

Length **19–23½in (48–60cm)**	Wingspan **30in (77cm)**	Weight **1¾–2¾lb (0.8–1.2kg)**
Social **Flocks/Pairs**	Lifespan **Unknown**	Status **Secure**

| Order **Anseriformes** | Family **Anatidae** | Species *Melanitta fusca* |

White-winged Scoter

white wing patch

ADULT

IN FLIGHT

appears all-black in flight

long, sloping head

blackish bill

two distinct pale patches on face

IMMATURE FEMALE

dark brown overall

feathers extend onto the bill

upturned white "comma" around white eye

FEMALE

all black with brownish sides

black knob at base of bill

pinkish red to yellow-orange bill

MALE

The White-winged Scoter is the largest of the three scoters. When visible, the white wing patch makes identification easy. Females are quite similar to immature male and female Surf Scoters and can be identified by head shape, extent of bill feathering, and shape of white areas on the face. When diving, this scoter leaps forward and up, arching its neck, and opens its wings when entering the water. Underwater, White-winged Scoters open their wings to propel and stabilize themselves.

VOICE Mostly silent; courting males emit a whistling note; female call a growly *karr*.

NESTING Depression lined with twigs and down in dense thickets, often far from water; 8–9 eggs; 1 brood; June–September.

FEEDING Dives for mollusks and crustaceans; sometimes eats fish and aquatic plants.

FLIGHT: direct with rapid wing beats; flies low over the water in small groups.

WHITE FLASH IN FLIGHT
Scoters often migrate or feed in mixed flocks. The white wing patches are striking in flight.

OCCURRENCE
Majority breed in dense colonies in interior Alaska and western Canada on large freshwater or brackish lakes or ponds, sometimes on saltwater lakes. Winters along both coasts, large bays, inlets, and estuaries. Rarely winters inland, except on the Great Lakes.

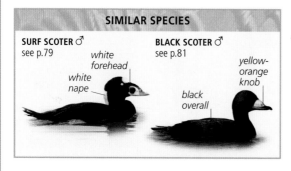

SIMILAR SPECIES

SURF SCOTER ♂
see p.79

white forehead

white nape

BLACK SCOTER ♂
see p.81

yellow-orange knob

black overall

| Length **19–23in (48–58cm)** | Wingspan **31in (80cm)** | Weight **2¾–4¾lb (0.9–1.9kg)** |
| Social **Flocks/Colonies** | Lifespan **Up to 18 years** | Status **Secure** |

| Order **Anseriformes** | Family **Anatidae** | Species *Melanitta nigra* |

Black Scoter

pale, silvery gray flight feathers

black lining on underwings

ADULT

IN FLIGHT

dark cap

pale brownish gray cheeks

black bill with small yellow patch

smaller bill

dark brown overall

FEMALE

dark brown eye

conspicuous yellow-orange knob on black bill

entirely black, heavily built body

MALE

Black Scoters, the most vocal of the scoters, are medium-sized sea ducks that winter along both coasts of North America. Riding high on the waves, they form dense flocks, often segregated by gender. While swimming, the Black Scoter sometimes flaps its wings and while doing so drops its neck low down, unlike the other two scoters. This scoter breeds in two widely separated sub-Arctic breeding areas and is one of the least studied ducks in North America. The Eurasian subspecies, known as the Common Scoter, has much less orange on its bill with a smaller knob at the base.

VOICE Male call a high-whistled *peeew*; female a low raspy *kraaa*.
NESTING Depression lined with grass and down, often in tall grass on tundra; 5–10 eggs; 1 brood; May–September.
FEEDING Dives in saltwater for mollusks, crustaceans, and plant matter; feeds on aquatic insects and freshwater mussels.

FLIGHT: strong wing beats; male's wings make whistling sound during takeoff.

SILVERY FLIGHT FEATHERS
The flight feathers of the male Black Scoters are more silvery in color than in the other scoters.

SIMILAR SPECIES

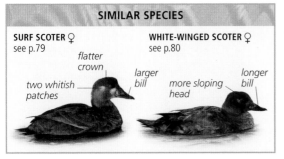

SURF SCOTER ♀
see p.79

WHITE-WINGED SCOTER ♀
see p.80

flatter crown

two whitish patches

larger bill

more sloping head

longer bill

OCCURRENCE
Breeding habitat is somewhat varied, but is generally close to fairly shallow, small lakes. Winters along both coasts. Populations wintering farther north prefer water over cobbles, gravel, or offshore ledges, whereas in southern locations, sandier habitats are chosen.

| Length **17–21in (43–53cm)** | Wingspan **31–35in (79–90cm)** | Weight **1¾–2¾lb (0.8–1.2kg)** |
| Social **Flocks** | Lifespan **Unknown** | Status **Declining** |

| Order **Anseriformes** | Family **Anatidae** | Species *Clangula hyemalis* |

Long-tailed Duck

MALE (WINTER)

chunky body

IN FLIGHT

FEMALE (WINTER)

short tail

whitish underparts

long dark tail

MALE (WINTER)

mostly dark brown back, flanks, head, and breast

small, dark bill

FEMALE (SUMMER)

dark back

brown breastband

FEMALE (WINTER)

all-dark wings

white shoulder feathers

smudgy face pattern

JUVENILE (WINTER)

gray face

blackish head, neck, and breast

MALE (SUMMER)

white head

white eye-ring

large, brown spot on side of head

pinkish band on bill

black breastband

The Long-tailed Duck, which used to be called the Oldsquaw is a small, pudgy sea duck. The male has two extremely long tail feathers, which are often held up in the air like a pennant. The male's loud calls are quite musical, and, when heard from a flock, have a chorus-like quality, hence the name *Clangula*, which is Latin for "loud." The Long-tailed Duck is capable of diving for a prolonged period of time, and can reach depths of 200ft (60m), making it one of the deepest diving ducks. Its three-part molt is more complex than that of other ducks.

VOICE Male call a *ang-ang-eeeooo* with yodelling quality; female barking *urk* or *uk* alarm call.

NESTING Shallow depression in ground lined with plant matter; 6–9 eggs; 1 brood; May–September.

FEEDING Dives to bottom of freshwater or saltwater habitats for mollusks, crustaceans, insects, fish, and roe.

FLIGHT: flies low over the water, somewhat erratically, with fast, fluttering wing beats.

UNMISTAKABLE MALE
In winter, dark wings, a white body with black breast-band, and a long tail make this male unmistakable.

OCCURRENCE
Breeds in Arctic and sub-Arctic, nesting in small groups on islands and peninsulas on lakes, less commonly on tundra and freshwater ponds on islands. Winters mostly along rocky coasts and headlands, protected bays, or on large freshwater lakes.

SIMILAR SPECIES

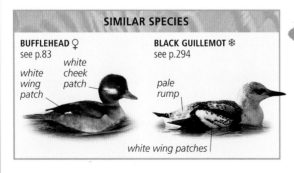

BUFFLEHEAD ♀
see p.83

white wing patch

white cheek patch

BLACK GUILLEMOT ❋
see p.294

pale rump

white wing patches

| Length **14–23in (35–58cm)** | Wingspan **28in (72cm)** | Weight **18–39oz (500–1,100g)** |
| Social **Flocks** | Lifespan **Up to 22 years** | Status **Secure** |

| Order **Anseriformes** | Family **Anatidae** | Species **Bucephala albeola** |

Bufflehead

black-and-white outer wings

MALE

gray underwings with white patch

pinkish orange legs

IN FLIGHT

oval, white cheek patch

dark, unmarked back

grayish brown sides

dark brown head

all-dark wings

FEMALE

large, triangular, white patch on head

black back

front part of head and neck has iridescent green-and-purple gloss

angled forehead

small, narrow, gray bill

white breast and flanks

MALE

The smallest diving duck in North America, the Bufflehead is a close relative of the Common and Barrow's Goldeneye. Males make a bold statement with their striking head pattern. In flight, males resemble the larger Common Goldeneye, yet the large white area on their head makes them easy to distinguish. The Common Goldeneye's wings create a whirring sound in flight whereas the Bufflehead's do not. The northern limit of the Bufflehead's breeding range corresponds to that of the Northern Flicker, as the ducks usually nest in abandoned Flicker cavities.
VOICE Male a low growl or squeal; chattering during breeding; female mostly silent except during courtship or calling to chicks.
NESTING Cavity nester, no nesting material added, near water; 7–9 eggs; 1 brood; April–September.
FEEDING Dives for aquatic invertebrates: usually insects in freshwater, mollusks and crustaceans in saltwater; also eats seeds.

FLIGHT: very rapid wing beats; no flight sound, unlike Goldeneyes.

IMMEDIATE TAKE OFF
Unlike other diving ducks, the small, compact Bufflehead can take off almost vertically.

SIMILAR SPECIES

HOODED MERGANSER ♂
see p.86

smaller, with white cheek patch

RUDDY DUCK ♂ ✳
see p.89

dark cap

longer bill

larger size

OCCURRENCE
Breeds in forest from Alaska to eastern Canada, in woodlands near small lakes and permanent ponds, where young are raised. Winters largely along the Pacific and Atlantic Coasts with lower densities scattered across the continent, south to northern Mexico, and in Bermuda.

| Length **12½–15½in (32–39cm)** | Wingspan **21½–24in (54–61cm)** | Weight **10–18oz (275–500g)** |
| Social **Flocks** | Lifespan **Up to 15 years** | Status **Secure** |

| Order **Anseriformes** | Family **Anatidae** | Species ***Bucephala clangula*** |

Common Goldeneye

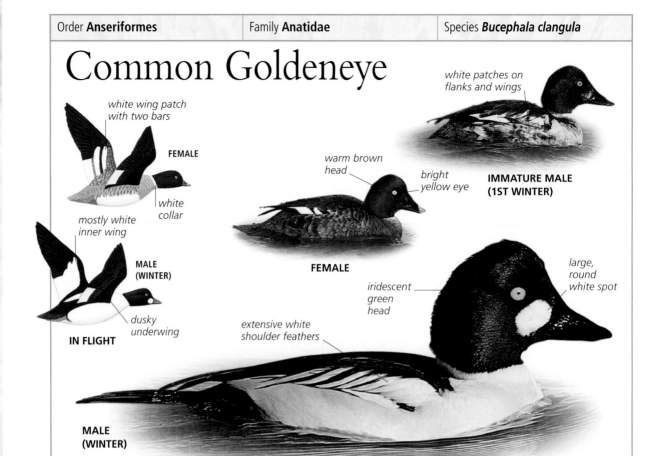

white wing patch with two bars

FEMALE

white collar

mostly white inner wing

MALE (WINTER)

dusky underwing

IN FLIGHT

white patches on flanks and wings

warm brown head

bright yellow eye

IMMATURE MALE (1ST WINTER)

FEMALE

iridescent green head

large, round white spot

extensive white shoulder feathers

MALE (WINTER)

Common Goldeneyes closely resemble Barrow's Goldeneyes. Found in North America and Eurasia, this is a medium-sized, compact, diving duck. It is aggressive and very competitive with members of its own species, as well as other cavity-nesting ducks. It regularly lays eggs in the nests of other species—a behavior that is almost parasitic. Before diving, the Common Goldeneye flattens its feathers in preparation for underwater foraging. The female's head shape changes according to her posture.

VOICE Courting males make a faint *peent* call; females a harsh *gack* or repeated *cuk* calls.

NESTING Cavity nester in holes made by other birds, including Pileated Woodpeckers, in broken branches or hollow trees; also commonly uses nest boxes; 4–13 eggs; 1 brood; April–September.

FEEDING Dives during breeding season for insects; in winter, mollusks and crustaceans; sometimes eats fish and plant matter.

FLIGHT: rapid with fast wing beats; male's wings make a tinkling sound in flight.

MALE TAKING OFF
Quite a long takeoff, involving energetically running on the water, leaves a trail of spray.

SIMILAR SPECIES

BUFFLEHEAD ♀
see p.83

white oval patch behind eye

smaller overall

BARROW'S GOLDENEYE ♂
see p.85

smaller bill

large crescent on face

OCCURRENCE
Breeds along wetlands, lakes, and rivers with clear water in northern forests, where large trees provide appropriate nest cavities. Winters across continent, with highest densities located from north New England to the mid-Atlantic on coastal bays and in the West from coastal southeast Alaska to British Columbia.

| Length **15½–20in (40–51cm)** | Wingspan **30–33in (77–83cm)** | Weight **19–44oz (550–1,300g)** |
| Social **Flocks** | Lifespan **Up to 15 years** | Status **Secure** |

Order **Anseriformes**	Family **Anatidae**	Species ***Bucephala islandica***

Barrow's Goldeneye

white wing patch

MALE

dark underwings

IN FLIGHT

narrow, white wing patch

FEMALE (BREEDING)

darker brown head

steep forehead

small, yellow bill

black head with purple gloss

sloping crown

grayish brown wing feathers

IMMATURE MALE (1ST WINTER)

white neck

white "piano key" markings on sides

bold, white facial crescent

MALE

Barrow's Goldeneye is a slightly larger, darker version of the Common Goldeneye. Although the female can be identified by its different head structure and bill color, the bill color varies seasonally and geographically. Eastern Barrow's have blacker bills with less yellow, and western populations have entirely yellow bills, which darken in summer. During the breeding season, the majority of Barrow's Goldeneyes are found in mountainous regions of northwest North America.

VOICE Males normally silent; courting males grunt *ka-KAA*; females *cuc* call, slightly higher pitched than Common Goldeneye.
NESTING Tree cavity in holes formed by Pileated Woodpeckers, often broken limbs or hollow trees; also uses nest boxes; 6–12 eggs; 1 brood; April–September.
FEEDING Dives in summer for insects, some fish, and roe; in winter, mainly mollusks and crustaceans; some plant matter.

FLIGHT: rapid flight with fast, deep wing beats; flies near water surface on short flights.

COURTING DISPLAY
A male thrusts his head back and gives a guttural call. His feet then kick back, driving him forward.

OCCURRENCE
Winters along the Pacific Coast between southeast Alaska and Washington, with small populations in east Canada. Smaller numbers found inland from the lower Colorado River to Yellowstone National Park. Eastern population is localized in winter with the highest count in St. Lawrence estuary.

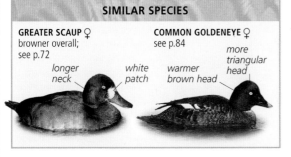

SIMILAR SPECIES

GREATER SCAUP ♀
browner overall; see p.72

longer neck

white patch

COMMON GOLDENEYE ♀
see p.84

more triangular head

warmer brown head

Length **17–19in (43–48cm)**	Wingspan **28–30in (71–76cm)**	Weight **17–46oz (475–1,300g)**
Social **Flocks**	Lifespan **Up to 18 years**	Status **Secure**

| Order **Anseriformes** | Family **Anatidae** | Species *Lophodytes cucullatus* |

Hooded Merganser

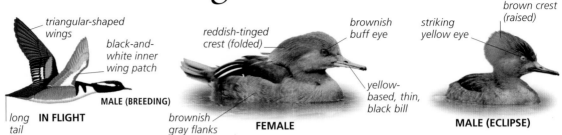

triangular-shaped wings

black-and-white inner wing patch

MALE (BREEDING)

long tail **IN FLIGHT**

reddish-tinged crest (folded)

brownish buff eye

yellow-based, thin, black bill

brownish gray flanks

FEMALE

small, gray-brown crest (raised)

striking yellow eye

MALE (ECLIPSE)

longish tail, often raised

crested black-and-white head (crest not raised)

black back

yellow eye

thin, black, serrated bill

white breast

MALE (BREEDING)

warm brown flanks

bold vertical bars

This dapper, miniature fish-eater is the smallest of the three mergansers. Both male and female Hooded Mergansers have crests that they can raise or flatten. When the male raises his crest, the thin horizontal white stripe turns into a gorgeous white fan, surrounded by black. Although easily identified when swimming, the Hooded Merganser and the Wood Duck can be confused when seen in flight since they both are fairly small with bushy heads and long tails.

VOICE Normally silent; during courtship, males produce a low, growly, descending *pah-hwaaaaa*, reminiscent of a frog; females give a soft *rrrep*.

NESTING Cavity nester; nest lined with down feathers in a tree or box close to or over water; 6–15 eggs; 1 brood; February–June.

FEEDING Dives for fish, aquatic insects, and crayfish, preferably in clear and shallow fresh waters, but also in brackish waters.

FLIGHT: low, fast, and direct; shallow wing beats; quiet whirring noise produced by wings.

FANHEAD SPECTACULAR
The male's magnificent black-and-white fan of a crest is like a beacon in the late afternoon light.

OCCURRENCE
Prefers forested small ponds, marshes, or slow-moving streams during the breeding season. During winter, occurs in shallow water in both fresh- and saltwater bays, estuaries, rivers, streams, ponds, freshwater marshes, and flooded sloughs.

SIMILAR SPECIES

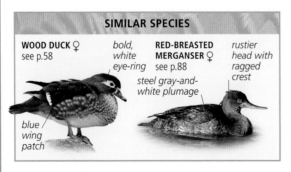

WOOD DUCK ♀ see p.58

bold, white eye-ring

blue wing patch

RED-BREASTED MERGANSER ♀ see p.88

rustier head with ragged crest

steel gray-and-white plumage

| Length **15½–19½in (40–49cm)** | Wingspan **23½–26in (60–66cm)** | Weight **16–31oz (450–875g)** |
| Social **Small flocks** | Lifespan **Unknown** | Status **Secure** |

Order **Anseriformes**	Family **Anatidae**	Species *Mergus merganser*

Common Merganser

dark outer wing

gray-and-white inner wing

reddish brown head

FEMALE

bright, rusty brown head

black-tipped red bill

silver-gray upperparts

FEMALE

small white spot above eye

short, ragged crest

JUVENILE

thin, black bar

gray rump and tail

MALE (NONBREEDING)

black head

all-white or tinged pink underparts

IN FLIGHT

iridescent blackish green head

black eye

reddish orange hooked bill

long nape feathers

black center

serrated sides on bill

white breast and underparts

MALE (BREEDING)

The largest of the three merganser species in North America, the Common Merganser is called a Goosander in the UK. This large fish-eater is common and widespread, particularly in the northern portion of its range. It is often found in big flocks on lakes or smaller groups along rivers. It spends most of its time on the water, using its serrated bill to catch fish underwater.

VOICE Mostly silent, except when alarmed or during courtship; females give a low-pitched harsh *karr* or *gruk*, the latter also given in series; during courtship, males emit a high-pitched, bell-like note and other twangy notes; alarm call a hoarse *grrr* or *wak*.

NESTING Cavity nester sometimes high in trees; uses nest boxes, nests on ground; 6–17 eggs; 1 brood; April–September.

FEEDING Eats mostly fish (especially fond of trout and salmon, but also carp and catfish), aquatic invertebrates, frogs, small mammals, birds, and plants.

FLIGHT: fast with shallow wing beats; often flying low over the water.

FEEDING ON THE MOVE
This female Common Merganser is trying to swallow, head-first, a rather large fish.

OCCURRENCE
Breeds in the northerly forests from Alaska to Newfoundland; winters south to north central Mexico. Being very hardy, it will winter farther north than most other waterfowl as long as water remains open. Prefers fresh- to saltwater locations.

SIMILAR SPECIES

COMMON GOLDENEYE ♂
see p.84

white patch

black-and-white pattern

RED-BREASTED MERGANSER ♀
see p.88

smaller, more lightly built

thinner bill

Length **21½–28in (54–71cm)**	Wingspan **34in (86cm)**	Weight **1¾–4¾lb (0.8–2.1kg)**
Social **Flocks**	Lifespan **Up to 13 years**	Status **Secure**

| Order **Anseriformes** | Family **Anatidae** | Species *Mergus serrator* |

Red-breasted Merganser

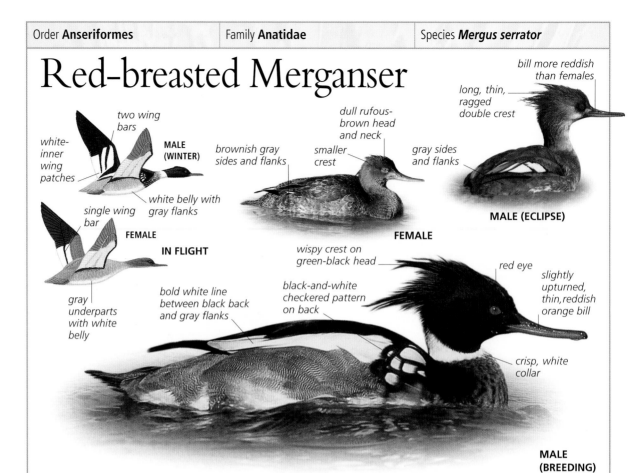

two wing bars

white-inner wing patches

MALE (WINTER)

white belly with gray flanks

single wing bar

FEMALE

IN FLIGHT

gray underparts with white belly

brownish gray sides and flanks

dull rufous-brown head and neck

smaller crest

FEMALE

bill more reddish than females

long, thin, ragged double crest

gray sides and flanks

MALE (ECLIPSE)

bold white line between black back and gray flanks

wispy crest on green-black head

black-and-white checkered pattern on back

red eye

slightly upturned, thin, reddish orange bill

crisp, white collar

MALE (BREEDING)

The Red-breasted Merganser, like the other saw-billed mergansers, is an elegant fish-eating duck. Both sexes are easily recognized by their long, sparse, somewhat ragged-looking double crest. Red-breasted Mergansers are smaller than Common Mergansers, but much larger than the Hooded. The Red-breasted Merganser, unlike the other two mergansers, nests on the ground, in loose colonies, often among gulls and terns, and is protected by its neighbors.

VOICE During courtship males make a raucous *yeow-yeow* call; females emit a raspy *krrr-krrr*.

NESTING Shallow depression on ground lined with down and plant material, near water; 5–11 eggs; 1 brood; May–July.

FEEDING Dives for small fish such as herring and minnows; also salmon eggs; at times flocks coordinate and drive fish together.

FLIGHT: fast flying duck with very rapid, regular, and shallow flapping.

KEEPING CLOSE
Red-breasted Mergansers are gregarious at all times of year, often feeding in loose flocks.

OCCURRENCE
Most northerly range of all the mergansers, nests across Arctic and sub-Arctic regions, tundra and northerly forests, along coasts, inland lakes, river banks, marsh edges, and coastal islands. Winters farther south than other mergansers, mostly in protected bays, estuaries, or on the Great Lakes.

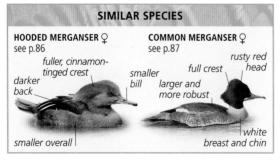

SIMILAR SPECIES

HOODED MERGANSER ♀
see p.86

fuller, cinnamon-tinged crest

darker back

smaller overall

COMMON MERGANSER ♀
see p.87

smaller bill

full crest

larger and more robust

rusty red head

white breast and chin

| Length **20–25in (51–64cm)** | Wingspan **26–29in (66–74cm)** | Weight **1¾–2¾lb (0.8–1.3kg)** |
| Social **Flocks/Colonies** | Lifespan **Up to 9 years** | Status **Secure** |

Order **Anseriformes**	Family **Anatidae**	Species *Oxyura jamaicensis*

Ruddy Duck

broad, short wings with whitish wing linings

pale belly

MALE (BREEDING)
IN FLIGHT

dull gray-brown two-tone body

duller head

blackish bill

MALE (NONBREEDING)

arched dark line on cheek

brownish upperparts

dark bill

paler flanks

FEMALE

black cap and nape

large head

rich cinnamon body and neck

long tail, often erect

bright blue bill, slightly knobby at base

large, white cheek patches

MALE (BREEDING)

Small and stiff-tailed, the Ruddy Duck is comical in both its appearance and behavior. Both sexes often hold their tail in a cocked position, especially when sleeping. During courtship displays, the male points its long tail skyward while rapidly thumping its electric blue bill against its chest, ending the performance with an odd, bubbling sound. In another display, males make a popping sound by slapping their feet on the water's surface. Large feet, on legs set far back on its body, make the Ruddy Duck an excellent swimmer and diver; however, on land it is perhaps one of the most awkward of diving ducks. Females are known to push themselves along instead of walking.

VOICE Females give a nasal *raanh* and high pitched *eeek*; males vocally silent, but make popping noises with feet.

NESTING Platform, bowl-shaped nest built over water in thick emergent vegetation, rarely on land; 6–10 eggs; 1 brood; May–September.

FEEDING Dives for aquatic insects, larvae, crustaceans, and other invertebrates, particularly when breeding; during winter, also eats plants.

FLIGHT: rapid and direct, with fast wing beats; not very agile in flight, which seems labored.

HEAVY HEAD
A female "sitting" on the water streamlines her body ready to dive, making her look large-headed.

OCCURRENCE
Breeds in the prairie pothole region in wetland habitats; marshes, ponds, reservoirs, and other open shallow water with emergent vegetation and open areas. Majority winter on freshwater habitats from ponds to large lakes; smaller numbers found on brackish coastal marshes, bays, and estuaries.

SIMILAR SPECIES

MASKED DUCK ♂
see p.704

black face

ruddy-colored back with black streaks

black tip to bill

Length **14–17in (35–43cm)**	Wingspan **22–24in (56–62cm)**	Weight **11–30oz (300–850g)**
Social **Flocks**	Lifespan **Up to 13 years**	Status **Secure**

Family **Gaviidae**

LOONS

ORLDWIDE THERE ARE ONLY five species of loon, comprising a single genus (*Gavia*), a single family (the Gaviidae), and a single order (the Gaviiformes). The five species are limited to the Northern Hemisphere, where they are found in both northern North America and northern Eurasia. One feature of loons is that their legs are positioned so far to the rear of their body that they must shuffle on their bellies when they go from water to land. Not surprisingly, therefore, loons are almost entirely aquatic birds. In summer they are found on rivers, lakes, and ponds, where they nest close to the water's edge. After breeding, they occur along coasts, often after flying hundreds of miles away from their freshwater breeding grounds.

Excellent swimmers and divers, loons are unusual among birds in that their bones are less hollow than those of other groups. Consequently, they can expel air from their lungs and compress their body feathers until they slowly sink beneath the surface. They can remain submerged like this for several minutes. A loons wings are relatively small in proportion to its body weight. This means that they have to run a long way across the surface of the water, flapping energetically, before they can get airborne. Once in the air, they keep on flapping, and can fly at up to 60mph (95kmh).

LOON RANGER
The Common Loon has a wider range than any other in North America, as its name suggests.

FLIGHT SHAPE
The humped back and drooping neck of this Red-throated Loon are typical of a loon in flight.

PROVIDING FOR THE FUTURE
A Red-throated Loon gives a fish to its chick to gulp down headfirst and whole.

Order **Gaviiformes**	Family **Gaviidae**	Species *Gavia stellata*

Red-throated Loon

white speckled back

white face

ADULT (NONBREEDING)

humped back

head lower than body

white underparts

ADULT (BREEDING)

ADULT (NONBREEDING)

IN FLIGHT

upturned bill

pale dusky face

IMMATURE

upturned gray bill

gray face and neck

striped gray nape

tapering dark reddish brown throat patch

all-brown back

ADULT (BREEDING)

Even when seen from a distance, this elegant loon is almost unmistakable, with a pale, slim body, upward tilted head, and a thin, upturned bill. Unlike other Loons, the Red-throated Loon can leap straight into the air from both land and water, although most of the time it needs a "runway." The Red-throated Loon has an elaborate breeding ritual—side by side, a pair of birds races upright across the surface of water. Downy chicks climb onto the parents back only when very young.

VOICE High gull-like or even cat-like wail and low goose-like growl; vocal on breeding grounds, otherwise silent.

NESTING Scrape with mud and vegetation added during incubation, placed at water's edge in coastal and lake bays, shallow ponds, often at high altitudes; 2 eggs; 1 brood; April–July.

FEEDING Mainly eats fish; also spiders, crustaceans, and mollusks; flies long distances from shallow ponds when food is scarce.

FLIGHT: very direct; fast, with constant wing beats; head held lower than other loons.

TAKING OFF
While this bird is using the water's surface to take off, it can leap directly into flight from water and land.

SIMILAR SPECIES

YELLOW BILLED LOON ❋
see p.95

massive, light-colored bill

larger overall

RED NECKED GREBE ❋
see p.119

yellow in bill

darker back

smaller overall

OCCURRENCE
Lives in open areas within northern boreal forest, muskeg, and tundra; in Canadian Arctic Archipelago, sometimes in areas almost devoid of vegetation. Winters on the Great Lakes, and both coasts southwards to Florida and northern Mexico.

Length **24–27in (61–69cm)**	Wingspan **3½ft (1.1m)**	Weight **3¼lb (1.5kg)**
Social **Solitary/Loose flocks**	Lifespan **Up to 23 years**	Status **Declining**

Order **Gaviiformes**	Family **Gaviidae**	Species *Gavia arctica*

Arctic Loon

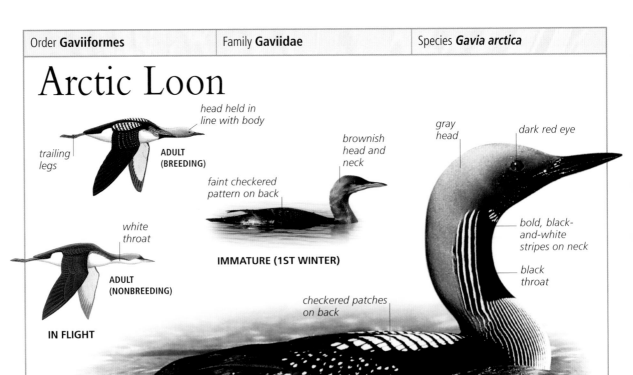

head held in line with body

trailing legs

ADULT (BREEDING)

brownish head and neck

faint checkered pattern on back

IMMATURE (1ST WINTER)

gray head

dark red eye

bold, black-and-white stripes on neck

black throat

white throat

ADULT (NONBREEDING)

IN FLIGHT

checkered patches on back

ADULT (BREEDING)

The Arctic Loon and the Pacific Loon had for a long time been considered to be members of a single species, with a geographically variable population across Eurasia and North America. There are a couple of color and pattern differences that distinguish the two species. In breeding plumage, the Arctic Loon has slightly more white on its flanks, a paler head and neck, and bolder stripes on the side of its neck. It is also slightly larger and shows green iridescence in its black throat patch, whereas the Pacific Loon shows purple. This species is not capable of taking off from the land, and finds it difficult to move around. Instead of walking, it will drop to its breast and slide along, propelling itself by pushing its feet backward.

VOICE Variety of calls; most common call repeated guttural yodeling or rapid cackling *kwuk;* also quieter, hoarse ravenlike croak, yelp, and plaintive cry.

NESTING Mound of mud and vegetation at water's edge in tundra lakes and marshy inlets; 1–3 eggs; 1 brood; June–July.

FEEDING Mainly eats fish, amphibians, aquatic insects, mollusks, and some plants.

FLIGHT: fast and direct with continuous wing beats; head and neck in line with body.

HIDDEN BUT ALERT
An adult incubates its eggs, hidden in low vegetation, but keeps ready to leave if disturbed.

OCCURRENCE
Breeds on freshwater tundra lakes and fairly large brackish coastal lakes. Forages on freshwater lakes up to 2,600ft (800m) inland. Believed to prefer calmer water than the Pacific Loon, such as sheltered bays.

SIMILAR SPECIES

PACIFIC LOON ☼
see p.93

lighter buff nape

PACIFIC LOON ❋
see p.93

less white on face

vertical neck stripes less bold

white breast

Length **30in (76cm)**	Wingspan **3ft 3in–4ft (1–1.2m)**	Weight **5–8¾lb (2.2–4kg)**
Social **Flocks**	Lifespan **Up to 25 years**	Status **Secure**

Order **Gaviiformes**	Family **Gaviidae**	Species *Gavia pacifica*

Pacific Loon

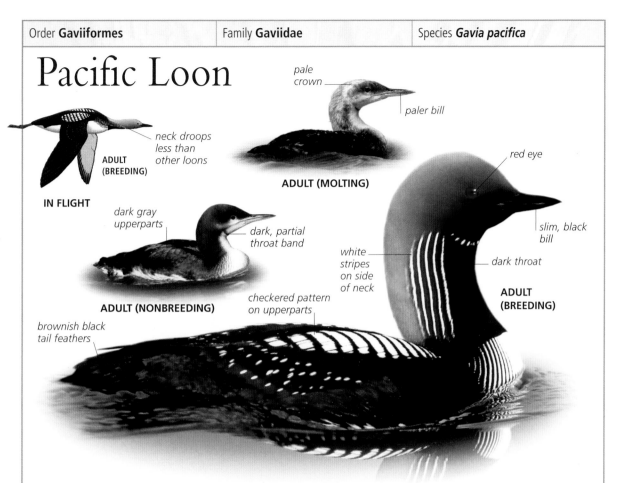

pale crown

paler bill

ADULT (MOLTING)

neck droops less than other loons

ADULT (BREEDING)

IN FLIGHT

dark gray upperparts

dark, partial throat band

ADULT (NONBREEDING)

brownish black tail feathers

checkered pattern on upperparts

white stripes on side of neck

red eye

slim, black bill

dark throat

ADULT (BREEDING)

Although the Pacific Loon's breeding range is about a third of that of the Common Loon, it is believed to be the most abundant loon species in North America. It shares its habitat in northern Alaska with the nearly identical, but slightly larger and darker Arctic Loon. It is a conspicuous migrant along the Pacific Coast in spring, but disappears to its remote breeding grounds in summer. The Pacific Loon is an expert diver and swimmer, capable of remaining underwater for sustained periods of time, usually in pursuit of fish. However, on its terrestrial nesting site, its chicks are vulnerable to a number of mammalian predators.

VOICE Deep barking *kowk*; high-pitched wail, croaks, and growls when breeding; makes a yelping noise when diving.

NESTING Simple scrape in flat area close to water, vegetation and mud added during incubation; 1-2 eggs; June-July.

FEEDING Eats fish, aquatic insects, and mollusks in breeding lake or nearby waters; may dip or dive, depending on the depth.

FLIGHT: swift and direct with constant wing beats; humped back, but head in line with body.

LEVEL GROUND
As loons cannot take off from land, nest sites need to be on flat land close to the water.

OCCURRENCE
Breeds across Arctic and sub-Arctic North America, from Alaska and northern Canadian provinces to Hudson Bay and on some of the islands of the Canadian Arctic; tundra lakes and muskeg. Small numbers in Great Lakes and along East coast from Quebec to Florida. Vagrant elsewhere.

SIMILAR SPECIES

ARCTIC LOON ☼
see p.92

darker nape

bolder black-and-white stripes on neck

ARCTIC LOON ❄
see p.92

heavier bill

brownish neck and head

Length **23–29in (58–74cm)**	Wingspan **2¾–4¼ft (0.9–1.3m)**	Weight **2½–5½lb (1–2.5kg)**
Social **Flocks**	Lifespan **Up to 25 years**	Status **Secure**

| Order **Gaviiformes** | Family **Gaviidae** | Species *Gavia immer* |

Common Loon

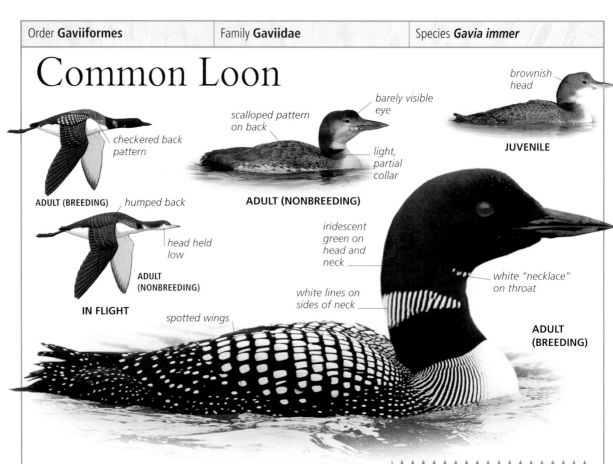

checkered back pattern

ADULT (BREEDING)   humped back

head held low

ADULT (NONBREEDING)

IN FLIGHT

spotted wings

scalloped pattern on back

barely visible eye

light, partial collar

ADULT (NONBREEDING)

brownish head

JUVENILE

iridescent green on head and neck

white lines on sides of neck

white "necklace" on throat

ADULT (BREEDING)

The Common Loon has the largest range of all loons in North America and is the only species to nest in a few of the northern states. It is slightly smaller than the Yellow-billed Loon but larger than the other three loons. It can remain underwater for well over 10 minutes, although it usually stays submerged for 40 seconds to 2 minutes while fishing, or a few more minutes if it is being pursued. Evidence shows that, occasionally, it interbreeds with its closest relative, the Yellow-billed Loon, in addition to the Arctic and Pacific Loons.

VOICE Most recognized call a 3–10 note falsetto yodel, rising, then fading; other calls similar in quality.

NESTING Simple scrape in large mound of vegetation, a few feet from open water; 2 eggs; 1 brood; April–June.

FEEDING Feeds primarily on fish underwater; also eats crustaceans, mollusks, amphibians, leeches, insects, and aquatic plants.

FLIGHT: fast, direct, with constant wing beats; head and neck held just above belly.

COZY RIDE
Downy Common Loon chicks climb up the backs of male and female adults for a safe ride.

BATHING RITUAL
Common Loons often shake their wings after bathing.

OCCURRENCE
Breeds across North America, Canada, and south to northern US. Winters on large ice-free lakes in Canada and the US, and along the Pacific and Atlantic Coasts, south to Baja California and Florida.

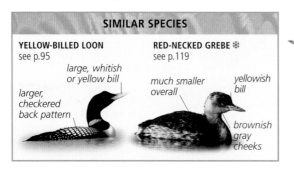

SIMILAR SPECIES

YELLOW-BILLED LOON
see p.95

large, whitish or yellow bill

larger, checkered back pattern

RED-NECKED GREBE ✳
see p.119

much smaller overall

yellowish bill

brownish gray cheeks

| Length **26–36in (66–91cm)** | Wingspan **4¼–5ft (1.3–1.5m)** | Weight **4½–18lb (2–8kg)** |
| Social **Family groups** | Lifespan **Up to 30 years** | Status **Vulnerable** |

Order **Gaviiformes**	Family **Gaviidae**	Species *Gavia adamsii*

Yellow-billed Loon

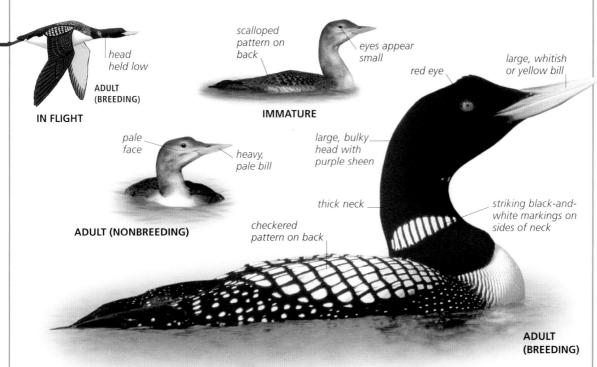

IN FLIGHT

head held low

ADULT (BREEDING)

scalloped pattern on back

eyes appear small

IMMATURE

red eye

large, whitish or yellow bill

pale face

heavy, pale bill

ADULT (NONBREEDING)

large, bulky head with purple sheen

thick neck

checkered pattern on back

striking black-and-white markings on sides of neck

ADULT (BREEDING)

The largest of the loons, the Yellow-billed Loon has the most restricted range and smallest global population. About three quarters of the estimated 16,000 birds live in North America. It makes the most of the short nesting season, arriving at its breeding grounds already paired and breeding immediately, although extensive ice formation can prevent it from breeding in some years. Yellow-billed Loons have more rugged proportions than other loons; their feet, for example, extend further away from their bodies.

VOICE Tremulous call much like Common Loon's, but louder, harsher, and even more "mournful"; yodels, wails, and "laughs" also part of repertoire.

NESTING Depression in mass of mud and vegetation, on shores of tundra lakes and ponds, and on river islands at high altitudes; 1–2 eggs; 1 brood; June–July.

FEEDING Dives underwater to catch small fish; also eats crustaceans, worms, and some vegetation.

FLIGHT: rapid and direct; head and neck held lower than body.

BOLDLY PATTERNED
The adult Yellow-billed Loon is strikingly patterned, like a checkerboard.

OCCURRENCE
Breeds from extreme northern edge of Alaska to eastern Northwest Territories and Nunavut. Also breeds in northern Siberia. Winters along the Pacific Coast of Alaska and British Columbia, and has been sighted in a number of US states.

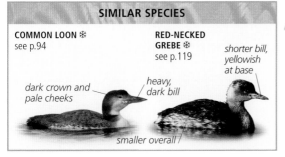

SIMILAR SPECIES

COMMON LOON ❄
see p.94

dark crown and pale cheeks

heavy, dark bill

RED-NECKED GREBE ❄
see p.119

shorter bill, yellowish at base

smaller overall

Length **30–36in (77–92cm)**	Wingspan **4–5ft (1.2–1.5m)**	Weight **8¾–14lb (4–6.5kg)**
Social **Solitary/Pairs/Family groups**	Lifespan **Up to 30 years**	Status **Vulnerable**

TUBENOSES

THE TUBENOSES ARE DIVIDED into everal families, but all are characterized by the tubular nostrils for which the order is named. These nostrils help to get rid of excess salt, and may enhance their of smell.

FLAP AND GLIDE
Shearwaters alternate stiff-winged flapping with gliding just over the ocean's surface.

Pacific Ocean is home to a greater variety of these seabirds than the Atlantic. During and after storms are the best times to look for these birds, as this is when they have been drifting away from the deep sea due to wind and waves.

ALBATROSSES
The long, narrow wings of albatrosses (family Diomedeidae) are perfectly suited for tackling the strong, constant winds which prevail on the southern oceans that form their main habitat. While they are expert gliders, albatrosses cannot takeoff from the ground without sufficient wing to give them lift.

SHEARWATERS
Shearwaters and gadfly petrels (family Procellariidae) are smaller than albatrosses. Like their larger cousins they are excellent gliders, but their lighter weight and proportionately shorter wings mean that they use more powered flight than Albatrosses. They range over all the world's oceans. With its far more numerous islands, the

STORM-PETRELS
The smallest tubenoses in North American waters, the storm-petrels (family Hydrobatidae) are also the most agile fliers. They often patter or "dance" as they fly low to the surface of the ocean in search of small fish, squid, and crustaceans. Storm-petrels spend most of their lives flying over the open sea, only visiting land in the breeding season, when they form huge colonies.

HOOKED BILL
In addition to the tubular nostrils all tubenoses have strongly hooked bills.

STRONG PAIR BOND
After elaborate courtship displays, albatrosses generally pair for life. The rituals are simpler in later years.

| Order **Procellariiformes** | Family **Diomedeidae** | Species *Phoebastria immutabilis* |

Laysan Albatross

stocky, tubular body

ADULT

pinkish legs and feet

very long wings

IN FLIGHT

white rump

dark tail

dark back and upperwings

white head

ADULT

long, thick pale bill with dark tip

white underwings with dark margins

white belly and underparts

ADULT

The Laysan Albatross generally stays far offshore, and is usually only ever seen from boats on the Pacific Ocean. This elegant, long-winged species breeds mainly in the Hawaiian Islands (as well as in Japan and the Pacific Coast of Mexico) and then travels thousands of miles to find food over the northern Pacific Ocean. Like many other albatross species, it takes a long time to reach sexual maturity—around eight to nine years. With its extraordinarily long wings and bold, black-and-white plumage, the Laysan Albatross is a remarkable sight, soaring low over the ocean.

VOICE A variety of calls given in colonies, including a range of squeaks, whinnies, whines, and moans.
NESTING Depression in ground, on sand beach or grass; twigs and leaves sometimes added; 1 egg; 1 brood; November–July.
FEEDING Floats over the ocean surface and forages for squid and other marine invertebrates; mostly at night.

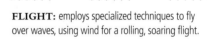

FLIGHT: employs specialized techniques to fly over waves, using wind for a rolling, soaring flight.

TRICKY TAKE OFF
Because of their bulk and long, thin wings, the birds run on water, flapping until they become airborne.

SIMILAR SPECIES

NORTHERN FULMAR (LIGHT FORM) see p.99

much paler wings

WESTERN GULL see p.255

shorter wings

small bill

slimmer body

much shorter bill

OCCURRENCE
Usually found far out to sea over the Pacific Ocean; localized breeder on isolated islands in the Pacific; when feeding, found throughout the north ocean, offshore from the western US.

| Length **31–32in (79–81cm)** | Wingspan **6¼–6½ft (1.9–2m)** | Weight **5¼–6½lb (2.4–3kg)** |
| Social **Colonies** | Lifespan **Up to 40 years** | Status **Vulnerable** |

| Order **Procellariiformes** | Family **Diomedeidae** | Species *Phoebastria nigripes* |

Black-footed Albatross

long, slender wings

less white around tail

less white around bill

IMMATURE

white rump patch

ADULT

IN FLIGHT

white patch above eye

brown eyes

dark bill

ADULT

dark upperparts

white ring at base of bill

dark legs and feet

ADULT

white undertail feathers

dark underparts

FLIGHT: uses specialized technique to minimize flapping; flies close to the water's surface.

The most frequently seen albatross in North American waters, this distinctive all-dark bird breeds mainly on the Hawaiian Islands, and regularly visits the Pacific Coast during the nonbreeding season. Unfortunately, a tendency to scavenge around fishing boats results in this and other species of albatross being drowned when they are accidentally hooked on long lines or tangled in drift nets—a major conservation concern for this particular species.

VOICE Generally silent outside the breeding season, but utters weak squeals while scavenging; variety of noises made during courtship.

NESTING Shallow depression in ground on higher reaches of sandy beaches; 1 egg; 1 brood; October–June.

FEEDING Dives for fish and squid, and picks floating masses of fish eggs from the ocean's surface with its bill.

TAKING OFF
Like other albatross species, the big-winged Black-footed Albatross takes off from water by running across the surface, heading into the wind.

OCCURRENCE
Breeds on sandy beaches, almost exclusively on remote, uninhabited islands in Hawaii; during the nonbreeding season, the Black-footed Albatross disperses across the whole northern Pacific Ocean.

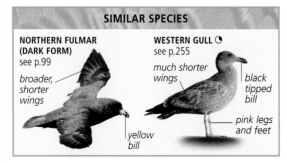

SIMILAR SPECIES

NORTHERN FULMAR (DARK FORM)
see p.99

broader, shorter wings

WESTERN GULL ○
see p.255

much shorter wings

black tipped bill

pink legs and feet

yellow bill

| Length **25–29in (64–74cm)** | Wingspan **6¼–7¼ft (1.9–2.2m)** | Weight **6¼lb (2.8kg)** |
| Social **Solitary/Flocks** | Lifespan **Up to 28 years** | Status **Endangered** |

| Order **Procellariiformes** | Family **Procellariidae** | Species *Fulmarus glacialis* |

Northern Fulmar

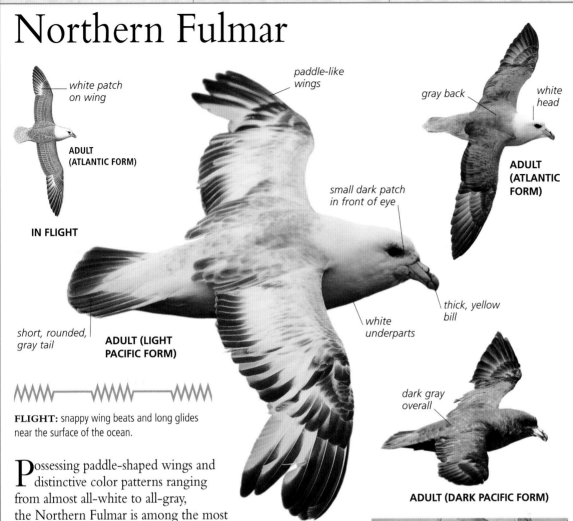

white patch on wing

ADULT (ATLANTIC FORM)

IN FLIGHT

paddle-like wings

gray back

white head

ADULT (ATLANTIC FORM)

small dark patch in front of eye

thick, yellow bill

white underparts

short, rounded, gray tail

ADULT (LIGHT PACIFIC FORM)

dark gray overall

ADULT (DARK PACIFIC FORM)

FLIGHT: snappy wing beats and long glides near the surface of the ocean.

Possessing paddle-shaped wings and distinctive color patterns ranging from almost all-white to all-gray, the Northern Fulmar is among the most common seabirds in places like the Bering sea. It breeds at high latitudes, then disperses south to offshore waters on both coasts of the continent. The Northern Fulmar can often be seen in large mixed flocks containing albatrosses, shearwaters, and petrels. Fulmars often follow boats, eager to pounce on the offal thrown overboard by fishermen.

VOICE Mostly silent at sea; occasionally utters cackles and grunts.
NESTING Scrape in rock or soil on edge of cliff; 1 egg; 1 brood; May–October.
FEEDING Picks fish and offal from the surface of the ocean; also dives underwater to catch fish.

FEEDING FRENZY
Large numbers of Northern Fulmars compete for the offal discarded by fishing trawlers.

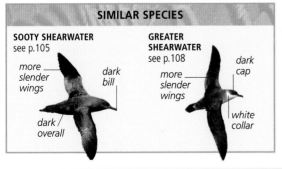

SIMILAR SPECIES

SOOTY SHEARWATER
see p.105

more slender wings

dark bill

dark overall

GREATER SHEARWATER
see p.108

more slender wings

dark cap

white collar

OCCURRENCE
Breeds on remote, high, coastal cliffs in Alaska and northern Canada; winters at sea in offshore Pacific and Atlantic waters, generally farther north than most other seabirds. Breeds in Europe, to Greenland, Svalbard; also parts of Russia.

| Length **17½–19½in (45–50cm)** | Wingspan **3¼–3½ft (1–1.1m)** | Weight **16–35oz (0.45–1kg)** |
| Social **Flocks** | Lifespan **Up to 50 years** | Status **Secure** |

| Order **Procellariiformes** | Family **Procellariidae** | Species *Pterodroma hasitata* |

Black-capped Petrel

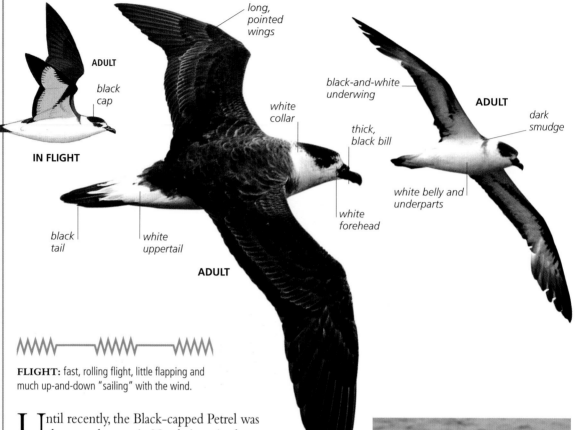

ADULT

black cap

IN FLIGHT

long, pointed wings

white collar

black-and-white underwing

ADULT

dark smudge

thick, black bill

white forehead

white belly and underparts

black tail

white uppertail

ADULT

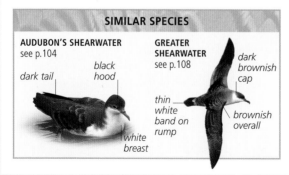

FLIGHT: fast, rolling flight, little flapping and much up-and-down "sailing" with the wind.

Until recently, the Black-capped Petrel was almost unknown in North America because its feeding grounds are located well offshore. After breeding in the West Indies, much of the population moves northwest to feed in the warm Gulf Stream during the summer, where the petrels are seen fairly commonly on deep-water birdwatching trips. The Black-capped Petrel's flight is characteristic of *Pterodroma* species, as it rockets up above the ocean and then drops back down while moving forward swiftly, using lift from the air currents above the water.

VOICE Silent at sea; quite vocal on breeding grounds.
NESTING Underground burrow on high-elevation forested slopes of tropical islands; 1 egg; 1 brood; December–April.
FEEDING Picks fish and squid from the surface of the ocean.

COMPARISON
Note the field marks that separate the Black-capped Petrel flying past a paddling Greater Shearwater.

SIMILAR SPECIES

AUDUBON'S SHEARWATER
see p.104

dark tail

black hood

white breast

GREATER SHEARWATER
see p.108

dark brownish cap

thin white band on rump

brownish overall

OCCURRENCE
When not breeding, forages at sea over the deep, warm water of the Gulf Stream off the southeastern US. Breeds in the West Indies, where dogs and rats are a serious threat to birds and their chicks.

| Length **13in (33cm)** | Wingspan **35in (88cm)** | Weight **17oz (475g)** |
| Social **Solitary/Flocks** | Lifespan **Unknown** | Status **Endangered** |

Order **Procellariiformes**	Family **Procellariidae**	Species *Calonectris diomedea*

Cory's Shearwater

long, pointed wings

pale rump

ADULT

IN FLIGHT

dark wingtip and trailing edge

clean white underwing

all white belly

ADULT

scalloped pattern

grayish head and chin

yellow bill with dark tip

ADULT

white breast, with sooty-gray sides

Close studies of a group of Cory's Shearwaters off the Atlantic coast suggest the presence of two forms. The more common form, *C. d. borealis*, nests in the eastern Atlantic and is chunkier, with less white in the wing from below. The other form, *C. d. diomedea*, breeds in the Mediterranean, has a more slender build (including a thinner bill), and has more extensive white under the wing. Cory's Shearwater has a distinctive, relatively languid flight style that is different from the other shearwaters regularly found in North American waters.

VOICE Mostly silent at sea; descending, lamb-like bleating.

NESTING Nests in burrow or rocky crevice; 1 egg; 1 brood; May–September.

FEEDING Dives into water or picks at surface for small schooling fish, and marine invertebrates such as squid.

FLIGHT: slow, deliberate wing beats interspersed with long glides; often arcs strongly on bent wings.

LAZY FLIERS
In calm weather Cory's Shearwaters look heavy and fly low, swooping higher in strong winds.

OCCURRENCE
This species breeds in the Mediterranean and on islands of the eastern Atlantic, including the Azores, the Salvages, Madeira, and the Canaries. When nonbreeding, Cory's Shearwaters disperse widely over the Atlantic Ocean.

SIMILAR SPECIES

AUDUBON'S SHEARWATER
see p.104

dark brown overall

GREATER SHEARWATER
see p.108

dark head

brownish overall

white neck

Length **18in (46cm)**	Wingspan **3½ft (1.1m)**	Weight **28oz (800g)**
Social **Flocks**	Lifespan **Unknown**	Status **Secure**

| Order **Procellariiformes** | Family **Procellariidae** | Species **_Puffinus puffinus_** |

Manx Shearwater

long, pointed wings

black edge of wing

IN FLIGHT

very dark brownish black upperparts

head is black above, white below

crisp white underwings

long, thin, hooked bill

white undertail feathers

snow white underparts

dark upperwings

small head

dark, hooked bill

short tail

white throat

Most shearwaters are little known because of their nocturnal and oceanic ways, but the Manx is an exception. It is common in the British Isles, and ornithologists have been studying it there for decades. Long-term banding programs revealed one bird that flew over 3,000 miles (4,800km) from Massachusetts to its nesting burrow in Wales in just 12½ days, and another that was captured 56 years after it was first banded, making its accumulated migration-only mileage around 600,000 miles (1,000,000km).
VOICE Usually silent at sea, but at breeding sites, produces loud and raucous series of cries, _kah-kah-kah-kah-kah-HOWW_.
NESTING In burrow, in peaty soil, or rocky crevice; 1 egg; 1 brood; April–October.
FEEDING Dives into water, often with open wings and stays underwater, or picks at surface for small schooling fish and squid.

FLIGHT: rapid, stiff wing beats interspersed with glides; arcs high in strong winds.

PITTER-PATTER
Unlike gulls, shearwaters have to patter along the surface with their feet to achieve lift-off speed.

SIMILAR SPECIES

BLACK-VENTED SHEARWATER
see p.103

AUDUBON'S SHEARWATER
see p.104

brownish upperparts

paler head

longer tail

slightly smaller overall

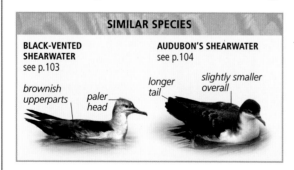

OCCURRENCE
Breeds on many islands in eastern North Atlantic; restricted to islands off Newfoundland in North America. Regularly occurs off US east coast as far south as Florida. Rare in Gulf of Mexico and off the West Coast. Rarely seen from shore; cold-water shearwater.

| Length **13½in (34cm)** | Wingspan **33in (83cm)** | Weight **14–20oz (400–575g)** |
| Social **Migrant flocks** | Lifespan **Up to 55 years** | Status **Secure** |

Order **Procellariiformes**	Family **Procellariidae**	Species *Puffinus opisthomelas*

Black-vented Shearwater

mostly white underwings

ADULT

IN FLIGHT

dark smudging on head and upper breast

ADULT

dark undertail feathers

short, relatively rounded wings

variable pale patch

long, dark tail

brownish overall

irregularly marked, pale face

dark eyes stand out on pale face

long, dark bill

ADULT

whitish underparts

The Black-vented Shearwater is one of the few species of tubenoses that can be seen from land. It is an inshore feeder, and flocks of hundreds are often seen from various vantage points along the southern and central coasts of California. Its presence in waters farther north is rare, and seems to be linked to seawater temperatures because this species favors warm waters. The plumage variation of this species is unique—birds range from ghostly pale beige (especially on the head) to very dark.

VOICE Silent at sea; breeding ground vocalizations unknown.
NESTING Burrow in soil or rocky crevice; 1 egg; 1 brood; February–July.
FEEDING Shallow dives to catch fish and squid at the surface; also catches fish while swimming.

FLIGHT: rapid, stiff wing beats interspersed with glides; arcs high in strong winds.

DINGY BROWN
This species' dull and muddy head coloration, and white body and wings aid identification.

OCCURRENCE
Breeds on islands off Baja California, Mexico; spends August–January off the Pacific coast from southern California south to Mexico (as far as Oaxaca). Northernmost and southernmost extent of post-breeding range not well known. A warm-water shearwater.

SIMILAR SPECIES

MANX SHEARWATER see p.102

SOOTY SHEARWATER see p.105

head black above, white below

very dark upperparts

upperparts entirely sooty black

Length **14in (36cm)**	Wingspan **34in (86cm)**	Weight **10–17oz (275–475g)**
Social **Flocks**	Lifespan **Unknown**	Status **Declining**

| Order **Procellariiformes** | Family **Procellariidae** | Species *Puffinus lherminieri* |

Audubon's Shearwater

ADULT

short, rounded wingtips

pale underwings

ADULT

ADULT

dark undertail feathers

white underparts

long tail

IN FLIGHT

dark brown upperparts

dark, hooked bill

dark tail

ADULT

white neck

white underparts

FLIGHT: low to water; fluttery, stiff wing beats interspersed with glides; arcs up in strong winds.

Audubon's Shearwater, also known as the Tropical Shearwater, is much smaller and more slender than all the other regularly occurring shearwaters in Northern American waters and comprises around 10 distinct subspecies. It has especially short wings that, when combined with its small size, make its flight similar to members of the Alcidae family (auks, murres, and puffins). In the northwestern Atlantic, the only really similar species is the Manx Shearwater, which has much longer, narrower, pointed wings. and white undertail feathers.

VOICE Occasional thin, high-pitched call; silent at sea; twittering and mewing calls at colonies.

NESTING Nests in burrow or rocky crevice; 1 egg; 1 brood; breeds year round.

FEEDING Dives into water and forages at surface for small schooling fish, such as sardines, and mollusks, such as squid.

RARE ON LAND
Audubon's Shearwater spends most of its life at sea, coming to land in the nesting season.

SIMILAR SPECIES

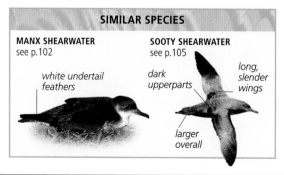

MANX SHEARWATER
see p.102

white undertail feathers

SOOTY SHEARWATER
see p.105

dark upperparts

long, slender wings

larger overall

OCCURRENCE
Breeds on Caribbean islands; widespread in tropical waters; spends warmer months feeding in the Gulf of Mexico and along the east coast of the US, as far north as Massachusetts. Depending on when they breed, nesting populations can be found at almost anytime of the year.

| Length **12in (31cm)** | Wingspan **27in (69cm)** | Weight **6oz (175g)** |
| Social **Flocks** | Lifespan **Unknown** | Status **Secure** |

Order **Procellariiformes**	Family **Procellariidae**	Species *Puffinus griseus*

Sooty Shearwater

silvery white patch along underwing

ADULT

ADULT

all-dark underparts

IN FLIGHT

long, slender wings

ADULT

all-dark upperparts

sooty head

long, hooked bill

FLIGHT: rapid, stiff wing beats, interspersed with glides; arcs up highly in strong winds.

Sooty Shearwaters are extremely long-distance migrants, with both Atlantic and Pacific populations undergoing lengthy circular migrations. Pacific birds in particular travel as far as 300 miles (480km) per day and an extraordinary 45,000 miles (72,500km) or more per year. Huge flocks of the bird are often seen off the coast of California. It is fairly easy to identify off the East Coast of the US, as it is the only all-dark shearwater found there.
VOICE Silent at sea; occasionally gives varied, agitated vocalizations when feeding, very loud calls at breeding colonies.
NESTING In burrow or rocky crevice; 1 egg; 1 brood; October–May.
FEEDING Dives and picks at surface for small schooling fish and mollusks such as squid.

HUGE FLOCKS
Sooty Shearwaters are often found in "rafts" numbering many thousands of birds.

TUBENOSE
Shearwaters are tubenoses, so-called for the salt-excreting tubes on their bills.

SIMILAR SPECIES

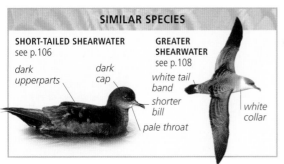

SHORT-TAILED SHEARWATER
see p.106

dark upperparts

dark cap

GREATER SHEARWATER
see p.108

white tail band

shorter bill

pale throat

white collar

OCCURRENCE
Sooty Shearwaters breed on islands in the southern Ocean and nearby waters, some colonies number thousands of pairs. Postbreeding movements take them north into the Pacific and Atlantic Ocean, on 8-shaped migrations.

Length **18in (46cm)**	Wingspan **3ft 3in (1m)**	Weight **27oz (775g)**
Social **Flocks**	Lifespan **Unknown**	Status **Secure**

| Order **Procellariiformes** | Family **Procellariidae** | Species *Puffinus tenuirostris* |

Short-tailed Shearwater

thin wing

ADULT

dark underwing with central paler line

IN FLIGHT

dark sooty brown overall

dark cap contrasts with paler cheeks and white throat

rounded crown

"bulb" at tip

dark, short bill

ADULT

FLIGHT: rapid, stiff wing beats interspersed with glides; will arch up high in strong winds.

S hort-tailed Shearwaters are abundant off the Alaskan coast in the summer, where they have been seen in gigantic groups numbering perhaps in the millions. The total world population may be about 50 million. The Short-tailed Shearwater spends most of its life at sea, and its migration route follows a huge figure 8 around the North Pacific. Field identification is difficult, as they look very similar to Sooty Shearwaters. However, the Short-tailed Shearwater has some distinguishing features. It is more compact overall, with a rounder crown, shorter bill, a dark head contrasting with a paler throat and breast, and more uniform underwings, that may include a pale part extending onto the outer wing feathers.

VOICE Silent at sea; varied, agitated vocalizations when feeding.
NESTING Burrow dug in peat; 1 egg; 1 brood; September–April.
FEEDING Dives and picks at surface for small schooling fish, squid, octopus, and crustaceans.

DARK BIRD
A rounded head, short bill, pale throat, and dark underwings identify this bird.

SIMILAR SPECIES

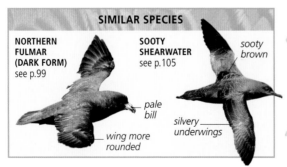

NORTHERN FULMAR (DARK FORM) see p.99

SOOTY SHEARWATER see p.105

sooty brown

pale bill

wing more rounded

silvery underwings

OCCURRENCE
Breeds on islands off eastern Australia from New South Wales to Tasmania; migrates north to spend its winter (US summer) in the Gulf of Alaska and the Bering Sea, where it is common; during spring migration (US fall and early winter) it passes along the West Coast of North America.

| Length **17in (43cm)** | Wingspan **3ft 3in (1m)** | Weight **19oz (550g)** |
| Social **Large flocks** | Lifespan **Unknown** | Status **Secure** |

Order **Procellariiformes**	Family **Procellariidae**	Species *Puffinus creatopus*

Pink-footed Shearwater

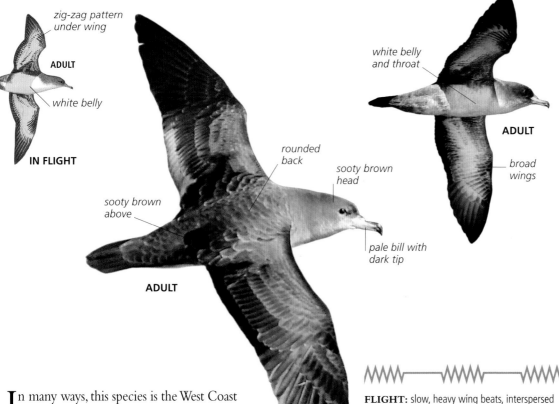

zig-zag pattern under wing

ADULT

white belly

IN FLIGHT

white belly and throat

ADULT

rounded back

sooty brown head

broad wings

sooty brown above

pale bill with dark tip

ADULT

In many ways, this species is the West Coast equivalent of Cory's Shearwater. The way it holds its wings (angled at the "wrist"), its size, and its flight style are all reminiscent of Cory's. Though Pink-footed Shearwaters are fairly variable in plumage, they are always rather dull, with little color variation. This plumage pattern is similar to that of the Black-vented Shearwater, and as both species are found off the California coast in fall and spring identification is difficult. However, the Pink-footed Shearwater can be distinguished by its larger size and distinctly pinkish bill.

VOICE Usually silent at sea, but may produce a horse-like whinny when feeding with other sea birds.

NESTING Burrows in peat; 1 egg; 1 brood; October–March.

FEEDING Like other shearwaters, makes shallow dives to catch squid, octopus, and fish.

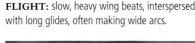

FLIGHT: slow, heavy wing beats, interspersed with long glides, often making wide arcs.

PINK FEET
This Pink-footed Shearwater, ready to alight on the water, shows off its pink legs and feet.

SIMILAR SPECIES

BLACK-VENTED SHEARWATER see p.103

SOOTY SHEARWATER see p.105

usually pale head

smaller overall

sooty brown overall

smaller overall

pale chest

OCCURRENCE
Breeds on a few islands off Chile, including Juan Fernandez. Spends its winter (US summer) off the coasts of the Americas, reaching as far north as British Columbia and southern Alaska. Found closer to shore than other shearwaters. On Juan Fernandez, population reduced by predation of introduced rats.

Length **19in (48cm)**	Wingspan **3½ft (1.1m)**	Weight **26oz (725g)**
Social **Flocks**	Lifespan **Unknown**	Status **Vulnerable**

| Order **Procellariiformes** | Family **Procellariidae** | Species *Puffinus gravis* |

Greater Shearwater

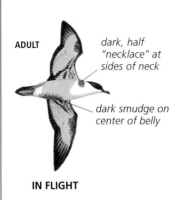

ADULT

dark, half "necklace" at sides of neck

dark smudge on center of belly

IN FLIGHT

darker outer wing feathers

brownish upperwings

white collar

dark cap

thin, black bill

thin, white band on rump

ADULT

A common species in North Atlantic waters, from northern Canada to Florida, the Greater Shearwater is similar in size to Cory's Shearwater and the birds scavenge together for scraps around fishing boats. However, their plumages and flight styles are quite different. While Cory's Shearwater has slow, labored wing beats, and glides high on broad, bowed, swept-back wings, Greater Shearwaters keep low, flapping hurriedly between glides on straight, narrow wings. The brown smudges on the belly (not always visible) and paler underwings of the Greater Shearwater also help distinguish the species.
VOICE Silent at sea; descending, lamb-like bleating at breeding sites.
NESTING Digs deep burrow in peaty or boggy soil; 1 egg; 1 brood; September–March.
FEEDING Feeds either from the surface, picking up items such as fish and squid, or makes shallow dives with open wings.

FLIGHT: fast, stiff wing beats interspersed with gliding; arcs high in windy conditions.

WHITE COLLAR
The Greater Shearwater's white collar is highly visible between its black cap and sooty back.

SIMILAR SPECIES

BLACK-CAPPED PETREL
see p.100

large, white rump

white forehead

MANX SHEARWATER
see p.102

darker plumage

smaller overall

OCCURRENCE
Nests on just a few islands in the middle of the South Atlantic. Total population probably well over 200 million. Postbreeding birds make a very long 8-shaped migration around the Atantic, spending late July–September in North Atlantic waters, usually offshore.

| Length **18in (46cm)** | Wingspan **3½ft (1.1m)** | Weight **30oz (850g)** |
| Social **Flocks** | Lifespan **At least 25 years** | Status **Secure** |

| Order **Procellariiformes** | Family **Hydrobatidae** | Species **Oceanites oceanicus** |

Wilson's Storm-Petrel

broad, pointed wings

white rump and lower flanks

pale bar on upperwing

ADULT

IN FLIGHT

"walking" on water

dark wings and body

small, black "tube nose"

ADULT

short, square tail

yellow webbing between toes

Named after Alexander Wilson, often called the "father of North American ornithology," Wilson's Storm-Petrel is the quintessential small oceanic petrel. It is an extremely abundant species and breeds in the many millions on the Antarctic Peninsula and islands in Antarctica. After breeding, many move north to spend the summer off the Atlantic coast of North America. Here, they are a familiar sight to fishermen and birders at sea. By August they can be seen lingering, but by October they have flown south.

VOICE At sea, soft rasping notes; at breeding sites a variety of *coos*, *churrs*, and twitters during the night.

NESTING Mostly in rock crevices; also burrows where there is peaty soil; 1 egg; 1 brood; November–March.

FEEDING Patters on the water's surface, legs extended, picking up tiny crustaceans; also carrion, droplets of oil.

FLIGHT: flutters, low to ocean's surface, often "stalling" to drop to the surface and glean food.

FEEDING FLOCK
While flying, this bird "walks" on water, simultaneously picking food from the surface.

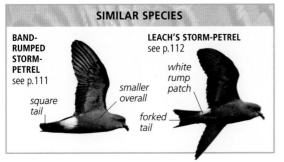

SIMILAR SPECIES

BAND-RUMPED STORM-PETREL see p.111

square tail

smaller overall

LEACH'S STORM-PETREL see p.112

white rump patch

forked tail

OCCURRENCE
Breeds on the Antarctic Peninsula, many sub-Antarctic islands, and islands in the Cape Horn Archipelago. April –September or October, moves north, and is abundant off the coasts of New England, New York, and New Jersey July– September. With inshore winds, can often be seen from land.

| Length **6¾in (17cm)** | Wingspan **16in (41cm)** | Weight **1¹⁄₁₆–1⁷⁄₁₆oz (30–40g)** |
| Social **Flocks** | Lifespan **Up to 10 years** | Status **Secure** |

| Order **Procellariiformes** | Family **Hydrobatidae** | Species *Oceanodroma microsoma* |

Least Storm-Petrel

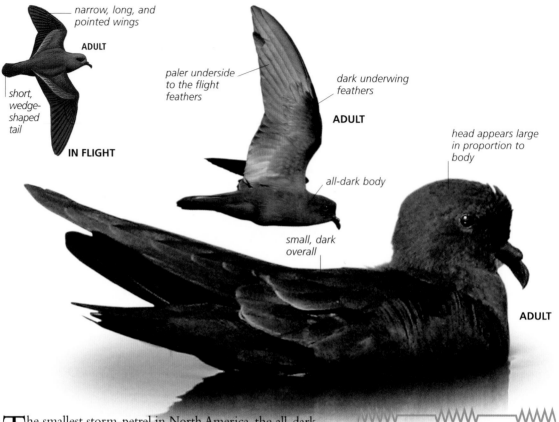

narrow, long, and pointed wings

ADULT

short, wedge-shaped tail

IN FLIGHT

paler underside to the flight feathers

dark underwing feathers

ADULT

all-dark body

small, dark overall

head appears large in proportion to body

ADULT

The smallest storm-petrel in North America, the all-dark Least Storm-Petrel is numerous in flocks of tubenoses off the southern California coast in fall. These tiny petrels are very susceptible to predation by introduced cats and rats on their Pacific nesting islands. Least Storm-Petrels are often blown inland by California's hurricanes; for example, hundreds appeared on Salton Sea after Hurricane Kathleen in 1976. The Least Storm-Petrel is dark and similar in appearance to the Black Storm-Petrel, but the latter flies with slower wing beats interrupted by glides.

VOICE Silent at sea; whirring and purring at breeding sites.

NESTING Under rock pile or crevice on island; 1 egg; 1 brood; July–September.

FEEDING Picks small crustaceans off the water while flying.

FLIGHT: rapid and jerky; low along the surface of the ocean with deep, quick wing beats.

BALANCING ACT
The Least Storm-Petrel forages on the sea's surface, often balancing on the water with its feet.

SIMILAR SPECIES

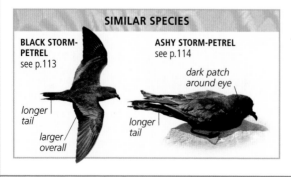

BLACK STORM-PETREL
see p.113

longer tail

larger overall

ASHY STORM-PETREL
see p.114

dark patch around eye

longer tail

OCCURRENCE
Breeds on a small number of islands along the Pacific and Gulf shores of Baja California, Mexico. After breeding season (August–October), many birds disperse north to warm waters off southern California and south along the Pacific coast of Mexico and Central America, south to Ecuador.

| Length **5½in (14cm)** | Wingspan **13in (33cm)** | Weight **¹¹⁄₁₆oz (20g)** |
| Social **Flocks** | Lifespan **Unknown** | Status **Secure** |

| Order **Procellariiformes** | Family **Hydrobatidae** | Species *Oceanodroma castro* |

Band-rumped Storm-Petrel

pale bars on upperwing

ADULT

IN FLIGHT

long, broad wings

all-dark underwing

ADULT

white extends to sides

feet do not extend beyond tail in flight

ADULT

narrow, white band on rump and rear flanks

square or shallowly notched tail

small, black bill

The Band-rumped Storm-Petrel is an uncommon summer visitor to warm offshore waters of the Gulf Stream and the Gulf of Mexico. It can be seen from boats about 25–35 miles (40–56km) offshore. Its origin is unclear, but it is likely that it comes from colonies in the eastern Atlantic. When compared to other Atlantic storm-petrels at sea, Band-rumped Storm-Petrels appear brawny, long-winged, and square-tailed, with the white at the base of the tail extending down to the belly. Their flight pattern is more direct and less erratic than the smaller Wilson's.

VOICE Silent at sea; squeaking and purring sounds at nest.
NESTING Underground burrow on island free of predators; 1 egg; 1 brood; timing variable depending on breeding location.
FEEDING Picks small fish and other small marine creatures, such as crustaceans, from the ocean surface.

FLIGHT: more direct than other Atlantic storm-petrels; less fluttering, more long, banking glides.

TAKE OFF
These petrels show off their namesake white rump band as they take off from the water.

SIMILAR SPECIES

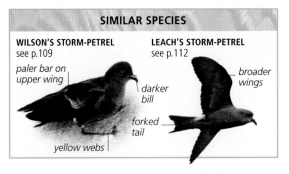

WILSON'S STORM-PETREL
see p.109

paler bar on upper wing

darker bill

yellow webs

LEACH'S STORM-PETREL
see p.112

broader wings

forked tail

OCCURRENCE
A warm-water petrel of the Gulf Stream and Gulf of Mexico. Breeds on islands of the tropical and subtropical parts of the Pacific (*O. c. bangsi*) and Atlantic (*O. c. castro*). Disperses throughout both oceans; most birds seen in North America probably breed in eastern Atlantic Ocean.

| Length **7½–8½ in (19–21cm)** | Wingspan **17–18½ in (43–47cm)** | Weight **1⁷⁄₁₆–1¾oz (40–50g)** |
| Social **Solitary/Small flocks** | Lifespan **Up to 6 years** | Status **Secure** |

Order **Procellariiformes**	Family **Hydrobatidae**	Species *Oceanodroma leucorhoa*

Leach's Storm-Petrel

IN FLIGHT

long, angled wings

ADULT

white rump with thin, dark line down center

ADULT

brown bar across blackish wings

dark sooty black underwings

dark smudge beside eye

forked tail

dark sooty brown underparts

ADULT

FLIGHT: buoyant, deep wing beats low over ocean's surface, interrupted by twists and turns.

Leach's Storm-Petrel is widespread in both the Atlantic and Pacific Oceans, unlike most other storm-petrels. It breeds in colonies on islands off the coasts, coming to land at night and feeding offshore during the day, often many miles from the colony. This wide-ranging storm-petrel has both geographical and individual variation; most populations show a white rump, but others have a dark rump that is the same color as the rest of the body. Leach's Storm-Petrel can be distinguished from the similar Band-rumped Storm-Petrel by its notched tail and swooping flight.

VOICE At nesting sites, often from burrows, calls are long series of soft purring and chattering sounds.

NESTING Underground burrow on island free of predators such as rats; 1 egg; 1 brood; May–November.

FEEDING Gleans small crustaceans and small fish from the water's surface while in flight.

BALANCING ACT
Leach's Storm-Petrel will often balance itself with its wings while walking.

OCCURRENCE
Breeds on islands in the Pacific Ocean from Alaska and the Aleutian Islands south to California; in the Atlantic Ocean, from Newfoundland to Maine. After breeding, it wanders widely on both oceans, keeping well out of sight of land.

SIMILAR SPECIES

BAND-RUMPED STORM-PETREL
see p.111

white of rump extends toward belly

BLACK STORM-PETREL
see p.113

dark rump

Length **7–8½in (18–22cm)**	Wingspan **17½–19in (45–48cm)**	Weight **1⁹⁄₁₆–1¾oz (45–50g)**
Social **Colonies**	Lifespan **Up to 36 years**	Status **Secure**

Order **Procellariiformes**	Family **Hydrobatidae**	Species *Oceanodroma melania*

Black Storm-Petrel

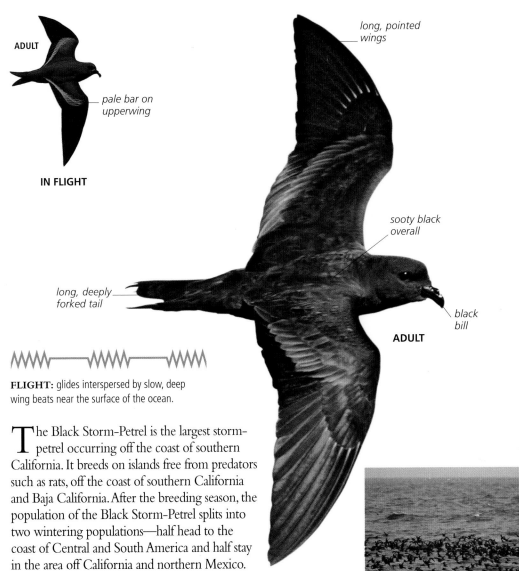

ADULT

IN FLIGHT

pale bar on upperwing

long, pointed wings

sooty black overall

long, deeply forked tail

black bill

ADULT

FLIGHT: glides interspersed by slow, deep wing beats near the surface of the ocean.

The Black Storm-Petrel is the largest storm-petrel occurring off the coast of southern California. It breeds on islands free from predators such as rats, off the coast of southern California and Baja California. After the breeding season, the population of the Black Storm-Petrel splits into two wintering populations—half head to the coast of Central and South America and half stay in the area off California and northern Mexico.

VOICE Silent at sea; in colonies, emits long, undulated, chattering and purring sounds.

NESTING Boulder crevice on small rocky island; 1 egg; 1 brood; May–November.

FEEDING Picks small crustaceans and fish from the surface.

FEEDING FLOCK
Large flocks of Black Storm-Petrels often feed far off the coast of southern California in the fall.

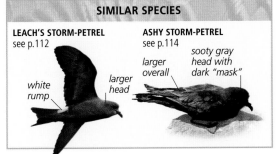

SIMILAR SPECIES

LEACH'S STORM-PETREL
see p.112

white rump

larger head

ASHY STORM-PETREL
see p.114

larger overall

sooty gray head with dark "mask"

OCCURRENCE
A warm-water species, breeding on a number of small islands off both the Pacific and Gulf Coasts of Baja California. Postbreeding dispersal takes birds northward to Oregon and southward along the Pacific coast to Mexico, Central and South America, as far as Peru.

Length **9in (23cm)**	Wingspan **19–21in (48–53cm)**	Weight **2⅛oz (60g)**
Social **Solitary/Flocks**	Lifespan **Unknown**	Status **Secure**

| Order **Procellariiformes** | Family **Hydrobatidae** | Species *Oceanodroma homochroa* |

Ashy Storm-Petrel

short wings

dark overall

darker smudge around eye

steep forehead

ADULT

pale upperwing bars

ADULT

forked tail

hooked black bill, with tube-shaped nostrils on top

dark legs and feet

IN FLIGHT

The Ashy Storm-Petrel is one of four all-dark storm-petrels that nest on islands in the offshore waters of California and Baja California. It is smaller than the Black Storm-Petrel and Leach's Storm-Petrel, but larger than the Least Storm-Petrel. Since it is non-migratory, it can afford to spend more time molting each year than the other three species, which are all migratory and fly south for the winter. The Ashy Storm-Petrel's molt overlaps with its breeding season, a phenomenon that requires more energy than most migratory species can dare to expend. Over the sea, it has rapid, shallow, fluttering wing beats but a fairly direct flight, and it looks noticeably long-tailed. It is paler and grayer overall than the Black Storm-petrel, but these small seabirds require good views and careful examination for accurate identification.

VOICE Usually silent at sea; coos and other calls at colonies.

NESTING Cavities and crevices in boulders, on slopes of rocky islands; 1 egg; 1 brood; May–January.

FEEDING Plucks small fish, squid, and shrimps from the surface of the ocean.

FLIGHT: abrupt, fluttering flight, low over the ocean surface; wings held below horizontal.

TRAVELLING TOGETHER
Ashy Storm-Petrels travel, feed, and roost in flocks, as do most other storm-petrels.

SIMILAR SPECIES

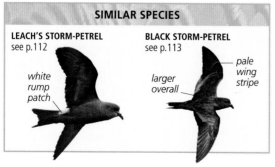

LEACH'S STORM-PETREL
see p.112

white rump patch

BLACK STORM-PETREL
see p.113

larger overall

pale wing stripe

OCCURRENCE
Breeds on islands off the coast of California (Farallon, San Miguel, Santa Barbara, Santa Clara, Santa Cruz), and northern Baja California (Los Coronados). Post-breeding dispersal takes some birds north to waters off Humboldt County, others south to waters off central Baja California.

| Length **7½in (19cm)** | Wingspan **16–18in (41–46cm)** | Weight **1⁷⁄₁₆oz (40g)** |
| Social **Colonies** | Lifespan **Unknown** | Status **Endangered** |

Order **Procellariiformes**	Family **Hydrobatidae**	Species *Oceanodroma furcata*

Fork-tailed Storm-Petrel

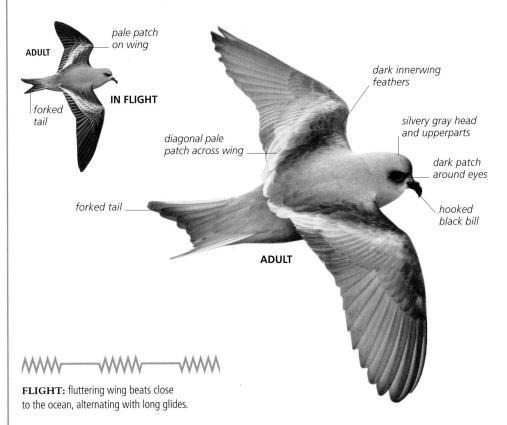

ADULT

pale patch on wing

IN FLIGHT

forked tail

dark innerwing feathers

silvery gray head and upperparts

diagonal pale patch across wing

dark patch around eyes

forked tail

hooked black bill

ADULT

FLIGHT: fluttering wing beats close to the ocean, alternating with long glides.

The Fork-tailed Storm-Petrel is one of the most distinctive of all storm-petrels in North American waters, with its ghostly silvery gray plumage, and forked tail. It is the most northerly breeding storm-petrel in the North Pacific, nesting all the way north to the Aleutian Islands. It incubates its eggs at lower temperatures than other petrels do, and its chicks can be left alone between feeding for a longer time—apparently an adaptation to northern conditions. Its chicks can also lower their body temperature, thereby conserving energy.

VOICE Silent at sea; various purring sounds at colonies.
NESTING Underground burrow on offshore island; 1 egg; 1 brood; March–November.
FEEDING Plucks shrimps, squids, and small fish from the surface of the ocean.

AERIAL SURVEY
Flying low over the ocean, the Fork-tailed Storm-Petrel looks out for fish below.

SIMILAR SPECIES

LEACH'S STORM-PETREL
see p.112

white rump patch

dark brown overall

ASHY STORM-PETREL
see p.114

slightly smaller

brown overall

OCCURRENCE
Breeds in colonies on offshore rocky islands from California northward to Alaska, mostly to the Aleutian Islands, and south to islands off British Columbia; also Washington and Oregon. Post-breeding dispersal takes birds to the Bering Sea and to offshore waters of California.

Length **8in (20cm)**	Wingspan **18in (46cm)**	Weight **2oz (55g)**
Social **Colonies**	Lifespan **At least 14 years**	Status **Secure**

Family **Podicipedidae**

GREBES

GREBES RESEMBLE LOONS and share many of their aquatic habits, but anatomical and molecular features show that they are actually unrelated; and they are placed in a different order: the Podicipediformes. Grebe bodies are streamlined, offering little resistance when diving and swimming. Underwater their primary means of propulsion is the sideways motion of their lobed toes. The legs are placed far back on the body, which greatly aids the bird when swimming above or below the surface. Grebes have short tails, and their trailing legs and toes serve as rudders when they fly. The position of the legs makes it impossible, however, for grebes to stand upright for long or easily walk on land. Thus, even when breeding they are tied to water; and their nests are usually partially floating platforms, built on beds of water plants. Grebes toes have broad lobes that splay when the bird thrusts forward through the water with its feet. They dive to catch fish with a short, forward arching spring. Unusually among birds, they swallow feathers, supposedly to trap fish bones and protect their stomachs, then periodically disgorge them. Like loons, grebes can control their buoyancy by exhaling air and compressing their plumage so that they sink quietly below the surface. They are strong fliers, and migratory.

PIED BILL
The black-and-white bill pattern clearly distinguishes this bird as the Pied-billed Grebe.

A FINE DISPLAY
This Horned Grebe reveals the colorful plumes on its head, as part of its elaborate courtship display.

SIDE BY SIDE
This pair of Western Grebes is displaying their elaborate courtship behavior.

Order **Podicipediformes**	Family **Podicipedidae**	Species *Tachybaptus dominicus*

Least Grebe

IN FLIGHT

neck held high

ADULT (SUMMER)

legs extend beyond tail

white flight feathers

brown head

paler bill

ADULT (WINTER)

gray head

yellowish orange eye

dark gray plumage

small, pointed bill

blackish gray cheeks and throat

pale, whitish gray puffy undertail

ADULT (SUMMER)

A tiny bird, this tropical and subtropical species is the most easily overlooked of the North American grebes. This is primarily because, in the continent, it breeds only in fresh or brackish water in southern Texas, often choosing temporary ponds. The Least Grebe is a great diver, capable of remaining submerged for over 25 seconds. When fleeing from danger, it has been known to hide underwater, with only its head poking above the water's surface. While adults are not seen on land, swimming chicks, when threatened, can clamber ashore.

VOICE Metallic, sputtering trill, accelerating at the start, then slowing and accelerating again; alarm call a single *beep*.

NESTING Floating nest of mostly decaying vegetation anchored to emergent plants, sometimes in the open; fresh plants and mud added as needed; 4–6 eggs; 2–3 broods; April–August.

FEEDING Primarily feeds on aquatic insects; also crustaceans, spiders, and other arthropods; small fish and tadpoles from shallow water or from above surface; also feeds on algae and other plant matter.

FLIGHT: short flight with strenuously quick wing beats; paddles rapidly during take-off.

UP FOR AIR
Fresh from its dive to catch prey, this Least Grebe has not had time to dry its plumage.

OCCURRENCE
Found in tropical and subtropical regions, temporary or permanent bodies of fresh and brackish water, such as mangrove swamps, marsh openings, small ponds, ditches, lakes, and slow-moving rivers, often with very little or no emergent vegetation.

SIMILAR SPECIES

PIED-BILLED GREBE
larger overall; see p.118

black-ringed, white bill

tawny brown sides

Length **9–10½in (23–27cm)**	Wingspan **19–21in (48–53cm)**	Weight **3½–6oz (100–175g)**
Social **Small flocks**	Lifespan **Unknown**	Status **Localized**

| Order **Podicipediformes** | Family **Podicipedidae** | Species *Podilymbus podiceps* |

Pied-billed Grebe

outstretched neck

ADULT (BREEDING)

lighter flight feathers

IN FLIGHT

yellowish bill

whitish throat

ADULT (NONBREEDING)

brown eye

whitish, hooked bill with a black ring

black throat patch

brownish gray body

reddish brown neck and breast

ADULT (BREEDING)

white undertail

The widest ranging of the North American grebes, the Pied-billed Grebe is tolerant of highly populated areas and is often seen breeding on lakes and ponds across North America. It is a powerful swimmer and can remain submerged for 16–30 seconds when it dives. In contrast to some of the elaborate displays from other grebe species, its courtship ritual is more vocal than visual and a pair usually duet-call in the mating season. Migration, conducted at night, is delayed until its breeding area ices up and food becomes scarce. The Pied-billed Grebe is capable of sustained flights of over 2,000 miles (3,200km).
VOICE Various grunts and wails; in spring, call a cuckoo-like repeated gobble *kup-kup-Kaow-Kaow-kaow*, gradually speeding up.
NESTING Floating nest of partially decayed plants and clipped leaves, attached to emergent vegetation in marshes and quiet waters; 4–7 eggs; 2 broods; April–October.
FEEDING Dives to catch a variety of crustaceans, fish, amphibians, insects, and other invertebrates; also picks prey from emergent vegetation, or catches them mid-air.

FLIGHT: strong, direct flight with rapid wing beats, but rarely seen.

BACK OFF
When alarmed, a Pied-billed Grebe will flap its wings in a defensive display.

SIMILAR SPECIES

LEAST GREBE ✿
see p.117

smaller bill

yellow eye

darker body

OCCURRENCE
Breeds on a variety of water bodies, including coastal brackish ponds, seasonal ponds, marshes, and even sewage ponds. Winters in the breeding area if food and open water are available, otherwise chooses still waters resembling its breeding habitat.

| Length **12–15in (31–38cm)** | Wingspan **18–24in (46–62cm)** | Weight **13–17oz (375–475g)** |
| Social **Family groups** | Lifespan **At least 3 years** | Status **Vulnerable** |

| Order **Podicipediformes** | Family **Podicipedidae** | Species ***Podiceps grisegena*** |

Red-necked Grebe

IN FLIGHT

head and neck in line with body

white-edged inner wing

ADULT (BREEDING)

pale, reddish brown crescent near ear

brownish cap

ADULT (NONBREEDING)

broad stripes on cheek and ear

mostly yellowish bill

JUVENILE

broad head with crest at rear

black cap

brown eye

grayish white cheeks and throat

chestnut brown neck and chest

gray flanks

ADULT (BREEDING)

The Red-necked Grebe is smaller than Western and Clark's Grebes, but larger than the other North American grebes. It migrates over short to medium distances and spends the winter along both coasts, where large flocks may be seen during the day. It runs along the water's surface to become airborne, although it rarely flies. This grebe doesn't come ashore often; it stands erect, but walks awkwardly, and prefers to sink to its breast and shuffle along.

VOICE Nasal, gull-like call on breeding grounds, evolves into bray, ends with whinny; also honks, rattles, hisses, purrs, and ticks.

NESTING Compact, buoyant mound of decayed and fresh vegetation in sheltered, shallow marshes and lakes, or artificial wetlands; 4–5 eggs; 1 brood; May–July.

FEEDING An opportunistic hunter, eats fish, crustaceans, aquatic insects, worms, mollusks, salamanders, and tadpoles.

FLIGHT: fast, direct, wing beats, with head and outstretched neck mostly level with line of body.

COURTSHIP DISPLAY
This courting pair face each other, with outstreched necks and raised chests.

SIMILAR SPECIES

RED-THROATED LOON ❋
see p.91

white spots on back

white neck

no yellow on bill

HORNED GREBE ❋
see p.120

reddish eye paler neck

OCCURRENCE
Breeds from northern prairies and forests, almost to the tree line in the northwest; limited to suitable interior bodies of water such as large marshes and small lakes. Winters primarily in estuaries, inlets, bays, and offshore shallows along Atlantic and Pacific Coasts; can also be found on the Great Lakes.

| Length **16½–22in (42–56cm)** | Wingspan **24–35in (61–88cm)** | Weight **1¾–3½lb (0.8–1.6kg)** |
| Social **Pairs/Loose flocks** | Lifespan **Up to 6 years** | Status **Vulnerable** |

| Order **Podicipediformes** | Family **Podicepedidae** | Species *Aechmophorus occidentalis* |

Western Grebe

black nape stripe

ADULT

whitish band on dark wing

IN FLIGHT

dark patch around eyes

light gray back

light white-gray neck

CHICK

black crown extends below eye

distinctive red eye

long, slender, slightly upturned greenish yellow bill

ADULT

brilliant white throat, breast, and belly

black nape stripe

dark gray back

Western and Clark's Grebes are strictly North American species. They share much of their breeding habitat and elaborate mating rituals, and were, until 1985, classified as different color forms of a single species. Interbreeding is uncommon, perhaps because of slight differences in calls, bill colors, and facial patterns. Although hybrids are rare, they appear to be fertile, and produce chicks of their own. Female Western Grebes are smaller than males and have smaller, thinner, slightly upturned bills. The Western Grebe dives more frequently than Clark's, and remains submerged for about 30 seconds.

VOICE Nine calls, each with a specific purpose, such as alarm, begging, and mating calls; advertising call a harsh, rolling two-noted *krrrikk krrreek*.

NESTING Floating pile of available plants, attached to thick growth of submerged vegetation; occasionally constructed on land; 2–3 eggs; 1 brood; May–July.

FEEDING Mainly catches a wide variety of freshwater or saltwater fish; also crustaceans, worms, occasionally insects.

FLIGHT: fast and direct with rapid wing beats; neck extended with feet stretched out behind.

SELF-DEFENSE
The posture of this the Western Grebe shows ready to defend itself when threatened.

SIMILAR SPECIES

CLARK'S GREBE
see p.123 bright orange-yellow bill

white between crown and eye

HIGHLY SOCIAL
Western Grebes, much like Clark's Grebes, are highly gregarious in all seasons.

OCCURRENCE
Western North America, breeds from southern Canada to Mexico, in freshwater lakes and marshes with open water and emergent vegetation; rarely on tidewater marshes; also man-made marshes and artificial habitats. Winters along Pacific Coast, in bays and estuaries in the southwest US and Mexico.

| Length **21½–30in (55–75cm)** | Wingspan **30–39in (76–100cm)** | Weight **1¾–4lb (0.8–1.8kg)** |
| Social **Flocks** | Lifespan **At least 15 years** | Status **Declining** |

Order **Podicipediformes**	Family **Podicipedidae**	Species *Aechmophorus clarkii*

Clark's Grebe

IN FLIGHT

outstretched neck

white throat, breast, and belly

ADULT

distinct white band on wings

red eye

black crown, slightly crested

white space between black crown and eye

very thin, black nape stripe

bright orange-yellow bill

long, thin, swan-like neck

ADULT

moderately dark, gray back

whitish flanks

Clark's and Western grebes are closely related and very difficult to distinguish. They rarely fly except when migrating at night. Both species seldom come to land, where their movement is awkward because their legs and toes are located so far back, although they have been reported to run upright rapidly. Their flight muscles suffer wastage after their arrival on the breeding grounds, which also inhibits their ability to travel, but during the incubation period adults may feed several miles from the colony by following continuous water trails.
VOICE Variety of different calls, including a harsh, reedy, grating, two-syllable, single, rising *kree-eekt* advertising call.
NESTING Floating pile of available plants, attached to thick growth of submerged vegetation; occasionally constructed on land; 2–3 eggs; 1 brood; May–July.
FEEDING Mainly catches saltwater or freshwater fish; also crustaceans.

FLIGHT: swift and direct with quick wing beats; neck extended with feet trailing.

HOW TO SWALLOW?
It is not unusual for grebes to catch large fish; they crush the head first before swallowing.

FORAGING IN DEEP WATER
Clark's Grebe has a distinctive white S-shaped neck and black crown.

SIMILAR SPECIES

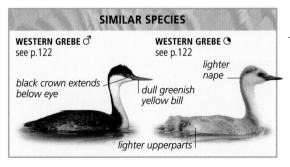

WESTERN GREBE ♂
see p.122

black crown extends below eye

dull greenish yellow bill

WESTERN GREBE ♀
see p.122

lighter nape

lighter upperparts

OCCURRENCE
Breeds in freshwater lakes and marshes with open water bordered by emergent vegetation; rarely tidewater marshes; has been nesting in man-made Lake Havasu marshes since 1960s. Winters along Pacific Coast, and in bays and estuaries in the southwest US and Mexico.

Length **21½–30in (55–75cm)**	Wingspan **32in (82cm)**	Weight **1½–3¾lb (0.7–1.7kg)**
Social **Flocks**	Lifespan **At least 15 years**	Status **Declining**

Families **Ciconiidae, Threskiornithidae, Ardeidae**

IBISES & HERONS

THESE ARE LARGE, WATER and wetland birds that have long legs and look rather similar, but have different habits. They eat fish and other aquatic prey as well as plants. Most breed in colonies.

IBISES

Birds of the waterside or dry land, ibises (Threskiornithidae) are characterized by rounded bodies, medium-long legs and strong feet that allow an easy, long-striding walk, short tails,

rounded wings, and small, often bare, heads on curved necks, merging into long, curved bills. Gregarious birds, they fly in long lines or "V" formation. Ibises feed mostly on insects, worms, small mollusks, and crustaceans, probing for them in the water and wet mud.

EYE-CATCHING IBIS
The White-faced Ibis has a distinctive white patch around its eye in the breeding season.

BITTERNS, HERONS, AND EGRETS

These are mostly waterside birds (Ardeidae) with long, slender toes, broad, rounded wings, very short tails, forward-facing eyes, and dagger-shaped bills. Bitterns and night-herons have a shawl of smooth, dense neck feathers, while an egret's long, slender neck is tightly feathered, with an obvious "kink" that allows a lightning-fast stab for prey. Bitterns, herons, and egrets fly with their legs trailing and their necks coiled back into their shoulders. Some make obvious bulky treetop nests and feed in the open, while others, especially bitterns, nest and feed secretively. In fact, often the only clue to a bittern's presence in a dense reedbed is the haunting, booming call it makes to keep in touch with its mate.

EVER ALERT
The Green Heron stalks fish by watching and waiting patiently until prey is near.

DANCING ON AIR
The Great Egret's courtship display often involves spreading its wings and leaping in a kind of aerial dance.

Order **Ciconiiformes**	Family **Ciconiidae**	Species **Mycteria americana**

Wood Stork

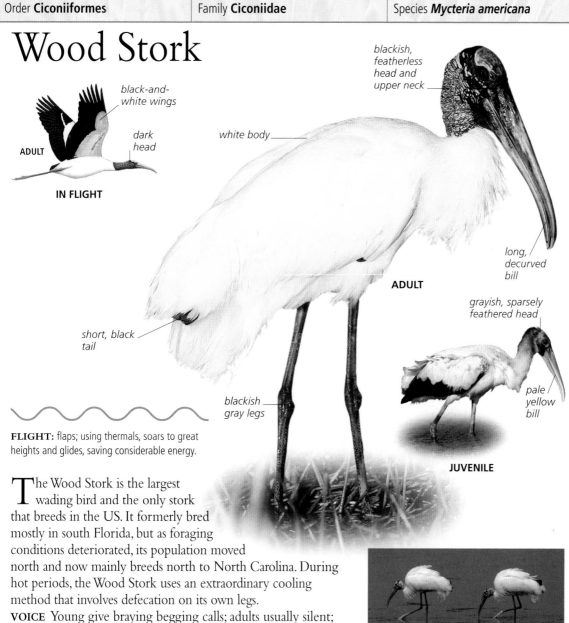

ADULT — black-and-white wings, dark head

IN FLIGHT

blackish, featherless head and upper neck

white body

long, decurved bill

ADULT

short, black tail

blackish gray legs

grayish, sparsely feathered head

pale yellow bill

JUVENILE

FLIGHT: flaps; using thermals, soars to great heights and glides, saving considerable energy.

The Wood Stork is the largest wading bird and the only stork that breeds in the US. It formerly bred mostly in south Florida, but as foraging conditions deteriorated, its population moved north and now mainly breeds north to North Carolina. During hot periods, the Wood Stork uses an extraordinary cooling method that involves defecation on its own legs.

VOICE Young give braying begging calls; adults usually silent; clatter bills during courting.

NESTING Large twig nest usually in swamps; colonial nesters, usually in trees over water for protection against predators; 2–4 eggs; 1 brood; December–August.

FEEDING Feeds on aquatic prey including fish, crabs, and insects; moves bill through water and detects prey movements.

FOOT STIRRING
Wood Storks often feed by stirring the bottom with their feet and feeling for prey with their bills.

OCCURRENCE
Forested freshwater and coastal areas, swamps, and marshes; feeds in shallow wetlands. In the US, a southeastern species, breeding in Florida to North Carolina. Birds in Texas and Louisiana are postbreeders dispersing from Mexico. A few birds have been seen in southern California.

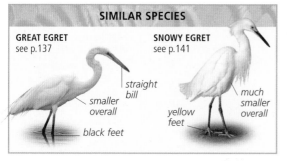

SIMILAR SPECIES

GREAT EGRET
see p.137

SNOWY EGRET
see p.141

straight bill

smaller overall

black feet

yellow feet

much smaller overall

Length **3ft 3in (100cm)**	Wingspan **5ft (1.5m)**	Weight **5½lb (2.5kg)**
Social **Flocks**	Lifespan **Up to 25 years**	Status **Endangered**

| Order **Ciconiiformes** | Family **Threskiornithidae** | Species *Eudocimus albus* |

White Ibis

trailing legs

long, white neck

ADULT (BREEDING)

black wing tips

IN FLIGHT

pale bluish eye

red or pink facial skin

white overall

curved, red bill with dark tip

short tail

streaked neck

mottled brown-and-white upperparts

curved, yellowish bill

white underparts

yellow legs

red legs and toes

ADULT (BREEDING)

IMMATURE (1ST SPRING)

It is the shape that hints at the close relationship between the White Ibis and the darker Glossy and White-faced Ibises. Depending on the season, the White Ibis has a pink or flesh-colored face, bill, and legs set against its white plumage and black wing tips. When breeding, however, the legs, bill, and bare facial skin turn a vivid red. The 20,000–30,000 birds living in the southeastern US breed from Florida north to South Carolina, and along the Gulf Coast to Louisiana and Texas. The population moves around within this area, as do other large waders, depending on the water level.

VOICE Hoarse, croaking *kraah*; high-pitched calls during courtship.
NESTING Platform of sticks placed in trees or shrubs, often mangroves, over water; 2–4 eggs; 1 brood; March–October.
FEEDING Eats small crustaceans such as crayfish, and small fish, frogs; feeds in flocks in both estuarine and freshwater wetlands.

FLIGHT: rapid wing beats alternating with glides; soars on thermals to save energy.

HIGHLY GREGARIOUS
White Ibises are extremely social birds, flying, breeding, feeding, and roosting in large flocks.

OCCURRENCE
Found in estuaries along the coast, also in freshwater marshes, swamps, and rice fields; breeds in colonies with other wading birds. Also occurs throughout Central America and northern South America from Venezuela to Colombia.

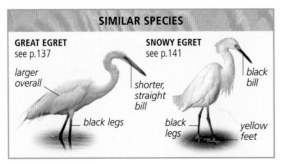

SIMILAR SPECIES

GREAT EGRET see p.137

SNOWY EGRET see p.141

larger overall

shorter, straight bill

black legs

black bill

black legs

yellow feet

| Length **25in (64cm)** | Wingspan **3ft 2in (96cm)** | Weight **32oz (900g)** |
| Social **Flocks/Colonies** | Lifespan **Up to 16 years** | Status **Secure** |

| Order **Ciconiiformes** | Family **Threskiornithidae** | Species *Plegadis falcinellus* |

Glossy Ibis

IN FLIGHT

outstretched neck

trailing legs

ADULT (BREEDING)

finely streaked head and neck

ADULT (NONBREEDING)

iridescent crown

dark brown eye

dark maroon neck

curved, gray-brown bill

iridescent bronze-green feathers on inner wing

chestnut or maroon underparts

ADULT (BREEDING)

gray-green legs and feet

FLIGHT: alternate wing beats and glides; flies with neck outstretched, legs extended beyond tail.

With its long, curved bill, the dark, long-legged Glossy Ibis is similar to the White-faced Ibis. It is well known for its wandering tendencies and can also be found in southern Europe, Asia, Australia, and Africa. Despite being found in the US in the mid-19th century, the Glossy Ibis was not discovered nesting in Florida until 1886. Confined to Florida until the mid-20th century, it then started spreading northward, eventually as far as New England.

VOICE Crow-like croak; subdued nasal chatter in flocks; mostly silent.

NESTING Platform of twigs and reeds in trees, shrubs, or reeds, on ground or over water; 3–4 eggs; 1 brood; April–July.

FEEDING Forages by feel, puts bill in soil and mud to catch prey, including snails, insects, leeches, frogs, and crayfish.

MARSH FEEDER
The Glossy Ibis regularly feeds in shallow pools and along the waterways of coastal marshes.

OCCURRENCE
Common from New England south to Florida. Occurs in brackish and freshwater marshes and in flooded or plowed fields; feeds with other waders in inland freshwater wetlands as well as coastal lagoons and estuaries.

SIMILAR SPECIES

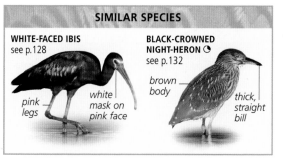

WHITE-FACED IBIS
see p.128

pink legs

white mask on pink face

BLACK-CROWNED NIGHT-HERON ◑
see p.132

brown body

thick, straight bill

| Length **23in (59cm)** | Wingspan **36in (92cm)** | Weight **13oz (375g)** |
| Social **Flocks/Colonies** | Lifespan **15–20 years** | Status **Secure (p)** |

| Order **Ciconiiformes** | Family **Ardeidae** | Species *Botaurus lentiginosus* |

American Bittern

dark outer wing feathers

ADULT

trailing legs

IN FLIGHT

rusty brown crown

long, straight bill

black streak on side of neck

brown back

duller crown

no large black patch on neck

short tail

brown streaks on chest

JUVENILE

greenish legs

ADULT

The American Bittern's camouflaged plumage and secretive behavior help it to blend into the thick vegetation of its freshwater wetland habitat. It is heard much more often than it is seen; its call is unmistakable and has given rise to many evocative colloquial names, such as "thunder pumper."

VOICE Deep, resonant *pump-er-unk, pump-er-unk*; calls mainly at dawn, dusk, and night time, but also during the day in the early mating season.

NESTING Platform or mound constructed of available marsh vegetation, usually over shallow water; 2–7 eggs; 1 brood; April–August.

FEEDING Stands still or moves slowly, then strikes downward with bill to catch prey; eats fish, insects, crustaceans, snakes, amphibians, and small mammals.

FLIGHT: steady, deep, slightly stiff wing beats; usually flies relatively low and direct.

LOOKING UP
Bitterns are secretive birds, but can occasionally be found walking slowly through reeds.

OCCURRENCE
Breeds in heavily vegetated freshwater wetlands across the northern US and southern Canada; also occasionally in estuarine wetlands; winters in southern and coastal wetlands where temperatures stay above freezing; can appear in any wetland habitat during migration.

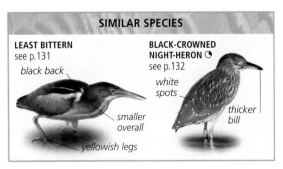

SIMILAR SPECIES

LEAST BITTERN
see p.131
black back
smaller overall
yellowish legs

BLACK-CROWNED NIGHT-HERON ☾
see p.132
white spots
thicker bill

| Length **23½–31in (60–80cm)** | Wingspan **3½–4¼ft (1.1–1.3m)** | Weight **13–20oz (375–575g)** |
| Social **Solitary** | Lifespan **At least 8 years** | Status **Declining** |

Order **Ciconiiformes**	Family **Ardeidae**	Species *Ixobrychus exilis*

Least Bittern

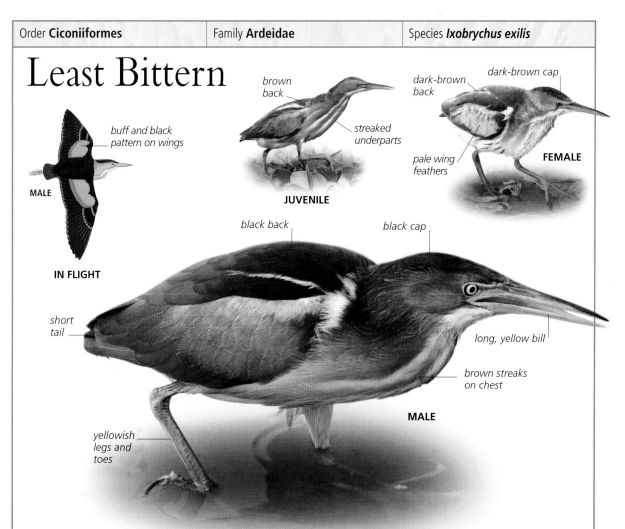

brown back

streaked underparts

JUVENILE

dark-brown back

dark-brown cap

pale wing feathers

FEMALE

buff and black pattern on wings

MALE

IN FLIGHT

black back

black cap

short tail

long, yellow bill

brown streaks on chest

MALE

yellowish legs and toes

The smallest heron in North America, the Least Bittern is also one of the most colorful, but its secretive nature makes it easy to overlook in its densely vegetated marsh habitat. A dark color form, which was originally described in the 1800s as a separate species named Cory's Bittern, has rarely been reported in recent decades.

VOICE Soft *ku, ku, ku, ku, ku* display call; year-round, a loud *kak, kak, kak*.

NESTING Platform of marsh vegetation with sticks and stems added, usually within 30ft (9m) of open water; 2–7 eggs; 1 brood; April–August.

FEEDING Feeds on small fish, insects including dragonflies; also crustaceans; clings quietly to vegetation before striking prey, or stalks slowly.

FLIGHT: rapid wing beats; weak, direct flight; flies low, around top of vegetation.

OCCURRENCE
Breeds in summer in lowland freshwater marshes; less commonly in brackish and rarely in saltwater marshes; frequents similar habitat on migration; winters in brackish and saltwater marshes. Wide distribution in the Americas, south to Argentina.

SIMILAR SPECIES

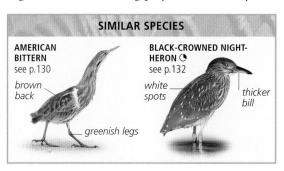

AMERICAN BITTERN
see p.130

brown back

greenish legs

BLACK-CROWNED NIGHT-HERON ◐
see p.132

white spots

thicker bill

REED CREEPER
With its small, thin body, this species easily creeps through dense reeds in search of prey.

Length **11–14in (28–36cm)**	Wingspan **15½–18in (40–46cm)**	Weight **2⅝–3⅜oz (75–95g)**
Social **Solitary/Small flocks**	Lifespan **Unknown**	Status **Secure**

| Order **Ciconiiformes** | Family **Ardeidae** | Species *Nycticorax nycticorax* |

Black-crowned Night-Heron

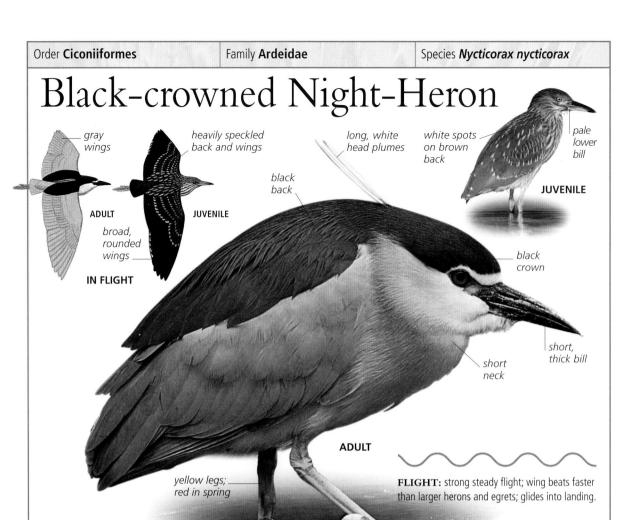

gray wings

heavily speckled back and wings

ADULT

JUVENILE

broad, rounded wings

IN FLIGHT

long, white head plumes

black back

white spots on brown back

pale lower bill

JUVENILE

black crown

short, thick bill

short neck

ADULT

yellow legs; red in spring

FLIGHT: strong steady flight; wing beats faster than larger herons and egrets; glides into landing.

The Black-crowned Night-Heron is chunky and squat. It is also one of the most common and widespread herons in North America and in the world. But because, as its name suggests, it is mainly active at twilight and at night, many people have never seen one. However, its distinctive barking call can be heard at night—even at the center of large cities.

VOICE Loud, distinctive *quark* or *wok*, often given in flight and around colonies.

NESTING Large stick nests built usually 20–40ft (6–12m) up in trees; 3–5 eggs; 1 brood; November–August.

FEEDING Feeds primarily on aquatic animals, such as fish, crustaceans, insects, and mollusks; also eggs and chicks of colonial birds, such as egrets, ibises, and terns.

LONG PLUMES
In breeding plumage, the plumes of the male of this species are longer than the female's.

SIMILAR SPECIES

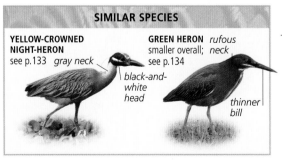

YELLOW-CROWNED NIGHT-HERON see p.133 *gray neck*

GREEN HERON *rufous neck* smaller overall; see p.134

black-and-white head

thinner bill

OCCURRENCE
Widespread; can be found wherever there are waterbodies, such as lakes, ponds, streams; generally absent from higher elevations. Colonies often on islands or in marshes; colony sites may be used for decades. In winter, found in areas where water remains open.

| Length **23–26in (58–65cm)** | Wingspan **3½–4ft (1.1–1.2m)** | Weight **1½–2½lb (0.7–1kg)** |
| Social **Colonies** | Lifespan **Up to 21 years** | Status **Secure** |

Order **Ciconiiformes**	Family **Ardeidae**	Species ***Nyctanassa violacea***

Yellow-crowned Night-Heron

short tail

ADULT

IN FLIGHT

uniform gray back and wings

long, white plumes extending from crown

white cheek patches

yellowish white crown

thick, black bill

slender neck

ADULT

long, yellow legs

no white on face

fine speckling on back and wings

brown streaks on underparts

JUVENILE

M ore slender and elegant than its more common cousin, the Black-crowned Night-Heron, the Yellow-crowned Night-Heron was unaffected by the plume hunting trade that decimated many heron species in the 19th century. It then expanded northward in the 20th century, but has retreated slightly from the northern edge of its range in recent decades. It can be seen in wooded areas.

VOICE Call an abrupt *quark* or *wok*, higher-pitched than Black-crowned Night-Heron; most vocal in mornings, evenings, and at night.

NESTING Platform of sticks in tree, tall shrubs, often 40–60ft (12–18m) above ground, away from main trunk; 2–6 eggs; 1 brood; March–August.

FEEDING Stands motionless or slowly stalks prey and then lunges; mostly eats crabs and crayfish; also insects, small mollusks, and fish.

FLIGHT: strong and steady, with neck drawn up close to body; legs trailing.

OCCURRENCE
Breeds near wetlands along the East Coast, across the Southeast and the Midwest; often nests and roosts near houses in wooded neighborhoods. Found in similar habitats during migration; mainly coastal in winter.

SIMILAR SPECIES

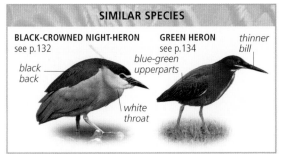

BLACK-CROWNED NIGHT-HERON
see p.132

black back

white throat

GREEN HERON
see p.134

blue-green upperparts

thinner bill

DARKER JUVENILE
A juvenile Yellow-crowned has darker plumage than its Black-crowned counterpart.

Length **19½–28in (50–70cm)**	Wingspan **3¼–3½ft (1–1.1m)**	Weight **23–28oz (650–800g)**
Social **Colonies**	Lifespan **At least 6 years**	Status **Secure (p)**

| Order **Ciconiiformes** | Family **Ardeidae** | Species ***Butorides virescens*** |

Green Heron

ADULT (BREEDING)

greenish back

IN FLIGHT

greenish black cap

short, rufous neck

white chin

cream streak extends from throat to belly

yellowish legs and feet

ADULT (NONBREEDING)

white speckles on wings

paler bill

JUVENILE

thin, straight, black bill

long back plumes

glossy orange legs

ADULT (BREEDING)

A small, solitary, and secretive bird of dense thicketed wetlands, the Green Heron can be difficult to observe. This dark, crested heron is most often seen flying away from a perceived threat, emitting a loud squawk. While the Green Heron of North and Central America has now been recognized as a separate species, it was earlier grouped with the Green-backed Heron (*B. striatus*), which is found in the tropics and subtropics throughout the world.

VOICE Squawking *keow* when flying from disturbance.

NESTING Nest of twigs often in bushes or trees, often over water but also on land; 1–2 broods; 3–5 eggs; March–July.

FEEDING Stands quietly on the shore or in shallow water and strikes quickly; mainly fish, but also frogs, insects, and spiders.

FLIGHT: direct, a bit plodding, and usually over short distances.

READY TO STRIKE
Green Herons usually catch their prey by lunging forward and downward with their whole body.

OCCURRENCE
An inhabitant of swampy thickets, but occasionally dry land close to water across much of North America, but missing in the plains, the Rocky Mountains, and the western deserts that do not provide appropriate wetlands. Winters in coastal wetlands.

SIMILAR SPECIES

BLACK-CROWNED NIGHT-HERON ☽
see p.132

larger overall

thicker bill

YELLOW-CROWNED NIGHT-HERON ☾
see p.133

larger overall

| Length **14½–15½ in (37–39cm)** | Wingspan **25–27in (63–68cm)** | Weight **7–9oz (200–250g)** |
| Social **Solitary/Pairs/Small flocks** | Lifespan **Up to 10 years** | Status **Secure** |

Order **Ciconiiformes**	Family **Ardeidae**	Species **Bubulcus ibis**

Cattle Egret

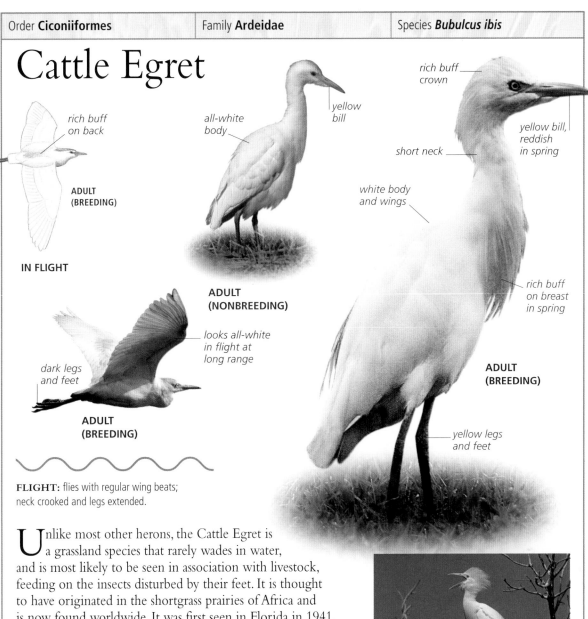

rich buff on back

ADULT (BREEDING)

IN FLIGHT

all-white body

yellow bill

ADULT (NONBREEDING)

rich buff crown

short neck

yellow bill, reddish in spring

white body and wings

rich buff on breast in spring

looks all-white in flight at long range

dark legs and feet

ADULT (BREEDING)

ADULT (BREEDING)

yellow legs and feet

FLIGHT: flies with regular wing beats; neck crooked and legs extended.

Unlike most other herons, the Cattle Egret is a grassland species that rarely wades in water, and is most likely to be seen in association with livestock, feeding on the insects disturbed by their feet. It is thought to have originated in the shortgrass prairies of Africa and is now found worldwide. It was first seen in Florida in 1941, but expanded rapidly and has now bred in over 40 US states.

VOICE Generally silent; vocal at the nest: *rick-rack* common.

NESTING Nest of branches or plants placed in trees over ground; also in trees or shrubs over water; 2–5 eggs; 1 brood; March–October.

FEEDING Eats in groups, consumes insects, spiders as well as larger animals such as frogs; insects stirred up in grasslands by cattle.

VOCAL BREEDERS
This bird almost never calls away from a breeding colony, but is vocal near its nests.

SIMILAR SPECIES

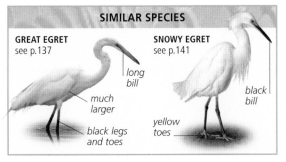

GREAT EGRET see p.137

long bill

much larger

black legs and toes

SNOWY EGRET see p.141

black bill

yellow toes

OCCURRENCE
Since the 1940s, it has expanded to many habitats in much of North America, primarily in grasslands and prairies, but also wetland areas. In tropical regions, the Cattle Egrets flock around the cattle feeding in shallow wetlands.

Length **20in (51cm)**	Wingspan **31in (78cm)**	Weight **13oz (375g)**
Social **Colonies**	Lifespan **Up to 17 years**	Status **Secure**

Order **Ciconiiformes**	Family **Ardeidae**	Species *Ardea herodias*

Great Blue Heron

dark wing tips

dark tail

brownish body

white face

dark bill

ADULT

crooked neck

IN FLIGHT

JUVENILE

gray neck

blue-gray body

yellowish bill

lighter-colored neck, almost beige

light bill

large, white bird

overall similar to Great Blue

shaggy plumes

light legs

WURDEMANN'S HERON (WHITE-HEADED FORM)

MALE

dark legs

GREAT WHITE HERON (WHITE FORM)

FLIGHT: deep-flapping, regular wing beats.

This is one of the three largest herons in the world—the Great Blue in North America, the Gray in Eurasia, and the Cocoi in South America—all of which are all interrelated, but classified separately. The Great Blue Heron is a common inhabitant of a variety of North American waterbodies, from marshes to swamps, as well as along sea coasts. Its majestic, deliberate flight is a highly wonderful sight to behold.

VOICE Mostly silent; gives a loud, barking squawk or *crank* in breeding colonies or when disturbed.

NESTING Nest of twigs and branches; usually in colonies, but also singly; in trees, often over water, but also over ground; 2–4 eggs; 1–2 broods; February–August.

FEEDING Catches prey with quick jab of bill; primarily fish.

LOFTY ABODE
Great Blue Herons nest in small colonies in trees, and often roost in them.

SIMILAR SPECIES

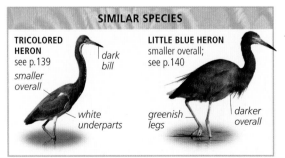

TRICOLORED HERON
see p.139

smaller overall

dark bill

white underparts

LITTLE BLUE HERON
smaller overall;
see p.140

greenish legs

darker overall

OCCURRENCE
Across southern Canada and the US in wetlands, such as marshes, lake edges, and along rivers and swamps; also in marine habitats, especially tidal grass flats. The Great White Heron is primarily found in marine habitats.

Length 2¾–4¼ft (0.9–1.3m)	Wingspan 5¼–6½ft (1.6–2m)	Weight 4¾–5½lb (2.1–2.5kg)
Social **Solitary/Flocks**	Lifespan **Up to 20 years**	Status **Secure**

| Order **Ciconiiformes** | Family **Ardeidae** | Species **Ardea alba** |

Great Egret

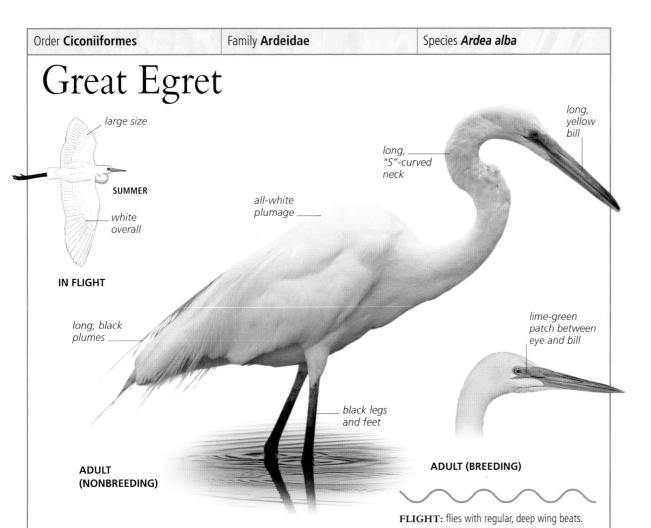

large size

SUMMER

white overall

IN FLIGHT

long, "S"-curved neck

long, yellow bill

all-white plumage

long, black plumes

lime-green patch between eye and bill

black legs and feet

ADULT (NONBREEDING)

ADULT (BREEDING)

FLIGHT: flies with regular, deep wing beats.

This large white heron is found on every continent except Antarctica. When feeding, the Great Egret would apparently rather forage alone than in flocks—it maintains space around itself, and will defend a territory of 10ft (3m) in diameter from other wading birds. This territory "moves" with the bird as it feeds. In years of scarce food supplies, a chick may kill a sibling, permitting the survival of at least one bird.

VOICE Largely vocal during courtship and breeding; otherwise, *kraak* or *cuk-cuk-cuk* when disturbed or in a combative encounter.

NESTING Nest of twigs in trees, over land or water; 2–4 eggs; 1 brood; March–July.

FEEDING Catches prey with quick thrust of bill; feeds on aquatic prey, primarily fish, also crustaceans.

TREE PERCHES
Great Egrets nest in trees and regularly perch in them when not feeding.

SIMILAR SPECIES

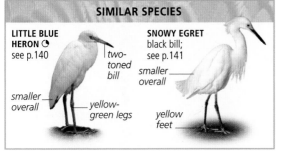

LITTLE BLUE HERON ◐
see p.140

smaller overall

two-toned bill

yellow-green legs

SNOWY EGRET
black bill;
see p.141

smaller overall

yellow feet

OCCURRENCE
Breeds in trees over water or on islands; forages in almost all types of freshwater and marine wetlands from marshes and ponds to rivers. Migratory over much of its North American range; more southerly populations resident. Distance migrated depends on severity of winter.

| Length **3¼ft (1m)** | Wingspan **6ft (1.8m)** | Weight **1¾–3¼ft (0.8–1.5kg)** |
| Social **Solitary** | Lifespan **Up to 25 years** | Status **Secure** |

| Order **Ciconiiformes** | Family **Ardeidae** | Species *Egretta rufescens* |

Reddish Egret

trailing legs

ADULT (DARK FORM)

gray wings

IN FLIGHT

shaggy, rufous head and neck

heavy, dark bill

heavy, pink bill with black tip

gray body

rufescent neck and chest

JUVENILE (WHITE FORM)

pink bill with black tip

shaggy neck

ADULT (DARK FORM)

gray legs

ADULT (WHITE FORM)

FLIGHT: strong, with steady, deep wing beats; may extended neck on short flights.

Endemic to the Americas, the Reddish Egret occurs in two color forms. The rufous head and neck of the dark form gives the species its name, while the all-white form resembles other egrets. The bird can be identified in any plumage by its highly active feeding habits. It runs back and forth in the shallow waters of mudflats, halting occasionally to stretch out its wings over its head, apparently to lure small fish into their shadow; a method of hunting known as "canopy feeding."
VOICE Occasional low, throaty grunt *aww-unh* or *aww-unh-unh*.
NESTING Stick nest lined with grass on ground, shrubs, or trees up to 30ft (10m) above ground, in colonies with other herons; 3–4 eggs; 1 brood; March–September.
FEEDING Almost exclusively eats small fish.

FISHING WITH OPEN WINGS
The Reddish Egret pounces on small fish with outspread wings when "canopy feeding."

SIMILAR SPECIES

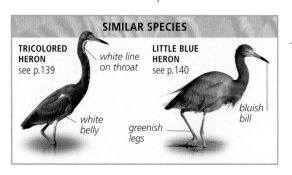

TRICOLORED HERON see p.139

white line on throat

white belly

LITTLE BLUE HERON see p.140

greenish legs

bluish bill

OCCURRENCE
Found year-round in coastal lagoons, mudflats, and keys around Florida and the Gulf Coast; mostly nonmigratory; sometimes seen in southern California in winter; vagrants and post-breeders seen inland and north along the Atlantic coast. Breeds in Mexico, the West Indies, south to Belize.

| Length **26–32in (66–81cm)** | Wingspan **3½–4ft (1.1–1.2m)** | Weight **25–30oz (700–850g)** |
| Social **Colonies** | Lifespan **Up to 12 years** | Status **Localized** |

| Order **Ciconiformes** | Family **Ardeidae** | Species *Egretta tricolor* |

Tricolored Heron

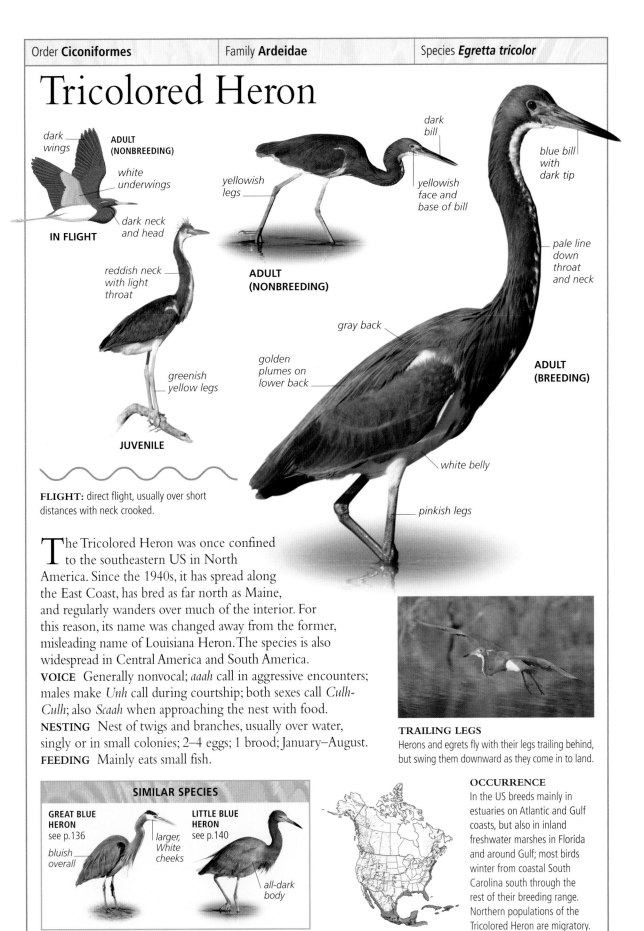

ADULT (NONBREEDING)
dark wings
white underwings
dark neck and head

IN FLIGHT

dark bill
yellowish legs
yellowish face and base of bill

ADULT (NONBREEDING)

blue bill with dark tip

reddish neck with light throat

pale line down throat and neck

gray back

golden plumes on lower back

greenish yellow legs

JUVENILE

ADULT (BREEDING)

white belly

pinkish legs

FLIGHT: direct flight, usually over short distances with neck crooked.

The Tricolored Heron was once confined to the southeastern US in North America. Since the 1940s, it has spread along the East Coast, has bred as far north as Maine, and regularly wanders over much of the interior. For this reason, its name was changed away from the former, misleading name of Louisiana Heron. The species is also widespread in Central America and South America.
VOICE Generally nonvocal; *aaah* call in aggressive encounters; males make *Unh* call during courtship; both sexes call *Culh-Culh*; also *Scaah* when approaching the nest with food.
NESTING Nest of twigs and branches, usually over water, singly or in small colonies; 2–4 eggs; 1 brood; January–August.
FEEDING Mainly eats small fish.

TRAILING LEGS
Herons and egrets fly with their legs trailing behind, but swing them downward as they come in to land.

SIMILAR SPECIES

GREAT BLUE HERON
see p.136
bluish overall

larger, White cheeks

LITTLE BLUE HERON
see p.140

all-dark body

OCCURRENCE
In the US breeds mainly in estuaries on Atlantic and Gulf coasts, but also in inland freshwater marshes in Florida and around Gulf; most birds winter from coastal South Carolina south through the rest of their breeding range. Northern populations of the Tricolored Heron are migratory.

| Length **26in (66cm)** | Wingspan **36in (92cm)** | Weight **11–15oz (325–425g)** |
| Social **Solitary** | Lifespan **Up to 20 years** | Status **Secure** |

| Order **Ciconiiformes** | Family **Ardeidae** | Species *Egretta caerulea* |

Little Blue Heron

ADULT (in flight diagram) — short tail, coiled neck

IN FLIGHT

JUVENILE — white plumage, pale, black-tipped bill, pale greenish legs

IMMATURE (1ST SPRING) — blotchy, blue-and-white plumage

ADULT — slate-gray back, purplish maroon neck, gray bill with black tip, long, slender neck, yellowish to greenish legs

The shy and retreating Little Blue Heron is often overlooked because of its blue-gray color and secretive eating habits. First-year birds, which may be mistaken for Snowy Egrets, are white, and gradually acquire blue-gray, mottled feathers before eventually molting into their all-dark adult plumage. Immature birds are seen feeding together in open wetlands while adults feed alone in denser habitats, such as swamps and thick wetlands.

VOICE Vocal during courtship; generally silent.
NESTING Uses sticks and twigs, in trees or reeds, in wetlands or terrestrial habitats nearby; 2–4 eggs; 1 brood; April–September.
FEEDING Eats small fish, amphibians, crustaceans, and insects; stalks its prey, wading slowly in shallow waters or along the water's edge.

FLIGHT: deep and continuous wing beats; glides when descending and landing.

UNIQUE TRANSFORMATION
No other heron species undergoes such a drastic change from an all-white juvenile to all-dark adult.

SIMILAR SPECIES

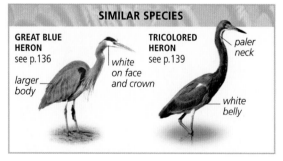

GREAT BLUE HERON see p.136 — larger body

TRICOLORED HERON see p.139 — paler neck, white on face and crown, white belly

OCCURRENCE
Breeds across much of southeast US in various wetlands, such as swamps, marshes, lakes, streams, rivers, and flooded fields, as well as estuarine and marine habitats, such as lagoons and tidal flats. Winters in similar habitat from southern California to Mexico and Central America.

| Length **24in (61cm)** | Wingspan **3ft 3in (100cm)** | Weight **11–13oz (325–375g)** |
| Social **Solitary** | Lifespan **10–20 years** | Status **Secure** |

Order **Ciconiiformes**	Family **Ardeidae**	Species *Egretta thula*

Snowy Egret

long, extended legs

ADULT

IN FLIGHT

red patch between eye and bill

paler patch of skin at base of bill

plumes on head

JUVENILE

greenish yellow legs

all-white plumage

yellow patch between eye and bill

black bill

wispy breast plumes

ADULT (HIGH BREEDING)

orangish legs

ADULT (BREEDING)

black legs

yellow feet

FLIGHT: flies with deep wing beats; gliding descent before landing.

A New World species, the Snowy Egret is similar to the Little Egret. It is very adaptable in estuarine and freshwater habitats. When foraging, it uses a wide variety of behaviors, including wing-flicking, foot-stirring, and foot-probing to get its prey moving, making it easier to capture.

VOICE High-pitched *Aargaarg* when flushed; low-pitched *Arg* and *Raah* aggressive calls; *Aarg* call during attacks and pursuits.

NESTING Small sticks, branches, and rushes over water or on land; also on ground, in shrubs, mangroves, and other trees; 3–5 eggs; 1 brood; March–August.

FEEDING Feeds on aquatic prey, from invertebrates, such as insects, shrimp, and prawns, to small fish, amphibians, and snakes.

WIDESPREAD SPECIES
Snowy Egrets feed in a wide variety of wetland habitats, using different foraging techniques.

SIMILAR SPECIES

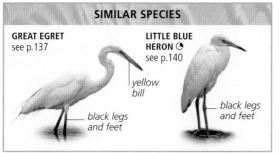

GREAT EGRET see p.137

LITTLE BLUE HERON see p.140

yellow bill

black legs and feet

black legs and feet

OCCURRENCE
Found in a wide variety of wetlands throughout North America: from mangroves in Florida to marshlands in New England and the western US. Highly adaptable and widely found. Sites of breeding colonies may change from year to year within a set range.

Length **24in (62cm)**	Wingspan **3½ft (1.1m)**	Weight **12oz (350g)**
Social **Solitary**	Lifespan **Up to 22 years**	Status **Secure**

PELICANS & RELATIVES

PELICANS AND THEIR relatives belong to an order of large to huge fish-eating birds, Pelecaniformes, with four toes connected by leathery webs, and with fleshy, elastic pouches beneath their bills.

PELICANS

The pelican family includes seven large species, two of which—the American White Pelican and the Brown Pelican—are North American. All pelicans are buoyant swimmers and excellent fliers, capable of great lift on their long, broad wings with wing feathers spread. Flocks can be seen soaring to great heights on migration and when flying to feeding grounds. They feed by sweeping with open bills for fish, often cooperatively, or by plunging from a height to scoop up fish and water in their large, flexible bill pouches.

CORMORANTS

With 36 species worldwide, these are medium to large waterbirds, some marine, others freshwater, with broad, long wings, rounded tails, short, strong legs and hook-tipped bills often tilted upward when swimming. In flight, the neck is extended but noticeably kinked.

DARK PLUMAGE
Grooming for this Neotropic Cormorant includes spreading its wings to dry them in the sun.

When hunting for fish, cormorants dive from the surface of the water, rolling smoothly under or with a noticeable forward leap, and then swim underwater with closed wings, using their webbed toes for propulsion. Most are dark birds, apart from some distinctive facial patterns on areas of bare skin which become more colorful in spring. Most cormorants nest on cliff ledges, although some prefer trees; others are happy to use both cliffs and trees. There is one flightless cormorant species in the Galapagos.

WATER BIRD
Webbed feet help Brown Pelicans negotiate water with ease, while strong wings mean easy takeoffs.

| Order **Pelecaniformes** | Family **Fregatidae** | Species *Fregata magnificens* |

Magnificent Frigatebird

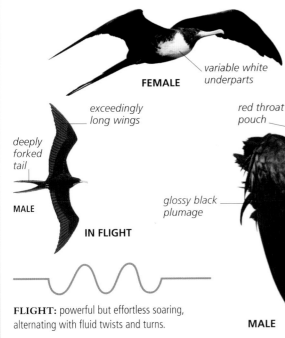

FEMALE — variable white underparts

exceedingly long wings

deeply forked tail

MALE

IN FLIGHT

glossy black plumage

dark head

JUVENILE

long, dark wings

white on head

very powerful, long, hooked bill

red throat pouch

white on head

MALE

FLIGHT: powerful but effortless soaring, alternating with fluid twists and turns.

Ｏne of North America's most-skilled aerialists, the Magnificent Frigatebird is never seen perched except when nesting in mangroves or roosting on buoys. It is usually seen flying gracefully above bays, lagoons, or open ocean, but it never alights on the water's surface. Identifying the different species of frigatebirds is exceedingly difficult, but only the Magnificent Frigatebird occurs regularly in North American waters. This species is well known for its in-flight piracy and aggressive behavior. It will pursue birds of its own species and others, stealing food from their bills.

VOICE Male call consists of whirring, rattling, and drumming sounds.

NESTING Flat or shallow depression in platform of twigs; 1 egg; 1 brood; November–May.

FEEDING Plucks small fish from water's surface, never wetting itself; sometimes steals food from other birds.

long tail

INFLATED POUCH
Breeding males display their gaudy, flapping throat pouches by inflating them.

OCCURRENCE
Breeds mainly in coastal mangroves, but in North America, frigatebirds are usually seen away from nest sites, flying high in the sky over open water. Sometimes found well north of its usual Florida and Gulf Coast range, especially after hurricanes, and a few wander inland every year.

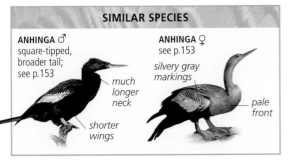

SIMILAR SPECIES

ANHINGA ♂
square-tipped, broader tail; see p.153

much longer neck

shorter wings

ANHINGA ♀
see p.153

silvery gray markings

pale front

| Length **3ft 3in (100cm)** | Wingspan **4½ft (1.4m)** | Weight **39–60oz (1.1–1.7kg)** |
| Social **Colonies** | Lifespan **Up to 30 years** | Status **Secure** |

Order **Pelecaniformes**	Family **Pelecanidae**	Species **Pelecanus erythrorhynchos**

American White Pelican

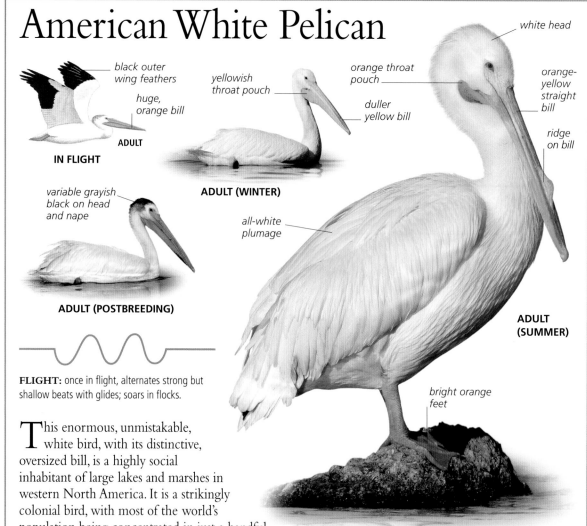

black outer
wing feathers

huge,
orange bill

ADULT

IN FLIGHT

yellowish
throat pouch

orange throat
pouch

duller
yellow bill

ADULT (WINTER)

white head

orange-
yellow
straight
bill

ridge
on bill

variable grayish
black on head
and nape

all-white
plumage

ADULT (POSTBREEDING)

**ADULT
(SUMMER)**

bright orange
feet

FLIGHT: once in flight, alternates strong but
shallow beats with glides; soars in flocks.

This enormous, unmistakable,
white bird, with its distinctive,
oversized bill, is a highly social
inhabitant of large lakes and marshes in
western North America. It is a strikingly
colonial bird, with most of the world's
population being concentrated in just a handful
of large colonies in isolated wetland complexes in deserts and
prairies. The American White Pelican forms foraging flocks,
which beat their wings in coordinated movements to drive fish
into shallow water, where they can be caught more easily.

VOICE Usually silent except around nesting colonies; around
the nest, young and adults exchange various grunts and hisses.

NESTING Depression in the ground, both sexes incubate;
1–2 eggs; 1 brood; April–August.

FEEDING . Mainly gulps down small fish, occasionally eats small
amphibians, and crayfish.

LARGE COLONIES
The White Pelican is highly social and is usually
seen feeding or roosting in large groups.

SIMILAR SPECIES

WOOD STORK
see p.125

bare
head

curved bill

long
thin
legs

**BROWN
PELICAN**
see p.145

gray bill

dark
underparts

OCCURRENCE
Breeds on islands in freshwater
lakes in south-central Canada,
mountainous areas of the
western US, and in coastal
northeast Mexico; an early spring
migrant, often returning to
breeding grounds in early March.
Winters in coastal regions from
California and Texas to Mexico
and Central America.

Length **4¼–5½ft (1.3–1.7m)**	Wingspan **7¾–9½ft (2.4–2.9m)**	Weight **12–20lb (5.5–9kg)**
Social **Colonies**	Lifespan **Up to 26 years**	Status **Vulnerable**

| Order **Pelecaniformes** | Family **Pelecanidae** | Species *Pelecanus occidentalis* |

Brown Pelican

ADULT

IN FLIGHT

bulky and dark

head mainly white

ADULT (NONBREEDING)

cream forehead and crown

dark stripe on nape

variable red on throat

unmarked brownish upperparts

whitish underparts

JUVENILE

huge bill

extensive white on wings

ADULT (BREEDING)

long neck

ADULT (POSTBREEDING)

ADULT (BREEDING)

black feet

FLIGHT: flies low over surface of the water; alternates glides with wingbeats.

This colossal and conspicuous inhabitant of warm coastal regions is an ungainly species on land but is amazingly graceful in flight. Sadly, numbers plummeted in the 1960s when DDT was used widely as a pesticide, but it rapidly recovered in recent decades, and is now expanding its range northwards along both coasts. The color of its throat varies according to geographic location.

VOICE Silent most of the time; vocal at nest colonies; adults and juveniles communicate with grunts and hisses; courting birds give a strange, deliberate *heart-hark*, repeated slowly.

NESTING Pile of debris, usually on ground; 2–3 eggs; 1 brood; February–August.

FEEDING Adults plunge headfirst into water to scoop up fish near the surface; does not herd fish, like the American White Pelican..

RESTING TOGETHER
Brown Pelicans are social most of the year, and can often be seen roosting in groups.

OCCURRENCE
Found in and around warm coastal waters, flying above the water's surface over the cresting waves; small numbers breed in the interior US; individuals and small flocks can be found around docks and marinas.

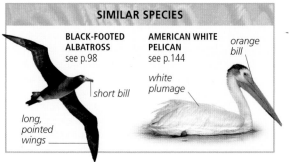

SIMILAR SPECIES

BLACK-FOOTED ALBATROSS
see p.98

AMERICAN WHITE PELICAN
see p.144

short bill

long, pointed wings

orange bill

white plumage

| Length **4–4¼ft (1.2–1.3m)** | Wingspan **6½–7ft (2–2.1m)** | Weight **4–8¾lb (1.8–4kg)** |
| Social **Colonies** | Lifespan **Up to 10 years** | Status **Secure** |

Order **Pelecaniformes**	Family **Sulidae**	Species **Morus bassanus**

Northern Gannet

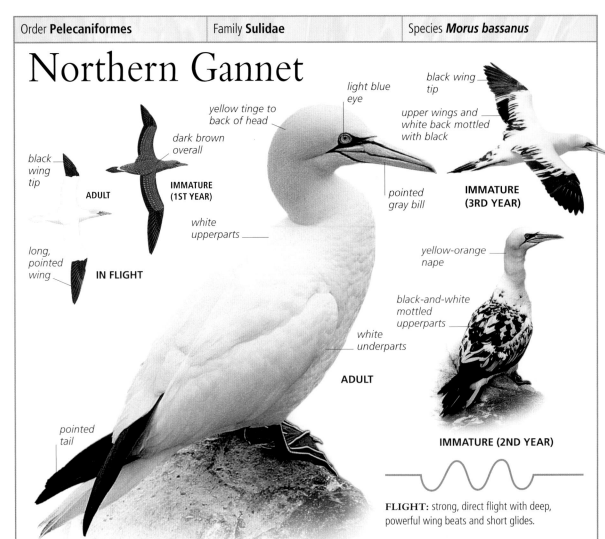

ADULT

black wing tip

long, pointed wing

IN FLIGHT

dark brown overall

IMMATURE (1ST YEAR)

white upperparts

yellow tinge to back of head

light blue eye

pointed gray bill

white underparts

ADULT

black wing tip

upper wings and white back mottled with black

IMMATURE (3RD YEAR)

yellow-orange nape

black-and-white mottled upperparts

IMMATURE (2ND YEAR)

pointed tail

FLIGHT: strong, direct flight with deep, powerful wing beats and short glides.

The Northern Gannet is known for its spectacular headfirst dives during frantic, voracious foraging in flocks of hundreds to thousands for surface-schooling fish. This bird nests in just six locations in northeastern Canada. The Northern Gannet was the first species to have its total world population estimated, at 83,000 birds in 1939. Numbers have since increased.

VOICE Loud landing call by both sexes *arrrr, arrah,* or *urrah rah rah*; hollow groan *oh-ah* uttered during take-off; *krok* call at sea.

NESTING Large pile of mud, seaweed, and rubbish, glued with guano, on bare rock or soil; 1 egg; 1 brood; April–November.

FEEDING Plunge-dives headfirst into water and often swims underwater to catch fish; eats mackerel, herring, capelin, and cod.

NESTING SITE
Northern Gannets prefer to nest in huge, noisy colonies on isolated rocky slopes or cliffs.

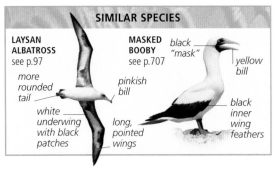

SIMILAR SPECIES

LAYSAN ALBATROSS see p.97

more rounded tail

white underwing with black patches

MASKED BOOBY see p.707

black "mask"

yellow bill

pinkish bill

long, pointed wings

black inner wing feathers

OCCURRENCE
Breeds on isolated rock stacks, on small uninhabited islands in the eastern North Atlantic, or on steep, inaccessible cliffs in marine areas of northeast North America; during migration and in winter, can be found in the waters of the continental shelf of the Gulf and Atlantic coast.

Length **2¾–3½ft (0.8–1.1m)**	Wingspan **5½ft (1.7m)**	Weight **5–8lb (2.2–3.6kg)**
Social **Flocks**	Lifespan **Up to 20 years**	Status **Localized**

Order **Pelecaniformes**	Family **Phalacrocoracidae**	Species *Phalacrocorax penicillatus*

Brandt's Cormorant

black overall — **ADULT (BREEDING)**

IN FLIGHT — *outstretched neck*

no facial whiskers — *lacks blue chin*

relatively short tail

ADULT (NONBREEDING)

rounded head — *long, dark bill*

white facial "whiskers" — *blue chin* — *pale brownish throat patch*

black upperparts with oily sheen

black underparts

ADULT (BREEDING)

FLIGHT: constant, rapid wing beats low over water in V-shaped flocks; glides while landing.

Brandt's Cormorant is the only cormorant with a blue chin, edged with a pale brownish patch at its lower end. Unlike the Double-crested Cormorant, most Brandt's fly with their necks straight. This species is found only along the Pacific Coast of North America. During the breeding season, it depends heavily on food from the nutrient-rich upwellings of the California Current. Named after a German who was the director of the zoological museum in St. Petersburg, Russia, this species is at risk from commercial fishing, pollution, and recreational disturbance.

VOICE Emits croaks, growls, gargles and coughing sounds.

NESTING Circular, drum-shaped nest of grass, moss, weeds, seaweed, sticks, and rubbish, on gentle slopes of islands or ledges on cliffs; 1–6 eggs; 1 brood; April–August.

FEEDING Dives and chases after surface- and bottom-dwelling fish; grasps fish in bill, crushes it, and swallows it head-first.

DRYING OUT
Like all cormorants, this species stretches its wings to drain its soggy feathers after diving for fish.

SIMILAR SPECIES

DOUBLE-CRESTED CORMORANT see p.149
lighter colored overall — *large yellow or orange throat pouch*

PELAGIC CORMORANT see p.151
slender neck — *very thin bill*

OCCURRENCE
Breeding colonies are found on offshore or near-shore islands or on mainland promontories on the Pacific coast of North America occasionally found in inshore lagoons; winters in sheltered inlets and other protected waters or on open ocean within a 1 mile (1.6km) of land.

Length **28–31in (70–79cm)**	Wingspan **3½ft (1.1m)**	Weight **3–6lb (1.4–2.7kg)**
Social **Flocks/Colonies**	Lifespan **Up to 18 years**	Status **Secure**

| Order **Pelecaniformes** | Family **Phalacrocoracidae** | Species *Phalacrocorax brasilianus* |

Neotropic Cormorant

ADULT

IN FLIGHT

long neck

long tail

gray at end of bill

brownish neck and breast

JUVENILE

long, slim, hooked bill

bluish eye

dull orange base to bill

patch of bare, yellowish skin

ADULT

blackish upperparts

long, slim body

black legs and feet

ADULT (NONBREEDING)

FLIGHT: strong flight with regular, fast wing beats interspersed with occasional glides.

The slender Neotropic Cormorant breeds widely in the Western Hemisphere. In the US, it breeds and winters along the Gulf Coast and in the lower Rio Grande Valley. Unlike other cormorant species, it tolerates human activities. In the 1960s, its numbers declined as a result of coastal development and pesticide use, but they have recovered in recent years.

VOICE Series of low, piglike grunts; croaks in alarm.
NESTING Platform of sticks lined with leaves, grass, and seaweed, cemented with guano; built on large branches of trees or bare ground; 3–4 eggs; 1 brood; February–December.
FEEDING Dives for fish and shrimp; also eats frogs and tadpoles; also plunge-dives, which is unusual for a cormorant.

SIMILAR SPECIES

DOUBLE-CRESTED CORMORANT
see p.149

longer body

shorter tail

COMMUNAL FEAST
Normally a solitary feeder, this species will gather at places where food is abundant.

OCCURRENCE
Breeds in coastal marshes, swamps, and inland reservoirs from southeast Texas and western Louisiana to the far south of South America; winters close inshore in protected bays, inlets, estuaries, and lagoons; found in a wide variety of wetlands in fresh, brackish, or saltwater.

| Length **24in (61cm)** | Wingspan **3¼ft (1m)** | Weight **2½–3¼lb (1–1.5kg)** |
| Social **Flocks** | Lifespan **Up to 12 years** | Status **Secure (p)** |

Order **Pelecaniformes**	Family **Phalacrocoracidae**	Species *Phalacrocorax auritus*

Double-crested Cormorant

ADULT (BREEDING)

long neck

no crest

pale neck and breast

browner plumage overall

JUVENILE

ADULT (NONBREEDING)

white crest

bluish eye

orange facial skin

black overall

pale throat and chest

JUVENILE

black underparts

blackish crest

IN FLIGHT

FLIGHT: regular wing beats, occasional glides; over water, flies close to the surface; often soars.

ADULT
P. a. auritus
(EASTERN; BREEDING)

ADULT
P. a. cincinatus
(WESTERN; BREEDING)

This species is the most widespread of the North American cormorants. It often flies high over land in V-shaped flocks, but is mostly seen swimming in the water with its head and neck visible, or resting on trees and rocks, sometimes with its wings spread. While fishing, it dives from the surface of the water and chases fish underwater, using its webbed toes for propulsion.

VOICE Deep gruntlike calls while nesting, roosting, and fishing; *t-t-t-t* call before taking off and *urg-urg-urg* before landing; prolonged *arr-r-r-r-t-t* while mating, and *eh-hr* as threat.

NESTING Nests of twigs and sticks, seaweed, and trash, lined with grass; built on ground, cliffs, or in trees usually in colonies; 3-5 eggs; 1 brood; April–August.

FEEDING Pursues slow-moving or schooling fish; feeds on insects, crustaceans, amphibians, and, rarely, on voles and snakes.

DRYING OFF
Like all cormorants, the Double-crested usually perches with wings spread, to dry its feathers.

SIMILAR SPECIES

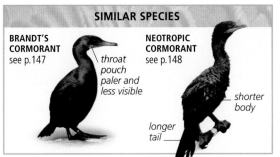

BRANDT'S CORMORANT
see p.147

throat pouch paler and less visible

NEOTROPIC CORMORANT
see p.148

shorter body

longer tail

OCCURRENCE
Breeds in a wide range of aquatic habitats, including ponds, artificial and natural lakes, slow-moving rivers, estuaries, lagoons, and seashores; winters on coastlines and sandbars in coastal inlets; roosts near catfish farms in some areas.

Length **28–35in (70–90cm)**	Wingspan **3½–4ft (1.1–1.2m)**	Weight **2¾–5½lb (1.2–2.5kg)**
Social **Flocks**	Lifespan **Up to 18 years**	Status **Secure**

| Order **Pelecaniformes** | Family **Phalacrocoracidae** | Species *Phalacrocorax carbo* |

Great Cormorant

JUVENILE

whitish gray belly

ADULT

outstretched head

neck kinked in flight

IN FLIGHT

brown neck

mostly white underparts

JUVENILE

large head with flat forehead

long, black neck

thick bill with hooked tip

orange-yellow patch of skin near bill

white throat

glossy black underparts with greenish scalloping

long body with glossy black upperparts

ADULT (SUMMER)

short, black legs and webbed feet

long, broad tail

FLIGHT: regular, shallow wing beats; sometimes glides and soars; flocks often fly in V-shape.

As its name suggests, the Great Cormorant is the largest of the North American cormorants and is also the most widely distributed cormorant species in the world. It sometimess breeds in mixed colonies with Double-crested Cormorants. From a distance, the two can be confused, especially outside breeding areas. However, Great Cormorants can be distinguished by their stouter bill, larger size, and, their white throat in summer. It is a coastal species in North America, but in Europe, it is more likely to be found inland. Like other cormorants, its plumage retains water, which effectively reduces buoyancy so that it is able to dive more easily. The Great Cormorant can dive to depths of 115ft (35m) to catch prey.

VOICE Deep, guttural calls at nesting and roosting site; otherwise silent.
NESTING Mound of seaweed, sticks, and debris added to previous year's nest, built on cliff ledges and flat tops of rocks above high-water mark on islands; 3–5 eggs; 1 brood; April–August.
FEEDING Dives to pursue fish and small crustaceans; smaller prey swallowed underwater, while larger prey brought to surface.

SIMILAR SPECIES

DOUBLE-CRESTED CORMORANT see p.149

thinner bill

black throat

RARE EVENT
Great Cormorants usually nest on sea cliffs; tree breeding is rare in North America.

OCCURRENCE
Breeds on cliff ledges of islands along rocky coasts, in northeast US and Maritimes of Canada; feeds in protected inshore waters. Winters in shallow coastal waters similar to breeding habitat, but not restricted to rocky shoreline; winter habitat extends to the Carolinas in the US.

| Length **33–35in (84–90cm)** | Wingspan **4¼–5¼ft (1.3–1.6m)** | Weight **5¾–8¼lb (2.6–3.7kg)** |
| Social **Colonies** | Lifespan **Up to 14 years** | Status **Secure** |

| Order **Pelecaniformes** | Family **Phalacrocoracidae** | Species *Phalacrocorax pelagicus* |

Pelagic Cormorant

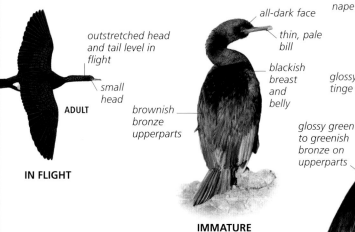

IN FLIGHT

outstretched head and tail level in flight

small head

ADULT

all-dark face

thin, pale bill

blackish breast and belly

brownish bronze upperparts

IMMATURE

tufts on crown and nape

red patch at base of bill

thin, dark bill with blunt or hooked end

glossy purple tinge on neck

long, thin neck with white flecks

glossy green to greenish bronze on upperparts

iridescent greenish black underparts

ADULT (BREEDING)

long, blackish tail

white patch on flank

FLIGHT: rapid with regular, steady wing beats; glides before landing.

The Pelagic Cormorant is the smallest cormorant species in North America. Although a marine bird, its English (and scientific) name, *pelagicus*, meaning "oceanic," is misleading because this bird mostly inhabits inshore waters. This bird is most visible at its roosting sites, where it spends much of its time drying its feathers. The Pelagic Cormorant has not been well studied, because it is more solitary than the other cormorant species in North America; however, like all cormorants, it is threatened by the disturbance of its nesting colonies, oil spills, entanglement in fishing nets, and pollution.

VOICE Female two-note call *igh-ugh*, similar to ticking grandfather clock; male call note *purring* or *arr-arr-arr*; both utter croaks, hisses, and low groans.

NESTING Saucer-shaped nest of grass, seaweed, sticks, feathers, and marine debris, cemented to cliff face with guano; 3–5 eggs; 1 brood; May–October.

FEEDING Dives from water's surface for any medium-sized fish, and also invertebrates, such as shrimps, worms, and hermit crabs.

SITTING LOW
Pelagic Cormorants sit low in the water with only their head, neck, and back visible.

SIMILAR SPECIES

BRANDT'S CORMORANT
see p.147

round head

thicker neck

shorter tail

larger overall

OCCURRENCE
Found in rocky habitat on outer coast, shallow bays, inlets, estuaries, harbors, and lagoons; nesting colonies found on steep cliffs on forested and grassy islands, and on rocky promontories along the shoreline; also seen on built structures such as wharf pilings, bridges, and harbor buoys.

| Length **20–30in (51–76cm)** | Wingspan **3¼–4ft (1–1.2m)** | Weight **2¾–5¼lb (1.3–2.4kg)** |
| Social **Solitary/Pairs** | Lifespan **Up to 17 years** | Status **Secure** |

| Order **Pelecaniformes** | Family **Phalacrocoracidae** | Species *Phalacrocorax urile* |

Red-faced Cormorant

prominent crest on crown of head

red bare skin on face

glossy black body with green and violet iridescence

ADULT

white patch near base of tail

IN FLIGHT

outstretched head and neck

brighter red face

mostly pale bill with dark tip

ADULT (BREEDING)

some individuals have orange-yellow face

ADULT (BREEDING)

dull brown wings and tail

ADULT (NONBREEDING)

black feet and legs

FLIGHT: rapid on vibrating wings, with head and tail stretched out in line with body.

The Red-faced Cormorant has the most restricted distribution of all North American cormorants. Often confused with the Pelagic Cormorant where their ranges overlap, the Red-faced Cormorant is distinguishable by its red facial skin when seen at close range. However, Red-faced Cormorants are occasionally spotted with orange-yellow bare skin on their face. Otherwise, it is a dark bird with an iridescent back, a small crest and a long tail. The shyest of all cormorants, this species nests far from potential human disturbance, and even though a few colonies are sizeable, most are small and scattered. As these breeding sites are remote, this species has not been well studied.

VOICE Low groans and croaks; alarmed birds hiss.

NESTING Oval compact nest made of grass, seaweeds, mosses, sticks, feathers, and debris, its rim cemented by guano on narrow ledges of high, steep cliffs facing the sea; 2–4 eggs; 1 brood; April–July.

FEEDING Dives from water surface to pursue young, bottom-dwelling schooling fish like herring and sandlance; typically swallows small prey underwater, but will bring larger prey to the surface.

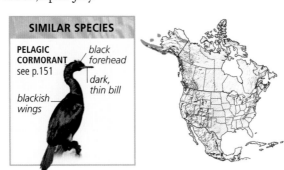

SIMILAR SPECIES

PELAGIC CORMORANT see p.151

black forehead

dark, thin bill

blackish wings

ON THE ROCKS
Usually solitary or in very small groups, this cormorant is mainly found along rocky ocean shores.

OCCURRENCE
Localized to the Aleutian Islands and the Pacific Coast of Alaska, south to British Columbia. Nests on steep cliffs on rocky marine islands and headlands; roosts on offshore rocks and protected but isolated rocky outcrops; seldom seen far out at sea.

| Length **30in–3ft 3in (75–100cm)** | Wingspan **3½ft (1.1m)** | Weight **4–5¼lb (1.8–2.4kg)** |
| Social **Colonies** | Lifespan **Unknown** | Status **Secure (p)** |

| Order **Pelecaniformes** | Family **Anhingidae** | Species *Anhinga anhinga* |

Anhinga

FEMALE

dark brown overall

long neck

JUVENILE

pale tan neck and head

dark underwings

IN FLIGHT

long tail

brown plumes on small, pointed head

dagger-like bill

blotchy, silver-white markings on upperparts

MALE

black underparts

variable white upperparts

pale tan breast and neck

FEMALE

long tail with horizontal ridges

This resident of the Southeast coastal plain, locally called "Water Turkey," may be found swimming in murky swamps, roosting on tall trees, or soaring high overhead. The Anhinga is also known as the "snake bird"—a reference to its habit of swimming with its body immersed so deeply that only its long, thin, sinuous neck, pointed head, and sharp bill stick out above the water. Although they superficially resemble cormorants, the two species of Anhingas stand apart in many ways—particularly their long tails with unusual horizontal ridges.

VOICE Silent most of the time, but pairs may give various calls around nest; these vocalizations consist of soft rattles and trills, but are sometimes quite noisy, repeated *Krah-Krah*.

NESTING Loose platform of sticks in trees above water; 3–5 eggs; 1 brood; February–June.

FEEDING Jabs suddenly with its dagger-like bill, mostly for fish in calm freshwater habitats; also eats insects and shrimp.

FLIGHT: strong flier; neck and tail outstretched and wings held flat.; often soars.

HANGING OUT TO DRY
Anhingas do not have waterproof plumage and so spend a lot of time drying off their wings.

SIMILAR SPECIES

DOUBLE-CRESTED CORMORANT see p.149

hooked bill

shorter tail

entirely black body

DOUBLE-CRESTED CORMORANT ☾ see p.149

dark upperwings

shorter tail

OCCURRENCE
An inhabitant of southeastern wetlands. Greatest concentrations in wooded wetlands, calm waters in swamps; often also seen in habitats far from open water.

| Length **35in (89cm)** | Wingspan **3½ft (1.1m)** | Weight **2¾lb (1.3kg)** |
| Social **Colonies** | Lifespan **Up to 10 years** | Status **Secure** |

Families **Cathartidae, Falconidae, Accipitridae**

BIRDS OF PREY

THE DEFINING FEATURES of all birds of prey, or raptors, are strong feet with sharp talons for catching and holding prey or carrying off a carcass, and a powerful, hooked bill for tearing the catch to pieces.

VULTURES

Of the seven New World species of vulture, three occur in North America: the Black Vulture, the smaller Turkey Vulture, which has an acute sense of smell that enables it to detect carrion hidden from sight beneath the forest canopy, and the rare California Condor, the continent's largest soaring land bird. All three can stay in the air for hours on end, using the lift provided by updrafts to minimize the energy spent on wing flapping.

WEAK TOOL
In spite of its sharp beak, the Turkey Vulture cannot always break the skin of carcasses.

FALCONS

Ranging in size from the diminutive American Merlin, with northern breeding habitats, to the large, powerful Gyrfalcon, which nests in the Arctic, this group also includes the Kestrel, the Prairie Falcon, and perhaps the best-known raptor of all—the fast-diving Peregrine Falcon. Falcon prey ranges from insects to large mammals and birds.

EAGLES AND HAWKS

This group covers a wide range of raptors of varying sizes, from the the iconic Bald Eagle and the majestic Golden Eagle to smaller birds, such as the Northern Harrier, and various hawks and kites. These birds use a wide range of hunting methods. Forest-dwelling hawks, for example, rely on speed and stealth to pounce on small birds among the trees in a sudden, short dash. The Osprey, by contrast, hovers over water until it sees a fish below, then dives steeply, pulling up at the last moment to pluck its prey clean out of the water with its talons.

DOUBLE SHOT
When there are lots of fish running in a tight school, the Osprey has the strength and skill to catch two with one dive.

Order **Ciconiiformes**	Family **Cathartidae**	Species *Cathartes aura*

Turkey Vulture

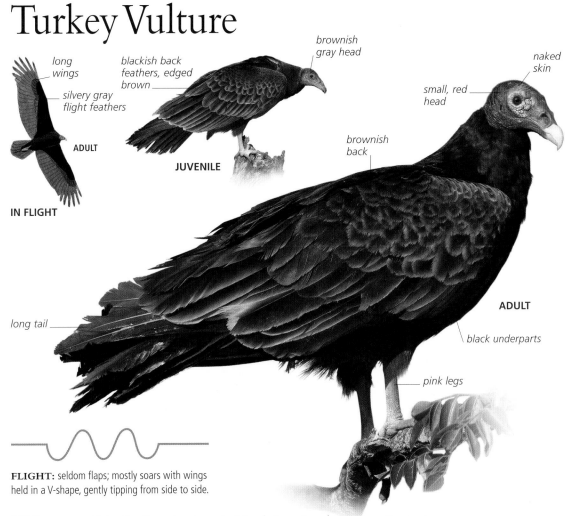

long wings

silvery gray flight feathers

ADULT

IN FLIGHT

blackish back feathers, edged brown

brownish gray head

JUVENILE

naked skin

small, red head

brownish back

ADULT

long tail

black underparts

pink legs

FLIGHT: seldom flaps; mostly soars with wings held in a V-shape, gently tipping from side to side.

The most widely distributed vulture in North America, the Turkey Vulture is found in most of the US and has expanded its range into southern Canada. It possesses a better sense of smell than the Black Vulture, which often follows it and displaces it from carcasses. The Turkey Vulture's habit of defecating down its legs, which it shares with the Wood Stork, may serve to cool it or to kill bacteria with its ammonia content.

VOICE Silent, but will hiss at intruders; also grunts.

NESTING Dark recesses, such as under large rocks or stumps, on rocky ledges in caves, and crevices, in mammal burrows and hollow logs, and abandoned buildings; 1–3 eggs; 1 brood; March–August.

FEEDING Feeds on a wide range of wild and domestic carrion, mostly mammals, also birds, reptiles, amphibians, and fish; occasionally takes live prey such as nestlings or trapped birds.

SOAKING UP THE SUN
Turkey Vultures often spread their wings to sun themselves and increase their body temperature.

SIMILAR SPECIES

BLACK VULTURE
see p.156

all-black body

shorter tail

OCCURRENCE
Generally forages and migrates over mixed farmland and forest; prefers to nest in forested or partly forested hillsides offering hidden ground protected from disturbance; roosts in large trees such as cottonwoods, on rocky outcrops, and on power line transmission towers; some winter in urban areas and near landfills.

Length **25–32in (64–81cm)**	Wingspan **5½–6ft (1.7–1.8m)**	Weight **4½lb (2kg)**
Social **Flocks**	Lifespan **At least 17 years**	Status **Secure**

| Order **Ciconiiformes** | Family **Cathartidae** | Species ***Coragyps atratus*** |

Black Vulture

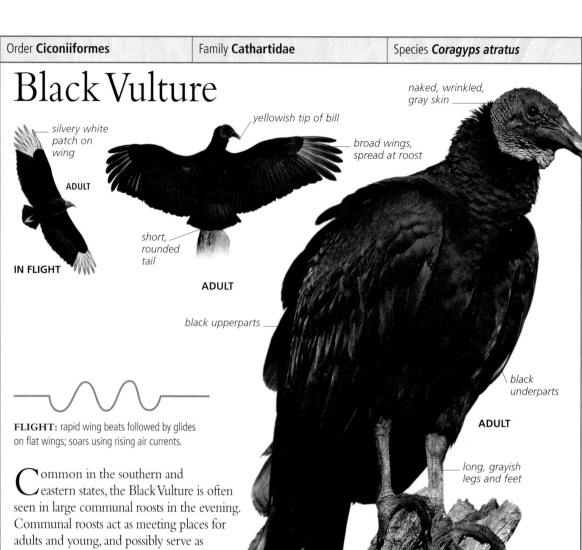

silvery white patch on wing

ADULT

IN FLIGHT

yellowish tip of bill

broad wings, spread at roost

short, rounded tail

ADULT

naked, wrinkled, gray skin

black upperparts

black underparts

ADULT

long, grayish legs and feet

FLIGHT: rapid wing beats followed by glides on flat wings; soars using rising air currents.

Common in the southern and eastern states, the Black Vulture is often seen in large communal roosts in the evening. Communal roosts act as meeting places for adults and young, and possibly serve as information centers, where food locations are communicated. Maintaining long pair-bonds, Black Vultures remain together year-round. According to one study, parents will continue to feed their young for as long as eight months after fledging. When not feeding on roadkills along highways, Black Vultures spend time soaring above the landscape, in search of carrion.
VOICE Usually silent; hisses and barks occasionally.
NESTING No nest; lays eggs on ground in thickets or under stumps, in piles of rocks, seldom in old buildings; 2 eggs; 1 brood; January–August.
FEEDING Generally eats carrion (mostly large mammals) on the ground; also consumes live prey.

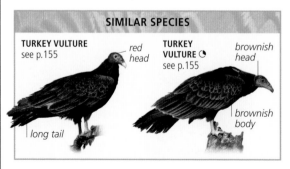

SIMILAR SPECIES

TURKEY VULTURE see p.155
red head
long tail

TURKEY VULTURE ☾ see p.155
brownish head
brownish body

DOMINANT SCAVENGER
The more aggressive Black Vultures often displace the Turkey Vultures at carcasses.

OCCURRENCE
Breeds in dense woodlands, caves, old buildings; forms roosts in stands of tall trees; forages in open habitats and near roads and highways; year-round resident throughout its range in southern and eastern states. Range expanding in the northeastern US.

| Length **24–27in (61–68cm)** | Wingspan **4½–5ft (1.4–1.5m)** | Weight **3½–5lb (1.6–2.2kg)** |
| Social **Loose colonies** | Lifespan **Up to 26 years** | Status **Secure** |

Order **Falconiformes**	Family **Falconidae**	Species *Caracara cheriway*

Crested Caracara

ADULT

- slightly bent wings
- black tail band
- white patch on wing

IN FLIGHT

- black crown and crest
- yellow-orange to red face
- thick, pale blue bill
- white cheek
- black back
- thin, dark bars on white breast and nape
- cream or whitish undertail feathers

ADULT

- long, yellow to orange legs

- blackish crest
- yellowish cheek
- streaked breast
- barred tail
- pale legs

JUVENILE

In North America, the hawk-like Crested Caracara is only found in Texas, southern Arizona, and central Florida, where there is a small, isolated population. Crested Caracara pairs are monogamous and highly territorial. Although known locally as the "Mexican Buzzard," the Crested Caracara is actually a member of the falcon family, rather than the hawk family.

VOICE Adults disturbed at nest emit cackles, hollow rattles, and high-pitched screams; nestlings utter high-pitched screams and raspy *swee-swee* calls.

NESTING Builds large nest in trees with a commanding view using vines, stems, twigs; 2–4 eggs; 1–2 broods; January–May.

FEEDING Eats live and dead prey, including mammals, birds, reptiles, and insects; raids nests for eggs; patrols roads for carrion.

FLIGHT: alternate flapping and soaring; low over tree tops; soars on thermals with vultures.

FEASTING TOGETHER
Regularly foraging in groups, together with vultures, Crested Caracaras feast on carcasses.

OCCURRENCE
Breeds and winters in open areas ranging from desert to grasslands with scattered tall trees. Also found around agricultural land, in addition to dumps and slaughterhouses. Occurs widely in Central and South America.

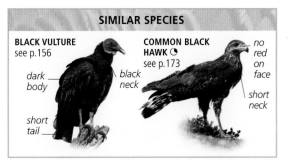

SIMILAR SPECIES

BLACK VULTURE
see p.156
- dark body
- black neck
- short tail

COMMON BLACK HAWK
see p.173
- no red on face
- short neck

Length **19–23in (48–58cm)**	Wingspan **4ft (1.2m)**	Weight **2½–2¾lb (1–1.3kg)**
Social **Pairs/Flocks**	Lifespan **Up to 22 years**	Status **Vulnerable**

| Order **Falconiformes** | Family **Falconidae** | Species *Falco sparverius* |

American Kestrel

gray crown with reddish cap

rufous upperparts

dark barring or spots on blue-gray wings

light undertail with partial barring

small head

FEMALE

MALE

IN FLIGHT

light undertail feathers

long wings

dark, outer flight feathers

MALE

bold "mustache"

tan to cinnamon breast

spotted underparts

yellow to yellowish orange legs and toes

barred, rufous upperparts

heavy checks on belly

dark, barred, rufous tail

FEMALE

IMMATURE MALE

The smallest of the North American falcons, the American Kestrel features long pointed wings, a "tooth and notch" bill structure, and the dark brown eyes typical of falcons, though kestrels have shorter toes than other falcons. This may be due to the fact that kestrels often dive into long grass to capture insects and small mammals, which would be more difficult with long, thin toes. Male and female American Kestrels show differences in plumage, and also in size.

VOICE Common call a high-pitched *killy-killy-killy*.
NESTING Natural cavities, crevices, holes in dead trees, woodpeckers' holes, crevices in barns, manmade nest boxes if constructed and located properly; 4–5 eggs; 1 brood; April–June.
FEEDING Plunges for grasshoppers and crickets in spring and summer; small birds and mice in fall and winter; lizards and snakes.

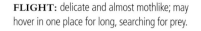

FLIGHT: delicate and almost mothlike; may hover in one place for long, searching for prey.

HIGH FLIER
A male American Kestrel hovers over a field, its sharp eyes scanning the ground for insects and rodents.

SIMILAR SPECIES

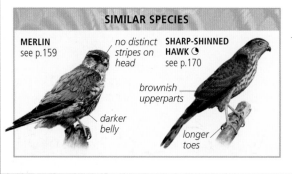

MERLIN
see p.159

no distinct stripes on head

SHARP-SHINNED HAWK ◗
see p.170

brownish upperparts

darker belly

longer toes

OCCURRENCE
From near the northern tree line in Alaska and Canada south, east, and west throughout most of North America. Occurs also in Central and South America. Habitat ranges from semi-open tree groves to grasslands, cultivated and fallow farmland, and open desert.

| Length **9in (23cm)** | Wingspan **22in (56cm)** | Weight **3½–4oz (100–125g)** |
| Social **Family groups** | Lifespan **10–15 years** | Status **Secure** |

| Order **Falconiformes** | Family **Falconidae** | Species *Falco columbarius* |

Merlin

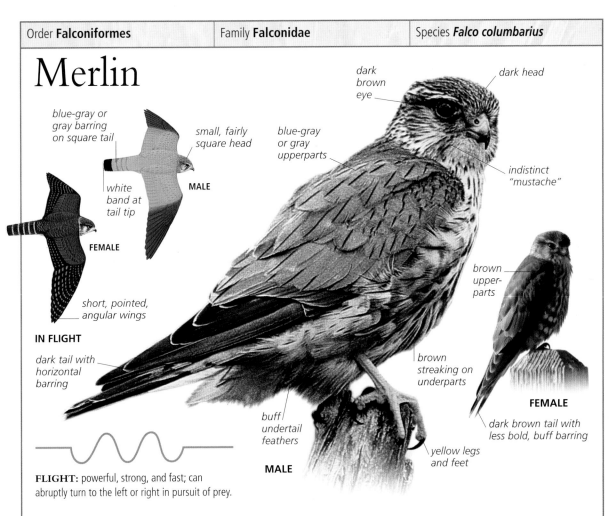

blue-gray or gray barring on square tail

small, fairly square head

MALE

white band at tail tip

FEMALE

short, pointed, angular wings

IN FLIGHT

dark tail with horizontal barring

dark brown eye

dark head

blue-gray or gray upperparts

indistinct "mustache"

brown upperparts

FEMALE

dark brown tail with less bold, buff barring

brown streaking on underparts

buff undertail feathers

yellow legs and feet

MALE

FLIGHT: powerful, strong, and fast; can abruptly turn to the left or right in pursuit of prey.

Merlins are small, fast-flying falcons that were formerly known as "pigeon hawks," because their shape and flight are similar to those strong fliers. Merlins can overtake and capture a wide variety of prey. They can turn on a dime, and use their long, thin toes, typical of falcons, to pluck birds from the air after launching a direct attack. Males are smaller than females, and different in color. Both males and females show geographical color variations.

VOICE Male call a high-pitched *ki-ki-ki-ki*; female call a low-pitched *kek-ek-ek-ek-ek*.

NESTING Small scrapes on ground in open country, or abandoned nests of other species, such as crows, in forested areas; 4–6 eggs; 1 brood; April–June.

FEEDING Catches small birds in midair, and occasionally birds as large as doves; also feeds on small mammals, including bats.

ABOUT TO ROUSE
An adult female Merlin sits on a moss-covered rock, about to "rouse," or fluff out and shake her feathers.

SIMILAR SPECIES

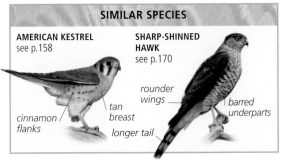

AMERICAN KESTREL
see p.158

cinnamon flanks

tan breast

SHARP-SHINNED HAWK
see p.170

rounder wings

barred underparts

longer tail

OCCURRENCE
Breeds from northern California east to Newfoundland, and south to Louisiana, Texas, and Mexico. Merlins can be seen hunting along coastlines, over marshlands and open fields, and in desert areas. Eastern birds migrate to southern areas.

| Length **10in (25cm)** | Wingspan **24in (61cm)** | Weight **5–7oz (150–200g)** |
| Social **Pairs/Family groups** | Lifespan **10–15 years** | Status **Secure** |

| Order **Falconiformes** | Family **Falconidae** | Species *Falco rusticolus* |

Gyrfalcon

pointed tips

dark brown to black all over

almost completely white

JUVENILE (GRAY FORM)

paler upperparts with brown barring

gray, barred upperparts

darker wing linings

ADULT (DARK FORM)

paler flight feathers

yellow bill

heavily streaked head

yellow patch of skin near bill

dark brown iris

ADULT (WHITE FORM)

IN FLIGHT

blue bill with dark tip

yellow toes and legs

ADULT (GRAY FORM)

long, barred tail

lighter underparts with spots

ADULT (GRAY FORM)

Arctic-bred, the Gyrfalcon is used to harsh environments. It is the largest of all the falcons and one of the most majestic species of bird in the world. For centuries, the Gyrfalcon has been sought by both the nobility and falconers for its power, beauty, and gentle nature; today, it is also the mascot of the US Air Force Academy. It uses its speed to pursue prey in a "tail chase," sometimes striking its quarry on the ground, but also in flight. Three forms are known, ranging from almost pure white to gray and dark.

VOICE Loud, harsh *KYHa-KYHa-KYHa*.
NESTING Scrape on cliff, or old Common Ravens' nests; 2–7 eggs; 1 brood; April–July.
FEEDING Feeds mostly on large birds such as ptarmigan, pigeons, grouse; may also hunt mammals, such as lemmings.

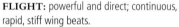

FLIGHT: powerful and direct; continuous, rapid, stiff wing beats.

SNOWY PLUMAGE
A Gyrfalcon stands on an Arctic hillside. From a distance, it might be mistaken for a patch of snow.

SIMILAR SPECIES

PRAIRIE FALCON light, brown-spotted underparts; see p.161

PEREGRINE FALCON see p.162

light, sandy brown upperparts

light, barred underparts

dark "hood" on head

smaller overall

OCCURRENCE
Found in Arctic North America. Sometimes found in northern regions of the US. A truly Arctic species found in the most barren regions of the tundra, high mountains and foothills of the tundra, and Arctic and sub-Arctic evergreen forests and woodlands. Not common outside its breeding range.

| Length **22in (56cm)** | Wingspan **4ft (1.2m)** | Weight **2¾–4lb (1.2–1.8kg)** |
| Social **Solitary/Pairs** | Lifespan **15–30 years** | Status **Localized** |

Order **Falconiformes**	Family **Falconidae**	Species *Falco mexicanus*

Prairie Falcon

yellow eye-ring

yellow patch of skin near bill

light head and "mustache"

white cheek

long, pointed wings

ADULT

light, sandy brown upperparts with incomplete barring

longish tail

distinctive, triangle-shaped patch on wingpit feathers

light underparts with brown spots

IN FLIGHT

ADULT

yellow legs and toes

light undertail feathers

Prairie Falcons are light-colored, buoyant residents of the arid regions of North America. They blend in well with their surroundings (cliff faces and dry grass), where they are invisible to their prey. Prairie Falcons chase their prey close to the ground and do not often dive or "stoop" on prey from a great height. Ground squirrels are important prey items in some areas, and breeding is often linked with the squirrels' emergence. The sexes are very similar in coloration, though juveniles have a streaked rather than spotted breast. The underwing pattern with almost black feathers in the "wingpits" is distinctive; no other North American falcon shows this mark.

VOICE Repeated shrill *kik-kik-kik-kik-kik*.

NESTING Slight, shallow scrapes, almost always located on high cliff ledges or bluffs; 3–6 eggs; 1 brood; March–July.

FEEDING Feeds on small to medium-sized birds and small mammals, such as ground squirrels.

FLIGHT: fast flight; capable of soaring and diving; usually chases prey low above the ground.

STRIKING MUSTACHE
An inquisitive Prairie Falcon stares at the camera. The white cheek is obvious from this angle.

SIMILAR SPECIES

MERLIN
see p.159

smaller overall

heavily streaked underparts

PEREGRINE FALCON ☾
see p.162

darker head

streaked underparts

yellow or bluish gray legs and toes

OCCURRENCE
Interior North America, from central British Columbia east to western North Dakota and south to southern California, and Mexico, Arizona, northern Texas. Found in open plains, prairies, and grasslands, dotted with buttes or cliffs. A partial migrant, it moves east of its breeding range in winter.

Length **16in (41cm)**	Wingspan **3¼ft (1m)**	Weight **22–30oz (625–850g)**
Social **Solitary/Pairs**	Lifespan **10–20 years**	Status **Localized**

Order **Falconiformes**	Family **Falconidae**	Species *Falco peregrinus*

Peregrine Falcon

long, pointed wings

streaked underparts

short tail

ADULT

IN FLIGHT

dark "hood" on head

yellow eye-ring

brown upperparts

JUVENILE

dark spots on light buff breast

bluish gray upperparts

light yellow or bluish gray legs and toes

barred underwings

barred undertail feathers

prominent dark "mustache"

light underparts with horizontal barring

ADULT

ADULT

yellow toes and legs

FLIGHT: powerful and direct; faster, deeper wing beats during pursuit; also soars.

Peregrine Falcons are distributed worldwide and are long-distance travelers—"Peregrine" means "wanderer." It has been shown to dive from great heights at speeds of up to 200mph (320kmph)—a technique known as "stooping." Like all true falcons, this species has a pointed "tooth" on its upper beak and a "notch" on the lower one, and it instinctively bites the neck of captured prey to kill it. From the 1950s–1980s, its breeding ability was reduced by the insecticide DDT, which resulted in thin eggshells that could easily be crushed by the parent. Peregrines were then bred in captivity, and later released into the wild. Their status is now secure.

VOICE Sharp *hek-hek-hek* when alarmed.

NESTING Shallow scrape on cliff or building (nest sites are used year after year); 2–5 eggs; 1 brood; March–June.

FEEDING Dives on prey—birds of various sizes in flight; now feeds on pigeons in cities.

PARENTAL CARE
An adult Peregrine gently feeds a hatchling bits of meat; the remaining egg is likely to hatch soon.

SIMILAR SPECIES

GYRFALCON
see p.160

larger and stockier

longer tail

less defined "hood"

PRAIRIE FALCON
see p.161

lighter head color

light sandy brown upperparts

OCCURRENCE
A variety of habitats across northern North America, ranging from open valleys to cities with tall buildings. Peregrines prefer to inhabit cliffs along sea coasts, in addition to inland mountain ranges, but also occur in open country such as scrubland and salt marshes.

Length **16in (41cm)**	Wingspan **3¼–3½ft (1–1.1m)**	Weight **22–35oz (620–1000g)**
Social **Solitary/Pairs**	Lifespan **15–20 years**	Status **Secure**

Order **Falconiformes**	Family **Accipitridae**	Species *Pandion haliaetus*

Osprey

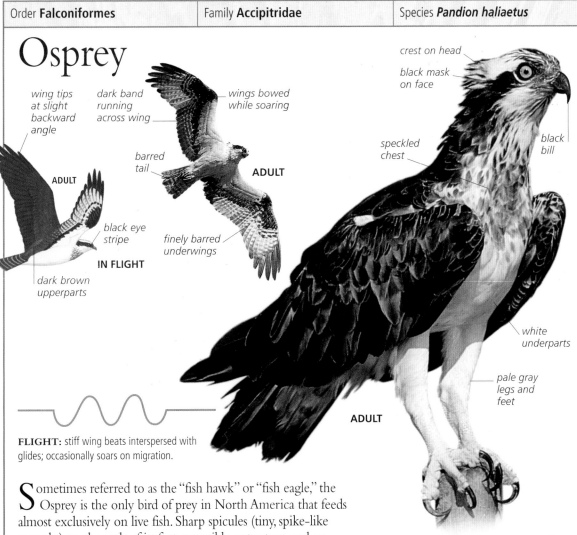

wing tips at slight backward angle

dark band running across wing

wings bowed while soaring

crest on head

black mask on face

barred tail

speckled chest

black bill

ADULT

ADULT

black eye stripe

finely barred underwings

IN FLIGHT

dark brown upperparts

white underparts

pale gray legs and feet

ADULT

FLIGHT: stiff wing beats interspersed with glides; occasionally soars on migration.

Sometimes referred to as the "fish hawk" or "fish eagle," the Osprey is the only bird of prey in North America that feeds almost exclusively on live fish. Sharp spicules (tiny, spike-like growths) on the pads of its feet, reversible outer toes, and an ability to lock its talons in place enable it to hold onto slippery fish. Some populations declined between the 1950s and 1980s due to the use of dangerous pesticides. However, the ban on use of these chemicals, along with availability of artificial nest sites and a tolerance of nearby human activity has allowed the Osprey to return to its former numbers.

VOICE Slow, whistled notes, falling in pitch: *tiooop, tioooop, tiooop*; also screams by displaying male.

NESTING Twig nest on tree, cliff, rock pinnacles, boulders, ground; 1–4 eggs; 1 brood; March–August.

FEEDING Dives to catch fish up to top 3ft (90cm) of water.

IMPROVING AERODYNAMICS
Once caught a fish is held with its head pointing forward reducing drag as the bird flies.

OCCURRENCE
Breeds in a wide variety of habitats: northern forests, near shallow reservoirs, along freshwater rivers and large lakes, estuaries and salt marshes, coastal deserts and desert saltflat lagoons. Migrates through and winters in similar habitats.

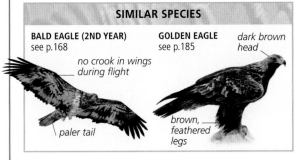

SIMILAR SPECIES

BALD EAGLE (2ND YEAR)
see p.168

GOLDEN EAGLE
see p.185

dark brown head

no crook in wings during flight

paler tail

brown, feathered legs

Length **21–23in (53–58cm)**	Wingspan **5–6ft (1.5–1.8m)**	Weight **3–4½lb (1.4–2kg)**
Social **Solitary/Pairs**	Lifespan **Up to 25 years**	Status **Secure**

| Order **Falconiformes** | Family **Accipitridae** | Species **Elanoides forficatus** |

Swallow-tailed Kite

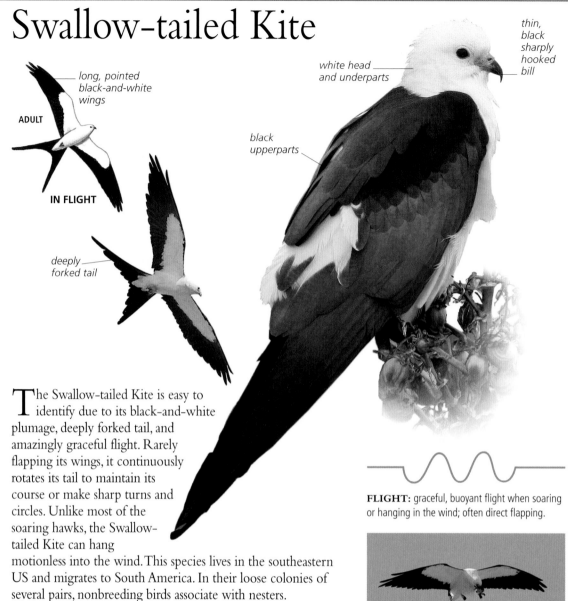

ADULT

IN FLIGHT

long, pointed black-and-white wings

deeply forked tail

white head and underparts

black upperparts

thin, black sharply hooked bill

The Swallow-tailed Kite is easy to identify due to its black-and-white plumage, deeply forked tail, and amazingly graceful flight. Rarely flapping its wings, it continuously rotates its tail to maintain its course or make sharp turns and circles. Unlike most of the soaring hawks, the Swallow-tailed Kite can hang motionless into the wind. This species lives in the southeastern US and migrates to South America. In their loose colonies of several pairs, nonbreeding birds associate with nesters.

VOICE Loud *klee-klee-klee* given by both sexes when excited or alarmed; a drawn-out *tew-whee* given during courtship.

NESTING Lined cup of small sticks, mostly in tall pine but also cypress and mangroves; 2 eggs; 1 brood; March–June.

FEEDING Feeds mainly on flying insects; also eats frogs, lizards, snakes, nestlings, and occasionally bats, fruit, and small fish.

FLIGHT: graceful, buoyant flight when soaring or hanging in the wind; often direct flapping.

AERIAL SNACK
Swallow-tailed Kites commonly eat smaller prey, such as insects, while on the wing.

SIMILAR SPECIES

WHITE-TAILED KITE
see p.165

red eye

gray back

SWAINSON'S HAWK (LIGHT FORM)
see p.179

streaked head

square tail

OCCURRENCE
In swamps, lowland forests, freshwater and brackish marshes of Florida and the southeastern US; avoids arid areas. Needs tall trees for nesting, with open areas for foraging for small prey nearby. Tropical populations are found from Central America south to Argentina.

| Length **20–25in (51–64cm)** | Wingspan **4ft (1.2m)** | Weight **13–21oz (375–600g)** |
| Social **Colonies** | Lifespan **Unknown** | Status **Secure** |

| Order **Falconiformes** | Family **Accipitridae** | Species *Elanus leucurus* |

White-tailed Kite

IN FLIGHT

dark gray wing tips

ADULT

square or notched tail tip

JUVENILE

pale eye

splashes of sandy rufous around neck and breast

dark wrist mark

gray upperparts, black triangle on shoulder

dusky wing tips

white head and neck

orange eye

thin, shapely black bill

dusky gray wingtips

whitish underside

white sided tail

ADULT

FLIGHT: fast, shallow wing beats interspersed with glides; hovers with tail down.

Formerly known as the Black-shouldered Kite, the White-tailed Kite almost disappeared from North America due to hunting and egg-collecting, but its numbers have rebounded in California. It is also found in Oregon, Washington, Florida, southern Texas, and from Mexico to Central and South America. These birds can be easily identified by their falcon-like shape, gray-and-white plumage, and hovering behavior when hunting for rodents in open grasslands. When not breeding, White-tailed Kites roost communally in groups of about 100. The species is largely sedentary, but dispersal takes place after breeding, especially of young birds.

VOICE Whistle-like *kewt* and an *eee-grack* call.

NESTING Twig nest lined with grass or hay; 4 eggs; 1–2 broods; February–August.

FEEDING Captures rodents such as voles and field mice; also birds, lizards, and insects from a hovering position.

A HIGH PERCH IS BEST
The White-tailed Kite like to perch as high up in trees as possible.

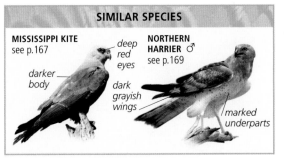

SIMILAR SPECIES

MISSISSIPPI KITE
see p.167

darker body

deep red eyes

NORTHERN HARRIER ♂
see p.169

dark grayish wings

marked underparts

OCCURRENCE
Limited range in the US, breeds and winters in a restricted range; found in open grassland areas, and over large agricultural fields, as well as in rough wetlands with low, reedy, or rushy growth, open oak woodland and light savanna woods. Especially fond of damp, riverside areas.

| Length **13–15in (33–38cm)** | Wingspan **3ft 3in–3½ft (1–1.1m)** | Weight **11–12oz (300–350g)** |
| Social **Colonies** | Lifespan **Up to 6 years** | Status **Secure** |

| Order **Falconiformes** | Family **Accipitridae** | Species *Rostrhamus sociabilis* |

Snail Kite

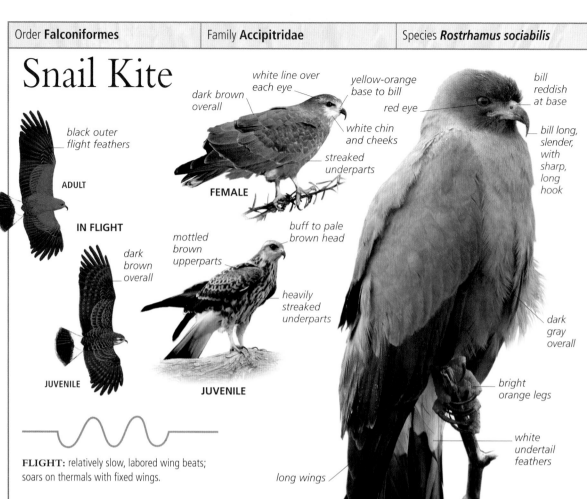

black outer
flight feathers

ADULT

IN FLIGHT

white line over
each eye

dark brown
overall

yellow-orange
base to bill

red eye

white chin
and cheeks

streaked
underparts

FEMALE

dark
brown
overall

JUVENILE

mottled
brown
upperparts

buff to pale
brown head

heavily
streaked
underparts

JUVENILE

bill
reddish
at base

bill long,
slender,
with
sharp,
long
hook

dark
gray
overall

bright
orange legs

white
undertail
feathers

MALE

long wings

white tip
to tail

FLIGHT: relatively slow, labored wing beats; soars on thermals with fixed wings.

In North America, the Snail Kite, formerly known as the Everglade Kite, is found only in peninsular Florida, where it was discovered in 1844. Snail Kites occur around shallow lakes and freshwater marshes. They are nomadic, following the apple snail and breeding in colonies when the snails are abundant. The pair bond is loose and males may breed with several females in one season, but sequentially, rather than all at one time.

VOICE Harsh, grating cackle given by both sexes: *ka-ka-ka-ka-ka-ka* or a harsh *krrrr*, variations of nasal, sheep-like bleating *k-a-a-a-a-a-a*, while being harassed or when begging for food.

NESTING Large nest of dry sticks on small trees, almost always over water; 2–4 eggs; 1–2 broods; January–July.

FEEDING Eats mainly apple snails (*Pomacea paludosa*); also crabs, crayfish, snakes, small turtles, small fish, and rodents.

SICKLE-SHAPED BILL
Snail Kites use their sharply hooked bills to extract apple snails from their shells.

SIMILAR SPECIES

NORTHERN HARRIER ♀
owl-like face;
see p.169

*slender
wings*

*shorter
bill*

NORTHERN HARRIER ♂
white rump patch;
see p.169

*no white
in tail*

*streaked, buff
underparts*

*reddish
underparts*

OCCURRENCE
In Florida, found very locally, year-round in inland freshwater marshes and along shallow lakes, where apple snails reside. In ilts tropical range, locally abundant, in many types of water habitats, including roadside ditches near towns.

| Length **14–16in (36–41cm)** | Wingspan **3½ft (1.1m)** | Weight **13–20oz (375–575g)** |
| Social **Colonies** | Lifespan **At least 9 years** | Status **Endangered** |

Order **Falconiformes**	Family **Accipitridae**	Species *Ictinia mississippiensis*

Mississippi Kite

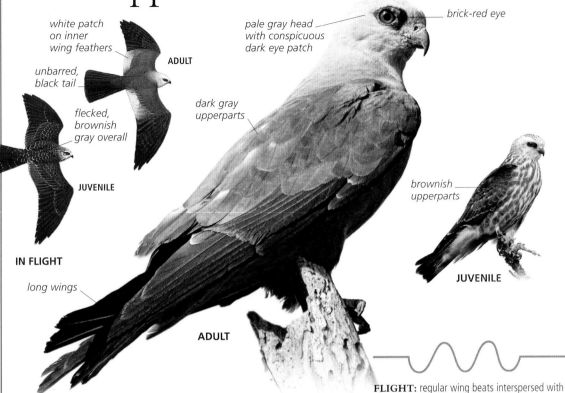

white patch on inner wing feathers

ADULT

unbarred, black tail

flecked, brownish gray overall

JUVENILE

IN FLIGHT

long wings

ADULT

pale gray head with conspicuous dark eye patch

brick-red eye

dark gray upperparts

brownish upperparts

JUVENILE

FLIGHT: regular wing beats interspersed with glides; often soars with flight feathers extended.

The Mississippi Kite is locally abundant and nests in colonies in the central and southern Great Plains, but is less common and less colonial in the southeastern US. Foraging flocks of 25 or more individuals are common, and groups of ten or more roost near nests. In the West, the species nests in urban habitats, including city parks and golf courses. These urban birds can be aggressive, even attacking humans who venture too close to their nest. This graceful bird pursues its insect prey in flight. Mississippi Kites are long-distance migrants, wintering in South America.

VOICE High-pitched *phee-phew*; also multisyllabled *phee-ti-ti*.
NESTING Circular to oval nest of dead twigs, built in dead or well-foliaged tree; 1–3 eggs; 1 brood; March–July.
FEEDING Eats medium to large insects; also frogs, toads, lizards, box turtles, snakes, small birds, terrestrial mammals, and bats.

HIGH FLYING
Despite their falcon-like shape, these birds spend much of their time soaring, rather than perched.

SIMILAR SPECIES

PEREGRINE FALCON
see p.162

dark head

larger overall

prominent black "mustache"

WHITE-TAILED KITE
see p.165

dark shoulder patch

white underparts

OCCURRENCE
In the East, mostly mature bottomland forest or riverside woodland with open habitat nearby for foraging. Birds in the central and southern Great Plains prefer areas with numerous shelterbelts (windbreaks). Western birds use both rural woodland and suburban or urban habitat.

Length **13–15in (33–38cm)**	Wingspan **35in (89cm)**	Weight **8–14oz (225–400g)**
Social **Colonies**	Lifespan **At least 8 years**	Status **Secure**

| Order **Falconiformes** | Family **Accipitridae** | Species *Haliaeetus leucocephalus* |

Bald Eagle

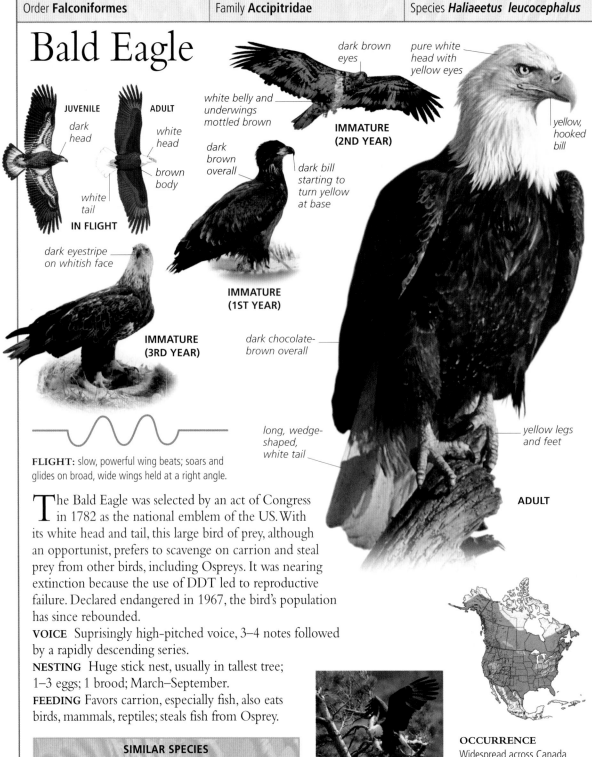

JUVENILE
dark head

ADULT
white head

brown body

white tail

IN FLIGHT

dark brown eyes

white belly and underwings mottled brown

IMMATURE (2ND YEAR)

pure white head with yellow eyes

yellow, hooked bill

dark brown overall

dark bill starting to turn yellow at base

IMMATURE (1ST YEAR)

dark eyestripe on whitish face

IMMATURE (3RD YEAR)

dark chocolate-brown overall

long, wedge-shaped, white tail

yellow legs and feet

ADULT

FLIGHT: slow, powerful wing beats; soars and glides on broad, wide wings held at a right angle.

The Bald Eagle was selected by an act of Congress in 1782 as the national emblem of the US. With its white head and tail, this large bird of prey, although an opportunist, prefers to scavenge on carrion and steal prey from other birds, including Ospreys. It was nearing extinction because the use of DDT led to reproductive failure. Declared endangered in 1967, the bird's population has since rebounded.

VOICE Suprisingly high-pitched voice, 3–4 notes followed by a rapidly descending series.

NESTING Huge stick nest, usually in tallest tree; 1–3 eggs; 1 brood; March–September.

FEEDING Favors carrion, especially fish, also eats birds, mammals, reptiles; steals fish from Osprey.

SIMILAR SPECIES

FERRUGINOUS HAWK
dark head; see p.183

whitish underparts

GOLDEN EAGLE ☾
white in flight feathers; see p.185

feathered legs

SUBSTANTIAL ABODE
Bald eagles make the largest stick nest of all raptors; it can weigh up to two tons.

OCCURRENCE
Widespread across Canada and much of the US. Breeds in forested areas near water; also shoreline areas ranging from undeveloped to relatively well-developed with marked human activity; winters along major river systems and in coastal areas and occasionally even in arid regions of southwest US.

| Length **28–38in (71–96cm)** | Wingspan **6½ft (2m)** | Weight **6½–14lb (3–6.5kg)** |
| Social **Solitary/Pairs** | Lifespan **Up to 28 years** | Status **Secure** |

Order **Falconiformes**	Family **Accipitridae**	Species *Circus cyaneus*

Northern Harrier

MALE black wing tips

wings held in v-shape

white rump

IN FLIGHT

FEMALE dark barring on silver-gray underwings

dark bill with yellow skin near bluish base

bluish gray upperparts

gray uppertail with light undertail feathers

MALE

bluish gray head

reddish underparts

JUVENILE

white ring around face

brown upperparts

white underparts with reddish brown markings

FEMALE

F ound nearly all over North America, the Northern Harrier is most often seen flying buoyantly low in search of food. A white rump, V-shaped wings, and tilting flight make this species easily identifiable. The blue-gray males are quite different to the dark-brown females. The bird's most recognizable characteristic is its owl-like face, which contains stiff feathers to help channel in sounds from prey. Northern Harriers are highly migratory throughout their range.

VOICE Call given by both sexes in rapid succession at nest: *kek* becomes more high-pitched when intruders are spotted.

NESTING Platform of sticks on ground in open, wet field; 4–6 eggs; 1 brood; April–September.

FEEDING Mostly hunts rodents like mice and muskrats; also birds, frogs, reptiles; occasionally takes larger prey such as rabbits.

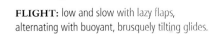

FLIGHT: low and slow with lazy flaps, alternating with buoyant, brusquely tilting glides.

WATERY DWELLING
To avoid predators, Northern Harriers prefer to raise their young on wet sites in tall, dense vegetation.

OCCURRENCE
Breeds in a variety of open wetlands: marshes, meadows, pastures, fallow fields across most of North America; winters in open habitats like deserts, coastal sand dunes, cropland, grasslands, marshy, and riverside areas.

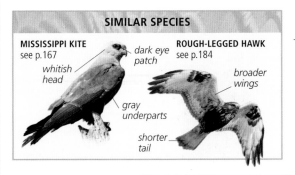

SIMILAR SPECIES

MISSISSIPPI KITE see p.167

whitish head

dark eye patch

gray underparts

ROUGH-LEGGED HAWK see p.184

broader wings

shorter tail

Length **18–20in (46–51cm)**	Wingspan **3½–4ft (1.1m–1.2m)**	Weight **11–26oz (300–750g)**
Social **Solitary/Pairs/Colonies**	Lifespan **Up to 16 years**	Status **Secure**

| Order **Falconiformes** | Family **Accipitridae** | Species *Accipiter striatus* |

Sharp-shinned Hawk

grayish blue crown

reddish yellow eye

square-tipped tail

short, rounded wings

head appears small

JUVENILE

grayish blue upperparts

slightly browner upperparts than male

yellow legs and toes

MALE

wide, dark, horizontal bars on gray tail

IN FLIGHT

dark brown upperparts

light yellowish eye

wide, brown streaks on underparts

ADULT

reddish brown bars on underparts

white, fluffy undertail feathers

FEMALE

JUVENILE FEMALE

This small and swift hawk is quite adept at capturing birds, occasionally even taking species larger than itself. The Sharp-shinned Hawk's short, rounded wings and long tail allow it to make abrupt turns and lightning-fast dashes in thick woods and dense shrubby terrain. With needle-like talons, long, spindle-thin legs, and long toes, this hawk is well adapted to snatching birds in flight. The prey is plucked before being consumed or fed to the nestlings.

VOICE High-pitched, repeated *kiu kiu kiu* call; sometimes makes squealing sound when disturbed at nest.

NESTING Sturdy nest of sticks lined with twigs or pieces of bark; sometimes an old crow or squirrel nest; 3–4 eggs; 1 brood; March–June.

FEEDING Catches small birds, such as sparrows and wood-warblers, on the wing, or takes them unaware while perched.

FLIGHT: rapid, direct, and strong; nimble enough to maneuver in dense forest; soars during migration.

HUNTING BIRDS
A Sharp-shinned Hawk pauses on the ground with a freshly captured sparrow in its talons.

SIMILAR SPECIES

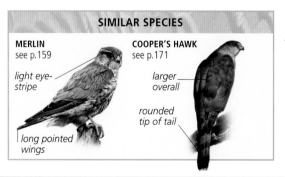

MERLIN
see p.159

light eye-stripe

long pointed wings

COOPER'S HAWK
see p.171

larger overall

rounded tip of tail

OCCURRENCE
Deep coniferous forests and mixed hardwood–conifer woodlands across North America from the tree limit in northern Canada to the Gulf states. During fall migration sometimes seen in flocks of hundreds of individuals. Winters in Central America from Guatemala to Panama.

| Length **11in (28 cm)** | Wingspan **23in (58cm)** | Weight **3½–6oz (100–175g)** |
| Social **Solitary/Flocks** | Lifespan **At least 10 years** | Status **Secure** |

Order **Falconiformes**	Family **Accipitridae**	Species *Accipiter cooperii*

Cooper's Hawk

broad, rounded wings

JUVENILE

long, barred tail with rounded tip

IN FLIGHT

dark crown

reddish eye

grayish blue upperparts

yellowish eyes

light underparts, with brown streaks

mottled dark brown upperparts

yellow legs and toes

brown tail

grayish blue overall

ADULT

JUVENILE

ADULT

gray tail with wide, dark bands

white band at tip of tail

FLIGHT: fast with rapid wing beats interspersed with glides; sometimes soars.

A secretive and inconspicuous bird, Cooper's Hawk, was named by Charles Bonaparte, nephew of French Emperor Napoleon Bonaparte, for William C. Cooper, a noted New York naturalist. It is a typical woodland hawk, capable of quickly maneuvering through dense vegetation. Although it prefers to stay close to cover, it will venture out in search of food. Should a human approach the nest of a Cooper's Hawk, the brooding adult will quietly glide down and away from the nest tree rather than attack the intruder.

VOICE Most common call a staccato *ca-ca-ca-ca*; other vocalizations include as many as 40 different calls.

NESTING Medium-sized, stick nest, usually in a large deciduous tree; 4–5 eggs; 1 brood; April–May.

FEEDING Catches birds, such as robins and blackbirds; larger females can capture grouse; also eats chipmunks, small squirrels, and even bats.

DENSE BARRING
This hawk has characteristic fine, reddish brown, horizontal barring on its undersides.

OCCURRENCE
Breeds in woodlands across northern North America, southern Canada, and the northern US, south to Florida, Texas, and northwestern Mexico. Likes mature deciduous forests with leaf cover, and also roosts in conifers. Winters in southwestern US and Mexico.

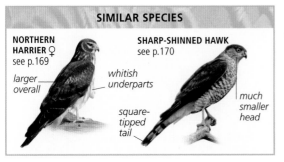

SIMILAR SPECIES

NORTHERN HARRIER ♀
see p.169

larger overall

whitish underparts

square-tipped tail

SHARP-SHINNED HAWK
see p.170

much smaller head

Length **15½–17½in (40–45cm)**	Wingspan **28–34in (70–86cm)**	Weight **13–19oz (375–525g)**
Social **Solitary/Pairs**	Lifespan **At least 10 years**	Status **Secure**

| Order **Falconiformes** | Family **Accipitridae** | Species *Accipiter gentilis* |

Northern Goshawk

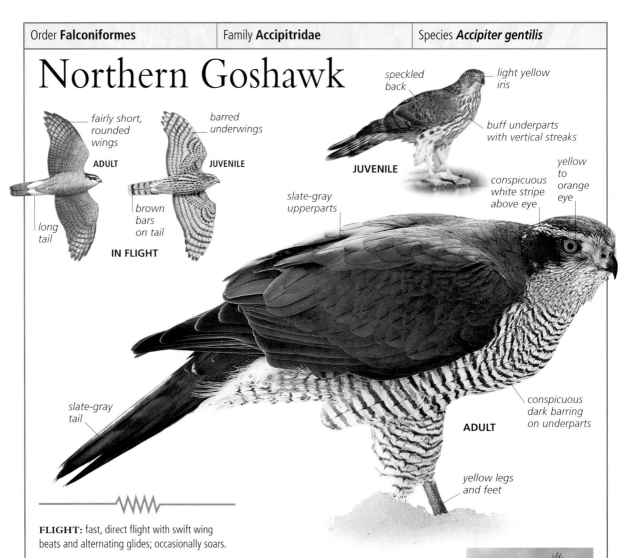

fairly short, rounded wings

barred underwings

ADULT

JUVENILE

long tail

brown bars on tail

IN FLIGHT

speckled back

light yellow iris

buff underparts with vertical streaks

JUVENILE

slate-gray upperparts

conspicuous white stripe above eye

yellow to orange eye

slate-gray tail

conspicuous dark barring on underparts

ADULT

yellow legs and feet

FLIGHT: fast, direct flight with swift wing beats and alternating glides; occasionally soars.

The powerful and agile Northern Goshawk is secretive by nature and not easily observed, even in regions where it is common. It has few natural enemies, but will defend its territories, nests, and young fiercely, by repeatedly diving and screaming at intruders that get too close. Spring hikers and turkey-hunters occasionally discover Northern Goshawks by wandering into their territory and being driven off by the angry occupants.

VOICE Loud, high-pitched *gek-gek-gek* when agitated.

NESTING Large stick structures lined with bark and plant matter in the mid- to lower region of tree; 1–3 eggs; 1 brood; May–June.

FEEDING Sits and waits on perch before diving rapidly; preys on birds as large as grouse and pheasants; also mammals, including hares and squirrels.

OCCASIONAL SOARER
A juvenile Northern Goshawk takes advantage of a thermal, soaring over its territory.

OCCURRENCE
Breeds in deep deciduous, coniferous, and mixed woodlands in northern North America, from the tundra–taiga border south to California, northern Mexico, and Pennsylvania in the eastern US, absent from east central US. The Northern Goshawk is widespread in northern Eurasia.

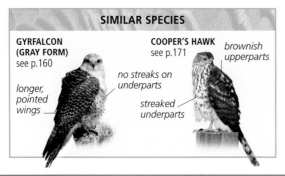

SIMILAR SPECIES

GYRFALCON (GRAY FORM) see p.160

longer, pointed wings

COOPER'S HAWK see p.171

brownish upperparts

no streaks on underparts

streaked underparts

| Length **21in (53cm)** | Wingspan **3½ft (1.1m)** | Weight **2–3lb (0.9–1.4kg)** |
| Social **Solitary/Pairs** | Lifespan **Up to 20 years** | Status **Secure** |

Order **Falconiformes**	Family **Accipitridae**	Species *Buteogallus anthracinus*

Common Black-hawk

small, pale patches near wing tips

ADULT

finely barred underparts

JUVENILE

short, barred tail

darker wing tips

IN FLIGHT

broad, white band on fan-shaped tail

white streaking on nape

dark brown upperparts

whitish tail band

long legs

IMMATURE

black head

black-tipped bill

dark, brownish black upperparts

long wings

ADULT

black underparts with some brownish markings

long, bright yellow legs and feet

short tail

FLIGHT: strong, slow wing beats with wings held flat when soaring, completely fanned tail.

This species is a poorly studied hawk because of its low numbers, secretiveness, and limited distribution north of Mexico. The Common Black-hawk is an opportunistic hunter, and can be most often seen hunting along forest-lined streams. It is considered to be either threatened or endangered by most state governments.
VOICE Complex, shrill calls when excited or alarmed; series of 8–14 piercing, whistle-sounding notes, increasing in speed.
NESTING Large shallow cup of dead twigs in tree, lined with leaves; 1–3 eggs; 1 brood; April–September.
FEEDING Hunts from a perch; eats crayfish, crabs, fish, frogs, non-venomous snakes, and lizards; also caterpillars and grasshoppers.

WINGS SPREAD
An immature Common Black-hawk flies through trees with wings and tail spread out.

OCCURRENCE
Mature forests of cottonwoods and willow along streams that offer hunting perches like low branches and boulders; US populations are migratory; resident throughout the rest of its range, in Central America and northern South America, and Cuba.

SIMILAR SPECIES

BLACK VULTURE
see p.156

ZONE-TAILED HAWK
see p.181

small head with no feathers

no white band on tail

longer tail

Length **21in (53cm)**	Wingspan **4¼ft (1.3m)**	Weight **1½–2¾lb (0.7–1.2kg)**
Social **Solitary/Pairs**	Lifespan **Up to 13 years**	Status **Vulnerable**

| Order **Falconiformes** | Family **Accipitridae** | Species *Parabuteo unicinctus* |

Harris's Hawk

yellow eye-ring

yellow base of bill

dark brown upperparts

rufous shoulders

dark brown chest and belly

ADULT

chestnut feathers

rufous shoulder feathers

ADULT

dark flight feathers

heavily streaked underparts

JUVENILE

light flight feathers

JUVENILE

IN FLIGHT

black tail with white tip

yellow legs and feet

FLIGHT: a few rapid wing beats followed by glide; occasionally soars, sometimes dives steeply.

Named by the renowned ornithologist John James Audubon in honor of his friend and patron, Edward Harris, Harris's Hawks nest in social units, unlike other North American birds of prey. These groups engage in cooperative hunting: members take turns leading the chase to wear down their prey and share in the kill. This species has become popular with falconers all over the world.
VOICE Main territorial alarm call a prolonged, harsh growl lasting about 3 seconds; also chirps, croaks, and screams.
NESTING Bulky nest of dead sticks lined with leaves in tall, sturdy trees; 3–4 eggs; 1–2 broods; March–August.
FEEDING Hunts in groups for mammals including cottontails, black-tailed jackrabbits, ground squirrels, gophers; also birds, snakes, and skinks.

SIT-AND-WAIT
Lone Harris's Hawks will often employ a sit-and-wait tactic, until prey moves.

OCCURRENCE
Forages and breeds year-round in semi-open desert scrub, savanna, grassland, and wetland containing scattered larger trees and cacti. Occasionally appears in suburban areas. Essentially a Central and South American species, small range north of the Rio Grande.

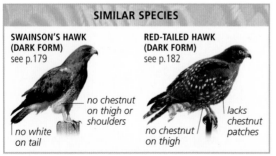

SIMILAR SPECIES

SWAINSON'S HAWK (DARK FORM)
see p.179

no chestnut on thigh or shoulders

no white on tail

RED-TAILED HAWK (DARK FORM)
see p.182

lacks chestnut patches

no chestnut on thigh

| Length **18–23in (46–59cm)** | Wingspan **3½–4ft (1.1–1.2m)** | Weight **18–35oz (500–1,000g)** |
| Social **Small flocks** | Lifespan **Up to 11 years** | Status **Localized** |

Order **Falconiformes**	Family **Accipitridae**	Species *Buteo nitidus*

Gray Hawk

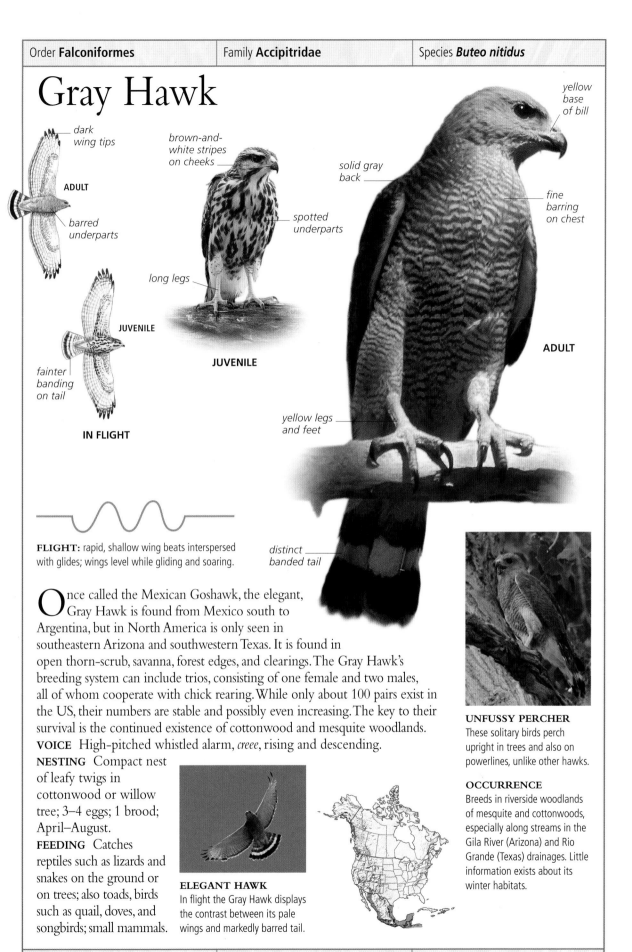

dark wing tips

ADULT

barred underparts

brown-and-white stripes on cheeks

spotted underparts

long legs

JUVENILE

JUVENILE

fainter banding on tail

IN FLIGHT

solid gray back

yellow base of bill

fine barring on chest

ADULT

yellow legs and feet

distinct banded tail

FLIGHT: rapid, shallow wing beats interspersed with glides; wings level while gliding and soaring.

Once called the Mexican Goshawk, the elegant, Gray Hawk is found from Mexico south to Argentina, but in North America is only seen in southeastern Arizona and southwestern Texas. It is found in open thorn-scrub, savanna, forest edges, and clearings. The Gray Hawk's breeding system can include trios, consisting of one female and two males, all of whom cooperate with chick rearing. While only about 100 pairs exist in the US, their numbers are stable and possibly even increasing. The key to their survival is the continued existence of cottonwood and mesquite woodlands.

VOICE High-pitched whistled alarm, *creee*, rising and descending.

NESTING Compact nest of leafy twigs in cottonwood or willow tree; 3–4 eggs; 1 brood; April–August.

FEEDING Catches reptiles such as lizards and snakes on the ground or on trees; also toads, birds such as quail, doves, and songbirds; small mammals.

ELEGANT HAWK
In flight the Gray Hawk displays the contrast between its pale wings and markedly barred tail.

UNFUSSY PERCHER
These solitary birds perch upright in trees and also on powerlines, unlike other hawks.

OCCURRENCE
Breeds in riverside woodlands of mesquite and cottonwoods, especially along streams in the Gila River (Arizona) and Rio Grande (Texas) drainages. Little information exists about its winter habitats.

Length **16–17in (41–43cm)**	Wingspan **35in (89cm)**	Weight **14–24oz (400–675g)**
Social **Solitary/Pairs**	Lifespan **Unknown**	Status **Vulnerable**

Order **Falconiformes**	Family **Accipitridae**	Species *Buteo lineatus*

Red-shouldered Hawk

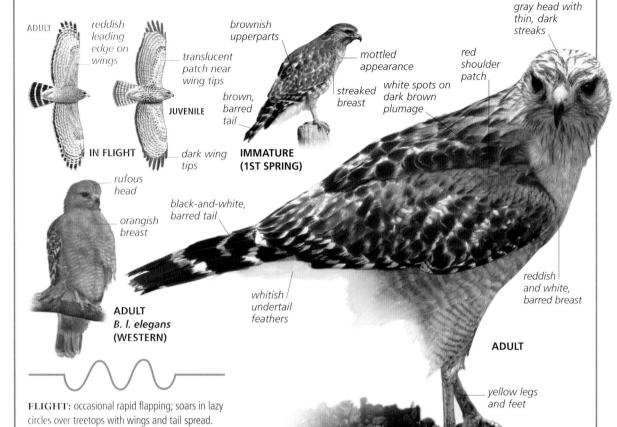

ADULT

reddish leading edge on wings

translucent patch near wing tips

brown, barred tail

JUVENILE

IN FLIGHT

dark wing tips

brownish upperparts

mottled appearance

streaked breast

white spots on dark brown plumage

IMMATURE (1ST SPRING)

gray head with thin, dark streaks

red shoulder patch

reddish and white, barred breast

rufous head

orangish breast

black-and-white, barred tail

whitish undertail feathers

ADULT
B. l. elegans
(WESTERN)

ADULT

yellow legs and feet

FLIGHT: occasional rapid flapping; soars in lazy circles over treetops with wings and tail spread.

The Red-shouldered Hawk has a remarkable distribution, with widespread populations in the East and northeast, and in the Midwest Great Plains and the West, from Oregon to Baja California, despite a geographical gap of 1,000 miles (1,600km) between the two regions. Eastern birds are divided into four subspecies; western populations belong to the subspecies *B. l. elegans*. The red shoulder patches are not always evident, but the striped tail and translucent "windows" in the wings are easily identifiable.

VOICE Call a whistled *kee-aah*, accented on first syllable, descending on second.
NESTING Platform of sticks, dried leaves, bark, moss, and lichens in trees not far from water; 3–4 eggs; 1 brood; March–July.
FEEDING Catches mice, chipmunks, and voles; also snakes, toads, frogs, crayfish, and small birds.

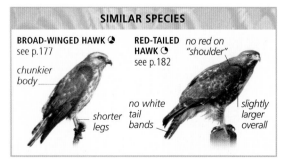

SIMILAR SPECIES

BROAD-WINGED HAWK ☹
see p.177

chunkier body

shorter legs

RED-TAILED HAWK ☾
see p.182

no red on "shoulder"

no white tail bands

slightly larger overall

CHESTNUT WING
When seen from below, the reddish forewing of this adult hawk is clearly visible.

OCCURRENCE
Eastern populations breed in woodlands and forest, deciduous or mixed, whereas those in the West occur in oak woodlands and eucalyptus groves. In Florida, this species also lives in mangroves. Eastern birds migrate to Mexico.

Length **17–24in (43–61cm)**	Wingspan **3–3½ft (0.9–1.1m)**	Weight **17–27oz (475–775g)**
Social **Solitary/Flocks**	Lifespan **Up to 18 years**	Status **Declining (p)**

| Order **Falconiformes** | Family **Accipitridae** | Species **Buteo platypterus** |

Broad-winged Hawk

indistinct "mustache"

dark border on edges of wings

one to two broad, white bands visible on tail

ADULT

ADULT

upperparts brown with white flecking

JUVENILE

pale tan wings with dark tips

IN FLIGHT

finely barred, all-brown tail

pale outer wing feathers

JUVENILE

pale underparts, with conspicuous, tear-shaped, brown spots

short, yellow feet

IMMATURE

One of the most numerous of all North American birds of prey, the Broad-winged Hawk migrates in huge flocks or "kettles," with thousands of birds gliding on rising thermals. Some birds winter in Florida, but the majority average about 70 miles (110km) a day to log more than 4,000 miles (6,500km) before ending up in Brazil, Bolivia, and even some of the Caribbean islands. Compared to its two cousins, the Red-shouldered and Red-tailed Hawks, the Broad-winged Hawk is slightly smaller, but stockier. Adults are easily identified by a broad, white-and-black band on their tails. Broad-winged Hawks have two color forms, the light one being more common than the dark, sooty brown one.

VOICE High-pitched *peeoweee* call, first note shorter and higher-pitched.

NESTING Platform of fresh twigs or dead sticks, often on old squirrel, hawk, or crow nest in tree; 2–3 eggs; 1 brood; April–August.

FEEDING Eats small mammals, toads, frogs, snakes, grouse chicks, insects, and spiders; crabs in winter.

FLIGHT: circles above forest canopy with wings and tail spread; short flights from branch to branch.

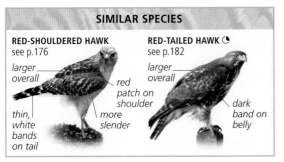

SIMILAR SPECIES

RED-SHOULDERED HAWK
see p.176

larger overall

thin, white bands on tail

red patch on shoulder

more slender

RED-TAILED HAWK ☾
see p.182

larger overall

dark band on belly

WATCHING FOR PREY
From an elevated perch, this hawk scans for vertebrate prey such as rodents.

OCCURRENCE
Breeds across Canada (but not the Rockies) and in the eastern US (not west of the 100th meridien), in forested areas with deciduous, conifers, and mixed trees, with clearings and water nearby. Concentrations of migrants can be seen at bottlenecks such as the Isthmus of Tehuantepec and Panama.

| Length **13–17in (33–43cm)** | Wingspan **32–39in (81–100cm)** | Weight **10–19oz (275–550g)** |
| Social **Flocks** | Lifespan **Up to 14 years** | Status **Secure** |

| Order **Falconiformes** | Family **Accipitridae** | Species ***Buteo brachyurus*** |

Short-tailed Hawk

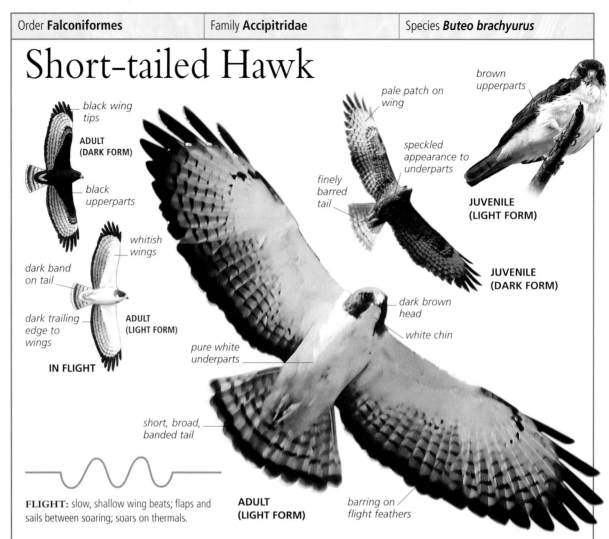

black wing tips

ADULT (DARK FORM)

black upperparts

whitish wings

dark band on tail

dark trailing edge to wings

ADULT (LIGHT FORM)

IN FLIGHT

pale patch on wing

speckled appearance to underparts

finely barred tail

JUVENILE (LIGHT FORM)

brown upperparts

JUVENILE (DARK FORM)

dark brown head

white chin

pure white underparts

short, broad, banded tail

FLIGHT: slow, shallow wing beats; flaps and sails between soaring; soars on thermals.

ADULT (LIGHT FORM)

barring on flight feathers

This species is widespread but not common in Central and South America, but in North America it is found only in peninsular Florida, where it numbers at most about 500 individuals. Like some other hawks, this species has light and dark forms, the latter more common. The Short-tailed Hawk is not easy to see, as it seldom perches in the open and soars quite high. Its habitat is dwindling, and population studies are needed to learn its status.

VOICE High-pitched cat-like *keeea*; also a variety of *keee* calls.

NESTING Stick or moss platform in cypress, mangrove swamps, open woodlands, or savanna; 2 eggs; 1 brood; March–June.

FEEDING Picks small birds from their perches: blackbirds, larks, quails, doves; also rodents, snakes, and frogs.

RARE SIGHT
The light form of this species is easily identified by its white underparts and dark upperparts.

SIMILAR SPECIES

RED-SHOULDERED HAWK see p.176

BROAD-WINGED HAWK ☺ see p.177

reddish underparts

black-and-white barred tail

shorter, more pointed wings

smaller overall

OCCURRENCE
Found in woodlands, flooded upland habitats, savanna, prairies, and open country. Nests in cypress or bay swamps with closed canopy; winters where mangrove forest meets tidal sawgrass marsh, in wet prairies, also in suburban areas with forest tracts. In tropical range prefers thin forests.

| Length **15½–17½in (39–44cm)** | Wingspan **33–39in (83–100cm)** | Weight **14–18oz (400–500g)** |
| Social **Solitary** | Lifespan **Unknown** | Status **Vulnerable** |

Order **Falconiformes**	Family **Accipitridae**	Species *Buteo swainsoni*

Swainson's Hawk

long pointed wings

ADULT (LIGHT FORM)

dark wing tips

JUVENILE (LIGHT FORM)

dark chest

IN FLIGHT

whitish head

spotted underparts

JUVENILE (LIGHT FORM)

white face and chin

reddish breast and belly

slender shape overall

ADULT (INTERMEDIATE FORM)

dark brown head and breast

spotted underparts

ADULT (DARK FORM)

pale reddish upper chest

white underbelly

longish tail

wing tips reach end of tail when perched

FLIGHT: soaring, buoyant flight with deep wing beats; will often hover and hang motionless.

ADULT (LIGHT FORM)

S wainson's Hawk is perhaps most famous for its spectacular 6,000-mile (9,650km) fall migration from the Canadian prairies to the lower regions of South America, when thousands can be observed soaring in the air at any one time. While migrating, this hawk averages 125 miles (200km) a day. There are three color forms: light, dark, and an intermediate form between the two.

VOICE Alarm call a shrill, plaintive scream *kreeeee* given by both sexes; high-pitched *keeeoooo* fading at the end.

NESTING Bulky, flimsy pile of sticks or various debris, in solitary tree or on utility poles; 1–4 eggs; 1 brood; April–July.

FEEDING Eats ground squirrels, pocket gophers, mice, voles, bats, rabbits; also snakes, lizards, songbirds.

SIMILAR SPECIES

HARRIS'S HAWK see p.174

RED-TAILED HAWK see p.182

bulkier overall

chestnut thighs and wing patches

long legs

white on tail

shorter wings

red tail

ON THE LOOKOUT
This slim, elegant species will perch before diving for its prey.

OCCURRENCE
Breeds in scattered trees along streams; found in areas of open woodland, sparse shrubland, grasslands, and agricultural land; winters in native Argentinian grassland, and in harvested fields where grasshoppers are found abundantly.

Length **19–22in (48–56cm)**	Wingspan **4½ft (1.4m)**	Weight **1½–3lb (0.7–1.4kg)**
Social **Solitary/Pairs/Flocks**	Lifespan **Up to 19 years**	Status **Declining (p)**

| Order **Falconiformes** | Family **Accipitridae** | Species **Buteo albicaudatus** |

White-tailed Hawk

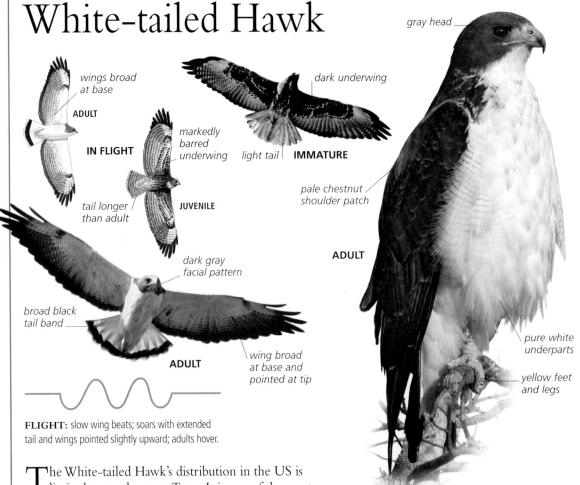

wings broad at base

ADULT

IN FLIGHT

gray head

dark underwing

markedly barred underwing

light tail   **IMMATURE**

tail longer than adult   **JUVENILE**

pale chestnut shoulder patch

ADULT

dark gray facial pattern

broad black tail band

ADULT

wing broad at base and pointed at tip

pure white underparts

yellow feet and legs

FLIGHT: slow wing beats; soars with extended tail and wings pointed slightly upward; adults hover.

The White-tailed Hawk's distribution in the US is limited to southeastern Texas. It is one of the most easily identifiable hawks, with its all-gray plumage, striking white breast, reddish shoulder patches, and black-banded white tail. Unlike other hawks, the adult's outer flight feathers extend noticeably beyond the tail. Although shy and secretive, the White-tailed Hawk is a versatile forager, capturing prey by soaring, hovering, or by still-hunting from a perch. It likes to hunt at the edges of river basins.

VOICE Series of scream-like calls *raa kad-ik kad-ik kad-ik kad-ik.*
NESTING Bulky platform of branches, twigs, and grasses in trees close to the ground; 2–3 eggs; 1 brood; January–August.
FEEDING Eats mammals such as wood rats, mice, and rabbits; birds, such as quails, rails, and doves; also snakes, lizards, and frogs.

EAGLE-LIKE HAWK
Its long head and legs make the White-tailed Hawk resemble a small eagle.

OCCURRENCE
In the US, lives in Texas, where it is found in savannah, prairie, and humid to arid grasslands at low elevations; also lightly grazed cattle pasture, open woodland; also areas with woody understory with yucca, mesquite, and introduced thorny shrubs.

SIMILAR SPECIES

SWAINSON'S HAWK ☾ **(LIGHT FORM)**
see p.179

dark spotting on breast

FERRUGINOUS HAWK ☾ **(LIGHT FORM)**
see p.183

no red on shoulder

no dark band on tail

| Length **18–23in (46–58cm)** | Wingspan **4¼ft (1.3m)** | Weight **2–2¾lb (0.9–1.2kg)** |
| Social **Solitary/Pairs** | Lifespan **Unknown** | Status **Localized** |

| Order **Falconiformes** | Family **Accipitridae** | Species ***Buteo albonotatus*** |

Zone-tailed Hawk

- dark head
- black upperparts
- grayish black underparts
- long, broad wings
- barred flight feathers
- yellow legs and feet
- long tail with white band
- tail with one or more white bars
- gray, barred tail

ADULT   IMMATURE

IN FLIGHT

ADULT

ADULT

The Zone-tailed Hawk is widely distributed throughout much of Central and South America, with its range creeping into parts of the southwestern US. It shares the same habitats used by the Common Black-hawk, which can lead to misidentification. The Zone-tailed Hawk is an amazing aerialist during courtship, flying up high, then rapidly plunging down. It is quite aggressive towards territorial intruders, even those as large as Golden Eagles. It has been suggested that the Zone-tailed Hawk mimics the Turkey Vulture, but it hunts live prey, whereas the Turkey Vulture eats carrion.

VOICE Harsh *kreeee*; also another harsh two-syllable *kreeee-arr*.
NESTING Bowl of long sticks in mid- to lower region of Ponderosa pine or oak; 1–3 eggs; 1 brood; March–August.
FEEDING Preys on small birds, ground squirrels, and chipmunks, amphibians, and lizards.

FLIGHT: soars with little flapping; wings held in a V-shaped—tipping eratically from side to side.

BANDED HAWK
A Zone-tailed Hawk's broad, white tail band is conspicuous when the bird is perched.

SIMILAR SPECIES

TURKEY VULTURE
see p.155
brownish black upperparts
small, unfeathered, red head

COMMON BLACK-HAWK
see p.173
broader wings
short tail with single white band

OCCURRENCE
Breeds in riverside forest and woodland, desert uplands, and mixed-conifer forest in mountains. Nests in mixed broadleaf and cottonwood or willow trees; winters in central South America. Occurs in South America all the way south to Paraguay.

| Length **17½–22in (45–56cm)** | Wingspan **4–4½ft (1.2–1.4m)** | Weight **22–29oz (625–825g)** |
| Social **Solitary/Pairs** | Lifespan **Unknown** | Status **Localized** |

Order **Falconiformes**	Family **Accipitridae**	Species **Buteo jamaicensis**

Red-tailed Hawk

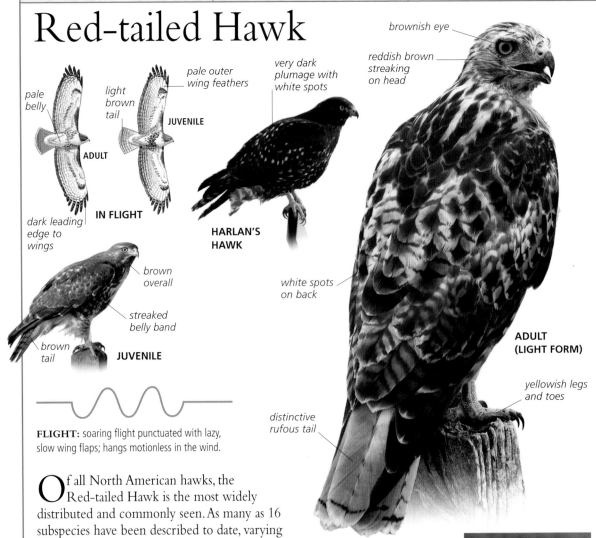

IN FLIGHT

pale belly

light brown tail

pale outer wing feathers

JUVENILE

ADULT

dark leading edge to wings

very dark plumage with white spots

HARLAN'S HAWK

brown overall

streaked belly band

brown tail

JUVENILE

brownish eye

reddish brown streaking on head

white spots on back

ADULT (LIGHT FORM)

yellowish legs and toes

distinctive rufous tail

FLIGHT: soaring flight punctuated with lazy, slow wing flaps; hangs motionless in the wind.

Of all North American hawks, the Red-tailed Hawk is the most widely distributed and commonly seen. As many as 16 subspecies have been described to date, varying in coloration, tail markings, and size. The very dark Harlan's Hawk, which breeds in Alaska and northwestern Canada, was at one time considered a subspecies, but genetic studies have since confirmed it as a separate species. While it occasionally stoops on prey, the Red-tailed Hawk usually adopts a sit-and-wait approach.

VOICE Call *kee-eee-arrr* that rises then descends over a period of 2–3 seconds.

NESTING Large platform of sticks, twigs on top of tall tree, cliff, building, ledge, or billboard; 2 eggs; 1 brood; February–September.

FEEDING Captures small mammals, such as voles, mice, rats; birds including pheasant, quail; small reptiles; carrion also eaten.

FLYING HIGH
A Red-tailed Hawk soaring over an open field is a very common sight in North America.

OCCURRENCE
Breeds, forages in open areas in wide range of habitats and altitudes: scrub desert, grasslands, agricultural fields and pastures, coniferous and deciduous woodland, and tropical rainforest. Prefers areas with tall perch sites; can be found in suburban woodlots.

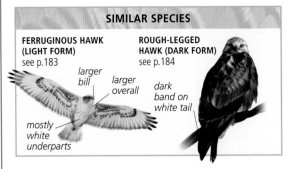

SIMILAR SPECIES

FERRUGINOUS HAWK (LIGHT FORM) see p.183

ROUGH-LEGGED HAWK (DARK FORM) see p.184

larger bill

larger overall

dark band on white tail

mostly white underparts

Length **18–26in (46–65cm)**	Wingspan **3½–4¼ft (1.1–1.3m)**	Weight **1½–3¼lb (0.7–1.5kg)**
Social **Solitary/Pairs**	Lifespan **Up to 21 years**	Status **Secure**

Order **Falconiformes**	Family **Accipitridae**	Species *Buteo regalis*

Ferruginous Hawk

ADULT (LIGHT FORM)

relatively long pointed wings

white undertail

large bill

dark brown overall

dark chocolate brown

brown and white contrast on wings

ADULT (DARK FORM)

ADULT (LIGHT FORM)

IN FLIGHT

reddish tinge to tail

all-white underparts

ADULT (LIGHT FORM)

JUVENILE (DARK FORM)

dark spots on belly

JUVENILE (LIGHT FORM)

fully feathered legs

FLIGHT: slow, deep wing beats alternating with lazy glides; soars high with thermals.

This inhabitant of open country is the largest North American hawk. Its Latin name *regalis* means kingly, and its English name refers to its rusty coloring. It is a versatile nester: it builds its stick nests on cliffs or nearly level ground, trees, and manmade structures like farm buildings. Regrettably, its preference for prairie dogs, which are declining because of habitat loss, shooting, and pesticide use, threatens Ferruginous Hawk populations.

VOICE Screaming *Kree-aa* or *kaah, kaah* during courtship; quieter, lower-pitched, longer alarm call.

NESTING Large stick nest of old sagebrush stems, sticks, and various debris, lined with bark strips; 2–4 eggs; March–August.

FEEDING Hunts mainly rabbits, hares, ground squirrels, and prairie dogs; rarely fledgling birds, amphibians, and reptiles.

PERCHED HUNTER
The Ferruginous Hawk usually hunts from a perch such as a rock or a branch.

OCCURRENCE
In western North America, breeds in low-elevation grasslands interrupted by cliffs or isolated trees for nesting; winters across southwestern US and Mexico in open terrain ranging from grassland to desert.

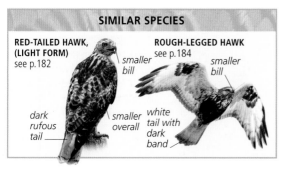

SIMILAR SPECIES

RED-TAILED HAWK, (LIGHT FORM)
see p.182

smaller bill

dark rufous tail

smaller overall

ROUGH-LEGGED HAWK
see p.184

smaller bill

white tail with dark band

Length **22–27in (56–69cm)**	Wingspan **4¼–4½ft (1.3–1.4m)**	Weight **2½–4½lb (1–2kg)**
Social **Solitary/Pairs**	Lifespan **Up to 20 years**	Status **Secure**

| Order **Falconiformes** | Family **Accipitridae** | Species **Buteo lagopus** |

Rough-legged Hawk

dark wing tips

bold black patch

FEMALE

ADULT

black trailing edge

dark tail band

one line before tail tip

IN FLIGHT

pale head

short, broad head

MALE

JUVENILE

barred underparts

black belly

thin bands near tail tip

FLIGHT: strong wing beats; usually soars on thermals; frequently hovers in one spot.

white tail with faint black band at tip

plain gray brown or frosty feather edges

MALE

The Rough-legged Hawk is known for its extensive variation in plumage—some individuals are almost completely black, whereas others are much paler, very nearly cream or white. The year to year fluctuation in numbers of breeding pairs in a given region strongly suggest that this species is nomadic, moving about as a response to the availiability of its rodent prey.

VOICE Wintering birds silent; breeding birds utter loud, cat-like mewing or thin whistles, slurred downward when alarmed.

NESTING Bulky mass of sticks, lined with grasses, sedges, feathers and fur from prey, constructed on cliff ledge; 2–6 eggs; 1 brood; April–August.

FEEDING Hovers in one spot over fields in search of prey; lemmings and voles in spring and summer; mice and shrews in winters; variety of birds, ground squirrels, and rabbits year-round.

ABUNDANT FOOD SUPPLY
When small mammals are abundant, these hawks produce large broods on cliff ledges in the tundra.

SIMILAR SPECIES

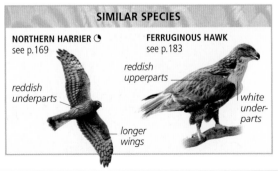

NORTHERN HARRIER ☾
see p.169

FERRUGINOUS HAWK
see p.183

reddish upperparts

reddish underparts

white underparts

longer wings

OCCURRENCE
Breeds in rough, open country with low crags and cliffs, in high subarctic and Arctic regions; found on the edge of extensive forest or forest clearings, and in treeless tundra, uplands, and alpine habitats. Winters in open areas with fields, marshes, and rough grasslands.

| Length **19–20in (48–51cm)** | Wingspan **4¼–4½ft (1.3–1.4m)** | Weight **1½–3lb (0.7–1.4kg)** |
| Social **Solitary** | Lifespan **Up to 18 years** | Status **Secure** |

Order | Species **Aquila chrysaetos**

C

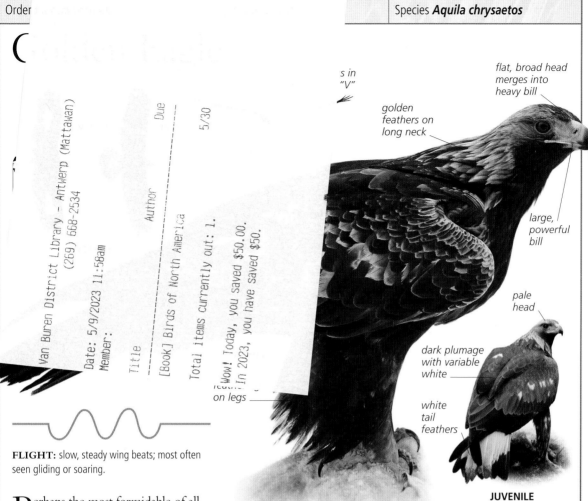

s in "V"

golden feathers on long neck

flat, broad head merges into heavy bill

large, powerful bill

pale head

dark plumage with variable white

white tail feathers

feathering on legs

JUVENILE

FLIGHT: slow, steady wing beats; most often seen gliding or soaring.

P erhaps the most formidable of all North American birds of prey, the Golden Eagle is found mostly in the western part of the continent. It defends large territories ranging from 8–12 square miles (20–30 square kilometers), containing up to 14 nests. Although its appears sluggish, it is amazingly swift and agile, and employs a variety of hunting techniques to catch specific prey. Shot and poisoned by ranchers and trappers, it is unfortunately also faced with dwindling habitat and food sources due to human development.

VOICE Mostly silent, but breeding adults yelp and mew.

NESTING Large pile of sticks and vegetation on cliffs, in trees, and on mademade structures; 1–3 eggs; 1 brood; April–August.

FEEDING Eats mammals, such as hares, rabbits, ground squirrels, prairie dogs, marmots, foxes, and coyotes; also birds.

POWER AND STRENGTH
The Golden Eagle symbolizes all birds of prey, with its sharp talons, hooked bill, and large size.

SIMILAR SPECIES

BALD EAGLE ♀
see p.168
white head and neck
some pale wing feathers

FERRUGINOUS HAWK ☾ **(DARK FORM)**
see p.183
no golden tinge
smaller overall

OCCURRENCE
In North America occurs mostly in grasslands, wetlands, and rocky areas; breeds south to Mexico, in open and semi-open habitats from sea level to 12,000ft (3,500m) including tundra, shrublands, grasslands, coniferous forests, farmland, areas close to streams or rivers; winters in open habitat.

Length **28–33in (70–84cm)**	Wingspan **6–7¼in (1.8–2.2m)**	Weight **6½–13lb (3–6kg)**
Social **Solitary/Pairs**	Lifespan **Up to 39 years**	Status **Declining (p)**

RAILS

THE RALLIDAE, OR RAIL family is a diverse group of small to medium-sized marsh birds. In the US and Canada, rallids, as they are known collectively, are represented by three rails, three crakes, two gallinules, and a coot. Rails and crakes inhabit dense marshland and are secretive, solitary, and inconspicuous, whereas coots and gallinules are seen on open water. Rallids are chicken-like birds with stubby tails and short, rounded wings. The rails of genus *Rallus* have drab, camouflage coloring, and are long-legged, long-billed, and narrow-bodied. The smaller crakes are similar, but with shorter necks and stout, stubby bills. Both rails and crakes walk and run on the ground in marsh vegetation, but can swim well. Colorful gallinules include the Common Moorhen and the Purple Gallinule. Rallids look like weak flyers, but many migrate great distances at night. None has a specialized diet; their food includes insects, small crabs, slugs, snails, and plant matter. Rallids nest in pairs, the birds keep in close contact by calling loudly and clearly.

THIN AS A RAIL
This marsh-dwelling Clapper Rail's narrow body enables it to slip easily through reedbeds.

FLAT LANDING
Purple Gallinules can safely land on lily pads, because their large toes spread their weight.

CRANES

CRANES ARE LARGE WADING BIRDS, superficially similar to storks and to the larger herons and egrets. However, several anatomical differences place them in a different family (Gruidae), within a different order (Gruiformes). The two North American species of cranes have much lighter bills than storks. Typically, too, long inner wing feathers form a "bustle" on a standing crane, giving it a different profile than a heron. Additionally, cranes fly with their necks straight out, rather than in the tight S-curve regularly seen in similar-sized herons.
The Whooping Crane is the tallest bird in North America, standing nearly 5ft (1.5m) high.

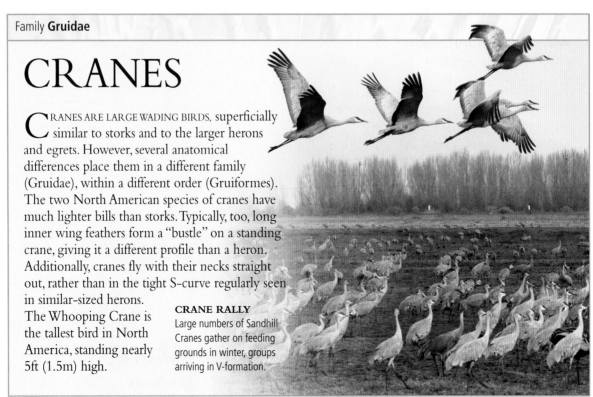

CRANE RALLY
Large numbers of Sandhill Cranes gather on feeding grounds in winter, groups arriving in V-formation.

Order **Gruiformes**	Family **Rallidae**	Species **Coturnicops noveboracensis**

Yellow Rail

dark brown crown

stubby yellow to olive-gray bill

dark stripe runs from cheek to bill

dangling legs

ADULT

white patch on inner wing feathers

IN FLIGHT

long tan stripes on blackish background

buff or yellow breast

ADULT

short tail

FLIGHT: low, weak, short, and direct with stiff wing beats; dangling legs.

Although widespread, the diminutive, secretive, nocturnal Yellow Rail is extremely difficult to observe in its dense, damp, grassy habitat, and is detected mainly by its voice. The Yellow Rail, whose Latin name of *noveboracensis* means "New Yorker," has a small head, almost no neck, a stubby bill, a plump, almost tail-less body, and short legs. The bill of the male turns yellow in the breeding season; for the rest of the year, it is olive-gray like the female's. Although the Yellow Rail tends to dart for cover when disturbed, when it does fly, it reveals a distinctive white patch on its inner wing.

VOICE Two clicking calls followed by three more given by males, usually at night, reminiscent of two pebbles being struck together; also descending cackles, quiet croaking, and soft clucking.

NESTING Small cup of grasses and sedges, on the ground or in a plant tuft above water, concealed by overhanging vegetation; 8–10 eggs; 1 brood; May–June.

FEEDING Plucks seeds, aquatic insects, various small crustaceans, and mollusks (primarily small freshwater snails) from vegetation or ground; forages on the marsh surface or in shallow water, hidden by grass.

CURIOUS LISTENER
Imitating the "tick" calls of the Yellow Rail is often an effective way to lure it out into the open.

OCCURRENCE
Breeds in brackish and freshwater marshes and wet sedge meadows in Canada and the north central US; there is an isolated breeding population in Oregon. Winters predominantly in coastal marshes along the eastern seaboard.

SIMILAR SPECIES

SORA
see p.192

black streaks on brown upperparts

gray underparts

Length **7¼in (18.5cm)**	Wingspan **11in (28cm)**	Weight **1¾oz (50g)**
Social **Pairs**	Lifespan **Unknown**	Status **Secure**

| Order **Gruiformes** | Family **Rallidae** | Species *Laterallus jamaicensis* |

Black Rail

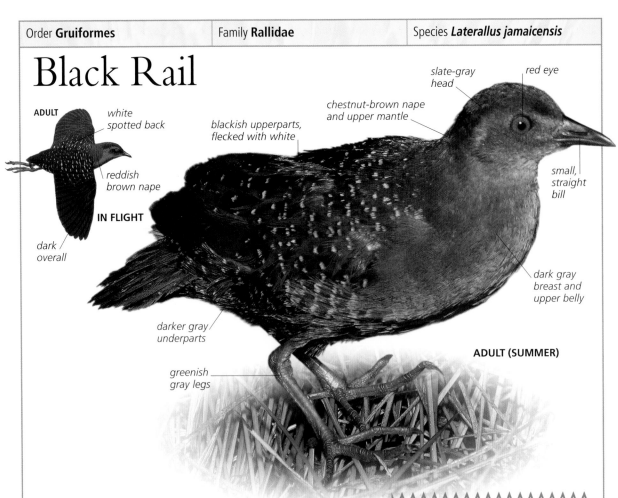

ADULT

white spotted back

reddish brown nape

IN FLIGHT

dark overall

slate-gray head

red eye

chestnut-brown nape and upper mantle

blackish upperparts, flecked with white

small, straight bill

dark gray breast and upper belly

darker gray underparts

greenish gray legs

ADULT (SUMMER)

This tiny, mouse-sized rail is so elusive that few people have ever seen it; consequently, much remains unknown about its life history and it is of great interest to birdwatchers. It is usually detected by its territorial call that is given during the breeding season from the cover of marsh grass. The best chance to see a Black Rail is when high tides force it to move to higher ground. Unfortunately, this is when it can fall prey to herons.

VOICE Distinctive, three-note *kik-kee-do* given by male, mostly at night, during breeding season; makes low growl when agitated.

NESTING Small, deep cup of grasses and sedges placed on the ground, with an overhanging canopy of woven plants; 5–9 eggs; 2 broods; March–July.

FEEDING Forages on the wet marsh surface beneath the cover of grass for snails, insects, spiders, and seeds of marsh plants.

FLIGHT: reluctant flier, short flights with dangling legs; longer flights; fast and direct.

ELUSIVE BIRD
The highly secretive Black Rail is almost never seen by birdwatchers, and is a prize find.

OCCURRENCE
The Black Rail has a disjointed distribution across the US. It is found among reeds in freshwater, salt, and brackish marshes or wet meadows. It also occurs patchily in the West Indies (its scientific name is *jamaicensis*, after the island Jamaica), Central America, and South America.

SIMILAR SPECIES

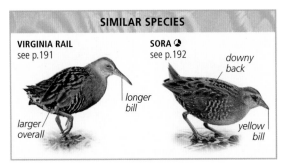

VIRGINIA RAIL see p.191

larger overall

longer bill

SORA ☾ see p.192

downy back

yellow bill

| Length **6in (15cm)** | Wingspan **9in (23cm)** | Weight **1¹⁄₁₆oz (30g)** |
| Social **Solitary** | Lifespan **Unknown** | Status **Secure** |

Order **Gruiformes**	Family **Rallidae**	Species *Rallus longirostris*

Clapper Rail

drab gray overall

gray cheeks

long, down-curved bill

ADULT (GULF COAST)

IN FLIGHT

brownish cheeks

cinnamon breast

long, slender bill

pale underparts

R. l. saturatus (GULF COAST)

long, thick legs

R. l. obsoletus (CALIFORNIA)

R. l. crepitans (ATLANTIC)

Closely related to the King Rail, the Clapper Rail is a common and widespread species on the Atlantic and Gulf coasts. The Clapper Rail can be found in a variety of habitats but it is closely tied to brackish and saltwater marshes dominated by *Spartina* cord grass. However, in southern Florida, this rail is found close to mangrove swamps. The "Yuma" subspecies (*yumanensis*) occupies freshwater marshes in the interior. The Clapper Rail's distinctive, insistent calls are the best way to recognize its presence, as it is rarely seen.

VOICE Grunting calls; repeated loud *kek* notes.

NESTING Bulky cup of grasses and plant stems lined with finer material; bends growing plants to form a canopy; 4–14 eggs; 1 brood; March–August.

FEEDING Forages by crouching low and stalking through marsh, eating snails, insects, spiders, clams, fish, bird eggs, and seeds.

FLIGHT: low and weak; flies with outstretched neck and dangling legs.

LOUD AND CLEAR
The repeated, insistent *kek* call may be heard more than a mile away.

SIMILAR SPECIES

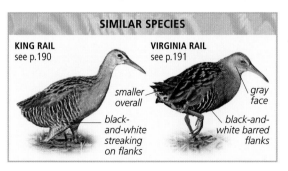

KING RAIL
see p.190

smaller overall

black-and-white streaking on flanks

VIRGINIA RAIL
see p.191

gray face

black-and-white barred flanks

OCCURRENCE
Found mostly in saltwater and brackish marshes along the Atlantic Seaboard. Isolated populations are found in coastal California and inland in southwest North America, along the lower Colorado River. The Clapper Rail winters south of its breeding range.

Length **14½in (37cm)**	Wingspan **19in (48cm)**	Weight **10oz (275g)**
Social **Solitary**	Lifespan **Up to 7 years**	Status **Localized**

Order **Gruiformes**	Family **Rallidae**	Species *Rallus elegans*

King Rail

ADULT

rufous upperwing

heavy down-curved bill

IN FLIGHT

reddish eye

brown stripe running down neck

long, curved, yellow-orange bill

boldly streaked upperparts

short tail

orangish breast

ADULT

boldly barred, black-and-white flanks

This chicken-like marsh bird is the freshwater version of the Clapper Rail. These two species are known to interbreed where their ranges overlap. A scattered and localized breeder across eastern North America, the King Rail depends on extensive freshwater marsh habitats with tall, emergent reeds and cattails. Concealed by this vegetation, the King Rail is rarely seen and is most often detected by its distinctive calls.

VOICE Male call similar to Clapper Rail but lower; emits a loud *kik kik kik* during breeding season.

NESTING Cup of vegetation, often hidden by bent stems that form a canopy; 6–12 eggs; 2 broods; February–August.

FEEDING Forages in concealed locations for insects, snails, spiders, and crustaceans such as shrimps, crabs, and barnacles; also fish, frogs, and seeds.

FLIGHT: somewhat clumsy and labored; legs dangling; prefers to run.

LARGEST RAIL
Easily confused with the closely related Clapper Rail, this is the largest North American rail.

OCCURRENCE
Mostly breeds in freshwater marshes in the eastern US and in extreme southern Ontario. Also found throughout the year along the southern coast of the US, including Florida, and in central Mexico and Cuba.

SIMILAR SPECIES

CLAPPER RAIL
see p.189

flank barring diffused

grayer overall

VIRGINIA RAIL
see p.191

gray face

red bill

smaller overall

Length **15in (38cm)**	Wingspan **20in (51cm)**	Weight **13oz (375g)**
Social **Pairs**	Lifespan **Unknown**	Status **Localized**

Order **Gruiformes**	Family **Rallidae**	Species *Rallus limicola*

Virginia Rail

gray cheeks

rufous upperwing

streaked black and brown upperparts

ADULT (BREEDING)

dark outer wing feathers

IN FLIGHT

white undertail

curved, red bill

reddish brown breast

black-and-white barring on flanks

reddish legs and toes

ADULT (BREEDING)

diffused streaking

dark bill

dark, blotchy breast

ADULT (NONBREEDING)

A smaller version of the King Rail, this freshwater marsh dweller is, similar to its other relatives, more often heard than seen. Distributed in a wide range, the Virginia Rail spends most of its time in thick, reedy vegetation, which it pushes using its "rail thin" body and flexible vertebrae. Although it spends most of its life walking, it can swim and even dive to escape danger. The Virginia Rail is a long-distance migrant that leaves its breeding grounds in winter.

VOICE Series of pig-like grunting *oinks* that start loud and sharp, becoming steadily softer; also emits a series of double notes *ka-dik ka-dik*.

NESTING Substantial cup of plant material, concealed by bent-over stems; 5–12 eggs; 1–2 broods; April–July.

FEEDING Actively stalks prey or may wait and dive into water; primarily eats snails, insects, and spiders, but may also eat seeds.

FLIGHT: weak and struggling with outstretched neck and legs trailing behind.

HARD TO SPOT
The secretive Virginia Rail is difficult to spot in its reedy habitat.

SIMILAR SPECIES

CLAPPER RAIL see p.189

KING RAIL see p.190

less gray face

larger overall

orange face

weak flank barring

dark undertail

yellow-orange bill

OCCURRENCE
Breeds in freshwater habitats across North America, though is found throughout the year along the West Coast of the US. In winter, moves to saltwater and freshwater marshes in the southern US, including Florida, and in northern and central Mexico.

Length **9½in (24cm)**	Wingspan **13in (33cm)**	Weight **3oz (85g)**
Social **Pairs**	Lifespan **Unknown**	Status **Secure**

| Order **Gruiformes** | Family **Rallidae** | Species *Gallinula chloropus* |

Common Moorhen

ADULT
(BREEDING)

duller frontal shield

less bright
bill

ADULT (NONBREEDING)

red frontal
shield

greenish
yellow legs

red
bill
with
yellow
tip

white undertail
feathers divided
with black stripe

IN FLIGHT

conspicuous
white stripe

white
flank
stripe

brownish
gray head

JUVENILE

ADULT
(BREEDING)

FLIGHT: rather weak and labored with legs trailing, seldom flies.

The Common Moorhen is fairly widespread in the eastern US, although its distribution is more scattered in the western states. It has similarities in behavior and habitat to both the true rails and coots. Equally at home on land and water, its long toes allow it to walk easily over floating vegetation and soft mud. When walking or swimming, the Common Moorhen nervously jerks its short tail, revealing its white undertail feathers, and bobs its head.

VOICE A variety of hen-like clucks and cackles, including an exlosive *krrooo*.

NESTING Bulky platform of aquatic vegetation with growing plants pulled over to conceal it, or close to water; 5–11 eggs, 1–3 broods; May–August, maybe year round in Florida.

FEEDING Forages mainly on aquatic and terrestrial plants and aquatic vegetation; also eats snails, spiders, and insects.

DUAL HABITAT
A walker and a swimmer, the Moorhen is equally at home on land and in water.

OCCURRENCE
Breeds in freshwater habitats in the eastern US and Canada; more localized in the West. Winters in warmer areas with open water, such as southern California and Mexico. Also found in Central and South America.

SIMILAR SPECIES

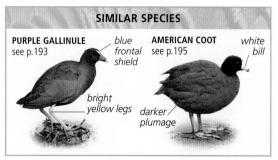

PURPLE GALLINULE
see p.193

blue
frontal
shield

bright
yellow legs

AMERICAN COOT
see p.195

white
bill

darker
plumage

| Length **14in (36cm)** | Wingspan **21in (53cm)** | Weight **11oz (325g)** |
| Social **Pairs** | Lifespan **Up to 10 years** | Status **Secure** |

Order **Gruiformes**	Family **Rallidae**	Species *Fulica americana*

American Coot

black head

red eye

ADULT (BREEDING)

dark gray body

black ring on bill

white bill

white-edged feathers

IN FLIGHT

dull grayish plumage

JUVENILE

long, greenish yellow legs

ADULT (BREEDING)

lobed toes

This duck-like species of rail is the most abundant and widely distributed of North American rails. Its lobed toes make it well adapted to swimming and diving, but somewhat of an impediment on land. Its flight is clumsy; it becomes airborne with difficulty, running along the water surface before taking off. American Coots form large flocks on open water in winter, often associating with ducks—an unusual trait for a member of the rail family.

VOICE Various raucous clucks, grunts, and croaks and an explosive *keek*.

NESTING Bulky cup of plant material placed in aquatic vegetation on or near water; 5–15 eggs; 1–2 broods; April–July.

FEEDING Forages on or under shallow water and feeds on land; primarily herbivorous, but also eats snails, insects, spiders, tadpoles, fish, and even carrion.

FLIGHT: low and labored; runs for quite a long distance to take off.

SWIMMING AWAY
The red-headed, baldish looking Americans Coot chicks leave the nest a day after hatching.

SIMILAR SPECIES

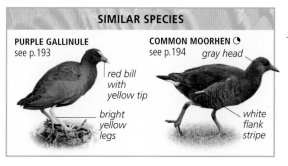

PURPLE GALLINULE
see p.193

red bill with yellow tip

bright yellow legs

COMMON MOORHEN ☾
see p.194

gray head

white flank stripe

OCCURRENCE
Breeds in open water habitats west of the Appalachians and in Florida. Moves from the northern parts of its range in winter to the southeastern US, where open water persists; also moves to western and southern Mexico.

Length **15½in (40cm)**	Wingspan **24in (61cm)**	Weight **16oz (450g)**
Social **Flocks**	Lifespan **Up to 22 years**	Status **Secure**

Order **Gruiformes**	Family **Gruidae**	Species **Grus canadensis**

Sandhill Crane

black wing tips

ADULT

head held straight

IN FLIGHT

trailing legs

brownish head

body with pale brown smudges

JUVENILE

red crown

long, black bill

pale cheek

long neck

ADULT

rusty body

shaggy feathers

"IRON-STAINED" PLUMAGE

long, black legs

FLIGHT: alternates slow, steady flapping with periods of gliding; flocks in single-file.

These large, slender, and long-necked birds are famous for their elaborate courtship dances, far-carrying vocalizations, and remarkable migrations. Their bodies are sometimes stained with a rusty color, supposedly because they probe into mud which contains iron; when a bird preens, this is transferred from the bill to its plumage. Sandhill Cranes are broadly grouped into "Lesser" and "Greater" populations that differ in the geographical location of their breeding grounds and migration routes.

VOICE Call loud, wooden, hollow bugling, audible at great distances; noisy in flight and courtship.

NESTING Mound of sticks and grasses placed on ground; 1 egg; 1 brood; April–September.

FEEDING Eats shoots, grain; also aquatic mollusks and insects.

MEMORABLE IMAGE
Its long neck, large wings, and distinctive red crown make it difficult to mistake.

OCCURRENCE
Breeds in muskeg, tundra, and forest clearings across northwestern North America, east to Quebec and the Great Lakes; large wintering and migratory flocks often densely packed, roosting in or near marshes. Winters south to northern Mexico.

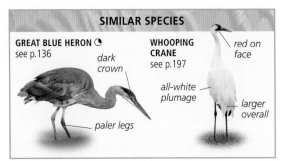

SIMILAR SPECIES

GREAT BLUE HERON ☾
see p.136

dark crown

WHOOPING CRANE
see p.197

red on face

all-white plumage

larger overall

paler legs

Length **2¾–4ft (0.8–1.2m)**	Wingspan **6–7½ft (1.8–2.3m)**	Weight **7¾–11lb (3.5–5kg)**
Social **Flocks**	Lifespan **Up to 25 years**	Status **Secure**

Order **Gruiformes**	Family **Gruidae**	Species **Grus americana**

Whooping Crane

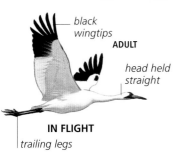

black wingtips

ADULT

head held straight

IN FLIGHT

trailing legs

very dark red "mask"

long, dark bill

long neck

ADULT

white overall

gray-black legs

brownish head

scattered brown feathers

JUVENILE

FLIGHT: slow and powerful wing beats; appears imposingly large in flight.

The colossal and majestic Whooping Crane is one of the most compelling success stories of the US Endangered Species Act. Thanks to an ambitious campaign of habitat protection, captive breeding and release, and public education, the species has rebounded from just a few dozen birds in the mid-20th century to hundreds of individuals in the early 21st century. However, it still remains endangered, because it reproduces slowly in a restricted range and additional intervention measures are required to help this fragile species continue its recovery.

VOICE Piercing and trumpeting, *kerloo!* and *kerleeyew*, audible from afar; bugling calls during courtship dances.

NESTING Mound of vegetation placed on ground; 2 eggs; 1 brood; April–August.

FEEDING Gleans animal and plant matter, such as frogs, mollusks, berries, and seeds, from the ground.

STATELY PROGRESS
Whooping Cranes move slowly and steadily through the shallows searching for prey.

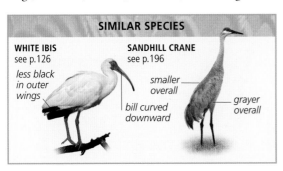

SIMILAR SPECIES

WHITE IBIS
see p.126

less black in outer wings

SANDHILL CRANE
see p.196

smaller overall

bill curved downward

grayer overall

PREPARING TO LAND
The Whooping Crane brakes by opening its outer wing feathers to let air flow through.

OCCURRENCE
Breeds in marshy country with scattered ponds and prairies in a very small region of Canada; birds migrate along a narrow route to winter in coastal estuaries in Texas; on migration, uses both agricultural fields and marshland. Small numbers of migrants found with large numbers of Sandhill Cranes.

Length **4–4½ft (1.2–1.4m)**	Wingspan **7¼ft (2.2m)**	Weight **15–18lb (7–8kg)**
Social **Solitary/Pairs**	Lifespan **Up to 30 years**	Status **Endangered**

Order **Gruiformes**	Family **Aramidae**	Species *Aramus guarauna*

Limpkin

dark wings

ADULT curved bill

IN FLIGHT

long, curvaceous neck

sparse white spotting on back

white speckles on neck

ADULT (SUMMER)

chocolate brown overall

long, gray legs

—WWW—

FLIGHT: direct and heavy flight; legs are either drawn up into the body or left dangling behind.

Similar to both herons and ibises, the Limpkin is actually related to the cranes, coots, and rails. It is at home in the swamps and marshes of southeastern North America, eating during the daylight, but remaining active at night. Individuals and small flocks tend to move slowly and deliberately, occasionally erupting into animated motions and wild wailing. This species's preferred food resource is threatened by habitat conversion and by competition from introduced species.
VOICE Call short whistles, abrupt barks, and medium length wails; often have an eerie quality.
NESTING Vegetation placed on ground or in tree; 5–6 eggs; 1–3 broods; February–July.
FEEDING Feeds in shallow water, on apple snails; also insects and spiders.

SNAILS FOR DINNER
Limpkins forage mainly for apple snails in quiet waterways in wooded southeastern swamps.

DEEP WADING
Although Limpkins often hide in vegetation, they sometimes wander into open water.

OCCURRENCE
Range limited to areas inhabited by apple snails. Breeds and forages in extensive marshes, wooded swamps, and swamp forests, but also ranges into disturbed habitats, including ditches, canals, and parks.

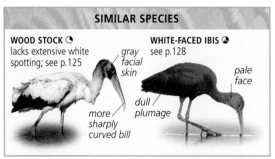

SIMILAR SPECIES

WOOD STOCK ◐
lacks extensive white spotting; see p.125

gray facial skin

more sharply curved bill

WHITE-FACED IBIS ◐
see p.128

pale face

dull plumage

Length **26in (66cm)**	Wingspan **3ft 3in (100cm)**	Weight **2–2¾lbs (0.9–1.2kg)**
Social **Solitary**	Lifespan **Up to 12 years**	Status **Declining**

SHOREBIRDS, GULLS, & AUKS

THE DIVERSE SHOREBIRD, gull, and auk families together form the order Charadriiformes. They are small to medium-sized, mostly migratory birds, associated with aquatic habitats. Over 100 species are found in North America.

TYPICAL GULL
Most large gulls, such as this Western Gull, have white heads and underparts with long dark wings and a bright sturdy bill.

SHOREBIRDS

The various species popularly known as shorebirds belong to several different families. In North America there are the oystercatchers (Haematopodidae), the avocets and stilts (Recurvirostridae), the plovers (Charadriidae), the sandpipers (Scolopacidae); and the Phalaropes (a subfamily Phalaropodinae, of Scolopacidae). They have long legs in proportion to their bodies, and a variety of bills, ranging from short to long, wthin, thick, straight, down-curved and up-curved.

GULLS

The over 20 species of North American gulls in the family Laridae all share a similar stout body shape, sturdy bills and webbed toes. Nearly all are scavengers. Closely associated with coastal areas, few gulls venture far out to sea. Some species are seen around fishing ports and harbors, or inland, especially in urban areas and garbage dumps.

TERNS

Terns are specialized, long-billed predators that dive for fish. More slender and elegant than gulls, nearly all are immediately recognizable when breeding, due to their black caps and long, pointed bills. The related but differently billed Black Skimmer also catches fish.

AUKS, MURRES, AND PUFFINS

Denizens of the northern oceans, these birds come to land only to breed. Most nest in colonies on sheer cliffs overlooking the ocean, but puffins excavate burrows in the ground, and some murrelets nest away from predators high up in treetops far inland.

COLOR-CHANGE BILL
The bright colors of a breeding Tufted Puffin's bill fade to more muted tones in winter, after the breeding season.

ON THE MOVE
Dunlins and other sandpipers gather in large, highly coordinated flocks on migration.

| Order **Charadriiformes** | Family **Haematopodidae** | Species *Haematopus bachmani* |

Black Oystercatcher

IN FLIGHT

ADULT

long, orange-red bill

broad, powerful wings

dark brown to black body

bright yellow eye

orange-red eye-ring

ADULT

thick, pink legs

dull orange eye-ring

dark eye

dark tip of bill

JUVENILE

This large, striking oystercatcher shares the typical round-bodied, hunch-backed, and squat-necked shape of other oystercatchers, as well as their typically thick legs and bill. But it is instantly obvious because of its all-dark plumage, making the pale eyes and colorful bill all the more conspicuous. It is restricted to rocky coasts, where it feeds in pairs or family groups, using well-defined territories in summer. In winter, the birds gather in larger flocks where they are numerous, sometimes in hundreds, where mussels are abundant. These are noisy, demonstrative birds, and always entertaining to watch.

VOICE Flight call a loud, whistled *wheeu*, with emphasis on first part of call; alarm call sharper *wheep*; courtship and posturing calls a series of whistles based on flight call, accelerating into descending piping calls.

NESTING Simple scrape just above high-tide line, often lined with broken shells and pebbles; 1–3 eggs; 1 brood; May–June.

FEEDING Feeds on slightly submerged shellfish beds; diet includes mollusks, particularly mussels and limpets; also eats a variety of crustaceans, such as crabs and barnacles; oysters are rarely consumed.

FLIGHT: strong, powerful flight with shallow wing beats.

MUSSEL LOVER
The Black Oystercatcher can often be spotted walking along mussel beds at low tide.

SIMILAR SPECIES

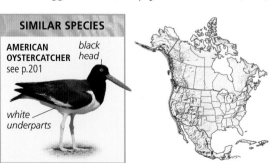

AMERICAN OYSTERCATCHER
see p.201

black head

white underparts

OCCURRENCE
Feeds in the area between the high and low tide marks on rocky shores of western North America, from Alaska southward to Baja California. Breeds just above high tide line on rocky headlands or sand, shell, and gravel beaches. In winter, also found on rocky jetties in southern part of range.

| Length **16½–18½ in (42–47cm)** | Wingspan **30–34in (77–86cm)** | Weight **18–25oz (500–700g)** |
| Social **Pairs/Flocks** | Lifespan **10–15 years** | Status **Secure** |

| Order **Charadriiformes** | Family **Haematopodidae** | Species *Haematopus palliatus* |

American Oystercatcher

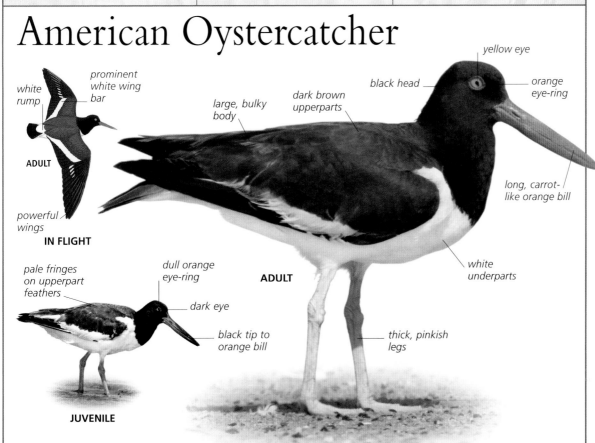

yellow eye

black head

orange eye-ring

dark brown upperparts

large, bulky body

white rump

prominent white wing bar

long, carrot-like orange bill

ADULT

powerful wings

IN FLIGHT

pale fringes on upperpart feathers

dull orange eye-ring

ADULT

white underparts

dark eye

black tip to orange bill

thick, pinkish legs

JUVENILE

This large and noisy shorebird is conspicuous on beachfront habitats along the Atlantic and Gulf of Mexico coastlines. It is the heaviest of all North American shorebirds, and often runs on its thick, powerful legs to escape danger. This species is found in flocks of a few to several hundred birds in winter at its preferred feeding and roosting locations. Up to eight birds can be seen together in synchronized courtship flights, with their heads and necks bowed and wings arched upwards

VOICE Whistled, loud, clear descending *wheeu* call; alarm call sharp *wheep*; flight display call several sharp whistles accelerating into a series of descending piping notes.

NESTING Simple scrape with shell debris on coastal sandy beaches, dunes, and salt marshes; 2–3 eggs; 1 brood; April–May.

FEEDING Forages on slightly submerged shellfish beds; feeds by probing in subsoil; also by stabbing or hammering open bivalve shells with powerful bill.

FLIGHT: powerful, fast, direct flight with rapid shallow wing beats.

OPENING UP
This species uses its long, powerful bill to pry open or smash bivalve mollusks on rocks.

SIMILAR SPECIES

BLACK OYSTERCATCHER
see p.200

all dark plumage

STRONG FLIER
Strong fliers, these birds use their long, powerful wings for swift, short-distance forays.

OCCURRENCE
Exclusive to saltwater coastal habitats; locally common from Massachusetts southward to Gulf Coast; also Caribbean south to Argentina, north from Chile to Baja California, Mexico. Occurs in southern California and recent nesting has been documented in Nova Scotia. Expanding northwards on Atlantic Coast.

| Length **15½–17½in (40–44cm)** | Wingspan **29–32in (73–81cm)** | Weight **14–25oz (400–700g)** |
| Social **Flocks** | Lifespan **Up to 17 years** | Status **Secure** |

| Order **Charadriiformes** | Family **Recurvirostridae** | Species *Himantopus mexicanus* |

Black-necked Stilt

ADULT

long, angular, black wings

no white spot above red eye

long, slender neck

IN FLIGHT

black upperparts

slender, tapered body

MALE

long, bright pink legs

white underparts

JUVENILE

scaly appearance

less contrasting head pattern than adult

shorter, stubbier bill

white spot above red eye

black mask encircles eye

long, needle-like black bill

brownish wash to back

duller legs than male

FEMALE

This tall, slender, elegant, and black-and-white shorebird is a familiar sight at ponds and lagoons in the western and southern US. Even among the shorebirds, it is remarkably long-legged, at times almost grotesquely so: in flight, it often crosses its trailing feet as if for extra control and support. Breeding takes place in small colonies, with several pairs sharing the same site. In winter, these tall birds are often seen in small flocks of about 25 individuals. These small groups feed quietly in sheltered areas, but they aggressively drive visitors away with their raucous calls, dog-like yips, and noisy communal protests. The increased use of pesticides and loss of wetland habitat could cause a decline in its numbers in the future.

VOICE Flight and alarm call a loud, continuous poodle-like *yip-yip-yip*, given in a long series when alarmed.

NESTING Simple scrape lined with grass in soft soil; 4 eggs; 1 brood; April–May.

FEEDING Walks slowly in shallow water, picking food off surface; diet includes tadpoles, shrimps, snails, flies, worms, clams, small fish, and frogs.

FLIGHT: direct, but somewhat awkward due to long, trailing legs; deep wing beats.

FRIENDLY BUNCH
Black-necked Stilts are gregarious by nature, and often roost together in shallow water.

OCCURRENCE
Breeds around marshes, shallow grassy ponds, lake margins, and manmade waterbodies, such as reservoirs; uses similar habitats during migration and winter, as well as shallow lagoons, flooded fields, and mangrove swamps. Southern birds migrate locally only.

| Length **14–15½in (35–39cm)** | Wingspan **29–32in (73–81cm)** | Weight **4–8oz (125–225g)** |
| Social **Small flocks** | Lifespan **Up to 19 years** | Status **Secure** |

| Order **Charadriiformes** | Family **Recurvirostridae** | Species *Recurvirostra americana* |

American Avocet

striking black-and-white pattern

ADULT (BREEDING)

IN FLIGHT

cinnamon-colored head

bold shoulder feathers

white underparts

white eye-ring

dark eye

long, thin, upturned bill

cinnamon-colored neck

FEMALE

less upturned bill

long, bluish legs

MALE

no cinnamon color on head and neck

white plumage

ADULT (NONBREEDING)

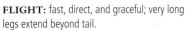

FLIGHT: fast, direct, and graceful; very long legs extend beyond tail.

With its long, thin, and upturned bill, this graceful, long-legged shorebird is unmistakable when foraging. When it takes off, its striking plumage pattern is clearly visible. It is the only one of the four avocet species in the world that changes plumage when breeding. Breeding birds have a cinnamon head and neck, and bold, patterns on their black-and-white wings and upperparts. The American Avocet forms large flocks during migration and in winter.

VOICE Flight call a variable melodic *kleet*, loud and repetitive, given when alarmed and by foraging birds.

NESTING Simple scrape in shallow depression; 4 eggs; 1 brood; May–June.

FEEDING Uses specialized bill to probe, scythe, or jab a variety of aquatic invertebrates, small fish, and seeds; walks steadily in belly-deep water to chase its prey.

TRICKY BALANCE
During mating, the male supports himself with raised wings as the female extends her neck.

FORAGING FLOCK
These birds walk through shallow water in flocks searching mainly for insects and crustaceans.

OCCURRENCE
Breeds in temporary wetlands, in dry to arid regions. During migration and in winter, found in shallow water habitats, including ponds, reservoirs, fresh- and saltwater marshes, tidal mudflats, and lagoons. Each year, flock of 10,000 birds winters at Bolivar Flats, Texas. Regular East Coast visitor.

| Length **17–18½in (43–47cm)** | Wingspan **29–32in (74–81cm)** | Weight **10–12oz (275–350g)** |
| Social **Large flocks** | Lifespan **Up to 9 years** | Status **Secure** |

| Order **Charadriiformes** | Family **Charadriidae** | Species *Pluvialis fulva* |

Pacific Golden Plover

long wings

ADULT (NON-BREEDING)

MALE (BREEDING)

black-and-white head

mostly white underparts

IN FLIGHT

variable white feathering on cheek and underparts

FEMALE (BREEDING)

tan face

tan, black, and white upperparts

off-white underparts

ADULT (NONBREEDING)

checkered tan-and-black upperparts

pale tan breast

JUVENILE

white band on forehead

tan-and-black upperparts

white undertail feathers

black underparts

MALE (BREEDING)

FLIGHT: fast and direct flight on powerful wings.

The Pacific Golden Plover and American Golden Plover were formerly considered to belong to the same species. Although the Pacific Golden Plover frequents grassy habitats, it is also regularly encountered on migration and it migrates over the ocean to wintering grounds on remote South Pacific islands. The species nests in the tundra of the Arctic, but it can adapt to human-altered environments away from the breeding grounds.

VOICE Flight call a clearly two-syllabled *chu-EEt*, with emphasis on second note; breeding song a clear, haunting, low whistle *pEE-prr-EE*.

NESTING Shallow depression lined with lichens on densely vegetated tundra; 4 eggs; 1 brood; May–July.

FEEDING Forages in run and stop manner on grasshoppers, beetles, wireworms; also eats spiders, small mollusks, crustaceans, small fish, berries, and seeds.

SIMILAR SPECIES

AMERICAN GOLDEN PLOVER ◑ see p.205

shorter bill

shorter legs

FLEDGLING
Vulnerable to predators, the downy chick is camouflaged well in its tundra habitat.

OCCURRENCE
Nests primarily on Arctic and sub-Arctic tundra; in migration and winter, found in a wide variety of habitats, including prairies, pastures, mudflats, shorelines, mangroves, parks, tiny lawns and gardens in urban areas, and roadsides. About 12 percent of the world's population nests in Alaska.

| Length **9–10½in (23–27cm)** | Wingspan **21–24in (53–61cm)** | Weight **3½–7oz (100–200g)** |
| Social **Solitary/Small flocks** | Lifespan **Up to 7 years** | Status **Localized** |

| Order **Charadriiformes** | Family **Charadriidae** | Species *Pluvialis dominica* |

American Golden Plover

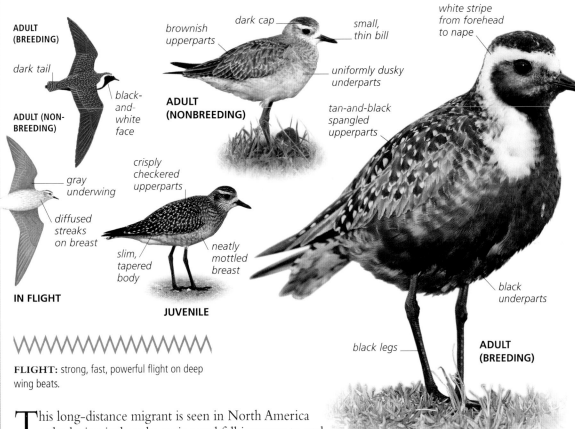

ADULT (BREEDING)

dark tail

black-and-white face

ADULT (NON-BREEDING)

gray underwing

diffused streaks on breast

IN FLIGHT

brownish upperparts

dark cap

small, thin bill

uniformly dusky underparts

tan-and-black spangled upperparts

ADULT (NONBREEDING)

crisply checkered upperparts

slim, tapered body

neatly mottled breast

JUVENILE

white stripe from forehead to nape

black underparts

black legs

ADULT (BREEDING)

FLIGHT: strong, fast, powerful flight on deep wing beats.

This long-distance migrant is seen in North America only during its lengthy spring and fall journeys to and from its high Arctic breeding grounds and wintering locations in southern South America. An elegant, slender, yet large plover, it prefers inland grassy habitats and plowed fields to coastal mudflats. The American Golden Plover's annual migration route includes a feeding stop at Labrador, then a 1,550–1,860 miles (2,500–3,000km) flight over the ocean to South America.

VOICE Flight call a whistled two-note *queE-dle*, or *klee-u*, with second note shorter and lower pitched; male flight song a strong, melodious whistled *kid-eek*, or *kid-EEp*.

NESTING Shallow depression lined with lichens in dry, open tundra; 4 eggs; 1 brood; May–July.

FEEDING Forages in run, pause, and pluck sequence on insects, mollusks, crustaceans, and worms; also berries and seeds.

DISTRACTION TECHNIQUE
This breeding American Golden Plover is feigning an injury to its wing to draw predators away from its eggs or chicks in its nest.

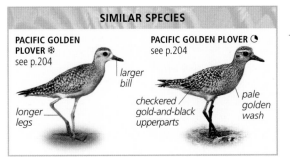

SIMILAR SPECIES

PACIFIC GOLDEN PLOVER ✳
see p.204

longer legs

larger bill

PACIFIC GOLDEN PLOVER ☾
see p.204

checkered gold-and-black upperparts

pale golden wash

OCCURRENCE
Breeds in Arctic tundra habitats. In migration, it occurs in prairies, tilled farmlands, golf courses, pastures, airports; also mudflats, shorelines, and beaches. In spring, seen in Texas and Great Plains; in fall, uncommon in northeast Maritimes and New England; scarce along the Pacific Coast.

| Length **9½–11in (24–28cm)** | Wingspan **23–28in (59–72cm)** | Weight **4–7oz (125–200g)** |
| Social **Solitary/Small flocks** | Lifespan **Unknown** | Status **Secure** |

| Order **Charadriiformes** | Family **Charadriidae** | Species *Pluvialis squatarola* |

Black-bellied Plover

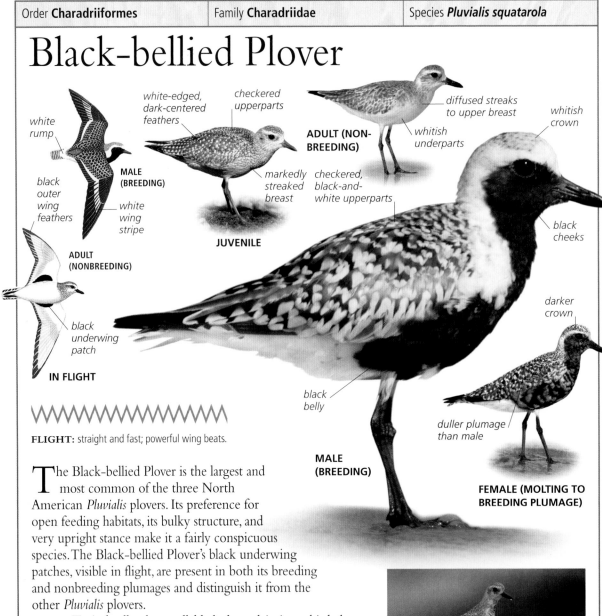

white rump

black outer wing feathers

white wing stripe

MALE (BREEDING)

white-edged, dark-centered feathers

checkered upperparts

ADULT (NON-BREEDING)

markedly streaked breast

JUVENILE

diffused streaks to upper breast

whitish underparts

whitish crown

black cheeks

checkered, black-and-white upperparts

ADULT (NONBREEDING)

black underwing patch

IN FLIGHT

black belly

MALE (BREEDING)

darker crown

duller plumage than male

FEMALE (MOLTING TO BREEDING PLUMAGE)

FLIGHT: straight and fast; powerful wing beats.

The Black-bellied Plover is the largest and most common of the three North American *Pluvialis* plovers. Its preference for open feeding habitats, its bulky structure, and very upright stance make it a fairly conspicuous species. The Black-bellied Plover's black underwing patches, visible in flight, are present in both its breeding and nonbreeding plumages and distinguish it from the other *Pluvialis* plovers.

VOICE Typical call a three-syllabled, clear, plaintive, whistled *whEE-er-eee*, with middle note lower; flight song of male during breeding softer, with accent on second syllable.

NESTING Shallow depression lined with mosses and lichens in moist to dry lowland tundra; 1–5 eggs; 1 brood; May–July.

FEEDING Forages mainly along coasts in typical plover style: run, pause, and pluck; eats insects, worms, bivalves, and crustaceans.

CASUAL WADING
The Black-bellied Plover wades in shallow water but does most of its foraging in mudflats.

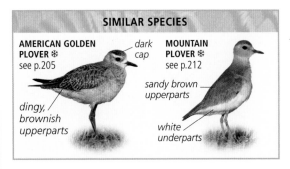

SIMILAR SPECIES

AMERICAN GOLDEN PLOVER ❊ see p.205

dark cap

MOUNTAIN PLOVER ❊ see p.212

sandy brown upperparts

dingy, brownish upperparts

white underparts

OCCURRENCE
Breeds in High Arctic habitats from western Russia across the Bering Sea to Alaska, and east to Baffin Island; winters primarily in coastal areas from southern Canada and US, south to southern South America. Found inland during migration. Migrates south all the way to South America.

| Length **10½–12in (27–30cm)** | Wingspan **29–32in (73–81cm)** | Weight **5–9oz (150–250g)** |
| Social **Flocks** | Lifespan **Up to 12 years** | Status **Secure** |

Order **Charadriiformes**	Family **Charadriidae**	Species *Charadrius semipalmatus*

Semipalmated Plover

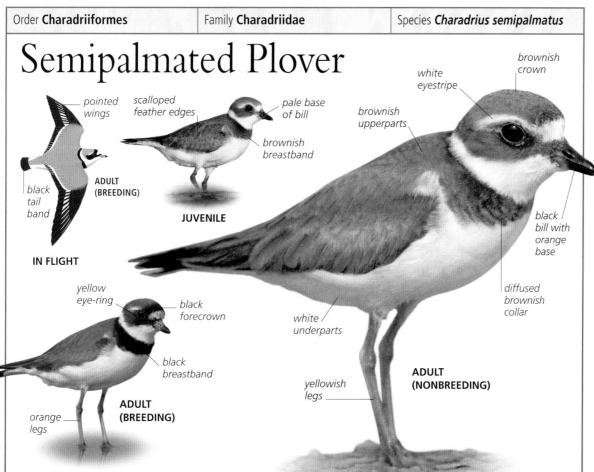

pointed wings

scalloped feather edges

pale base of bill

brownish breastband

ADULT (BREEDING)

JUVENILE

black tail band

IN FLIGHT

white eyestripe

brownish crown

brownish upperparts

black bill with orange base

diffused brownish collar

white underparts

ADULT (NONBREEDING)

yellow eye-ring

black forecrown

black breastband

yellowish legs

orange legs

ADULT (BREEDING)

Similar in appearance to the Eurasian Common Ringed Plover, the Semipalmated Plover is a small bird with a tapered shape. It is a familiar sight in a wide variety of habitats during migration and in winter, when these birds gather in loose flocks. A casual walk down a sandy beach between fall and spring might awaken up to 100 Semipalmated Plovers, sleeping in slight depressions in the sand, though flocks of up to 1,000 birds may also be encountered.

VOICE Flight call a whistled abrupt *chu-WEEp*, with soft emphasis on second syllable; courtship display song quick version of flight call followed by rough *r-r-r-r-r-r-r*, ending with a slurred, descending *yelp*.

NESTING Simple scrape on bare or slightly vegetated ground in Arctic tundra; 3–4 eggs; 1 brood; May–June.

FEEDING Forages in typical plover style: run, pause, and pluck; eats aquatic mollusks, crustaceans, flies, beetles, and spiders.

FLIGHT: straight, fast; with fluttering wing beats.

BY SIGHT AND TOUCH
Semipalmated Plovers locate prey by sight or through the sensitive soles of their feet.

SIMILAR SPECIES

WILSON'S PLOVER
see p.208

heavier, dark bill

pinkish legs

RINGED PLOVER
see p.708

wider breastband

OCCURRENCE
Breeding habitat is Arctic or sub-Arctic tundra well-drained gravel, shale, or other sparsely vegetated ground. During migration, mudflats, saltwater marshes, lake edges, tidal areas, and flooded fields. During winter, coastal or near coastal habitats.

Length **6¾–7½in (17–19cm)**	Wingspan **17–20½in (43–52cm)**	Weight **1¹⁄₁₆–2½oz (30–70g)**
Social **Solitary/Flocks**	Lifespan **Up to 6 years**	Status **Secure**

Order **Charadriiformes**	Family **Charadriidae**	Species *Charadrius wilsonia*

Wilson's Plover

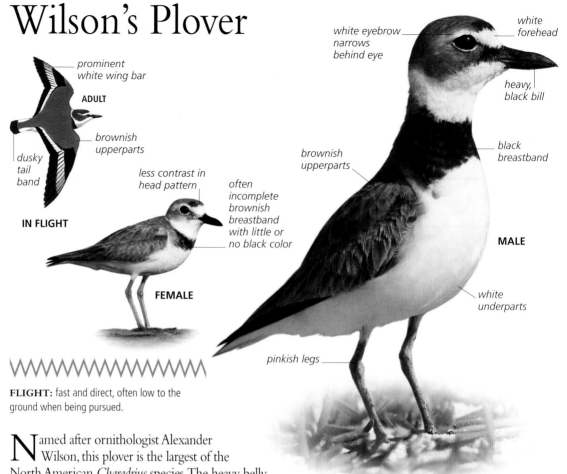

prominent white wing bar

ADULT

brownish upperparts

dusky tail band

IN FLIGHT

white eyebrow narrows behind eye

white forehead

heavy, black bill

brownish upperparts

black breastband

MALE

white underparts

less contrast in head pattern

often incomplete brownish breastband with little or no black color

FEMALE

pinkish legs

FLIGHT: fast and direct, often low to the ground when being pursued.

Named after ornithologist Alexander Wilson, this plover is the largest of the North American *Charadrius* species. The heavy belly of the Wilson's Plover gives it a very upright posture when it pauses, and its distinctive habit of running horizontally, low to the ground, is a familiar sight on beaches. The subspecies *C. w. beldingi* (Gulf of California and Mexico's Pacific coast) is smaller and darker, with a darker face. Wilson's Plover was listed as a species of "high concern" in 2000.

VOICE Flight call a short *pip*, or *pi-dit;* alarm calls include slurred whistle *tweet*, and short whistled *peet;* common distraction call a descending buzzy rattle, given in series.

NESTING Simple scrape in sand, dunes, and other coastal habitats; 3–4 eggs; 1 brood; April–June.

FEEDING Forages in typical plover style: run, pause, and pluck; mainly eats crustaceans, including fiddler crabs; also insects.

STRICTLY COASTAL
Wilson's Plover is strongly associated with coastal areas, where it forages during low tide.

OCCURRENCE
Found primarily in coastal habitats, including open beaches, vegetated sand dunes, coastal lagoons, saltwater flats, and overwash areas. Located only in North American coastal regions of the southeast Atlantic and Gulf Coasts.

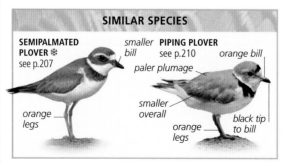

SIMILAR SPECIES

SEMIPALMATED PLOVER ✳ see p.207

smaller bill

PIPING PLOVER see p.210

paler plumage

orange bill

orange legs

smaller overall

orange legs

black tip to bill

Length **6½–8in (16–20cm)**	Wingspan **15½–19½in (39–49cm)**	Weight **2–2½oz (55–70g)**
Social **Flocks**	Lifespan **Unknown**	Status **Declining**

Order **Charadriiformes**	Family **Charadriidae**	Species *Charadrius vociferus*

Killdeer

long wings

white wing bar

ADULT

reddish orange tail and rump

IN FLIGHT

brownish upperparts

black collar encircling neck

red eye-ring

brownish crown

small, thin, black bill

rufous wash to back and wings

MALE

long tail

second neck band crosses upper breast

white underparts

pinkish legs, sometimes with yellowish tinge

FLIGHT: fast, twisting flight with fluid wing beats.

This loud and vocal shorebird is the most widespread plover in North America, nesting in all southern Canadian provinces and across the US. The Killdeer's piercing call carries for long distances, sometimes causing other birds to fly away in fear of imminent danger. These birds often nest near human habitation, allowing a close observation of their vigilant parental nature with young chicks.

VOICE Flight call a rising, drawn out *deeee*; alarm call a loud, penetrating *dee-ee*, given repetitively; agitated birds also give series of *dee* notes, followed by rising trill.

NESTING Scrape on ground, sometimes in slight depression; 4 eggs; 1 brood (north), 2–3 broods (south); March–July.

FEEDING Forages in typical plover style: run, pause, and pick; eats a variety of invertebrates such as worms, snails, grasshoppers, and beetles; also small vertebrates and seeds.

CLEVER MANEUVER
The Killdeer lures intruders away from its nest with a "broken wing" display.

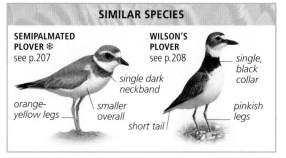

SIMILAR SPECIES

SEMIPALMATED PLOVER ❃
see p.207

WILSON'S PLOVER
see p.208

single, black collar

single dark neckband

orange-yellow legs

smaller overall

short tail

pinkish legs

OCCURRENCE
Widespread across Canada and the US, the Killdeer occurs in a wide variety of habitats. These include shorelines, mudflats, lake and river edges, sparsely grassy fields and pastures, golf courses, roadsides, parking lots, flat rooftops, driveways, and other terrestrial habitats.

Length **9–10in (23–26cm)**	Wingspan **23–25in (58–63cm)**	Weight **2¼–3⅛ oz (65–90g)**
Social **Small flocks**	Lifespan **Up to 10 years**	Status **Secure**

Order **Charadriiformes**	Family **Charadriidae**	Species *Charadrius melodus*

Piping Plover

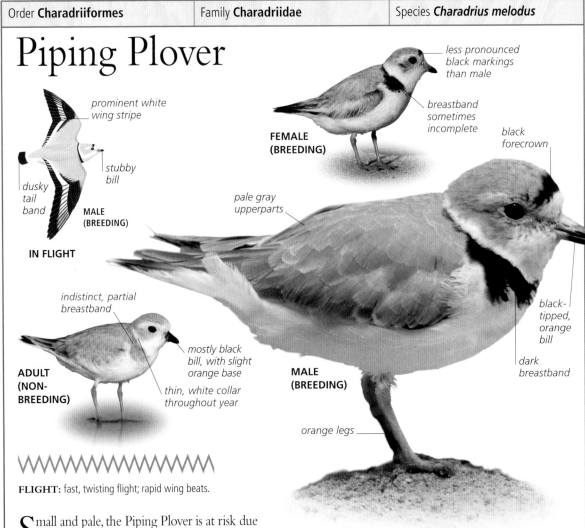

prominent white wing stripe

stubby bill

dusky tail band

MALE (BREEDING)

IN FLIGHT

less pronounced black markings than male

breastband sometimes incomplete

FEMALE (BREEDING)

black forecrown

pale gray upperparts

black-tipped, orange bill

dark breastband

indistinct, partial breastband

mostly black bill, with slight orange base

thin, white collar throughout year

ADULT (NON-BREEDING)

MALE (BREEDING)

orange legs

FLIGHT: fast, twisting flight; rapid wing beats.

Small and pale, the Piping Plover is at risk due to eroding coastlines, human disturbance, and predation by foxes, raccoons, and cats. With its pale gray back, it is well camouflaged along beaches or in dunes, but conservation measures, such as fencing off nesting beaches and control of predators, are necessary to restore populations. Two subspecies of the Piping Plover are recognized; one nests on the Atlantic Coast, and the other inland.

VOICE Clear, whistled *peep* call in flight; quiet *peep-lo* during courtship and contact; high-pitched *pipe-pipe-pipe* song.

NESTING Shallow scrape in sand, gravel, dunes, or salt flats; 4 eggs; 1 brood; April–May.

FEEDING Typical run, pause, and pluck plover feeding style; diet includes marine worms, insects, and mollusks.

VULNERABLE NESTS
The fragile nature of their preferred nesting sites has led to this species becoming endangered.

OCCURRENCE
Found along beaches, in saline sandflats, and adjacent mudflats; during winter, found exclusively along the Atlantic and Gulf Coasts, sandflats, and mudflats. Inland subspecies nests on sand or gravel beaches adjacent to large lakes, rivers, and saline lakes.

SIMILAR SPECIES

SEMIPALMATED PLOVER ✳
see p.207

dark, brown upperparts

SNOWY PLOVER ✳
see p.211

narrow, white collar

black bill

darker legs

Length **6½–7in (17–18cm)**	Wingspan **18–18½in (45–47cm)**	Weight **1⅝–2⅜ oz (45–65g)**
Social **Small flocks**	Lifespan **Up to 11 years**	Status **Vulnerable**

Order **Charadriiformes**	Family **Charadriidae**	Species *Charadrius alexandrinus*

Snowy Plover

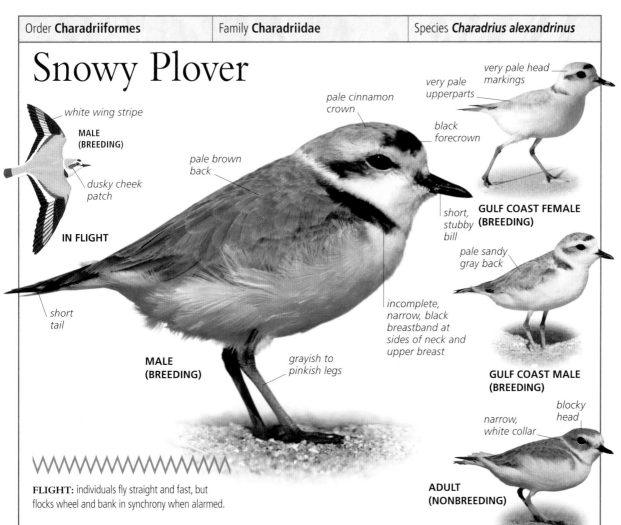

white wing stripe

MALE (BREEDING)

dusky cheek patch

IN FLIGHT

pale cinnamon crown

pale brown back

short tail

MALE (BREEDING)

grayish to pinkish legs

very pale head markings

very pale upperparts

black forecrown

short, stubby bill

GULF COAST FEMALE (BREEDING)

pale sandy gray back

incomplete, narrow, black breastband at sides of neck and upper breast

GULF COAST MALE (BREEDING)

blocky head

narrow, white collar

ADULT (NONBREEDING)

FLIGHT: individuals fly straight and fast, but flocks wheel and bank in synchrony when alarmed.

The smallest and palest of all North American plovers, the Snowy Plover's cryptic coloration blends in so well with its beach and dune habitat that it often remains unnoticed. This bird often runs faster and covers longer distances than other beach plovers, sprinting along the sand for extended spurts, like sanderlings. Nests are frequently destroyed by weather, disturbance, or predators, but the birds readily construct new nests, even up to six times in the face of regular losses. Nevertheless, habitat destruction has resulted in shrinking populations, and the species is designated as threatened along the Pacific Coast.

VOICE Repeated *tow-heet*; *purrt* and single *churr*; typically silent when not breeding, tinkling *ti* at roosts or before flight.

NESTING Shallow scrape in sand; 2–3 eggs; 2–3 broods; March–June.

FEEDING Feeds in run, pause, and pluck style on terrestrial and aquatic invertebrates, such as snails and clams.

TRULY SNOWY
The Snowy Plover breeds in sandy areas that are as pale as snow.

OCCURRENCE
Breeds on open beach and dune habitats on the Pacific and Gulf Coasts, and inland on brackish lakes in the Great Basin and southern Great Plains region. Coastal birds are only partially migratory, but most inland birds winter at the coast.

SIMILAR SPECIES

SEMIPALMATED PLOVER ☾ see p.207

brown breastband

PIPING PLOVER ♂ see p.210

plumper overall

orange legs

Length **6–6½in (15–17cm)**	Wingspan **16–18in (41–46cm)**	Weight **1¼–2⅛ oz (35–60g)**
Social **Large flocks**	Lifespan **Up to 4 years**	Status **Declining**

Order **Charadriiformes**	Family **Charadriidae**	Species *Charadrius montanus*

Mountain Plover

subtle, white wing stripe

chunky body

ADULT (BREEDING)

IN FLIGHT

sandy brown upperparts

small, thin bill

white throat

flesh-colored legs

ADULT (NONBREEDING)

uniformly brown plumage

scaly crown

white belly

JUVENILE

white forehead

black crown patch

large dark eyes

black stripe between eye and bill

rounded body shape

tan colored overall

ADULT (BREEDING)

This dainty, rather plain-looking plover is rarely found near water, unlike most other North American shorebirds. It can be hard to see against ploughed land, sandy soils, and on short, dry grassland. Unusually wary by nature, the Mountain Plover often faces away from danger and squats motionless on the ground, virtually disappearing into the landscape and earning its nickname "Prairie Ghost." It has the usual plover feeding action of run, stop, tilt forward, then scan for danger. It is declining, and endangered due to habitat loss from overgrazing and pesticides.

VOICE Generally silent; flight call grating *kirrp*; wintering birds in flight give short *kip* call; courtship song rolling, drawled, whistled *wee-wee*.

NESTING Simple scrape, often lined with grass, roots; dummy nests built; 3 eggs; 1-2 broods; May–June.

FEEDING Runs, pauses, and plucks while feeding; eats a variety of insects, such as grasshoppers, crickets, and beetles.

FLIGHT: strong, direct, and swift with powerful wing beats.

FEEDING FLOCKS
Mountain Plovers form feeding flocks during migration and winter that can be quite large.

SIMILAR SPECIES

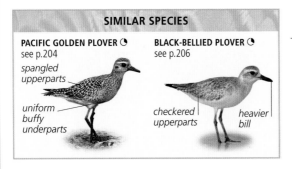

PACIFIC GOLDEN PLOVER ◑
see p.204

spangled upperparts

uniform buffy underparts

BLACK-BELLIED PLOVER ◑
see p.206

checkered upperparts

heavier bill

OCCURRENCE
Localized to patchy areas in west–central North America. Breeds in dry, flat, short grass prairies, semi-desert areas with short, sparse vegetation; during migration and in winter prefers plowed fields, grazed grasslands, turf farms, and dried-up lakes in arid regions. Winters south to Mexico.

Length **8½–9½ in (21–24cm)**	Wingspan **21½–23½in (54–60cm)**	Weight **3⅛–3½oz (90–100g)**
Social **Flocks**	Lifespan **Up to 10 years**	Status **Vulnerable**

| Order **Charadriiformes** | Family **Scolopacidae** | Species *Scolopax minor* |

American Woodcock

IN FLIGHT

two pale bands across back

long bill

plump body

short, rusty tail

ADULT

large, black eye

long bill, wide at base with slightly drooping tip

black, gray, and buff upperparts

rich orange-buff underparts

round, plump body

ADULT

short, rusty tail

pinkish legs and feet

FLIGHT: twisting, slow and clumsy; wings twitter when flushed.

This forest-dwelling member of the sandpiper family bears little resemblance in behavior to its water-favoring relatives, but slightly resembles Wilson's Snipe and the dowitchers. Although widespread, the American Woodcock is very secretive and seldom seen, except during its twilight courtship displays. It is largely nocturnal, and feeds in mature fields or woodlands. Its noisy, repetitive display flights are a welcome sign of spring in northern breeding areas.

VOICE Low, nasal *peen* call by male during dawn and dusk display; variety of chirping and twittering sounds given by male in display flight, made by air passing through narrow outer wing feathers.

NESTING Shallow depression in existing leaf and twig litter in young, mixed growth woodlands; 4 eggs; 1 brood; January (southern populations) and April (northern populations).

FEEDING Probes deep in damp soil or mud; mostly for earthworms, but also insects, snails, and some plants.

STAYING PUT
A foraging American Woodcock "caught" in an open field will freeze before it flies off.

SIMILAR SPECIES

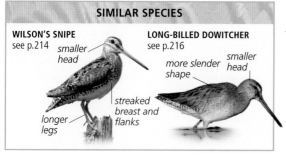

WILSON'S SNIPE
see p.214

smaller head

longer legs

streaked breast and flanks

LONG-BILLED DOWITCHER
see p.216

more slender shape

smaller head

OCCURRENCE
Breeds from southern Canada to southeastern US states, in damp, second growth forest, overgrown fields and bogs. In winter, found in similar habitat; also found along marsh edges, swamps, and damp, grassy roadsides in Texas and Florida in the southern US.

| Length **10–12in (25–31cm)** | Wingspan **16–20in (41–51cm)** | Weight **4–7oz (125–200g)** |
| Social **Solitary** | Lifespan **Up to 9 years** | Status **Secure** |

| Order **Charadriiformes** | Family **Scolopacidae** | Species *Gallinago delicata* |

Wilson's Snipe

long, pointed, angled wings

long bill

short tail

ADULT

IN FLIGHT

high-set large, dark eye

streaked face

long, thick, tapered bill, slightly drooping at tip

white, vertical streaks

mostly brown upperparts

brown spots on breast and neck

white underparts with barring on flanks

short russet tail

MALE

WWWWWWWWWW

FLIGHT: extremely fast and zig-zagging, rapid wing beats; erratic-looking changes of direction.

RUSSET TAIL
Wilson's Snipe's russet colored tail is usually hard to see, but it is evident on this preening bird.

Also known as the Common Snipe, this secretive and well camouflaged member of the sandpiper family has an unsettled taxonomic history, but is now classified individually. On its breeding grounds Wilson's Snipe produces rather eerie sounds during its aerial, mainly nocturnal, display flights. The birds fly up silently from the ground, then, from about 330 feet (100m) up, they descend quickly, with their tail feathers spread, producing a unique, loud and vibrating sound through modified feathers.

VOICE Alarm and overhead flight call raspy *kraitsch*; perched and low flying breeding birds give repetitive, monotonous *kup-kup-kup-kup* in alarm or aggression; distinctive whistling sound during territorial displays.

NESTING Elaborate woven nest lined with fine grass on ground, sedge, or moss; 4 eggs; 1 brood; May–June.

FEEDING Forages in mud or shallow water; probes deep into subsoil; diet includes mostly insect larvae, but also crustaceans, earthworms, and mollusks.

OCCURRENCE
Widespread from Alaska to Quebec and Labrador south of the tundra zone; breeds in a variety of wetlands, including marshes, bogs, and open areas with rich soil. Winters further south, where it prefers damp areas with vegetative cover, such as marshes, wet fields, and other bodies of water.

SIMILAR SPECIES

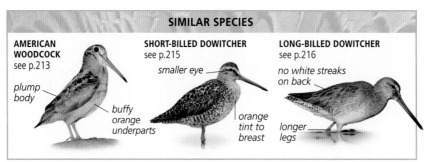

AMERICAN WOODCOCK
see p.213

plump body

buffy orange underparts

SHORT-BILLED DOWITCHER
see p.215

smaller eye

orange tint to breast

LONG-BILLED DOWITCHER
see p.216

no white streaks on back

longer legs

| Length **10–11in (25–28cm)** | Wingspan **17–19in (43–48cm)** | Weight **2⅞–5oz (80–150g)** |
| Social **Solitary** | Lifespan **Up to 10 years** | Status **Secure** |

Order **Charadriiformes**	Family **Scolopacidae**	Species *Limnodromus griseus*

Short-billed Dowitcher

white slash from rump to mid-back

ADULT (BREEDING)

long, pointed wings

IN FLIGHT

orange-fringed feathers

flanks less heavily streaked

JUVENILE

orange wash to face, neck, breast, and underparts

long, stout bill

dark-centered upperpart feathers

ADULT *L. g. griseus*

variable spotting on upper breast

ADULT *L. g. hendersoni*

slightly larger bill

streaked flanks

greenish yellow legs

plain gray upperparts

white belly

ADULT (NONBREEDING)

ᗺᗺᗺᗺᗺᗺᗺᗺᗺ

FLIGHT: swift, powerful with quick wing beats.

The Short-billed Dowitcher is a common visitor along the Atlantic, Gulf, and Pacific Coasts. Its remote and bug-infested breeding areas in northern bogs have hindered the study of its breeding behavior until recent years. There are three subspecies (*L. g. griseus, L. g. hendersoni,* and *L. g. caurinus,*) which differ in plumage, size, and respective breeding areas. Recent knowledge about shape and structure has helped ornithologists distinguish the Short-billed from the Long-billed Dowitcher.

VOICE Flight call low, plaintive *tu-tu-tu*, 3–4 notes; flight song *tu-tu, tu-tu, toodle-ee, tu-tu*, ending with low *anh-anh-anh*.

NESTING Simple depression, typically in sedge hummock; 4 eggs; 1 brood; May–June.

FEEDING Probes in "sewing machine" feeding style with water up to belly for aquatic mollusks, crustaceans, and insects.

ORANGE UNDERPARTS
In complete breeding plumage, the Short-billed Dowitcher is orange, even in late afternoon light.

SIMILAR SPECIES

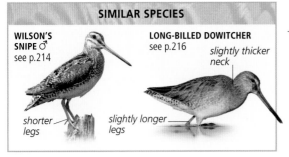

WILSON'S SNIPE ♂
see p.214

shorter legs

LONG-BILLED DOWITCHER
see p.216

slightly thicker neck

slightly longer legs

OCCURRENCE
Breeds mostly in sedge meadows or bogs with interspersed spruce and tamaracks between subarctic tundra and boreal forest. Migrates south to Central and South America, preferring coastal mudflats, saltmarshes or adjacent freshwater pools.

Length **9–10in (23–25cm)**	Wingspan **18–20in (46–51cm)**	Weight **2½–5½oz (70–155g)**
Social **Pairs/Flocks**	Lifespan **Up to 20 years**	Status **Secure (p)**

| Order **Charadriiformes** | Family **Scolopacidae** | Species *Limnodromus scolopaceus* |

Long-billed Dowitcher

bands on tail

ADULT (BREEDING)

dark upperparts with reddish markings

ADULT (BREEDING)

white rump patch

long, pointed wings

IN FLIGHT

brick-red underparts

lightly streaked head

white belly

black-centered feathers

JUVENILE

mostly dusky gray upperparts

short but distinct white eyebrow

long, stout bill

dark patch between eye and bill

variable dark barring on flanks

white belly

ADULT (NONBREEDING)

It was not until 1950 that museum and field studies identified two seperate species of dowitcher in North America. The Long-billed Dowitcher is usually slightly larger, longer-legged, and heavier in the chest and neck than the Short-billed Dowitcher. The breeding ranges of the two species are separate, but their migration and en route stop-over areas overlap. The Long-billed Dowitcher is usually found in freshwater wetlands, and in the fall most of its population occurs west of the Mississippi River.

VOICE Flight and alarm call sharp, whistled *keek*, given singly or in series when agitated; song buzzy *pipipipipipi-chi-drrr*.

NESTING Deep sedge or grass-lined depression in sedge or grass; 4 eggs; 1 brood; May–June.

FEEDING Probes wet ground with "sewing-machine" motion for spiders, snails, worms, insects, and seeds.

FLIGHT: swift, direct flier with fast, powerful wing beats.

TOUCHY FEELY
Sensitive touch-receptors at the tip of the bird's bill enable it to feel in the mud for food.

SIMILAR SPECIES

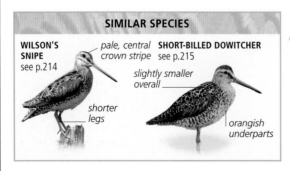

WILSON'S SNIPE see p.214

pale, central crown stripe

SHORT-BILLED DOWITCHER see p.215

shorter legs

slightly smaller overall

orangish underparts

OCCURRENCE
Breeds in wet, grassy meadows or coastal sedge tundra near freshwater pools. Migrates to Mexico and Central America, south to Panama, when found in freshwater habitats, including ponds, flooded fields, lake shores, also sheltered lagoons, saltmarsh pools, and tidal mudflats.

| Length **9½–10in (24–26cm)** | Wingspan **18–20½in (46–52cm)** | Weight **3–4oz (85–125g)** |
| Social **Pairs/Flocks** | Lifespan **Unknown** | Status **Secure** |

| Order **Charadriiformes** | Family **Scolopacidae** | Species *Limosa haemastica* |

Hudsonian Godwit

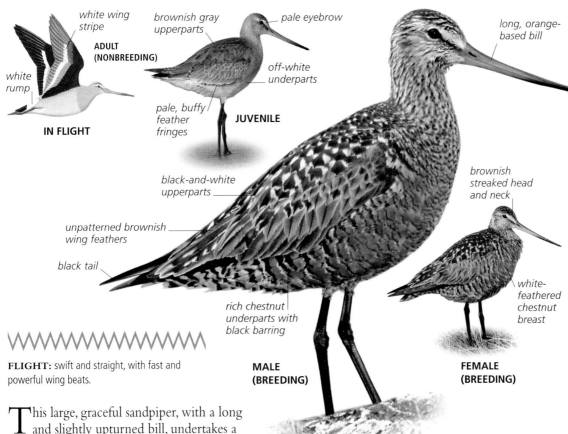

white wing stripe

ADULT (NONBREEDING)

white rump

IN FLIGHT

brownish gray upperparts

pale eyebrow

off-white underparts

pale, buffy feather fringes

JUVENILE

black-and-white upperparts

unpatterned brownish wing feathers

black tail

long, orange-based bill

brownish streaked head and neck

white-feathered chestnut breast

rich chestnut underparts with black barring

MALE (BREEDING)

FEMALE (BREEDING)

FLIGHT: swift and straight, with fast and powerful wing beats.

This large, graceful sandpiper, with a long and slightly upturned bill, undertakes a remarkable annual migration from its tundra breeding grounds in Alaska and Canada all the way to extreme southern South America, a distance probably close to 10,000 miles (16,000km) in one direction, with very few stopovers. The number of breeding birds is unknown, but counts in Tierra del Fuego indicate totals of perhaps 30,000 to 40,000 birds, all found in two areas of tidal mudflats. Between the far North and the far South, North American stops are few, and only in the spring, along a central route mid-continent. Hudsonian Godwits spend six months wintering, two months breeding, and four flying between the two locations.

VOICE Flight call emphatic *peed-wid*; also high *peet* or *kwee*; display song *to-wida to-wida to-wida*, or *to-wit, to-wit, to-wit*.

NESTING Saucer-shaped depression on dry hummock or tussocks under cover; 4 eggs; 1 brood; May–July.

FEEDING Probes in mud for insects, insect grubs, worms, crustaceans and mollusks; also eats plant tubers in fall.

SIMILAR SPECIES

BAR-TAILED GODWIT ↻
see p.218   *more streaks*

shorter legs   *longer bill*

LONG-HAUL BIRD
Hudsonian Godwits only make a few stops on their long flights to and from South America.

OCCURRENCE
Breeds in the High Arctic, in sedge meadows and bogs in scattered tundra; scarce along the Atlantic Coast in fall near coastal freshwater reservoirs; but locally common in flooded rice fields, pastures, and reservoirs in spring. Winters in extreme southern Chile and Argentina.

| Length **14–16in (35–41cm)** | Wingspan **27–31in (68–78cm)** | Weight **7–12oz (200–350g)** |
| Social **Flocks** | Lifespan **Up to 29 years** | Status **Declining** |

| Order **Charadriiformes** | Family **Scolopacidae** | Species *Limosa lapponica* |

Bar-tailed Godwit

black wing patch

long, slightly upturned bill

MALE (SUMMER)

IN FLIGHT

streaked head and upper breast

dull buff underparts

FEMALE (SUMMER)

bill longer than male's

streaked head and breast

off-white underparts

ADULT (WINTER)

dark crown with orange eyebrow

black-and-white spangled upperparts

orange breast

diffused upper flank streaks

orange belly

MALE (SUMMER)

pink-based bill

white underparts

buff breast

JUVENILE

dark gray legs and feet

FLIGHT: direct, powerful, with rapid wing beats.

This large, primarily Eurasian sandpiper is a summer visitor in tundra regions of northern and western Alaska. During its remarkable nonstop migration flight, it covers a huge distance, from western Alaska to Australia and New Zealand, a distance of over 7,000 miles (11,250km). Before this marathon journey, the Bar-tailed Godwit more than doubles its body weight with fat reserves and shrinks its digestive tract as weight-saving measures. Almost 100,000 birds make this journey in September or early October, and rely on favorable tailwinds along the way for a free ride of up to 1,500 miles (2,400km), without which they would not physically be able to complete the trip.

VOICE Flight call a slightly nasal *kirruc, kurruc* or *kirrik*; display song *ta-WEA, ta-WEA, ta-WEA*.

NESTING Depression in tundra, lined with grasses, leaves, moss; 2–4 eggs; 1 brood; May–June.

FEEDING Probes for berries, beetles, crane flies, larvae, marine bivalves, earthworms, marine worms, seeds, crustaceans, and small fish.

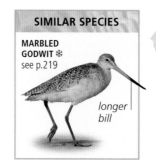

SIMILAR SPECIES

MARBLED GODWIT ✳ see p.219

longer bill

DEFIANT DEFENSE
Standing guard over its eggs, this mate will defend its nest fiercely if threatened.

OCCURRENCE
Breeds in lowland tundra, coastal wetlands, foothills, and uplands of Arctic and sub-Arctic regions. During migration and winter months, found in coastal mudflats between the high-and low-tide marks, estuaries, shorelines, and in the interior wetlands.

| Length **14½–15½in (37–39cm)** | Wingspan **28–32in (72–81cm)** | Weight **8–16oz (225–450g)** |
| Social **Flocks** | Lifespan **Up to 10 years** | Status **Secure** |

Order **Charadriiformes**	Family **Scolopacidae**	Species *Limosa fedoa*

Marbled Godwit

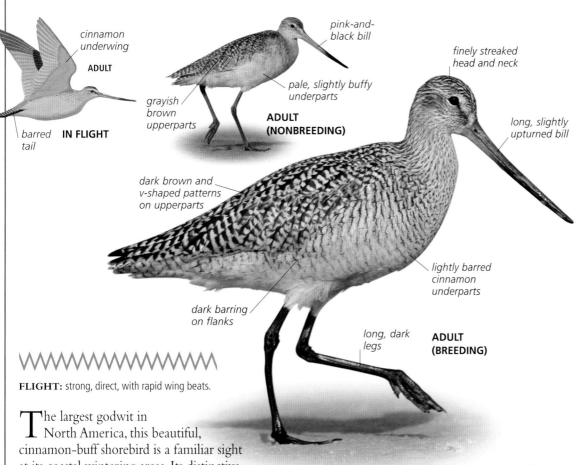

cinnamon underwing
ADULT

barred tail **IN FLIGHT**

pink-and-black bill

grayish brown upperparts

pale, slightly buffy underparts

ADULT (NONBREEDING)

finely streaked head and neck

long, slightly upturned bill

dark brown and v-shaped patterns on upperparts

lightly barred cinnamon underparts

dark barring on flanks

long, dark legs

ADULT (BREEDING)

FLIGHT: strong, direct, with rapid wing beats.

The largest godwit in North America, this beautiful, cinnamon-buff shorebird is a familiar sight at its coastal wintering areas. Its distinctive brown-and-cinammon plumage and the fact that it chooses open habitats, such as mudflats and flooded plains, to feed and roost, make the Marbled Godwit a conspicuous species. A monogamous bird, the Marbled Godwit is also long-lived—the oldest bird recorded was 29 years old.

VOICE Call a nasal *ah-ahk*, and single *ahk*; breeding call, *goddWhit, wik-wik*; other calls include *rack-a, karatica, ratica, ratica.*

NESTING Depression in short grass in Alaska; also nests on vegetation in water; 4 eggs; 1 brood; May–July.

FEEDING Probes mudflats, beaches, short grass for insects, especially grasshoppers; also crustaceans, mollusks, and small fish.

EASILY RECOGNIZED
Its large size and buffy to cinnamon color make this godwit a very distinctive shorebird.

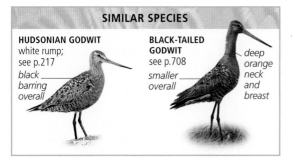

SIMILAR SPECIES

HUDSONIAN GODWIT
white rump;
see p.217
black barring overall

BLACK-TAILED GODWIT
see p.708
smaller overall
deep orange neck and breast

OCCURRENCE
Breeds in the grassy marshes of the Great Plains. During migration and in winter, prefers sandy beaches and coastal mudflats with adjoining meadows or savannas in California and the Gulf of Mexico. Also seen on inland wetlands and lake edges.

Length **16½–19in (42–48cm)**	Wingspan **28–32in (70–81cm)**	Weight **10–16oz (275–450g)**
Social **Winter flocks**	Lifespan **Up to 29 years**	Status **Secure**

| Order **Charadriiformes** | Family **Scolopacidae** | Species **_Numenius phaeopus_** |

Whimbrel

IN FLIGHT

ADULT

long, pointed wings

all-dark rump

coarsely streaked face, neck, and breast

striped crown

long, decurved, mostly black bill; orange base in winter

brownish patterned upperparts

finely streaked neck, breast, and underparts

light brown spotting to upper breast

large, heavy body

brownish tail and rump

ADULT

long, grayish legs

FLIGHT: steady and moderate wing beats; often glides.

This large, conspicuous shorebird is the most widespread of the curlew species, with four subspecies across North America and Eurasia. Its bold head stripes and clearly streaked face, neck, and breast make the species distinctive. The Whimbrel's fairly long, decurved bill allows it to probe into fiddler crab burrows, a favorite food item.

VOICE Characteristic call is a loud, staccato _pi-pi-pi-pi-pi_; flight song a series of haunting melodious whistles, followed by long trill.

NESTING Depression in hummock, mound, grass, sedge, or gravel; 4 eggs; 1 brood; May–August.

FEEDING Probes for crabs, in addition to worms, mollusks, and fish; also eats insects and berries.

LARGE MOUTHFUL
The Whimbrel often rinses muddy crabs in water before swallowing them whole.

UP CLOSE
A close look at the Whimbrel shows this bird's beautiful, fine patterning.

OCCURRENCE
Several populations breed in northern, sub-Arctic, and low-Arctic regions of North America; during migration and in winter, found mostly in coastal marshes, tidal creeks, flats, and mangroves; also at inland Salton Sea, California. Winters along rocky coasts in South America.

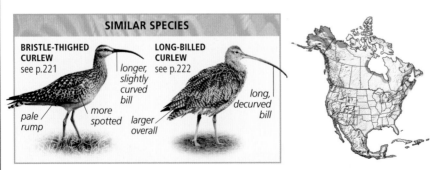

SIMILAR SPECIES

BRISTLE-THIGHED CURLEW see p.221

longer, slightly curved bill

pale rump

more spotted

LONG-BILLED CURLEW see p.222

long, decurved bill

larger overall

| Length **15½–16½in (39–42cm)** | Wingspan **30–35in (76–89cm)** | Weight **11–18oz (300–500g)** |
| Social **Flocks** | Lifespan **Up to 19 years** | Status **Secure** |

| Order **Charadriiformes** | Family **Scolopacidae** | Species **Numenius tahitiensis** |

Bristle-thighed Curlew

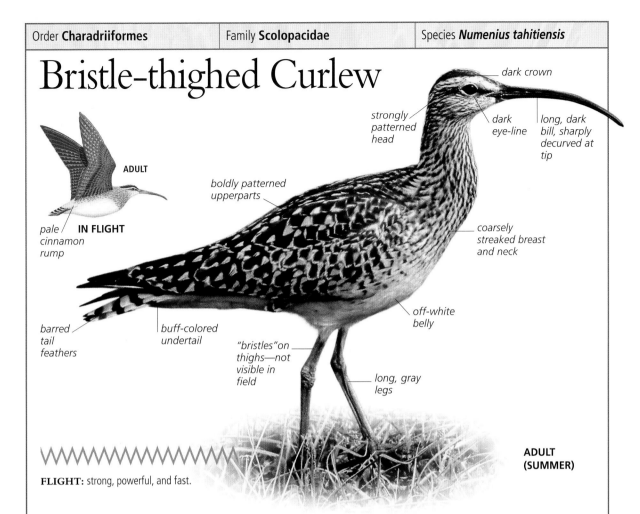

dark crown

strongly
patterned
head

dark
eye-line

long, dark
bill, sharply
decurved at
tip

ADULT

boldly patterned
upperparts

coarsely
streaked breast
and neck

pale
cinnamon
rump

IN FLIGHT

off-white
belly

barred
tail
feathers

buff-colored
undertail

"bristles"on
thighs—not
visible in
field

long, gray
legs

**ADULT
(SUMMER)**

FLIGHT: strong, powerful, and fast.

This rare, localized curlew is one of the world's most unusual shorebirds. It winters exclusively on oceanic islands, becomes flightless during its molting period in wintering grounds, and uses "tools" when foraging, even using rocks to break open albatross eggs. Nesting in just two small areas of western Alaska, the world population of Bristle-thighed Curlews, which could be as few as 3,000 pairs, migrates 2,500–4,000 miles (4,000–6,500km) over open Pacific waters to reach its wintering grounds on South Pacific islands. During winter, the birds will sometimes demonstrate their remarkable technique of picking up pieces of coral with their bills and throwing them at bird eggs in order to break them.

VOICE Flight call a clear whistle *ee-o-weet*; flight song a whistled phrase, *wiwiwi-chyooo*.

NESTING Shallow depression in moss on rolling, hilly tundra; 4 eggs; 1 brood; May–June.

FEEDING Eats insects at breeding grounds; in winter, eats seabird eggs, crustaceans, and snails, uses "tools" for foraging.

SIMILAR SPECIES

WHIMBREL
see p.220

plainer
brown
upperparts

whitish
tail

RESTRICTED RANGE
The Bristle-thighed Curlew has the most restricted breeding range of all North American shorebirds. It is rarely ever seen away from its breeding area.

OCCURRENCE
Breeds in hilly tundra with scattered vegetation in two small locations in western Alaska; winters on remote South Pacific islands, using open habitats, including beaches, lagoons, salt-pans, grassy areas, and coral reefs. Has occasionally been found in California.

| Length **16–17½in (41–45cm)** | Wingspan **30–35in (75–90cm)** | Weight **11–28oz (300–800g)** |
| Social **Flocks** | Lifespan **Up to 22 years** | Status **Vulnerable** |

| Order **Charadriiformes** | Family **Scolopacidae** | Species ***Numenius americanus*** |

Long-billed Curlew

ADULT
bright cinnamon underwing
cinnamon flight feathers
buff underparts
IN FLIGHT

black-and-buff spangled upperparts

very long, curved bill

pale pink base of bill

upper breast, neck, and head finely streaked

bill slightly shorter than adult

head less patterned than adult

ADULT (SUMMER)

pale, bluish gray legs

narrow, pointed wing feathers

JUVENILE

The Long-billed Curlew has the southernmost breeding range and northernmost wintering range of the four North American curlews. It is also one of nine species of birds that are endemic to the grasslands of the Great Plains. Its large size and tame behavior on its wintering grounds in North America add to its mystique. The curvature of its bill is adapted to probe for food in soft mud and sand.

VOICE Flight call a 2-note *cur-LUoo*, often accompanied by rapid *qui-pi-pi-pi-pi*; flight song consists of haunting whistles, trills *werr-EEEer*.

NESTING Shallow depression in sparsely vegetated prairie habitat; 4 eggs; 1 brood; April–May.

FEEDING Picks insects on the surface or probes in soft mud for insects, crustaceans, mollusks, and worms; also eats fish.

FLIGHT: graceful and strong series of flaps alternating with a glide.

APTLY NAMED
The Long-billed Curlew is the longest billed shorebird in North America.

OCCURRENCE
Breeds in prairies, short grass and mixed-grass habitats of the Great Basin and Great Plains. Winters in wet pastures, marshes, beaches, and tidal mudflats primarily of California, Texas, and Mexico, with some stragglers occurring in Florida. Generally not a "shorebird" found along shores.

SIMILAR SPECIES

MARBLED GODWIT
see p.219
straight bill
more rounded body shape
darker, grayish legs

WHIMBREL
smaller; see p.220
streaks on face, neck, and breast
brownish upperparts

| Length **20–26in (51–65cm)** | Wingspan **30–39in (75–100cm)** | Weight **16–28oz (450–800g)** |
| Social **Solitary/Winter flocks** | Lifespan **At least 8 years** | Status **Vulnerable** |

| Order **Charadriiformes** | Family **Scolopacidae** | Species *Bartramia longicauda* |

Upland Sandpiper

ADULT
long tail
long, narrow wings
IN FLIGHT

pale head
speckled breast
JUVENILE

large, dark eye
small, pigeon-like head
short, straight mostly yellow bill
mostly brownish upperparts
buff feather fringes

long tail extends beyond wings
yellow legs
ADULT (BREEDING)

Unlike other sandpipers, this graceful bird spends most of its life away from water in grassy habitats. The Upland Sandpiper's coloration helps it camouflage itself in the grasslands, especially while nesting on the ground. It is well known for landing on fence posts and raising its wings while giving its tremulous, whistling call. The bird is currently listed as endangered in many of its breeding states due to the disappearance of its grassland habitat.

VOICE Flight call a low *qui-pi-pi-pi*; song consists of gurgling notes followed by long, descending "wolf whistle" *whooooleeeeee, wheeelooooo-ooooo*.

NESTING Simple depression in ground among grass clumps; 4 eggs; 1 brood; May.

FEEDING Feeds with head-bobbing motion on adult and larval insects, spiders, worms, centipedes; occasionally seeds.

FLIGHT: strong and swift; rapid, fluttering flight in breeding display.

DRY GROUND WADER
A true grassland species, the Upland Sandpiper is rarely found away from these habitats.

OCCURRENCE
Breeds in native tallgrass or mixed-grass prairies. Airports make up large portion of its breeding habitat in the northeast US. During migration and in winter it prefers shortgrass habitats such as grazed pastures, turf farms, cultivated fields.

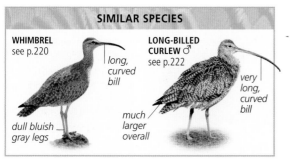

SIMILAR SPECIES

WHIMBREL see p.220
long, curved bill
dull bluish gray legs

LONG-BILLED CURLEW ♂ see p.222
very long, curved bill
much larger overall

WHIMBREL see p.220 · LONG-BILLED CURLEW see p.222

| Length **11–12½in (28–32cm)** | Wingspan **25–27in (64–68cm)** | Weight **4–7oz (150–200g)** |
| Social **Migrant flocks** | Lifespan **Unknown** | Status **Declining** |

| Order **Charadriiformes** | Family **Scolopacidae** | Species *Tringa melanoleuca* |

Greater Yellowlegs

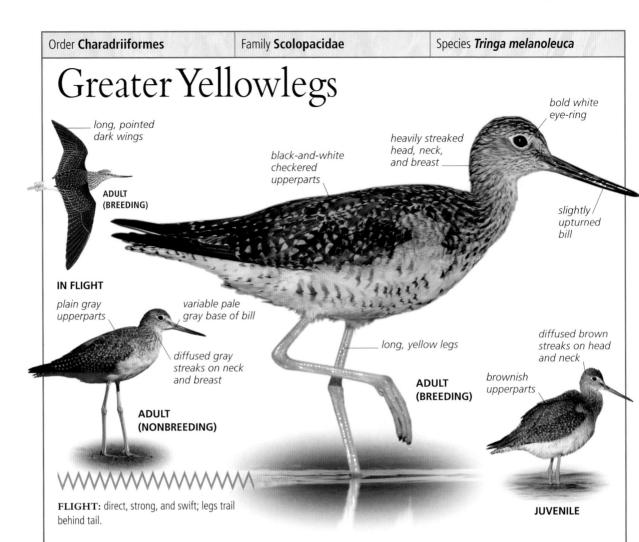

long, pointed dark wings

ADULT (BREEDING)

IN FLIGHT

bold white eye-ring

heavily streaked head, neck, and breast

black-and-white checkered upperparts

slightly upturned bill

plain gray upperparts

variable pale gray base of bill

diffused gray streaks on neck and breast

long, yellow legs

ADULT (BREEDING)

ADULT (NONBREEDING)

diffused brown streaks on head and neck

brownish upperparts

JUVENILE

FLIGHT: direct, strong, and swift; legs trail behind tail.

This fairly large shorebird often runs frantically in many directions while pursuing small prey. It is one of the first northbound spring shorebird migrants, and one of the first to return south in late June or early July. Its plumage, a mixture of brown, black, and white checkered upperparts, and streaked underparts, is more streaked during the breeding season.
VOICE Call a loud, penetrating *tew-tew-tew*; agitated birds make repetitive *keu* notes; song a continuous *too-whee*.
NESTING Simple scrape in moss or peat, usually close to water; 4 eggs; 1 brood; May–June.
FEEDING Picks water surface and mud for small aquatic and terrestrial crustaceans and worms; also eats small fish, frogs, seeds, and berries.

EFFECTIVE METHOD
The Greater Yellowlegs often catches small fish by sweeping its bill sideways through water.

OCCURRENCE
Breeds in openings in northerly forests with bogs and wet meadows, a habitat called muskegs. In migration and winter, uses a wide variety of shallow water habitats, including freshwater and saltwater marshes, reservoirs, and tidal mudflats.

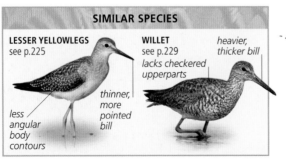

SIMILAR SPECIES

LESSER YELLOWLEGS
see p.225

less angular body contours

thinner, more pointed bill

WILLET
see p.229

lacks checkered upperparts

heavier, thicker bill

| Length **11½–13in (29–33cm)** | Wingspan **28–29in (70–74cm)** | Weight **4–8oz (125–225g)** |
| Social **Solitary/Flocks** | Lifespan **Unknown** | Status **Secure** |

| Order **Charadriiformes** | Family **Scolopacidae** | Species *Tringa flavipes* |

Lesser Yellowlegs

small head

ADULT (BREEDING)

long, pointed, dark wings

IN FLIGHT

gray back with delicate scalloping pattern

dark, slender bill

diffused, pale streaks on breast

white underparts

diffused spots on neck

brownish upperparts

crisp whitish spotting on wings

JUVENILE

black-and-brown upperparts with white spotting

heavily streaked head, neck, and breast

ADULT (BREEDING)

long, yellow-orange legs

ADULT (NONBREEDING)

yellow legs

FLIGHT: straight and fast; with gliding and sideways banking; legs trail behind body.

With its smaller head, thinner bill, and smoother body shape, the Lesser Yellowlegs has a more elegant profile than the Greater Yellowlegs. It prefers smaller, freshwater, or brackish pools to open saltwater habitats, and it walks quickly and methodically while feeding. Although this species is a solitary feeder, it is often seen in small to large loose flocks in migration and winter.

VOICE Low, whistled *tu*, or *tu-tu* call; series of *tu* or *cuw* notes when agitated; display song a *pill-e-wee, pill-e-wee, pill-e-wee*.

NESTING Depression in ground or moss, lined with grass and leaves; 4 eggs; 1 brood; May–June.

FEEDING Eats a wide variety of aquatic and terrestrial insects, mollusks, and crustaceans, especially flies and beetles; also seeds.

BALANCING ACT
The Lesser Yellowlegs uses its long, raised wings for balance while feeding in soft mud.

SIMILAR SPECIES

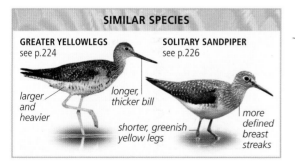

GREATER YELLOWLEGS see p.224

larger and heavier

longer, thicker bill

SOLITARY SANDPIPER see p.226

shorter, greenish yellow legs

more defined breast streaks

OCCURRENCE
Breeds in northerly forest with clearings, and where forest meets tundra. In migration and in winter, uses wide variety of shallow wetlands, including flooded pastures and agricultural fields, swamps, lake and river shores, tidal creeks, and brackish mudflats. Winters from Mexico to Argentina.

| Length **9–10in (23–25cm)** | Wingspan **23–25in (58–64cm)** | Weight **2–3⅜oz (55–95g)** |
| Social **Flocks** | Lifespan **Unknown** | Status **Secure** |

| Order **Charadriiformes** | Family **Scolopacidae** | Species *Tringa solitaria* |

Solitary Sandpiper

long, pointed wings

ADULT (BREEDING)

dark flight feathers

IN FLIGHT

brown-and-white checkered upperparts

brownish streaked crown and head

JUVENILE

dark-and-white checkered upperparts

conspicuous white eye-ring

roundish forehead

straight, dark, tapered bill

ADULT (BREEDING)

finely streaked breast

greenish olive legs

FLIGHT: graceful and strong, with deep, stiff wing beats.

Alexander Wilson described this species in 1813, naming it, quite appropriately, "Solitary." This Sandpiper seldom associates with other shorebirds as it moves nervously along margins of wetlands. When feeding, the Solitary Sandpiper constantly bobs its head like the Spotted Sandpiper. When disturbed, the Solitary Sandpiper often flies directly upward, and when landing, it keeps its wings upright briefly, flashing the white underneath, before carefully folding them to its body.

VOICE Flight and alarm call a high-pitched *weet-weet-weet* or *pit*; display song a *pit-pit-pit-pit*; *kik-kik-kik*.
NESTING Abandoned nests in trees (a unique behavior for a North American shorebird); 4 eggs; 1 brood; May–June.
FEEDING Eats insects, small crustaceans, snails, and small frogs.

LONE RANGER
This sandpiper is often solitary and is found in quiet, sheltered habitats and along river shores.

SIMILAR SPECIES

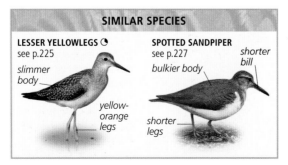

LESSER YELLOWLEGS ◑
see p.225

slimmer body

yellow-orange legs

SPOTTED SANDPIPER
see p.227

bulkier body

shorter bill

shorter legs

OCCURRENCE
Breeds primarily in bogs in northern forests; in winter and during migration, occurs in sheltered pools or muddy areas near forests. Winters from Mexico down to South America, sometimes in tiny pools at high alititude in the Andes; also riverbanks, streams, rain pools, and ditches.

| Length **7½–9in (19–23cm)** | Wingspan **22–23in (56–59cm)** | Weight **1¹⁄₁₆–2¼oz (30–65g)** |
| Social **Solitary/Small flocks** | Lifespan **Unknown** | Status **Secure** |

| Order **Charadriiformes** | Family **Scolopacidae** | Species *Actitis macularia* |

Spotted Sandpiper

darker flight feathers

ADULT (BREEDING)

white wing stripe

IN FLIGHT

thin, white eyestripe

straight, orange bill with dark tip

brownish gray upperparts

dark barring on back

ADULT (BREEDING)

bold, white eye-ring

brownish gray upperparts

buff barring on wings and back

white underparts with bold, dark spots

JUVENILE

orange-yellow legs

plain brownish-gray upperparts

straight, dark bill

white wedge on breast

ADULT (NONBREEDING)

One of only two species of the genus *Actitus*, from the Latin meaning "a coastal inhabitant," this small, short-legged sandpiper is the most widespread shorebird in North America. It is characterized by its quick walking pace, its habit of constantly teetering and bobbing its tail, and its unique style of flying low over water. Spotted Sandpipers have an unusual mating behavior, in which the females take on an aggressive role, defending territories and mating with three or more males per season.

VOICE Call a clear, ringing note *tee-tee-tee-tee*; flight song a monotonous *cree-cree-cree*.

NESTING Nest cup shaded by or scrape built under herbaceous vegetation; 3 eggs; 1–3 broods; May–June.

FEEDING Eats many items, including adult and larval insects, mollusks, small crabs, and worms.

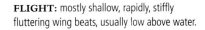

FLIGHT: mostly shallow, rapidly, stiffly fluttering wing beats, usually low above water.

BEHAVIORAL QUIRKS
This sandpiper "teeters," raising and lowering its tail while walking along the water's edge.

OCCURRENCE
Breeds across North America in a wide variety of grassy, brushy, forested habitats near water, but not High Arctic tundra. During migration and in winter found in habitats near freshwater, including lake shores, rivers, streams, beaches, sewage ponds, ditches, seawalls, sometimes estuaries.

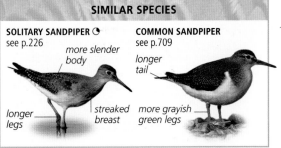

SIMILAR SPECIES

SOLITARY SANDPIPER ☾
see p.226

more slender body

longer legs

streaked breast

COMMON SANDPIPER
see p.709

longer tail

more grayish green legs

| Length **7¼–8in (18.5–20cm)** | Wingspan **15–16in (38–41cm)** | Weight **1⁹⁄₁₆–1¾oz (45–50g)** |
| Social **Small flocks** | Lifespan **Up to 12 years** | Status **Secure** |

Order **Charadriiformes**	Family **Scolopacidae**	Species *Tringa incana*

Wandering Tattler

long, pointed wings

dark gray flight feathers

fairly long, straight bill

ADULT (BREEDING)

IN FLIGHT

grayish upperparts

thin, pale feather edges

white stripe above eye

dark patch between eye and bill

barring on gray breast

IMMATURE (1ST FALL)

dull yellow-green legs

plain gray upperparts

straight, dark bill

yellow legs

fine, dark barring on underparts

ADULT (BREEDING)

While "Wandering" refers to this species' widespread annual migration, "Tattler" highlights the loud nature of its calls and songs, which it makes in its mountainous breeding haunts in the Northwest. There is still much to learn about this mostly solitary species, including its remote wintering range, especially given its small world population numbers (10–25,000 birds). Seen singly or occasionally in small groups on the rocky Pacific Coast shoreline from late summer to spring, this enigmatic species is often overlooked.

VOICE Flight call a ringing, trilled *didididididi*; song a sharp, 3–4 note whistle *treea-treea-treea-tree*.

NESTING Depression on rocks in mountain tundra; 4 eggs; 1 brood; May–July.

FEEDING Picks worms, mollusks, and crustaceans from intertidal habitats; also eats insects, sand fleas, and fish.

FLIGHT: swift and direct, can also be buoyant, may dip, soar, nose-dive, and glide.

DISTINCTIVE WALKING
This bird may be seen walking with a teetering motion on rocky shores away from breeding habitats.

OCCURRENCE
Breeds in shrubby mountainous Alaskan tundra close to water bodies formed as a result of glaciers melting. During migration and winter, uses rocky coastlines, particularly in the area between the high and low tide marks; also reefs, jetties, and piers.

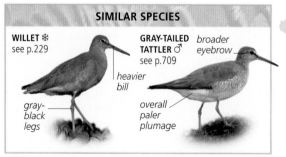

SIMILAR SPECIES

WILLET ❋ see p.229

GRAY-TAILED TATTLER ♂ see p.709

broader eyebrow

heavier bill

gray-black legs

overall paler plumage

Length **10½–12in (27–30cm)**	Wingspan **20–22in (51–56cm)**	Weight **3½–5oz (100–150g)**
Social **Solitary/Pairs**	Lifespan **Unknown**	Status **Secure**

| Order **Charadriiformes** | Family **Scolopacidae** | Species *Tringa semipalmata* |

Willet

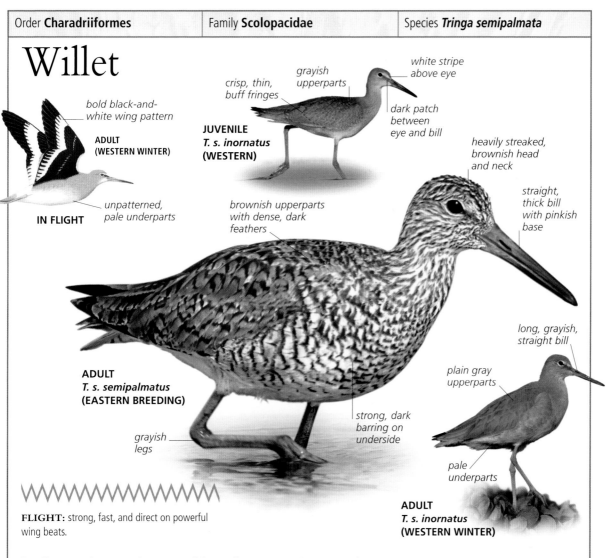

bold black-and-white wing pattern

ADULT (WESTERN WINTER)

unpatterned, pale underparts

IN FLIGHT

crisp, thin, buff fringes

grayish upperparts

white stripe above eye

dark patch between eye and bill

JUVENILE T. s. inornatus (WESTERN)

heavily streaked, brownish head and neck

straight, thick bill with pinkish base

brownish upperparts with dense, dark feathers

ADULT T. s. semipalmatus (EASTERN BREEDING)

grayish legs

strong, dark barring on underside

long, grayish, straight bill

plain gray upperparts

pale underparts

ADULT T. s. inornatus (WESTERN WINTER)

FLIGHT: strong, fast, and direct on powerful wing beats.

The two distinct subspecies of the Willet, Eastern (*T. s. semipalmata*) and Western (*T. s. inornata*), differ in breeding habit, plumage coloration, vocalizations, and migratory habits. The Eastern Willet leaves North America from September to March; whereas the Western Willet winters along southern North American shorelines south to South America.

VOICE Flight call a loud *kyah-yah*; alarm call a sharp, repeated *kleep*; song an urgent, rapid *pill-will-willet*.

NESTING Depression in vegetated dunes, wetlands, prairies, or salt marshes; 4 eggs; 1 brood; April–June.

FEEDING Picks, probes, or swishes for crustaceans such as fiddler and mole crabs, aquatic insects, marine worms, small mollusks, and fish.

EXPOSED PERCH
Willets roost on exposed perches at breeding grounds.

OCCURRENCE
Eastern subspecies breeds in coastal saltwater habitats: salt marshes, barrier islands, beaches, mangroves; winters in similar habitats. Western subspecies breeds near sparsely vegetated prairie wetlands or adjacent semiarid grasslands; winters in coastal regions.

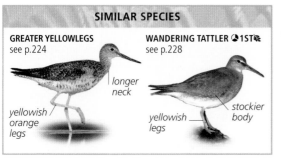

SIMILAR SPECIES

GREATER YELLOWLEGS see p.224

longer neck

yellowish orange legs

WANDERING TATTLER 1ST see p.228

stockier body

yellowish legs

| Length **12½–16½in (32–42cm)** | Wingspan **21½–28½in (54–72cm)** | Weight **7–12oz (200–350g)** |
| Social **Flocks** | Lifespan **Up to 10 years** | Status **Secure** |

Order **Charadriiformes**	Family **Scolopacidae**	Species **Arenaria interpres**

Ruddy Turnstone

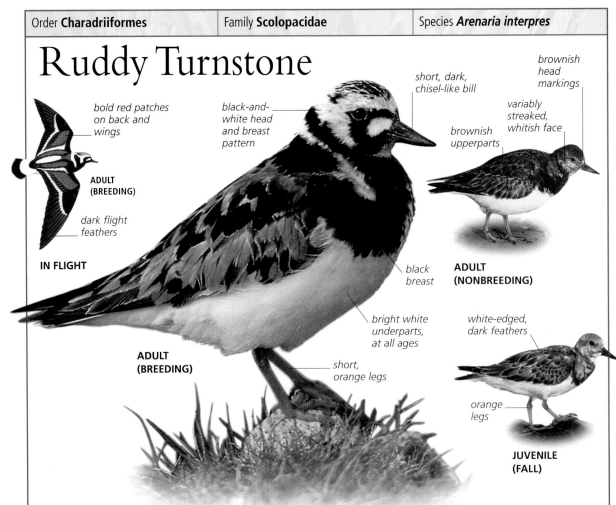

bold red patches on back and wings

ADULT (BREEDING)

dark flight feathers

IN FLIGHT

black-and-white head and breast pattern

short, dark, chisel-like bill

brownish head markings

variably streaked, whitish face

brownish upperparts

black breast

ADULT (NONBREEDING)

ADULT (BREEDING)

bright white underparts, at all ages

short, orange legs

white-edged, dark feathers

orange legs

JUVENILE (FALL)

This tame, medium-sized, and stocky sandpiper with a chisel-shaped bill is a common visitor along the shorelines of North and South America. On its high-Arctic breeding grounds, it is bold and aggressive and is able to drive off predators as large as the Glaucous Gull and Parasitic Jaeger. The Ruddy Turnstone was given its name due to its reddish back color and because of its habit of flipping and overturning items like mollusk shells and pebbles, or digging in the sand and looking for small crustaceans and other marine invertebrates. Two subspecies live in Arctic North America: *A. i. interpres* in northeast Canada and *A. i. morinellas* elsewhere in Canada and Alaska.

VOICE Rapid chatter on breeding ground: *TIT-wooo TIT-woooRITitititititit*; flight call a low, rapid *kut-a-kut*.

NESTING Simple scrape lined with lichens and grasses in dry, open areas; 4 eggs; 1 brood; June.

FEEDING Forages along shoreline for crustaceans, insects, including beetles, spiders; also eats plants.

SIMILAR SPECIES

BLACK TURNSTONE see p.231

darker overall

no rust color in plumage

duller legs

FLIGHT: swift and strong flight, with quick wing beats.

WINTER GATHERINGS
Ruddy Turnstones often congregate in large winter flocks on rocky shorelines.

OCCURRENCE
Breeds in high Arctic: wide-open, barren, and grassy habitats and rocky coasts, usually near water. In winter, on sandy or gravel beaches and rocky shorelines, from northern California to South America, and from northern Massachusetts south along Atlantic and Gulf Coasts.

Length **8–10½in (20–27cm)**	Wingspan **20–22½in (51–57cm)**	Weight **3½–7oz (100–200g)**
Social **Flocks**	Lifespan **Up to 7 years**	Status **Secure**

| Order **Charadriiformes** | Family **Scolopacidae** | Species *Arenaria melanocephala* |

Black Turnstone

dark chocolate-brown head and breast

short, blackish, chisel-like bill

stocky, pointed wings

white patch on back

brownish upperparts, with scattered black feathers

black tail band

ADULT (NONBREEDING)

IN FLIGHT

ADULT (NONBREEDING)

pale edges to some feathers

yellowish legs

white belly

black head and breast with white flecking

white patch

blackish back

darker legs

ADULT (BREEDING)

The Black Turnstone is found along the entire North American Pacific coastline in winter, from Kodiak Island, Alaska, to the Gulf of California. Highly dependent on rocky shorelines, the zebralike but cryptic plumage of this species blends in well, and it becomes almost invisible when it forages or roosts on dark, rocky surfaces. Although the Black Turnstone flips stones and beach litter in search of food, it uses its chisel-like bill to pry loose or crack tougher prey, particularly mussels and barnacles. On its breeding grounds, this species is a vocal and aggressive defender of the nesting community, even physically attacking predators such as jaegars.

VOICE Flight call a *breerp*, often continued as rapid chattering; variety of trills, purrs, and a *tu-whit* call.

NESTING Hollow depression in tundra; 4 eggs; 1 brood; May–June.

FEEDING Eats invertebrates such as mussels, barnacles, limpets, snails, and crabs, also seeds, small bird eggs, and carrion.

FLIGHT: swift and direct, with strong, shallow wing beats.

CRACKING IT
Black Turnstones use their chisel-shaped bills to break open barnacles on rocks.

SIMILAR SPECIES

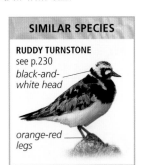

RUDDY TURNSTONE
see p.230
black-and-white head

orange-red legs

OCCURRENCE
Breeds in tundra of western Alaska; also inland along rivers and lakes. It is strictly coastal during migration and winter where it is found in the tidal zone of rocky shorelines, on sand and gravel beaches, mudflats, and rocky jetties of the West Coast, south to Baja, California.

| Length **8½–10½in (22–27cm)** | Wingspan **20–22½in (51–57cm)** | Weight **3⅛–6oz (90–175g)** |
| Social **Flocks** | Lifespan **At least 4 years** | Status **Secure** |

| Order **Charadriiformes** | Family **Scolopacidae** | Species **Aphriza virgata** |

Surfbird

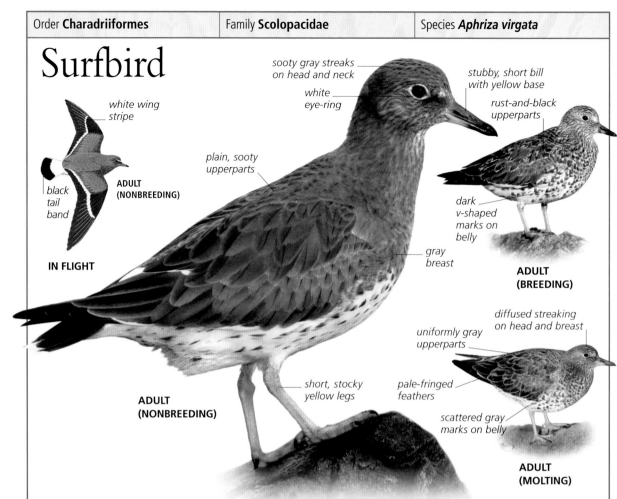

sooty gray streaks on head and neck

white eye-ring

white wing stripe

black tail band

ADULT (NONBREEDING)

IN FLIGHT

plain, sooty upperparts

gray breast

stubby, short bill with yellow base

rust-and-black upperparts

dark v-shaped marks on belly

ADULT (BREEDING)

short, stocky yellow legs

ADULT (NONBREEDING)

diffused streaking on head and breast

uniformly gray upperparts

pale-fringed feathers

scattered gray marks on belly

ADULT (MOLTING)

The chunky, stubby-billed Surfbird has a dual lifestyle—it breeds in the high mountain tundra of Alaska and then migrates to the rocky Pacific coasts of both North and South America. Some individuals migrate as far as southern Chile, a round trip of about 19,000 miles (30,500km) each year. This remarkable wintering range is among the largest of all North American shorebirds. The extent of the rust color on the upperparts of breeding Surfbirds is variable.

VOICE Flight call a soft *whiff-if-if*; feeding flocks soft, chattering *whiks*; display call *kree, kree…ki-drr ki-drr*, and *quoy quoy quoy*.
NESTING Shallow lined depression on vegetated or bare ground; 4 eggs; 1 brood; May–June.
FEEDING Eats mainly insects, especially beetles; also aquatic mollusks and crustaceans, such as mussels and barnacles.

FLIGHT: swift and direct, with strong, powerful wing beats.

COASTAL PROXIMITY
Except when breeding, Surfbirds spend their lives along rocky intertidal shores.

OCCURRENCE
Breeds in low to high-elevation steep, rocky slopes of ridges and mountains; the rest of the year it spends exclusively on rocky Pacific coastlines, typically within 6½ft (2m) of the high-tide line (the narrowest range of all North American shorebirds).

SIMILAR SPECIES

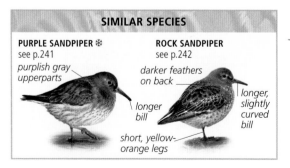

PURPLE SANDPIPER ✳
see p.241

purplish gray upperparts

longer bill

ROCK SANDPIPER
see p.242

darker feathers on back

longer, slightly curved bill

short, yellow-orange legs

| Length **9½–10½in (24–27cm)** | Wingspan **25–27in (63–68cm)** | Weight **4–8oz (125–225g)** |
| Social **Small flocks** | Lifespan **Unknown** | Status **Secure** |

Order **Charadriiformes**	Family **Scolopacidae**	Species *Calidris canutus*

Red Knot

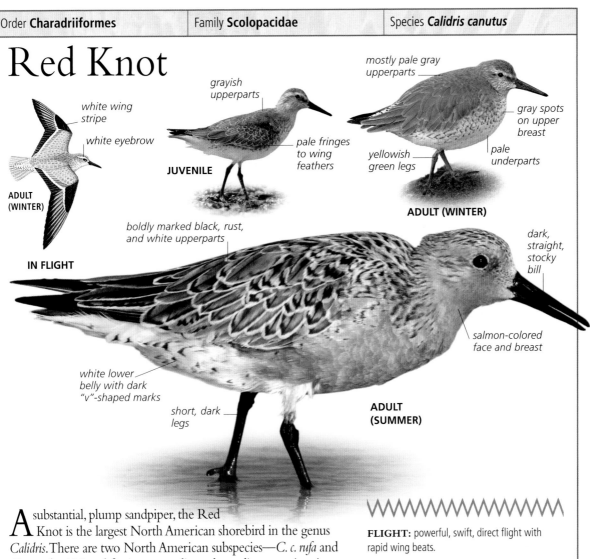

white wing stripe

white eyebrow

ADULT (WINTER)

IN FLIGHT

grayish upperparts

pale fringes to wing feathers

JUVENILE

mostly pale gray upperparts

gray spots on upper breast

yellowish green legs

pale underparts

ADULT (WINTER)

boldly marked black, rust, and white upperparts

dark, straight, stocky bill

salmon-colored face and breast

white lower belly with dark "v"-shaped marks

short, dark legs

ADULT (SUMMER)

A substantial, plump sandpiper, the Red Knot is the largest North American shorebird in the genus *Calidris*. There are two North American subspecies—*C. c. rufa* and *C. c. roselaari*. Noted for its extraordinary long-distance migration, *C. c. rufa* flies about 9,300 miles (15,000km) between its high-Arctic breeding grounds and wintering area in South America, especially in Tierra del Fuego, at the tip of South America. Recent declines have occurred in this population, attributed to over-harvesting of horseshoe crab eggs—its critical food source. With the population of *C. c. rufa* having declined from over 100,000 birds in the mid-1980s to below 15,000 today, the Red Knot is now listed as endangered in New Jersey, and faces possible extinction.

VOICE Flight call a soft *kuEEt* or *kuup*; display song *eerie por-meeee por-meeee*, followed by *por-por por-por*.

NESTING Simple scrape in grassy or barren tundra, often lined; 4 eggs; 1 brood; June.

FEEDING Probes mud or sand for insects, plant material, small mollusks, crustaceans, especially small snails, worms, and other invertebrates.

FLIGHT: powerful, swift, direct flight with rapid wing beats.

STAGING AREAS
Red Knots form colossal flocks during migration and on their wintering grounds.

SIMILAR SPECIES

BLACK-BELLIED PLOVER
see p.206 *large, dark eye*

longer, dark legs

OCCURRENCE
Breeds in flat, barren tundra in high-Arctic islands and peninsulas. Mostly coastal during migration and winter, preferring sandbars, beaches, and tidal flats, where it congregates in huge flocks.

Length **9–10in (23–25cm)**	Wingspan **23–24in (58–61cm)**	Weight **3⅜–8oz (95–225g)**
Social **Large flocks**	Lifespan **Unknown**	Status **Declining**

Order **Charadriiformes**	Family **Scolopacidae**	Species *Calidris alba*

Sanderling

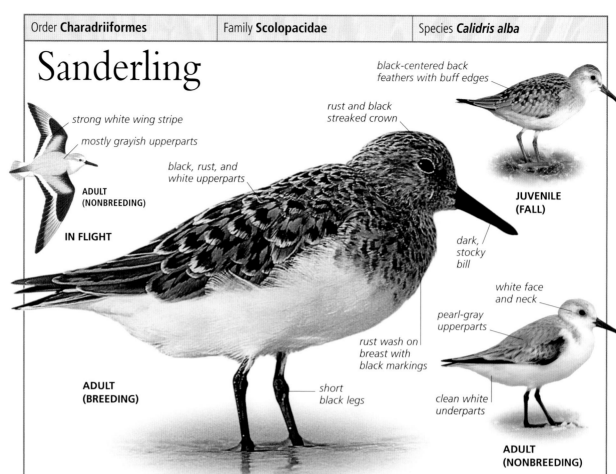

strong white wing stripe

mostly grayish upperparts

ADULT (NONBREEDING)

IN FLIGHT

black-centered back feathers with buff edges

rust and black streaked crown

black, rust, and white upperparts

JUVENILE (FALL)

dark, stocky bill

white face and neck

pearl-gray upperparts

rust wash on breast with black markings

ADULT (BREEDING)

short black legs

clean white underparts

ADULT (NONBREEDING)

The Sanderling is probably the best-known shorebird in the world. It breeds in some of the most remote, high-Arctic habitats, from Greenland to Siberia, but occupies just about every temperate and tropical shoreline in the Americas when not breeding. Indeed, its wintering range spans both American coasts, from Canada to Argentina. Feeding in flocks, it is a common sight in winter on sandy beaches. In many places, though, the bird is declining rapidly, with pollution of the sea and shore, and the disturbance caused by people using beaches for various recreational purposes, the main causes.

VOICE Flight call squeaky *pweet*, threat call *sew-sew-sew*; display song harsh, buzzy notes and chattering *cher-cher-cher*.

NESTING Small, shallow depression on dry, stony ground; 4 eggs; 1–3 broods; June–July.

FEEDING Probes along the surf-line in sand for insects, small crustaceans, small mollusks, and worms.

FLIGHT: rapid, free-form; birds in flocks twisting and turning as if they were one.

CHASING THE WAVES
The sanderling scampers after retreating waves to pick up any small creatures stranded by the sea.

OCCURRENCE
Breeds in barren high-Arctic coastal tundra of northernmost Canada, including the islands, north to Ellesmere Island. During winter months and on migration, found along all North American coastlines, but especially sandy beaches; inland migrants found along lake and river edges.

SIMILAR SPECIES

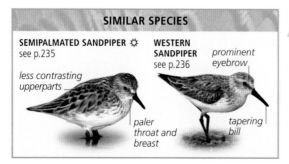

SEMIPALMATED SANDPIPER ☼
see p.235

less contrasting upperparts

paler throat and breast

WESTERN SANDPIPER see p.236

prominent eyebrow

tapering bill

Length **7½–8in (19–20cm)**	Wingspan **16–18in (41–46cm)**	Weight **1⁷⁄₁₆–3½oz (40–100g)**
Social **Small flocks**	Lifespan **Up to 10 years**	Status **Declining**

Order **Charadriiformes**	Family **Scolopacidae**	Species *Calidris pusilla*

Semipalmated Sandpiper

SUMMER

white eyebrow

crisp, pale fringed feathers

short, straight bill with blunt tip

pale grayish black legs

dark-centered back feathers with buff fringes

slightly paler grayish nape

streaked black and rust crown

JUVENILE

pale wing stripe along flight feathers

IN FLIGHT

short, dark bill

wing tips extend to tail tip

ADULT (SUMMER)

lightly streaked breast

This is the most abundant of the so-called "peep" *Calidiris* sandpipers, especially in the eastern US. Flocks of up to 300,000 birds gather on migration staging areas. As a species, though, it can be hard to identify, due to plumage variation between juveniles and breeding adults, and a bill that varies markedly in size and shape from west to east. Semipalmated sandpipers from northeasterly breeding grounds may fly nonstop to their South American wintering grounds in the fall.

VOICE Flight call *chrrk* or higher, sharper *chit*; display song monotonous, droning trill, often repeated for minutes at a time.

NESTING Shallow, lined scrape in short grass habitat; 4 eggs; 1 brood; May–June.

FEEDING Probes mud for aquatic and terrestrial invertebrates such as mollusks, worms, and spiders.

FLIGHT: fast and direct on narrow, pointed, wings; flies in large flocks in winter.

SLEEPING TOGETHER
Semipalmated Sandpipers form large feeding or resting flocks on migration and in winter.

OCCURRENCE
Breeds in Arctic and sub-Arctic tundra habitats near water; in Alaska, on outer coastal plain. Migrants occur in shallow fresh- or saltwater and open muddy areas with little vegetation, such as intertidal flats or lake shores. Winters in Central and South America, south to Brazil and Peru.

SIMILAR SPECIES

SANDERLING
see p.234
more contrasting upperparts

darker breast

WESTERN SANDPIPER ❄
see p.236

puffier head

usually longer legs

usually more pointed bill

LEAST SANDPIPER ❄
see p.237

yellowish legs

smaller overall

Length **5¼–6in (13.5–15cm)**	Wingspan **13½–15in (34–38cm)**	Weight **½–1⁷⁄₁₆oz (14–40g)**
Social **Large flocks**	Lifespan **Up to 12 years**	Status **Secure**

| Order **Charadriiformes** | Family **Scolopacidae** | Species *Calidris mauri* |

Western Sandpiper

reddish-edged upper shoulder feathers

JUVENILE

mostly uniform brown or grayish upperparts

grayish, streaked crown, nape, and face

white tail

ADULT

dusky tail band

narrow, white wing stripe

long, narrow, pointed wing

IN FLIGHT

dark patch between eyes and bill

white belly

partial grayish, streaked collar

ADULT (NONBREEDING)

bright, rusty cap and cheek patch

grayish, streaked nape and neck

medium-length black legs

ADULT (BREEDING)

Despite its restricted breeding range in western Alaska, the Western Sandpiper is one of the most common shorebirds in the Western Hemisphere. During its spring migration, spectacularly large flocks are seen at several Pacific coast locations: at the Copper River Delta in Alaska, over four million Western Sandpipers stop on their way to their tundra breeding grounds to fatten up and refuel for the last hop northward. Many of these migrate over relatively short distances to winter along US coastlines, so the timing of their molt in fall is earlier than that of the similar Semipalmated Sandpiper, which migrates later in winter.
VOICE Flight call loud *chir-eep*; flushed birds make *sirp* call, or *chir-ir-ip*; song *tweer, tweer, tweer*, followed by descending trill.
NESTING Shallow depression on drained Arctic and sub-Arctic tundra; 4 eggs; 1 brood; May–June.
FEEDING Probes mud for insect larvae, crustaceans, and worms.

FLIGHT: direct, rapid flight on narrow, pointed wings; in large flocks.

FORAGING FOR FOOD
The Western Sandpiper feels for hidden prey with the touch-sensitive tip of its bill.

OCCURRENCE
Breeds in wet sedge, grassy habitats with well-drained microhabitats; in migration and in winter, prefers shallow freshwater or saltwater habitats with open muddy or sandy areas and little vegetation, such as intertidal mudflats and lake shores.

SIMILAR SPECIES

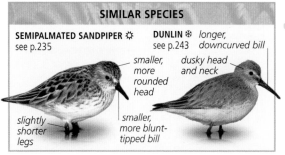

SEMIPALMATED SANDPIPER ☼ see p.235

smaller, more rounded head

slightly shorter legs

DUNLIN ❋ see p.243

longer, downcurved bill

dusky head and neck

smaller, more blunt-tipped bill

| Length **5½–6½in (14–16cm)** | Wingspan **14–15in (35–38cm)** | Weight **¹¹⁄₁₆–1¼oz (19–35g)** |
| Social **Flocks** | Lifespan **Up to 9 years** | Status **Secure** |

| Order **Charadriiformes** | Family **Scolopacidae** | Species *Calidris minutilla* |

Least Sandpiper

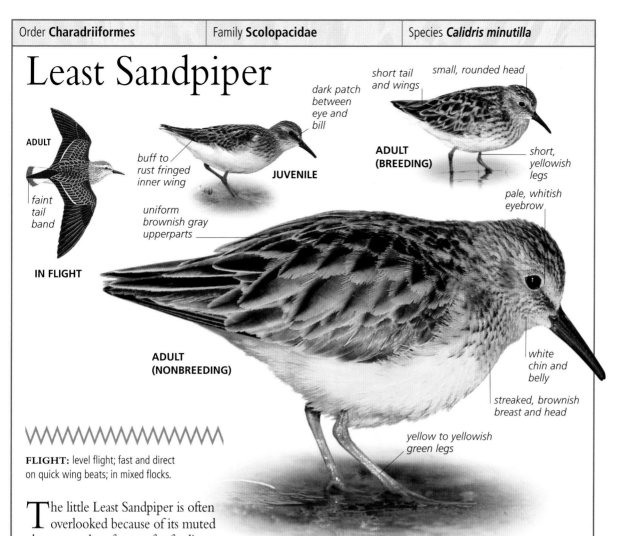

short tail and wings

small, rounded head

dark patch between eye and bill

ADULT (BREEDING)

short, yellowish legs

buff to rust fringed inner wing

JUVENILE

pale, whitish eyebrow

ADULT

faint tail band

uniform brownish gray upperparts

IN FLIGHT

white chin and belly

ADULT (NONBREEDING)

streaked, brownish breast and head

yellow to yellowish green legs

FLIGHT: level flight; fast and direct on quick wing beats; in mixed flocks.

The little Least Sandpiper is often overlooked because of its muted plumage and preference for feeding unobtrusively near vegetative cover. With its brown or brownish gray plumage, the Least Sandpiper virtually disappears in the landscape when feeding crouched down on wet margins of water bodies. The bird is often found in small to medium flocks, members of which typically are nervous when foraging, and frequently burst into flight, only to alight a short way off.
VOICE Its flight call, *kreeeep*, rises in pitch, often repeated two-syllable *kree-eep*; display call trilled *b-reeee, b-reeee, b-reeee.*
NESTING Depression in open, sub-Arctic habitat near water; 4 eggs; 1 brood; May–June.
FEEDING Forages for variety of small terrestrial and aquatic prey, especially sand fleas, mollusks, and flies.

FLOCK IN FLIGHT
The narrow pointed wings of the Least Sandpiper allow it to fly fast and level.

SIMILAR SPECIES

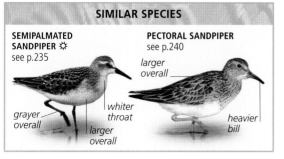

SEMIPALMATED SANDPIPER ☼
see p.235

grayer overall

larger overall

whiter throat

PECTORAL SANDPIPER
see p.240

larger overall

heavier bill

OCCURRENCE
Breeds in wet low-Arctic areas from Alaska and the Yukon to Quebec and Newfoundland. During migration and in winter, uses muddy areas such as lake shores, riverbanks, flooded fields, and tidal flats. Winters from southern North America south to Peru and Brazil.

| Length **4¾in (12cm)** | Wingspan **13–14in (33–35cm)** | Weight **⁵⁄₁₆–1oz (9–27g)** |
| Social **Flocks** | Lifespan **Up to 16 years** | Status **Secure** |

Order **Charadriiformes**	Family **Scolopacidae**	Species *Calidris fuscicollis*

White-rumped Sandpiper

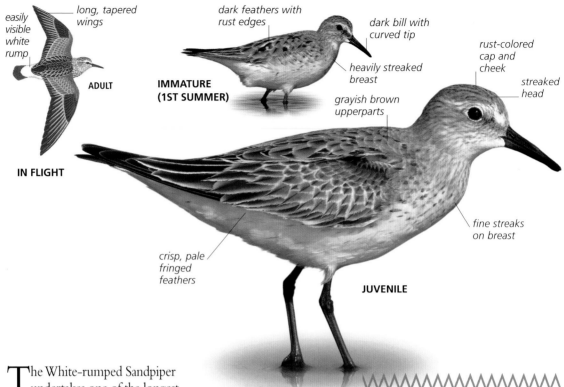

easily visible white rump

long, tapered wings

ADULT

IN FLIGHT

dark feathers with rust edges

IMMATURE (1ST SUMMER)

dark bill with curved tip

heavily streaked breast

grayish brown upperparts

rust-colored cap and cheek

streaked head

fine streaks on breast

crisp, pale fringed feathers

JUVENILE

The White-rumped Sandpiper undertakes one of the longest migrations of any bird in the Western Hemisphere. From its High Arctic breeding grounds in Alaska and Canada, it migrates in several long jumps to extreme southern South America—about 9,000–12,000 miles (14,500–19,300km), twice a year. Almost the entire population migrates through the central US in spring, with several stopovers, which are critical to the success of its journey. While associating with other shorebird species during migration and winter, it can be overlooked in the crowd. Its insect-like call and white rump aid identification.

VOICE Call a very high-pitched, insect-like *tzeet*; flight song an insect-like, high-pitched, rattling buzz, interspersed with grunts.

NESTING Shallow depression in usually wet but well-vegetated tundra; 4 eggs; 1 brood; June.

FEEDING Picks and probes for insects, spiders, earthworms, and marine worms; also some plant matter.

FLIGHT: fast, strong, and direct flight with deep wing beats.

WING POWER
Long narrow wings enable this species to migrate to and from the Arctic and Tiera del Fuego.

OCCURRENCE
Breeds in wet but well-vegetated tundra, usually near ponds, lakes, or streams. In migration and winter, grassy areas: flooded fields, grassy lake margins, rivers, ponds, grassy margins of tidal mudflats, and roadside ditches. On wintering grounds, often associates with Baird's Sandpiper.

SIMILAR SPECIES

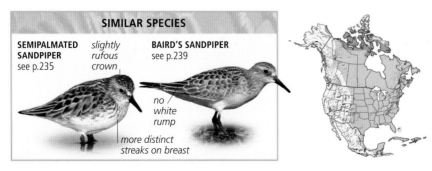

SEMIPALMATED SANDPIPER see p.235

slightly rufous crown

BAIRD'S SANDPIPER see p.239

no white rump

more distinct streaks on breast

Length **6–6¾in (15–17cm)**	Wingspan **16–18in (41–46cm)**	Weight **⅞–1¾oz (25–50g)**
Social **Flocks**	Lifespan **Unknown**	Status **Secure**

| Order **Charadriiformes** | Family **Scolopacidae** | Species *Calidris bairdii* |

Baird's Sandpiper

long, pointed wings

finely streaked head

ADULT

blackish upperparts with silver-edged feathers

dark patch between eye and bill

straight, fine-tipped dark bill

ADULT

clean, white underparts

IN FLIGHT

scalloped look to upperparts

streaked back

indistinct, pale eye-line

wings extend beyond tail

buff, finely streaked upper breast

JUVENILE

blackish legs

FLIGHT: strong and direct, with deep, quick wing beats.

Baird's Sandpiper is less well known than the other North American *Calidris* sandpipers. It was described in 1861, later than its relatives, by the famous North American ornithologist Elliott Cowes, a former surgeon in the US Army, in honor of Spencer Fullerton Baird. Both men were founding members of the AOU (the American Ornithologists' Union). From its High Arctic, tundra habitat, Baird's Sandpiper moves across North America and the Western USA, into South America, and all the way to Tierra del Fuego, a remarkable biannual journey of 6,000–9,000 miles (9,700–14,500km).

VOICE Flight call a low, dry *preep*; song on Arctic breeding ground: *brraay, brray, brray*, followed by *hee-aaw, hee-aaw, hee-aaw*.

NESTING Shallow depression in coastal or upland tundra; 4 eggs; 1 brood; June.

FEEDING Picks and probes for insects and larvae; also spiders and pond crustaceans.

FEEDING IN FLOCKS
Flocks of this sandpiper rush about in search of food in shallow water and muddy areas.

SIMILAR SPECIES

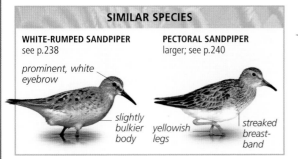

WHITE-RUMPED SANDPIPER
see p.238

prominent, white eyebrow

slightly bulkier body

PECTORAL SANDPIPER
larger; see p.240

yellowish legs

streaked breast-band

OCCURRENCE
Breeds in tundra habitats of High Arctic Alaska and Canada. During migration and winter, inland freshwater habitats: lake and river margins, wet pastures, rice fields; also tidal flats at coastal locations. In winter, common in the high Andes of South America, and sometimes all the way to Tierra del Fuego.

| Length **5¾–7¼in (14.5–18.5cm)** | Wingspan **16–18½in (41–47cm)** | Weight **1¹⁄₁₆–2oz (30–55g)** |
| Social **Flocks** | Lifespan **Unknown** | Status **Secure** |

| Order **Charadriiformes** | Family **Scolopacidae** | Species *Calidris melanotos* |

Pectoral Sandpiper

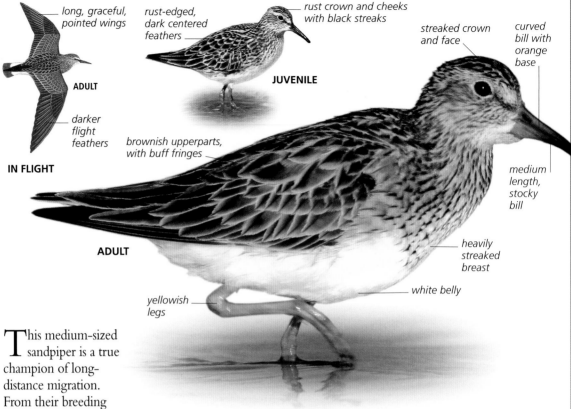

long, graceful, pointed wings

ADULT

darker flight feathers

IN FLIGHT

rust-edged, dark centered feathers

rust crown and cheeks with black streaks

JUVENILE

streaked crown and face

curved bill with orange base

brownish upperparts, with buff fringes

medium length, stocky bill

heavily streaked breast

ADULT

white belly

yellowish legs

This medium-sized sandpiper is a true champion of long-distance migration. From their breeding grounds in the high-Arctic to their wintering grounds on the pampas of southern South America, some birds travel up to 30,000 miles (48,000km) each year. The Pectoral Sandpiper is a promiscuous breeder, with males keeping harems of females in guarded territories. Males mate with as many females as they can attract with a display that includes a deep, booming call, and flights, but take no part in nest duties. Males migrate earlier than females, with both sexes prefer wet, grassy habitats during migration and in winter.

VOICE Flight call low, trilled *chrrk*; display song deep, hollow, hooting: *whoop, whoop, whoop*.

NESTING Shallow depression on ridges in moist to wet sedge tundra; 4 eggs; 1 brood; June.

FEEDING Probes or jabs mud for larvae, and forages for insects and spiders on tundra.

FLIGHT: fast and direct, with rapid, powerful wing beats; flocks zig-zag when flushed.

LONG JOURNEYS
This species migrates long distances to arrive in southern South American for the winter.

SIMILAR SPECIES

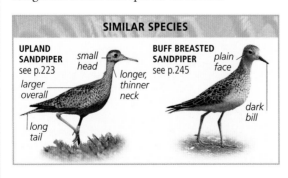

UPLAND SANDPIPER see p.223

small head

longer, thinner neck

larger overall

long tail

BUFF BREASTED SANDPIPER see p.245

plain face

dark bill

OCCURRENCE
In North America, breeds in northern Alaska, northern Yukon, Northern Territories, and some islands of the Canadian Arctic Archipelago, in wet, grassy tundra, especially near coasts. On migration and in winter favors wet pastures, the grassy margins of ponds and lakes, and saltmarshes.

| Length **7½–9in (19–23cm)** | Wingspan **16½–19½in (42–49cm)** | Weight **1¾–4oz (50–125g)** |
| Social **Migrant flocks** | Lifespan **Up to 4½ years** | Status **Secure** |

Order **Charadriiformes**	Family **Scolopacidae**	Species *Calidris maritima*

Purple Sandpiper

brownish gray
upperparts

buff-fringed
feathers

heavily streaked
head

long bill with
drooping tip

dark brownish
wash to breast

short, thick
neck

thin
white
wing
stripe

**ADULT
(NONBREEDING)**

JUVENILE

**ADULT
(BREEDING)**

IN FLIGHT

grayish wash
to head and neck

compact body
shape overall

gray inner
wing feathers

bill yellow at
base, dark at
drooping tip

white belly and
flanks, with thin
streaking

yellow legs
and toes

**ADULT
(NONBREEDING)**

FLIGHT: reluctant; rapid, low,
and direct with full wing beats.

A medium-sized, stocky bird, the Purple Sandpiper shares the most northerly wintering distribution of all North American shorebirds with its close relative, the Rock Sandpiper. The dark plumage and low, squat body of the Purple Sandpiper often disguise its presence on dark tidal rocks, until a crashing wave causes a previously invisibvle flock to explode into flight.

VOICE Flight call low *kweesh*; when disturbed, *eh-eh-eh*; breeding *kwi-ti-ti-ti-bli-bli-bli* followed by *dooree-dooree-dooree*.

NESTING Simple lined scrape in high-alpine-like or barren low-lying Arctic tundra; 4 eggs; 1 brood; June.

FEEDING Feeds on various invertebrates, including crustaceans, snails, insects, spiders, and worms.

SIMILAR SPECIES

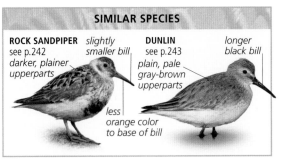

ROCK SANDPIPER
see p.242
*darker, plainer
upperparts*

*slightly
smaller bill*

*less
orange color
to base of bill*

DUNLIN
see p.243
*plain, pale
gray-brown
upperparts*

*longer
black bill*

WINTER EXPOSURE
The Purple Sandpiper winters mainly on exposed rocky shores along the eastern seaboard.

OCCURRENCE
On breeding grounds, found on barren Arctic and alpine tundra habitats in the Canadian Arctic Archipelago. On migration and in winter, predominantly found on rocky, wave-pounded shores on the eastern seaboard.

Length **8–8½in (20–21cm)**	Wingspan **16½–18½in (42–47cm)**	Weight **1¾–3½oz (50–100g)**
Social **Small flocks**	Lifespan **Up to 20 years**	Status **Declining**

| Order **Charadriiformes** | Family **Scolopacidae** | Species *Calidris ptilocnemis* |

Rock Sandpiper

ADULT (NONBREEDING)

IN FLIGHT

bold white wing stripe

dark gray head, neck, and upper breast

greenish yellow on base of bill

slightly darker, uniform gray upperparts

variable gray streaks on breast

ADULT (NONBREEDING)

crisply fringed white, rust, and buff upperparts

JUVENILE

white belly

gray-streaked nape

reddish and black feathers on upperparts

rust and black cheek patch

rounded head

rusty cap

medium-length, dark bill

diffused black streaks on upper breast

white throat

**ADULT
C. p. couesi
(ALEUTIAN; BREEDING)**

variable black belly patch

FLIGHT: strong, swift, and direct flight, often low, with clipped wing beats.

dull, yellowish legs

**ADULT
C. p. ptilocnemis
(PRIBILOF; BREEDING)**

All three regularly occurring North American subspecies of this bird breed in the Bering Sea region. The Rock Sandpiper is the western, and closely related, counterpart of the Purple Sandpiper, and the two species have the most northerly wintering range of any shorebird in North America. Only one subspecies, *C. p. tschuktschorum*, migrates to the Pacific coast of North America.

VOICE Call short squeaking *chreet*, *cheet*, or *cheerrt*; song *di-jerr, di-jerr, di-jerr* and more melodic *quida-se-quida-we-quida*.

NESTING Simple scrape in coastal lowland and mountain tundra; 4 eggs; 1 brood; May–June.

FEEDING Probes for clams and snails in seaweed; in breeding season eats mainly land insects, especially beetles.

CLOSE ENCOUNTER
The Rock Sandpiper is not easily frightened, allowing it to be clearly identified.

OCCURRENCE
Breeds in Arctic lowland coastal heath tundra or mountain tundra. On migration and in winter can be found in a variety of habitats including rocky headlands, gravel beaches, mudflats, and sandflats, but perhaps commonest along rocky shores south to southern California.

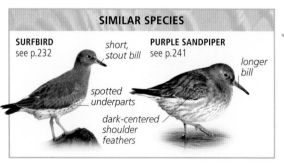

SIMILAR SPECIES

SURFBIRD
see p.232

short, stout bill

PURPLE SANDPIPER
see p.241

longer bill

spotted underparts

dark-centered shoulder feathers

| Length **7¼–9½in (18.5–24cm)** | Wingspan **13–18½in (33–47cm)** | Weight **2½–4oz (70–125g)** |
| Social **Large flocks** | Lifespan **Unknown** | Status **Secure** |

Order **Charadriiformes**	Family **Scolopacidae**	Species *Calidris alpina*

Dunlin

black-and-cream stripes on back

JUVENILE

black streaks on buff underside

JUVENILE

dull gray-brown head and back

white sided rump

thin white wing bar

IN FLIGHT

long, tapered, black bill

dull, gray-streaked breast

ADULT (NONBREEDING)

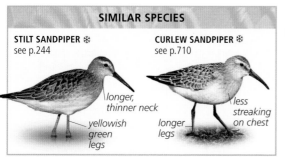

rich chestnut-and-black back

fine dark streaks on whitish breast

large, squarish, black belly patch

ADULT (BREEDING)

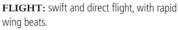

FLIGHT: swift and direct flight, with rapid wing beats.

The Dunlin is one of the most abundant and widespread of North America's shorebirds, but of the ten officially recognized subspecies, only three breed in North America: *C. a. arcticola*, *C. a. pacifica*, and *C. a. hudsonia*. The Dunlin is unmistakable in its striking, red-backed, black-bellied breeding plumage. In winter it sports much drabber colors, but more than makes up for this by gathering in spectacular flocks of many thousands of birds on its favorite, coastal mudflats.

VOICE Call accented trill, *drurr-drurr*, that rises slightly, then descends; flight call *jeeezp*; song *wrraah-wrraah*.

NESTING Simple cup lined with grasses, leaves, and lichens in moist to wet tundra; 4 eggs; 1 brood; June–July.

FEEDING Probes for marine, freshwater, terrestrial invertebrates: clams, worms, insect larvae, crustaceans; also plants and small fish.

OLD RED BACK
The Dunlin was once known as the Red-backed Sandpiper due to its distinct breeding plumage.

OCCURRENCE
Breeds in Arctic and sub-Arctic moist, wet tundra, often near ponds, with drier islands for nest sites. In migration and winter, prefers coastal areas with extensive mudflats and sandy beaches; also feeds in flooded fields and seasonal inland wetlands.

SIMILAR SPECIES

STILT SANDPIPER ❋
see p.244

longer, thinner neck

yellowish green legs

CURLEW SANDPIPER ❋
see p.710

less streaking on chest

longer legs

Length **6½–8½in (16–22cm)**	Wingspan **12½–17½in (32–44cm)**	Weight **1⁹⁄₁₆–2¼oz (45–65g)**
Social **Large flocks**	Lifespan **Up to 24 years**	Status **Declining**

Order **Charadriiformes**	Family **Scolopacidae**	Species *Calidris himantopus*

Stilt Sandpiper

white rump

long, pointed wing

dusky tail band

ADULT (NONBREEDING)

IN FLIGHT

plain grayish brown upperparts

greenish leg

whitish belly

ADULT (NONBREEDING)

whitish eyebrow extends behind eye

scaly look to upperparts

crisp, white-and-rust-fringed upperparts

long, dark, straight bill

slightly diffused gray streaks to breast and neck

rusty cap

rusty cheek patch

long wings and tail

JUVENILE (FALL)

long, yellowish legs

ADULT (BREEDING)

chocolate-brown barring on white underparts

The slender Stilt Sandpiper is uncommon and unique to North America, where it breeds in several small areas of northern tundra. It favors shallow, freshwater habitats, where it feeds in a distinctive style, walking slowly through belly-deep water with its neck outstretched and bill pointed downward. It either picks at the surface, or submerges itself, keeping its tail raised up all the while. During migration it forms dense, rapidly moving flocks that sometimes include other sandpiper species.

VOICE Flight or alarm call low, muffled *chuf*; also *krrit* and sharp *kew-it*; display call *xxree-xxree-xxree-xxree-ee-haw, ee-haw*.

NESTING Shallow depression on raised knolls or ridges in tundra; 4 eggs; 1 brood; June.

FEEDING Eats mostly adult and larval insects; also some snails, mollusks, and seeds.

FLIGHT: fast and direct, with rapid beats of its long wings.

SIMILAR SPECIES

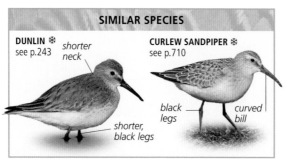

DUNLIN ❄ see p.243

shorter neck

shorter, black legs

CURLEW SANDPIPER ❄ see p.710

black legs

curved bill

PALE BELOW
Wading through shallow water, this Stilt Sandpiper displays its whitish underparts.

OCCURRENCE
Breeds in moist to wet coastal tundra on well-drained, raised knolls or ridges in Alaska, Yukon, and northwestern territories and Hudson Bay. During migration and in winter, prefers freshwater habitats, such as flooded fields, marsh pools, reservoirs, and sheltered lagoons to tidal mudflats.

Length **8–9in (20–23cm)**	Wingspan **17–18½in (43–47cm)**	Weight **1¾–2⅛oz (50–60g)**
Social **Pairs/Flocks**	Lifespan **At least 3 years**	Status **Secure**

Order **Charadriiformes**	Family **Scolopacidae**	Species *Tryngites subruficollis*

Buff-breasted Sandpiper

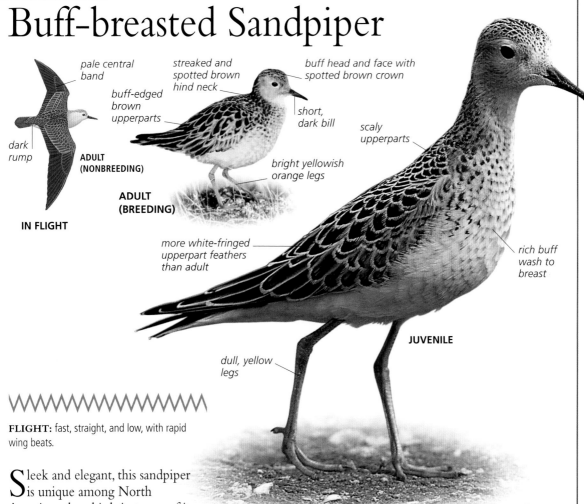

pale central band

streaked and spotted brown hind neck

buff head and face with spotted brown crown

buff-edged brown upperparts

short, dark bill

scaly upperparts

dark rump

ADULT (NONBREEDING)

bright yellowish orange legs

ADULT (BREEDING)

IN FLIGHT

more white-fringed upperpart feathers than adult

rich buff wash to breast

JUVENILE

dull, yellow legs

FLIGHT: fast, straight, and low, with rapid wing beats.

Sleek and elegant, this sandpiper is unique among North American shorebirds in terms of its mating system. On the ground in the Arctic, each male flashes his white underwings to attract females for mating. After mating, the female leaves to perform all nest duties alone, while the male continues to display and mate with other females. Once nesting is over, the Buff-breasted Sandpiper migrates an astonishing 16,000 miles (26,000km) from its breeding grounds to winter in temperate South America.

VOICE Flight call soft, short *gert*, or longer, rising *grriit*.

NESTING Simple depression on well-drained moss or grass hummock; 4 eggs; 1 brood; June.

FEEDING Forages on land for insects, insect larvae, and spiders; occasionally eats seeds.

LANDLUBBER
The Buff-breasted Sandpiper is very much a shorebird of dry land, it doesn't swim or dive.

OCCURRENCE
Breeds in moist to wet, grassy or sedge coastal tundra; during migration, favors short grass areas such as pastures, sod farms, meadows, rice fields, or agricultural areas. Winters in the pampas region of South America in short, wet grass habitats.

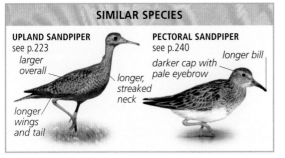

SIMILAR SPECIES

UPLAND SANDPIPER see p.223
larger overall
longer, streaked neck
longer wings and tail

PECTORAL SANDPIPER see p.240
longer bill
darker cap with pale eyebrow

Length **7¼–8in (18.5–20cm)**	Wingspan **17–18½in (43–47cm)**	Weight **1⁷⁄₁₆–3³⁄₈oz (40–95g)**
Social **Large flocks**	Lifespan **Unknown**	Status **Declining**

| Order **Charadriiformes** | Family **Scolopacidae** | Species *Phalaropus tricolor* |

Wilson's Phalarope

reddish brown markings on sides of back

FEMALE (BREEDING)

grayish brown wings

IN FLIGHT

plain gray upperparts

largely white face

white cheek

yellowish legs

white underparts

JUVENILE (MOLTING TO 1ST WINTER)

plain gray-and-black upperparts

paler head markings

MALE

white eyebrow

fairly long, straight bill

gray and reddish brown back

black stripe from bill to nape

rust neck and throat

FEMALE (BREEDING)

A truly American phalarope, Wilson's is the largest of the three phalarope species. Unlike its two relatives, it does not breed in the Arctic, but in the shallow wetlands of western North America, and winters mainly in continental habitats of Bolivia and Argentina instead of in the ocean. This species can be found employing the feeding technique of spinning in shallow water to churn up adult and larval insects, or running in various directions on muddy wetland edges with its head held low to the ground while chasing and picking up insects. This bird is quite tolerant of humans on its breeding grounds, but this attitude changes immediately before migration, as it has gained weight and its movement is sluggish.

VOICE Flight call a low, nasal *werpf*; also higher, repetitive *emf, emf, emf, emf*, or *luk, luk, luk*.

NESTING Simple scrape lined with grass; 4 eggs; 1 brood; May–June.

FEEDING Eats brine shrimp, various insects, and insect larvae.

FLIGHT: fast and direct with quick wing beats.

ODD ONE OUT
Unlike its two essentially oceanic cousins, Wilson's Phalarope is also found in freshwater habitats.

OCCURRENCE
Breeds in shallow, grassy wetlands of interior North America; during migration and winter, occurs in salty lakes and saline ponds as well as inland waterbodies. In winter, tens of thousands can be seen in the middle of Titicaca Lake in Bolivia.

SIMILAR SPECIES

LESSER YELLOWLEGS
see p.225

darker, spotted back

streaked head and neck

RED-NECKED PHALAROPE ❍
see p.247

black cheek patch

shorter bill

| Length **8½–9½in (22–24cm)** | Wingspan **15½–17in (39–43cm)** | Weight **1¼–3oz (35–85g)** |
| Social **Large flocks** | Lifespan **Up to 10 years** | Status **Secure** |

| Order **Charadriiformes** | Family **Scolopacidae** | Species *Phalaropus lobatus* |

Red-necked Phalarope

pointed wings

narrow, white wing stripe

FEMALE (BREEDING)

IN FLIGHT

dark cap and cheek patch

black back with dull, white lines

JUVENILE (WORN PLUMAGE)

dark upperparts with buff stripes

JUVENILE

white throat

dark gray crown and face

needle-like, dark bill

rust neck and upper breast

FEMALE (BREEDING)

dark upperparts with buff or rust feather edges

white underparts with dusky streaked flanks

This aquatic sandpiper spends much of its life in deep ocean waters feeding on tiny plankton; each year, after nine months at sea, it comes to nest in the Arctic. Its Latin name *lobatus* reflects the morphology of its feet, which are webbed (lobed). Both the Red-necked Phalarope and the Red Phalarope are oceanic birds that are found in large flocks or "rafts" far from shore. However, both species are occasionally found swimming inland, in freshwater habitats. Like the other two phalaropes, the Red-necked has a fascinating and unusual reversal of typical sex roles. The female is more brightly colored and slightly larger than the male; she will also pursue the male, compete savagely for him, and will migrate shortly after laying her eggs.

VOICE Flight call a hard, squeaky *pwit* or *kit*; on breeding grounds, vocalizations include variations of flight call notes.
NESTING Depression in wet sedge or grass; 3–4 eggs; 1–2 broods; May–June.
FEEDING Eats plankton; also insects, brine shrimp, and mollusks.

FLIGHT: fast and direct, with rapid wing beats.

SINGLE FATHER
Male phalaropes perform all nesting and rearing duties after the female lays the eggs.

SIMILAR SPECIES

WILSON'S PHALAROPE see p.246

RED PHALAROPE see p.248 slightly thicker bill

paler face

larger overall

larger head and thicker neck

OCCURRENCE
Breeds in wet tundra, on raised ridges, or hummocks, but during migration and in winter, occurs far out to sea and away from shores, although sometimes found in a number of freshwater habitats.

| Length **7–7½in (18–19cm)** | Wingspan **12½–16in (32–41cm)** | Weight **1¹⁄₁₆–1⁹⁄₁₆oz (30–45g)** |
| Social **Flocks** | Lifespan **Unknown** | Status **Secure** |

| Order **Charadriiformes** | Family **Scolopacidae** | Species *Phalaropus fulicarius* |

Red Phalarope

bold white wing bar

FEMALE (BREEDING)

white rump with black line in center, and white edges

broad, pointed wings

IN FLIGHT

dull rust crown with black streaks

buff feather fringes

scalloped upperparts

brick-red underparts; paler than female

MALE (BREEDING)

black cheek patch and nape

mostly gray upperparts

white neck and head

white underparts

ADULT (NONBREEDING)

bold white cheek patch

black crown

stout, yellow bill with black tip

deep brick-red neck, throat, and underparts

tan-fringed feathers on upperparts

FEMALE (BREEDING)

The Red Phalarope spends over ten months each year over deep ocean waters. It also migrates across the ocean, which explains why few birds of this species are ever seen inland. Many Red Phalaropes winter in tropical waters, with concentrations in the Humboldt Current off Peru and Chile, and in the Benguela current off southwestern Africa. During migration over Alaskan waters, flocks of Red Phalaropes feed on crustaceans in the mud plumes that are created by the foraging of gray and bowhead whales on the ocean floor.

VOICE Flight call a sharp *psip* or *pseet*, often in rapid succession; alarm call a drawn-out, 2-syllabled *sweet*.

NESTING Depression on ridge or hummock in coastal sedge; 3–4 eggs; 1 brood; June.

FEEDING Plucks prey from sea; marine crustaceans, fish eggs, larval fish; adult or larval insects.

FLIGHT: direct with rapid wing beats, birds in flocks often synchronize.

DIFFERENT COLOR
In nonbreeding plumage, phalaropes are gray and white.

NO TIES
After breeding, female Red Phalaropes leave the male and play no role in raising young.

OCCURRENCE
Breeds in coastal Arctic tundra; during migration and in winter, occurs in deep ocean waters; small numbers are seen near the shore in coastal California in fall and winter. The Red Phalarope is rare inland.

SIMILAR SPECIES

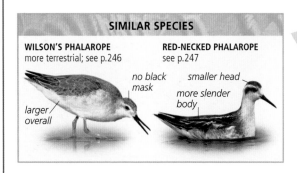

WILSON'S PHALAROPE
more terrestrial; see p.246

RED-NECKED PHALAROPE
see p.247

larger overall

no black mask

smaller head

more slender body

| Length **8–8½in (20–22cm)** | Wingspan **16–17½in (41–44cm)** | Weight **1¼–2⅝oz (35–75g)** |
| Social **Large flocks** | Lifespan **Unknown** | Status **Secure** |

Order **Charadriiformes**	Family **Laridae**	Species *Larus heermanni*

Heermann's Gull

ADULT (BREEDING)

IMMATURE (1ST WINTER)

white trailing edge feathers

all-dark wings

IN FLIGHT

gray underparts

dark brown body

chocolate-brown body

pale base to bill

IMMATURE (1ST WINTER)

red eye-ring

white head

gray body

red bill with black tip

duller bill

mottled head

black legs

ADULT (BREEDING)

ADULT (NONBREEDING)

FLIGHT: flight strong, direct, and a bit heavy.

In North America, the breeding Heermann's Gull is the only gull with a dark gray body and white head. These features, along with its bright red bill, make this gull unmistakable. In nonbreeding plumage, the head is mottled dark and the bill is black-tipped. Juveniles are generally dark brown, with pale patches at the base of their bills. These gulls have black legs in all plumages, unlike any other North American gull, except the Black-legged Kittiwake.

VOICE Nasal *caw* or *cow-awk* call; not very vocal away from breeding grounds.

NESTING Depression lined with dead grass or twigs in sand, small rocks, or grass; usually nests with terns; 1–3 eggs; 1 brood; March–July.

FEEDING Feeds on fish, crustaceans, mollusks, squid, and lizards; in breeding colonies, takes eggs of terns and gulls; also scavenges.

WHITE EDGES
The white trailing edge of the wing and the white tip of the tail are obvious in flight.

OCCURRENCE
A truly western North American gull, it nests on islands off Baja California; over 90 percent of the world's population nests on Isla Raza; occasionally in California; after breeding spreads north along coast to British Columbia, uncommon north of Monterey; rare inland and accidental elsewhere.

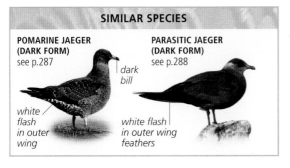

SIMILAR SPECIES

POMARINE JAEGER (DARK FORM)
see p.287

PARASITIC JAEGER (DARK FORM)
see p.288

dark bill

white flash in outer wing

white flash in outer wing feathers

Length **18–21in (46–53cm)**	Wingspan **4¼ft (1.3m)**	Weight **13–23oz (375–650g)**
Social **Colonies**	Lifespan **Up to 13 years**	Status **Secure**

Order **Charadriiformes**	Family **Laridae**	Species *Larus canus*

Mew Gull

IMMATURE (1ST WINTER)

barred rump

brownish gray wings

IN FLIGHT

ADULT (BREEDING)

white spot on wing tip

dark gray back

all-yellow bill

yellow legs

ADULT (BREEDING)

small bill, often with dusky ring

streaks on rounded head

dusky mottling

prominent gray back

IMMATURE (1ST SUMMER)

dull pink legs and feet

small head

black tip to bill

brown belly

IMMATURE (1ST WINTER)

ADULT (NONBREEDING)

yellow to green legs

The Mew Gull was given its English name due to the sound of its call. Its small bill and rounded head give it a rather dove-like profile. It can be confused with the widespread Ring-billed Gull, which it resembles in all plumages. Some taxonomists split the Mew Gull into four species—the European "Common Gull" (*L. c. canus*), the northeast Asian species (*L. c. heinei*), the "Kamchatka Gull" (*L. c. kamtschatschensis*), and the North American "Short-billed Gull" (*L. c. brachyrhynchus*).
VOICE Shrill mewing calls; higher pitched than other gulls.
NESTING Platform of mainly dry vegetation in trees or on ground; 1–5 eggs; 1 brood; May–August.
FEEDING Eats aquatic crustaceans and mollusks, insects, fish, bird eggs, chicks; scavenges trash and steals food from other birds.

FLIGHT: wing beats faster than larger, similar-looking gulls.

PLAIN YELLOW BILL
Although back color and bill size vary in different forms, all adult Mew Gulls have plain yellow bills.

SIMILAR SPECIES

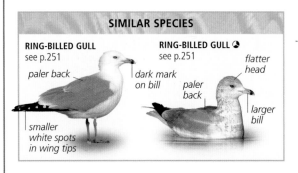

RING-BILLED GULL
see p.251

paler back

dark mark on bill

smaller white spots in wing tips

RING-BILLED GULL ♀
see p.251

flatter head

paler back

larger bill

OCCURRENCE
Breeds in Alaska, except extreme north and northwest Canada south along coast to British Columbia; winters along the Pacific Coast south to Baja California and inland on major river systems. Casual to accidental across the continent to Atlantic Coast.

Length **15–16in (38–41cm)**	Wingspan **3ft 3in–4ft (1–1.2m)**	Weight **13–18oz (375–500g)**
Social **Pairs/Colonies**	Lifespan **Up to 24 years**	Status **Secure**

| Order **Charadriiformes** | Family **Laridae** | Species *Larus delawarensis* |

Ring-billed Gull

white wing spots

ADULT (BREEDING)

black-tipped, pink bill

dark eye

mottled gray back

white neck

IMMATURE (1ST WINTER)

heavily mottled back

mottled underparts

pink legs

JUVENILE

black band on yellow bill

fine streaks on head

IN FLIGHT

gray back

olive-yellow legs

ADULT (NONBREEDING)

pale gray back

IMMATURE (2ND WINTER)

white markings on outer wing feathers

pale eye, with red eye-ring

pale gray back

ADULT (BREEDING)

white underparts

yellowish or greenish legs

FLIGHT: quick, deep wing beats; strong, direct flight, soaring on thermals.

One of the most common birds in North America, the medium-sized Ring-billed Gull is distinguished by the black band on its yellow bill. From the mid-19th to the early 20th century, population numbers crashed due to hunting and habitat loss. Protection allowed the species to make a spectacular comeback, and in the 1990s, there were an estimated 3–4 million birds. It can often be seen scavenging in parking lots at malls.

VOICE Call a slightly nasal and whiny *kee-ow* or *meee-ow*; series of 4−6 *kyaw* notes, higher pitched than Herring Gull.
NESTING Shallow cup of plant matter on ground in open areas, usually near low vegetation; 1–5 eggs; 1 brood; April–August.
FEEDING Picks food while walking; also dips and plunges in water; eats small fish, insects, grain, small rodents; also scavenges.

BLACK WING MARKING
The sharply demarcated black wing tips are prominent from both above and below.

SIMILAR SPECIES

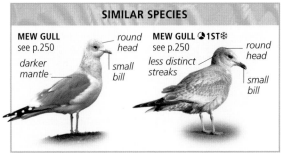

MEW GULL
see p.250

darker mantle

round head

small bill

MEW GULL ♂1ST✳
see p.250

less distinct streaks

round head

small bill

OCCURRENCE
Breeds in freshwater habitats in the interior of the continent. In winter, switches to mostly saltwater areas and along both the East and West Coasts; also along major river systems and reservoirs. Found year-round near the southern Great Lakes.

| Length **17–21½in (43–54cm)** | Wingspan **4–5ft (1.2–1.5m)** | Weight **11–25oz (300–700g)** |
| Social **Colonies** | Lifespan **Up to 32 years** | Status **Secure** |

Order **Charadriiformes**	Family **Laridae**	Species *Larus californicus*

California Gull

black wing tips
with white
terminal spot

**ADULT
(NONBREEDING)**

IN FLIGHT

red eye-
ring

white head
and neck

gray back

black line
and red spot
on bill

brownish mottling
on head
and neck

**IMMATURE
(2ND WINTER)**

white trailing
edge to
feathers

white
underparts

gray
legs

**IMMATURE
(3RD SUMMER)**

black-
tipped
wings

greenish yellow
legs and toes

**ADULT
(BREEDING)**

dark streaks
on nape of
neck

**ADULT
(NONBREEDING)**

Slightly smaller than the Herring Gull, the medium-sized California Gull has a darker back and longer wings. In breeding plumage, it can also be distinguished by the black and red coloration on its bill and its greenish yellow legs. In winter and on young birds, dark streaks are prominent on the nape of the neck. A common interior gull, it is honored by a large, gilded statue in Salt Lake City that commemorates the birds rescue of the settlers' crops from a plague of grasshoppers in 1848.
VOICE Call a repeated *kee-yah, kee-yah, kee-yah*.
NESTING Shallow scrape, lined with feathers, bones, and vegetation, usually on islands; 2–3 eggs; 1 brood; May–July.
FEEDING Forages around lakes for insects, mollusks; hovers over cherry trees dislodging fruits with its wings.

FLIGHT: strong and direct, but somewhat stiff, with deep wing beats.

AGGRESSIVE POSTURE
This California Gull is displaying signs of aggression—possibly against another bird.

OCCURRENCE
Breeds at scattered locations across interior western Canada and the US. Some of the largest colonies are on the highly saline Mono Lake and the Great Salt Lake; winters along the Pacific Coast from British Columbia to Mexico; strays increasingly reported in the East.

SIMILAR SPECIES

**HERRING
GULL** ☼
see p.260

paler
back

pink legs

larger
body

**HERRING
GULL** ❈
see p.260

heavy
streaking
on head

paler back

Length **17½–20in (45–51cm)**	Wingspan **4–4½ft (1.2–1.4m)**	Weight **18–35oz (0.5–1kg)**
Social **Colonies**	Lifespan **Up to 30 years**	Status **Secure**

Order **Charadriiformes**	Family **Laridae**	Species *Larus marinus*

Great Black-backed Gull

red eye-ring

white underwings

white head and neck

yellow bill with red spot

large white spot on wing tips

ADULT (BREEDING)

white head with faint streaks

ADULT (BREEDING)

black upperparts

IN FLIGHT

ADULT (NONBREEDING)

white underparts

white tips to outer feathers

whitish head

black bill

ADULT (BREEDING)

speckled back

pale pink legs and feet

IMMATURE (1ST WINTER)

The largest gull in North America, the Great Black-backed Gull is known for its bullying dispostion. In breeding colonies, it is especially aggressive in the morning and early evening, and after chicks hatch; adults dive at ground predators and strike them with their wings and feet. Other birds benefit from this forceful behavior, for example eiders nesting in Great Black-backed Gull colonies suffer a low rate of nest predation.

VOICE Low, growling flight call, often repeated, low-pitched *heyaa…heyaa…heyaa…heyaa*, similar to the Herring Gull.

NESTING Shallow bowl on ground, lined with vegetation, feathers, and trash; 2–3 eggs; 1 brood; April–August.

FEEDING Scavenges and hunts fish, marine invertebrates, small mammals, eggs, chicks, adult seabirds, and waterfowl.

FLIGHT: heavy lumbering with deep wing beats.

SOLITARY BIRDS
While all gulls are social animals, the Great Black-breasted Gull is the most solitary.

OCCURRENCE
Breeds on natural and artificial islands, barrier beaches, salt marshes, sand dunes; during winter, found along the coast, near shore water, major rivers, landfills, and harbors; in all seasons, often found together with Herring Gulls and Ring-billed Gulls. Also occurs also in Europe.

SIMILAR SPECIES

LESSER BLACK-BACKED GULL ✻
see p.261

smaller body

slate-gray back

yellow legs

SLATY-BACKED GULL
see p.711

gray back

bright pink legs

Length **28–31in (71–79cm)**	Wingspan **5–5¼ft (1.5–1.6m)**	Weight **2¾–4½lb (1.3–2kg)**
Social **Pairs/Colonies**	Lifespan **Up to 27 years**	Status **Secure**

Order **Charadriiformes**	Family **Laridae**	Species *Larus glaucescens*

Glaucous-winged Gull

pale tan overall

IMMATURE (1ST WINTER)

uniform gray-brown plumage

gray mantle

pale base of dark bill

string of white spots in outer feathers

white head

thick bill

light brown tail

IMMATURE (1ST WINTER)

IN FLIGHT

ADULT (BREEDING)

pale gray mantle

IMMATURE (2ND WINTER)

very faint to dark markings on head and neck

pale blue-gray wings

ADULT (BREEDING)

white underparts

pale pink legs

ADULT (NONBREEDING)

The Glaucous-winged Gull, the most common large gull on the north Pacific coast, is found around towns and cities, even nesting on the roofs of shorefront buildings. This species commonly interbreeds with Western Gulls in the southern part of its range, and with Herring and Glaucous Gulls in the north, producing intermediate birds that are more difficult to identify.
VOICE Call a slow, deep *aah-aah-aah*; many types of calls heard around colonies; voice lower pitched than Herring Gull.
NESTING Scrape surrounded by ring of torn up grass or other vegetation; forms colonies usually on small, low islands; 2–3 eggs; 1 brood; May–August.
FEEDING Snatches fish, aquatic mollusks, and crustaceans while walking, swimming, or diving; also scavenges carrion and trash.

FLIGHT: strong and graceful; shallow wing beats; also soars.

PALE WINGS
The Glaucous-winged Gull is named for its delicate, pale, bluish gray wings.

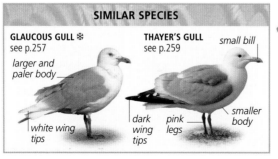

SIMILAR SPECIES

GLAUCOUS GULL ❋
see p.257

larger and paler body

white wing tips

THAYER'S GULL
see p.259

small bill

dark wing tips

pink legs

smaller body

OCCURRENCE
Breeds along coast of northwest Oregon northward to the Bering Sea coast of Alaska; winters within its breeding range and southward, to Gulf of California; primarily a coastal and offshore gull (farther offshore in winter); it is very rare inland and accidental to central US.

Length **23–24in (58–62cm)**	Wingspan **4½–5ft (1.4–1.5m)**	Weight **2–2¾lb (0.9–1.3kg)**
Social **Colonies**	Lifespan **Up to 32 years**	Status **Secure**

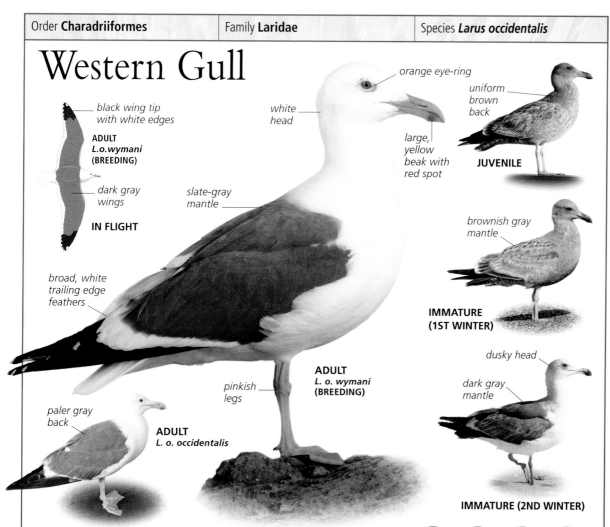

| Order **Charadriiformes** | Family **Laridae** | Species *Larus occidentalis* |

Western Gull

black wing tip with white edges

ADULT
L.o.wymani
(BREEDING)

dark gray wings

IN FLIGHT

white head

orange eye-ring

large, yellow beak with red spot

uniform brown back

JUVENILE

slate-gray mantle

brownish gray mantle

**IMMATURE
(1ST WINTER)**

broad, white trailing edge feathers

dusky head

dark gray mantle

pinkish legs

**ADULT
L. o. wymani
(BREEDING)**

paler gray back

**ADULT
L. o. occidentalis**

IMMATURE (2ND WINTER)

The Western Gull is the only dark-backed gull found regularly within its normal range and habitat. However, identification is complicated due to two subspecies: the paler *occidentalis* in the north, and the darker *wymani* in the south. Western Gulls interbreed with Glaucous-winged Gulls, producing confusing hybrids. The total population of these gulls is small, and the small number of nesting colonies makes conservation a concern.

VOICE Shrill, repeated *heyaa…heyaa…heyaa* similar to Herring Gull, but lower in pitch, harsher; very vocal at breeding sites.

NESTING Scrape filled with vegetation, usually next to bush or rock; 3–4 eggs; 1 brood; April–August.

FEEDING Eats crabs, squid, insects, fish, bird eggs, and chicks; also eats sea lion pups; scavenges.

FLIGHT: strong, slow with heavy wing beats; also commonly soars.

DARK UNDERWINGS
The undersides of the outer wing feathers are much darker in this bird than in similar species.

SIMILAR SPECIES

YELLOW-FOOTED GULL
see p.256

darker back

yellow legs

SLATY-BACKED GULL
see p.711

thinner bill

OCCURRENCE
Nests on offshore islands along West Coast; about one third of the total population breeds on Southeast Farallon Island, west of San Francisco; nonbreeders and wintering birds occur along the coast and in major bays and estuaries southward to Baja California; very rare inland or far offshore.

| Length **22–26in (56–66cm)** | Wingspan **4¼–4½ft (1.3–1.4m)** | Weight **1¾–2¾lb (0.8–1.2kg)** |
| Social **Colonies** | Lifespan **Up to 28 years** | Status **Secure** |

| Order **Charadriiformes** | Family **Laridae** | Species *Larus livens* |

Yellow-footed Gull

black outer wings

ADULT

white spot on wing tips

IN FLIGHT

pinkish bill with black tip

IMMATURE (2ND WINTER)

brownish wing feathers

white head

large yellow bill

large red spot

blackish bill

brown wing feathers

IMMATURE (1ST WINTER)

slate-gray back

plain white underparts

streaky face

dark bill with pink base

IMMATURE (1ST SUMMER)

long wings

ADULT

pale to deep yellow legs

FLIGHT: strong glider and flier, with relatively slow and heavy wing beats.

Once upon a time, considered a subspecies of the Western Gull, the Yellow-footed Gull was first described as a species in 1919. It is now thought to be related to the Kelp Gull of South America. Unlike the Western Gull, it has long, yellow legs and takes three years to reach adult plumage rather than four. If its leg color is not visible, it is hard to distinguish it from the Western Gull. The only place outside of the Sea of Corez, Mexico, to see the Yellow-footed Gull is the Salton Sea in southern California, where it first appeared on August 22, 1965.

VOICE Call a *keow*, repeated in series, speeding up slightly towards the end; lower pitched, more nasal, and slower than the Western Gull's voice.

NESTING Scrape on the ground made with sargassum seaweed, and other material, within 100ft (30m) of high-tide line; 1–5 eggs; 1 brood; March–June.

FEEDING Forages alone or in small groups for fish, crustaceans, mollusks, eggs, and carrion; territorial around scavenged carcasses.

BRIGHT LEGS
The bright yellow legs that give this bird its name are particularly obvious in bright sunshine.

OCCURRENCE
Breeding birds endemic to the Sea of Cortez, Mexico, on offshore islands and rocks close to high-tide line; in the US, nonbreeders found at California's Salton Sea, mainly June–September, where it frequents rocky areas and beaches with barnacles.

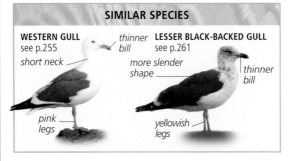

SIMILAR SPECIES

WESTERN GULL
see p.255
short neck
pink legs

thinner bill

LESSER BLACK-BACKED GULL
see p.261
more slender shape
thinner bill
yellowish legs

| Length **21½–28in (55–72cm)** | Wingspan **5ft (1.5m)** | Weight **2–3¼lb (0.9–1.5kg)** |
| Social **Colonies** | Lifespan **Unknown** | Status **Secure** |

| Order **Charadriiformes** | Family **Laridae** | Species **_Larus hyperboreus_** |

Glaucous Gull

ADULT (WINTER)

streaking on head

mottled white plumage

IMMATURE (1ST WINTER, FADED)

IN FLIGHT

light brownish plumage

white wing tips

IMMATURE (1ST WINTER)

mottled, pale brown back

IMMATURE (1ST WINTER)

pale brown underparts

pale gray upperparts

yellow bill with distinct red spot

white head

white underparts

pink legs

ADULT (SUMMER)

FLIGHT: heavy, slow, and powerful; often glides and soars.

The Glaucous Gull is the largest of the "white-winged" gulls. Its large, pale shape is immediately apparent in a group of gulls as it appears like a large white spectre among its smaller, darker cousins. In the southern part of its US winter range, pale immatures are encountered more frequently than adults. In the Arctic, successful pairs of Glaucous Gulls maintain the bonds with their mates for years, often returning to the same nest site year after year.

VOICE Similar to that of the Herring Gull, but slightly harsher and deeper; hoarse, nasal *ku-ku-ku*.

NESTING Shallow cup lined with vegetation on ground, at edge of tundra pools, on cliffs and ledges and islands; 1–3 eggs; 1 brood; May–July.

FEEDING Eats fish, crustaceans, mollusks; also eggs and chicks of waterfowl, small seabirds, and small mammals.

NORTHERN VISITOR
This large gull is an uncommon visitor over most of North America during the winter months.

SIMILAR SPECIES

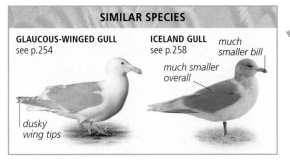

GLAUCOUS-WINGED GULL
see p.254

dusky wing tips

ICELAND GULL
see p.258

much smaller bill

much smaller overall

OCCURRENCE
Breeds along the high-Arctic coast, rarely inland; winters along northern Atlantic and Pacific coasts and the Great Lakes; frequently seen at Niagara Falls. Strays, usually immatures, can occur inland anywhere where concentrations of gulls are found, such as trash sites dumps.

| Length **26–30in (65–75cm)** | Wingspan **5–6ft (1.5–1.8m)** | Weight **2¾–6lb (1.2–2.7kg)** |
| Social **Colonies** | Lifespan **Up to 21 years** | Status **Secure** |

Order **Charadriiformes**	Family **Laridae**	Species *Larus glaucoides*

Iceland Gull

gray wing tips

pale brown plumage

ADULT (WINTER)

IMMATURE (1ST WINTER)

IN FLIGHT

pale or gray wing tip

short, pale yellow bill with red spot

markedly streaked head

gray back

white belly

pink legs

brown barred plumage

blackish bill

head mostly white

pale, barred underparts

IMMATURE (1ST WINTER)

IMMATURE (2ND WINTER)

ADULT (WINTER)

The Iceland Gull is the smallest "white-winged" gull. Similar to the larger Glaucous Gull, it is a common sight in winter, and immatures are seen more often than adults. North American breeding birds have gray wing tips, and have been considered a separate species called the "Kumlien's Gull." The subspecies *L. g. glaucoides* is distinguishable as it possesses white wing tips; it breeds in Greenland, and winters in Greenland and Iceland, but a few birds travel to the western North Atlantic.
VOICE Call a *clew, clew, clew* or *kak-kak-kak*; vocal around breeding colonies; virtually silent on wintering grounds.
NESTING Loose nest of moss, vegetation, and feathers, usually on narrow rock ledge; 2–3 eggs; 1 brood; May–August.
FEEDING Grabs small fish from surface while in flight; also eats small fish, crustaceans, mollusks, carrion, and garbage.

FLIGHT: light and graceful; wings long in proportion to body.

WING TIP COLOR VARIATION
Some adult Iceland Gulls found in North America have wing tips that are almost pure white.

SIMILAR SPECIES

GLAUCOUS GULL
see p.257

much larger body

white wing tips

THAYER'S GULL
see p.259

larger bill

dark eye

slightly larger and darker overall

OCCURRENCE
Uncommon far from sea coast; usually nests on ledges on vertical cliffs overlooking the sea; winters where it finds regions of open water in frozen seas and along coast. A few wander to open water areas in the interior, such as the Great Lakes and major rivers; Niagara Falls.

Length **20½–23½in (52–60cm)**	Wingspan **4½–5ft (1.4–1.5m)**	Weight **21–39oz (600–1,100g)**
Social **Colonies**	Lifespan **Up to 33 years**	Status **Secure**

Order **Charadriiformes**	Family **Laridae**	Species *Larus thayeri*

Thayer's Gull

pale patch on outer flight feathers

IMMATURE (1ST WINTER)

IN FLIGHT

medium-gray upperparts

reddish purple eye-ring

gray to mottled brown eyes

white head and neck

small, yellow bill with red spot

white underparts

ADULT (SUMMER)

variable gray on head and neck forms a hood sometimes

dark pink legs

uniformly scaly appearance on upperparts

ADULT (WINTER)

black wing tips

IMMATURE (1ST WINTER)

The classification of Thayer's Gull as a species is still slightly puzzling. After it was described in 1915, it was classified as a subspecies of the Herring Gull, but in the 1970s, it was considered a full species. Although it is still usually treated as a separate species, many authorities now consider the Thayer's Gull to be a subspecies of the Iceland Gull. When standing with the Herring and Iceland Gulls, this bird is difficult to identify. Positive identification is complicated further by the existence of hybrid gulls of various parentages.

VOICE Mewing squeals, like herring gulls familiar *kee-yow*; calls more on breeding grounds than on wintering grounds.

NESTING On cliff ledges; 2–3 eggs; 1 brood; May–August.

FEEDING Picks fish, mollusks, and crustaceans from the water's surface; swallows food while in flight.

FLIGHT: steady and direct, but wing beat varies greatly with wind conditions.

TWO-TONED WINGS
Immature birds have two-toned wings, with a prominent pale patch on the outer flight feathers.

SIMILAR SPECIES

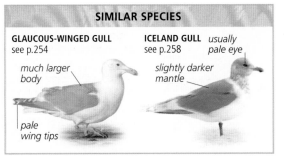

GLAUCOUS-WINGED GULL see p.254

much larger body

pale wing tips

ICELAND GULL see p.258 *usually pale eye*

slightly darker mantle

OCCURRENCE
Nests on cliff ledges of fiords facing the Canadian High Arctic. Winter movements not fully understood; occurs mainly along the Pacific Coast, but is also found across the interior and along the East Coast.

Length **22½–25in (57–64cm)**	Wingspan **4¼–5ft (1.3–1.5m)**	Weight **25–39oz (700–1,100g)**
Social **Colonies**	Lifespan **Unknown**	Status **Secure (p)**

Order **Charadriiformes**	Family **Laridae**	Species *Larus argentatus*

Herring Gull

white spots near wing tips

ADULT (BREEDING)

light head

barred gray-brown overall

gray wings

IMMATURE (2ND WINTER)

mottled brown back

barred brown body

white head and neck

IMMATURE (1ST WINTER)

large, yellow bill with red spot

gray back

streaked head

ADULT (NONBREEDING)

black outer wing feathers

IN FLIGHT

white underparts

pink legs

ADULT (BREEDING)

streaked head and neck

ADULT (NONBREEDING)

The Herring Gull is the archetypal, large "white-headed" gull that nearly all other gulls are compared with. When people mention "seagulls" they usually refer to the Herring Gull. The term "seagull" is actually misleading because the Herring Gull, like most other gulls, does not commonly go far out to sea—it is a bird of near-shore waters, coasts, lakes, rivers, and inland waterways. Now very common, the Herring Gull was nearly wiped out in the late 19th and early 20th century by plumage hunters and egg collectors.

VOICE Typical call a high-pitched, shrill, repeated *heyaa… heyaa…heyaa…heyaa*; vocal throughout the year.

NESTING Shallow bowl on ground lined with feathers, vegetation, detritus; 2–4 eggs; 1 brood; April–August.

FEEDING Eats fish, crustaceans, mollusks, worms; eggs and chicks of other seabirds; scavenges carrion, garbage; steals from other birds.

FLIGHT: steady, regular, slow wing beats; also commonly soars and glides.

MASTER SCAVENGER
A common sight near any water body, the Herring Gull is an expert scavenger of carrion and trash.

OCCURRENCE
Found throughout North America along coasts and inland on lakes, rivers, and reservoirs; also frequents garbage dumps. Breeds in northeastern US and across Canada. Migrates southward across much of the continent to winter in coastal areas and along lakes and major rivers.

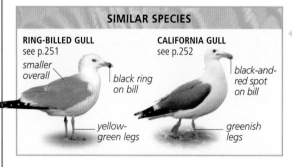

SIMILAR SPECIES

RING-BILLED GULL see p.251
smaller overall

black ring on bill

yellow-green legs

CALIFORNIA GULL see p.252

black-and-red spot on bill

greenish legs

Length **22–26in (56–66cm)**	Wingspan **4–5ft (1.2–1.5m)**	Weight **28–42oz (800–1200g)**
Social **Colonies**	Lifespan **At least 35 years**	Status **Secure**

Order **Charadriiformes**	Family **Laridae**	Species *Larus fuscus*

Lesser Black-backed Gull

black wing tips with white spot

ADULT (NONBREEDING)

IN FLIGHT

mottled, dark brown body

black bill

IMMATURE (1ST WINTER)

yellow eye

streaked head and neck

slate-gray back

back turns dark gray

IMMATURE (2ND WINTER)

white head

white underparts

yellow bill with red spot

dull yellow legs

ADULT (NONBREEDNG)

bright yellow legs

ADULT (BREEDING)

This European visitor was first discovered in North America on the New Jersey coast on September 9, 1934 and in New York City a few months later. In recent decades, it has become an annual winter visitor. Nearly all the Lesser Black-backed Gulls found in North America are of the Icelandic and western European subspecies *L. f. graellsii*, with a slate-gray back. Another European subspecies, with a much darker back, has rarely been reported in North America, but it is probably only a matter of time before it nests here.

VOICE A *kyow…yow…yow…yow* call, similar to that of Herring Gull; also a deeper and throaty, repeated *gah-gah-gah-gah*.

NESTING Scrape on ground lined with dry lichens, dry grass, and feathers; 3 eggs; 1 brood; April–September.

FEEDING Eats mollusks, crustaceans, and various insects; also scavenges carrion and garbage.

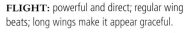

FLIGHT: powerful and direct; regular wing beats; long wings make it appear graceful.

OCCURRENCE
Regular and increasingly common winter visitor to eastern North America, usually along the coast, but also in the interior; wherever gulls commonly concentrate such as harbors, lakeshores, landfills, and around fishing boats.

SIMILAR SPECIES

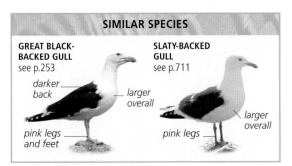

GREAT BLACK-BACKED GULL
see p.253

darker back

larger overall

pink legs and feet

SLATY-BACKED GULL
see p.711

larger overall

pink legs

EXCITING FIND
In recent years, gull enthusiasts and birdwatchers have found these birds visiting from Europe.

Length **20½–26in (52–67cm)**	Wingspan **4¼–5ft (1.3–1.5m)**	Weight **22–35oz (625–1000g)**
Social **Colonies**	Lifespan **Up to 26 years**	Status **Secure**

| Order **Charadriiformes** | Family **Laridae** | Species *Larus ridibundus* |

Black-headed Gull

white flash on outer wings

black trailing edge of wing

ADULT (NONBREEDING)

IN FLIGHT

black-tipped, red bill

brownish "crown-collar"

dark "ear" spot

gray back

reddish bill

white underparts

bright red legs

ADULT (NONBREEDING)

brown spots on feathers

black-tipped orange bill

white nape

very pale gray back

chocolate brown hood

dark red bill

black tail tip

dark red legs

IMMATURE (1ST WINTER)

ADULT (BREEDING)

An abundant breeder in Eurasia, the Black-headed Gull colonized North America in the 20th century. It was first seen in the 1920s, not long after nests were discovered in Iceland in 1911. It has become common in Newfoundland after being found nesting there in 1977, and has nested as far south as Cape Cod. However, it has not spread far to the West and remains an infrequent visitor or stray over most of the continent.

VOICE Loud laughing (its French name is Laughing Gull) or a chattering *kek kek keeaar*; very vocal at breeding sites.

NESTING Loose mass of vegetation, on ground or on top of other vegetation; may be a large mound in wet areas; 2–3 eggs; 1 brood; April–August.

FEEDING Picks insects, small crustaceans, and mollusks off water's surface while flying or hovering; eats some vegetation; also forages in plowed farm fields; raids garbage dumps.

FLIGHT: graceful, light, and buoyant; agile.

BEAUTIFUL BREEDING PLUMAGE
Most American birders never see the elegant summer plumage of the Black-headed Gull.

SIMILAR SPECIES

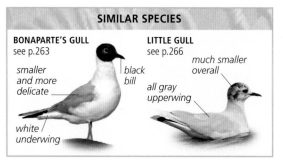

BONAPARTE'S GULL
see p.263

smaller and more delicate

white underwing

black bill

LITTLE GULL
see p.266

much smaller overall

all gray upperwing

OCCURRENCE
Rare breeder in northeastern North America; singles or a few individuals may be found along the coast, often with Bonaparte's Gulls, at harbors, inlets, bays, rivers, lakes, sewage outlets, or garbage dumps; strays may occur anywhere. One of the most common European gulls.

| Length **13½–14½in (34–37cm)** | Wingspan **3ft 3in–3½ft (1–1.1m)** | Weight **7–14oz (200–400g)** |
| Social **Colonies** | Lifespan **Up to 18 years** | Status **Localized** |

Order **Charadriiformes**	Family **Laridae**	Species *Larus philadelphia*

Bonaparte's Gull

black wing tips

ADULT (NONBREEDING)

white flash on outer wings

IN FLIGHT

white head

blackish "ear" spot

gray neck

ADULT (NONBREEDING)

black hood

short bill

gray back and wings

gray back

brown patches on wing

IMMATURE (1ST WINTER)

white wedge on wing

orange-red legs

white underparts

ADULT (BREEDING)

Lighter and more delicate than the other North American gulls, Bonaparte's Gull is commonly distinguished in winter by the blackish smudge behind each eye and the large, white wing patch. It is one of America's most abundant gulls. In 1989, for example, more than 120,000 were estimated to have occured in one harbor near Cleveland, Ohio. This species was named after the French ornithologist Charles Lucien Bonaparte (nephew of Napoleon), who lived in New Jersey in the 1820s.

VOICE Harsh *keek, keek*; can be vocal in feeding flocks, *kew, kew, kew.*

NESTING Stick nest of twigs, branches, tree bark, lined with mosses or lichens; usually in conifers 5–20ft (1.5–6m) above ground; also in rushes over water; 1–4 eggs; 1 brood; May–July.

FEEDING Catches insects in flight on breeding grounds; picks crustaceans, mollusks, and small fish from water's surface; also plunge-dives.

FLIGHT: graceful, light, and agile; rapid wing beats; can be mistaken for a tern in flight.

TERN-LIKE GULL
Bonaparte's Gulls are very social and, flying in flocks, these pale, delicate birds look like terns.

WHITE UNDERWINGS
In all plumages, Bonaparte's Gull have white underwings, unlike other similar small gulls.

OCCURRENCE
During breeding season, found in northern forest zone, in lakes, ponds, or bogs; on migration, may be found anywhere where there is water: ponds, lakes, sewage pools, or rivers. Winters on Great Lakes and along the coast; often found in large numbers at coastal inlets.

SIMILAR SPECIES

BLACK-HEADED GULL
see p.262
dark outer wing feathers

larger overall

red bill

LITTLE GULL
see p.266

smaller overall

uniform gray upperwing

Length **11–12in (28–30cm)**	Wingspan **35in–3ft 3in (90–100cm)**	Weight **6–8oz (175–225g)**
Social **Flocks**	Lifespan **Up to 18 years**	Status **Secure**

| Order **Charadriiformes** | Family **Laridae** | Species *Larus atricilla* |

Laughing Gull

dark gray wings

ADULT (WINTER)

IN FLIGHT

brown wing feathers

white forehead

IMMATURE (1ST WINTER)

broken white eye-ring

black head

long, slightly drooped bill

white neck

dark gray back

black wing tips

long, dark legs

white underparts

ADULT (BREEDING)

gray nape

ADULT (WINTER)

The distinctive call of the Laughing Gull is a familiar sound in spring and summer along the East Coast. Already abundant when the Europeans arrived in North America, it was greatly reduced in the 19th century by egg collectors and the millinery trade. Its numbers increased in the 1920s, following protection, but declined again due to competition with larger gulls from the North. With the closing of landfills however, the Laughing Gull population has recovered.

VOICE Typical call strident laugh, *ha…ha…ha…ha…ha*; very vocal in breeding season; quiet in winter.

NESTING Mass of grass on dry land with heavy vegetation, sand, rocks, and salt marshes; 2–4 eggs, 1 brood; April–July.

FEEDING Picks from surface while walking and swimming; feeds on various invertebrates: insects, earthworms, squid, crabs, crab eggs, and larvae; also eats small fish, garbage, and berries.

FLIGHT: strong and direct; graceful for a gull; agile enough to catch flying insects.

DARK WING TIPS
Unlike many gulls, the Laughing Gull usually shows little or no white in the wing tips.

SIMILAR SPECIES

FRANKLIN'S GULL
see p.265

white band in wing tips

short, straight bill

FRANKLIN'S GULL ☽ ☼
see p.265

short, straight bill

darker head

pink blush on underparts

OCCURRENCE
During breeding season usually found near saltwater. Post-breeders and juveniles wander widely; strays can turn up anywhere. Rare in winter in the Northeast. Small numbers once nested at the Salton Sea but only a visitor there for the last 50 years.

| Length **15½–18in (39–46cm)** | Wingspan **3¼–4ft (1–1.2m)** | Weight **7–13oz (200–375g)** |
| Social **Colonial** | Lifespan **Up to 20 years** | Status **Secure** |

Order **Charadriiformes**	Family **Laridae**	Species *Larus pipixcan*

Franklin's Gull

black wing tips set-off by white band

dark gray wings

ADULT (WINTER)

IN FLIGHT

dark back of head

gray back

short, straight bill

ADULT (WINTER)

partial hood

IMMATURE (1ST SUMMER)

broken white eye crescent

black head

red bill

dark gray back

white in outer wing feathers

pink blush underneath

ADULT (SUMMER)

FLIGHT: stiff and direct; relatively fast wing beats; agile flier.

Since its discovery, Franklin's Gull has carried a number of names: Prairie Dove, Rosy Dove, and Franklin's Rosy Gull—"Dove" alluding to its dainty appearance and "rosy" to the pink blush of its undersides. Its official name honors British Arctic explorer, John Franklin, on whose first expedition, the bird was discovered in 1823. Unlike other gulls, this species has two complete molts each year. As a result, its plumage usually looks fresh and it rarely has the scruffy look of some other gulls.

VOICE Nasal *weeh-a, weeh-a*; shrill *kuk kuk kuk kuk*; extremely vocal around breeding colonies.

NESTING Floating mass of bulrushes or other plants; material added as nest sinks; 2–4 eggs; 1 brood; April–July.

FEEDING Feeds mainly on earthworms and insects during breeding and some seeds, taken while walking or flying; opportunistic feeder during migration and winter.

PROMINENT EYES
In all plumages, Franklin's Gull has much more prominent white eye-crescents than similar species.

OCCURRENCE
In summer, a bird of the high prairies; always nests over water. On migration often found in agricultural areas; large numbers frequent plowed fields or follows plows. Winters mainly along the Pacific Coast of South America.

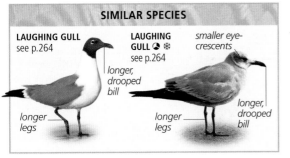

SIMILAR SPECIES

LAUGHING GULL see p.264

longer, drooped bill

longer legs

LAUGHING GULL ◑ ❄ see p.264

smaller eye-crescents

longer legs

longer, drooped bill

Length **12½–14in (32–36cm)**	Wingspan **33in–3ft 1in (85–95cm)**	Weight **8–11oz (225–325g)**
Social **Colonial**	Lifespan **At least 10 years**	Status **Secure**

| Order **Charadriiformes** | Family **Laridae** | Species *Larus minutus* |

Little Gull

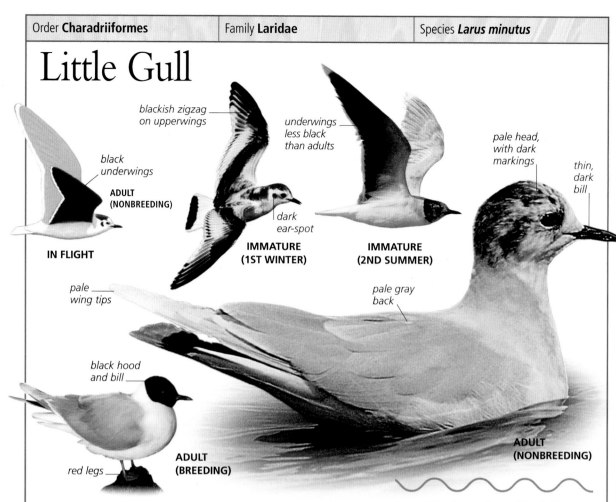

blackish zigzag
on upperwings

underwings
less black
than adults

black
underwings

**ADULT
(NONBREEDING)**

IN FLIGHT

dark
ear-spot

**IMMATURE
(1ST WINTER)**

**IMMATURE
(2ND SUMMER)**

pale head,
with dark
markings

thin,
dark
bill

pale
wing tips

pale gray
back

black hood
and bill

red legs

**ADULT
(BREEDING)**

**ADULT
(NONBREEDING)**

FLIGHT: quick wing beats; light, nimble, and agile.

SIMPLE ELEGANCE
Its long, pale gray wings with a thin white border place this bird among the most elegant of gulls.

A Eurasian species distributed from the Baltic to China, the Little Gull is the smallest gull in the world. Whether it is a recent immigrant to North America or has actually been here, unnoticed, in small numbers for many years remains a mystery. It was first recorded in North America in the early 1800s, but a nest was not found until 1962, in Ontario, Canada. Known nesting areas are still few, but winter numbers have been increasing steadily in recent decades.
VOICE Nasal *kek, kek, kek, kek*, reminiscent of a small tern.
NESTING Thick, floating mass of dry cattails, reeds, or other vegetation, in marshes and ponds; 3 eggs; 1 brood; May–August.
FEEDING Seizes prey from water's surface, while swimming or plunge-diving; typical prey includes flying insects, aquatic invertebrates such as shrimps, and small fish.

OCCURRENCE
Breeds in extensive freshwater marshes in Hudson Bay and Great Lakes region, but the full extent of its breeding range in North America is unknown; can appear almost anywhere while migrating. Winters primarily along sea coasts, at sewage outfalls; often with groups of Bonaparte's Gulls.

SIMILAR SPECIES

BLACK-HEADED GULL
see p.262

white flash
in wing

red
bill

BONAPARTE'S GULL
see p.263

larger
overall

white flash
in wing

| Length **10–12in (25–30cm)** | Wingspan **23½–26in (60–65cm)** | Weight **3½–5oz (100–150g)** |
| Social **Colonies** | Lifespan **Up to 6 years** | Status **Secure** |

| Order **Charadriiformes** | Family **Laridae** | Species *Xema sabini* |

Sabine's Gull

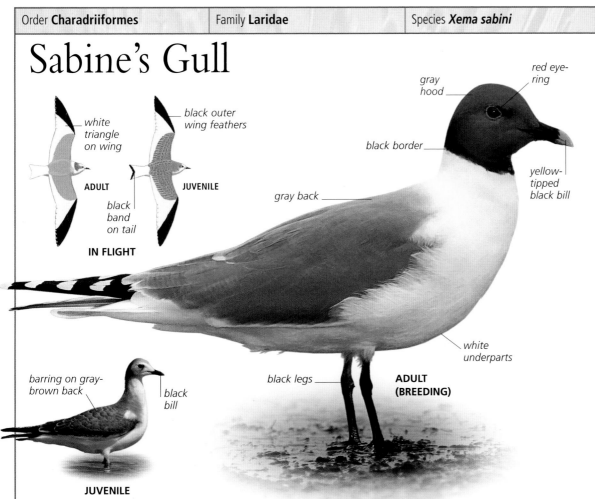

IN FLIGHT

white triangle on wing

black outer wing feathers

ADULT

JUVENILE

black band on tail

gray hood

red eye-ring

black border

gray back

yellow-tipped black bill

white underparts

black legs

ADULT (BREEDING)

barring on gray-brown back

black bill

JUVENILE

This strikingly patterned gull was discovered in Greenland by the English scientist Edward Sabine during John Ross's search for the Northwest Passage in 1818 (it was described in 1819). The distinctive wing pattern and notched tail make it unmistakable in all plumages—only juvenile kittiwakes are superficially similar. Previously thought to be related to the larger, but similarly patterned, Swallow-tailed Gull of the Galapagos, recent research indicates that Sabine's Gull is more closely related to the Ivory Gull. This species breeds in the Arctic and winters at sea, off the coasts of the Americas (south to Peru) and Africa (south to the Cape region).

VOICE Raucous, harsh *kyeer, kyeer, kyeer*; tern-like.

NESTING Shallow depression in marsh or tundra vegetation usually near water, lined with grass or unlined; 3–4 eggs; 1 brood; May–August.

FEEDING Catches aquatic insects from the water surface while swimming, wading, or flying during breeding season; winter diet mainly includes crustaceans, small fish, and plankton.

FLIGHT: wing beats shallow and stiff; tern-like, buoyant.

STRIKING WING PATTERN
Juvenile Sabine's Gulls have a muted version of the distinctive triangular wing pattern seen in the adults.

BLACK-LEGGED KITTIWAKE ◐ see p.268

SIMILAR SPECIES

partial black collar

black wing bar

OCCURRENCE
In the summer, breeds near the Arctic coast and on wet tundra in freshwater and brackish habitats, but also occurs near saltwater. Winters far off-shore in tropical and subtropical waters; widespread in Pacific and Atlantic oceans on migration.

| Length **13–14in (33–36 cm)** | Wingspan **35in–3ft 3in (90–100cm)** | Weight **5–9oz (150–250g)** |
| Social **Colonies** | Lifespan **At least 8 years** | Status **Secure** |

| Order **Charadriiformes** | Family **Laridae** | Species *Rissa tridactyla* |

Black-legged Kittiwake

IN FLIGHT

pale outer wing feathers

black "M" pattern in wings

pale gray upperparts

black tip to tail

black bill

ADULT

JUVENILE

black wing tip

yellow bill

white head

pale gray back feathers

ADULT

black legs and feet

dark neck collar

dark wing bar

JUVENILE

A kittiwake nesting colony is an impressive sight, with sometimes thousands of birds lined up along steep cliff ledges overlooking the sea. The ledges are often so narrow that the birds' tails stick out over the edge. Kittiwakes have sharper claws than other gulls, probably to give them a better grip on their ledges. In the late 20th century, the Black-legged Kittiwake population expanded greatly in the Canadian maritime provinces, with numbers doubling in the Gulf of St. Lawrence.

VOICE Repeated, nasal *kit-ti-wake, kit-ti-wake* call; vocal near nesting cliffs; usually silent in winter.

NESTING Mound of mud and vegetation on narrow cliff ledge; 1–3 eggs; 1 brood; April–August.

FEEDING Snatches small marine fish and invertebrates from the surface, or dives just below the water's surface; feeds in flocks.

FLIGHT: very stiff-winged; rapid, shallow wing beats; overall more buoyant than most gulls.

LIVING ON THE EDGE
Young and adult kittiwakes pack together tightly on their precariously narrow cliff ledges.

SIMILAR SPECIES

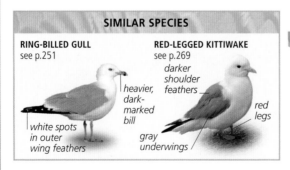

RING-BILLED GULL see p.251

white spots in outer wing feathers

heavier, dark-marked bill

RED-LEGGED KITTIWAKE see p.269

darker shoulder feathers

red legs

gray underwings

OCCURRENCE
Rarely seen far from the ocean; common in summer around sea cliffs, with ledges suitable for nesting, and nearby offshore waters; winters at sea; most likely to be seen from land during and after storms; strays have appeared throughout the interior.

| Length **15–16in (38–41cm)** | Wingspan **3ft 1in–4ft (0.95m–1.2m)** | Weight **11–18oz (300–500g)** |
| Social **Colonies** | Lifespan **Up to 26 years** | Status **Secure** |

Order **Charadriiformes**	Family **Laridae**	Species *Rissa brevirostris*

Red-legged Kittiwake

medium gray upper wing

ADULT

gray underwing

IN FLIGHT

gray neck collar

JUVENILE

black outer wing feathers

white head

small, yellow bill

medium gray shoulder feathers

black wing tips

red legs and feet

ADULT

FLIGHT: stiff-winged; similar to Black-legged Kittiwake, but wing beats often faster.

This small, distinctive gull is found mainly on the remote Pribilof Islands in the Bering Sea, with over 75 percent of the world's Red-legged Kittiwake population nesting on St. George Island. Research has indicated that this species was once more widespread in the Aleutians than it is today. It is also found accidentally south to Oregon. The Red-legged Kittiwake is often mistaken for the Black-legged Kittiwake outside its normal range since the latter may also, occasionally, have red legs.
VOICE Calls similar to Black-legged Kittiwake, but higher pitched; vocal at breeding colony, generally silent elsewhere.
NESTING Mound of mud and vegetation, usually grass or kelp, on narrow sea cliff ledge; 1–2 eggs; 1 brood; May–September.
FEEDING Shallow plunges or dips to capture small fish, squid, and zooplankton from ocean surface or just below the surface.

JOINT VENTURE
Red-legged Kittiwakes nest on vertical cliff ledges, where both birds help build the nests.

SIMILAR SPECIES

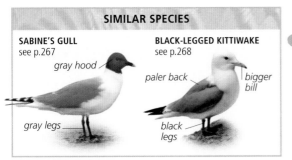

SABINE'S GULL
see p.267

gray hood

gray legs

BLACK-LEGGED KITTIWAKE
see p.268

paler back

bigger bill

black legs

OCCURRENCE
Spends life out at sea, mostly found over deep waters. Restricted almost totally to the Bering Sea and vicinity. Nesting colonies occur on near vertical seacliffs up to 975ft (300m). During the breeding season rarely seen more than 93 miles (150km) from nesting colonies.

Length **14–15½in (35–39cm)**	Wingspan **33–36in (84–92cm)**	Weight **11–17oz (300–475g)**
Social **Colonies**	Lifespan **Up to 27 years**	Status **Localized**

| Order **Charadriiformes** | Family **Laridae** | Species *Gelochelidon nilotica* |

Gull-billed Tern

white crown

small black "mask"

black cap

dark trailing edges on outer wing feathers

ADULT (BREEDING)

IN FLIGHT

ADULT (NONBREEDING)

thick, black bill

pale gray upperparts

ADULT (BREEDING)

white underparts

black legs and toes

With its relatively heavy build, thick bill, and broad wings, the Gull-billed Tern is more gull-like than any other North American tern. Also, unlike most other terns, it does not feed only on fish, and has a notably varied diet that requires foraging in a variety of different habitats, ranging from mudflats to desert scrub. It often nests in colonies with other terns—particularly Common and Caspian terns—and skimmers, and will occasionally hunt their chicks and steal their prey. During the 19th century, Gull-billed Terns were hunted ruthlessly for their eggs and feathers. Their numbers have at least partially recovered, but increasing human disturbance at nesting sites is a long-term conservation concern.

VOICE Short, two-noted, nasal yapping, *kay-wek, kay-wek*.

NESTING Simple, camouflaged scrape on ground, usually on sand, shell bank, or bare rock; shells and other debris used to build up nest; 2–3 eggs; 1 brood; April–July.

FEEDING Eats insects, lizards, small fish, and chicks. Catches insects in flight; plucks prey from ground or water's surface.

FLIGHT: buoyant and graceful; stiff-winged with shallow wing beats.

LONG WINGS
The Gull-billed Tern has very long, pointed wings with a dusky edge on the outer feathers.

OCCURRENCE
Rarely found away from saltwater. Historically considered a species of saltmarshes, but now breeds primarily on sandy beaches and barrier islands; most birds leave the US to winter in Central America, where they favor mudflats or flooded fields.

SIMILAR SPECIES

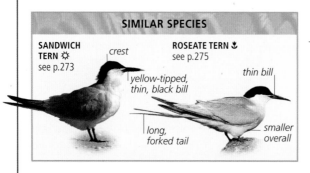

SANDWICH TERN ☼
see p.273

crest

yellow-tipped, thin, black bill

ROSEATE TERN ☙
see p.275

thin bill

long, forked tail

smaller overall

| Length **13–15in (33–38cm)** | Wingspan **3¼–4ft (1–1.2m)** | Weight **5–7oz (150–200g)** |
| Social **Colonies** | Lifespan **Up to 16 years** | Status **Localized** |

Order **Charadriiformes**	Family **Laridae**	Species *Hydroprogne caspia*

Caspian Tern

streaked dark crown

ADULT (BREEDING)

short tail

dark-tipped outer wing feathers

IN FLIGHT

ADULT (NONBREEDING)

dark markings on upperparts

JUVENILE

slightly crested black cap

light gray back

thick, red bill with dark tip

ADULT (BREEDING)

white underparts

black legs and feet

FLIGHT: strong, swift flier; heavy, powerful wing beats; the most gull-like of North American terns.

Rivalling some of the gulls in size, the Caspian Tern is the world's largest tern. Unlike other "black-capped" terns, it never has a completely white forehead, even in winter. In non-breeding plumage, when the cap is very heavily streaked. The Caspian Tern is known for its predatory habits, stealing prey from other seabirds, as well as snatching eggs from, and hunting the chicks of, other gulls and terns. It is aggressive in defending its nesting territory, giving hoarse alarm calls, and rhythmically opening and closing its beak in a threatening display to intruders.

VOICE Hoarse, deep *kraaa, kraaa*; also barks at intruders; male's wings vibrate loudly in courtship flight.

NESTING Shallow scrape on ground; 2–3 eggs; 1 brood; May–August.

FEEDING Plunges into water to snatch fish, barnacles, and snails.

AGRESSIVE BIRDS
The Caspian Tern is one of the most aggressive terns, though actual physical contact is rare.

SIMILAR SPECIES

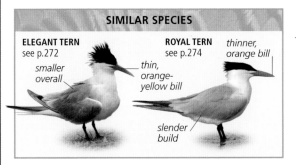

ELEGANT TERN
see p.272

smaller overall

thin, orange-yellow bill

ROYAL TERN
see p.274

thinner, orange bill

slender build

OCCURRENCE
Found in a variety of aquatic habitats, freshwater and marine; rare offshore; breeds on interior lakes, saltmarsh, and on coastal barrier islands; winters on and near the coast. May be seen on marshes and wetlands during migration.

Length **18½–21½in (47–54cm)**	Wingspan **4¼–5ft (1.3–1.5m)**	Weight **19–27oz (525–775g)**
Social **Colonies/Pairs**	Lifespan **Up to 30 years**	Status **Declining**

Order **Charadriiformes**	Family **Laridae**	Species *Thalasseus elegans*

Elegant Tern

long bill

short forked tail

IN FLIGHT

ADULT (BREEDING)

white forehead

ADULT (NONBREEDING)

shaggy black crest

black cap

gray back and wings

slender, orange-bill with yellow tip

white underparts

ADULT (BREEDING)

FLIGHT: stiff-winged, but strong, graceful flight; wing beats generally faster than other large terns.

The Elegant Tern is not a widespread species. By the mid-20th century its population had declined due to the demand for its eggs and the impact of introduced predators (cats, dogs, and rats); at one point it was confined to only five known nesting colonies. This bird nests in tight groups within colonies of Heermann's Gulls and Caspian Terns, taking advantage of the other birds' aggressive defense against potential predators. Nesting Elegant Terns are highly synchronized, with the majority making nests and laying eggs within 24 hours of each other.

VOICE Nasal *karrreeek, karrreeek*; very vocal at nesting colonies.

NESTING Shallow scrape on ground, may be lined with debris, pebbles, and shells; sometimes rim of fecal matter around nest; 1–2 eggs; 1 brood; April–July.

FEEDING Almost exclusively eats fish, mainly the Northern Anchovy; hovers over schools of fish before plunging into water; also eats crustaceans, such as crabs, shrimp, and barnacles.

VOICE RECOGNITION
Parent and young Elegant Terns are able to identify each other by voice, even within dense colonies.

OCCURRENCE
Handful of colonies in southern California and Baja California; over 90 percent of world's population nest on Isla Raza in the Gulf of California. After breeding, many fly to central Californian coast, rarely north to British Columbia; accidental elsewhere.

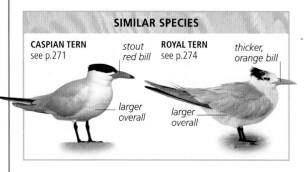

SIMILAR SPECIES

CASPIAN TERN see p.271 — stout red bill — larger overall

ROYAL TERN see p.274 — thicker, orange bill — larger overall

Length **15½–16½in (39–42cm)**	Wingspan **30–32in (76–81cm)**	Weight **7–11oz (200–325g)**
Social **Colonies**	Lifespan **Up to 16 years**	Status **Vulnerable**

Order **Charadriiformes**	Family **Laridae**	Species *Thalasseus sandvicensis*

Sandwich Tern

JUVENILE
- dark-edged tail
- indistinct barring above

ADULT (BREEDING)
- long, slender wings
- dark wedge in outer feathers

IN FLIGHT

ADULT (NONBREEDING)
- white forehead
- no shaggy crest

IMMATURE (1ST WINTER)
- dark spots on wings
- pale forehead

ADULT (BREEDING)
- black cap
- shaggy crest
- very pale gray back
- long, yellow-tipped black bill
- white underparts
- black legs and toes

FLIGHT: shallow, relatively rapid wing beats; strong and agile.

The Sandwich Tern is the only North American tern to possess both a crest and a mostly black bill. Up-close it is possible to spot the yellow tip on its black bill, which is also a unique feature among North American terns. This species nests in dense breeding colonies along with Royal Terns and Laughing Gulls. It is not an aggressive species and, like the Elegant Tern, is thought to benefit from the protection the other, more aggressive species offer it from potential predators. Worldwide, there are three subspecies of Sandwich Tern, but only one of these inhabits North America.

VOICE Loud, harsh two-syllabled *kirr-ick*; vocal when breeding, less elsewhere.

NESTING Shallow scrape on bare ground in open area, often alongside other tern species; debris added during incubation, but sometimes unlined; 1–2 eggs; 1 brood; April–August.

FEEDING Plunge-dives from medium height to catch fish, squid, and crustaceans; also snatches prey from surface and catches insects in flight.

SIMILAR SPECIES

GULL-BILLED TERN see p.270
- more compact body
- stout, all black bill

ROSEATE TERN see p.275
- no yellow tip on bill
- smaller overall

CLOSE NESTING
Sandwich Terns often nest in extremely dense colonies with nests packed closely together.

OCCURRENCE
An East Coast and Caribbean species, it is rarely far from saltwater; breeds on barrier beaches, barrier islands, and man-made dredge islands. Winters in similar areas; roosts on sandbars. May occur north of normal range after tropical storms and hurricanes.

Length **13½–17½in (34–45cm)**	Wingspan **3ft 1in–3ft 4in (95–105cm)**	Weight **6–11oz (175–300g)**
Social **Colonies**	Lifespan **Up to 22 years**	Status **Secure**

| Order **Charadriiformes** | Family **Laridae** | Species *Thalasseus maximus* |

Royal Tern

white underwings
white flanks
shaggy crest
black forehead and crown

ADULT (BREEDING)

darker gray tips on outer flight feathers

darker pattern on wings

ADULT (BREEDING)

pale gray wings

IN FLIGHT

JUVENILE

light gray upperparts

strong, orange bill

ADULT (BREEDING)

forked tail

white underparts

black legs

white forehead

shaggy coat

ADULT (NONBREEDING)

FLIGHT: wing beats shallow, but powerful; less rapid and buoyant than other large terns.

Royal Terns have a full black cap for only a very short time at the beginning of the breeding season; for most of the year, they have white foreheads. The color of a Royal Tern's bill is quite variable, ranging from yellowish orange to red. Some possess a reddish bill similar to that of the Caspian Tern, but the latter does not have a pure white forehead and its bill is thicker. Perhaps it was these red-billed Royal Terns that caused the renowned ornithologist, John James Audubon, to confuse the two species.

VOICE Call *keer-reet*, usually during courtship; higher pitched and less raspy than Caspian Tern; more vocal around colonies.

NESTING Shallow scrape on bare ground, usually unlined, rim of guano reinforces nest; 1 egg; 1 brood; April–August.

FEEDING Mostly plunge-dives, but also plucks prey from surface while flying; sometimes skims surface; almost exclusively eats fish and crustaceans, such as crabs and barnacles.

BREEDING HABITS
Royal Terns appear monogamous, but it is unclear whether the pair bond is kept between seasons.

OCCURRENCE
Normally restricted to warm saltwater habitats. Breeds in dense colonies, often on barrier islands; post-breeders wander north of regular breeding range; some are carried north by tropical storms and hurricanes, and may be found in the interior of the US.

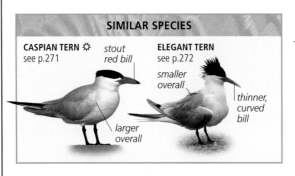

SIMILAR SPECIES

CASPIAN TERN ☼
see p.271

stout red bill

larger overall

ELEGANT TERN
see p.272

smaller overall

thinner, curved bill

| Length **17½–19½in (45–50cm)** | Wingspan **4–4¼ft (1.2–1.3m)** | Weight **12–16oz (350–450g)** |
| Social **Colonies** | Lifespan **Up to 29 years** | Status **Secure** |

Order **Charadriiformes**	Family **Laridae**	Species ***Sterna dougallii***

Roseate Tern

scalloped appearance
to upperparts

long tail
feathers

red base to
black bill

**ADULT
(LATE SUMMER)**

IN FLIGHT

pale gray
underwings

**ADULT
(SPRING)**

dark legs

JUVENILE

black
cap

pale gray
upperparts

black
bill

long,
forked tail

**ADULT
(SPRING)**

white
underparts

FLIGHT: strong and fairly swift; stiffer-winged
than terns of similar size.

Mostly found nesting with Common Tern, the Roseate Tern
is paler and more slender. Its slim bill is black only for a
short time in the spring before turning at least half red during
the nesting season. At breeding colonies, these terns engage in
distinctive courtship flights, with pairs gliding down from
hundreds of feet in the air, swaying side to side with each other.
Some birds nest as trios—two females and a male—all taking
part in incubating the eggs and raising the young.

VOICE Most common calls *keek* or *ki-rik* given in flight and
around nesting colony.

NESTING Simple scrape, often under vegetation or large rocks;
adds twigs and dry grass during incubation; 1–3 eggs; 1 brood;
May–August.

FEEDING Catches small fish with its bill by diving from a height
of 3–20ft (1–6m); carries whole fish to young.

GRACEFUL COURTSHIP
Roseate Tern pairs engage in elegant, graceful
courtship displays before mating.

SIMILAR SPECIES

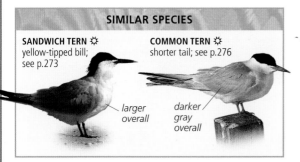

SANDWICH TERN ☼
yellow-tipped bill;
see p.273

COMMON TERN ☼
shorter tail; see p.276

larger
overall

darker
gray
overall

OCCURRENCE
Breeds almost exclusively in
coastal areas in the Northeast
from Long Island, New York, to
Nova Scotia, with another small
population in the outer Florida
Keys. Typically nests on beaches
and off-shore islands. Not often
seen far from breeding sites.

Length **13–16in (33–41cm)**	Wingspan **28in (70cm)**	Weight **3–5oz (85–150g)**
Social **Colonies**	Lifespan **Up to 26 years**	Status **Endangered**

| Order **Charadriiformes** | Family **Laridae** | Species **Sterna hirundo** |

Common Tern

dark wedge on outer feathers

ADULT (BREEDING)

IN FLIGHT

whitish forehead

brown bars on upperparts

dark bill with red-orange base

black wing bar

JUVENILE

white forehead

bill mostly dark

blackish leg

ADULT (NONBREEDING)

black cap

gray upperparts

black-tipped red bill

forked tail

pale gray-white underparts

red leg

ADULT (BREEDING)

FLIGHT: graceful, steady and strong; wing beats relatively deep.

One of North America's most widespread terns, the Common Tern was nearly wiped out in the late 19th century by hunters seeking its feathers. The 1918 Migratory Bird Treaty helped protect it, and numbers increased, but populations have declined again in recent decades due to human disturbance, habitat loss, and pollution.
VOICE Common call loud *keee-aarr* descending at end; emits *kek-kek-kek-kek* call when attacking intruders; vocal in colonies; also calls elsewhere.
NESTING Shallow scrape on bare sand, often gravel or similar surface, dry vegetation and debris used during incubation; 2–3 eggs; 1 brood; May–August.
FEEDING Plunges for prey, snatches from water's surface, catches insects in flight; mainly eats fish but also crustaceans, squid, and insects.

SIMILAR SPECIES

ARCTIC TERN ☼
see p.277

shorter red bill

shorter neck

shorter legs

FORSTER'S TERN
see p.278

paler wings

longer tail

FEEDING FLOCK
A flock of Common Terns focus on a school of fish, diving to catch them. Fisherman watch for such flocks to locate fish.

OCCURRENCE
Found almost anywhere with water during migration. Winters in Central and South America. One population breeds along the barrier beaches and coasts northwards from the Carolinas; a second population occurs around lakes and wet areas in the northern interior.

| Length **12–14in (31–35cm)** | Wingspan **30–31in (75–80cm)** | Weight **3⅜–5oz (95–150g)** |
| Social **Colonies** | Lifespan **Up to 26 years** | Status **Declining** |

Order **Charadriiformes**	Family **Laridae**	Species *Sterna paradisaea*

Arctic Tern

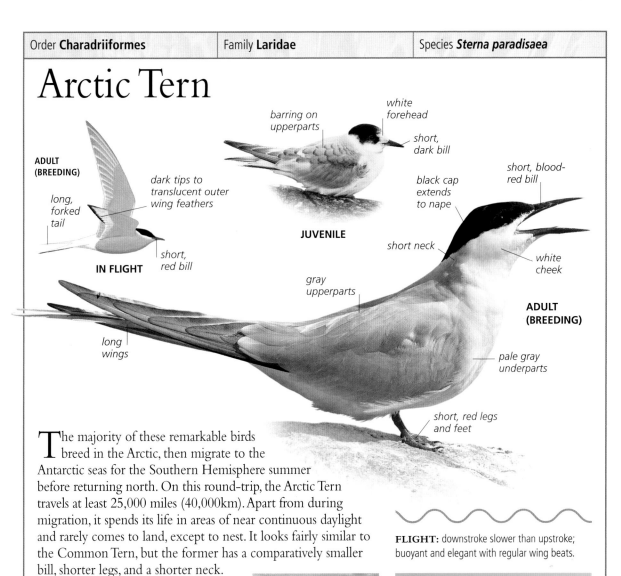

barring on upperparts

white forehead

short, dark bill

JUVENILE

ADULT (BREEDING)

long, forked tail

dark tips to translucent outer wing feathers

IN FLIGHT

short, red bill

long wings

short, blood-red bill

black cap extends to nape

short neck

white cheek

gray upperparts

ADULT (BREEDING)

pale gray underparts

short, red legs and feet

The majority of these remarkable birds breed in the Arctic, then migrate to the Antarctic seas for the Southern Hemisphere summer before returning north. On this round-trip, the Arctic Tern travels at least 25,000 miles (40,000km). Apart from during migration, it spends its life in areas of near continuous daylight and rarely comes to land, except to nest. It looks fairly similar to the Common Tern, but the former has a comparatively smaller bill, shorter legs, and a shorter neck.

VOICE Descending *keeyaar* call; nearly all calls similar to Common Tern, but higher-pitched and harsher.

NESTING Shallow scrape on bare ground or low vegetation in open areas; 2 eggs; 1 brood; May–August.

FEEDING Mostly plunge-dives for small fish and crustaceans, including crabs and shrimps; will also take prey from surface, sometimes catches insects in flight.

FLIGHT: downstroke slower than upstroke; buoyant and elegant with regular wing beats.

FEEDING THE YOUNG
Both parents feed chicks—males bring more food than females, especially right after hatching.

TRANSLUCENT FEATHERS
The translucent outer wing feathers of the Arctic Tern are evident on these two flying birds.

SIMILAR SPECIES

COMMON TERN ☼
see p.276

longer neck

longer bill

longer legs

FORSTER'S TERN
see p.278

longer, orange bill

longer legs

OCCURRENCE
Breeds in far North, mostly in open, unforested areas near water and along the coast; generally migrates far off-shore. Spends more time away from land than other northern terns. Winters on edge of pack ice in Antarctica.

Length **11–15½in (28–39cm)**	Wingspan **26–30in (65–75cm)**	Weight **3⅛–4oz (90–125g)**
Social **Colonies**	Lifespan **Up to 34 years**	Status **Vulnerable**

| Order **Charadriiformes** | Family **Laridae** | Species *Sterna forsteri* |

Forster's Tern

deeply forked tail

gray wings with slightly darker wing tips

IN FLIGHT

ADULT (NONBREEDING)

large, black ear patch

shorter tail

JUVENILE

plain gray wings

dark bill

ADULT (NONBREEDING)

black cap and nape

pale gray upperparts

orange-red bill with dark tip

long, gray tail with white outer margins

snowy white underparts

ADULT (BREEDING)

FLIGHT: graceful and agile, with shallow wing beats.

This medium-sized tern is very similar in appearance to the Common Tern. The features that differentiate it from the Common Tern are its lighter outer wing feathers and longer tail. Early naturalists could not tell the two species apart until 1834 when English botanist Thomas Nuttall made the distinction. He named this tern after Johann Reinhold Forster, a naturalist who accompanied the English explorer Captain Cook on his epic second voyage (1772-75).
VOICE Harsh, descending *kyerr*; more nasal than Common Tern.
NESTING Shallow scrape in mud or sand, but occasionally nests on top of muskrat lodge or on old grebe nest; sometimes constructs raft of floating vegetation; 2–3 eggs; 1 brood; May–August.
FEEDING Catches fish and crustaceans with shallow plunge-diving, often only head submerges; also catches insects in flight.

BLACK EARS
With its black ear patch, Foster's Tern is more distinctive in nonbreeding than breeding plumage.

OCCURRENCE
Breeds in northeastern Mexico, in freshwater and saltwater marshes with large stretches of open water. Winters on both coasts and across southern US states, unlike the Common Tern, which primarily winters in South America.

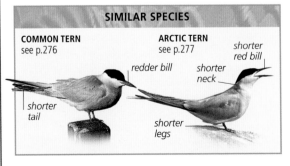

SIMILAR SPECIES

COMMON TERN
see p.276

shorter tail

ARCTIC TERN
see p.277

redder bill

shorter neck

shorter red bill

shorter legs

| Length **13–14in (33–36cm)** | Wingspan **29–32in (73–82cm)** | Weight **4–7oz (125–190g)** |
| Social **Colonies** | Lifespan **Up to 16 years** | Status **Secure** |

| Order **Charadriiformes** | Family **Laridae** | Species ***Sternula antillarum*** |

Least Tern

IN FLIGHT

dark outer wing feathers

forked tail

ADULT (BREEDING)

streaked crown

patterned back

mostly dark bill

JUVENILE

black cap with white forehead

yellow bill

pale gray back

two dark outer wing feathers

white underparts

yellow legs

ADULT (BREEDING)

FLIGHT: extremely agile with stiff-winged, deep, rapid wing beats; frequently hovers.

The Least Tern is the smallest of the North American terns and, in summer, its distinctive black cap and white forehead distinguish it from other members of its family. In the 19th century the population of Least Terns declined rapidly as its feathers were prized fashion accessories. Protected by the Migratory Bird Treaty of 1916, its numbers grew again, but it is still threatened by ongoing habitat loss.

VOICE Extremely vocal during breeding; a high-pitched *ki-deek, ki-deek*; also a rapid, almost non-stop chatter.

NESTING Shallow scrape on ground lined with dry vegetation, broken shells, and pebbles; 2–3 eggs; 1 brood; April–September.

FEEDING Plunge-dives, often after hovering, for fish and aquatic invertebrates, does not submerge completely; also skims surface for food; catches insects in flight.

COURTSHIP FEEDING
As with many other species of tern, Least Tern males offer fish to females during courtship.

SIMILAR SPECIES

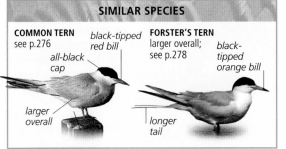

COMMON TERN see p.276

all-black cap

larger overall

black-tipped red bill

FORSTER'S TERN larger overall; see p.278

black-tipped orange bill

longer tail

OCCURRENCE
Breeds along both coasts, major rivers, lakes, reservoirs, and in Great Plains wetlands; favors sandy areas such as barrier islands, beaches, sandbars, and nearby waters. Winters from Mexico to South America. Also breeds in the West Indies and Mexico.

| Length **8½–9in (21–23cm)** | Wingspan **19–21in (48–53cm)** | Weight **1¼–2oz (35–55g)** |
| Social **Colonies** | Lifespan **Up to 24 years** | Status **Endangered** |

| Order **Charadriiformes** | Family **Laridae** | Species **_Sterna fuscata_** |

Sooty Tern

JUVENILE

ADULT
(BREEDING)

white spots on
underwing

white spots on
back and wings

dark bill

sooty brown
breast and
head

JUVENILE

extensive
white
forehead
reaches eye

forked
black
tail

white leading
edge of wing

black
bill

dark
underparts

IN FLIGHT

brown tinged
black upperparts

white outer edge
on black tail

white
underparts

black legs
and toes

ADULT
(BREEDING)

FLIGHT: stiff-winged with deep wing beats;
often soars and glides.

Except when nesting, the Sooty Tern spends almost its entire life flying over the tropical and subtropical oceans of the world. After fledging, the young do not return to land until they breed, usually six to eight years later. The Sooty Tern's plumage is not particularly waterproof so the bird rarely settles on water. It sometimes lands briefly on calm seas, and occasionally perches on floating debris or even sea turtles. An old common name for the bird is "Wide-awake," due to its distinctive nasal call.

VOICE High nasal call: _wide-a-wake, wide-a-wake_; vocal throughout year, particularly at breeding colonies.

NESTING Directly on sand or shallow scrape in open, lightly vegetated areas; 1 egg; 1 brood; March–July.

FEEDING Picks fish and squid from water while flying; snatches leaping fish; forages in flocks, often with other seabirds.

ROMANTIC REUNION
A pair of Sooty Terns will mate again in subsequent years if both birds return to the same nesting site.

SIMILAR SPECIES

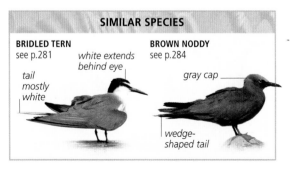

BRIDLED TERN
see p.281

white extends
behind eye

tail
mostly
white

BROWN NODDY
see p.284

gray cap

wedge-
shaped tail

OCCURRENCE
Lives out at sea and only comes to land to nest. There is a large colony at Dry Tortugas, off the Florida Keys. Small numbers breed along the coast of Texas and near the mouth of the Mississippi River. In summer, is found in the Gulf Stream north to Virginia; may be seen farther north after hurricanes.

| Length **14–17½in (36–45cm)** | Wingspan **32–37in (82–94cm)** | Weight **6–7oz (175–200g)** |
| Social **Colonies** | Lifespan **Up to 36 years** | Status **Localized** |

Order **Charadriiformes**	Family **Laridae**	Species *Chlidonias niger*

Black Tern

dark gray wings

dark gray tail

ADULT (BREEDING)

IN FLIGHT

ADULT (NONBREEDING)

whitish underparts

white forehead

dark smudge on sides

gray upperparts

black head

black bill

black breast

black legs and toes

ADULT (BREEDING)

white rump

FLIGHT: very agile, but somewhat erratic-looking, bouncy flight; strong, deep wing beats.

The Black Tern is a small, elegant, marsh-dwelling tern that undergoes a remarkable change in appearance from summer to winter—more so than any other regularly occurring North American tern. The Black Tern's breeding plumage can cause the bird to be confused with the closely related White-winged Tern, which is an accidental visitor to North America. The Black Tern's nonbreeding plumage is much paler than its breeding plumage—the head turns white with irregular black streaks, and the neck, breast, and belly become whitish gray.

VOICE Call nasal and harsh *krik*, *kip*, or *kik*; most vocal during breeding, but calls throughout the year.

NESTING Shallow cup on top of floating mass of vegetation, sometimes on top of muskrat lodges; usually 3 eggs; 1 brood; May–August.

FEEDING Picks prey off water's surface or vegetation; rarely plunge dives; in summer, feeds on mainly insects, caught from the air or ground, also freshwater fish; in winter, eats mainly small sea fish.

FLOATING NEST
A floating nest is a dry place to lay eggs and raise chicks in a watery environment.

SIMILAR SPECIES

SOOTY TERN ☾
see p.282

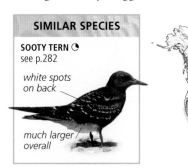

white spots on back

much larger overall

OCCURRENCE
Freshwater marshes in summer, but nonbreeding plumaged birds—probably young—occasionally seen along the coast. During migration, can be found almost anywhere near water. Winters in the marine coastal waters of Central and South America.

Length **9–10in (23–26cm)**	Wingspan **25–35in (63–88cm)**	Weight **1¾–2½ oz (50–70g)**
Social **Colonies**	Lifespan **Up to 9 years**	Status **Vulnerable**

| Order **Charadriiformes** | Family **Laridae** | Species *Anous stolidus* |

Brown Noddy

ADULT

IN FLIGHT

long tail

white forehead

indistinct, gray cap

JUVENILE

gray cap and grayish white forehead

dark brown upperparts

slender, dark bill

ADULT

wedge-shaped tail with slight notch

dark legs, paler webbing

FLIGHT: strong, direct flight; rapid wing beats; rarely higher than 10ft (3m) over ocean.

The Brown Noddy resembles a typical tern species with the colors reversed, its pale gray forehead and crown contrasting with a dark body. Noddies nest on rocks and islands in warm, tropical ocean waters around the world. The Brown Noddy has earned its place on the list of North American breeding birds because of a single colony a few miles off the Florida Keys. It is very tame and shows little fear of humans: hence its scientific name, *Anous stolidus*, which is Latin for "foolish" and "slow-witted."

VOICE Variety of crow-like *caw* or *kark* calls given around nesting colonies; usually silent.

NESTING Nests of twigs and debris on bare rock, sand, gravel, or vegetation; 1–2 eggs; 1 brood; February–July.

FEEDING Snatches small fish and squid while flying over or swimming in the ocean; also baitfish driven to surface by larger fish.

ROCK NESTER
When Brown Noddies nest in the open, the birds use their bodies to shade their eggs.

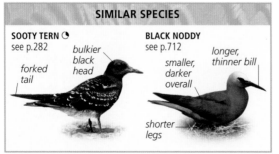

SIMILAR SPECIES

SOOTY TERN ◖
see p.282

forked tail

bulkier black head

BLACK NODDY
see p.712

smaller, darker overall

longer, thinner bill

shorter legs

OCCURRENCE
Only nesting site in the US is at Dry Tortugas, off the Florida Keys; during summer occurs offshore in Gulf of Mexico and as far north as the Outer Banks, North Carolina; found very rarely farther north to offshore southern New England, usually after tropical storms. Widely distributed in tropical seas.

| Length **15½–17½in (40–45cm)** | Wingspan **30–33in (77–85cm)** | Weight **5–8oz (150–225g)** |
| Social **Colonies** | Lifespan **Up to 27 years** | Status **Localized** |

| Order **Charadriiformes** | Family **Laridae** | Species *Rynchops niger* |

Black Skimmer

long wing

ADULT (BREEDING)

short, forked tail **IN FLIGHT**

mottled brown upperparts

bill duller than adult

JUVENILE

white forehead

orange-red and black bill

lower half of bill longer than upper

long, thick neck

black upperparts

ADULT (BREEDING)

white underparts

orange-red legs

With its long, orange-red and black bill, the Black Skimmer is quite unmistakable. Compressed laterally into a knife-like shape, the bill's lower mandible is about 1in (2.5cm) longer than the upper part. The unique bill and feeding behavior of the world's three skimmer species have led some to place them in their own family, although they are usually grouped with gulls and terns. When disturbed, Black Skimmer chicks kick sand up with their feet, forming a depression and throwing sand over their backs, which helps to camouflage them.

VOICE Calls given by both sexes, more often at night; distinctive sound like the yapping of a small dog.

NESTING Shallow scrape or depression on sandy beach or dead saltmarsh vegetation, also on gravel rooftops; 1–5 eggs; 1 brood; May–August.

FEEDING Skims surface with the lower part of its bill in water; bill snaps shut when prey is within reach; catches small fish in relatively calm waters.

FLIGHT: mostly low with slow wing beats; often glides when feeding.

GREGARIOUS BIRDS
The Black Skimmer is often seen in flocks on sandy beaches and mudflats.

SLICING THE SURFACE
The unique way in which skimmers such as the Black Skimmer feed gave rise to the old common name for these birds—Cutwaters.

OCCURRENCE
Breeds on East Coast from Massachusetts south to Mexico; West Coast only in southern California, including Salton Sea; rarely found far from saltwater. Found on beaches; feeds in bays, estuaries, lagoons, and areas with relatively calm waters. Winters in Central America.

| Length **15½–19½in (40–50cm)** | Wingspan **3½–4¼ft (1.1–1.3m)** | Weight **8–14oz (225–400g)** |
| Social **Colonies** | Lifespan **Up to 20 years** | Status **Vulnerable** |

| Order **Charadriiformes** | Family **Stercorariidae** | Species *Stercorarius maccormicki* |

South Polar Skua

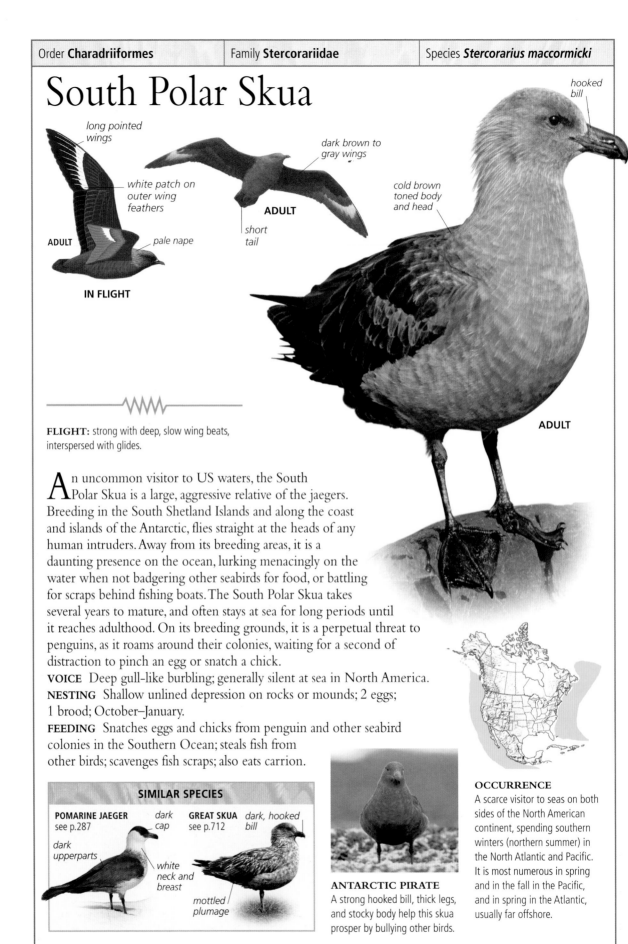

long pointed wings

white patch on outer wing feathers

ADULT

pale nape

IN FLIGHT

dark brown to gray wings

ADULT

short tail

hooked bill

cold brown toned body and head

ADULT

FLIGHT: strong with deep, slow wing beats, interspersed with glides.

An uncommon visitor to US waters, the South Polar Skua is a large, aggressive relative of the jaegers. Breeding in the South Shetland Islands and along the coast and islands of the Antarctic, flies straight at the heads of any human intruders. Away from its breeding areas, it is a daunting presence on the ocean, lurking menacingly on the water when not badgering other seabirds for food, or battling for scraps behind fishing boats. The South Polar Skua takes several years to mature, and often stays at sea for long periods until it reaches adulthood. On its breeding grounds, it is a perpetual threat to penguins, as it roams around their colonies, waiting for a second of distraction to pinch an egg or snatch a chick.

VOICE Deep gull-like burbling; generally silent at sea in North America.

NESTING Shallow unlined depression on rocks or mounds; 2 eggs; 1 brood; October–January.

FEEDING Snatches eggs and chicks from penguin and other seabird colonies in the Southern Ocean; steals fish from other birds; scavenges fish scraps; also eats carrion.

SIMILAR SPECIES

POMARINE JAEGER see p.287

dark cap

dark upperparts

white neck and breast

GREAT SKUA see p.712

dark, hooked bill

mottled plumage

ANTARCTIC PIRATE
A strong hooked bill, thick legs, and stocky body help this skua prosper by bullying other birds.

OCCURRENCE
A scarce visitor to seas on both sides of the North American continent, spending southern winters (northern summer) in the North Atlantic and Pacific. It is most numerous in spring and in the fall in the Pacific, and in spring in the Atlantic, usually far offshore.

| Length **21in (53cm)** | Wingspan **4¼ft (1.3m)** | Weight **2½lb (1kg)** |
| Social **Solitary** | Lifespan **Unknown** | Status **Secure** |

Order **Charadriiformes**	Family **Stercorariidae**	Species ***Stercorarius pomarinus***

Pomarine Jaeger

ADULT (BREEDING: PALE FORM)

prominent white "flash" in feathers

white wing flash

barred flanks

ADULT (NONBREEDING; PALE FORM)

dusky breastband

ADULT (DARK FORM)

dark overall

blunt tail spike

IN FLIGHT

twisted, spoon-like central tail feathers

all-dark body

deep, barrel breast

JUVENILE (FALL; DARK FORM)

blackish cap

pale based, thick bill

cream cheeks

gray-brown back

dusky breast-band

ADULT (BREEDING; PALE FORM)

The intimidating Pomarine Jaeger uses its size and strength to overpower larger seabirds, such as gulls and shearwaters, in order to steal their food. Thought to be nomadic during the breeding season, it only nests opportunistically, when populations of lemmings are at their peak to provide food for its young. Although larger and more powerful than the Parasitic Jaeger, the Pomarine Jaeger is not as acrobatic in the air and is readily driven away from breeding territories by the more dynamic Parasitic Jaeger. Interestingly, research suggests that the Pomerine Jaeger is actually more closely related to the large skuas—such as the Great and South Polar Skuas—than to other jaegers.

VOICE Nasal *cow-cow-cow* and various sharp, low whistles.

NESTING Shallow unlined depression on a rise or hummock in open tundra; 2 eggs; 1 brood; June–August.

FEEDING Hunts lemmings and other rodents; eats fish or scavenges refuse from fishing boats during nonbreeding season; often steals fish from other seabirds, such as gulls.

FLIGHT: powerful, deep, quick wing beats, with glides; rapid twists and turns in pursuit of prey.

OCCURRENCE
Breeds on open tundra in the Canadian Arctic. Migrates north in spring and south in fall, along coasts and also far offshore. Most often seen when brought close to land by gales. Storm-driven birds very occasionally found inland. More commonly seen on West Coast than East Coast; winters far out at sea.

OBVIOUS FEATURE
The twisted, spoon-like central tail feathers are clearly visible when the Pomerine Jaeger flies.

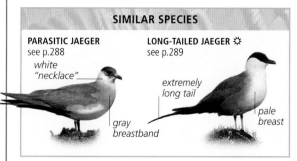

SIMILAR SPECIES

PARASITIC JAEGER
see p.288

white "necklace"

gray breastband

LONG-TAILED JAEGER ☼
see p.289

extremely long tail

pale breast

Length **17–20in (43–51cm)**	Wingspan **4ft (1.2m)**	Weight **23–26oz (650–750g)**
Social **Solitary**	Lifespan **Unknown**	Status **Secure**

Order **Charadriiformes**	Family **Stercorariidae**	Species *Stercorarius parasiticus*

Parasitic Jaeger

barring on wings

white wing patch

IN FLIGHT

ADULT (PALE FORM)

ADULT (DARK FORM)

pale cheek patch

ADULT (DARK FORM)

mostly dark brown overall

dark cap

pale cheek

dark upperparts

long, pointed, central feathers

ADULT (PALE FORM)

dark legs and toes

white wing patch

gray breastband

FLIGHT: swift wing beats interspersed with fast glides, interrupted by twisting and climbing.

A true avian pirate of the high seas, the Parasitic Jaeger routinely seeks food by chasing, bullying, and forcing other seabirds to drop or regurgitate fish or other food they have caught. Unlike most jaegers, the Parasitic Jaeger is adaptable in its feeding habits so that it can forage and raise its young under a wide range of environmental conditions. Breeding on the Arctic tundra, it migrates to offshore areas during the nonbreeding season.

VOICE Variety of terrier-like yelps and soft squeals, often during interactions with other jaegers or predators, usually around nesting territories.

NESTING Shallow unlined depression on a rise or hummock in open tundra; 2 eggs; 1 brood; May–August.

FEEDING Steals fish and other aquatic prey from gulls and terns; catches small birds, eats eggs, or hunts small rodents on breeding grounds.

PARASITIC PIRATE
This Parasitic Jaeger is harrying a gull by pecking at it, to make it disgorge its hard-won meal.

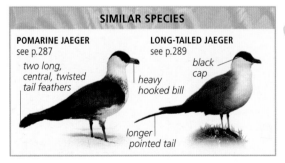

SIMILAR SPECIES

POMARINE JAEGER
see p.287

two long, central, twisted tail feathers

LONG-TAILED JAEGER
see p.289

black cap

heavy hooked bill

longer pointed tail

OCCURRENCE
Breeds on tundra in northern Canada and Alaska (breeds farther south than other jaegers); during migration and in winter, uses both nearshore and offshore waters; rarely found inland in the US outside the breeding season.

Length **16–18½in (41–47cm)**	Wingspan **3ft 3in–3½ ft (1–1.1m)**	Weight **13–18oz (375–500g)**
Social **Solitary/Small flocks**	Lifespan **Up to 18 years**	Status **Secure**

Order **Charadriiformes**	Family **Stercorariidae**	Species *Stercorarius longicaudus*

Long-tailed Jaeger

gray-and-black upperwing

ADULT (BREEDING)

IN FLIGHT

thin wings

slim, long body

IMMATURE (2ND SUMMER)

dark cap

yellowish cream cheeks

dark, grayish back

grayish brown

JUVENILE (DARK FORM)

extremely long tail streamers

ADULT (BREEDING)

pale breast, with no breastband

FLIGHT: direct, swift glides with rapid wing beats; more buoyant and light than other jaegers.

This elegant and striking species is a surprisingly fierce Arctic and marine predator. Though the Long-tailed Jaeger occasionally steals food from small gulls and terns, it is much less proficient at such piracy than its larger relatives, and usually hunts for its own food. Indeed, the Long-tailed Jaeger is so dependent on there being an abundance of lemmings in the Arctic that in years when lemming numbers dip low, the bird may not even attempt to nest, because there would not be enough lemmings with which to feed its chicks.

VOICE Calls include a chorus of *kreek*, a loud *kreer* warning call, whistles, and high-pitched, sharp clicks.

NESTING Shallow, unlined depression on a rise or hummock in open tundra; 2 eggs; 1 brood; May–August.

FEEDING Hunts lemmings on tundra breeding grounds; takes fish, beetles, and mayflies from water surface; occasionally steals small fish from terns.

DEFENSIVE MOVES
This species protects its territory with angry calls, aggressive swoops, and distraction displays.

SIMILAR SPECIES

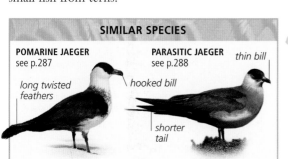

POMARINE JAEGER see p.287

long twisted feathers

PARASITIC JAEGER see p.288

thin bill

hooked bill

shorter tail

OCCURRENCE
Breeds on tundra in northern Canada and Alaska—generally the most northern breeding jaeger; on migration and in winter uses mostly offshore waters; very rarely seen inland in winter.

Length **19–21in (48–53cm)**	Wingspan **3½ft (1.1m)**	Weight **10–11oz (275–300g)**
Social **Solitary/Flocks**	Lifespan **Up to 8 years**	Status **Secure**

| Order **Charadriiformes** | Family **Alcidae** | Species *Alle alle* |

Dovekie

short, dark tail

dark wings

ADULT (BREEDING)

IN FLIGHT

dark head and upper breast

white triangle on side of breast

ADULT (BREEDING)

dark back

white collar at back of head

dark crown

small bill

white throat

white undertail

ADULT (NONBREEDING)

A lso known widely as the Little Auk, the stocky and diminutive black-and-white Dovekie is a bird of the High Arctic. Most Dovekies breed in Greenland in large, noisy, crowded colonies (the largest one containing 15–20 million birds), but some breed in northeastern Canada, and others on a few islands in the Bering Sea off Alaska. On their breeding grounds, both adult and immature Dovekies are hunted ruthlessly by Glaucous Gulls, as well as mammalian predators, such as the Arctic Fox. Vast numbers of Dovekies winter on the Low Arctic waters off the northeastern North American seaboard, in immense flocks. Occasionally, severe onshore gales cause entire flocks to become stranded along the East Coast of North America.

VOICE Variety of calls at breeding colony, including high-pitched trilling that rises and falls; silent at sea.

NESTING Pebble nest in crack or crevice in boulder field or rocky outcrop; 1 egg; 1 brood; April–August.

FEEDING Mostly picks tiny crustaceans from just below the sea's surface.

FLIGHT: rapid, whirring wing beats; flies in flocks low over the water's surface.

SOCIABLE LITTLE AUK
After initial squabbles over nest sites, Dovekies in breeding colonies become highly sociable.

OCCURRENCE
Breeds on islands inside the Arctic Circle; in Greenland, mostly, but also in northeastern Canada and the Bering Sea. Many birds remain just south of the Arctic pack ice throughout the winter; others fly south to winter off the northeastern seaboard of North America.

SIMILAR SPECIES

BLACK GUILLEMOT ☾
see p.294

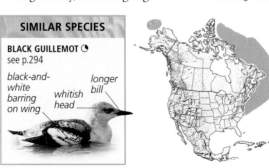

black-and-white barring on wing

whitish head

longer bill

| Length **8½in (21cm)** | Wingspan **15in (38cm)** | Weight **6oz (175g)** |
| Social **Colonies** | Lifespan **Unknown** | Status **Secure** |

Order **Charadriiformes**	Family **Alcidae**	Species ***Uria lomvia***

Thick-billed Murre

ADULT (BREEDING)

IN FLIGHT

hunched in flight

short, black tail

brownish black sides of head

white line along bill

white breast and underparts

all-blackish upperparts

ADULT (BREEDING)

reduced or absent white line on bill

more extensive white on throat

ADULT (NONBREEDING)

FLIGHT: near the water surface with strong, rapid wing beats.

Large and robust, the Thick-billed Murre is one of the most abundant seabirds in the whole of the Northern Hemisphere. Its dense, coastal cliff breeding colonies can be made up of around a million birds each. Chicks leave the colony when they are only about 25 percent of the adult's weight. Their growth is completed at sea, while being fed by the male parent alone. The Thick-billed Murre can dive to a remarkable 600ft (180m) to catch fish and squid.

VOICE Roaring, groaning, insistent sounding *aoorrr*; lower-pitched than the Common Murre.

NESTING Rocky coast or narrow sea cliff ledge in dense colony; 1 egg; 1 brood; March–September.

FEEDING Cod, herring, capelin, and sand lance in summer; also crustaceans, worms, and squid.

SIMILAR SPECIES

COMMON MURRE see p.292

more upright posture

longer, thinner bill

RAZORBILL see p.293

flat, dark bill

thick neck

CLIFF HANGER
Thick-billed Murres breed in dense colonies on steep cliffs, often in very remote areas.

OCCURRENCE
Breeds on rocky shorelines, using the same nest each year. Winters at sea, spending extended periods of time on very cold, deep, and often remote ocean waters and pack ice edges or openings.

Length **18in (46cm)**	Wingspan **28in (70cm)**	Weight **34oz (975g)**
Social **Colonies**	Lifespan **At least 25 years**	Status **Secure**

| Order **Charadriiformes** | Family **Alcidae** | Species *Cepphus grylle* |

Black Guillemot

ADULT (BREEDING)
- broad, rounded wings
- oval, snowy white upperwing patch

IN FLIGHT

gray bars in white wing patch
gray cap
gray neck

JUVENILE

thin, straight bill

large white patch

dark belly

scarlet legs and feet

ADULT (BREEDING)

round, black body

Black Guillemots, also known as "sea pigeons," are medium-sized auks with distinctive black plumage and white wing patches. Their striking scarlet legs and mouth lining help attract a mate during the breeding season. Like the other two species of the *Cepphus* genus, Black Guillemots prefer shallow, inshore waters to the open ocean. They winter near the shore, sometimes moving into the mouths of rivers.

VOICE Very high-pitched whistles and squeaks given on land and water near nesting habitat that resonate like an echo.

NESTING Shallow scrape in soil or pebbles within cave or crevice, site may be reused; 1–2 eggs; 1 brood; May–August.

FEEDING Dives under water near shore to hunt small, bottom-dwelling fish, such as rock eels, sand lance, and sculpin; propels down to depths of 59ft (18m) using partly opened wings, webbed feet as a rudder; feeds close to nesting islands.

FLIGHT: flies low over the water with very rapid wing beats.

FOOD FOR CHICKS
The birds carry food for the chicks in their bills and often pause near the nest before dashing home.

SIMILAR SPECIES

DOVEKIE ❄
see p.290
smaller
dark back
white patch behind eye

PIGEON GUILLEMOT ☼
dusky underwings in flight; see p.295
black bar on white wing patch

OCCURRENCE
Primarily an Atlantic species. Breeds in crevices on remote rocky islands and cliffs that provide protection from predators. At sea prefers shallow waters, close to rocky coasts. At end of breeding season, adults and young move closer to shore to avoid pack ice.

| Length **13in (33cm)** | Wingspan **21in (53cm)** | Weight **15oz (425g)** |
| Social **Colonies** | Lifespan **At least 20 years** | Status **Localized** |

| Order **Charadriiformes** | Family **Alcidae** | Species *Cepphus columba* |

Pigeon Guillemot

oval, snowy white upperwing patch

dusky neck and face

dusky crown

black upperparts

ADULT

JUVENILE

ADULT (BREEDING)

broad, rounded wings

IN FLIGHT

feet and legs trail in flight

stocky, round body

dark bar across white wing patch

dark rump

bright red-orange legs and feet

The Pigeon Guillemot, a North Pacific seabird, is found along rocky shores in small colonies or isolated pairs. This auk nests in burrows or under rocks, often on small islands that provide protection from land-bound predators. The male excavates a burrow, or chooses an abandoned burrow or crevice, to build a nest. During the breeding season, the bird's striking red-orange legs and mouth lining are used in courtship displays to attract a mate.

VOICE Excited, squeaky whistles, and twitters; nesting birds give a weak whistle *peeeee*.

NESTING Shallow scrape in burrow or crevice; 2 eggs; 1 brood; May–August.

FEEDING Feeds near shore; dives to seabed, then uses bill to forage for small rock eels, sculpin, crabs, shrimp, marine worms, and mollusks; carries food for chicks in beak.

FLIGHT: flies close to water surface with very rapid, fluttering wing beats.

PREDATOR BECOMES PREY
Predatory gulls can kill adult Pigeon Guillemots and sometimes eat their chicks and eggs.

OCCURRENCE
Breeds on rocky islands, coastlines, and cliffs where it is less accessible to predators. At sea, it generally remains close to rocky coasts, except in the Bering Sea, where it is found further out along the edges of the pack ice. In winter, some populations are forced south by sea ice.

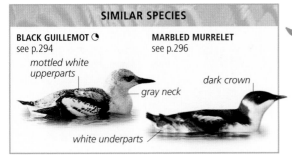

SIMILAR SPECIES

BLACK GUILLEMOT ☾ see p.294

MARBLED MURRELET see p.296

mottled white upperparts

gray neck

dark crown

white underparts

| Length **13½in (34cm)** | Wingspan **23in (58cm)** | Weight **18oz (500g)** |
| Social **Colonies** | Lifespan **Up to 14 years** | Status **Localized** |

| Order **Charadriiformes** | Family **Alcidae** | Species **Brachyramphus marmoratus** |

Marbled Murrelet

ADULT (NONBREEDING)

white patches on side of rump

IN FLIGHT

dark overall

ADULT (BREEDING)

dark face patch

white collar

ADULT (NONBREEDING)

dark brown head

dark tail

speckled upperparts

dark brown back

spotted chin, throat, and chest

ADULT (BREEDING)

mottled underparts

The breeding habits of the Marbled Murrelet, a bird of both sea and forest, remained a mystery until 1974, when the first nest was discovered high in a Douglas Fir in a California park. Unlike most auks and their relatives, which have black and white breeding plumage, the Marbled Murrelet's breeding plumage is brown, to camouflage the bird on its nest in the branches of trees or, in places, on the ground. Ornithologists are eager to learn more about this secretive seabird, even as its numbers decline due to clear-cutting of old-growth conifer forests, where it nests, entanglement of the bird in fishing gear, and oil pollution out at sea, where it feeds.

VOICE Flight call series of high-pitched, squealing, slightly descending *kleeer* notes.

NESTING In northern part of its range, on island mountainsides; in the south, on tree limbs in old-growth forests; 1 egg; 1 brood; April–September.

FEEDING Short dives to catch small fish and crustaceans in shallow offshore waters, "flying" underwater; feeds at night, in pairs.

FLIGHT: straight, fast, and low over water, with extremely rapid wing beats.

RUNNING ON WATER
The Marbled Murrelet flaps its wings energetically and runs across the surface to become airborne.

OCCURRENCE
Relies on marine and forested habitats for both feeding and breeding, on Pacific coasts from Alaska to California; at sea, usually found near coast, in relatively shallow waters. In the breeding season, travels back and forth between the sea and inland breeding grounds.

SIMILAR SPECIES

KITTLITZ'S MURRELET
see p.297

white above eyes

white undertail

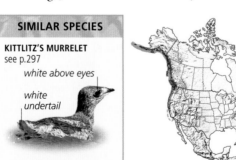

| Length **10in (26cm)** | Wingspan **16in (41cm)** | Weight **8oz (225g)** |
| Social **Pairs/Small groups** | Lifespan **Unknown** | Status **Vulnerable** |

Order **Charadriiformes**	Family **Alcidae**	Species ***Brachyramphus brevirostris***

Kittlitz's Murrelet

dark underwing

ADULT (NONBREEDING)

white face

white underparts

complete dark collar

ADULT (BREEDING)

IN FLIGHT

dark upper wing feathers

mottled brown and white upperparts

white above eye

short bill

white outer tail

ADULT (BREEDING)

FLIGHT: low and rapid, with very fast beats of its long, pointed wings.

D ue to the remote, far-north habitat of Kittlitz's Murrelet, even the basic facts of this little seabird's life cycle are shrouded in mystery. Fewer than 30 of its nests have been found in North America. These nests were found in crevices of talus slopes and other rocky habitats, also near glaciers, on steep, barren hillsides on both islands and the mainland. The bird's breeding behavior is little known, but it is a permanent resident except where the ocean freezes over in winter. This species is declining at an alarming rate, most likely due to climate change warming the sea, and so affecting the bird's food supply. Kittlitz's Murrelet is sometimes seen with other birds, such as the Marbled Murrelet, with which it can be easily confused.

VOICE Quiet, low, groaning *urrrrn* call; also short quacking.

NESTING Scrape on rocky mountain slopes near coast; 1 egg; 1 brood; April–September.

FEEDING Dives primarily in the nutrient-rich glacial outflow areas along coasts for crustaceans and fish such as capelin, sandlance, and herring.

GLACIAL HOME
Frigid waters at the mouth of glaciers are the favorite feeding places of Kittlitz's Murrelet.

TAKING OFF
Frantic wing flapping and kicking precede this bird's lift-off from icy water.

SIMILAR SPECIES

MARBLED MURRELET
see p.296

darker face and crown

dark undertail

OCCURRENCE
Thrives in areas where glaciers meet ocean. During breeding season feeds at sea around icebergs or closer to coast in icy fiords and bays; after breeding moves farther out to sea, although exact winter location unknown; small numbers reported in openings in the pack ice.

Length **9½in (24cm)**	Wingspan **17in (43cm)**	Weight **8oz (225g)**
Social **Pairs/Small groups**	Lifespan **Unknown**	Status **Vulnerable**

| Order **Charadriiformes** | Family **Alcidae** | Species *Synthliboramphus hypoleucus* |

Xantus's Murrelet

ragged margin between black and white on face

slender, black bill

gray upperparts

white throat, to base of bill

broken, white eye-ring

dark margin to wing lining

white wing lining

ADULT

IN FLIGHT

ADULT

short tail, frequently raised

white underparts

WWWWWWWWWWWWW

FLIGHT: swift and direct with rapid wing beats; close to the water's surface.

This small bird of coastal Pacific waters is among the world's most threatened seabirds, nesting in as few as 10 locations. Rarely seen from the coast, Xantus's Murrelet prefers deep, warm, offshore waters. It breeds much farther south than other members of its family, in southern California and Baja California. Chicks leave the nest two days after fledging, leaping into the waters below from cliffs as high as 200ft (60m), in the dark of night. Parent birds then rear their young on the water, where they stay in family groups. Xantus's Murrelets in Baja California are distinguished from those in southern California by a white patch in front of each eye.

VOICE Series of several high pitched *seeep* notes by southern Californian birds; Baja California birds give a rattling call.
NESTING On ground, usually in rocky area concealed by vegetation; 2 eggs; 1 brood; April–August.
FEEDING Dives underwater for small fish such as anchovies, and crustaceans, propelling itself through the sea with its powerful wings.

INSTANT LIFTOFF
Powerful wings enable Xantus's Murrelet to leap straight into the air from water.

OFFSHORE FEEDER
Xantus's Murrelet forages in offshore waters beyond the continental shelf.

OCCURRENCE
Prefers warm water. During breeding, entire US population nests in California's Channel Islands, on protected lands. Nests on steep slopes and cliffs of rocky offshore islands; sufficient vegetation for cover preferred. In winter birds move far out to sea.

SIMILAR SPECIES

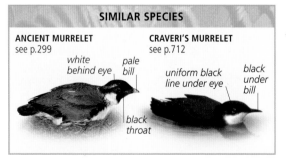

ANCIENT MURRELET
see p.299

white behind eye

pale bill

black throat

CRAVERI'S MURRELET
see p.712

uniform black line under eye

black under bill

| Length **10in (25cm)** | Wingspan **15in (38cm)** | Weight **6oz (175g)** |
| Social **Pairs/Family groups** | Lifespan **At least 15 years** | Status **Endangered** |

Shorebirds, Gulls, and Auks

Order **Charadriiformes**	Family **Alcidae**	Species **Synthliboramphus antiquus**

Ancient Murrelet

ADULT (BREEDING)

white under wing

IN FLIGHT

white underparts with gray sides

lacks distinctive white plumes behind eyes

lacks black throat

ADULT (NONBREEDING)

uniform gray upperparts

distinctive white plumes behind eyes

black face and throat

pale bill tip

distinctive white collar on side of neck

ADULT (BREEDING)

Of the five murrelets that occur regularly in North America, this little species is the most numerous. Like its close relatives, Xantus's Murrelet and Craveri's Murrelet, the Ancient Murrelet usually raises two chicks, and takes them out to sea when they are just a few days old, usually under the cover of darkness. The Ancient Murrelet can also leap straight out of the sea and into flight. White eyebrow-like plumes on the head, combined with a shawl-like gray back, give the bird its supposedly "ancient" appearance.

VOICE Short, high-pitched trills and rattles given by nesting birds while perched in trees.

NESTING Burrow in soft soil, often among forest tree roots; 2 eggs; 1 brood; June–August.

FEEDING Dives for prey in groups, often at the same time, driving schools of small fish to the surface; Euphansiid shrimps, which are about 1in (2.5cm) long, are its primary diet.

FLIGHT: flies fast, low, and straight with rapid wing beats; capable of quick take-off from water.

GROUP FEEDER
The Ancient Murrelet flies low to the water in flocks on the lookout for food.

OCCURRENCE
Lives in the north Pacific, and Bering Sea. Concentrates where food is abundant—most often in straits, sounds, and coastal waters—where it often feeds quite close to shore. Nests on coastal islands, mainly on forest floor but also where there is proper cover and sufficient peaty soil to dig burrows.

SIMILAR SPECIES

XANTUS'S MURRELET
see p.298

lacks white head plumes
gray back
white throat

CRAVERI'S MURRELET
see p.712

dark in front of eye
white throat

Length **10in (26cm)**	Wingspan **17in (43cm)**	Weight **7oz (200g)**
Social **Colonies**	Lifespan **At least 4 years**	Status **Localized**

| Order **Charadriiformes** | Family **Alcidae** | Species **Ptychoramphus aleuticus** |

Cassin's Auklet

rounded wing tips

ADULT (NONBREEDING)

dark underwing with pale stripe

whitish belly

IN FLIGHT

pale gray underparts

white patch

ADULT (NONBREEDING)

sooty overall

thin, white eyebrow

pale eyes

short, thick, gray bill

pale patch at base of bill

ADULT (BREEDING)

This secretive little seabird usually nests in an underground burrow, which can take a breeding pair many weeks to scratch out. Parent birds fish by day, returning to the nest in the safety of darkness to avoid gulls and other predators. Nestlings encourage regurgitation by nibbling at a white spot at the base of the parent's lower mandible. Uniquely for a member of the alcid family, Cassin's Auklet has been known to raise more than one brood in a season.

VOICE Hoarse, rhythmic night calls in colonies; squeals and peeps when in burrow; silent at sea.

NESTING On offshore islands, in crevices or burrows; 1 egg; 1–2 broods; March–September.

FEEDING Dives and swims underwater using wings to pursue small crustaceans, fish, and squid.

FLIGHT: low over the surface of the sea, with rapid wing beats.

RUNNING ON WATER
After a long run and some energetic wing beating, Cassin's Auklet eventually takes off from the water.

OCCURRENCE
Pacific distribution; breeds on cliffs, grassy plains, or slopes on coastal islands. During the nonbreeding season, northern birds found in deep waters beyond the continental shelf, where upwelling currents bring food from the depths. Southern birds remain near their colonies year-round.

SIMILAR SPECIES

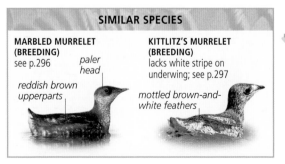

MARBLED MURRELET (BREEDING)
see p.296

paler head

reddish brown upperparts

KITTLITZ'S MURRELET (BREEDING)
lacks white stripe on underwing; see p.297

mottled brown-and-white feathers

| Length **9in (23cm)** | Wingspan **15in (38cm)** | Weight **6oz (175g)** |
| Social **Colonies** | Lifespan **At least 6 years** | Status **Localized** |

Order **Chradriiformes**	Family **Alcidae**	Species **Aethia psittacula**

Parakeet Auklet

uniformly dark wing

ADULT (NONBREEDING)

bright white underparts / **IN FLIGHT**

short tail

ADULT (BREEDING)

dark throat

pale flanks

white eye

single white plume behind each eye

conical orange bill

pale patch

whitish throat

white flanks

ADULT (NONBREEDING)

FLIGHT: strong and direct, but fluttering, with rapid wing beats.

This robust, potbellied little auklet has a bright orange, conical bill—a feature that makes it unique among alcids. It has the widest range of any auklet species, spanning the North Pacific, but breeding is concentrated at localized colonies. Parakeet Auklets live in small, isolated groups on remote islands, usually nesting together with Least and Crested Auklets, although they are always far less abundant than these two species. Like other auklets, Parakeet Auklets are monogamous, and pairs perform conspicuous vocal and visual courtship displays at their colonies.

VOICE Whinnying by males to attract a mate, followed by duet-whinnying by a mated pair during courtship; squeal calls given when birds are alarmed and take flight.

NESTING In crevices along rocky cliff faces, rocky beaches, and grassy slopes; 1 egg; 1 brood; May–August.

FEEDING Pursues soft-bodied prey, such as jellyfish, using wings for propulsion underwater; food regurgitated to young by both parents.

OUT OF REACH
On islands that have foxes, a ledge high up on a cliff is the safest place for the birds to nest.

OCCURRENCE
Breeding range spans rocky habitats, especially cliffs and grassy slopes, on islands of the northern Gulf of Alaska, Bering Sea, and the Pacific coast south of the Aleutians. After breeding, birds go south to winter at sea far from land; their distribution depends upon the location and abundance of food.

SIMILAR SPECIES

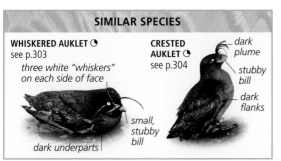

WHISKERED AUKLET ☾
see p.303

three white "whiskers" on each side of face

dark underparts

small, stubby bill

CRESTED AUKLET ☾
see p.304

dark plume

stubby bill

dark flanks

Length **10in (25cm)**	Wingspan **18in (46cm)**	Weight **11oz (300g)**
Social **Pairs/Colonies**	Lifespan **Unknown**	Status **Localized**

Order **Charadriiformes**	Family **Alcidae**	Species *Aethia pusilla*

Least Auklet

pale center of underwing visible on upstroke

ADULT (NONBREEDING)

IN FLIGHT

strikingly white eye

black wings and back

BREEDING (PALE FORM)

white underparts

pale eye

small, dark bill with reddish tip

white facial stripe behind eye

well-defined white throat

spotted underparts, with variable density of spots

BREEDING (DARK FORM)

FLIGHT: low over water with very rapid beats of small wings; circles over nesting colonies.

The smallest of the auks, the Least Auklet often occurs in vast flocks, roosting on boulders along the edge of nesting islands, where the birds give chirping calls. In the air, flocks swirl with great coordination over the ocean near nesting islands. The Least Auklet's underparts vary greatly from white to spotted or even solid gray. This variable plumage may function as a status signal in the breeding season. Despite being one of the most abundant seabirds species in North America, the Least Auklet has a low survival rate compared with other auks. It is vulnerable to rats and foxes, which threaten some colonies, and highly sensitive to human disturbance, refusing to return to its nesting site until the danger has passed.

VOICE Pulsing series of high, grating trills, chirps, or chatters; silent at sea.

NESTING Huge colonies nest on boulder fields or talus slopes in rock crevices; 1 egg; 1 brood; April–September.

FEEDING Forages for tiny swarming prey including shrimp; cannot dive deeply, but fast and agile underwater.

SIMILAR SPECIES

CASSIN'S AUKLET ◐
see p.300

gray flanks

SPRIGHTLY ROCK DWELLER
This plump little bird is surprisingly agile on rocks and cliffs, and can climb almost vertical surfaces.

OCCURRENCE
Huge colonies thrive on Bering Sea islands, where flocks perch on rock piles or circle overhead. Forages in areas with turbulent waters and concentrated food sources, either near shore or far out at sea. Winters at sea near breeding sites, as far north as open water permits.

Length **6½in (16.5cm)**	Wingspan **12in (31cm)**	Weight **3oz (85g)**
Social **Colonies**	Lifespan **Up to 4½ years**	Status **Localized**

Order **Charadriiformes**	Family **Alcidae**	Species *Aethia pygmaea*

Whiskered Auklet

pointed wings

black underwing

ADULT (NONBREEDING)

thin, white lines on face

dark gray undertail

IN FLIGHT

dark brown overall

three white, V-shaped "whiskers"

thin, black crest

dull, orange bill

ADULT (BREEDING)

This dark-plumaged little auk lives on very remote coasts, principally in Alaska. Compared with other North Pacific auks, it is relatively scarce and lives in smaller colonies. During the pre-laying season, pairs come ashore in daylight and congregate on rock piles with Crested, Least, and Parakeet Auklets. Later in the nesting season, the birds become largely nocturnal, with huge numbers appearing at the same time soon after dark. The long head plumes may assist the birds as they feel their way to their underground nests. This nocturnal arrival may help to avoid predation by birds such as large gulls and falcons. Crevice-nesting protects the eggs and chicks against predation during daylight hours, but the introduced Norway rat could have a devastating effect on auklet populations, as this rodent is able to access the nests.

VOICE Kitten-like *meew* and rapid, sharp *beedeer, beedeer, beedeer* call; silent at sea.

NESTING Egg laid on rock, or soil in rock crevices; 1 egg; 1 brood; May–July.

FEEDING Forages for small crustaceans, marine worms, and mollusks near nesting islands in shallow, often rough tidal waters.

FLIGHT: rapid with deep wing strokes; wings used underwater for chasing prey.

DEEP WING BEATS
Auklets need to flap their short, stubby wings with deep, rapid strokes to achieve takeoff speed.

SIMILAR SPECIES

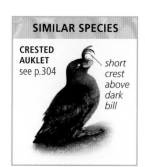

CRESTED AUKLET see p.304

short crest above dark bill

OCCURRENCE
Limited to remote areas of the Aleutian Islands. It forages in shallow water off rocky coasts, areas of rapid tidal currents, and open ocean within range of nesting islands. Nests under boulders on talus slopes. Also breeds in eastern Russia.

Length **8in (20cm)**	Wingspan **14in (36cm)**	Weight **4oz (125g)**
Social **Colonies**	Lifespan **Unknown**	Status **Vulnerable**

Order **Charadriiformes**	Family **Alcidae**	Species *Aethia cristatella*

Crested Auklet

black wing

ADULT (NONBREEDING)

white plume extending back from below eye

bushy tuft that curls forward

thick, stubby orange bill with paler tip

thickset body shape

IN FLIGHT

dark undertail feathers

black upperparts

grayish underparts

dark toes

ADULT (BREEDING)

This small, dark seabird is only found in the Bering Sea. Males and females have a forward-curling tuft of feathers on the forehead that varies in size among individuals. When choosing a breeding partner, both sexes prefer mates with large tufts. Pairs are typically monogamous and compete intensely for nest sites. Crested Auklets fly in large, tight flocks, sometimes circling in the air near their colonies; they are usually active only at night at the colonies. Similar to their close relative, the Whiskered Auklet, their plumage has a distinctive citrus-like odor.

VOICE In colonies, variable barking *kyow* call, reminiscent of small dog; rapid series of honks; silent at sea.

NESTING Shallow depression in soil or pebbles, underground in rock crevices, or several feet under piles of boulders; 1 egg; 1 brood; May–July.

FEEDING Forages in less than 100ft (30m) of water with strong currents, mainly on plankton and small crustaceans near nesting islands; both parents carry food for the young in a special throat pouch.

FLIGHT: swift, direct flight with rapid wing beats, often in tightly packed flocks.

SIMILAR SPECIES

WHISKERED AUKLET see p.303

single curly plume

plumes form v-shape

COURTING PAIR
During courtship, pairs make honking sounds, touch beaks, and intertwine necks.

OCCURRENCE
Forages in turbulent water, caused by nutrient-rich upwellings and tidal rips, near its nesting sites in the Aleutian Islands and other remote islands northward through the Bering Sea. Remains all year where water is ice-free, otherwise winters in the Gulf of Alaska.

Length **10½in (27cm)**	Wingspan **17in (43cm)**	Weight **10oz (275g)**
Social **Colonies**	Lifespan **Up to 8 years**	Status **Vulnerable**

| Order **Charadriiformes** | Family **Alcidae** | Species *Cerorhinca monocerata* |

Rhinoceros Auklet

dark wings

ADULT (NONBREEDING)

IN FLIGHT

white belly

lacks facial plumes

smaller bill

ADULT (NONBREEDING)

horny structure at base of upper bill

dark upperparts

thin, white plumes curving back

ADULT (BREEDING)

This robust bird is closely related to puffins, and is the only auk with a prominent "horn" on top of its bill; it is this structure that gives the bird its common name. The Rhinoceros Auklet forages closer to shore than its puffin relatives, and usually returns to its nesting colonies at night. This trusting seabird often allows boats to approach very closely. It became locally extinct, but re-established its population on California's Farallon Islands in the 1970s when non-native rabbits that were competing for nesting burrows were removed. When fishing, it carries its catch in its beak, rather than in a throat pouch like other auks.

VOICE Adults give series of low, mooing calls, as well as short barks and groans.

NESTING Cup of moss or twigs on islands, under vegetation, in crevice or long, soil burrow; 1 egg; 1 brood; April–September.

FEEDING Forages underwater during breeding season, looks for small schooling fish for nestlings; also eats crustaceans; powerful diver and swimmer.

FLIGHT: swift, direct with quick wing beats; takeoff appears labored.

SUBMARINE-LIKE
Its body nearly submerged and its head looking behind, this Rhinoceros Auklet is ready to dive.

OCCURRENCE
Throughout temperate North Pacific waters, generally south of puffin habitat. Typically lives far out at sea, but may feed near shore where currents concentrate food; usually forages and returns to nesting colonies by night.

SIMILAR SPECIES
PARAKEET AUKLET ♂ see p.301

paler breast

| Length **15in (38cm)** | Wingspan **22in (56cm)** | Weight **16oz (450g)** |
| Social **Colonies** | Lifespan **Unknown** | Status **Localized** |

| Order **Charadriiformes** | Family **Alcidae** | Species *Fratercula arctica* |

Atlantic Puffin

dusky gray face

dull bill

ADULT (NONBREEDING)

black back, collar, and underwings

blue-gray, orange, and red stripes on bill

short tail

ADULT (BREEDING)

IN FLIGHT

orange legs and feet

ADULT (BREEDING)

gray face

red eye-ring

thick black line

stocky, rounded body

large, colorful, triangular bill

white breast

ADULT (BREEDING)

With its black-and-white "tuxedo," ungainly upright posture, and enormous, colorful bill, the Atlantic Puffin is often known as the "clown of the sea." Certainly it looks comical, whether strutting about or simply bobbing on the sea. It is seen in summer, when large breeding colonies gather on remote, rocky islands. To feed itself and its young, it can dive down to 200ft (60m) with partly folded wings, essentially "flying" underwater in pursuit of small schooling fish.

VOICE Rising and falling buzzy growl, resembling a chainsaw.
NESTING Underground burrow or deep rock crevice lined with grass and feathers; 1 egg; 1 brood; June–August.
FEEDING Dives deep for capelin, herring, hake, sand lance, and other small fish, which it swallows underwater, or stores crossways in its bill to take back to its chicks.

FLIGHT: swift and direct, with rapid wing beats; often circles breeding islands.

CATCH AND CARRY
When returning to breeding colonies to feed chicks, most birds carry more than one fish in their bill.

SIMILAR SPECIES

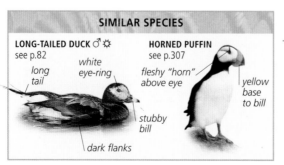

LONG-TAILED DUCK ♂ ☼
see p.82

long tail

white eye-ring

HORNED PUFFIN
see p.307

fleshy "horn" above eye

yellow base to bill

stubby bill

dark flanks

OCCURRENCE
This northern North Atlantic seabird (found on both sides of the ocean) breeds in colonies on small, rocky, offshore islands, where it excavates nesting burrows or nests under boulders. Between breeding seasons, it heads for the high seas and remains far offshore, favoring cold, open waters.

| Length **12½in (32cm)** | Wingspan **21in (53cm)** | Weight **12oz (350g)** |
| Social **Colonies** | Lifespan **At least 30 years** | Status **Localized** |

Order **Charadriiformes**	Family **Alcidae**	Species *Fratercula corniculata*

Horned Puffin

dark wing

no fleshy "horn" above eye

brown base to bill

gray face

ADULT (NONBREEDING)

IN FLIGHT

fleshy "horn" above eye

white face

black neck collar

large, yellow bill, with orange tip

dark upperparts

white underparts

ADULT (BREEDING)

bright orange legs and toes

FLIGHT: swift and direct, with rapid wing beats; usually near the water's surface.

This hardy alcid is similar to the Atlantic Puffin in appearance and behavior, but the Horned Puffin is larger and lives on the other side of North America, in the northern Pacific and Bering Sea. Here it nests on even more remote rocky offshore islands than its Atlantic relative. Outside the breeding season, Horned Puffins spend month after month far out at sea, hundreds of miles from the nearest land. When the birds return to their breeding grounds, pairs often head straight for the same rock crevice they nested in the year before.

VOICE Low-pitched, rumbling growls in rhythmic phrases.

NESTING Deep rock crevices lined with grass and feathers; 1 egg; 1 brood; May–August.

FEEDING Dives for herring, sand lance, capelin, smelt, and other small fishes to feed to chicks; adults consume squid, crustaceans, and marine worms underwater.

SIMILAR SPECIES

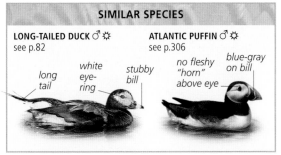

LONG-TAILED DUCK ♂ ☼
see p.82

long tail

white eye-ring

ATLANTIC PUFFIN ♂ ☼
see p.306

stubby bill

no fleshy "horn" above eye

blue-gray on bill

BACK AND FORTH
Parent birds fly repeatedly to and from the nest to catch fish for their chicks.

OCCURRENCE
Breeds on rocky islands off Alaskan coast (where crevices for nesting are plentiful); feeds close to these shores. Often found with Tufted Puffins, but generally farther north. Rarely wanders as far south as California in the nonbreeding season. Winters on ocean waters far from land.

Length **15in (38cm)**	Wingspan **23in (59cm)**	Weight **23oz (650g)**
Social **Colonies**	Lifespan **At least 20 years**	Status **Localized**

Order **Charadriiformes**	Family **Alcidae**	Species *Fratercula cirrhata*

Tufted Puffin

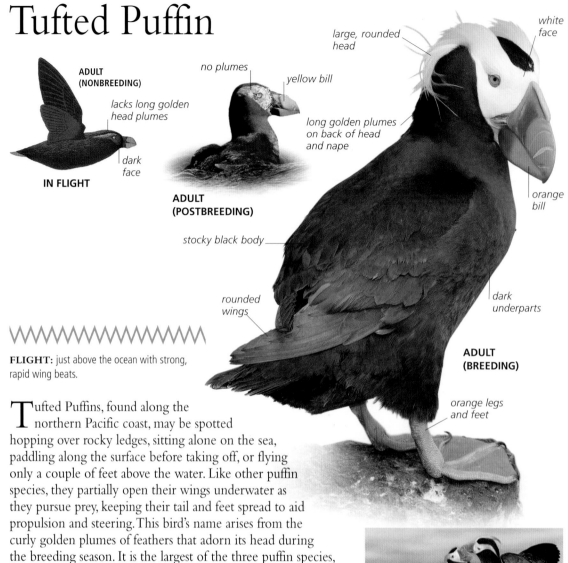

ADULT (NONBREEDING)

lacks long golden head plumes

dark face

IN FLIGHT

no plumes

yellow bill

long golden plumes on back of head and nape

ADULT (POSTBREEDING)

large, rounded head

white face

orange bill

stocky black body

rounded wings

dark underparts

ADULT (BREEDING)

orange legs and feet

WWWWWWWWWWWWW

FLIGHT: just above the ocean with strong, rapid wing beats.

Tufted Puffins, found along the northern Pacific coast, may be spotted hopping over rocky ledges, sitting alone on the sea, paddling along the surface before taking off, or flying only a couple of feet above the water. Like other puffin species, they partially open their wings underwater as they pursue prey, keeping their tail and feet spread to aid propulsion and steering. This bird's name arises from the curly golden plumes of feathers that adorn its head during the breeding season. It is the largest of the three puffin species, and can be distinguished from the Horned Puffin by its dark underparts, and from the Atlantic Puffin by its distribution.
VOICE Low, moaning growl given from burrow.
NESTING Chamber, lined with grass or feathers, at end of tunnel, under rocks, or in burrow; 1 egg; 1 brood; May–August.
FEEDING Dives deep to capture small fish, especially sand lance, juvenile pollock, and capelin; adults consume prey underwater, or take it ashore to feed their chicks.

TUFTED PAIR
These distinctive and popular birds breed in colonies and usually mate for life.

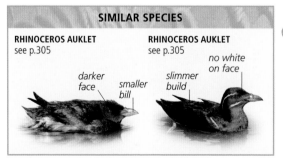

SIMILAR SPECIES

RHINOCEROS AUKLET
see p.305

darker face

smaller bill

RHINOCEROS AUKLET
see p.305

slimmer build

no white on face

OCCURRENCE
Breeds on rocky islands, and coastal cliffs of the North Pacific, especially treeless offshore islands with sea cliffs or grassy slopes; elevation may help them take flight. Found over unusually wide geographic and climatic range. Winters at sea, usually over deep waters of the central North Pacific.

Length **15in (38cm)**	Wingspan **25in (64cm)**	Weight **27oz (775g)**
Social **Colonies**	Lifespan **Up to 30 years**	Status **Localized**

PIGEONS AND DOVES

THE LARGER SPECIES WITHIN the family Columbidae are known as pigeons, and the smaller ones as doves, although there is no actual scientific basis for the distinction. They are all fairly heavy, plump birds with relatively small heads and short necks. They also possess slender bills with their nostrils positioned in a bumpy mound at the base. Among other things, members of this family have strong wing muscles, making them powerful and agile fliers. When alarmed, they burst into flight with their wings emitting a distinctive clapping or swishing sound. Pigeons and doves produce a nutritious "crop-milk," which they secrete to feed their young. Despite human activity having severely affected members of this family in the past (the leading cause of the Passenger Pigeon's extinction in the 19th century is thought to be over hunting), the introduced Rock Pigeon has adapted and proliferated worldwide, as has the recently introduced Eurasian Collared-Dove, albeit on a smaller scale. The introduced Spotted Dove has not shown a similar tendency for explosive expansion, however, and remains limited to southern California and the islands of Hawaii. Among the species native to North America, only the elegant Mourning Dove is as widespread as the various species of introduced birds.

NATIVE PIGEON
A native species, the Band-tailed Pigeon is sadly declining through much of its range.

DOVE IN THE SUN
The Mourning Dove sun bathes each side of its body in turn, its wings and tail outspread.

| Order **Columbiformes** | Family **Columbidae** | Species *Columba livia* |

Rock Pigeon

black wing bars

white underwings

white rump

ADULT

IN FLIGHT

iridescence on neck

gray back

short bill

no wing bars

variably colored body

two black wing bars

ADULT (FERAL)

dark-tipped tail

ADULT (ANCESTRAL FORM)

The Rock Pigeon was introduced to the Atlantic coast of North America by 17th century colonists. Now feral, this species is found all over the continent, especially around farms, cities, and towns. This medium-sized pigeon comes in a wide variety of plumage colors and patterns, including bluish gray, checkered, rusty red, and nearly all-white. Its wings usually have two dark bars on them—unique among North American pigeons. The variability of the Rock Pigeon influenced Charles Darwin as he developed his theory of natural selection.

VOICE Soft, gurgling *coo*, *roo-c'too-coo*, for courtship and threat.

NESTING Twig nest on flat, sheltered surface, such as caves, rocky outcrops, and buildings; 2 eggs; several broods; year-round.

FEEDING Eats seeds, fruit, and rarely insects; human foods such as popcorn, bread, peanuts; various farm crops in rural areas.

FLIGHT: strong, direct; can reach speeds up to around 60mph (95kph.)

CITY PIGEONS
Most Rock Pigeons in North America descend from domesticated forms and exhibit many colors.

SIMILAR SPECIES

WHITE-CROWNED PIGEON mangroves; see p.311

white crown

dark gray overall

BAND-TAILED PIGEON western; see p.312

yellow bill with dark tip

white band on nape

OCCURRENCE
Across southern Canada and North America; nests in human structures of all sorts; resident. Original habitat in the Old World was (and still is) sea cliffs and inland canyons; found wild in some places, such as dry regions of North Africa, but feral in much of the world.

| Length **11–14in (28–36cm)** | Wingspan **20–26in (51–67cm)** | Weight **9–14oz (250–400g)** |
| Social **Solitary/Flocks** | Lifespan **Up to 6 years** | Status **Secure** |

Order **Columbiformes**	Family **Columbidae**	Species **Columba leucocephala**

White-crowned Pigeon

white crown

dark gray overall

ADULT

IN FLIGHT

bright white crown

white eye ring

purple nape

reddish bill with yellowish tip

slate-gray back and wings

all-dark tail

ADULT

FLIGHT: strong, direct flight with fast wing beats at elevations under 300ft (90m).

The large White-crowned Pigeon is similar in size and shape to the Rock Pigeon, but with a distinctive white crown, slate-gray back, and slightly longer tail. In North America it is only found in the Florida Keys and the southern tip of the Florida, in the Everglades. While it is often more nervous around humans than the Rock Pigeon, it does feed in areas around hotels and suburban backyards. It subsists almost solely on fruit, and fruit trees are central to its survival. Habitat loss and its popularity as a game species have put this species under threat.

VOICE Loud, deep *coo-curra-coo*, repeated 5–8 times; also low, purring growl.
NESTING Frail twig platform in dense mangrove vegetation, often over water; 2 eggs; 1–4 broods; May–August.
FEEDING Mainly eats fruit and berries, rarely wasps and flies, small land snails, seeds, and mangrove flowers; feeds in mainland forests containing plenty of fruit-bearing trees.

UNMISTAKABLE
The bright, white crown of the male White-crowned Pigeon is unique among the pigeons.

OCCURRENCE
Nests on both red and black mangrove islands. Winters in seasonal deciduous forests of Florida Keys and Everglades National Park. Birds may travel some distance each day to visit key feeding sites. Widespread in Bahamas, West Indies, islands off Mexico, Central American birds winter on the mainland.

SIMILAR SPECIES

ROCK PIGEON
see p.310

variable plumage

darker crown

smaller overall

BAND-TAILED PIGEON
western; see p.312

dark-tipped yellow bill

white nape

larger overall

Length **13–14in (33–35cm)**	Wingspan **23in (59cm)**	Weight **8–10oz (225–275g)**
Social **Solitary**	Lifespan **Unknown**	Status **Vulnerable**

Order **Columbiformes**	Family **Columbidae**	Species **Patagioenas fasciata**

Band-tailed Pigeon

wide tail band

dark gray outer wings

light gray inner wings

tip of tail pale

ADULT

IN FLIGHT

dark-tipped yellow bill

white band on nape

iridescence on hind neck

ADULT

blue-gray upperparts

uniform blue-gray underparts

yellow legs and toes

gray tail

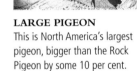

LARGE PIGEON
This is North America's largest pigeon, bigger than the Rock Pigeon by some 10 per cent.

WWWWWWWWWW

FLIGHT: direct, strong flight with powerful, regular wing beats.

The Band-tailed Pigeon is similar to the Rock Pigeon in its size, posture, body movements, and breeding and feeding behavior. However, in North America the Band-tailed Pigeon's distribution is limited to the dry, mountainous forests of four southwestern states, and the wet coastal forests of the West Coast, from the southeastern tip of Alaska south to Baja California. The distinguishing features of the Band-tailed Pigeon are its yellow bill and legs, a white band just above the iridescent green patch on the back of its neck—and its eponymous banded tail.
VOICE Often silent, but emits series of two-noted, low-frequency *whooos* punctuated with a pause.
NESTING Flat, saucer-shaped, rather flimsy platform of twigs, needles, and moss in a variety of trees; 1 egg; 1 brood; April–October.
FEEDING Forages on the ground for grain, seeds, fruit, acorns, and pine nuts; hangs upside down by its toes from the branches of shrubs and trees to eat dangling nuts and flowers that are otherwise out of reach.

UNIFORMITY
Unlike flocks of Rock Pigeons, Band-tailed Pigeon flocks have very uniform plumage.

SIMILAR SPECIES

ROCK PIGEON
see p.310

two wing bars

dark bill

OCCURRENCE
Breeds and winters in temperate conifer rainforest along the Pacific coast, and in mountain conifer and mixed-species forests in the interior. Lives in urban and rural areas where there are evergreen trees and access to grains, fruit, and feeders. Some populations are resident, others migratory.

Length **13–16in (33–41cm)**	Wingspan **26in (66cm)**	Weight **12–13oz (350–375g)**
Social **Flocks**	Lifespan **Up to 18 years**	Status **Declining**

Order **Columbiformes**	Family **Columbidae**	Species ***Streptopelia decaocto***

Eurasian Collared-Dove

ADULT

dark outer wing feathers

gray wing feathers

IN FLIGHT

dark bill

black collar on hind neck

pale gray body

ADULT

square tail

gray undertail wing feathers

A stocky bird, the Eurasian Collared-Dove is easily recognized by the black collar on the back of its neck and its square tail. First released at New Providence, Bahamas, in the mid-1970s, this species is spreading rapidly across the continental mainland, thanks to multiple local releases, the planting of trees in urban and suburban habitats, the popularity of bird feeders making food readily available, and the bird's extraordinarily high reproductive rate. This species soon becomes very confiding and tolerant of humans, regularly nesting and feeding in urban areas. One consequence of this is that it often falls prey to domestic cats, but this has little effect on the expanding population. Based on sightings from locations all over North America—and on the evidence from Europe, throughout which it has spread since only the 1940s—it is highly likely that the Eurasian Collared-Dove will soon become a common species in North America.

VOICE Repeated four-note *coo-hoo-HOO-cook* that is quick and low-pitched; also harsh, nasal *krreeew* in flight.

NESTING Platform of twigs, stems, and grasses in trees or on buildings; 2 eggs; multiple broods; March–November.

FEEDING Eats seed and grain, plant stems and leaves, berries, and some invertebrates; feeds on the ground for seed, but also visits elevated feeders.

FLIGHT: strong, stiff flight reminiscent of hawks; occasional swoops and dives.

COLLARED COLONIZER
The Eurasian Collared-Dove has spread throughout Europe in just a few decades, and now looks set to do the same in North America.

OCCURRENCE
Can be seen almost anywhere in North America south of the northern forest zone, but occurs mainly in suburban and urban areas (though not large cities) and agricultural areas with seeds and grain for food and deciduous trees for nesting and roosting. May roost in man-made structures such as barns.

SIMILAR SPECIES

MOURNING DOVE
see p.314

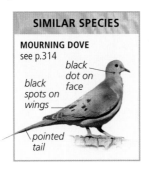

black dot on face

black spots on wings

pointed tail

Length **11½–12in (29–30cm)**	Wingspan **14in (35cm)**	Weight **5–6oz (150–175g)**
Social **Large flocks**	Lifespan **Up to 13 years**	Status **Localized**

313

| Order **Columbiformes** | Family **Columbidae** | Species ***Zenaida macroura*** |

Mourning Dove

mostly uniform gray wings

pointed tail

ADULT

IN FLIGHT

faint mottling on neck and underparts

JUVENILE

blue eye-ring

thin, dark bill

black dot on side of face

dark spots on wings

plump, gray body

long, pointed tail

pink legs and toes

ADULT

One of the most familiar, abundant, and widespread of North American birds, the Mourning Dove is a long, plump, medium-sized dove with an undersized head. It has a grayish tan body with a pale, rosy breast and black spots on folded wings. While coveted by hunters—as many as 70 million are shot annually—the Mourning Dove is also well known to those who live on farms and in suburbia. Found all across North America, the species is divided into two subspecies—the larger grayish brown *Z. m. carolinensis*, east of the Mississippi River, and the smaller, paler *Z. m. marginella* in the west.

VOICE Mellow, owl-like call: *hoO-Oo-oo, hoo-hoo-hoo.*
NESTING Flat, flimsy twig platform, mostly in trees, sometimes on the ground; 2 eggs; 2 broods; February–October.
FEEDING Forages mainly for seeds on the ground; obtains food quickly and digests it later at roost.

FLIGHT: swift, direct flight, with fairly quick wing beats; twists and turns sometimes.

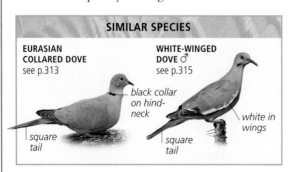

SIMILAR SPECIES

EURASIAN COLLARED DOVE
see p.313

WHITE-WINGED DOVE ♂
see p.315

black collar on hind-neck

square tail

white in wings

square tail

see p.313 ... see p.315

FAMILIAR SIGHT
The Mourning Dove is North America's most widespread member of this family.

OCCURRENCE
Breeds in a wide variety of habitats but shuns extensive forests; human-altered vegetation favored for feeding, including farmland and suburbia. Winters in small to medium sheltered woodland while feeding in grain fields; winters in southern Mexico and Central America.

| Length **9–13½in (23–34cm)** | Wingspan **14½–17½in (37–45cm)** | Weight **3–6oz (85–175g)** |
| Social **Pairs/Winter flocks** | Lifespan **Up to 19 years** | Status **Secure** |

| Order **Columbiformes** | Family **Columbidae** | Species **Zenaida asiatica** |

White-winged Dove

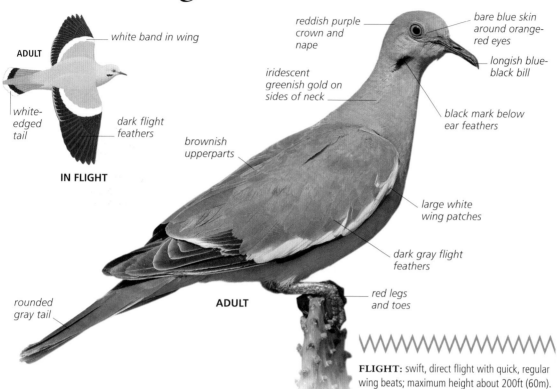

white band in wing

ADULT

white-edged tail

dark flight feathers

IN FLIGHT

reddish purple crown and nape

iridescent greenish gold on sides of neck

brownish upperparts

rounded gray tail

ADULT

bare blue skin around orange-red eyes

longish blue-black bill

black mark below ear feathers

large white wing patches

dark gray flight feathers

red legs and toes

FLIGHT: swift, direct flight with quick, regular wing beats; maximum height about 200ft (60m).

As one of the larger gray-colored dove species in North America, the White-winged Dove is best identified in flight by the conspicuous white bands on its wings. When perched, this bird displays bright blue skin around its orange eyes and a longish, square tail with a white tip. This species has been expanding its population northwards in recent decades, though not as progressively as the Eurasian Collared Dove. Increased farmland habitat and ornamental trees, both favorite roosting places, are the most likely cause. In common with many other doves, the nest is a somewhat flimsy structure, and eggs or nestlings frequently fall to their end if the nest is disturbed, or when there are high winds.

VOICE Distinctive, drawn-out cooing: *who-cooks-for-you*; also makes five-note variation from the nest: *la-coo-kla-coo-kla*.

NESTING Frail platform of twigs, moss, and grasses, on a sturdy branch in dense-canopied trees; 2 eggs; 2 broods; March–September.

FEEDING Forages for seeds, wild nuts, and fruit on the ground and in elevated locations; prefers corn, sorghum, wheat, and sunflower.

DESERT DWELLER
The White-winged Dove is much more at home in semi-arid and desert areas than the Mourning Dove.

SIMILAR SPECIES

MOURNING DOVE
see p.314

smaller, rounder head

no white wing patch

longer tail

see p.314

OCCURRENCE
Breeds and winters in dense, thorny woodlands dominated by mesquite and Texas Ebony; deserts with cactus, palo verde, and other scrub plants; riverine woodlands, orchards, and residential areas. Formerly only abundant in the US in the Rio Grande Valley, it has now expanded north to Oklahoma.

| Length **11½in (29cm)** | Wingspan **19in (48cm)** | Weight **5oz (150g)** |
| Social **Solitary/Flocks** | Lifespan **Up to 21 years** | Status **Localized** |

| Order **Psittaciformes** | Family **Psittacidae** | Species *Aratinga holochlora* |

Green Parakeet

long, pointed tail

pointed wings

green overall

IN FLIGHT

maroon skin around eye

green upperparts and wings

hooked bill

yellow-green breast and belly

long, pointed tail

As with other parrots in the US, this bright green bird is a native of Mexico and northern South America, and most probably an escapee from the cage-bird trade: it appeared in southern Texas in the late 1970s and early 1980s. The number of Green Parakeets in Texas has greatly increased in recent years, and is thought to have reached 2,000 or more. In Florida, where several species of *Aratinga* parakeets occur together, there are now around 100 Green Parakeets. Some birds have scattered yellow, orange, or red feathers either on the head, on the breast, or even all three colors combined.

VOICE Typical parakeet high-pitched screech notes; also shrill chattering.

NESTING Cavity in tree (often palm), which has previously been excavated by a woodpecker, rock crevice, or, in the tropics, termite mound; 4 eggs; 1 brood; March–July.

FEEDING Eats a variety of fruits, nuts, and seeds; also visits bird feeders.

FLIGHT: usually in flocks; swift and direct; also with rapid changes in course.

PERCHING VERTICALLY
Strong claws and feet allow parakeets to perch with ease on vertical surfaces.

OCCURRENCE
Breeds and winters in suburban and urban areas in Texas and Florida, including parks and gardens typically planted with exotic trees and shrubs. In their native range in Mexico and Central America, they are usually found in evergreen and deciduous forests up to 6,500 ft (2,000m).

SIMILAR SPECIES

MONK PARAKEET ♂
see p.321

dark wings

gray face and cap

bluish outer wing feathers

| Length **13in (33cm)** | Wingspan **21in (53cm)** | Weight **8oz (225g)** |
| Social **Flocks** | Lifespan **Up to 6 years** | Status **Localized** |

| Order **Psittaciformes** | Family **Psittacidae** | Species *Myiopsitta monachus* |

Monk Parakeet

long, pointed tail

green inner wing feathers

gray face

dark blue-black outer wing feathers

IN FLIGHT

green upperparts

hooked, orangish bill

gray face and forehead

gray breast

yellowish belly

two forward- and two backward-pointing toes

long green tail

Monk Parakeets, native to Bolivia, Argentina, Paraguay, and Brazil, have been introduced to a number of places in the United States. They are the most abundant and widespread species of introduced parrot in North America, locally breeding in huge colonies. Their large communal nests of sticks are unique among parrots and parakeets. These nests are used both for breeding and for roosting. If food is abundant, Monk Parakeets are perfectly capable of surviving cold winters in places such as Chicago or New York City, although supplementary food from feeders is welcome.

VOICE Wide variety of calls, mostly loud and grating squawks, can mimic human voice and other sounds.

NESTING Large, bulky stick nests placed in trees, palms, or on man-made structures; 5–8 eggs; 2 broods; March–July.

FEEDING Eats seeds, buds, flowers, fruits, nuts; occasionally eats insects; visits bird feeders.

FLIGHT: swift and direct; short glides on bowed wings; often changes direction, usually in flocks.

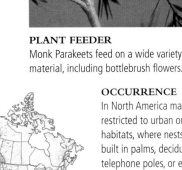

PLANT FEEDER
Monk Parakeets feed on a wide variety of plant material, including bottlebrush flowers.

SIMILAR SPECIES

GREEN PARAKEET
see p.320

green breast and face

green upper-parts and flight feathers

ACROBATIC FLIGHT
Flocks of vivdly colored Monk Parakeets twist and turn in flight, and are notoriously vocal.

OCCURRENCE
In North America mainly restricted to urban or suburban habitats, where nests can be built in palms, deciduous trees, telephone poles, or electrical substations. Common in southern Florida; found in several other areas, north to New York City, Chicago, and Portland, Oregon.

| Length **11½in (29cm)** | Wingspan **21in (53cm)** | Weight **3½oz (100g)** |
| Social **Flocks/Colonies** | Lifespan **Up to 6 years** | Status **Localized** |

| Order **Psittaciformes** | Family **Psittacidae** | Species *Amazona viridigenalis* |

Red-crowned Parrot

MALE

rounded wings

IN FLIGHT

conspicuous red patches on inner wings

yellow tip to tail

green back and wings

blue hind crown

red crown

large, pale, hooked bill

ADULT

red patch on wings

short tail

green underparts

A ny member of the family Psittacidae can be called a parrot, but to most people, parrots are the bulky-bodied ones with short, rounded wings and tails, and largely green plumage. One parrot species is well established in North America and, like other psittacids now found here, its presence is the result of releases or escapes from the pet trade. Red-crowned Parrots are becoming increasingly rare in their native range in northeastern Mexico due to habitat destruction and capture as pets. Ironically, the naturalized population in California may now exceed in size that of the native Mexican population. Red-crowned Parrots forage and roost in flocks and often breed in loose nesting colonies.

VOICE Variety of loud squawks or shrieks; can mimic human speech and other sounds.
NESTING Cavity in palm or tree; 2–5 eggs; 1 brood; March–July.
FEEDING Feeds on a variety of fruits, nuts, seeds, flowers, and leaves; chicks are also fed insects.

FLIGHT: fast, with rapid, shallow wing beats; often flocks.

CAVITY NESTER
Most parrots nest in cavities in telephone poles, trees, or in the case of these birds, in palms.

SIMILAR SPECIES

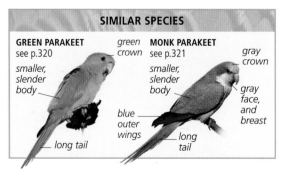

GREEN PARAKEET
see p.320

smaller, slender body

green crown

long tail

MONK PARAKEET
see p.321

smaller, slender body

blue outer wings

long tail

gray crown

gray face, and breast

OCCURRENCE
Nonmigratory species, native to northeastern Mexico; locally common in southern California and uncommon in southern Florida, southern Texas, and Puerto Rico. Prefers deciduous tropical rainforests in its native range. Texas population may be a mix of escaped birds and those from nearby Mexico.

| Length **12in (30cm)** | Wingspan **25in (63cm)** | Weight **11oz (300g)** |
| Social **Flocks** | Lifespan **Up to 10 years** | Status **Localized** |

CUCKOOS AND RELATIVES

Cuckoos are notorious for laying eggs in other birds' nests, but of the three species in North America, one never does this, and two seldom do so. Their close relatives on the continent are the Greater Roadrunner, and two species of Ani.

CUCKOOS

Generally shy and reclusive, the Black-billed Cuckoo, Yellow-billed Cuckoo, and Mangrove Cuckoo all favor dense, forested habitats. All three species usually build a nest and raise their own offspring. However, sometimes the Black-billed Cuckoo and the Yellow-billed Cuckoo lay their eggs in other birds' nest, including each other's, and even the nests of their own kind. In flight, cuckoos are often mistaken for small birds of prey. They do sometimes pounce on lizards, frogs, and other small animals—even small birds—but mostly they glean insects from the foliage of trees. Much, though, remains to be learned about these birds.

WEATHER BIRD
Folklore has it that the Yellow-billed Cuckoo, or "Raincrow," calls most on cloudy days.

ANIS

In North America both the Groove-billed Ani and the Smooth-billed Ani are at the northern edge of their known range, being much more widespread in open country in tropical and subtropical regions farther south. Anis are typically weak, short-distance fliers, but, like the Greater Roadrunner, they are sturdy on their feet and often run and hop after their insect prey. They breed communally, several pairs of birds laying their eggs in one nest, then all help to raise the young.

STRONG STOMACH
The Black-billed Cuckoo can safely eat caterpillars that are poisonous to other birds.

GREATER ROADRUNNER

An inhabitant of the arid Southwest, this large, ground-based member of the Cuckoo family is capable of running at over 15mph (25kph). It is one of the few species of bird that actively hunts rattlesnakes, and does so in pairs. The Greater Roadrunner has been seen pulling small birds out of mist nets set by scientists for research purposes. It does not fly often, and rarely above a few meters.

PERCHED TO KILL
After catching a lizard, the Greater Roadrunner bashes it repeatedly against a rock before gulping it down.

Order **Cuculiformes**	Family **Cuculidae**	Species *Coccyzus erythropthalmus*

Black-billed Cuckoo

long tail

small white spots on tips of tail feathers

long wings

ADULT

IN FLIGHT

bare red skin around eye

grayish brown back

long, black, decurved bill

ADULT

pale grayish white underparts

grayish feet

long tail

Although common, the Black-billed Cuckoo is usually difficult to spot because of its secretive nature and dense, leafy habitat. This species feeds mainly on spiny caterpillars, but the spines of these insects can become lodged in the cuckoo's stomach, obstructing digestion, so the bird periodically empties its stomach to clear any such blockage. The decline of this species is probably an indirect result of the chemical control of caterpillar outbreaks in forests throughout their range. During the breeding season, the birds call throughout the night, which leads some to believe erroneously that the cuckoo is nocturnal.

VOICE Series of 2–5 repeatedly whistled notes, *coo-coo-coo-coo*, with short breaks between series.

NESTING Shallow cup of sticks lined with moss, leaves, grass, and feathers; 2–4 eggs; 1 brood; May–July.

FEEDING Almost exclusively eats caterpillars, especially tent caterpillars and gypsy moths.

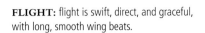

FLIGHT: flight is swift, direct, and graceful, with long, smooth wing beats.

SEARCHING FOR FOOD
These cuckoos spend a lot of their time in trees as they search for their favorite hairy caterpillars.

OCCURRENCE
Widespread northern and eastern North American species, lives in thickly wooded areas close to water, but can also be found in brushy forest edges and evergreen woods. Winters in South America in evergreen woodlands, scrub, and humid forests.

SIMILAR SPECIES

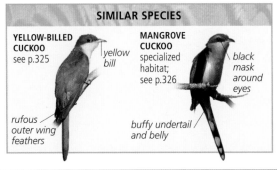

YELLOW-BILLED CUCKOO
see p.325

yellow bill

rufous outer wing feathers

MANGROVE CUCKOO
specialized habitat; see p.326

black mask around eyes

buffy undertail and belly

Length **11–12in (28–31cm)**	Wingspan **16–19in (41–48cm)**	Weight **1 9/16–2oz (45–55g)**
Social **Solitary**	Lifespan **Up to 5 years**	Status **Secure (p)**

Order **Cuculiformes**	Family **Cuculidae**	Species **Coccyzus americanus**

Yellow-billed Cuckoo

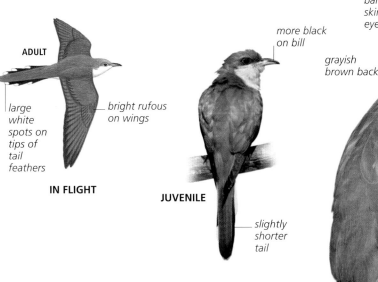

ADULT

large white spots on tips of tail feathers

bright rufous on wings

IN FLIGHT

more black on bill

JUVENILE

slightly shorter tail

bare yellow skin around eye

grayish brown back

mostly yellow bill

ADULT

rufous outer wing feathers

long tail

FLIGHT: flight is swift using long strokes to maintain level pattern.

The Yellow-billed Cuckoo is a shy, slow-moving bird, with a reputation for fairly odd behaviors, including its habit of calling more often on cloudy days. This tendency has earned it the nickname "rain crow" in some areas. In addition to raising young in its own nest, females often lay eggs in the nests of more than a dozen other species, especially during years with abundant food. The host species may be chosen on the basis of how closely the color of its eggs matches those of the cuckoo's. This brood parasitism is the rule in the Yellow-billed Cuckoo, which is an Old World species, and occurs in North America as a widespread vagrant.

VOICE Call a series of 10–12 low notes that slow down as it progresses, *ca ca ca ca coo coo coo cowl cowl cowl.*

NESTING Flimsy oval-shaped platform of small sticks and branches, often lined with leaves and strips of plants; 2–4 eggs; 1–2 broods; May–August.

FEEDING Mostly consumes insects such as grasshoppers, crickets, katydids, and caterpillars of several moth species; also eats seeds.

RARE SIGHT
Given the habitat they prefer and their skittish nature, a clear view of a Yellow-billed Cuckoo is rare.

OCCURRENCE
Has a wide range in the US. Found primarily in open forests with a mix of openings and thick understory cover, especially those near water. Winters in similar habitats in Central and South America.

SIMILAR SPECIES

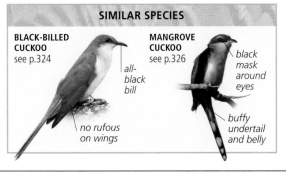

BLACK-BILLED CUCKOO see p.324

all-black bill

no rufous on wings

MANGROVE CUCKOO see p.326

black mask around eyes

buffy undertail and belly

Length **10–12in (26–30cm)**	Wingspan **17–20in (43–51cm)**	Weight **2–2¼oz (55–65g)**
Social **Small winter flocks**	Lifespan **Up to 4 years**	Status **Secure (p)**

| Order **Cuculiformes** | Family **Cuculidae** | Species *Cocczyus minor* |

Mangrove Cuckoo

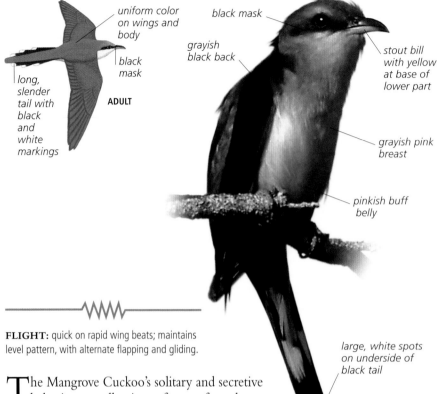

uniform color on wings and body

black mask

long, slender tail with black and white markings

black mask

ADULT

grayish black back

stout bill with yellow at base of lower part

grayish pink breast

pinkish buff belly

FLIGHT: quick on rapid wing beats; maintains level pattern, with alternate flapping and gliding.

large, white spots on underside of black tail

The Mangrove Cuckoo's solitary and secretive behavior, as well as its preference for a dense, nearly inaccessible mangrove habitat, make it one of the least studied birds of all North American birds. This, combined with the continued human development of coastal mangrove areas in Florida makes the future of this cuckoo uncertain in the US. The bird's black mask distinguishes it from the other two cuckoo species of North America.

VOICE Series of up to 2 dozen harsh, froglike notes resembling *aarhm aarhm aarrhmmm*; also fast *coo coo coo*.

NESTING Shallow oval platform of loosely assembled sticks, sparsely lined with softer plant material; 2–4 eggs; 1 brood; April–July.

FEEDING Consumes a variety of insects and their larvae, especially spiders, grasshoppers, and moth caterpillars.

TOUGH PREDATOR
The elusive Mangrove Cuckoo has a thick bill that it uses to take larger prey such as lizards as it skulks through coastal mangrove forests.

OCCURRENCE
Found in Florida, in coastal areas from Tampa Bay southward and in the Florida Keys, almost exclusively in mangrove swamps, but also locally in a wide range of habitats.

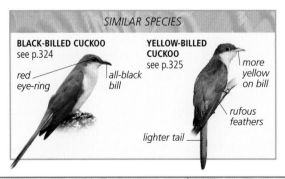

SIMILAR SPECIES

BLACK-BILLED CUCKOO
see p.324

red eye-ring

all-black bill

YELLOW-BILLED CUCKOO
see p.325

more yellow on bill

rufous feathers

lighter tail

| Length **11–12½in (28–32cm)** | Wingspan **16in (41cm)** | Weight **2¼–2½oz (65–70g)** |
| Social **Solitary** | Lifespan **Up to 5 years** | Status **Vulnerable (p)** |

Order **Cuculiformes**	Family **Cuculidae**	Species *Crotophaga sulcirostris*

Groove-billed Ani

ADULT

short, rounded wings

black overall

long tail trailing behind body

grooves on upper bill

black eyes

all-black body

short wings

high, narrow black bill

"unkempt" appearance

specialized toes for grasping

FLIGHT: short; begins with quick flaps, then alternates with short glides; tail dangles in flight.

long tail

A nis are members of the cuckoo family, with black plumage, long tails, and high, but narrow, blackish bills. Their disheveled appearance—as if their feathers are about to fall off— is most noticeable when they are in flight. Like parrots and woodpeckers, they have two toes pointing forward and two backward. These extremely social birds exhibit unusual communal nesting behavior—several females lay eggs in the same nest, and both males and females share incubation.

VOICE Most common call a liquid *Tee-ho*, accented on first syllable, given in flight and when perched, chorus like when many birds call at same time.

NESTING Large bulky nest in shrub or tree; 3–4 eggs; 1 brood; June–October.

FEEDING Pursues insects, spiders, and small vertebrates.

FLOCK OF THREE
Anis are among the few birds that are truly communal. Females share nesting tasks and will alternate brooding and incubation duties.

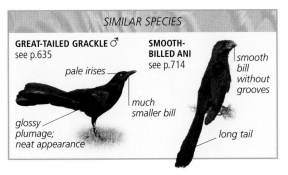

SIMILAR SPECIES

GREAT-TAILED GRACKLE ♂
see p.635

pale irises

glossy plumage; neat appearance

SMOOTH-BILLED ANI
see p.714

smooth bill without grooves

much smaller bill

long tail

OCCURRENCE
Breeds in brushy fields, hedgerows, or areas with clumps of trees in southern Texas; also Mexico, Central, and South America. Most birds return southward during fall, but a few travel as far east as Florida during late fall and winter. Resident elsewhere.

Length **13½in (34cm)**	Wingspan **17in (43cm)**	Weight **3oz (85g)**
Social **Flocks**	Lifespan **7 years**	Status **Localized**

| Order **Cuculiformes** | Family **Cuculidae** | Species *Geococcyx californianus* |

Greater Roadrunner

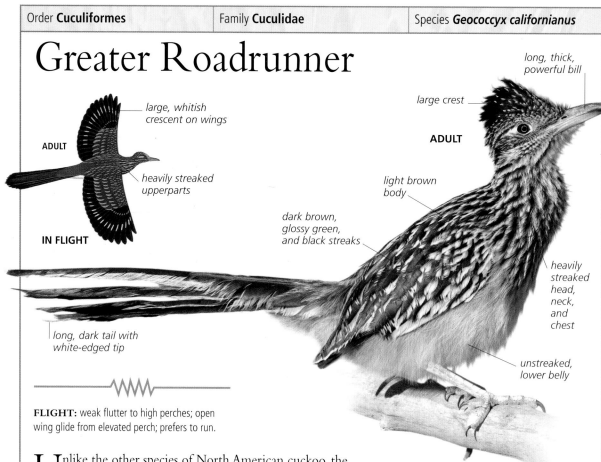

large, whitish crescent on wings

ADULT

IN FLIGHT

heavily streaked upperparts

long, thick, powerful bill

large crest

ADULT

light brown body

dark brown, glossy green, and black streaks

heavily streaked head, neck, and chest

unstreaked, lower belly

long, dark tail with white-edged tip

FLIGHT: weak flutter to high perches; open wing glide from elevated perch; prefers to run.

Unlike the other species of North American cuckoo, the Greater Roadrunnder is a ground bird, but it can fly, despite preferring to run. Its speed enables it to overcome and chase prey on foot, especially lizards and small birds. Its generalized feeding habits allow this bird to take advantage of whatever food resources it comes across. This may be one of the main reasons roadrunners are expanding their range.

VOICE Cooing *coo-coo-coo-cooo-cooooo* series of 4–5 descending notes.

NESTING Shallow, loosely organized cup of twigs and branches, lined with grass, animal hair, and feathers; 3–5 eggs; 2 broods; April–September.

FEEDING Eats a wide variety of insects, small reptiles such as lizards, birds, and mammals; also eggs and carrion.

DRINKING
Roadrunners obtain much of their moisture from the food they eat, but will take full advantage of water whenever it's available.

LOFTY ABODE
This species nests off the ground, and can occasionally be seen occupying elevated perches.

OCCURRENCE
Widespread across southeastern US, from California to Louisiana, and north to Utah, Colorado, Kansas, and Arkansas; lives at low elevations in open brushy areas mixed with thorn scrub such as mesquite; also pinyon-juniper shrubbery, and deserts and chaparral. Resident.

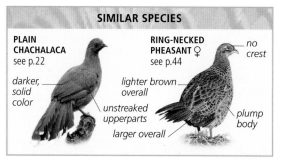

SIMILAR SPECIES

PLAIN CHACHALACA
see p.22

darker, solid color

RING-NECKED PHEASANT ♀
see p.44

no crest

lighter brown overall

unstreaked upperparts

larger overall

plump body

| Length **21in (53cm)** | Wingspan **23in (58cm)** | Weight **11oz (300g)** |
| Social **Solitary/Pairs** | Lifespan **Up to 6 years** | Status **Secure** |

Family **Tytonidae, Strigidae**

OWLS

PARTLY BECAUSE OF THEIR nocturnal habits and eerie cries, owls have fascinated humans throughout history. They are placed in the order Strigiformes, and two families are represented in North America: the Barn Owl is classified in Tytonidae, while the rest of the owl species are the Strigidae. Most owls are active primarily at night and have developed adaptations for living in low-light environments. Their large eyes are sensitive enough to see in the dark and face forward to maximize binocular vision. Since the eyes are fixed in their sockets, a flexible neck helps owls

BIG HORNS
The "ear" tufts of the Great Horned Owl are taller than those of other "tufted" owls.

turn the head almost 180° toward a direction of interest. Ears are offset on each side of the head to help identify the source of a sound; "ear tufts" on some species, however, are for visual effect and unrelated to hearing. Many owls have serrations on the forward edges of their flight feathers to cushion airflow, so their flight is silent while stalking prey. All North American owls are predatory to some degree and they inhabit most areas of the continent. The Burrowing Owl is unique in that it hunts during the day and nests underground.

OWL IN DAYLIGHT
The habits of the Barn Owl remain secretive, because it is not often seen in daylight.

SNOW SWOOP
The Great Gray Owl can hunt by sound alone, allowing it to locate and capture prey hidden even beneath a thick snow cover.

Order **Strigiformes**	Family **Tytonidae**	Species *Tyto alba*

Barn Owl

barring on wings and tail

ADULT

IN FLIGHT

head lacks "ear" tufts

long wings

ADULT

dark eyes

ruff surrounds facial disk

ADULT

relatively small eyes

rounded, heart-shaped facial disc

pale buff upperparts

gray and black spots

white underparts

feathered legs

FLIGHT: irregular bursts of flapping, interspersed with short glides, banking, doubling back, fluttering.

Aptly named, the Barn Owl inhabits old sheds, sheltered rafters, and empty buildings in rural fields. With its affinity for human settlement, and 32 subspecies, this owl has an extensive range covering every continent except Antarctica. Although widespread, the Barn Owl is secretive. Primarily nocturnal, it can fly undetected until its screeching call pierces the air. The Barn Owl is endangered in several Midwestern states due to modern farming practices, which have cut prey populations as well as the number of old barns for nesting.
VOICE Typical call loud, raspy, screeching shriek, *shkreee,* often given in flight; also clicking sounds associated with courtship.
NESTING Unlined cavity in tree, cave, building, hay bale, or nest box; 5–7 eggs; 1–2 broods; March–September.
FEEDING Hunts on the wing for small rodents such as mice; research reveals it can detect the slightest rustle made by prey even in total darkness.

NOCTURNAL HUNTER
The Barn Owl hunts at night for small rodents, but may be seen before sunset feeding its young.

OCCURRENCE
In North America breeds from northwestern and northeastern US south to Mexico. Resident in all except very north of range. Prefers open habitats, such as desert, grassland, and fields, wherever prey and suitable nest sites are available. Generally not found in mountainous or heavily forested areas.

SIMILAR SPECIES

SNOWY OWL
see p.335

black markings on female and juvenile

SHORT-EARED OWL
see p.347

dark patches on outer wing

dark barring on underparts

Length **12½–15½in (32–40cm)**	Wingspan **3ft 3in (100cm)**	Weight **14–25oz (400–700g)**
Social **Solitary**	Lifespan **Up to 8 years**	Status **Declining**

Order **Strigiformes**	Family **Strigidae**	Species *Otus flammeolus*

Flammulated Owl

long, rounded wings

ADULT

tawny underwings

short tail **IN FLIGHT**

small "ear" tufts, often hidden

dark eyes

reddish brown facial disc

grayish brown body

dark streaks on underparts

tawny "shoulder" bar

smaller in size than gray form

ADULT (RED FORM)

ADULT (GRAY FORM)

FLIGHT: straight flight with steady wing beats; often hovers while foraging.

The tiny Flammulated Owl nests in dry mountain pine forests from British Columbia to Mexico, moving south to Central America for the winter months. Its dark, watery-looking eyes distinguish it from other species of small North American owls. Entirely nocturnal, it is heard more often than seen. When the Flammulated Owl is visible, its trademark reddish brown plumage blends quite well with the color of pine tree bark. This species appears to breed in loose colonies, although this may reflect patchiness in habitat quality. Like some other owls, it has a "red" and "gray" form.

VOICE Series of soft low-frequency toots, often difficult to locate, can continue for hours; barks and screams when disturbed at nest site.

NESTING Cavity in tree, woodpecker hole, nest box; 3–4 eggs; 1–2 broods; May–August.

FEEDING Hunts from stationary perch, from which it flies to capture insects—mostly moths, and beetles—from branches, foliage, or ground.

BLENDING IN
If this owl peeks out of a tree-hole, its plumage blends in remarkably well with the bark.

OCCURRENCE
Breeds in semiarid mountain forests, especially Ponderosa and Yellow Pine, open wooded areas at middle elevations with scattered clearings, older trees, and groves of saplings. Winters in habitat similar to breeding season, primarily in southern Mexico, Guatemala, and El Salvador.

SIMILAR SPECIES

WESTERN SCREECH-OWL see p.333
yellow eyes

NORTHERN SAW-WHET OWL see p.345
yellow eyes
different streaking

Length **6–6¾in (15–17cm)**	Wingspan **16in (41cm)**	Weight **1⁹⁄₁₆–2¼oz (45–65g)**
Social **Solitary**	Lifespan **Up to 8 years**	Status **Secure**

Order **Strigiformes**	Family **Strigidae**	Species *Otus asio*

Eastern Screech-Owl

dark gray bars on short, rounded wings

ADULT

short tail

streaked underparts

IN FLIGHT

"ear" tufts

yellow eyes

white spots on inner wing feathers

ADULT (GRAY FORM)

feathered legs

FLIGHT: direct, purposeful flight; straight with steady wing beats, typically below tree cover.

This widespread little owl has adapted to suburban areas, and its distinctive call is a familiar sound across the eastern US at almost any time of the year. Although it is an entirely nocturnal species, it may be found roosting during the day in a birdhouse or tree cavity. With gray and red color forms, this species shows more plumage variation than the Western Screech-Owl. The relatively high mortality rate of Eastern Screech-Owls, especially juveniles, is caused in part by predation by Great Horned Owls and collisions with motor vehicles.

VOICE Most familiar call a descending whinny and often used in movie soundtracks; also an even trill; occasional barks and screeches; female higher-pitched than male.

NESTING No nest; lays eggs in cavity in tree, woodpecker hole, rotted snag, nest box; 2–6 eggs; 1 brood; March–August.

FEEDING Captures prey with toes; eats insects, earthworms, rodents, songbirds, crayfish, small fish, tadpoles, snakes, and lizards.

STANDING OUT
The striking red color form of the Eastern Screech-Owl is less common than the gray.

SIMILAR SPECIES

BOREAL OWL
see p.344

brown back

no ear tufts

NORTHERN SAW-WHET OWL
see p.345

white spots

long brown streaks

OCCURRENCE
In the US and south Canada, breeds in a variety of different lowland wooded areas east of the Rockies. Also breeds south to northeast Mexico. Can be found in suburban and urban parks and gardens; usually avoids mountain forests.

Length 6½–10in (16–25cm)	Wingspan **19–24in (48–61cm)**	Weight **5–7oz (150–200g)**
Social **Solitary**	Lifespan **Up to 13 years**	Status **Secure**

Order **Strigiformes**	Family **Strigidae**	Species **Otus kennicottii**

Western Screech-Owl

dark gray bars on rounded wings

ADULT

short tail — **IN FLIGHT**

small "ear" tufts

yellow eyes

gray to brown upperparts

heavily streaked underparts

ADULT

feathered legs and feet

The Western Screech-Owl is tolerant of human presence, and lives in a wide variety of wooded areas, including suburban habitats. Because of its nocturnal habits, the Western Screech-Owl is heard more often than it is seen; its "bouncing ball" call, sometimes repeated for hours, is a familiar sound in much of western North America. This species exhibits significant differences in plumage color, and size, depending on its geographical location.

VOICE Series of toots accelerating and descending in pitch; also occasional trills, barks, chirps; female higher-pitched.

NESTING Hole in a tree, nest box, woodpecker cavity; 2–5 eggs; 1 brood; March–July.

FEEDING Sits quietly under canopy waiting to spot small prey below, then pounces; eats small birds and mammals, insects, crayfish, and worms.

FLIGHT: straight, steady flight, seldom over long distances; rarely hovers or glides.

GOOD CAMOUFLAGE
This roosting Western Screech-Owl blends in perfectly with the bark color of a tree.

OCCURRENCE
Breeds from British Columbia southward to Baja California and continental Mexico. Favors riverside and mixed deciduous woodlands, but uses many types of woodlands, parks, and gardens in residential areas; most common at lower elevations. Nonmigratory.

SIMILAR SPECIES

FLAMMULATED OWL
see p.331
— dark eyes
smaller overall

WHISKERED SCREECH-OWL
see p.334
smaller overall
heavily barred

Length **7½–10in (19–25cm)**	Wingspan **21–22in (53–56cm)**	Weight **3½–11oz (100–300g)**
Social **Family groups**	Lifespan **Up to 13 years**	Status **Secure**

| Order **Strigiformes** | Family **Strigidae** | Species *Otus trichopsis* |

Whiskered Screech-Owl

ADULT

thin black bar on underwing

mottled gray-brown upperparts

IN FLIGHT

heavily streaked underparts

small "ear" tufts

yellow eyes

large white spots on inner wing feathers

bold wavy barring

ADULT

Although it is smaller than the similar-looking Western Screech-Owl, the nocturnal Whiskered Screech-Owl more often heard than seen, and is most easily identified by its distinctive voice. In North America this little owl can be heard calling on still nights in mountain canyons in southeastern Arizona and southwestern New Mexico. Here the owl is found in its gray form, but there is a reddish form in the cloud forests of Mexico.

VOICE Series of toots and trills; also single hoots, barks, screeches; pairs may sing duets; female higher-pitched.

NESTING No nest; lays eggs in cavity in tree, woodpecker hole; 2–4 eggs; 1 brood; April–July.

FEEDING Preys mainly on beetles, crickets, katydids, caterpillars, and other insects and insect larvae; also occasionally pounces on small rodents and lizards.

FLIGHT: short, quick, straight flights, usually under cover; sometimes hovers while hunting.

READY TO HUNT
The Whiskered Screech-Owl perches on a branch at night, alert and waiting to spot its small prey.

OCCURRENCE
Lives year-round, up to around 8,000ft (2,400m), in oak-pine woodlands in canyons, and along rivers, and in deciduous woodlands with a patchy or closed canopy, in southeastern Arizona and northwestern New Mexico, and southward through Mexico to Nicaragua.

SIMILAR SPECIES

FLAMMULATED OWL
see p.331

dark eyes

WESTERN SCREECH-OWL
see p.333

larger overall

| Length **6–7½in (15–19cm)** | Wingspan **17½in (44cm)** | Weight **2½–4oz (70–120g)** |
| Social **Solitary** | Lifespan **Up to 4 years** | Status **Secure** |

| Order **Strigiformes** | Family **Strigidae** | Species **Bubo scandiacus** |

Snowy Owl

IMMATURE

flecked gray-brown

white face

IN FLIGHT

variably barred underparts

JUVENILE

dusky barring

large round head

yellow eyes

variable barring on wings

nearly all-white breast

feathered legs

ADULT

FLIGHT: slow, steady flight with strong, deep wing beats; flaps interspersed with glides.

An icon of the far north, the Snowy Owl has gained celebrity status for its occasional winter forays into northern US states. This is a bird of the open tundra, where it hunts from headlands or hummocks and nests on the ground. In such a harsh environment, the Snowy Owl largely depends on lemmings for prey. It is fiercely territorial, and will valiantly defend its young in the nest even against larger animals, such as the Arctic Fox.

VOICE Deep hoots, doubled or given in a short series, usually by male; also rattles, whistles, and hisses.

NESTING Scrape in ground vegetation or dirt, with no lining; 3–12 eggs; 1 brood; May–September.

FEEDING Mostly hunts lemmings, but takes whatever other small mammals, birds, and occasionally fish, it can find.

SNOWY MALE
Some adult males display no barring at all and have entirely pure white plumage.

SIMILAR SPECIES

BARN OWL
see p.330

black eyes

golden brown

SHORT-EARED OWL
see p.347

mottled brown markings

larger overall

OCCURRENCE
Breeds in the tundra of Eurasia and northern North America, north to Ellesmere Island; North American birds winter south to the Great Plains. In some years, many North American birds winter south of their normal range, including in dunes, marshes, and airfields, as far south as Idaho and New Jersey.

| Length **20–27in (51–68cm)** | Wingspan **4¼–5¼ft 1.3–1.6m)** | Weight **3½–6½lb (1.6–2.9kg)** |
| Social **Solitary** | Lifespan **Up to 9 years** | Status **Vulnerable** |

Order **Strigiformes**	Family **Strigidae**	Species **_Strix varia_**

Barred Owl

rounded wings

ADULT

IN FLIGHT

large, round head

dark eyes

conspicuously yellowish bill

brown upperparts

heavy white spotting

barring on breast

streaking on belly

ADULT

barred tail

ADULT

FLIGHT: glides silently among trees, interspersed with flaps; rarely hovers.

The Barred Owl is more adaptable and aggressive than its close relative, the Spotted Owl. Recent range expansions have brought the two species into closer contact, which has resulted in the Barred Owl displacing the Spotted Owl, as well as occasional interbreeding. The Barred Owl is mostly nocturnal, but may also call or hunt during the day.

VOICE Series of hoots in rhythm: _who-cooks-for-you_, _who-cooks-for-you-all_; also pair duetting (at different pitches), cawing, cackling, and guttural sounds.

NESTING No nest; lays eggs in broken-off branches, cavities, old stick nests; 1–5 eggs; 1 brood; January–September.

FEEDING Perches quietly and waits to spot prey below, then pounces; eats small mammals, birds, amphibians, reptiles, insects, and spiders.

WOODED HABITATS
The Barred Owl is very much at home in deep woodlands, including conifer forests.

OCCURRENCE
Widespread, though not evenly so, across North America from British Columbia across to the Maritimes and much of the eastern US. Found in a variety of wooded habitats—from cypress swamps in the south to conifer rainforest in the northwest—and in mixed hardwoods.

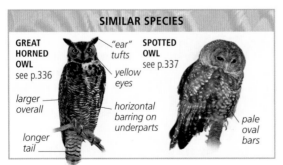

SIMILAR SPECIES

GREAT HORNED OWL see p.336

"ear" tufts

yellow eyes

larger overall

horizontal barring on underparts

longer tail

SPOTTED OWL see p.337

pale oval bars

Length **17–19½in (43–50cm)**	Wingspan **3½ft (1.1m)**	Weight **17–37oz (475–1,050g)**
Social **Solitary**	Lifespan **Up to 18 years**	Status **Secure**

Order **Strigiformes**	Family **Strigidae**	Species **Strix nebulosa**

Great Gray Owl

white crescents between small yellow eyes

gray and white facial disks

long wings

round facial pattern

long tail

ADULT

black and white chin

mottled gray upperparts

heavily streaked underparts

long wings

ADULT

thickset body

IN FLIGHT

ADULT

FLIGHT: deep, methodical wing beats, interspersed with glides; hovers while hunting.

With a thick layer of feathers that insulate it against cold northern winters, the Great Gray Owl is North America's tallest owl, although it weighs less than the Great Horned Owl or Snowy Owl. Its excellent hearing makes it an efficient rodent hunter. Often able to detect prey by sound alone, it will often plunge through deep snow, or into a burrow, to snatch unseen prey. This bird is primarily nocturnal, but may also hunt by daylight, usually at dawn or dusk.

VOICE Slow series of deep hoots, evenly spaced; also variety of hisses and chattering noises around nest site.

NESTING Reuses old eagle or hawk nests, broken-off trees; 2–5 eggs; 1 brood; March–July.

FEEDING Eats rodents and other small mammals; waits to pounce from perch or hunts in flight.

SIMILAR SPECIES

GREAT HORNED OWL see p.336

"ear" tufts

barring on belly

BARRED OWL see p.338

dark eyes

barring on breast

MAKESHIFT NEST
The Great Gray Owl often utilizes hollow snags as nesting sites, besides reusing deserted nests.

OCCURRENCE
In North America, resident across northern forests from Alaska to Quebec, south to Montana and Wyoming. Also resident in Eurasia from Scandinavia to the Russian Far East. Found in taiga, and muskeg (peat bogs), in fir, spruce, and pine forests.

Length **24–33in (61–84cm)**	Wingspan **4½ft (1.4m)**	Weight **1½–3¾lb (0.7–1.7kg)**
Social **Solitary**	Lifespan **Up to 14 years**	Status **Secure**

Order **Strigiformes**	Family **Strigidae**	Species *Aegolius funereus*

Boreal Owl

usually flat-topped head, with fine white spots

yellow eyes

pale bill

ADULT

rounded wings

finely spotted crown

IN FLIGHT

black border around face

white and brown streaked underparts

ADULT

short tail

ADULT

FLIGHT: quick, strong wing beats; adept at maneuvering; glides down to attack prey.

Unusually, the female Boreal Owl is much bigger than the male. Males will mate with two or three females in years when voles and other small rodents are abundant. The Boreal Owl roosts on an inconspicuous perch by day and hunts at night, detecting its prey by sound. In the US it is elusive and rarely seen, since it breeds at high elevations in isolated western mountain ranges. White spotting on the crown, a grayish bill, and a black facial disk distinguish the Boreal Owl from the Northern Saw-whet Owl.

VOICE Prolonged series of whistles, usually increasing in volume and intensity toward the end; also screeches and hisses; can be heard from afar.

NESTING Natural and woodpecker-built tree cavities, also nest boxes; 3–6 eggs; 1 brood; March–July.

FEEDING Mainly eats small mammals, occasionally birds and insects; pounces from elevated perch; sometimes stores prey.

DAYTIME ROOSTING
The Boreal Owl roosts in dense vegetation by day, even when the branches are laden with snow.

OCCURRENCE
Breeds in northern forests from Alaska to Newfoundland and Quebec, south into the Rockies to Colorado and New Mexico. Largely sedentary, but irregular movements take place south of the breeding range, southward to New England and New York.

SIMILAR SPECIES

NORTHERN PYGMY-OWL
see p.341
black streaks on belly

longer tail

NORTHERN SAW-WHET OWL
see p.345
lacks dark frame to facial disk

dark bill

Length **8½–11in (21–28cm)**	Wingspan **21½–24in (54–62cm)**	Weight **3⅜–8oz (90–225g)**
Social **Solitary**	Lifespan **Up to 11 years**	Status **Secure**

Order **Strigiformes**	Family **Strigidae**	Species *Aegolius acadicus*

Northern Saw-whet Owl

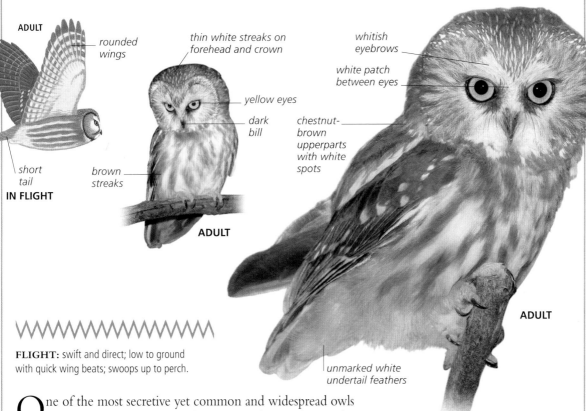

ADULT

rounded wings

thin white streaks on forehead and crown

whitish eyebrows

white patch between eyes

yellow eyes

dark bill

chestnut-brown upperparts with white spots

short tail

IN FLIGHT

brown streaks

ADULT

ADULT

FLIGHT: swift and direct; low to ground with quick wing beats; swoops up to perch.

unmarked white undertail feathers

One of the most secretive yet common and widespread owls in North America, the Northern Saw-whet Owl is much more often heard than seen. Strictly nocturnal, it is concealed as it sleeps by day in thick vegetation, usually in conifers. Although the same site may be used for months if it remains undisturbed, it is never an easy bird to locate and, like most owls, it is elusive, even though it sometimes roosts in large garden trees. When it is discovered, the Northern Saw-whet Owl "freezes," and relies on its camouflage rather than flying off. At night it watches intently from a perch, before swooping down to snatch its prey.

VOICE Series of rapid whistled notes, on constant pitch; can continue for minutes on end; also whines and squeaks.

NESTING Unlined cavity in tree, usually old woodpecker hole or nest box; 4–7 eggs; 1 brood; March–July.

FEEDING Hunts from elevated perch; eats small mammals, including mice and voles; also eats insects and small birds.

RARE SIGHT
Despite being abundant in its range, this species is quite shy and is rarely seen by humans.

OCCURRENCE
Breeds from Alaska and British Columbia to Maritimes; in west, south to Mexico; in east, south to Appalachians; coniferous and mixed deciduous forests, swampy forests, wooded wetlands, bogs. Winters in south to central states, in open woodlands, pine plantations, shrubby areas.

SIMILAR SPECIES

ELF OWL
see p.342

gray back

smaller overall

BOREAL OWL
see p.344

spotted crown

darker face

black facial border

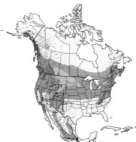

Length **7–8½in (18–21cm)**	Wingspan **16½–19in (42–48cm)**	Weight **3½oz (100g)**
Social **Solitary**	Lifespan **Up to 10 years**	Status **Secure**

Order **Strigiformes**	Family **Strigidae**	Species *Asio otus*

Long-eared Owl

tan patch on outer wing

long "ear" tufts

rusty face disks

dark wrist patch

gray tips

IN FLIGHT

slender body

finely streaked underparts

ADULT

white "eyebrows"

dark eye-ring

yellow eye

black bill

mottled upperwings

ADULT

FLIGHT: quick, deep wing beats and long glides; often hovers while hunting.

Although widely distributed across North America, the Long-eared Owl is seldom seen, being secretive and nocturnal. By day it roosts high up and out of sight in thick cover. Only at nightfall does it fly out to hunt on the wing over open areas, patrolling for small mammals. Its wing feathers, like those of many other owls, have sound-suppressing structures that allow it to fly almost silently, so it can hear the slightest rustle on the ground below.

VOICE Evenly spaced *hooo* notes, continuously repeated, about 3 seconds apart, typically 10–50 per series, sometimes more; barks when alarmed.

NESTING Old stick nests of ravens, crows, magpies, and hawks; 2–7 eggs; 1 brood; March–July.

FEEDING Preys mainly on mice and other small rodents, occasionally small birds.

OWL ON THE WING
In flight this birds "ear" tufts are flattened back and not visible, but the face and underwing markings are clearly revealed.

SIMILAR SPECIES

GREAT HORNED OWL see p.336

tufts farther apart

much larger overall

horizontal barring on underparts

SHORT-EARED OWL see p.347

patterned buffy above

pale below

larger overall

OCCURRENCE
Breeds in old nests, especially in dense stands of cottonwood, willow, juniper, and conifers by open areas suitable for hunting. Occasionally uses old nests in tree holes, cliffs, or on ground in dense vegetation; in winter, up to 100 birds in roosts. Northern birds move south for winter; some western birds resident.

Length **14–15½in (35–40cm)**	Wingspan **34–39in (86–98cm)**	Weight **8–15oz (225–425g)**
Social **Solitary/Winter flocks**	Lifespan **Up to 27 years**	Status **Secure**

Order **Strigiformes**	Family **Strigidae**	Species *Asio flammeus*

Short-eared Owl

short ear tufts

large, round head

blackish eye-ring

yellow eyes

pale face disks

black wing tips

row of pale spots along sides of back

whitish underwing

narrow, dark bar

complex, buff marbling on upperparts

dark wrist patch

orange-buff to yellowish outer wings

white belly

ADULT

IN FLIGHT

black wing tips

fine dark streaks

whitish buff underparts

ADULT

FLIGHT: light, slow, buoyant, harrier-like, maneuverable; often hovers, sometimes soars.

This owl is often seen on cloudy days or toward dusk, floating above and patrolling low back and forth over open fields, looking and listening for prey, sometimes with Northern Harriers. Although territorial in the breeding season, it sometimes winters in communal roosts of up to 200 birds, occasionally alongside Long-eared Owls. About 10 subspecies are widely distributed across five continents and numerous islands, including the Greater Antilles, Galápagos, the Falklands and Hawaii. Unlike other North American owls, the Short-eared Owl builds its own nest.

VOICE Usually silent; male courtship call a rapid *hoo hoo hoo*, often given during display flights; about 16 notes in 3 seconds; also barking, *chee-oww*.

NESTING Scrape lined with grass and feathers on ground; 4–7 eggs; 1–2 broods; March–June.

FEEDING Eats small mammals and some birds.

LOOKOUT POST
Perched on a branch, a Short-eared Owl keeps a wary eye on any intruder on its territory.

OCCURRENCE
Breeds in open areas, including prairie, grasslands, tundra, fields, and marshes, across northern North America, from Alaska, the Yukon, and British Columbia to Quebec, and Newfoundland, south to the western and central prairies, and east to New England. Partial migrant.

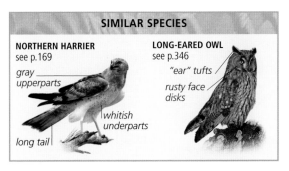

SIMILAR SPECIES

NORTHERN HARRIER
see p.169

gray upperparts

whitish underparts

long tail

LONG-EARED OWL
see p.346

"ear" tufts

rusty face disks

Length **13½–16in (34–41cm)**	Wingspan **2¾–3½ft (0.9–1.1m)**	Weight **11–13oz (325–375g)**
Social **Solitary/Winter flocks**	Lifespan **Up to 13 years**	Status **Vulnerable**

NIGHTJARS

Although widespread and common throughout North America, species of the family Caprimulgidae are heard more often than they are seen. The exceptions to this rule are the two species of Common Nighthawks that regularly forage for insects at dawn and dusk. All members of this group are medium-sized birds that use their long wings and wide tails to make rapid and graceful turns to capture their insect prey in the air. They feed predominantly on large flying insects such as moths. Their wide, gaping mouths are surrounded by bristles that greatly aid in foraging efforts. They have very small legs and toes. Both nightjars and nighthawks are similar in coloration and pattern, having a mottled mixture of various browns, grays, and blacks that provides impeccable camouflage when they remain hidden during daylight hours. This ability to hide in plain sight is useful during the nesting season when all nightjars lay their patterned eggs directly on the ground, without any nest material. The nature of the camouflage pattern of their feathers makes it difficult to distinguish between species when they rest in trees or on the ground. The most reliable means of telling species apart is their voice. If seen, the placement and nature of white markings, combined with the style of flight are the best means of identification. Most members of the family migrate and move southward as insects become dormant in the North.

Nightjars are also known as "Goatsuckers," because it was believed in ancient Greece that these birds sucked blood from goats.

PART OF THE LITTER
Not many bird species match the leaf litter of the forest floor as well as nightjars—as this Chuck-will's-widow shows.

SITTING PRETTY
Unusually for birds, members of the nightjar family, such as this Common Nighthawk, often perch lengthwise on branches.

ELEGANT HUNTER
This Lesser Nighthawk male soars through the air, hunting for insects, which it catches on the wing.

| Order **Caprimulgiformes** | Family **Caprimulgidae** | Species *Chordeiles acutipennis* |

Lesser Nighthawk

MALE

white band across tail

IN FLIGHT

buff barring on underwings

cream band close to wing tips

FEMALE

buff underparts with dark brown bars

cream throat

white band close to wing tips

MALE

white throat

huge eye

tiny bill

MALE

gray, black, and light brown plumage

Well camouflaged while resting on the ground during daytime, the Lesser Nighthawk is a wide-ranging airborne forager. It is most active at dusk and dawn, swooping low over water, bush, and desert in pursuit of insect prey, which it tracks with agile and abrupt changes in direction. The Lesser Nighthawk was formerly known as the Trilling Nighthawk because of its distinctive call. This call distinguishes the similar-looking Common Nighthawk from the Lesser Nighthawk.
VOICE Low, trilled whistle lasting up to 12 seconds and resembling calling toad.
NESTING Eggs laid directly on gravel strewn ground; 2 eggs; 1–2 broods; April–July.
FEEDING Almost exclusively catches insects in mid-air, especially emerging swarms of flies; also mosquitoes, beetles.

FLIGHT: elegant, with much bobbing and banking; frequently shifts from flapping to gliding.

AERIAL FEEDING
The Lesser Nighthawk uses its huge mouth to capture insects while flying through the air.

SIMILAR SPECIES

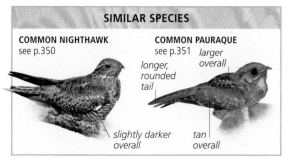

COMMON NIGHTHAWK
see p.350

slightly darker overall

COMMON PAURAQUE
see p.351

longer, rounded tail

larger overall

tan overall

OCCURRENCE
Breeds in desert scrub and open scrub and along watercourses. Widespread in the Americas, the Lesser Nighthawk occurs from the southern US to Central and South America as far south as Paraguay and Peru.

| Length **8–9in (20–23cm)** | Wingspan **21–23in (53–58cm)** | Weight **1⁹⁄₁₆oz (45g)** |
| Social **Flocks** | Lifespan **Unknown** | Status **Secure** |

| Order **Caprimulgiformes** | Family **Caprimulgidae** | Species *Chordeiles minor* |

Common Nighthawk

MALE
- pointed wings
- white bars on outer wing feathers
- narrow wings
- long wings

IN FLIGHT

white wing patch / **MALE**

- white throat
- very small bill
- large, dark eye
- delicate, gray-black pattern overall
- barring on gray underparts

FEMALE

FLIGHT: erratic flight with deep wing beats interrupted by banking glides.

Common Nighthawks are easy to spot as they swoop over parking lots, city streets, and athletics fields during the warm summer months. They are more active at dawn and dusk than at night, pursuing insect prey up to 250ft (76m) in the air. The species once took the name Booming Nighthawk, a reference to the remarkable flight display of the male birds, during which they dive rapidly towards the ground, causing their feathers to vibrate and produce a characteristic "booming" sound.
VOICE Nasal *peeent*; also soft clucking noises from both sexes.
NESTING Nests on ground on rocks, wood, leaves, or sand, also on gravel-covered rooftops in urban areas; 2 eggs; 1 brood; May–July.
FEEDING Catches airborne insects, especially moths, mayflies, and beetles, also ants; predominantly active at dusk and dawn.

A RARE SIGHT
Common Nighthawks are seen in flight more often than other caprimulgids, and it is a rare treat to see one resting on a perch.

SIMILAR SPECIES

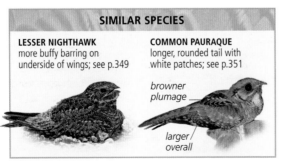

LESSER NIGHTHAWK
more buffy barring on underside of wings; see p.349

COMMON PAURAQUE
longer, rounded tail with white patches; see p.351

browner plumage

larger overall

OCCURRENCE
Wide variety of open habitats such as cleared forests, fields, grassland, beaches, and sand dunes; also common in urban areas, including cities. The most common and widespread North American nighthawk, this species also occurs in Central and South America.

| Length **9–10in (23–26cm)** | Wingspan **22–24in (56–61cm)** | Weight **2⅞oz (80g)** |
| Social **Solitary/Flocks** | Lifespan **Up to 9 years** | Status **Declining** |

| Order **Caprimulgiformes** | Family **Caprimulgidae** | Species *Nyctidromus albicollis* |

Common Pauraque

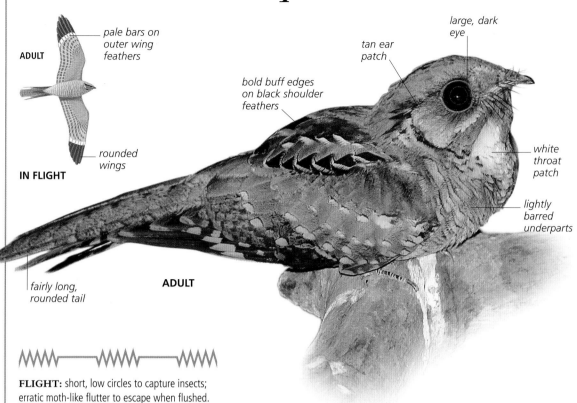

ADULT

pale bars on outer wing feathers

IN FLIGHT

rounded wings

bold buff edges on black shoulder feathers

tan ear patch

large, dark eye

white throat patch

lightly barred underparts

fairly long, rounded tail

ADULT

FLIGHT: short, low circles to capture insects; erratic moth-like flutter to escape when flushed.

The only year-round nightjar to be found north of Mexico, the Common Pauraque, is a nonmigratory bird, and Texas is currently the northern extent of its range. It is possible to get quite close to this bird during the day, as it relies on its effective camouflage for protection. Its feeding habits are strictly nocturnal; this large nightjar chooses to perch in open locations and ambush passing insects with sudden bursts of flight, rather than actively searching while in flight like nighthawks. This bird is culturally significant in many areas south of the US.

VOICE Strange, slurred, or buzzed *p' wheeerr* whistle; also various other harsh-sounding calls.

NESTING Lays eggs directly on bare soil or leaf litter; 2 eggs; 1 brood; March–July.

FEEDING Mostly eats flying insects, especially beetles.

CRYPTIC COLORATION
Their camouflage usually makes it difficult to spot these birds on the ground; they often startle humans when they flap away, resembling giant moths.

OCCURRENCE
Rests during the day in open scrub, sparsely wooded forests, and hedgerows; feeds in open fields, forest clearings, and even roads. In North America, found breeding in southern Texas, but its distribution includes all of Central and South America.

SIMILAR SPECIES

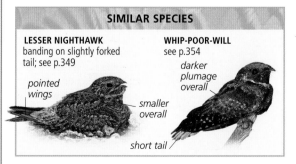

LESSER NIGHTHAWK
banding on slightly forked tail; see p.349

pointed wings

smaller overall

WHIP-POOR-WILL
see p.354

darker plumage overall

short tail

| Length **10–11in (25–28cm)** | Wingspan **21–23in (53–58cm)** | Weight **1¾oz (50g)** |
| Social **Solitary/Family groups** | Lifespan **Unknown** | Status **Secure** |

| Order **Caprimulgiformes** | Family **Caprimulgidae** | Species *Phalaenoptilus nuttallii* |

Common Poorwill

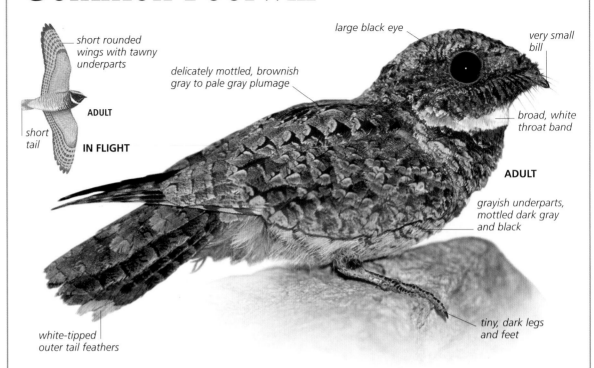

short rounded wings with tawny underparts

ADULT

short tail

IN FLIGHT

delicately mottled, brownish gray to pale gray plumage

large black eye

very small bill

broad, white throat band

ADULT

grayish underparts, mottled dark gray and black

tiny, dark legs and feet

white-tipped outer tail feathers

This nocturnal bird is the smallest North American nightjar, with much shorter wings than its relatives, and a stubbier tail, but a comparatively large head. In 1946 scientists discovered that it was able to go into a state of torpor, similar to mammalian hibernation. During "hibernation" its body temperature is about 64°F (18°C) instead of the usual 106°F (41°C), and it may remain in this state for several weeks during cold weather when food is unavailable. This may account for its colloquial name, "sleeping one," among the Hopi of the Southwest. Males and females are similar in appearance, but the male has whitish corners to its tail, while the female's are more buffy.

VOICE Call low *purr-WHEEOO* or *pooor-WEELLUP*, whistled at night when perched in the open.

NESTING Eggs laid on the ground among rocks, sometimes under shrubs; 2 eggs; 2 broods; May–August.

FEEDING Jumps up from the ground and flies briefly to capture night-flying insects, such as moths and beetles.

FLIGHT: brief, erratic; with slow and deep wing beats.

GRAVEL ROADS
The Common Poorwill uses gravel roads as a convenient place from which to jump at flying insects.

SIMILAR SPECIES

CHUCK-WILL'S-WIDOW
see p.353

larger overall

browner upperparts

WHIP-POOR-WILL
see p.354

larger bill

large white patches on tail

OCCURRENCE
Breeds from the western US southwards into Mexico, in arid habitats with much bare ground and sparse vegetation, such as grasses, shrubs, and cacti. Winters in northern Mexico.

| Length **7½–8½in (19–21cm)** | Wingspan **15½–19in (40–48cm)** | Weight **1¼–2oz (35–55g)** |
| Social **Solitary** | Lifespan **Up to 3 years** | Status **Secure** |

Order **Caprimulgiformes**	Family **Caprimulgidae**	Species ***Caprimulgus carolinensis***

Chuck-will's-widow

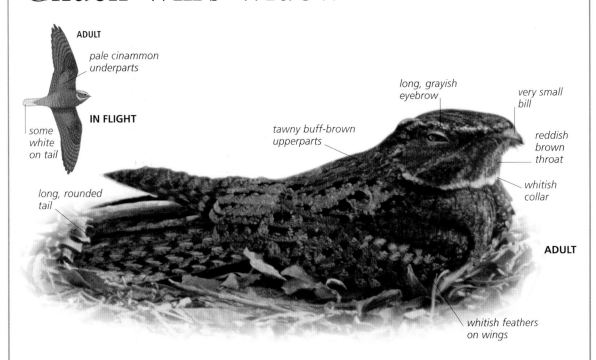

ADULT

pale cinammon underparts

IN FLIGHT

some white on tail

long, rounded tail

tawny buff-brown upperparts

long, grayish eyebrow

very small bill

reddish brown throat

whitish collar

ADULT

whitish feathers on wings

The larger of the two species of North American nightjar, the Chuck-will's-widow is also one of the least known. This species is very tolerant of human development and nests in suburban and urban areas. Unlike other nighjars it often feeds by hawking—flying continuously and capturing its prey in the air. It is also known to forage on the ground under streetlights and has occasionally been observed chasing down and swallowing bats and small birds, such as warblers, whole. Chuck-will's-widow is crepuscular, meaning that it hunts mostly at dawn and dusk. It is also active whenever there is a full moon, possibly because levels of light are similar to its preferred foraging times.
VOICE Whistled *chuck-will's-wid-ow*; begins softly, then increases in volume with emphasis on the two middle syllables.
NESTING Eggs laid directly on ground litter, including evergreen needles and fallen leaves; 2 eggs; 1 brood; May–June.
FEEDING Primarily catches flying insects, especially moths and beetles; usually hunts at dusk and dawn.

FLIGHT: alternation of slow flapping flight with eratic glides

DAYTIME SLEEPER
Well-camouflaged on the forest floor, this species of nightjar sleeps during the day.

OCCURRENCE
Breeds in habitats of forests composed of a mixture of deciduous and evergreen trees, and in open fields. A truly North American species, it is found mainly in the eastern US. Winters in Mexico and in northern Central America.

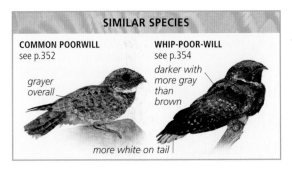

SIMILAR SPECIES

COMMON POORWILL
see p.352

grayer overall

WHIP-POOR-WILL
see p.354

darker with more gray than brown

more white on tail

Length **11–12½in (28–32cm)**	Wingspan **25–28in (63–70cm)**	Weight **3½oz (100g)**
Social **Solitary**	Lifespan **Up to 14 years**	Status **Secure**

| Order **Caprimulgiformes** | Family **Caprimulgidae** | Species *Caprimulgus vociferus* |

Whip-poor-will

rounded wings

MALE

IN FLIGHT

buffy throat stripe

FEMALE

buffy corners to tail

black-and-gray bands across back

flat, wide bill with long bristles

huge eye

tawny patch on cheeks

whitish throat stripe

MALE

cinnamon barring on dark wings

white corners to tail

As with many of the nightjars, the Whip-poor-will is heard more often than seen. Its camouflage makes it extremely difficult to spot on the forest floor and it usually flies away only when an intruder is very close—sometimes within a few feet. This species apparently has an unusual breeding pattern—while the male feeds the first brood until fledging, the female lays eggs for a second brood. The two eggs from each brood may hatch simultaneously during full moon, when there is most light at night, allowing the parents more time to forage for their young.

VOICE Loud, three-syllable whistle *WHIP-perrr-WIIL*.

NESTING Lays eggs on leaf litter on forest floor, often near overhead plant cover; 2 eggs; 2 broods; April–July.

FEEDING Flies upward quickly from perch to capture passing moths and other insects, such as mosquitoes.

FLIGHT: slow, erratic flight, with alternating bouts of flapping and gliding.

WAITING IN AMBUSH
Like other nightjars, this species waits in ambush for its prey from a perch on the forest floor.

SIMILAR SPECIES

COMMON POORWILL
see p.352

smaller, grayer overall

square tail

CHUCK-WILL'S WIDOW
see p.353

cinnamon-brown chin

larger overall

OCCURRENCE
Mixed mature forests with open understory, especially oak and pine forests on dry upland sites. Breeds north to southern Canada and south to El Salvador. Eastern and southwestern populations are widely separated.

| Length **9–10in (23–26cm)** | Wingspan **17–20in (43–51cm)** | Weight **1⁹⁄₁₆–2¼oz (45–65g)** |
| Social **Solitary** | Lifespan **Up to 15 years** | Status **Secure** |

SWIFTS

Family **Apodidae**

SWIFTS SPEND VIRTUALLY ALL their daylight hours and many night hours as well, plying the skies. The most aerial birds in North America—if not the world—swifts eat, drink, court, mate, and even sleep on the wing. Unsurprisingly, swifts also are some of the fastest and most acrobatic flyers of the bird world. Several species have been clocked at over 100mph (160kph). They feed on insects caught in zooming, zigzagging and dashing pursuits. The family name, based on the Greek *apous*, which means "without feet," originates from the ancient belief that swifts had no feet and lived their entire lives in the air.

ACROBATIC FLOCKS
White-throated Swifts are usually seen in groups of a handful to hundreds of birds.

HUMMINGBIRDS

Family **Trochilidae**

FOUND ONLY IN THE AMERICAS, hummingbirds are sometimes referred to as the crown jewels of the bird world. The first sight of a glittering hummingbird can be a life-changing experience. The amount of iridescence in their plumages varies from almost none to seemingly every feather. Most North American male hummingbirds have a colorful throat patch called a gorget, but most females lack this gorgeous attribute. Because iridescent colors are structural and not pigment-based, a gorget can often appear blackish until seen at the correct angle towards the light. Hummingbirds are the only birds that can fly backwards, an adaptation that allows them to move easily between flowers. Flying sideways, up, down, and hovering are also within hummingbirds' abilities, and all are achieved by their unique figure-eight, rapid wing strokes and reduced wing bone structure. Their long, thin bills allowing them access to nectar in tubular flowers.

AGGRESSIVE MALES
This male Ruby-throated Hummingbird defends his territory from a perch.

NECTAR FEEDERS
All North American hummingbirds, such as this Blacked-chinned, subsist on nectar from wildflowers.

Order **Apodiformes**	Family **Apodidae**	Species *Cypseloides niger*

Black Swift

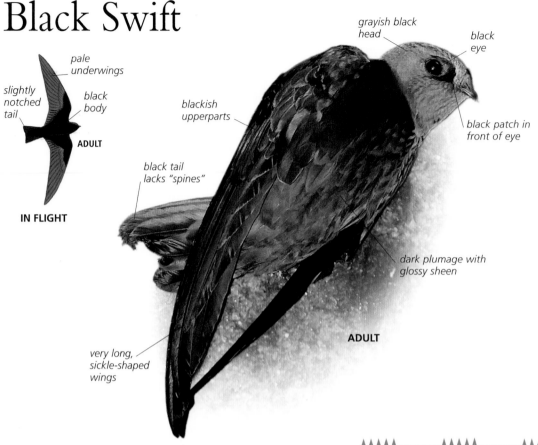

pale underwings

slightly notched tail

black body

ADULT

IN FLIGHT

grayish black head

black eye

blackish upperparts

black patch in front of eye

black tail lacks "spines"

dark plumage with glossy sheen

ADULT

very long, sickle-shaped wings

The largest of the North American swifts, the Black Swift is also the most enigmatic. It forages at high altitudes and nests on sea cliffs or behind waterfalls in mountainous terrains, and therefore can be difficult to observe. On cold and cloudy days, when their aerial insect prey occurs closer to the ground, Black Swifts also forage lower, and are easier to see. Like other swifts, the Black Swift often forms large feeding flocks, particularly in areas where swarms of winged ants occur.

VOICE Generally silent, but gives twittering chips, sometimes in fast series, during interactions with other swifts; sharp *cheep* when approaching nest.

NESTING Shallow cup of moss and mud on ledge or in rocky niche, often behind waterfalls; 1 egg; 1 brood; June–September.

FEEDING Catches airborne flies, beetles, bees, spiders, and other arthropods on the wing.

FLIGHT: shallow, rapid wing beats; often soars; acrobatic, looping flight when feeding.

TOTAL COMMITMENT
The female incubates her egg for up to a month, then both parents feed the nestling for seven weeks.

OCCURRENCE
Breeds from British Columbia in Canada, south to Mexico, Costa Rica, and the West Indies. Found in mountains from May or June to early October, feeding high over any habitat near nesting sites. Occasionally seen elsewhere during migration, often in flocks. Wintering areas still largely unknown.

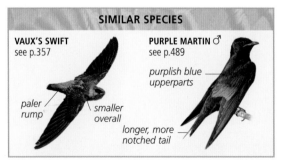

SIMILAR SPECIES

VAUX'S SWIFT see p.357

PURPLE MARTIN ♂ see p.489

purplish blue upperparts

paler rump

smaller overall

longer, more notched tail

Length **7in (18cm)**	Wingspan **18in (46cm)**	Weight **1⁷⁄₁₆–2oz (40–55g)**
Social **Flocks**	Lifespan **Up to 16 years**	Status **Localized**

Order **Apodiformes**	Family **Apodidae**	Species *Chaetura vauxi*

Vaux's Swift

pale throat
and breast

ADULT

short
wings

short tail

IN FLIGHT

sickle-shaped
wings

very
short
bill

cylindrical
body shape

ADULT

dark gray-
brown back

paler rump
and uppertail

black eye

spiny
tail

paler cheek
patch

ADULT

dark gray-
brown wings

This acrobatic and fast-flying bird is North America's smallest swift; it is slightly shorter than its eastern counterpart, the Chimney Swift. Its western range, small size, rapid and fluttering flight, and distinctive shape help distinguish this species from others. Vaux's Swifts are typically found foraging in flocks over mature forest and can be easily spotted on cold, cloudy days, often mixed with other swifts. Very large flocks are also sighted seemingly "pouring" into communal roost sites at dusk. It is fairly reliant on mature forest, and areas where this habitat has diminished have seen a corresponding decline in populations of Vaux's Swift. They may wander more widely in search of food in poor weather, even over towns.

VOICE High, insect-like chips and twittering in flight, often ending in buzzy trill.

NESTING Shallow cup of twigs, needles, and saliva attached to inside of hollow tree, rarely on chimneys; 4–6 eggs; 1 brood; June–September.

FEEDING Catches a wide variety of flying insects on the wing, including flies, moths, bees, beetles, and many others.

FLIGHT: swift, erratic flight; shallow, fluttering wing beats; acrobatic and bat-like when feeding.

AERIAL ACROBAT
Vaux's Swifts rarely land, spending all day hawking insects and even mating in flight.

OCCURRENCE
Occurs in North America from southeastern Alaska to California, where it breeds primarily in coniferous forests, nesting in large, hollow trunks; forages widely throughout many habitats. Resident population in Mexico, North American migrants move to Central America.

SIMILAR SPECIES

BLACK SWIFT
see p.356

larger
overall

blackish
body

longer, notched
tail

CHIMNEY SWIFT
see p.358

longer
tail and
wings

Length **4¾in (12cm)**	Wingspan **12in (30cm)**	Weight **½–⅞oz (15–25g)**
Social **Migrant flocks**	Lifespan **Up to 7 years**	Status **Declining**

Order **Apodiformes**	Family **Apodidae**	Species **Chaetura pelagica**

Chimney Swift

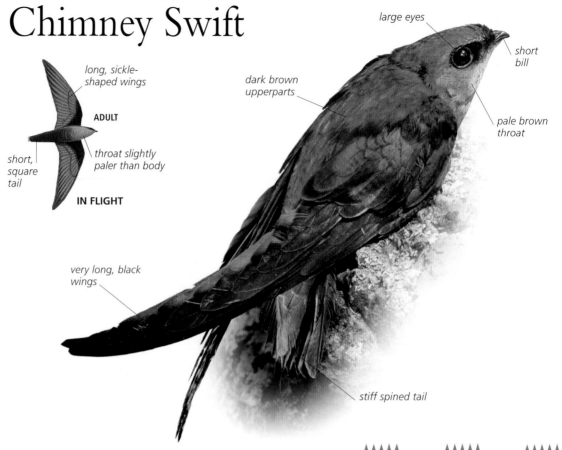

long, sickle-shaped wings

ADULT

short, square tail

throat slightly paler than body

IN FLIGHT

large eyes

short bill

dark brown upperparts

pale brown throat

very long, black wings

stiff spined tail

Nicknamed "spine-tailed," the Chimney Swift is a familiar summer sight and sound, racing through the skies east of the Rockies, its rolling twitters often heard. These birds do almost everything on the wing—feeding, drinking, and even bathing. Chimney Swifts have adapted to nest in human structures, including chimneys, although they once nested in tree holes. It remains a common bird, although local populations have declined; and it has expanded its range west and south.

VOICE High, rapid chips and twittering; notes from individuals in a flock run together into a rapid, descending chatter.

NESTING Shallow cup of twigs and saliva attached to inside of chimney or other artificial structure, rarely hollow tree; 4–5 eggs; 1 brood; April–August.

FEEDING Pursues a large variety of small aerial insects.

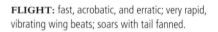

FLIGHT: fast, acrobatic, and erratic; very rapid, vibrating wing beats; soars with tail fanned.

HIGH FLYER
Swifts feed at heights on sunny days, and only feed near the ground when it is cold and cloudy.

SIMILAR SPECIES

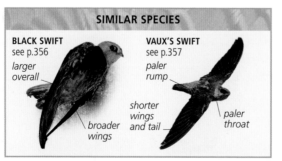

BLACK SWIFT
see p.356
larger overall

broader wings

VAUX'S SWIFT
see p.357
paler rump

shorter wings and tail

paler throat

OCCURRENCE
Widespread in eastern North America, over many habitats: urban and suburban areas, small towns; in sparsely populated areas nests in hollow trees and caves; regular in summer in southern California, present late March to early November. Winters in Amazonian South America.

Length **5in (13cm)**	Wingspan **14in (36cm)**	Weight **⅝–1¹⁄₁₆oz (17–30g)**
Social **Flocks**	Lifespan **Up to 15 years**	Status **Secure**

Order **Apodiformes**	Family **Apodidae**	Species *Aeronautes saxatalis*

White-throated Swift

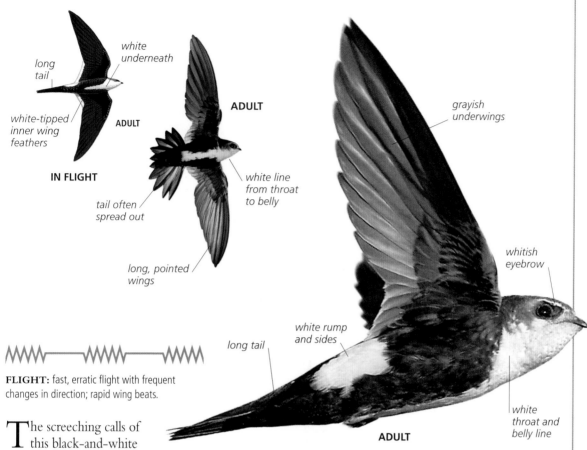

long tail

white underneath

long tail

white-tipped inner wing feathers

ADULT

IN FLIGHT

ADULT

tail often spread out

white line from throat to belly

long, pointed wings

grayish underwings

whitish eyebrow

white rump and sides

long tail

white throat and belly line

ADULT

FLIGHT: fast, erratic flight with frequent changes in direction; rapid wing beats.

The screeching calls of this black-and-white swift is a familiar sound in canyon country. Often seen racing around the cliffs on which they nest, White-throated Swifts are distinguished from other North American swifts by their black-and-white plumage and longer tail. This is also the only swift that winters in North America in large numbers. This species has become increasingly common in urban areas, as it has adapted to nesting in human structures that resemble its natural nest sites, such as bridges and quarries. As with other swifts, huge flocks of White-throated Swifts can be seen rushing into communal roosts at dusk, particularly outside the breeding season.

VOICE Drawn-out, descending, shrill twitter, *tee-tee-tee-ter-ter-ter-trr-trr-trr*, commonly given by flocks; occasionally gives two-note call in flight or sharp single note.

NESTING Shallow cup of feathers and saliva in rock, wall, crevice, or human structure; 3–6 eggs; 1 brood; March–August.

FEEDING Forages on a variety of aerial insects.

"AIR SAILOR"
These swifts—the aeronauts—were named to emphasize their mastery of the air.

SIMILAR SPECIES

VIOLET-GREEN SWALLOW ♂
slower flight and wing beats; see p.488

greenish upperparts

smaller overall

broader, shorter wings

OCCURRENCE
Breeds in western North America, from British Columbia to California, eastward to the Dakotas, and south to New Mexico. Prefers hilly and mountainous areas; forages over wide variety of habitats winters in the extreme southwest of North America, in communal roosts in canyons.

Length **6¾in (17cm)**	Wingspan **15in (38cm)**	Weight **1¹⁄₁₆–1⁹⁄₁₆oz (30–45g)**
Social **Flocks**	Lifespan **Unknown**	Status **Secure**

| Order **Apodiformes** | Family **Trochilidae** | Species *Amazilia violiceps* |

Violet-crowned Hummingbird

dark crown

MALE

notched tail

IN FLIGHT

blue-violet crown and forehead

long, red bill with black tip

bronze-green upperparts

white throat and underparts

dull greenish blue crown

all-dark tail

bright white underparts

FEMALE

MALE

FLIGHT: rapid flight with very fast wing beats; hovers at flowers; darts after insects.

This rather large and elegant species of the extreme southwest US is perhaps North America's most distinctive hummingbird, due to its white underparts, red bill, and blue-violet crown. The Violet-crowned Hummingbird is very aggressive, constantly chasing other species away from its territory and nectar sources. In the northernmost part of its range, it is not as common as some other hummingbirds, such as the Blue-throated and Magnificent Hummingbirds, because it is still largely restricted to its natural breeding habitat of sycamore woods, and has not adapted to urban gardens as much as the other hummingbird species. The Violet-Crowned Hummingbird's range is mostly Mexican.

VOICE Call a hard, dry *tek*, often in short series; chase call a squeaky series of *twi* notes; song a steady series of descending *chew* notes.

NESTING Tiny cup of twigs and lichens, bound with spider's silk and lined with plant down in tree; 2 eggs; 1 brood; May–September.

FEEDING Drinks nectar from a variety of flowers; eats small insects and spiders caught aerially or gleaned from foliage.

STRIKING UNDERPARTS
The Violet-crowned's white underparts are very striking, even when the bird is only glimpsed.

OCCURRENCE
Breeds in a small number of mountainous localities in Arizona and New Mexico. Lives near riversides in woody areas. Occasionally forages away from breeding habitat, particularly at feeders. Few birds remain in the US year-round, but in Mexico, the species is more of a resident. Vagrant in California and Texas.

| Length **4¼in (11cm)** | Wingspan **6in (15cm)** | Weight ³⁄₁₆–⁷⁄₃₂**oz (5–6g)** |
| Social **Solitary** | Lifespan **Unknown** | Status **Secure** |

Order **Apodiformes**	Family **Trochilidae**	Species *Lampornis clemenciae*

Blue-throated Hummingbird

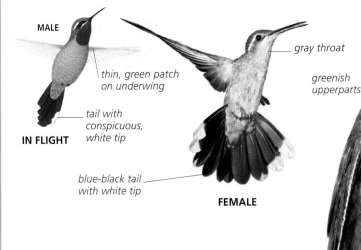

MALE

thin, green patch
on underwing

IN FLIGHT

tail with
conspicuous,
white tip

blue-black tail
with white tip

FEMALE

gray throat

greenish
upperparts

white
"mustache"

white
eyestripe

black ear
patch

long, dark,
slightly
curved bill

blue
throat

blue-gray
underparts

MALE

long tail, with
white tip

FLIGHT: rapid flight with very fast wing beats;
hovers at flowers; darts after insects.

The largest hummingbird found in North
America, the Blue-throated, strikes an imposing
figure when seen near one of its smaller relatives.
Large size and a two-striped facial pattern
distinguish it from other hummingbirds in its range.
Other hummingbird species in the *Lampornis* genus
are given the English name "Mountain gem," to reflect
their elevation preferences. The Blue-throated is no exception; it is a
specialist of the isolated "sky island" mountaintops of the Southwest.
VOICE Call a loud, high squeak, *seep*; common song a steady,
slow series of *seep* notes given by perched male; song a whisper
of mechanical hissing notes.
NESTING Tiny cup of plant fibers and moss, bound with spider's
silk and lined with plant down, built on branches and also man-
made structures; 2 eggs; 1–3 broods; February–September.
FEEDING Drinks nectar from variety of flowers; eats small
insects and spiders, caught aerially or gleaned from foliage.

SLOWER WING BEATS
The Blue-throated Hummingbird beats its wings
considerably slower than smaller species.

SIMILAR SPECIES

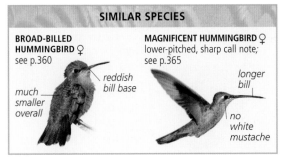

**BROAD-BILLED
HUMMINGBIRD** ♀
see p.360

much
smaller
overall

reddish
bill base

MAGNIFICENT HUMMINGBIRD ♀
lower-pitched, sharp call note;
see p.365

longer
bill

no
white
mustache

OCCURRENCE
Breeds locally in the extreme
southwest US (Arizona, New
Mexico, Texas), where it prefers
mid- to high-elevation moist,
shady canyons; on migration,
can be spotted feeding from
flowers in gardens: winters in
Mexico, sometimes winters at
feeding stations in the
southwest US.

Length **5in (13cm)**	Wingspan **8in (20cm)**	Weight **⁷⁄₃₂–⁵⁄₁₆oz (6–9g)**
Social **Solitary**	Lifespan **Up to 8 years**	Status **Secure**

| Order **Apodiformes** | Family **Trochilidae** | Species *Hylocharis leucotis* |

White-eared Hummingbird

purple throat

green breast and flanks

MALE

white undertail feathers

square tail

IN FLIGHT

straight bill

bold white stripe extends from eye to neck

black cheek patch

mottled green flanks and throat

FEMALE

white ear patch

red base of bill

iridescent purple chin and crown

green throat patch

green upperparts

MALE

The bold, black-and-white face pattern of this striking species (*leucotis* means "white-eared") distinguishes it from the other hummingbirds in its limited US range. The males are unmistakable, but the females can be confused with female Broad-billed Hummingbirds, although the latter's face pattern is more subtle. Although it is abundant in neighboring Mexico, the White-eared Hummingbird did not establish itself in the US until 1989. Aggressive even for a hummingbird, it often staunchly defends nectar sources and chases away larger species. The male is very vocal during the breeding season, singing and calling all day.

VOICE Call a metallic *tchink*, often doubled; chase call a rapid series of high chip notes; song a fast series of chips with upslurred rattles.

NESTING Cup of plant matter, lichens, and bark in shrubs; 2 eggs; 1–2 broods; April–July.

FEEDING Drinks nectar from a variety of flowers; eats small insects and spiders caught in flight or gleaned from foliage.

FLIGHT: very fast forward flight with fast wing beats; hovers at flowers and darts after insects.

AGGRESSIVE MALES
From conspicuous perches, males of this species constantly monitor and defend their territories.

OCCURRENCE
Rare but regular, breeder in mountain forests of mixed pine-oak and pure coniferous trees in southeastern Arizona and southwestern New Mexico. Rare vagrant (and possible breeder) in west Texas and also north of breeding areas, usually in late summer.

SIMILAR SPECIES

BROAD-BILLED HUMMINGBIRD ♀
wags tail constantly; see p.360

tail more forked

gray under-parts

white tail markings

| Length **3¾in (9.5cm)** | Wingspan **5½in (14cm)** | Weight **³/₃₂–⁵/₃₂oz (3–4g)** |
| Social **Solitary** | Lifespan **Unknown** | Status **Secure** |

Order **Apodiformes**	Family **Trochilidae**	Species *Eugenes fulgens*

Magnificent Hummingbird

MALE *(IN FLIGHT)*

dark tail

dusky undertail feathers

IN FLIGHT

emerald-green throat and chin

violet-purple crown

MALE

white spot behind eye

long, straight black bill

dark green upperparts

black breast and belly

MALE

greenish mottled throat and flanks

green uppertail feathers

grayish underparts

FEMALE

gray-white corners

A close second in size to the Blue-throated Hummingbird, the male Magnificent Hummingbird is far more spectacular. Characteristic of the "sky islands" of Arizona and New Mexico, this species is less territorial and aggressive than other hummingbirds, often utilizing more nectar sites. This species was previously named Rivoli's Hummingbird in honor of the second Duke of Rivoli—a French ornithologist and bird collector of the mid-19th century.

VOICE Call a loud, sharp *chip*; chase call an accelerating series of squeaky *dee* or *dik* notes; song a quiet, buzzy warbling.

NESTING Cup of plant fibers, lichens, moss, bound with spider's silk, lined with plant down; 2 eggs; 1 brood; April–September.

FEEDING Drinks nectar from a variety of flowers; eats small insects caught aerially or gleaned from foliage.

FLIGHT: very fast forward flight with fast wing beats; hovers at flowers; darts after insects.

NECTAR CHASING
Magnificent Hummingbirds are "trapliners" moving along from flower to flower to feed.

OCCURRENCE
Breeds in the extreme Southwest, where it prefers mid- to high-elevation riverside areas and pine-oak or oak woodlands; forages and migrates in drier habitats away from breeding areas as well; mostly present March–October, but sometimes winters at feeding stations.

SIMILAR SPECIES

BLUE-THROATED HUMMINGBIRD ♀
see p.363

clean gray throat

ANNA'S HUMMINGBIRD ♀
see p.369

much smaller overall

shorter bill

Length **5in (13cm)**	Wingspan **7½in (19cm)**	Weight **¼–⅜oz (7–10g)**
Social **Solitary**	Lifespan **Up to 8 years**	Status **Secure**

Order **Apodiformes**	Family **Trochilidae**	Species *Calothorax lucifer*

Lucifer Hummingbird

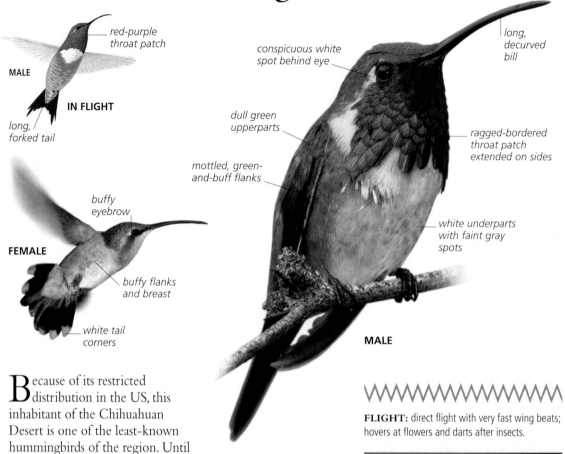

MALE

red-purple
throat patch

IN FLIGHT

long,
forked tail

conspicuous white
spot behind eye

long,
decurved
bill

dull green
upperparts

ragged-bordered
throat patch
extended on sides

mottled, green-
and-buff flanks

buffy
eyebrow

FEMALE

buffy flanks
and breast

white underparts
with faint gray
spots

white tail
corners

MALE

Because of its restricted distribution in the US, this inhabitant of the Chihuahuan Desert is one of the least-known hummingbirds of the region. Until recently, the Lucifer Hummingbird was thought to breed only in the Chisos Mountains of Big Bend National Park in west Texas, where it is easily spotted near flowering agave plants. However, it can now also be regularly seen at feeding stations further afield in Arizona and New Mexico. Recognizing a Lucifer Hummingbird is easy, as its curved bill is unique among North American hummingbirds (some tropical species also have long, curved bills). Males perform an impressive display in front of females at the nest, diving repeatedly near her, each dive being accompanied by the vibrating sound produced by their wings. *Lucifer*, the Latin name of this hummingbird, means "bringing light."

VOICE Call a dry, hard *chit*, often doubled or rolled into series when agitated; also makes sweeter *chi-chip* in territorial interactions; chase call a rapid series of sharp *chit* notes.

NESTING Tiny cup of plant fibers and down, twigs, leaves, and lichen, bound with spider's silk, built in shrubs; 2 eggs; 1–2 broods; April–August.

FEEDING Drinks nectar from a variety of flowers; feeds on small insects and spiders, caught aerially or taken from foliage.

FLIGHT: direct flight with very fast wing beats; hovers at flowers and darts after insects.

BACKYARD VISITOR
Although partial to agave plants, Lucifer Hummingbirds also love backyard feeders.

OCCURRENCE
Breeding range in the US barely reaches Arizona, New Mexico, and Texas, where birds are found April–September. Rocky hillsides, canyons, and washes in high areas of the Chihuahuan desert, particularly areas with flowering agaves are favored. Mexico is the true home of this species.

Length **3½in (9cm)**	Wingspan **4in (10cm)**	Weight **³⁄₃₂– ⁵⁄₃₂oz (3–4g)**
Social **Solitary**	Lifespan **At least 4 years**	Status **Secure**

Order **Apodiformes**	Family **Trochilidae**	Species *Archilochus colubris*

Ruby-throated Hummingbird

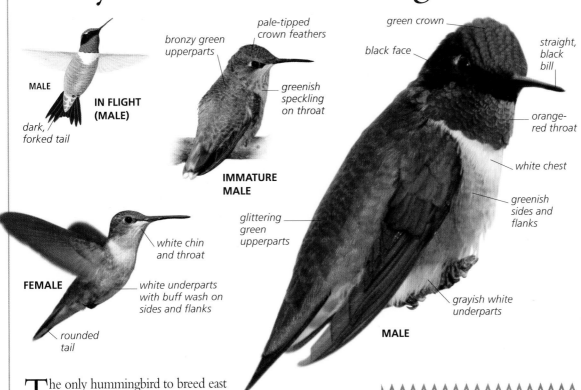

MALE

IN FLIGHT (MALE)

dark, forked tail

pale-tipped crown feathers

bronzy green upperparts

greenish speckling on throat

IMMATURE MALE

green crown

black face

straight, black bill

orange-red throat

white chest

greenish sides and flanks

glittering green upperparts

white chin and throat

FEMALE

white underparts with buff wash on sides and flanks

rounded tail

grayish white underparts

MALE

The only hummingbird to breed east of the Mississippi River, the Ruby-throated Hummingbird is a welcome addition to gardens throughout its range. It is easily identified in most of its range, though more difficult to distinguish in areas where other species are found, particularly during migration. Males perform a deep diving display for females. Before migration, these birds add about ⅟₁₆oz (2g) of fat to their weight to provide enough fuel for their nonstop 800-mile (1,300km) flight across the Gulf of Mexico.

VOICE Call a soft, thick *chic*, sometimes doubled; twittered notes in interactions; chase call a fast, slightly buzzy *tsi-tsi-tsi-tsi-tsi-tsi-tsi-tsi*; soft, rattling song very rarely heard.

NESTING Tiny cup of plant down, with bud scales and lichen on the exterior, bound with spider's silk, usually in deciduous trees; 2 eggs; 1–2 broods; April–September.

FEEDING Drinks nectar from many species of flowers; feeds on small insects and spiders, caught aerially or gleaned from foliage.

FLIGHT: swift, forward flight with very fast wing beats; hovers at flowers and darts after insects.

CATCHING THE LIGHT
Although the throat patch often appears all black, the right lighting sets it afire with color.

SIMILAR SPECIES

BLACK-CHINNED HUMMINGBIRD ♀
see p.368

broader outer feathers

longer bill

ANNA'S HUMMINGBIRD ♀
harder, sharper call notes;
see p.369

thicker neck

grayer underparts

OCCURRENCE
Favors a variety of woodlands, and gardens; earliest migrants appear in the South as early as late February; most leave by November; regular in winter in south Florida; small numbers winter elsewhere on the Gulf Coast; vagrant to the West. The bulk of the population migrates to Central America in winter.

Length **3½in (9cm)**	Wingspan **4¼in (11cm)**	Weight **⅟₁₆–⁷⁄₃₂oz (2–6g)**
Social **Solitary**	Lifespan **Up to 9 years**	Status **Secure**

| Order **Apodiformes** | Family **Trochilidae** | Species *Archilochus alexandri* |

Black-chinned Hummingbird

MALE — violet iridescence on lower part of throat

IN FLIGHT

notched tail

IMMATURE (MALE)

lighter gray-green crown

purple-and-black throat feathers

greenish upperparts

white tips to tail feathers

dusky flanks

whitish underparts

FEMALE

slightly curved, black bill

black throat

white collar below throat

dusky green sides and flanks

MALE

notched greenish tail with darker outer feathers

The Black-chinned Hummingbird is widespread across the western US, mainly due to its ability to adapt to a number of different environments. It readily accepts offerings of sugar water from birdfeeders. During courtship, the males perform a distinctive dive display comprising several broad arcs in addition to a short, back-and-forth shuttle display. The latter is accompanied by a droning noise produced by the bird's wings.

VOICE Call a soft, thick *chic*; fast, buzzy *tsi-tsi-tsi-tsi-tsi-tsi-tsi-tsi* is used to chase off other birds; song soft, warbling, very rarely heard.

NESTING Tiny cup of plant down, with leaves or lichen on the exterior, bound with spider's silk; usually built in a deciduous tree; 2 eggs; 1–2 broods; April–August.

FEEDING Drinks nectar from flowers; eats small insects and spiders, caught aerially or gleaned from foliage.

FLIGHT: rapid with very fast wing beats; hovers at flowers and darts after insects.

TAIL WAGGER
Black-chinned Hummingbirds regularly wag their tails from side to side while feeding.

SIMILAR SPECIES

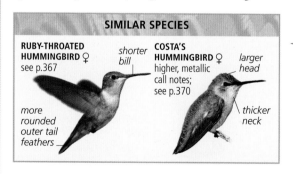

RUBY-THROATED HUMMINGBIRD ♀
see p.367

shorter bill

more rounded outer tail feathers

COSTA'S HUMMINGBIRD ♀
higher, metallic call notes; see p.370

larger head

thicker neck

OCCURRENCE
Widespread in a variety of habitats, particularly scrub and woodlands close to rivers and streams, and irrigated urban areas; also found in drier habitats; forages away from breeding habitat where nectar sources are found. Winters on the Pacific Coast of Mexico.

| Length **3½in (9cm)** | Wingspan **4¾in (12cm)** | Weight **¹⁄₁₆–³⁄₁₆oz (2–5g)** |
| Social **Solitary** | Lifespan **Up to 8 years** | Status **Secure** |

| Order **Apodiformes** | Family **Trochilidae** | Species *Calypte anna* |

Anna's Hummingbird

green crown
and nape

short,
straight,
black bill

green
upperparts

reddish
spots or
flecks on
throat

pale gray
underparts

FEMALE

rose-red head,
sides of neck,
and throat

pale throat

MALE

square tail

IN FLIGHT

iridescent green
upperparts

slightly
notched,
dark green
tail

grayish
underparts

MALE

greenish sides
and flanks

rounded,
green tail

mottled
rosy crown

**IMMATURE
(MALE)**

The most common garden hummingbird along the Pacific Coast from British Columbia to Baja California, the iridescent rose-red helmet of a male Anna's Hummingbird is spectacular and distinctive. The females are rather drab by comparison. This adaptable hummingbird has expanded its range dramatically in the last century because of the availability of garden flowers and feeders. It previously bred only in areas of dense evergreen shrubs along the coast of southern California. The males perform an impressive diving display to court females.
VOICE Call a hard, sharp *tsit*, often doubled or given in series when perched; fast, buzzy chatter used to chase off other birds; song variable series of thin, high, buzzing, warbled notes.
NESTING Tiny cup of mostly plant down, with lichen on the exterior, bound with spider's silk, built in trees or shrubs; 2 eggs; 2 broods; December–July.
FEEDING Drinks nectar from flowers; eats small insects and spiders, caught aerially or gleaned from foliage.

FLIGHT: rapid flight with very fast wing beats; hovers at flowers and darts after insects.

VARIABLE THROAT
Mature female Anna's Hummingbirds often show small iridescent patches on their throats.

SIMILAR SPECIES

BLACK-CHINNED HUMMINGBIRD ♀
see p.368

thinner
neck

whiter
underparts

COSTA'S HUMMINGBIRD ♀
see p.370

smaller
overall

paler,
cleaner
underparts

OCCURRENCE
Primary breeding habitat is coastal dense shrubs and open woodland; also utilizes human areas. Habitat during migration and in winter largely dependent on available nectar sources; range expands northward and eastward during this time. Some birds winter in northwest Mexico; vagrant in the East.

| Length **4in (10cm)** | Wingspan **5in (13cm)** | Weight **³⁄₃₂–⁷⁄₃₂oz (3–6g)** |
| Social **Solitary** | Lifespan **Up to 8 years** | Status **Secure** |

| Order **Apodiformes** | Family **Trochilidae** | Species *Calypte costae* |

Costa's Hummingbird

MALE

short, square tail

IN FLIGHT

violet crown

straight, black bill

violet throat patch extends to sides of neck

dusky, streaked throat with a purple center

mostly whitish underparts

IMMATURE MALE

greenish sides and flanks

MALE

gray-green cap and upperparts

white underparts

FEMALE

A specialty of the Sonoran and Mojave deserts, Costa's Hummingbird is one of North America's most enigmatic species, as its recent range changes and its partially migratory behavior remain unexplained. The male Costa's Hummingbird performs an acrobatic dive display, which includes up to 40 narrow vertical loops that are accompanied by a whistled song. Following this, they often perform a back-and-forth shuttle display for the female.

VOICE Call a soft, metallic *tik*; chase call rapid series of *tik*, often mixed with high, buzzy *tssrr* notes; song a thin, high-pitched, buzzing whistle *tseee-seeeeeeew.*

NESTING Cup of plant matter, feathers, bound with spider's silk, lined with plant down, built in shrubs, trees, or dead cacti; 2 eggs; 1–2 broods; February–July.

FEEDING Drinks nectar from flowers; small insects and arthropods, caught in air or gathered from foliage.

FLIGHT: rapid flight with very fast wing beats; hovers at flowers; darts after insects.

HUNGRY NESTLINGS Like its relatives, the Costa's Hummingbird feeds its young through regurgitation.

OCCURRENCE Largely restricted to desert scrub, sage scrub, and dense shrubs in southern California; generally prefers drier habitat than other western hummingbirds; North American range contracts in fall and early winter with most birds migrating to Mexico. Very rare vagrant north and east of breeding range.

SIMILAR SPECIES

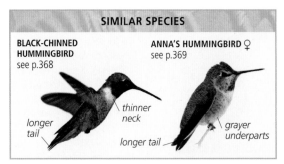

BLACK-CHINNED HUMMINGBIRD see p.368

ANNA'S HUMMINGBIRD ♀ see p.369

longer tail

thinner neck

longer tail

grayer underparts

| Length **3¼in (8.5cm)** | Wingspan **4¾in (12cm)** | Weight **³⁄₃₂oz (3g)** |
| Social **Solitary** | Lifespan **Unknown** | Status **Secure** |

Order **Apodiformes**	Family **Trochilidae**	Species *Selasphorus platycercus*

Broad-tailed Hummingbird

MALE

IN FLIGHT

mostly grayish underparts

FEMALE

spotted throat

buffy flanks

bluish green upperparts

green crown

long, straight bill

rose-red throat patch

green-and-buff flanks

MALE

The trilling sound generated by the male Broad-tailed Hummingbird's wings in flight is common throughout the alpine meadows of the Rocky Mountains. This distinctive noise is likely to be a substitute for song during displays. Birds may arrive on their breeding grounds before the snow melts or flowers bloom, and they survive on insects and tree sap. During courtship, males perform spectacular dives, with their wings trilling loudly during the descent. They also have a buzzing display, bobbing back and forth in front of females.

VOICE Call a sharp *chik*; also short, buzzy warning call, *tssrr*; chase call variable, squeaky twittering.

NESTING Tiny cup of plant down, with lichen and leaves on exterior, bound with spider's silk, and built in trees; 1–2 eggs; 1–2 broods; April–August.

FEEDING Drinks flower nectar; insects and arthropods caught in air or on foliage.

FLIGHT: rapid flight with extremely fast wing beats; hovers at flowers; darts after insects.

LOUD APPROACH
Whirring and trilling wings often announce the presence of a male Broad-tailed Hummingbird.

GUARDING TERRITORY
The male is characteristically seen strongly defending its territory from a high perch.

OCCURRENCE
Inhabits a variety of mid- to high-elevation forest types; early migrants arrive in March in southern states and most leave by September; some individuals winter on the Gulf Coast. Winters mostly in fairly arid habitats in northeastern Mexico. Also breeds in northern Mexico.

SIMILAR SPECIES

RUFOUS HUMMINGBIRD ♀
lower-pitched call;
see p.372

CALLIOPE HUMMINGBIRD ♀
see p.374

rufous flanks and under-tail

more graduated tail

shorter tail

Length **4in (10cm)**	Wingspan **5in (13cm)**	Weight $^{3}/_{32}$–$^{5}/_{32}$**oz (3–4g)**
Social **Solitary**	Lifespan **Up to 12 years**	Status **Secure**

| Order **Apodiformes** | Family **Trochilidae** | Species **Selasphorus rufus** |

Rufous Hummingbird

MALE

IN FLIGHT

rufous tail base with dark tips

white spot near eye

green to bronze-green crown

straight, smooth bill

rufous upperparts

white patch on breast

rich, rufous underparts

wrinkled top bill

mostly green back

rufous uppertail feathers

IMMATURE

MALE

buff face coloration

whitish underparts

FEMALE

One of the most aggressive hummingbirds, the Rufous Hummingbird packs quite a punch, despite its small size; it often chases other hummingbirds away from nectar sources. This bird also breeds farther north than any other North American species of hummingbird and undertakes a lengthy migration. Males are recognizable by their overall fiery orange-rufous color, but females and immature birds are difficult to distinguish from Allen's Hummingbirds.

VOICE Call a hard *chuk*, sometimes in steady series or doubled; also short, buzzy warning call, *tssrr*; chase call a fast, raspy twitter, *tzzerr tichupy tichupy*.

NESTING Tiny cup of plant down, lichen, and other plant matter on exterior, bound with spider's silk, in shrubs or trees; 2 eggs; 1–2 broods; April–July.

FEEDING Drinks nectar from flowers and sap from trees; catches small insects and other arthropods in the air or gleans them off foliage.

FLIGHT: fast flight with extremely rapid wing beats; hovers at flowers; darts after insects.

FIERY MALE
With temperaments matching their bold, flame-like color, males aggressively defend territories.

OCCURRENCE
Breeds in old-growth forest clearings, bushy country, as well as urban gardens; early migrants appear in March; most leave by August; it has become a regular winter inhabitant along the Gulf Coast and southern California; fall or winter vagrants are becoming more common in the East.

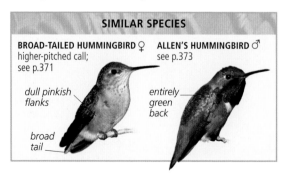

SIMILAR SPECIES

BROAD-TAILED HUMMINGBIRD ♀
higher-pitched call;
see p.371

dull pinkish flanks

broad tail

ALLEN'S HUMMINGBIRD ♂
see p.373

entirely green back

| Length **3½in (9cm)** | Wingspan **5in (13cm)** | Weight **³⁄₃₂–⁷⁄₃₂oz (3–6g)** |
| Social **Solitary** | Lifespan **Up to 12 years** | Status **Secure** |

Order **Apodiformes**	Family **Trochilidae**	Species *Selasphorus sasin*

Allen's Hummingbird

straight,
black bill

rufous patch
on sides of
head

MALE

rufous
underparts

IN FLIGHT

dark tips
on tail

iridescent
green back

orange-red
throat patch

white patch
on breast

warm face
coloration

rufous
underparts

rufous
uppertail with
dark tail band

whitish
underparts with
rufous flanks

green to bronze-
green crown

FEMALE

white-tipped
outer tail feathers

MALE

rufous tail
base and
uppertail

green to green-
bronze back

rufous rump

MALE

narrow,
pointed tail

FLIGHT: fast forward flight with extremely rapid
wing beats; hovers at flowers; darts after prey.

A llen's Hummingbird is a close relative of the similarly colored
Rufous Hummingbird. In some plumages, individuals of these
two species are hard, or even impossible, to tell apart. The range of
this species is limited to the Pacific Coast and the adjacent interior
of the western US from Oregon to California. Male Allen's
Hummingbirds perform a spectacular flight display near females,
which includes dives and a pendulum-like side-to-side motion,
during which they make odd, buzzy, almost metallic sounds.
VOICE Call a hard *chuk*, in steady series or doubled; short, buzzy
warning call, *tssrr*; chase call a fast, raspy twitter, *tzzerr tichupy tichupy*.
NESTING Tiny cup of plant matter and lichen, lined with plant
down, bound with spider's silk, built in shrubs or trees; 2 eggs;
2 broods; February–July.
FEEDING Drinks nectar from a variety of flowers; catches small
insects and spiders aerially or picks them off foliage.

EARLY BREEDER
Males may arrive on the California coast and
establish territories there as early as January.

SIMILAR SPECIES

RUFOUS HUMMINGBIRD ♂
see p.372

CALLIOPE HUMMINGBIRD ♀
softer call; see p.374

mostly
rufous
back

smaller
overall

shorter
tail

dull buffy
flanks

OCCURRENCE
S. s. sasin subspecies breeds in
a narrow belt of fog-affected
habitat along the US west coast
January–August; the second
subspecies (*S. s. sedentarius*)
breeds in dense shrubs on
the Channel Islands, southern
California and parts of the
mainland and is resident;
very rare east to Gulf Coast.

Length **3½in (9cm)**	Wingspan **5in (13cm)**	Weight **1⁄16–5⁄32oz (2–4g)**
Social **Solitary**	Lifespan **Up to 5 years**	Status **Secure**

Order **Apodiformes**	Family **Trochilidae**	Species *Stellula calliope*

Calliope Hummingbird

streaked, rose
throat patch

MALE

short,
square tail

IN FLIGHT

small, dark
streaks on
throat

bronzy
green
above

buffy
flanks

FEMALE

short,
straight bill

purple, beard-like
throat patch

pale
breast

iridescent
greenish
upperparts

MALE

short tail

FLIGHT: rapid with very fast wing beats;
hovers at flowers and darts after insects.

The Calliope Hummingbird is North America's
smallest bird. Despite its diminutive size, it is
just as territorial as other hummingbird species;
the females even attack squirrels trying to rob their nests. The
streaky, purplish throat patch of the males is unique, but the plainer
females can be confused with other hummingbird species when
their small size is not evident in a direct comparison. The male
courtship display includes a number of J-shaped dives, which are
accompanied by a high *tzzt-zing* at the bottom, in addition to
a buzzing hover display in front of a female.

VOICE Relatively silent for a hummingbird; call a soft, high *chip*,
sometimes doubled or repeated; series of high
buzzes and chips used to chase off other birds.

NESTING Tiny cup of plant material and lichen,
bound with spider's silk and lined with plant
down, usually under an overhanging conifer
branch; 2 eggs; 1 brood; May–August.

FEEDING Catches small insects aerially or gleans
insects and spiders from foliage; also drinks nectar.

ATTRACTED TO SAP
The Calliope Hummingbird
commonly feeds on sap and the
insects attracted to it.

MOUNTAIN GEM
Like other hummingbirds, this
mountain dweller hovers to
take nectar from flowers.

OCCURRENCE
Present in western mountains
primarily March–September;
breeds mostly in coniferous
mountainous forests, meadows,
and thickets; spring migrants
found in a variety of lower
elevation habitats; fall migrants
are found at higher elevations;
very rare in winter along the
Gulf Coast.

SIMILAR SPECIES

**BROAD-TAILED
HUMMINGBIRD** ♀
sharper call note;
see p.371

*larger
overall*

longer, more
graduated
tail

RUFOUS HUMMINGBIRD ♀
harder call note;
see p.372

*more rufous
flanks*

*longer, more
graduated tail*

Length **3¼in (8cm)**	Wingspan **4¼in (10.5cm)**	Weight **¹⁄₁₆–⁵⁄₃₂oz (2–4g)**
Social **Solitary**	Lifespan **Up to 12 years**	Status **Secure**

Family **Trogonidae**

TROGONS

TROGONS ARE WIDESPREAD birds of the tropical and subtropical forests of the world, but only one, the Elegant Trogon, regularly occurs north of Mexico. Like woodpeckers, parrots, and some other arboreal birds, they have four toes arranged in opposing pairs for grasping branches. Uniquely in trogons, the inner toe is reversed, instead of the outer toe as in other birds. Most species have long, square tails with distinctive black-and-white bands on the underside. Trogons have a slow, undulating flight pattern similar to that of woodpeckers, although they can easily outpace a predator if necessary. Trogons are also famously thin-skinned—to such an extent that their feathers are poorly anchored and easily fall out when they fly.

SIT AND WAIT
This Elegant Trogon spends most of its time sitting quietly while waiting for prey.

Family **Alcedinidae**

KINGFISHERS

KINGFISHERS ARE PRIMARILY a tropical family that apparently originated in the Australasian region. Three species are found in the US and Canada, but only one, the Belted Kingfisher, is widespread. Like most species of kingfishers, these birds are large-headed and large-billed but have comparatively short legs and toes. Although North American kingfishers lack the array of bright blues, greens, and reds associated with their tropical and European counterparts, they are striking birds, distinguished by chestnut-colored chest bands and white underparts. While they also eat frogs and crayfish, North American species are primarily fish-eaters. After catching a fish, they routinely stun their prey by beating it against a perch before turning the fish around so that it can be eaten head first. Smaller species such as the Green Kingfisher are shy and not often seen.

FISH DINNER
A Belted Kingfisher uses its large bill to catch and hold slippery prey.

DAZZLING GEM
The tropical Green Kingfisher, which is only found in Texas, is a small but striking species.

Order **Coraciiformes**	Family **Alcedinidae**	Species ***Ceryle torquata***

Ringed Kingfisher

barred tail
white collar
MALE
white underwing patches
white undertail feathers
IN FLIGHT

blue breast
white band between breast and chestnut belly
barred undertail
FEMALE

blue-gray head with shaggy crest
white spot on face
thick, powerful bill
white collar
chestnut breast and belly
MALE

deep blue upperparts
barred tail
white undertail

FLIGHT: strong, direct, with two or three deep, slow wing beats interrupted by one hurried beat.

The largest of the three species of North American kingfishers, the Ringed Kingfisher is easily identified by its size and color. It lives in the Lower Rio Grande Valley, where it perches conspicuously on trees and branches over the water. However, its shyness is such that it is not seen as often as its bright colors might suggest, and it flies off at the least suspicion of intrusion, with a loud rattle that signals where it was. Like other kingfishers it nests in a burrow, which it digs in a muddy or sandy riverbank.

VOICE Loud rattle; also loud, double-syllablled *ktok-ktok* in flight.

NESTING Excavates horizontal tunnel in sand or mud bank along rivers, ponds, or lagoons; eggs laid on layer of fish bones and scales; 3–6 eggs; 1 brood; March–July.

FEEDING Plunge-dives from perch or hovers, snatches fish; also eats crustaceans, small birds, and mammals.

SIMILAR SPECIES

BELTED KINGFISHER ♀
see p.379
smaller overall
pale blue slate tinted
white belly

FISHERMAN
The Ringed Kingfisher is mainly a fish hunter, but also feeds on birds and small mammals.

OCCURRENCE
Ranges from southern Texas to southern South America. At northernmost Texas range occurs along the Rio Grande Valley, where it breeds along wooded banks, and at ponds and lagoons. Resident throughout range. Found in a large variety of habitats south of the US.

Length **16in (41cm)**	Wingspan **25in (63cm)**	Weight **11oz (325g)**
Social **Solitary/Pairs**	Lifespan **Unknown**	Status **Localized**

Order **Coraciiformes**	Family **Alcedinidae**	Species **Ceryle alcyon**

Belted Kingfisher

MALE

large head

single blue breastband

barred tail

IN FLIGHT

bluish gray head with shaggy crest

white collar

bluish slate upperparts

white belly

MALE

prominent crest

long, thick, powerful bill

chestnut band across breast

chestnut flanks

FEMALE

double crest

white collar

single dark breastband

IMMATURE MALE

FLIGHT: strongly flaps its wings and then glides after two or three beats; frequently hovers.

Its stocky body, double-pointed crest, large head, and contrasting white collar distinguish the Belted Kingfisher from other species in its range. This kingfisher's loud and far-carrying rattles are heard more often than the bird is seen. Interestingly, it is one of the few birds in North America in which the female is more colorful than the male. The Belted Kingfisher can be found in a large variety of aquatic habitats, both coastal and inland, vigorously defending its territory, all year round.

VOICE Harsh mechanical rattle given in flight or from a perch; sometimes emits screams or trill-like warble during breeding.

NESTING Unlined chamber in subterranean burrow 3–6ft (1–2m) deep, excavated in earthen bank usually over water, but sometimes in ditches, sand, or gravel pits; 6–7 eggs; 1 brood; March–July.

FEEDING Plunge-dives from branches or wires to catch a wide variety of fish near the surface, including sticklebacks and trout; also takes crustaceans, such as crayfish.

SIMILAR SPECIES

RINGED KINGFISHER ♂ see p.378

larger overall

chestnut belly

CATCH OF THE DAY
The female's chestnut belly band and flanks are clearly visible here as she perches with her catch.

OCCURRENCE
Breeds and winters around clear, open waters of streams, rivers, lakes, estuaries, and protected marine shorelines, where perches are available and prey is visible. Avoids water with emergent vegetation. Northern populations migrate south to Mexico, Central America, and the West Indies.

Length **11–14in (28–35cm)**	Wingspan **19–23in (48–58cm)**	Weight **5–6oz (150–175g)**
Social **Solitary**	Lifespan **Unknown**	Status **Secure**

Family **Picidae**

WOODPECKERS

THE THREE GROUPS of closely related species that constitute the family Picidae are found throughout North America. They are a physically striking group adapted to living on tree trunks.

WOODPECKERS

The species that constitute the typical woodpeckers of North America share a distinct set of physical characteristics and behaviors. Their pecking and drumming, which they use for purposes of constructing nest cavities and communication, is made possible by a very thick skull, adapted to withstand the shock that results from continual pecking on wood. Woodpeckers nest in cavities in dead trees, and they are vulnerable to the loss of their specialized habitats as well as forest clearing.

SAPSUCKERS

This group of bird feed on tree sap as a primary source of nourishment for both adults and their young. Sapsuckers have tongues tipped with stiff hairs to allow sap that stick to them. The holes the birds create in trees in order to extract the sap also attract insects, which make up the main protein source in the sapsucker diet. Because they damage living trees, some orchard growers consider sapsuckers to be pests.

BALANCING ACT
The Yellow-bellied Sapsucker rests its stiff tail against a tree to maintain its balance.

FLICKERS

Flickers are relatively large members of the family Picidae and spend more time feeding on the ground than other woodpeckers, consuming ants and other insects. Flickers often forage in open areas around human habitation. They are notable for their colorful underwing feather plumages and their distinctive white rump.

RED ALERT
With its crimson head, the Red-headed Woodpecker is an instantly recognizable bird in North America.

COMMON FLICKER
The Northern Flicker can be found across the entire North American continent.

Order **Piciformes**	Family **Picidae**	Species *Melanerpes lewis*

Lewis' Woodpecker

long, broad wings

ADULT

blackish green rump

very dark upperparts

IN FLIGHT

blackish green head

black bill

dark red forehead and cheek

silvery and rosy red underparts

dull brown head

broad silvery gray collar

no gray collar

black upperparts with glossy green sheen

blackish brown upperparts

JUVENILE

ADULT (SUMMER)

blackish green tail

FLIGHT: rather slow, deep wing beats; flight is level rather than undulating.

The iridescent dark green back and the salmon-red abdomen of Lewis' Woodpecker distinguishes it from any other bird in North America. Juveniles, however, have a brownish head and underparts and lack the gray collar, red face, and pink belly. Lewis' Woodpecker is also notably quieter than other woodpeckers, but it aggressively defends its food sources from other woodpeckers, especially in the winter. During flight, the bird accomplishes acrobatic maneuvers in pursuit of flying insects, sallying out from a perch in order to catch them. Alexander Wilson, the founder of North American ornithology, named this species in 1811, to honor Meriwether Lewis, because it was collected during the Lewis and Clark expedition.

VOICE *Churrs* sound; drumming not loud.

NESTING Cavity nester, usually in dead tree trunks, with preference for natural cavities and previously used nest holes; 6–7 eggs; 1 brood; May–August.

FEEDING Eats a variety of flying insects during breeding season; acorns, other nuts, and fruits, at other times.

FAVORITE HANGOUT
This bird is found in a variety of habitats, but is most common in Ponderosa pine forests.

LOVE NEST
Lewis' Woodpecker excavates cavities in dead trees for nesting purposes.

OCCURRENCE
Prefers open Ponderosa pine forests for breeding, especially old growth stands that have been modified by burning. Also found in riverside woodlands with cottonwood trees. Gravitates to open canopy; in winter, oak woodlands and nut and fruit orchards.

Length **10–11in (25–28cm)**	Wingspan **19–20in (48–51cm)**	Weight **3¼–5oz (90–150g)**
Social **Solitary**	Lifespan **Unknown**	Status **Localized**

Order **Piciformes**	Family **Picidae**	Species ***Melanerpes erythrocephalus***

Red-headed Woodpecker

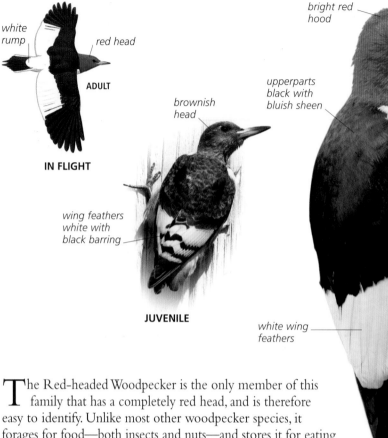

white rump

red head

ADULT

IN FLIGHT

brownish head

wing feathers white with black barring

JUVENILE

bright red hood

bluish gray bill

upperparts black with bluish sheen

narrow black "necklace"

ADULT

white wing feathers

The Red-headed Woodpecker is the only member of this family that has a completely red head, and is therefore easy to identify. Unlike most other woodpecker species, it forages for food—both insects and nuts—and stores it for eating at a later time. It is one of the most skilled flycatchers in the woodpecker family. Its numbers have declined, largely because of the destruction of its habitat, especially the removal of dead trees in urban and rural areas, and clearing and cutting of trees for firewood in rural areas. The Red-headed Woodpecker is a truly North American bird, not extending south of the Rio Grande.

VOICE Primary call a extremely harsh and loud *churr*, also produces breeding call and alarm; no song; active drummer.

NESTING Excavates cavity in dead wood; 3–5 eggs; 1–2 broods; May–August.

FEEDING Forages in flight, on ground, and in trees; feeds on a variety of insects, spiders, nuts seeds, berries, and fruit, and, in rare cases, small mammals such as mice.

WORK IN PROGRESS
The Red-headed Woodpecker excavates its breeding cavities in tree trunks and stumps.

FLIGHT: strong flapping; undulation not as marked as in other woodpecker species.

OCCURRENCE
Breeds in a variety of habitats, especially open deciduous woodlands, including riverine areas, orchards, municipal parks, agricultural areas, forest edges, and forests affected by fire. Uses the same habitats during the winter as in the breeding season.

Length **8½–9½in (22–24cm)**	Wingspan **16–18in (41–46cm)**	Weight **2–3oz (55–85g)**
Social **Solitary**	Lifespan **At least 10 years**	Status **Declining**

Order **Piciformes**	Family **Picidae**	Species ***Melanerpes formicivorus***

Acorn Woodpecker

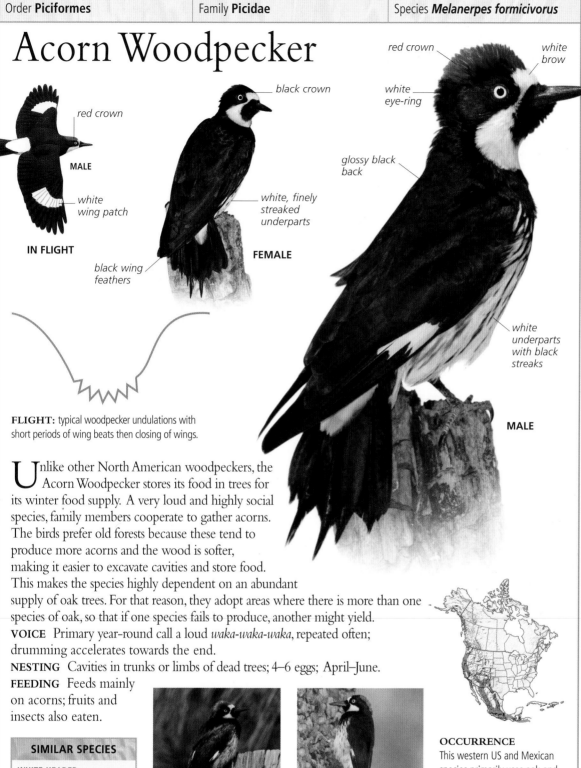

MALE

red crown

white wing patch

IN FLIGHT

black crown

white, finely streaked underparts

black wing feathers

FEMALE

red crown

white brow

white eye-ring

glossy black back

white underparts with black streaks

MALE

FLIGHT: typical woodpecker undulations with short periods of wing beats then closing of wings.

Unlike other North American woodpeckers, the Acorn Woodpecker stores its food in trees for its winter food supply. A very loud and highly social species, family members cooperate to gather acorns. The birds prefer old forests because these tend to produce more acorns and the wood is softer, making it easier to excavate cavities and store food. This makes the species highly dependent on an abundant supply of oak trees. For that reason, they adopt areas where there is more than one species of oak, so that if one species fails to produce, another might yield.

VOICE Primary year-round call a loud *waka-waka-waka*, repeated often; drumming accelerates towards the end.

NESTING Cavities in trunks or limbs of dead trees; 4–6 eggs; April–June.

FEEDING Feeds mainly on acorns; fruits and insects also eaten.

SIMILAR SPECIES

WHITE-HEADED WOODPECKER see p.397

white face

black back

TREE CAVITIES
A nest site may contain several cavities for breeding, typically in a large tree.

STORING FOOD
An obsessive acorn storer, it drills holes in oaks and accumulates large numbers of acorns.

OCCURRENCE
This western US and Mexican species primarily uses oak and pine-oak woodlands for its breeding and wintering habitat. Also found in urban parks and suburban areas where oak trees are present. Will use areas with other kinds of trees as long as oak trees are also present in the vicinity.

Length **7–9in (17.5–23cm)**	Wingspan **14–17in (36–43cm)**	Weight **2¼–3oz (65–85g)**
Social **Family groups**	Lifespan **Up to 16 years**	Status **Secure**

Order **Piciformes**	Family **Picidae**	Species *Melanerpes uropygialis*

Gila Woodpecker

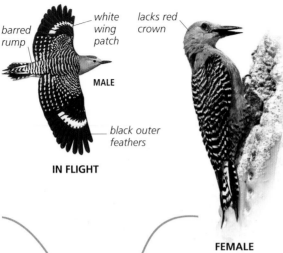

barred rump

white wing patch

lacks red crown

MALE

black outer feathers

IN FLIGHT

small, red crown patch

tan-rust head

tan-rust neck and underparts

MALE

FEMALE

black-and-white barred upperparts

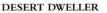

FLIGHT: typically undulating and swift wing beats, alternating with close-winged glides.

The Gila Woodpecker is distinctive in appearance and behavior. It can be identified by the barred rump, wings, and back and brownish head and underparts. It is well known for its use of live cacti, in which it bores holes for nests. Both male and female birds excavate the nest. This is done without injuring the plants, which benefits the woodpecker, as it can eat the fruit of the cacti. However, the cactus hole will not be used for several months, or even a year, until a hard casing has formed. Once the woodpeckers have abandoned their nest, other species of birds, including owls and flycatchers, find the holes attractive places to build their own nests.

VOICE Noisy, loud *churr-churr* and a series of *pip-pip* or *yip-yip* notes; drumming is prolonged.

NESTING Excavates nests in Saguaro cactus as well as trees; 3–5 eggs; 1–2 broods; April–July.

FEEDING Eats insects, fruit (such as Saguaro and other cacti), berries, bird eggs, and corn in fields or storage.

DESERT DWELLER
Gila Woodpeckers are year-round residents of their desert habitat.

OCCURRENCE
From its northernmost range in the southwestern US to its southern distribution in central Mexico, this desert species is attracted to cacti and large dead trees, but also lives in riverside woodlands. It has adapted quite well to suburban areas.

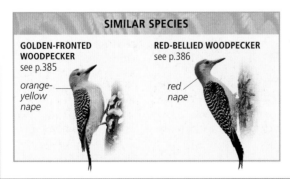

SIMILAR SPECIES

GOLDEN-FRONTED WOODPECKER
see p.385

orange-yellow nape

RED-BELLIED WOODPECKER
see p.386

red nape

Length **8–10in (20–25cm)**	Wingspan **16–17in (41–43cm)**	Weight **2¼–2⅝oz (65–75g)**
Social **Solitary**	Lifespan **Up to 8 years**	Status **Secure**

Order **Piciformes**	Family **Picidae**	Species *Melanerpes aurifrons*

Golden-fronted Woodpecker

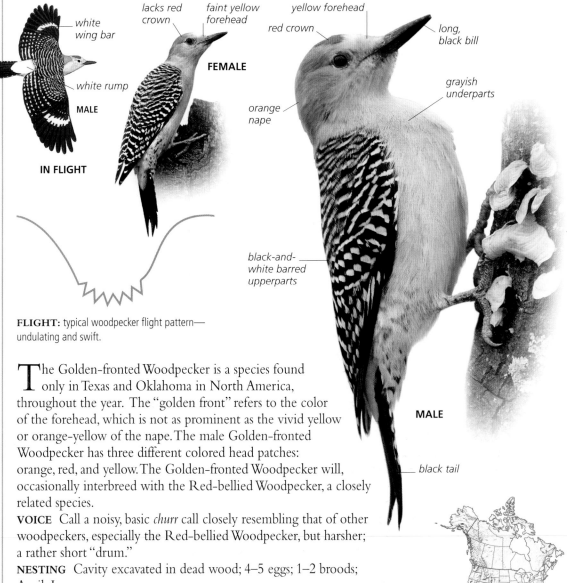

white wing bar

white rump

MALE

IN FLIGHT

lacks red crown

faint yellow forehead

FEMALE

yellow forehead

red crown

orange nape

long, black bill

grayish underparts

black-and-white barred upperparts

MALE

black tail

FLIGHT: typical woodpecker flight pattern—undulating and swift.

The Golden-fronted Woodpecker is a species found only in Texas and Oklahoma in North America, throughout the year. The "golden front" refers to the color of the forehead, which is not as prominent as the vivid yellow or orange-yellow of the nape. The male Golden-fronted Woodpecker has three different colored head patches: orange, red, and yellow. The Golden-fronted Woodpecker will, occasionally interbreed with the Red-bellied Woodpecker, a closely related species.

VOICE Call a noisy, basic *churr* call closely resembling that of other woodpeckers, especially the Red-bellied Woodpecker, but harsher; a rather short "drum."

NESTING Cavity excavated in dead wood; 4–5 eggs; 1–2 broods; April–June.

FEEDING Feeds on a diverse diet of insects, spiders, and vegetable matter, such as nuts, beans, and fruit; also probably bird eggs.

SIMILAR SPECIES

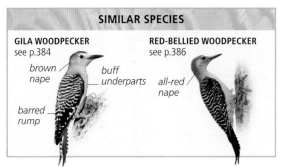

GILA WOODPECKER
see p.384

brown nape

buff underparts

barred rump

RED-BELLIED WOODPECKER
see p.386

all-red nape

HIDDEN RUMP
Note the distinctive white rump patch, which is partially hidden by finely barred plumage.

OCCURRENCE
This permanent resident of the US (southern Oklahoma, Texas), Mexico, and Central America, south to Nicaragua, occurs in a variety of open woodlands, including riverside groves, tropical scrub and forests, and brushlands. The mesquite tree is important to its breeding success.

Length **10–12in (25–30cm)**	Wingspan **17in (43cm)**	Weight **2¼–3½oz (65–100g)**
Social **Pairs**	Lifespan **Up to 5½ years**	Status **Secure**

Order **Piciformes**	Family **Picidae**	Species *Melanerpes carolinus*

Red-bellied Woodpecker

white patches at base of outer wing

MALE

gray crown   red crown

pale grayish tan face

pale grayish tan underparts

red nape

IN FLIGHT

FEMALE

regular black-and-white barring

MALE

FLIGHT: undulating flight, as with other woodpecker species.

This attractive, abundant woodpecker is found throughout the eastern half of the US, and has expanded its range both northward and westward in the last decade or two. Despite its common name, it does not actually possess a red belly. The male is distinguished by its red forehead, crown, and nape, while the female only has a red nape; both have pale-colored underparts and regularly barred upperparts. Male Red-bellied Woodpeckers excavate several holes in trees, one of which the female chooses. They also use previously available cavities, but often lose them to aggressive starlings. Unlike many woodpecker species, although the Red-bellied eats insects, it does not excavate trees to find them.

VOICE Rather soft, clearly rolling, slightly quivering *krrurrr* call.

NESTING Cavity nester; 4–5 eggs; 1–3 broods; May–August.

FEEDING Eats insects, fruit, seeds, acorns, and other nuts; in winter, eats mainly vegetable matter.

SIMILAR SPECIES

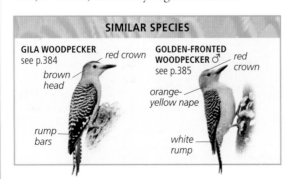

GILA WOODPECKER
see p.384

red crown

brown head

rump bars

GOLDEN-FRONTED WOODPECKER ♂
see p.385

red crown

orange-yellow nape

white rump

SUBURBAN SPECIES
These birds can be seen and heard on tree trunks in suburban and urban woods.

OCCURRENCE
Resident in the eastern and southeastern US, where it breeds in a wide range of habitats; found in forests, swamps, suburban wooded areas, open woodlands, and parks. Winter habitats resemble the breeding areas.

Length **9–10½ in (23–27cm)**	Wingspan **16in (41cm)**	Weight **2½ oz (70g)**
Social **Solitary/Pairs**	Lifespan **Up to 12 years**	Status **Secure**

Order **Piciformes**	Family **Picidae**	Species *Sphyrapicus thyroideus*

Williamson's Sapsucker

white rump

black wings with white patches

FEMALE

black tail

MALE

IN FLIGHT

dark bill

red throat

white head stripe

black back

barred flanks

MALE

brown head

brown overall with barred plumage

FEMALE

dark back

white wing patch

JUVENILE MALE

The Williamson's Sapsucker is one of the four sapsucker species occurring in North America. Unlike other sapsuckers, the male and female plumages are so dissimilar that it is difficult to believe they belong to the same species. The species has very specific habitat needs, partly because of its dependence on the sap and phloem, the innermost bark layer of trees. This secretive sapsucker can be located in the breeding season by its rather hesitant drumming, which occurs in an uneven series. With its white rump the female looks like a flicker in flight.

VOICE Primary call nasal *churr;* also a mewing call.
NESTING Excavates cavity in dead wood; 5–6 eggs; 1 brood; May–July.
FEEDING Mainly eats tree sap and ants during the breeding season; nonbreeding birds feed on the sap, phloem, and fruit of trees.

DRILLING FOR FOOD
These birds drill holes in tree barks and then eat the sap and insects that emerge.

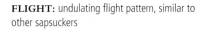

FLIGHT: undulating flight pattern, similar to other sapsuckers

OCCURRENCE
A species of the Intermountain West, breeding in coniferous forest. Winters at lower elevations, where it mainly occupies pine-oak woodlands, in the southeastern US and in Mexico.

Length **9in (23cm)**	Wingspan **17in (43cm)**	Weight **1¾oz (50g)**
Social **Pairs**	Lifespan **Unknown**	Status **Declining**

| Order **Piciformes** | Family **Picidae** | Species **Sphyrapicus varius** |

Yellow-bellied Sapsucker

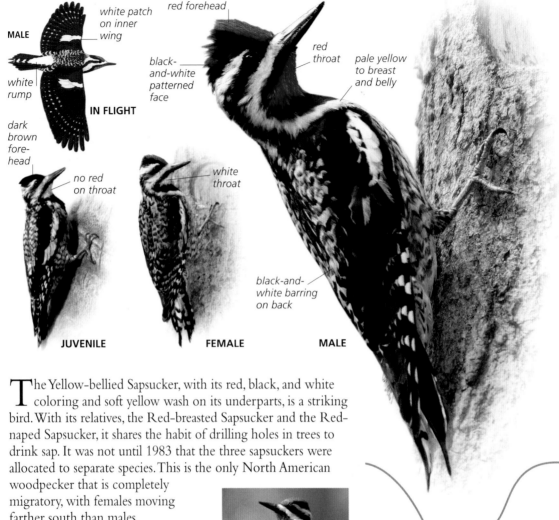

MALE

white patch on inner wing

white rump

IN FLIGHT

dark brown fore-head

red forehead

black-and-white patterned face

red throat

pale yellow to breast and belly

no red on throat

white throat

black-and-white barring on back

JUVENILE

FEMALE

MALE

The Yellow-bellied Sapsucker, with its red, black, and white coloring and soft yellow wash on its underparts, is a striking bird. With its relatives, the Red-breasted Sapsucker and the Red-naped Sapsucker, it shares the habit of drilling holes in trees to drink sap. It was not until 1983 that the three sapsuckers were allocated to separate species. This is the only North American woodpecker that is completely migratory, with females moving farther south than males.

VOICE Primary call a mewing *wheer-wheer-wheer.*

NESTING Cavities in dead trees; 5–6 eggs; 1 brood; May–June.

FEEDING Drinks sap; eats ants and other small insects; feeds on the inner bark of trees, also a variety of fruit.

FLIGHT: typical woodpecker, undulating flight pattern with intermittent flapping and gliding.

STRIKING SPECIES
The Yellow-bellied Sapsucker's white rump and black-and-white forked tail are clearly evident here.

OCCURRENCE
Breeds in eastern Alaska, Canada, and south to the Appalaichans. Prefers either deciduous forests or mixed deciduous-coniferous forests; prefers young forests. In winter, it is found in open wooded areas in southeastern states, Caribbean islands, and Central America.

SIMILAR SPECIES

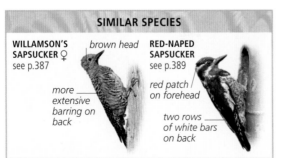

WILLAMSON'S SAPSUCKER ♀
see p.387

brown head

more extensive barring on back

RED-NAPED SAPSUCKER
see p.389

red patch on forehead

two rows of white bars on back

| Length **8–9in (20–23cm)** | Wingspan **16–18in (41–46cm)** | Weight **1¾oz (50g)** |
| Social **Solitary/Pairs** | Lifespan **Up to 7 years** | Status **Secure** |

Order **Piciformes**	Family **Picidae**	Species *Sphyrapicus nuchalis*

Red-naped Sapsucker

white rump

ADULT

red throat patch

black and white bars on tail

IN FLIGHT

red forehead and crown

red patch on nape

extensive red on throat

white stripe on face

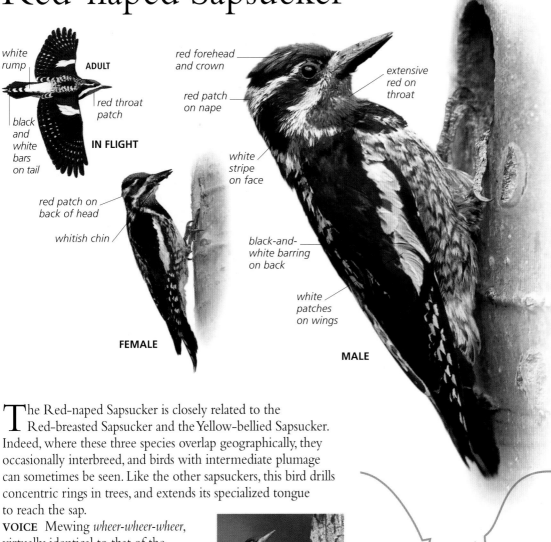

red patch on back of head

whitish chin

FEMALE

black-and-white barring on back

white patches on wings

MALE

The Red-naped Sapsucker is closely related to the Red-breasted Sapsucker and the Yellow-bellied Sapsucker. Indeed, where these three species overlap geographically, they occasionally interbreed, and birds with intermediate plumage can sometimes be seen. Like the other sapsuckers, this bird drills concentric rings in trees, and extends its specialized tongue to reach the sap.

VOICE Mewing *wheer-wheer-wheer*, virtually identical to that of the Red-breasted and Yellow-bellied sapsuckers.

NESTING Cavity nester; 4–5 eggs; 1 brood; May–August.

FEEDING Feeds on sap and seeds; fruit and other vegetable matter; also insects and spiders.

FLIGHT: typical woodpecker, undulating flight pattern, with intermittent flapping and gliding.

ASPEN DWELLER
The Red-naped Sapsucker excavates its nest cavities in live aspens.

SIMILAR SPECIES

YELLOW-BELLIED SAPSUCKER see p.388

less red on throat

no red on nape

RED-BREASTED SAPSUCKER see p.390

all-red head

red breast

OCCURRENCE
Breeds in coniferous forest, intermixed with aspen, in the Rocky Mountains from Canada to California; but also riverside woodlands. Winter habitats include forests, open woodlands, parks, and orchards in the Southeast.

Length **8–9in (20–23cm)**	Wingspan **17in (43cm)**	Weight **2⅛oz (60g)**
Social **Solitary/Migrant flocks**	Lifespan **Up to 3 years**	Status **Localized**

| Order **Piciformes** | Family **Picidae** | Species *Sphyrapicus ruber* |

Red-breasted Sapsucker

yellowish spots on back

white rump

MALE (S. r. ruber)

IN FLIGHT

duller head

red head

thick bill

large white patch on wing

red breast

pale yellowish belly

black back with white feathers

deep red head

heavy white markings on upperparts

ADULT (S. r. ruber)

ADULT (S. r. daggetti)

ADULT (S. r. daggetti)

FLIGHT: undulating flight pattern with intermittent flapping and gliding.

Apart from its distinctive red head and breast, the Red-breasted Sapsucker resembles other sapsuckers—so much so that the interrelated Red-breasted, Red-naped, and Yellow-bellied Sapsuckers were once all considered to belong to the same species. Like its relatives, the Red-breasted Sapsucker drills holes in tree trunks to extract sap. Other birds and mammals, such as squirrels and bats, obtain food from these holes. The northern form, *S. r. ruber,* occurs from Alaska to Oregon, and has a back lightly marked with gold spots and a brightly colored head. It's southern counterpart, *S. r. daggetti,* has a back more heavily marked with white.

VOICE Call reminiscent of a mewing cat; normally does not vocalize outside the breeding season.

NESTING Excavates cavity in deciduous trees such as aspen and willow, but will also nest in conifers if deciduous trees are not available; 4–5 eggs; 1 brood; May–July.

FEEDING Mainly drills for sap from a number of plants; also eats the insects that have become trapped in the sap.

SIMILAR SPECIES

RED-NAPED SAPSUCKER see p.389

red crown

more white on back

RED-HEADED DRILLER
Red-breasted Sapsuckers drill holes in trees to drink sap and eat the insects attracted to it.

OCCURRENCE
Breeds in a wide range of habitats, including coniferous forests, but may also select deciduous forests and habitats along rivers. Prefers areas with dead trees. A partial migrant, it winters within its breeding range, but also moves south, as far as northern Baja California.

| Length **8–9in (20–23cm)** | Wingspan **15–16in (38–41cm)** | Weight **2oz (55g)** |
| Social **Solitary** | Lifespan **2–3 years** | Status **Localized** |

| Order **Piciformes** | Family **Picidae** | Species ***Picoides scalaris*** |

Ladder-backed Woodpecker

MALE

IN FLIGHT

barred wings

buffy forehead patch

black crown

red crown

straight, black bill

fine streaking

FEMALE

barred back

MALE

black-and-white bars on back

MALE

white-barred outer tail feathers

A bird of the southwestern US, the Ladder-backed Woodpecker has conspicuous, zebra-like black-and-white barring on its back, and a wide black-and-white striped facial pattern. The male, like many North American woodpeckers, has a red crown. This nonmigratory species can be seen year-round in its range. The Ladder-backed Woodpecker occasionally hybridize with its closest relative, the Nuttall's Woodpecker. Desert cacti are used both as a place to breed and as a food source.

VOICE Two main calls: short *peek* call, and rattle- or whinny-like call of many notes; call descends at end.

NESTING Excavates cavity in dead or dying wood; 4–5 eggs; 1 brood; May–July.

FEEDING Males forage lower and on the ground, probing for insects, sometimes around cactus roots; females forage higher, gleaning insects from bark; also feeds on fruits of cactus.

FLIGHT: undulating and swift.

SIMILAR SPECIES

NUTTALL'S WOODPECKER ♂
see p.392

red on rear of crown only

TREE GRUB
This male Ladder-backed Woodpecker has just extracted a beetle larva from a tree trunk.

OCCURRENCE
Breeds in arid scrub, montane shrubbery, wooded canyons, and pine-oak woodlands. In southern Arizona, the bird is seen in grasslands, but in Colorado it is found in pinyon-juniper woodlands. Winters in same habitats as a nonmigratory species.

| Length **7¼in (18.5cm)** | Wingspan **11–12in (28–30cm)** | Weight **1¹⁄₁₆–1¼oz (30–35g)** |
| Social **Unknown** | Lifespan **Up to 4 years** | Status **Declining** |

| Order **Piciformes** | Family **Picidae** | Species *Picoides nuttallii* |

Nuttall's Woodpecker

finely barred plumage

MALE

IN FLIGHT

black crown

white stripe from eye to neck

FEMALE

bright red crown and nape

white breast with dark spots

MALE

barred back

unbarred tail

FLIGHT: undulating flight pattern with deep dips and bursts of wing beats.

Named for the famous British naturalist Thomas Nuttall, Nuttall's Woodpecker is found in the state of California, where it resides year-round. It is closely related to the Ladder-backed Woodpecker, although the two species do not overlap geographically. It resembles the Ladder-backed Woodpecker, with black-and-white barring on the back, and the male's red crown. Interestingly, although Nuttall's Woodpecker prefers oak woodlands, acorns are not part of its diet. It excavates a new nest cavity each year and it is likely that earlier nest sites are used by other species.

VOICE Two calls; single note contact call *pweek* and two-note call *pir-it-pir-it-pir-it*.

NESTING Excavates cavity in dead wood; 4–5 eggs; 1 brood; April–July.

FEEDING Forages by tapping and probing tree trunks, primarily in oaks and riverside trees; also forages on the ground for insects, especially beetles. Males more often forage on the trunks, and females prefer branches.

SIMILAR SPECIES

LADDER-BACKED WOODPECKER ♂ see p.391

red crown and forehead

OAKS ARE IT
Nuttall's Woodpecker prefer to feed in oak trees, but will also forage on cottonwoods.

OCCURRENCE
Lives mainly in oak woodlands, but also pine-oak and woodlands near rivers. It is highly eclectic as regards the species of oak that it chooses. It also uses willows, sycamores, maple, and certain pine trees. Sedentary, but occasionally found in Oregon.

| Length **7–7½in (18–19cm)** | Wingspan **16in (41cm)** | Weight **1¹⁄₁₆oz (30g)** |
| Social **Unknown** | Lifespan **Unknown** | Status **Secure** |

Order **Piciformes**	Family **Picidae**	Species ***Picoides pubescens***

Downy Woodpecker

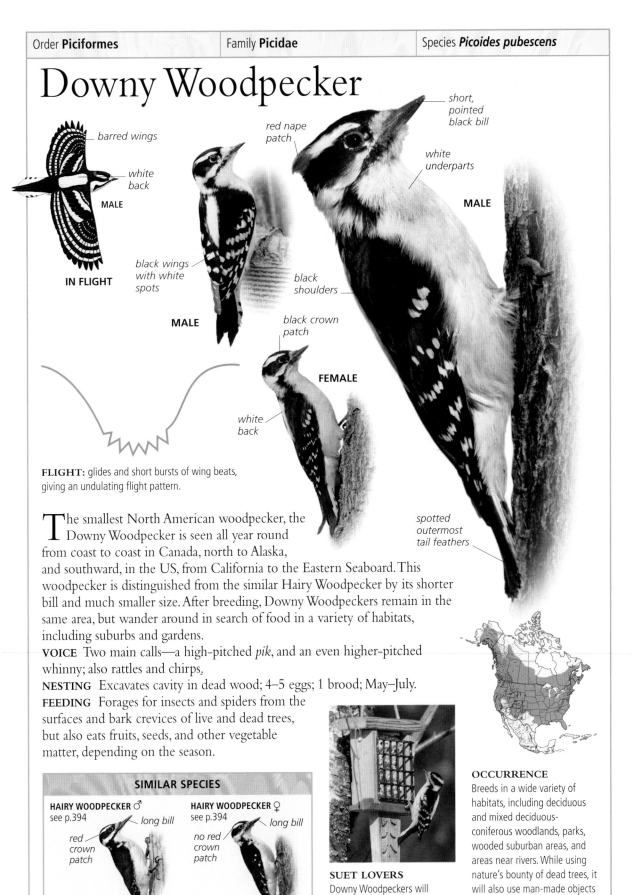

barred wings

white back

MALE

IN FLIGHT

red nape patch

black wings with white spots

MALE

black crown patch

white back

FEMALE

short, pointed black bill

white underparts

MALE

black shoulders

spotted outermost tail feathers

FLIGHT: glides and short bursts of wing beats, giving an undulating flight pattern.

The smallest North American woodpecker, the Downy Woodpecker is seen all year round from coast to coast in Canada, north to Alaska, and southward, in the US, from California to the Eastern Seaboard. This woodpecker is distinguished from the similar Hairy Woodpecker by its shorter bill and much smaller size. After breeding, Downy Woodpeckers remain in the same area, but wander around in search of food in a variety of habitats, including suburbs and gardens.

VOICE Two main calls—a high-pitched *pik*, and an even higher-pitched whinny; also rattles and chirps.

NESTING Excavates cavity in dead wood; 4–5 eggs; 1 brood; May–July.

FEEDING Forages for insects and spiders from the surfaces and bark crevices of live and dead trees, but also eats fruits, seeds, and other vegetable matter, depending on the season.

SIMILAR SPECIES

HAIRY WOODPECKER ♂
see p.394

long bill

red crown patch

HAIRY WOODPECKER ♀
see p.394

long bill

no red crown patch

SUET LOVERS
Downy Woodpeckers will feed on suet provided in feeders during the winter.

OCCURRENCE
Breeds in a wide variety of habitats, including deciduous and mixed deciduous-coniferous woodlands, parks, wooded suburban areas, and areas near rivers. While using nature's bounty of dead trees, it will also use man-made objects such as fence posts. Resident, but local movements occur.

Length **6–7in (15–18cm)**	Wingspan **10–12in (25–30cm)**	Weight **1¹⁄₁₆oz (30g)**
Social **Solitary/Flocks**	Lifespan **Up to 11 years**	Status **Secure**

| Order **Piciformes** | Family **Picidae** | Species *Plcoides villosus* |

Hairy Woodpecker

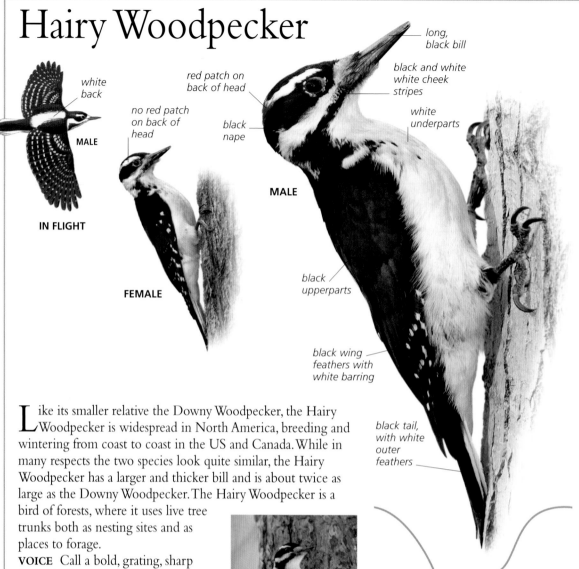

long, black bill

black and white white cheek stripes

white underparts

MALE

white back

MALE

IN FLIGHT

red patch on back of head

no red patch on back of head

black nape

black upperparts

FEMALE

black wing feathers with white barring

black tail, with white outer feathers

Like its smaller relative the Downy Woodpecker, the Hairy Woodpecker is widespread in North America, breeding and wintering from coast to coast in the US and Canada. While in many respects the two species look quite similar, the Hairy Woodpecker has a larger and thicker bill and is about twice as large as the Downy Woodpecker. The Hairy Woodpecker is a bird of forests, where it uses live tree trunks both as nesting sites and as places to forage.

VOICE Call a bold, grating, sharp *Peek,* similar to that of the Downy Woodpecker, but lower in pitch, and louder. Drumming a rather loud, even series of taps.

NESTING Excavates cavity in live trees; 4 eggs; 1 brood; May–July.

FEEDING Eats mainly insects and their larvae; also nuts and seeds.

FLIGHT: undulating; short glides alternating with wing beats.

HOME SWEET HOME
The Hairy Woodpecker is generally found in forests and prefers mature woodland areas, using both deciduous and coniferous trees.

OCCURRENCE
Breeds primarily in forests, both deciduous and coniferous, but also in more open woodlands, swamps, suburban parks, and wooded areas. Resident in North America all the year-round, though in the far north of its range it may move south for the winter.

| SIMILAR SPECIES | | |

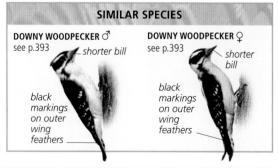

DOWNY WOODPECKER ♂
see p.393

shorter bill

black markings on outer wing feathers

DOWNY WOODPECKER ♀
see p.393

shorter bill

black markings on outer wing feathers

| Length **9–9½in (23–24cm)** | Wingspan **15–16in (38–41cm)** | Weight **2½oz (70g)** |
| Social **Solitary/Winter flocks** | Lifespan **At least 16 years** | Status **Secure** |

Order **Piciformes**	Family **Picidae**	Species *Plcoides arizonae*

Arizona Woodpecker

small white spots

head appears pale

MALE

IN FLIGHT

FEMALE

red nape patch

large white neck patch

scaly looking brown back

short, thin, pointed bill

brown barring on underparts

plain brown back

MALE

FLIGHT: undulating flight typical with lengthy dips, wings closed.

barred outer tail feathers

The Arizona Woodpecker, formerly considered to be the same species as Strickland's Woodpecker, is a year-round resident of southeastern Arizona and southwestern New Mexico. Its plumage is distinctive: it is the only brown-backed woodpecker species in North America. It also has a conspicuous white neck patch, and brown-and-white spots and bars on its underparts. This species is difficult to observe in the wild, as it inhabits inaccessible areas, is well camouflaged, and is remarkably secretive during the nesting period. It is often almost silent during this time, but otherwise the species has an exceptionally large repertoire of calls. Consequently information regarding breeding behavior was, until recently, often anecdotal and inaccurate.

VOICE Main call long *peep* or *peep*; also lengthy, loud, and harsh rattling call; also *kweek* call similar to that given by the Hairy Woodpecker.

NESTING Excavates cavity in dead deciduous trees; 2–4 eggs; 1 brood; March–June.

FEEDING Eats insects and insect larvae; mainly forages in oak trees in its Arizona habitats, extracting larvae from tree trunks.

NOW YOU SEE IT...
The brown plumage of the Arizona Woodpecker blends in well with tree bark.

OCCURRENCE
Found in oak and pine-oak woodlands, also deciduous sycamore–walnut woods near rivers. Oak woodlands in the mountainous areas where it breeds from 4,000–7,000ft (1,200–2,150m). May descend to lower elevations during winter if food is scarce.

Length **7–8in (18–20cm)**	Wingspan **14in (36cm)**	Weight **1⁹⁄₁₆–1¾oz (45–50g)**
Social **Solitary**	Lifespan **Unknown**	Status **Localized**

Order **Piciformes**	Family **Picidae**	Species *Picoides borealis*

Red-cockaded Woodpecker

black rump and upper tail

MALE

white outer tail feathers

black wings with fine white barring

IN FLIGHT

no red spot

FEMALE

white eyebrow

small red spot behind eye (cockade)

white cheek

black-and-white barred back

black cheek stripe

finely streaked underparts

white spots and bars on black wings

whitish undertail feathers

MALE

FLIGHT: typical undulating flight pattern of woodpeckers.

The Red-cockaded Woodpecker's population has been severely affected by the fragmentation of its southeastern US old-growth pine forest habitat, as trees have been cut down for timber and cleared for farmland. The bird breeds in small family groups, or clans, and takes up to three years to drill its nest cavity in a live tree. During incubation, parent birds are often helped by other clan members, usually males born in previous years.

VOICE Primary calls include a rolled *shrit* or *shiff;* also a rattle resembling a kingfisher; very vocal, chattering much of the day.

NESTING Excavates cavity in live, mature longleaf and Loblolly pines; 3–5 eggs; 1 brood; April–June.

FEEDING Forages and drills for insects, especially ants, and insect larvae on trunks of pine trees; eats some seeds and fruits occasionally, including pine seeds, grapes, and blueberries.

FINDING A MEAL
The bird works its way up and around a tree trunk in its search for insects and grubs.

OCCURRENCE
Widespread in pine forests of southeastern US, but localized; absent from some suitable-looking forest stands, common in others. Needs open pine forests maintained without much understory by regular forest fires. Resident.

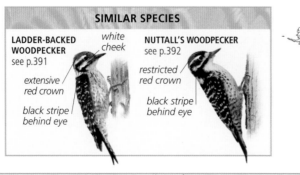

SIMILAR SPECIES

LADDER-BACKED WOODPECKER see p.391

white cheek

extensive red crown

black stripe behind eye

NUTTALL'S WOODPECKER see p.392

restricted red crown

black stripe behind eye

Length **7½–8½in (19–22cm)**	Wingspan **14–15in (36–38cm)**	Weight **1⁷⁄₁₆–1⁹⁄₁₆oz (40–45g)**
Social **Family groups**	Lifespan **12 years**	Status **Endangered**

| Order **Piciformes** | Family **Picidae** | Species *Picoides albolarvatus* |

White-headed Woodpecker

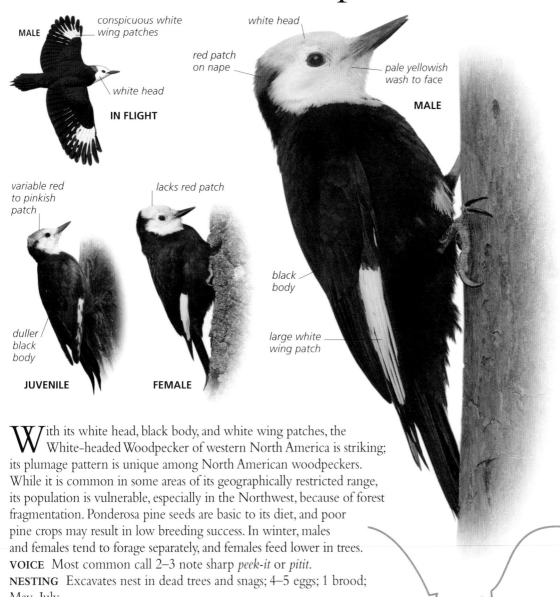

MALE

conspicuous white wing patches

IN FLIGHT

white head

white head

red patch on nape

pale yellowish wash to face

MALE

variable red to pinkish patch

lacks red patch

duller black body

JUVENILE

FEMALE

black body

large white wing patch

With its white head, black body, and white wing patches, the White-headed Woodpecker of western North America is striking; its plumage pattern is unique among North American woodpeckers. While it is common in some areas of its geographically restricted range, its population is vulnerable, especially in the Northwest, because of forest fragmentation. Ponderosa pine seeds are basic to its diet, and poor pine crops may result in low breeding success. In winter, males and females tend to forage separately, and females feed lower in trees.

VOICE Most common call 2–3 note sharp *peek-it* or *pitit*.
NESTING Excavates nest in dead trees and snags; 4–5 eggs; 1 brood; May–July.
FEEDING Eats arthropods, including ants, beetles, and spiders; also berries, and seeds, particularly pine seeds.

FLIGHT: undulating flight pattern typical of woodpeckers.

SIMILAR SPECIES

ACORN WOODPECKER see p.383
white forehead patch
red crown

PARENTING CHORES
This bird is carrying food back to the nest to feed its young.

OCCURRENCE
A strictly western North American bird, occurs from British Columbia to California in mountainous pine forests, especially with Ponderosa pines. Habitat specialist, but many birds move to lower elevations in winter, can be seen in deserts of Montana, Wyoming, and California.

| Length **9–9½in (23–24cm)** | Wingspan **16–17in (41–43cm)** | Weight **2oz (55g)** |
| Social **Solitary** | Lifespan **Unknown** | Status **Localized** |

Order **Piciformes**	Family **Picidae**	Species **Picoides dorsalis**

American Three-toed Woodpecker

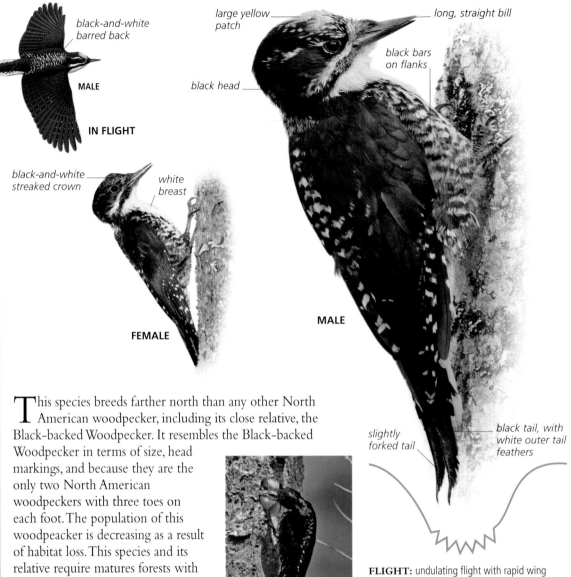

black-and-white barred back

MALE

IN FLIGHT

large yellow patch

long, straight bill

black bars on flanks

black head

black-and-white streaked crown

white breast

FEMALE

MALE

slightly forked tail

black tail, with white outer tail feathers

This species breeds farther north than any other North American woodpecker, including its close relative, the Black-backed Woodpecker. It resembles the Black-backed Woodpecker in terms of size, head markings, and because they are the only two North American woodpeckers with three toes on each foot. The population of this woodpeacker is decreasing as a result of habitat loss. This species and its relative require matures forests with old or dead trees.

VOICE Call notes *queep*, *quip*, or *pik*; generally quiet, likened to the Yellow-bellied Sapsucker.

NESTING Excavates cavity mainly in dead or dying wood, sometimes in live wood; 4 eggs; 1 brood; May–July.

FEEDING Flakes off bark and eats insects underneath, mainly the larvae of Bark Beetles.

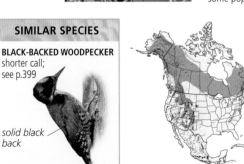

SIMILAR SPECIES

BLACK-BACKED WOODPECKER
shorter call; see p.399

solid black back

FLIGHT: undulating flight with rapid wing beats typical of other woodpeckers.

COLOR VARIATION
The streaks on this species' back are highly variable; some populations have nearly all-white backs.

OCCURRENCE
Breeds in mature northerly coniferous forests across Canada and through the Rockies. Since it is largely nonmigratory, this is also the winter habitat for most populations, although it is found in more open areas in winter.

Length **8–9in (20–23cm)**	Wingspan **15in (38cm)**	Weight **2¼–2½ oz (65–70g)**
Social **Solitary/Pairs**	Lifespan **Unknown**	Status **Vulnerable**

Order **Piciformes**	Family **Picidae**	Species *Picoides arcticus*

Black-backed Woodpecker

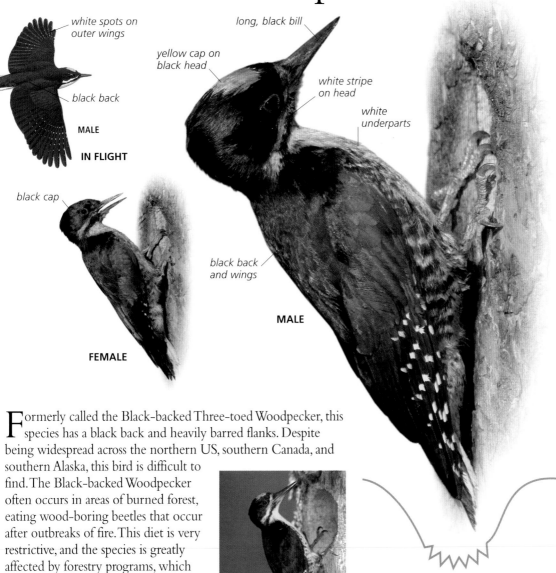

white spots on outer wings

long, black bill

yellow cap on black head

white stripe on head

black back

white underparts

MALE

IN FLIGHT

black cap

black back and wings

MALE

FEMALE

Formerly called the Black-backed Three-toed Woodpecker, this species has a black back and heavily barred flanks. Despite being widespread across the northern US, southern Canada, and southern Alaska, this bird is difficult to find. The Black-backed Woodpecker often occurs in areas of burned forest, eating wood-boring beetles that occur after outbreaks of fire. This diet is very restrictive, and the species is greatly affected by forestry programs, which prevent the spread of fire. Although it overlaps geographically with the American Three-toed Woodpecker, the two are rarely found together in the same locality.

VOICE Main call a single *pik*.

NESTING Cavity excavated in tree; 3–4 eggs; 1 brood; May–July.

FEEDING Eats beetles, especially larvae of wood-boring beetles, by flaking off bark.

FLIGHT: typical undulating flight of woodpeckers.

FREQUENT MOVING
This bird excavates a new nest cavity each year, rarely returning in subsequent years.

OCCURRENCE
Inhabitant of northerly and mountainous coniferous forests that require fire for renewal. Breeding occurs soon after sites are burned as new colonies are attracted to the habitat. In Michigan's Upper Peninsula, the bird uses trees similar to those in its northern habitat.

SIMILAR SPECIES

AMERICAN THREE-TOED WOODPECKER
see p.398

black-and-white barred upperparts

Length **9–9½in (23–24cm)**	Wingspan **15–16in (38–41cm)**	Weight **2½oz (70g)**
Social **Pairs**	Lifespan **Unknown**	Status **Secure**

| Order **Piciformes** | Family **Picidae** | Species *Colaptes auratus* |

Northern Flicker

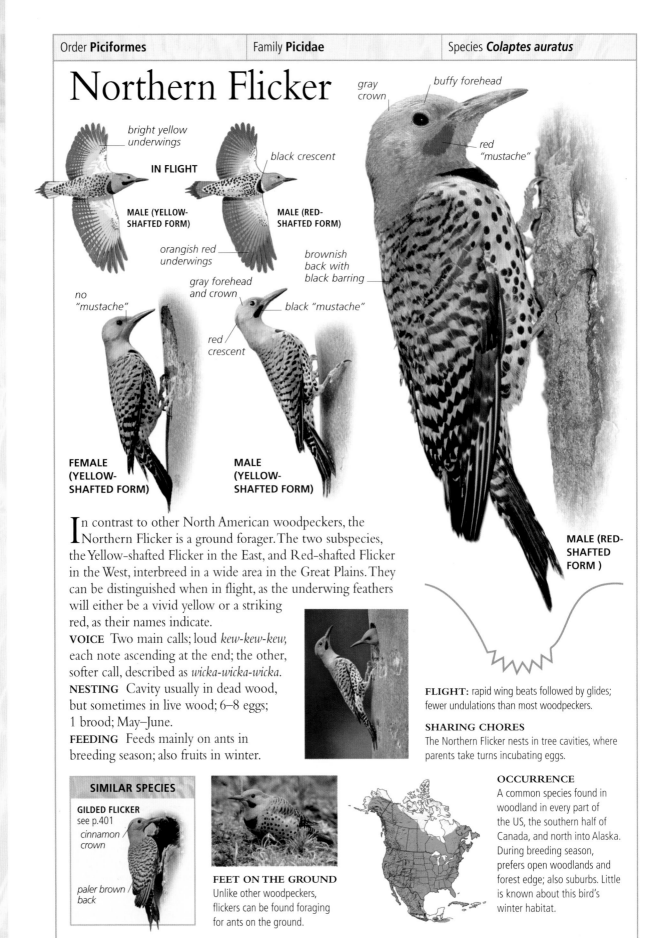

gray crown

buffy forehead

red "mustache"

bright yellow underwings

IN FLIGHT

MALE (YELLOW-SHAFTED FORM)

black crescent

MALE (RED-SHAFTED FORM)

orangish red underwings

brownish back with black barring

gray forehead and crown

no "mustache"

black "mustache"

red crescent

FEMALE (YELLOW-SHAFTED FORM)

MALE (YELLOW-SHAFTED FORM)

MALE (RED-SHAFTED FORM)

In contrast to other North American woodpeckers, the Northern Flicker is a ground forager. The two subspecies, the Yellow-shafted Flicker in the East, and Red-shafted Flicker in the West, interbreed in a wide area in the Great Plains. They can be distinguished when in flight, as the underwing feathers will either be a vivid yellow or a striking red, as their names indicate.

VOICE Two main calls; loud *kew-kew-kew*, each note ascending at the end; the other, softer call, described as *wicka-wicka-wicka*.

NESTING Cavity usually in dead wood, but sometimes in live wood; 6–8 eggs; 1 brood; May–June.

FEEDING Feeds mainly on ants in breeding season; also fruits in winter.

FLIGHT: rapid wing beats followed by glides; fewer undulations than most woodpeckers.

SHARING CHORES
The Northern Flicker nests in tree cavities, where parents take turns incubating eggs.

OCCURRENCE
A common species found in woodland in every part of the US, the southern half of Canada, and north into Alaska. During breeding season, prefers open woodlands and forest edge; also suburbs. Little is known about this bird's winter habitat.

SIMILAR SPECIES

GILDED FLICKER
see p.401

cinnamon crown

paler brown back

FEET ON THE GROUND
Unlike other woodpeckers, flickers can be found foraging for ants on the ground.

| Length **12–13in (31–33cm)** | Wingspan **19–21in (48–53cm)** | Weight **4oz (125g)** |
| Social **Solitary** | Lifespan **9 years** | Status **Secure** |

| Order **Piciformes** | Family **Picidae** | Species *Colaptes chrysoides* |

Gilded Flicker

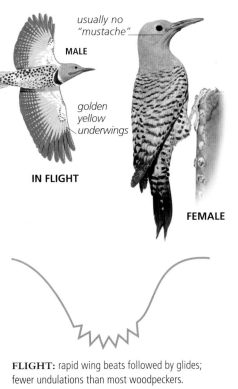

usually no
"mustache"

MALE

golden
yellow
underwings

IN FLIGHT

FEMALE

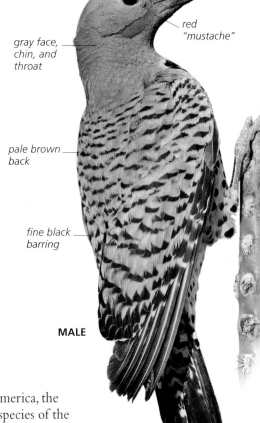

cinnamon
cap

red
"mustache"

gray face,
chin, and
throat

pale brown
back

fine black
barring

MALE

black tip
of tail

FLIGHT: rapid wing beats followed by glides;
fewer undulations than most woodpeckers.

One of two flicker species in North America, the
Gilded Flicker was considered a subspecies of the
Northern Flicker for a long time. The ranges of these two flicker
species overlap in the southwest US, where they interbreed. Both
male and female Gilded Flickers show a golden yellow undertail,
yellow underwings, and a white rump in flight. The Gilded Flicker
is known for its specific choice of nesting site.
VOICE Two common calls, loud *kew-kew-kew* with each note
ascending at end, and softer *wicka-wicka-wicka*; calls
are identical to those of the Northern Flicker.
NESTING Excavates cavity in Saguaro cactus, rarely
lined; 3–8 eggs; 1 brood; April–May.
FEEDING Forages on
the ground for ants; fruit
and seeds in winter.

SHARP DEFENSE
The Gilded Flicker typically
excavates its nest in a
Saguaro cactus, which protects
its young from predators.

SIMILAR SPECIES

**NORTHERN FLICKER (RED-
SHAFTED)**
see p.400

gray
crown

slightly
darker
back

GOLDEN PLUMAGE
The vivid golden yellow on its
undertail and underwings give
this species its name.

OCCURRENCE
In the US, found year-round,
almost exclusively in the giant
cactus deserts of Arizona and
southeastern California. Also
found throughout the year in
Baja California and other parts
of northwestern Mexico.

| Length **11–11½in (28–29cm)** | Wingspan **18–19in (46–48cm)** | Weight **3½oz (100g)** |
| Social **Unknown** | Lifespan **Unknown** | Status **Secure** |

Order **Piciformes**	Family **Picidae**	Species ***Dryocopus pileatus***

Pileated Woodpecker

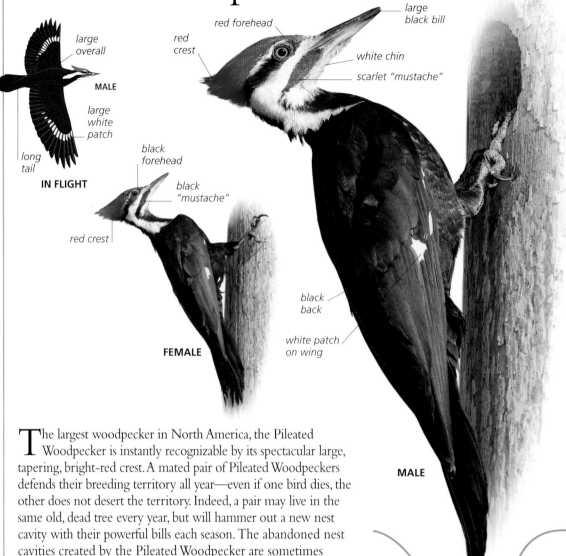

IN FLIGHT

large overall

MALE

large white patch

long tail

red forehead

red crest

large black bill

white chin

scarlet "mustache"

black forehead

black "mustache"

red crest

FEMALE

black back

white patch on wing

MALE

The largest woodpecker in North America, the Pileated Woodpecker is instantly recognizable by its spectacular large, tapering, bright-red crest. A mated pair of Pileated Woodpeckers defends their breeding territory all year—even if one bird dies, the other does not desert the territory. Indeed, a pair may live in the same old, dead tree every year, but will hammer out a new nest cavity with their powerful bills each season. The abandoned nest cavities created by the Pileated Woodpecker are sometimes reused by other birds, and occasionally inhabited by mammals.

VOICE Two primary calls, both high-pitched and quite loud— *yuck-yuck-yuck*, and *yuka-yuka-yuka*.

NESTING Excavates cavity, usually in dead tree; 3–5 eggs; 1 brood; May–July.

FEEDING Bores deep into trees and peels off large strips of bark to extract carpenter ants and beetle larvae; also digs on ground and on fallen logs, and opportunistically eats fruit and nuts.

EASY PICKINGS
This Pileated Woodpecker readily visits feeders to supplement its natural diet.

FLIGHT: slow, deep wing beats, with occasional undulation when wings briefly folded.

OCCURRENCE
Breeds and lives year-round in northwestern North America and throughout the eastern half of the US, in deciduous and coniferous forest and woodlands; also found in swampy areas. In some areas, chooses young forests with dead trees but in other places, old-growth conifers.

Length **16–18in (41–46cm)**	Wingspan **26–30in (66–76cm)**	Weight **10oz (275g)**
Social **Pairs**	Lifespan **Up to 9 years**	Status **Secure**

Family **Tyrannidae**

FLYCATCHERS

Birds popularly known as flycatchers occur in many parts of the world, however several different families of songbird have this name. With the exception of some Old World species that may stray into into Alaska, the North American species are all members of a New World family—the Tyrant Flycatchers (Tyrannidae). With about 400 species, this is the largest bird family in the New World. The North American species are fairly uniform in appearance with only a hint of the family's diversity in Central and South America. Most are drab colored, olive-green or gray birds, sometimes with yellow on the underparts. The Vermilion Flycatcher is a striking exception, as is the gray and salmon pink Scissor-tailed Flycatcher, which also has elongated outer tail feathers. The members of the genus *Empidonax* include some of the most difficult birds to identify in North America, and they are best distinguished by their songs.

Typical flycatcher feeding behavior is to sit on a branch or exposed perch sallying forth to catch flying insects. Tyrannid flycatchers are found across North America, except in Arctic regions. They are in wooded habitats, though the kingbirds (genus *Tyrannus*) prefer woodland edges and deserts. Nearly all flycatchers are long distance migrants and spend the winter in Central and South America.

TYRANT BEHAVIOR
Such aggressive display by Couch's Kingbird reflects its English and generic names.

ERECT STANCE
A large headed look and erect posture are typical of this Eastern Phoebe.

BIG MOUTHS
Young Dusky Flycatchers display the wide bills that help them to catch flying insects as adults.

| Order **Passeriformes** | Family **Tyrannidae** | Species *Camptostoma imberbe* |

Northern Beardless-Tyrannulet

ADULT

faint buff
wing bars

IN FLIGHT

brownish, ragged
crest makes head
look large

pale
eyebrow

stubby bill;
orange-based
lower mandible

grayish
back

brownish
wings

dull, whitish
underparts

ADULT

blackish
brown legs

This tiny, rare Central American flycatcher is found along the Rio Grande in southern Texas, in southeastern Arizona, and southwestern New Mexico. Typically detected by its calls, this bird has a distinctive tail-dip, frequently flopping its tail up and down while hopping through foliage. The word "beardless" refers to the lack of bristles at the base of its bill. It earns its name of "tyrannulet" (diminutive tyrant) by aggressively chasing away small potential predators. It is much more active than most other flycatchers, feeding among leaves and flitting about in the manner of a kinglet.

VOICE Calls include clear, piping *peeeuu* and *peeut di-i-i-i*; song *pee-pee-pee-pee*, a descending series of whistles given by males.

NESTING Domed plant fiber nest with side entrance in tree fork; 2 eggs; 1–3 broods; March–August.

FEEDING Feeds on small insects, spiders, larvae, and berries; gleans insects from foliage; rarely hovers.

FLIGHT: short, hopping flights with buzzy wing beats; can hover to glean food.

TINY BIRD
The small size of this flycatcher can be judged by the thorns that are about one inch long.

OCCURRENCE
Found in wooded areas, cultivated regions and gardens, and especially near streams flowing through sycamore, mesquite, or cottonwood groves; from southeastern Arizona and in the lower Rio Grande Valley of Texas, southward through Mexico to northwestern Costa Rica.

SIMILAR SPECIES

VERDIN ☾
see p.485

no crest

sharp,
pointed
bill

RUBY CROWNED KINGLET ♀
see p.499

lacks
ragged
crest

shorter
tail

| Length 4½–5½in (11.5–14cm) | Wingspan **7in (18cm)** | Weight ¼oz (7.5g) |
| Social **Solitary/Small flocks** | Lifespan **Up to 10 years** | Status **Secure** |

| Order **Passeriformes** | Family **Tyrannidae** | Species *Sayornis phoebe* |

Eastern Phoebe

round, dark-capped head

ADULT

rounded wings with two faint wing bars

white throat

IN FLIGHT

dark eye

ADULT (FALL)

yellowish tint on lower belly

long, dark tail

ADULT (BREEDING)

olive tint to sides and breast

FLIGHT: direct, with steady wing beats; hovers occasionally; approaches nest with a low swoop.

The Eastern Phoebe is an early spring migrant that tends to nest under bridges, culverts, and on buildings, in addition to rocky outcroppings. Not shy, it is also familiar because of its *fee-bee* vocalization and constant tail wagging. By tying a thread on the leg of several Eastern Phoebes, ornithologist John James Audubon established that individuals return from the south to a previously used nest site. Although difficult to tell apart, males tend to be slightly larger and darker than females.

VOICE Common call a clear, weak *chip*; song an emphatic *fee-bee* or *fee-b-be-bee*.

NESTING Open cup of mud, moss, and leaves, almost exclusively on manmade structures; 3–5 eggs; 2 broods; April–July.

FEEDING Feeds mainly on flying insects; also consumes small fruits from fall through winter.

PALE EDGES
Perched on a twig, a male shows off the pale margins of his wing feathers.

LIGHTER FEMALE
They are difficult to distinguish, but the female is slightly lighter overall than the male.

OCCURRENCE
Found in open woodland and along deciduous or mixed forest edges, in gardens and parks, near water. Breeds across Canada from the Northwest Territories south of the tundra belt and in the eastern half of the US. Winters in the southeast US and Mexico.

SIMILAR SPECIES

EASTERN WOOD-PEWEE
lacks tail-wag; see p.411

distinct wing bars

WILLOW FLYCATCHER
flicks tail upwards; see p.414

more distinct wing bars

often has eye-ring

smaller overall

| Length **5½–7in (14–17cm)** | Wingspan **10½in (27cm)** | Weight **¹¹⁄₁₆oz (20g)** |
| Social **Solitary** | Lifespan **Up to 9 years** | Status **Secure** |

| Order **Passeriformes** | Family **Tyrannidae** | Species *Sayornis nigricans* |

Black Phoebe

two pale wing bars

ADULT

rounded wings

IN FLIGHT

grayish brown head and chest

rusty wing bars

JUVENILE

black upperparts

black head

fairly short, black bill

sooty black breast and throat

white belly

ADULT

black tail

black legs and feet

North America's only black-and-white Flycatcher, the distinctive Black Phoebe is found in the southwestern part of the continent, where it is a year-round resident. This area is the northernmost part of the bird's range, which extends southward to Argentina. This species is commonly found close to water, where it conducts most of its foraging. It has even been known to dive into ponds to capture minnows—an unusual foraging method for a flycatcher. In the breeding season the male shows his mate potential nest sites by hovering in front of a likely spot, with the female deciding where the nest will eventually be.

VOICE Simple *tsip* call; also *tweedle-deedle-eek* during courting or when chasing rivals; song a *tee-hee, tee-hoo* or *sisee, sitsew*.

NESTING Open cup of mud mixed with grass, cemented to wall, or under bridge, cliff, or eave; 2–5 eggs; 2–3 broods; March–June.

FEEDING Mainly catches flying insects, but will also pick insects from ground; occasionally dives for small fish; also eats berries.

FLIGHT: direct with steady wing beats; hovers while foraging; vertical zig-zag courting display.

PERCHED AND ALERT
The Black Phoebe perches in an upright position, with its tail dipping and fanning.

SIMILAR SPECIES

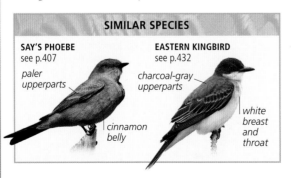

SAY'S PHOEBE
see p.407

paler upperparts

cinnamon belly

EASTERN KINGBIRD
see p.432

charcoal-gray upperparts

white breast and throat

OCCURRENCE
In the US, breeds and winters in Oregon, California, Nevada, Utah, Arizona, New Mexico, and Texas, in areas close to water, such as coastal cliffs, banks of rivers, streams, lakes, and ponds. Also seen at fountains and cattle troughs. Forages in open areas over water or grassland.

| Length **6in (15.5cm)** | Wingspan **11in (28cm)** | Weight **½–¹¹⁄₁₆oz (15–20g)** |
| Social **Solitary** | Lifespan **Up to 8 years** | Status **Secure** |

Order **Passeriformes**	Family **Tyrannidae**	Species *Sayornis saya*

Say's Phoebe

IN FLIGHT

faint wing bars

black tail

ADULT

grayish brown back

sooty gray cap

dark eye

small, black bill

pale sooty gray neck and breast

ADULT

black feet and legs

rufous undertail and lower belly

Say's Phoebe breeds farther north than any other flycatcher in its family. Although it is a bird of open country, it is not particularly shy around people, and from early spring to late fall is a common sight on ranches and farms. Its contrasting dark cap is conspicuous even at a distance as it perches on bushes, boulders, or power lines, often wagging its tail. Shortly after a pair is formed on the breeding grounds, the male will hover in front of potential nest sites, in a manner similar to the Black Phoebe. The pair bond among Say's Phoebes is relatively weak, though, and does not last through the summer.

VOICE Call a *pee-ee* or *pee-ur*; also a whistled *churr-eep*, which may be integrated with a chatter; primary song a *pit-see-eur* and *pit-eet*.

NESTING Shallow cup of twigs, moss, or stems on ledge or in rocky crevice; 3–7 eggs; 1–2 broods; April–July.

FEEDING Catches insects in flight, such as beetles, wasps, grasshoppers, and crickets; also eats berries.

FLIGHT: direct, with regular wing beats; chases may be erratic; hovers while foraging.

PALE WING FEATHERS
Say's Phoebe's pale underwings are clearly visible from below as it hovers.

SIMILAR SPECIES

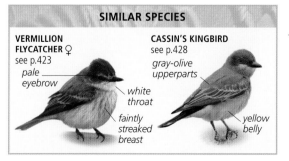

VERMILLION FLYCATCHER ♀
see p.423
pale eyebrow
white throat
faintly streaked breast

CASSIN'S KINGBIRD
see p.428
gray-olive upperparts
yellow belly

OCCURRENCE
Breeds in dry, open, or semi-open country, such as desert canyons, sagebrush ranch, and agricultural areas; generally avoids watercourses. Birds in the southwestern US are resident year-round, but those breeding farther north fly south for the winter.

Length **7in (17.5cm)**	Wingspan **13in (33cm)**	Weight **11/16oz (20g)**
Social **Solitary**	Lifespan **At least 3–4 years**	Status **Secure**

| Order **Passeriformes** | Family **Tyrannidae** | Species ***Contopus cooperi*** |

Olive-sided Flycatcher

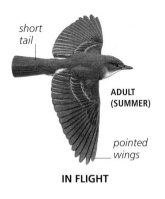

short tail

ADULT (SUMMER)

pointed wings

IN FLIGHT

large, dark head

lower base of bill often dull orange

brownish gray back

dull white throat

brownish olive flanks

white belly

ADULT (SUMMER)

FLIGHT: fast and direct, with deep, rapid wing beats; turns sharply to chase prey.

The Olive-sided Flycatcher is identified by its distinctive song, large size, and contrasting belly and flank colors, which make its underside appear like a vest with the buttons undone. Both members of a breeding pair are known to aggressively defend their territory. This flycatcher undertakes a long journey from northern parts of North America to winter in Panama and the Andes.

VOICE Call an evenly spaced *pip-pip-pip*; song a loud 3-note whistle: *quick-THREE-BEERS* or *whip-WEE-DEER*.

NESTING Open cup of twigs, rootlets, lichens; 2–5 eggs; 1 brood; May–August.

FEEDING Sits and waits for prey to fly past its perch before swooping after it; eats flying insects, such as bees, wasps, and flying ants.

BUILDING THE NEST
The female Olive-sided Flycatcher usually constructs the nest on her own.

EXPOSED PERCH
This species can often be found singing from an exposed twig emerging from the canopy.

OCCURRENCE
Breeds in mountainous, northern coniferous forests at edges or openings around ponds, bogs, meadows where standing dead trees occur. Also found in post-fire forests with abundant stumps. Winters in forest edges with tall trees and stumps.

SIMILAR SPECIES

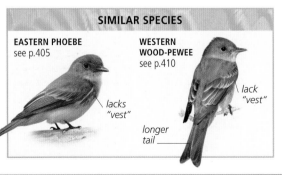

EASTERN PHOEBE
see p.405

lacks "vest"

WESTERN WOOD-PEWEE
see p.410

lack "vest"

longer tail

| Length **7–8in (18–20cm)** | Wingspan **13in (33cm)** | Weight **1¹⁄₁₆–1¼oz (30–35g)** |
| Social **Solitary** | Lifespan **Up to 7 years** | Status **Declining** |

Order **Passeriformes**	Family **Tyrannidae**	Species **Contopus pertinax**

Greater Pewee

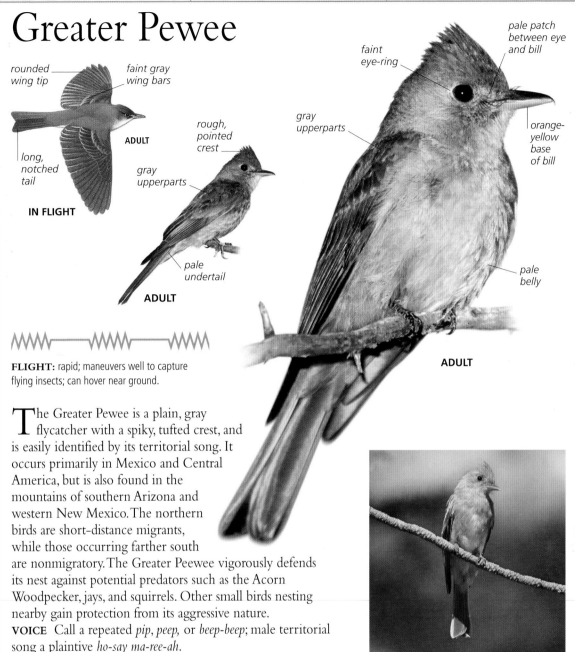

rounded wing tip

faint gray wing bars

ADULT

long, notched tail

IN FLIGHT

rough, pointed crest

gray upperparts

pale undertail

ADULT

faint eye-ring

pale patch between eye and bill

gray upperparts

orange-yellow base of bill

pale belly

ADULT

FLIGHT: rapid; maneuvers well to capture flying insects; can hover near ground.

The Greater Pewee is a plain, gray flycatcher with a spiky, tufted crest, and is easily identified by its territorial song. It occurs primarily in Mexico and Central America, but is also found in the mountains of southern Arizona and western New Mexico. The northern birds are short-distance migrants, while those occurring farther south are nonmigratory. The Greater Peewee vigorously defends its nest against potential predators such as the Acorn Woodpecker, jays, and squirrels. Other small birds nesting nearby gain protection from its aggressive nature.

VOICE Call a repeated *pip, peep,* or *beep-beep;* male territorial song a plaintive *ho-say ma-ree-ah.*

NESTING Cup of grass, bark, pine needles at fork of large branch near trunk; 3–4 eggs; 1 brood; May–July.

FEEDING Eats mainly flying insects; also berries.

SITTING AND WAITING
The bird sits upright, keeping a watchful eye over any insects that might fly by.

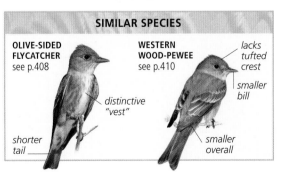

SIMILAR SPECIES

OLIVE-SIDED FLYCATCHER see p.408

distinctive "vest"

shorter tail

WESTERN WOOD-PEWEE see p.410

lacks tufted crest

smaller bill

smaller overall

OCCURRENCE
Breeds in open pine woodland with oak understory at heights of 7,000–10,000ft (2,100–3,000m); nests on slopes or steep-sided canyons. Primarily associated with high-elevation waterside trees such as sycamore or walnut.

Length **7in (18cm)**	Wingspan **13in (33cm)**	Weight **⅞oz (25g)**
Social **Solitary**	Lifespan **Unknown**	Status **Secure**

| Order **Passeriformes** | Family **Tyrannidae** | Species **Contopus sordidulus** |

Western Wood-pewee

slight crest

dark brown eye

dark gray back and head

two pale wing bars

pale gray underparts

ADULT

short legs

pale throat

ADULT

pointed wings

IN FLIGHT

ADULT

FLIGHT: flurries of rapid wing beats; returns to open perch with quivering wings.

This species is a widespread breeder in many forested habitats of western North America. Where its range overlaps that of the Eastern Wood-pewee, it shows no evidence of interbreeding. It vocalizes from high perches, principally during the breeding season, but also during winter and while on migration. The Western Wood-pewee forages aerially on insects in much the same way as swallows do. Adults are very aggressive toward laying parasitic intruders, however, they accept Brown-headed Cowbird eggs, though few fledge successfully from their nests. The Western Wood-pewee is a migrant that winters in the Andes from Colombia to Bolivia.

VOICE Calls burry *bzew* and infrequent *chip*; male's dawn song *pee-pip-pip* or *tswee-tee-teet*, given alternately with *pee-er*.

NESTING Shallow cup of woven grasses in fork of horizontal branch; 2–4 eggs; 1 brood; May–August.

FEEDING Sit-and-wait hunter; primarily eats flies, bees, wasps, ants, beetles, and moths; also forages for flying insects.

PERCHED AND ALERT
The crest is apparent in this alert bird probably on the look-out for prey.

OCCURRENCE
Open woodlands, forest edges and beside rivers and other water bodies; also in dry forests. Absent from dense forests. Large-diameter trees, open understory, stumps, and woodland edges are important. Winters in mature tropical forests. Breeds in Mexico and Central America to Nicaragua.

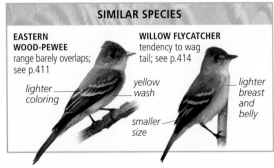

SIMILAR SPECIES

EASTERN WOOD-PEWEE
range barely overlaps; see p.411

lighter coloring

WILLOW FLYCATCHER
tendency to wag tail; see p.414

yellow wash

lighter breast and belly

smaller size

| Length **6¼in (16cm)** | Wingspan **10½in (27cm)** | Weight **⅜–½oz (11–14g)** |
| Social **Solitary** | Lifespan **Up to 6 years** | Status **Secure** |

| Order **Passeriformes** | Family **Tyrannidae** | Species **Contopus virens** |

Eastern Wood-pewee

slightly ragged crest

pointed wings

ADULT

IN FLIGHT

partial eye-ring

pale gray

thin, white wing bars

thin, white edges to wing feathers

yellow lower mandible

pale throat

yellowish wash on underparts

ADULT

FLIGHT: flies out from perch to catch flying insects; direct, steady wing beats.

The Eastern Wood-pewee is found in many types of woodland in the eastern US and southern and eastern Canada. The male is slightly larger than the female, but their plumage is practically identical. Recent population declines in this species have been attributed to heavy browsing by White-tailed Deer. This has been compounded by the Eastern Wood-pewee's susceptibility to brood parasitism by Brown-headed Cowbirds.

VOICE Call terse *chip*; song slurred *pee-ah-wee*, plaintive *wee-ooo*, or *wee-ur*, and slurred *ah di dee*.
NESTING Shallow cup of grass, lichens on horizontal limb; 2–4 eggs; 1 brood; May–September.
FEEDING Consumes mainly flying insects, such as flies, beetles, and bees; occasionally forages for insects on foliage on the ground.

SEARCHING FOR PREY
Holding its tail perfectly still, this Wood-pewee is perched upright, scanning for prey.

COLORATION
The Eastern Wood-pewee has yellowish underparts and a yellow lower mandible.

OCCURRENCE
Widely distributed in eastern US and adjacent Canadian provinces. Breeds in deciduous and coniferous forests, often near clearings or edges; uses waterside areas in Midwest, less so in the East. Late-arriving migrant. Winters in shrubby, second-growth forests of South America.

SIMILAR SPECIES

WESTERN WOOD-PEWEE range barely overlaps; see p.410
dark gray back

WILLOW FLYCATCHER tendency to wag tail; see p.414
stronger eye-ring
lighter breast and head
smaller size

| Length **6in (15cm)** | Wingspan **9–10in (23–26cm)** | Weight **⅜–¹¹⁄₁₆oz (10–19g)** |
| Social **Solitary** | Lifespan **Up to 7 years** | Status **Secure** |

| Order **Passeriformes** | Family **Tyrannidae** | Species *Empidonax traillii* |

Willow Flycatcher

IN FLIGHT

square tail
two buff to yellow wing bars
ADULT

dark upper mandible
thin eye-ring
brown eye
paler lower mandible
grayish green upperparts
yellow-tinged flanks
whitish belly
ADULT
dark legs and toes

FLIGHT: weak and fluttering; swoops and hovers when pursuing insects.

The Willow Flycatcher is only distinguished from the nearly identical Alder Flycatcher by its song. It is a strongly territorial bird, spreading its tail and flicking it upward during aggressive encounters. The Willow Flycatcher is, however, a frequent victim of brood parasitism by the Brown-headed Cowbird, which lays its eggs in the flycatcher's nest and removes the eggs that were already inside. Compounded by loss of suitable breeding habitat, this may be a major reason for the Willow Flycatcher's decline, especially in the case of the southwestern subspecies, *E. t. extimus*, which is now considered endangered.

dark tail

VOICE Calls include soft, dry *whit* and several buzzy notes; song sharp *fitz-bew* with accent on the first syllable; also *creet*.
NESTING Rather loose and untidy cup in base of shrub near water; 3–4 eggs; 1 brood; May–August.
FEEDING Eats insects, mostly caught in flight; eats fruit in winter.

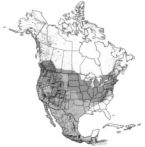

UNEVEN WORKLOAD
Although both parents feed their young, the female Willow Flycatcher does so the most.

SIMILAR SPECIES

ALDER FLYCATCHER
different song; see p.415
bolder wing bars

LEAST FLYCATCHER
see p.416
larger head
bold white eye-ring

OCCURRENCE
Breeds from southern Canada to eastern and southwestern US, mainly in willow thickets and other moist shrubby areas along watercourses. On winter grounds, it favors lighter woodland, shrubby clearings, and brush near water in coastal areas.

| Length **5–6¾in (13–17cm)** | Wingspan **7½–9½in (19–24cm)** | Weight **⅜–⁹⁄₁₆oz (11–16g)** |
| Social **Solitary** | Lifespan **Up to 11 years** | Status **Declining** |

Order **Passeriformes**	Family **Tyrannidae**	Species *Empidonax alnorum*

Alder Flycatcher

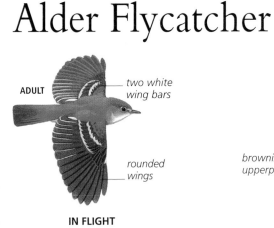

ADULT

two white
wing bars

rounded
wings

IN FLIGHT

brownish
olive head

white eye-ring

dark upper
mandible

paler
lower mandible

brownish olive
upperparts

whitish throat
and breast

ADULT

dark legs
and toes

long,
dark tail

FLIGHT: weak with shallow wing beats;
swoops and hovers when pursuing prey.

Until 1973 the Alder Flycatcher
and the Willow Flycatcher were
considered to be one species called
Traill's Flycatcher. The two species
cannot be reliably identified by sight,
but they do have distinctive songs.
The Alder Flycatcher also breeds
farther north than the Willow
Flycatcher, arriving late in spring
and leaving early in fall. Its nests
are extremely hard to locate, and
much remains to be learned about this bird's breeding habits.
VOICE Calls include flat *pit* or *pip-peep-tip*, also *wee-oo* and *churr*;
male sings characteristic *fee-bee-o* song while breeding, and
occasionally during spring migration.
NESTING Coarse and loosely structured nest low in fork
of deciduous shrub; 3–4 eggs; 1 brood; June–July.
FEEDING Mostly eats insects, caught mainly in flight, but
some gleaned from foliage; eats fruit in winter.

ON THE ALERT
Attentive to potential meals, an Alder Flycatcher
will swiftly pursue prey as soon as it flies by.

OCCURRENCE
Breeds at low density across
northern North America, in wet
shrubby habitats with alder or
willow thickets, often close to
streams. Winters at low
elevations in South America
in tropical second-growth
forest and forest edges.

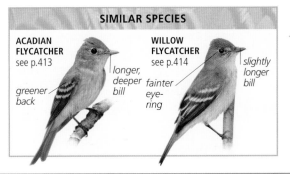

SIMILAR SPECIES

**ACADIAN
FLYCATCHER**
see p.413

greener
back

longer,
deeper
bill

**WILLOW
FLYCATCHER**
see p.414

fainter
eye-
ring

slightly
longer
bill

Length **5¾in (14.5cm)**	Wingspan **8½in (22cm)**	Weight **½oz (14g)**
Social **Solitary**	Lifespan **At least 3 years**	Status **Secure**

Order **Passeriformes**	Family **Tyrannidae**	Species ***Empidonax minimus***

Least Flycatcher

short, narrow tail

ADULT

large head

two wing bars

IN FLIGHT

short, broad-based bill

pale throat

buffy wing bars

JUVENILE

marked, white eye-ring

greenish brown back

short wings

ADULT

pale yellow belly

FLIGHT: direct, short forays with rapid wing beats to catch prey; sometimes hovers briefly.

The smallest eastern member of the *Empidonax* genus is a solitary bird and is very aggressive towards intruders encroaching upon its breeding territory, including other species of flycatcher. This combative behavior reduces the likelihood of acting as unwitting host parents to eggs laid by the Brown-headed Cowbird. The Least Flycatcher is very active, and frequently flicks its wings and tail upward. Common in the eastern US in mixed and deciduous woodland, especially at the edges, it spends a short time—up to only two months—on its northern breeding grounds before migrating south. Adults molt in winter, while young molt before and during fall migration.

VOICE Call soft, short *whit*; song frequent, persistent, characteristic *tchebeck*, sings during spring migration and breeding season.

NESTING Compact cup of tightly woven bark strips and plant fibers in fork of deciduous tree; 3–5 eggs; 1 brood; May–July.

FEEDING Feeds principally on insects, such as flies, midges, beetles, ants, butterflies, and larvae; occasionally eats berries and seeds.

YELLOW TINGE
The subtle yellow tinge to its underparts and white undertail feathers are evident here.

OCCURRENCE
Breeds in coniferous and mixed deciduous forests across North America, east of Rockies to East Coast; occasionally in conifer groves or wooded wetlands, often near openings or edges. Winters in Central America in varied habitat from second-growth evergreen woodland to arid scrub.

SIMILAR SPECIES

WILLOW FLYCATCHER
see p.414

larger body

longer bill

ALDER FLYCATCHER
see p.415

larger overall

wider tail

Length **5¼in (13.5cm)**	Wingspan **7¾in (19.5cm)**	Weight **⁹⁄₃₂–⁷⁄₁₆oz (8–13g)**
Social **Solitary**	Lifespan **Up to 6 years**	Status **Secure**

| Order **Passeriformes** | Family **Tyrannidae** | Species **Empidonax hammondii** |

Hammond's Flycatcher

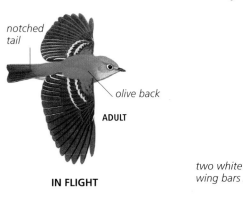

notched tail

olive back

ADULT

IN FLIGHT

gray head

small, dark bill

tear-shaped spot behind eye

grayish white throat and upper breast

olive breast and flanks

two white wing bars

ADULT

yellow tinge to lower belly

notched tail

FLIGHT: short, direct flights to pursue prey; occasionally hovers.

Hammond's Flycatcher is a small, gray migrant from Central and South America. It is generally silent on its wintering grounds, but starts performing its distinctive song shortly after arriving on its breeding grounds. In the breeding season, males are competitive and aggressive, and are known to lock together in mid-air to resolve their territorial squabbles. Since this species is dependent on mature old-growth forest, logging is thought to be adversely affecting its numbers.

VOICE Calls *peek* or *wheep*; song of 3 elements—dry, brisk *se-put*, low, burry *tsurrt*, or *greep*, and drawn-out *chu-lup*.

NESTING Compact open cup of plant fibers and fine grass saddled on large branch; 3–4 eggs; 1 brood; May–August.

FEEDING Sit-and-wait predator; pursues flying insects from perch.

DISTINCTIVE EYE-RING
Hammond's Flycatcher's white tear-shaped spot behind the eye is only visible in good lighting.

SIMILAR SPECIES

DUSKY FLYCATCHER
distinctive "whit" call; see p.418

mouse gray overall

wider, longer bill

GRAY FLYCATCHER
wags tail; see p.419

smaller body

paler overall

OCCURRENCE
Breeds in mature coniferous and mixed woodland in from Alaska to California. Inhabits primarily dense firs or conifers, but also occurs in aspen and other broadleaf mixed forests. Winters in oak-pine forests and dry shrubbery in the highlands of Mexico and Central America.

| Length **5–6in (12.5–15cm)** | Wingspan **9in (22cm)** | Weight **⁹⁄₃₂–⁷⁄₁₆oz (8–12g)** |
| Social **Solitary** | Lifespan **Up to 7 years** | Status **Secure** |

Order **Passeriformes**	Family **Tyrannidae**	Species **Empidonax oberholseri**

Dusky Flycatcher

ADULT

wing bars

faint, white edge to tail

IN FLIGHT

rounded head

less defined markings than adult

narrow tail

JUVENILE

inconspicuous eye-ring

dark gray upperparts

grayish olive above

wide wing bars

notched or square tail

ADULT

long tail

FLIGHT: flies out or hovers for prey; also drops to the ground.

The Dusky Flycatcher waits on a perch to locate a flying insect, flies out to catch it, and then returns to its position to consume it, often wiping its bill on the perch after completing its meal. It lives in mountainous areas of the western US and Canada, where it is vulnerable to storms that can severely impact a local breeding population by flattening the trees. The Dusky Flycatcher prefers shrubby habitats, and can benefit from forestry practices that open up dense stands of conifers.

VOICE Call a soft *whit*, vocal in early morning; song a two-syllabled rising *prll-it*, rough, low-pitched *prrdrrt*, high, clear *pseet*.
NESTING Tight, open grass cup in upright fork of shrub or low tree; 3–5 eggs; 1 brood; May–August.
FEEDING Catches insects in flight; sometimes from bark, rarely from ground; also eats caterpillars, wasps, bees, moths, butterflies.

FEEDING TIME
This adult Dusky Flycatcher is feeding three hungry nestlings in an open cupped nest.

SIMILAR SPECIES

HAMMOND'S FLYCATCHER
see p.417

GRAY FLYCATCHER
see p.419

eye-ring expands behind eye

longer wings

shorter, thinner, darker bill

distinctive downward tail dip

OCCURRENCE
Breeds in west North America, through west US into Mexico, in open coniferous forest, mountain thickets, aspen groves, water-side thickets, open brush, and chaparral. Winters in the highlands of Mexico, south to Oaxaca, in oak scrub and pine-oak; also in open riverside woods, and semi-arid scrub.

Length **5–6in (13–15cm)**	Wingspan **8–9in (20–23cm)**	Weight **⁵⁄₁₆–³⁄₈oz (9–11g)**
Social **Solitary**	Lifespan **Up to 8 years**	Status **Secure**

Order **Passeriformes**	Family **Tyrannidae**	Species ***Empidonax wrightii***

Gray Flycatcher

inconspicuous
eye-ring

weak wing bars

long, narrow bill

ADULT

pale gray
upperparts

pinkish yellow
lower mandible
with dark tip

pale throat

rounded
crown

brownish gray
upperparts

IN FLIGHT

buffy
wing bars

long tail

pale belly

short wings

JUVENILE

ADULT

FLIGHT: direct flight; mild and leisurely chases
between members of a pair.

This small flycatcher is easily
recognized by its habit of slowly
wagging its tail downward. It is very
similar to the Dusky Flycatcher and
was not recognized as a separate
species in North America until early in the 20th century. The Gray
Flycatcher is a monogamous bird, and a territorial pair occupies an area
of 8.15–13 acres (3.3–5.3ha). Like many other flycatchers, it is another host
to the Brown-headed Cowbird.

VOICE Call an upwardly inflected *prit*; song a rough, two-note *chlup, chlup*;
singing is sporadic during territory establishment.

NESTING Open cup at fork or top of branch in pines, junipers; 3–4 eggs;
2 broods; May–August.

FEEDING Sit-and-wait hunting techniques; eats mainly insects taken in air or
from ground, foliage, bark or branches.

IDENTITY
As it sits on a low perch, the
gentle downward wag of its tail
helps establish the bird's identity.

OCCURRENCE
Breeds in American West, from
southern British Columbia
south to Arizona, New Mexico,
and Texas; common in arid
woodland, sagebush, Pinyon
Pine, juniper, Ponderosa Pine,
oak-pine woods, riverside and
mountainous thickets, and
forests lacking high shrubs.
Winters from Arizona to Mexico.

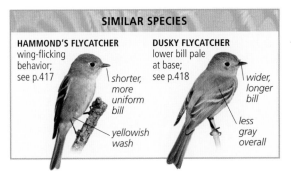

SIMILAR SPECIES

HAMMOND'S FLYCATCHER
wing-flicking
behavior;
see p.417

shorter,
more
uniform
bill

yellowish
wash

DUSKY FLYCATCHER
lower bill pale
at base;
see p.418

wider,
longer
bill

less
gray
overall

Length **6in (15cm)**	Wingspan **9in (23cm)**	Weight **⅜–½oz (11–14g)**
Social **Solitary**	Lifespan **Unknown**	Status **Secure**

| Order **Passeriformes** | Family **Tyrannidae** | Species *Empidonax difficilis* |

Pacific-slope Flycatcher

ADULT

yellow-washed throat

rounded wings

IN FLIGHT

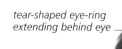

slight crest

wide bill

tear-shaped eye-ring extending behind eye

yellow-orange lower mandible

olive back and head

brown-washed breast

yellowish belly

ADULT

FLIGHT: sallies forth from a perch to hawk or glean insects.

The Pacific-slope Flycatcher is virtually identical to the Cordilleran Flycatcher— both were formerly considered to be one species called the Western Flycatcher. Differences in song led researchers to find genetic and behavioral differences between the two species. A population of Pacific-slope Flycatchers found on the Channel Islands off California may also be a distinct species, larger than mainland forms. The Pacific-slope Flycatcher is a short-distance migrant that winters in Mexico. The female is active during nest-building and incubation, but the male provides food for nestlings.

VOICE Call *chrrip, seet, zeet*; song 3 squeaky, repeated syllables *ps-SEET, ptsick, seet,* or *TSEE-wee, pttuck, tseep.*

NESTING Open cup, often with shelter above, in fork of tree or shelf on bank or bridge; 2–4 eggs; 2 broods; April–July.

FEEDING Feeds on insects caught in air or gleaned from foliage: beetles, wasps, bees, flies, moths, caterpillars, spiders; rarely berries.

DISTINCT MARKINGS
The Pacific-slope Flycatcher has distinct buffy wing bars and a streaked breast and belly.

SIMILAR SPECIES

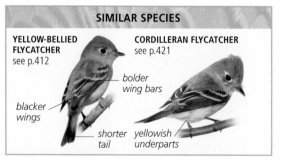

YELLOW-BELLIED FLYCATCHER
see p.412

CORDILLERAN FLYCATCHER
see p.421

bolder wing bars

blacker wings

shorter tail

yellowish underparts

OCCURRENCE
Breeds to west of mountains from northern British Columbia to southern California in humid coastal coniferous forest, Pine Oak forest, and dense second-growth forest. Resides in well-shaded woods, along stream bottoms, and steep-walled ravines.

| Length **6–7in (15–17.5cm)** | Wingspan **8–9in (20–23cm)** | Weight **⁹/₃₂–⁷/₁₆oz (8–12g)** |
| Social **Solitary** | Lifespan **Up to 6 years** | Status **Declining** |

Order **Passeriformes**	Family **Tyrannidae**	Species *Empidonax occidentalis*

Cordilleran Flycatcher

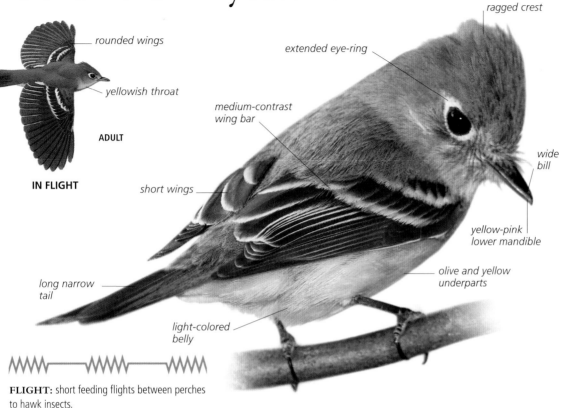

ragged crest

extended eye-ring

rounded wings

yellowish throat

medium-contrast wing bar

ADULT

IN FLIGHT

short wings

wide bill

yellow-pink lower mandible

long narrow tail

olive and yellow underparts

light-colored belly

FLIGHT: short feeding flights between perches to hawk insects.

The Cordilleran Flycatcher is virtually indistinguishable from the Pacific-slope Flycatcher; even their songs are difficult to differentiate. The Cordilleran, however, has slightly larger and darker upperparts and more olive and yellow underparts than its Pacific-slope cousin. Often nesting in man-made structures, this bird is found east of the Rocky Mountains, from central British Columbia south to the Arizona border. The sexes look alike and are monogamous, behaving territorially during the breeding season. Most molting occurs when the birds are wintering.

VOICE Call *seet*, vocalizes principally on breeding grounds, with occasional calls at other times; song *ps-SEET, ptsick, seet*.

NESTING Cup on rocky outcrop, in natural cavity or root mass; 2–5 eggs; 2 broods; April–July.

FEEDING Feeds on insects; waits on perch to fly out for hunt.

READY TO HUNT
The Cordilleran Flycatcher often adopts a sit-and-wait hunting posture before chasing insects.

SIMILAR SPECIES

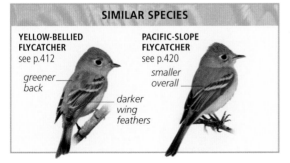

YELLOW-BELLIED FLYCATCHER
see p.412

greener back

PACIFIC-SLOPE FLYCATCHER
see p.420

smaller overall

darker wing feathers

OCCURRENCE
Breeds in cool, arid, relatively dense forests of pine, fir, and spruce, at mid- to high elevation, often associated with watercourses and openings. Winters in the mountains of Mexico.

Length **6–7in (15–17.5cm)**	Wingspan **9in (23cm)**	Weight **⅜–⁷⁄₁₆oz (11–13g)**
Social **Solitary**	Lifespan **Unknown**	Status **Secure**

| Order **Passeriformes** | Family **Tyrannidae** | Species *Empidonax fulvifrons* |

Buff-breasted Flycatcher

large gray head

pale area around eye

buffy wash

grayish brown back

two wing bars

short bill, with pale, yellowish lower mandible

rusty buff breast

pale yellow belly

ADULT

broad wing bars

buffy wash underneath

ADULT

IN FLIGHT

white on outer tail feathers

FLIGHT: short feeding flights, often returning to a favoured perch.

This flycatcher, the smallest of the genus *Empidonax*, is a partial migrant, residing year-round in the southern parts of its range in Central America. It molts on its breeding grounds before moving south for the winter. The Buff-breasted Flycatcher appears to benefit from periodic forest fires, which open up dense undergrowth in sparse pine or oak woodland, creating open understory, this bird's preferred habitat.

VOICE Call *pit,* and alarm call *quit-quit-qui-r-r*; song on breeding grounds *chee-lick* or *chee-lick-chou* by both sexes.

NESTING Open cup of webs, rootlets, and leaves against a trunk or in the fork of a branch; 2–3 eggs; 1 brood; May–July.

FEEDING Takes insects on the wing or from ground; gleans wasps, ants, bugs, beetles from branches, bushes, and weed stems.

MOLTING
This Buff-breasted Flycatcher appears to be undergoing a molt of belly feathers.

HIGH PERCH
This bird hunts by looking for prey in flight from an open perch, sometimes high up.

OCCURRENCE
Breeds in wide mountain canyons with pine-oak woodlands at 2,000–9,500ft (600–3,000m) where it prefers open understory. Occurs from southern Arizona and New Mexico to Mexico, and south to Honduras. US populations migratory, Mexican and Central American birds resident.

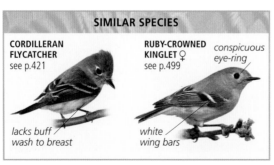

SIMILAR SPECIES

CORDILLERAN FLYCATCHER see p.421

lacks buff wash to breast

RUBY-CROWNED KINGLET ♀ see p.499

conspicuous eye-ring

white wing bars

| Length **5in (13cm)** | Wingspan **8½in (22cm)** | Weight **¼–⁵⁄₁₆oz (7–9g)** |
| Social **Solitary** | Lifespan **At least 2 years** | Status **Secure** |

Order **Passeriformes**	Family **Tyrannidae**	Species *Pyrocephalus rubinus*

Vermilion Flycatcher

rounded wings

ADULT
appears black above

IN FLIGHT

brownish nape

brown back

red crown and forehead

patchy red underparts

IMMATURE MALE (1ST SUMMER)

grayish brown crown

dark eye-line

narrow, white eyebrow

white throat and breast with dusky streaks

peach belly and undertail feathers

FEMALE (BREEDING)

short, square, black tail

red crown

thin, slightly hooked bill

dark brown upperparts

orange-red breast

MALE (BREEDING)

black legs and toes

FLIGHT: direct, fast flight; swift maneuvering while foraging; hovers briefly to glean prey.

This species resides year-round throughout most of its vast range, which includes Mexico, Central America, and South America, south to Argentina. Only the male is a vibrant red; the female is rather drab by comparison. Males often present a showy insect to attract a female. Breeding territories are defended by vocalizations during spectacular flight displays; intruders are chased vigorously and if one fails to depart, a fight may ensue.
VOICE Contact call *peeent*; male song an excited *p-p-pik-zee*, *pit-a-zee*, or *ching-tink-a-link*.
NESTING Shallow open cup of twigs, grasses, and fibers on fork of horizontal branch; 2–4 eggs; 1–2 broods; March–July.
FEEDING Locates insect prey from perch, then pursues and usually catches it in the air.

RED STUNNER
Perching for many hours of its day, this tame flycatcher dips and spreads its tail.

SIMILAR SPECIES

SAY'S PHOEBE
see p.407

uniform, dark back

cinnamon-brown belly

larger overall

OCCURRENCE
In the US (its northern range) found in California, Nevada, Arizona, New Mexico, and Texas, where it is a partial migrant. Breeds in riverside woodlands with cottonwoods, willows, and sycamores; also in drier areas with mesquite; scrubland, semi-desert, and farmland. US birds winter as far south as Honduras.

Length **5–6in (13–15cm)**	Wingspan **10in (25cm)**	Weight **⅜–½oz (11–14g)**
Social **Solitary**	Lifespan **Up to 5 years**	Status **Secure**

| Order **Passeriformes** | Family **Tyrannidae** | Species **Pitangus sulphuratus** |

Great Kiskadee

chestnut sides to tail

black-and-white face

ADULT

broad wings

IN FLIGHT

black crown

white stripe from forehead to nape

brownish olive back

largely chestnut wing feathers

thick, black, powerful bill

white throat

bright yellow underparts

ADULT

FLIGHT: alternates strong wing beats and brief dips with quick shallower wing beats.

The Great Kiskadee is named after its strident song, which, along with its black mask, yellow belly, large size, and habit of perching in the open, makes it a quite conspicuous bird. In Spanish it is called the Benteveo, which means "I see you well." Aggressive in defense of its nest, in the tropics the Great Kiskadee readily attacks large birds of prey, snakes, toucans, and even monkeys.

VOICE Calls include loud exclamatory *reeee* or *weeer*, *Chik-reee*, and harsh *Reep*, or *ick*; distinctive 3-syllable song *KIK-Chi-wee,*or *Kiss-ka-dee*, is most common during breeding season; highly vocal year-round.
NESTING Domed mass of vines, twigs, weeds, and Spanish moss, with side entrance, in fork of tree, or on utility pole, 20–30ft (6–9m) above ground; 2–5 eggs; 1–2 broods; April–July.
FEEDING Sallies out from open perch to capture insects, or pounce on rodents, frogs, and lizards; also eats seeds, fruit, and berries; dives for small fish, and tadpoles, in shallow water.

ANY FOOD WILL DO
The Great Kiskadee is a highly opportunistic feeder; almost anything edible will do.

GREAT BIG SHOW-OFF
Some flycatchers are quiet and secretive, but the Great Kiskadee shows offs with color and voice.

OCCURRENCE
In North America, occurs only in southern Texas, but has a very wide range, from Mexico and Central America south to most of South America to Argentina. In Texas, occurs in woodlands along rivers, shady plantations, thorn scrub, and woodland edges. Resident year-round.

| Length **8½–10in (21–26 cm)** | Wingspan **15in (38cm)** | Weight **2oz (60g)** |
| Social **Solitary** | Lifespan **At least 7 years** | Status **Secure** |

| Order **Passeriformes** | Family **Tyrannidae** | Species *Myiodynastes luteiventris* |

Sulphur-bellied Flycatcher

— broad wings

ADULT

IN FLIGHT

rufous undertail

streaked chest

ADULT

dark brown with streaks

mask-like streak

thick bill, hooked at tip

distinctly streaked breast and flanks

ADULT

chestnut outer tail feathers

yellow wash to belly and undertail feathers

FLIGHT: makes spectacular leaping flights; shorter darts to scoop prey from under a leaf.

In North America, this large and boldly patterned flycatcher breeds only in southeastern Arizona, especially in mountain canyons. It is widely distributed in Mexico and southward to Costa Rica. A long-distance migrant, it winters in equatorial South America, where it can be distinguished from other streaked flycatchers by its squeaky *weel-yum*, or "William," call. The Sulphur-bellied Flycatcher nests in a tree cavity or nestbox, which may be filled up with however much material it takes for the female to be able to look out of the hole for any approaching danger while brooding her eggs.

VOICE Calls *p'p'pe-ya, p'p'p'pe-ya, weel-yum, weel-yum, chu-eer*; male song soft *tre-le-re-re, tre-le-re-re, chu-eer, chee-a-leet s-lik*.

NESTING In natural tree cavity, on deep loose mass of broken twigs, pine needles, and other matter; 3–4 eggs; 1 brood; May–July.

FEEDING Consumes mostly insects while breeding, and eats fruit outside breeding season. Prey captured during flight or by gleaning.

HIGH UP OUT OF SIGHT
The Sulphur-bellied Flycatcher likes high perches, but always below the canopy of the forest.

OCCURRENCE
Sycamore and other trees in woodlands along rivers in canyons of southeastern Arizona. In Mexico and Central America from Guatemala to Costa Rica, breeds in deciduous and evergreen forest, forest edge, and gallery forest. Winters by rivers and forest edges from Ecuador to Bolivia and Brazil.

| Length **8–9in (20–23cm)** | Wingspan **14½in (37cm)** | Weight **1⁹⁄₁₆oz (45g)** |
| Social **Solitary** | Lifespan **Unknown** | Status **Secure** |

| Order **Passeriformes** | Family **Tyrannidae** | Species *Tyrannus melancholicus* |

Tropical Kingbird

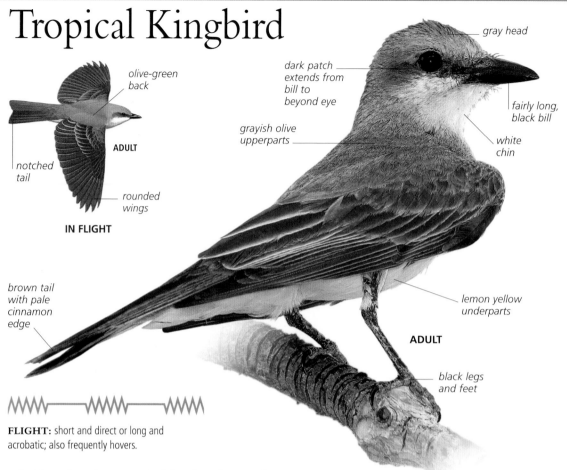

olive-green back

ADULT

notched tail

rounded wings

IN FLIGHT

gray head

dark patch extends from bill to beyond eye

grayish olive upperparts

fairly long, black bill

white chin

brown tail with pale cinnamon edge

lemon yellow underparts

ADULT

black legs and feet

FLIGHT: short and direct or long and acrobatic; also frequently hovers.

Although native to tropical South and Central America, the Tropical Kingbird can also be found in limited areas of the southern US during its breeding season. Additionally, immature Tropical Kingbirds are regular fall visitors to the Pacific coast of California and British Columbia. This species is comfortable around people and can be often found in residential areas. Like many flycatchers, it is a frequent host to several parasitic cowbird species, which lay their eggs in the Tropical Kingbird's nest.

VOICE Twittering calls given throughout day and all year; song tremulous *tere-ee-ee-tril-il-iil-l* or *tre-e-e-e-eip*.

NESTING Flimsy open cup of vines, rootlets, twigs, dry grasses in high fork of isolated tree; 2–3 eggs; 1 brood; May–July.

FEEDING Captures flying insects, including beetles, bees, dragonflies, grasshoppers, and wasps; also eats berries and fruit.

ATTENTION GRABBER
The Tropical Kingbird often sings its high-pitched song from a conspicuous perch.

SIMILAR SPECIES

COUCH'S KINGBIRD
see p.427

shallower notched tail

broader bill

WESTERN KINGBIRD
see p.430

smaller bill

darker upperparts

squarer tail

paler yellow belly

OCCURRENCE
In Arizona breeds in open country with scattered trees and shrubs; also gardens, golf courses, roadsides, farmland, and forest edges; in Tropical America in semi-open mangroves or cactus forests; and in woods near ponds and streams. Avoids dense forest. Found in similar habitats further south in winter.

| Length **7–9in (18–23cm)** | Wingspan **14½in (37cm)** | Weight **1¹⁄₁₆–1⁹⁄₁₆oz (30–45g)** |
| Social **Solitary/Flocks** | Lifespan **Unknown** | Status **Localized** |

Order **Passeriformes**	Family **Tyrannidae**	Species *Tyrannus couchii*

Couch's Kingbird

greenish back

ADULT

IN FLIGHT

gray head

olive breast

yellow belly

square or lightly notched tail

ADULT

short, thick bill

dark patch extends from bill to beyond eye

olive green upperparts

white chin

brownish gray wings

ADULT

black legs and feet

notched tail

This brightly-colored kingbird was once thought to belong to the same species as the Tropical Kingbird, but their vocalizations readily distinguish the two birds. Males and females are similar in appearance but juveniles are slightly duller in color.

This species aggressively chases Bronzed Cowbirds and is able to identify Brown-headed Cowbird eggs and remove them, so it is rarely parasitized. However, in south Texas, the bird needs to watch out for fox squirrels, which may be nest predators.

VOICE Calls include *dzzh*, *queer*, *bereeeer*, or *kip*; dawn song *tuwit*, *tuwit*, *tuwitchu* or nasal *pik-pik-pik-pitweeer*, given in April–July.

NESTING Untidy, lined, open bowl of twigs, bark strips, near treetop; 2–4 eggs; 1–2 broods; April–August.

FEEDING Forages around from treetops, mainly on flying insects; obtains fruit from trees and vines.

FLIGHT: strong, direct fight with stiff wing beats; hovers to glean insects from foliage.

TIGHT MANEUVER
The Couch's Kingbird is able to maneuver easily in quite dense foliage.

SIMILAR SPECIES

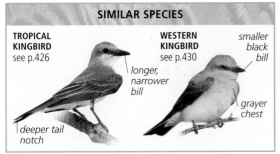

TROPICAL KINGBIRD see p.426

longer, narrower bill

deeper tail notch

WESTERN KINGBIRD see p.430

smaller black bill

grayer chest

OCCURRENCE
In the US, breeds in south Texas in thorn scrub, shrubby farm fields, bushy clearings in forest, scrubby woodland, and suburban and waterside areas. Avoids very dense foliage. Texas populations migrate to Mexico, but Mexican and Central American ones are resident.

Length **8–9in (20–23cm)**	Wingspan **15½in (39cm)**	Weight **1⁷⁄₁₆oz (40g)**
Social **Solitary/Flocks**	Lifespan **Unknown**	Status **Secure**

| Order **Passeriformes** | Family **Tyrannidae** | Species ***Tyrannus vociferans*** |

Cassin's Kingbird

IN FLIGHT

blackish tail

brownish wings

ADULT

buffy tail tip

dark gray head

small bill, hooked at tip

grayish olive back

white below eye

pale edge to feathers

grayish white chin

grayish breast

yellow belly

ADULT

L arge and highly vocal, Cassin's Kingbird is easily identified by its preference for territorial behavior and open perches, from where it swoops on insect prey. Courting birds impress each other in a display in which they hover in unison over a favorite perch. Cassin's Kingbird overlaps in range with the Western Kingbird, although there appears to be minimal competition between the two species. However, the nesting success of Cassin's Kingbird's is lower in areas where both birds occur.
VOICE Calls *ch-tuur* and low, nasal *chi-beer* or *chi-queer*; dawn song 1–2 rasping sounds followed by a prolonged *keecyur*.
NESTING Large, bulky open cup of twigs and rootlets; on branch high in deciduous tree; 3–5 eggs; 1 brood; April–August.
FEEDING Mainly insectivorous; feeds on beetles, bees, wasps, ants, flies, aphids, and grasshoppers; also eats fruit.

FLIGHT: direct, strong; males engage in "tumble flight"—fly up, stall, twist, pitch, tumble down.

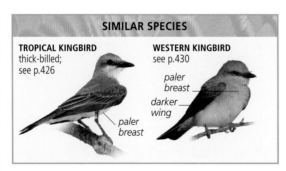

SIMILAR SPECIES

TROPICAL KINGBIRD
thick-billed; see p.426

WESTERN KINGBIRD
see p.430

paler breast

darker wing

paler breast

HIGH ALERT
This gray-breasted Cassin's Kingbird is perched and alert in mature riverside woodland.

OCCURRENCE
Breeds in Wyoming, Montana, South Dakota, Oklahoma, Texas, Arizona, California, and New Mexico in waterside woodland, Pinyon pine, juniper forests, grassland, desert scrub, rural, and suburban habitats. US population winters south to Mexico and Guatemala, overlapping with resident population.

| Length **8–9in (20–23cm)** | Wingspan **16in (41cm)** | Weight **1 9⁄16 oz (45g)** |
| Social **Solitary** | Lifespan **Unknown** | Status **Secure** |

| Order **Passeriformes** | Family **Tyrannidae** | Species *Tyrannus crassirostris* |

Thick-billed Kingbird

brown head

long, thick hooked bill

concealed yellow central crown patch

thick neck

white throat

all dark tail

dark gray back

gray-brown back

pale gray breast

ADULT

dark brown wings

IN FLIGHT

rufous edges to wing feathers

pale yellow belly and flanks

ADULT

The Thick-billed Kingbird is a year-round resident over most of its range in Mexico but was not found breeding in the US until 1958. The North American population inhabits the "sky islands" of southern Arizona—so named because the forested mountains are separated by inhospitable habitats, such as deserts, that are an obstacle to distribution—and migrates south for the winter. While hawking for insects from elevated perches, it takes off in its flight to capture food, quivering its wings while keeping its crown feathers erect.

VOICE Harsh and raspy *tch tchee* and *tch-uhreeeE* calls; vocal through the day while breeding; dawn song consists of two phrases *T-t-t-t-t, t-T-tt-rwheeuh-t-t-t*, or a loud whistled *pwaareeet*.

NESTING Open cup of small twigs, grass stems on high tree branch or close to trunk; 3–4 eggs; 1 brood; June–July.

FEEDING Hunts from topmost perches of trees or bushes to catch insects in the air; also known to consume large seeds.

FLIGHT: strong direct flight; display in flight with wings extended laterally and fluttering.

PERCHING HIGH
This Thick-billed Kingbird, seen from below, is perched high in a tree, its preferred habitat.

SIMILAR SPECIES

TROPICAL KINGBIRD
see p.426

dark tail

darker yellow

COUCH'S KINGBIRD
see p.427

thinner, shorter bill

more yellow on belly

different tail pattern

OCCURRENCE
Breeds in dry areas in Arizona, New Mexico, and southern California (rarely). Prefers wooded canyons close to water, inhabiting the upper branches of sycamore or cottonwood trees.

| Length **9–9½in (23–24cm)** | Wingspan **16in (41cm)** | Weight **2oz (55g)** |
| Social **Solitary** | Lifespan **Up to 10 years** | Status **Localized** |

| Order **Passeriformes** | Family **Tyrannidae** | Species ***Tyrannus verticalis*** |

Western Kingbird

olive-gray back

strong, dark eye-line

small bill

ADULT

white chin

white-edged tail

dark wing with no wing bars

IN FLIGHT

gray chest

gray head

gray back

white edge to outer tail feathers

yellow belly

notched tail

ADULT

ADULT

A conspicuous summer breeder in the US, the Western Kingbird occurs in open habitats in much of western North America. The white outer edges on its outer tail feathers distinguish it from other kingbirds. Its population has expanded eastward over the last 100 years. A large, loosely defined territory is defended against other kingbirds when breeding begins in spring; a smaller core area is defended as the season progresses.

VOICE Calls include *whit*, *pwee-t*, and chatter; song, regularly repeated sharp *kip* notes and high-pitched notes.

NESTING Open, bulky cup of grass, rootlets, and twigs in tree, shrub, utility pole; 2–7 eggs; 1 brood; April–July.

FEEDING Feeds on a wide variety of insects; also berries and fruit.

FLIGHT: agile, fast, direct, flapping flight; flies to catch insects; hovers to pick bugs on vegetation.

FENCE POST
A favorite place for the Western Kingbird to perch, and look around, is on fenceposts.

QUENCHING THIRST
A juvenile Western Kingbird drinks at the edge of a shallow pools of water.

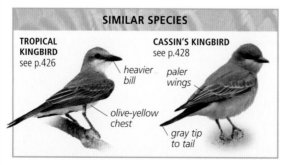

SIMILAR SPECIES

TROPICAL KINGBIRD
see p.426

heavier bill

olive-yellow chest

CASSIN'S KINGBIRD
see p.428

paler wings

gray tip to tail

OCCURRENCE
Widespread in southern Canada and the western US, in open habitats such as grasslands, savannah, desert shrub, pastures, and cropland, near elevated perches; particularly near water. Winters in similar habitats and in tropical forest and shrubbery from Mexico to Costa Rica.

| Length **8–9in (20–23cm)** | Wingspan **15–16in (38–41cm)** | Weight **1¼–1⁹⁄₁₆oz (35–45g)** |
| Social **Solitary** | Lifespan **Up to 6 years** | Status **Secure** |

| Order **Passeriformes** | Family **Tyrannidae** | Species *Tyrannus forficatus* |

Scissor-tailed Flycatcher

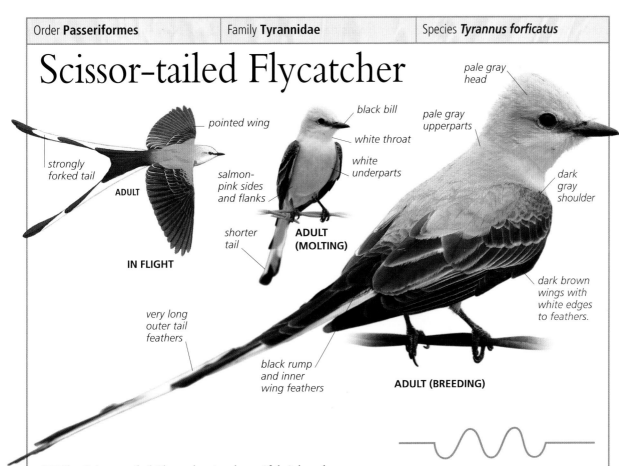

pale gray head

black bill

white throat

white underparts

pale gray upperparts

pale gray head

dark gray shoulder

pointed wing

strongly forked tail

ADULT

salmon-pink sides and flanks

shorter tail

ADULT (MOLTING)

dark brown wings with white edges to feathers.

IN FLIGHT

very long outer tail feathers

black rump and inner wing feathers

ADULT (BREEDING)

The Scissor-tailed Flycatcher is a beautiful sight when observed flying or when perched on a wire or fence in the south–central US. Its aerial courtship display, with its long tail streaming behind it, is rather spectacular. The Scissor-tailed Flycatcher's nest incorporates many human products, such as string, cloth, paper, and wrapping material. High winds or thunderstorms may be responsible for many nest failures in some years. This flycatcher forms impressive pre-migratory roosts in large trees during late summer. Flocks usually consist of more than 100 individuals, but groups of over 1,000 birds have been recorded.

VOICE Males vocalize in breeding territories and communal roosts; song variable number of *pups* followed by *perleep* or *peroo*.

NESTING Open cup of plant stems or strings, in small isolated tree or large shrub; 3–6 eggs; 1 brood; March–August.

FEEDING Catches insects in midair, also from trees or from ground; eats fruits and berries in winter.

FLIGHT: rapid wing beats, flies with folded tail, hovers with spread tail; abrupt, midair turns.

MALE IN FLIGHT
The male bird's tail seems to float behind him in flight and vivid pink can be seen under the wings.

OCCURRENCE
Breeds in southern states and northeast Mexico; savanna, open grasslands, agricultural fields, pastures, golf courses, and wherever occasional trees and shrubs give perches or nest sites. Winters in similar habitats and at edges of tropical forests in southern Mexico and Central America south to Costa Rica.

SIMILAR SPECIES

WESTERN KINGBIRD
see p.430

wider body

shorter tail

LOVES TO PERCH
Fenceposts, wires, and barbed-wire fences are all excellent perches for these birds.

| Length **9–15in (23–38cm)** | Wingspan **15in (38cm)** | Weight **1¼–2oz (35–55g)** |
| Social **Flocks** | Lifespan **Unknown** | Status **Secure** |

| Order **Passeriformes** | Family **Tyrannidae** | Species *Myiarchus tuberculifer* |

Dusky-capped Flycatcher

rufous edged outer wing feathers

ADULT

plain grayish olive upperparts

long tail

rounded wings

IN FLIGHT

crested, dark brown cap

brown, bushy crest

brown ear patch

grayish olive back

faint wing bars

large, straight bill

pale gray throat and breast

pale yellow belly

blackish legs and feet

rufous edges to wing feathers

narrow rusty edges to tail

ADULT

The Dusky-capped Flycatcher is one of the four species of flycatchers of the genus *Myiarchus* breeding in North America. These are not easy to identify, but their English names help with identification. The Dusky-capped barely reaches the US, inhabiting only Arizona and New Mexico, where it inhabits dense woodlands, preferring the foliage below the canopy to forage for insects. As in other *Myiarchus* species, the sexes are similar, with juveniles slightly darker than adults. The Dusky-capped Flycatcher is mainly silent, except when it sings at dawn.
VOICE Dawn song *whit, peeur,* or *wheeeeu* alternated with *huit* notes; vocalizes mostly in daylight during breeding season.
NESTING Twigs with moss, grass, and feathers in natural tree cavity or old woodpecker hole; 3–4 eggs; 1 brood; May–July.
FEEDING Picks insects from leaves and twigs; flies from perch to capture flying prey; also eats a variety of berries.

FLIGHT: short and direct with shallow wing beats; also frequently hovers.

BELOW THE CANOPY
The Dusky-capped Flycatcher prefers the shade of the canopy to the treetops.

SIMILAR SPECIES
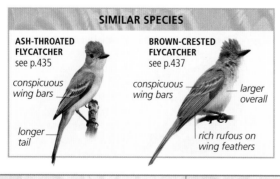
ASH-THROATED FLYCATCHER see p.435
conspicuous wing bars
longer tail

BROWN-CRESTED FLYCATCHER see p.437
conspicuous wing bars
larger overall
rich rufous on wing feathers

OCCURRENCE
In North America found only in southeast Arizona and southwest New Mexico. Breeds in pine-oak woodlands up to 11,200ft (3,400m), often along waterways with sycamore and live oak; also juniper woodlands at low elevation. Migrates to Mexico. Resident populations in South America.

| Length **7¼in (18.5cm)** | Wingspan **10in (25cm)** | Weight **¹¹⁄₁₆oz (20g)** |
| Social **Solitary** | Lifespan **Unknown** | Status **Secure** |

Order **Passeriformes**	Family **Tyrannidae**	Species *Myiarchus cinerascens*

Ash-throated Flycatcher

rusty outer edges to outer flight feathers

bushy gray-brown crest

short, relatively thin bill

all dark bill

pale gray throat

ADULT

brown outer tail feathers

rounded wings

IN FLIGHT

ADULT

grayish white chest

white wing bars

rusty edges to outer tail feathers

pale yellow belly

ADULT

FLIGHT: continuous flapping; rapid and direct; acrobatic maneuvers; hovers.

long tail

Of the three western species of *Myiarchus* flycatchers in the US, this is the most widespread and versatile, although it does prefer dry country. Deserts, mesquite, riverside and open woodlands, and juniper scrub are among its breeding habitats, though higher densities are found by rivers than in the open. Man-made structures such as pipes, the eaves of houses, and nest boxes often replace natural cavities for nesting. This species often fills cavities with material such as hair and feathers, to create a smaller chamber.

VOICE Call *huit* also *wheer*, *whip*, or *prrt;* dawn song *ha-wheer* or burry *ka-brick.*

NESTING Any natural or artificial cavity, adds dry grass, stems, twigs, and other materials such as hair or feathers; 2–7 eggs; 1–2 broods; March–July.

FEEDING Eats mainly insects; occasionally fruit, small reptiles, and mammals.

RUSTY FIELD MARKS
Rufous outer tail and wing feathers are useful field marks in identifying this species.

OCCURRENCE
Widespread in western North America. Breeds in lowland to mid-elevation habitats, in arid and semi-arid scrub, open woodland, or waterside forests. Migrates to Mexico and Central America to Costa Rica. Resident in Mexico.

SIMILAR SPECIES

GREAT CRESTED FLYCATCHER
eastern;
see p.436

bulkier overall

yellow belly

BROWN-CRESTED FLYCATCHER
different habitat;
see p.437

darker gray above

lighter yellow below

Length **7–8in (18–20cm)**	Wingspan **12–13in (30–33cm)**	Weight **1¹⁄₁₆–1⁷⁄₁₆oz (20–40g)**
Social **Solitary**	Lifespan **Up to 11 years**	Status **Secure**

| Order **Passeriformes** | Family **Tyrannidae** | Species *Myiarchus crinitus* |

Great Crested Flycatcher

ADULT

rusty edges
to outer wing
feathers

whitish
wing bars

IN FLIGHT

brown
crest

olive-brown
back

long,
thin
bill

gray breast
and face

ADULT

yellow
belly

brownish legs
and feet

long
tail

The Great Crested Flycatcher is locally common and geographically quite widespread from Alberta and the Maritimes to Florida and Texas, but is often overlooked because it remains in the forest canopy, though it visits the ground for food and nest material. Its presence is usually given away by its loud, sharp, double-syllabled notes. It lines its nest with shed snakeskins like other *Myiarchus* flycatchers.

FLIGHT: fast and direct; can glide between perches; will also hover.

VOICE Principal call a loud, abrupt *purr-it* given by both sexes; male song repeated *whee-eep*, occasionally *wheeyer*.

NESTING In deep cavity, usually woodpecker hole, lined with leaves, bark, trash, and snakeskins; 4–6 eggs; 1 brood; May–July.

FEEDING Picks flying insects, moths, and caterpillars mainly from leaves and brances in the canopy; also small berries and fruits.

OCCURRENCE
Widespread in eastern North America, from Alberta to the Maritimes in Canada, and, in the US, south to Texas and Florida. Migrates to Mexico, Central America, and northern South America. Breeds in deciduous and mixed woodlands with clearings.

TRICOLORED SPECIES
Viewed from the front, the eastern Great Crested Flycatcher is tricolored.

SIMILAR SPECIES

ASH-THROATED FLYCATCHER
see p.435

silvery
white
throat

paler
yellow
belly

BROWN-CRESTED FLYCATCHER
see p.437

more
rufous
wings

heavier
bill

paler
yellow
belly

| Length **7–8in (18–20cm)** | Wingspan **13in (33cm)** | Weight **⅞–1⁷⁄₁₆oz (25–40g)** |
| Social **Solitary** | Lifespan **Up to 13 years** | Status **Secure** |

| Order **Passeriformes** | Family **Tyrannidae** | Species **Myiarchus tyrannulus** |

Brown-crested Flycatcher

ADULT

thin, rusty edges to tail feathers

rusty edges to outer wing feathers

IN FLIGHT

black bill

ragged brown crest

faint wing bars

gray breast and throat

ADULT

pale yellow belly

blackish legs and toes

FLIGHT: rapid and direct; acrobatic while pursuing prey, courting, and in territorial chases.

This is the largest of the three western *Myiarchus* species, as large as the eastern Great Crested. It is a slender-looking, long-tailed flycatcher, with a thick bill and a ragged-looking, tan-brown crest. In flight, the rufous outer tail feathers are quite noticeable. Although mostly an insect catcher, it will sometimes pluck a hummingbird from a perch. In the Southwest, the territories of this species are larger than elsewhere.

long tail

VOICE Call *huit* singly or repeated, also distinctive *rasp*; dawn song loud *come-here, come-here* or *whit-will-do, whit-will-do*.
NESTING Cavities in trees or large cacti, often woodpecker holes, lined with snakeskin; 3–6 eggs; 1 brood; March–July.
FEEDING Omniverous, but during breeding season, eats insects like cicadas, grasshoppers, and beetles.

VOCAL ADVERTISING
This Brown-crested Flycatcher advertises its territory from a high perch in a Mesquite tree.

OCCURRENCE
A tropical species that reaches the US only in the Southwest, north to Nevada and south to Texas; breeds in riverside woodlands and giant cacti. Migrates south to Mexico and Guatemala, resident populations south to Honduras.

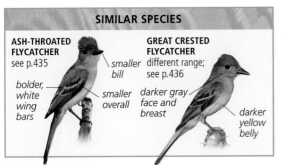

SIMILAR SPECIES

ASH-THROATED FLYCATCHER
see p.435

smaller bill

bolder, white wing bars

smaller overall

GREAT CRESTED FLYCATCHER
different range; see p.436

darker gray face and breast

darker yellow belly

| Length **8½in (22cm)** | Wingspan **13in (33cm)** | Weight **1⁹⁄₁₆oz (45g)** |
| Social **Solitary** | Lifespan **Up to 11 years** | Status **Secure** |

VIREOS

Vireos are a family of songbirds restricted to the New World, with 15 species occurring in the United States and Canada. The classification of vireos has long been problematic—traditionally they were associated with warblers, but recent

SEPARATE SPECIES
The Blue-headed Vireo is one of three species, formerly known as just one species, the Soltary Vireo.

molecular studies suggest that they are actually related to crow-like birds. Vireo plumage is drab, often predominantly greenish or grayish above and whitish below, augmented by eye-rings, "spectacles," eyestripes, and wing bars. Most vireos have a preference for broadleaved habitats, where they move about deliberately, hopping and climbing as they slowly forage for their prey. Because they are mainly insect-eaters, most are mid- to long-distance migrants, retreating to warmer climes in winter, when insects are dormant. Vireos are most often detected by the male's loud and clear territorial song, which is repetitive and persistent.

KEEN SONGSTER
The White-eyed Vireo sings almost continuously, even on the hottest of summer days.

JAYS & CROWS

Although jays and crows belong to a highly diverse family, the corvids, most members share some important characteristics. They are remarkably social, some species even breeding cooperatively, but at the same time they can be quiet and stealthy. Always the opportunists, corvids use strong bills and toes to obtain a varied, omnivorous diet. Ornithologists have shown that ravens, magpies, and crows are among the most intelligent birds. They exhibit self-awareness when looking into mirrors, can make tools, and successfully tackle difficult counting and problem-solving. As a rule, most corvid plumage comes in shades of blue, black, and white. The plumage of adult corvids does not vary by season. Corvidae are part of an ancient bird lineage (Corvoidea) that originated in Australasia. Crows and jays were among the birds most affected by the spread of West Nile virus in the early 2000s, but most populations seem to have recovered quickly.

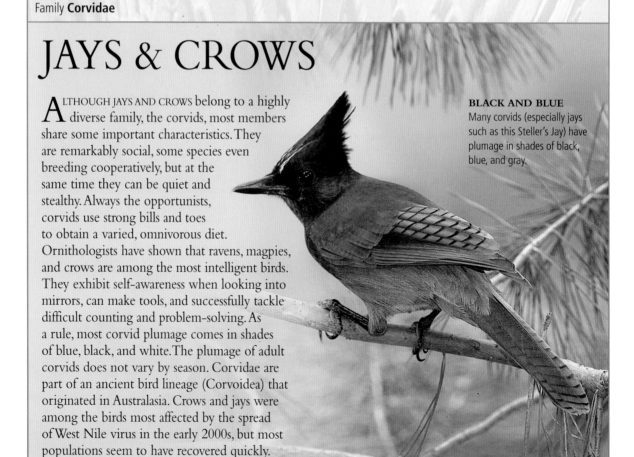

BLACK AND BLUE
Many corvids (especially jays such as this Steller's Jay) have plumage in shades of black, blue, and gray.

| Order **Passeriformes** | Family **Laniidae** | Species *Lanius ludovicianus* |

Loggerhead Shrike

ADULT

white flash in wings

IN FLIGHT

white edges to tail

gray crown

hooked bill

black "mask"

black wings

pale undertail feathers

JUVENILE

unstreaked, gray underparts

ADULT

FLIGHT: fast with rapid wing beats, sometimes interspersed with glides; swoops from perches.

rounded tail

Although a songbird, the Loggerhead Shrike is superficially raptor-like in several ways, particularly its prominent black face mask and powerful, hooked bill. It sits atop posts or tall trees, swooping down to catch prey on the ground. It has the unusual habit of then impaling its prey on thorns, barbed wire, or sharp twigs, which is thought to be the reason for the nickname "butcher bird." Unfortunately, the Loggerhead Shrike is declining, principally because of human alteration of its habitat.

VOICE Quiet warbles, trills, and harsh notes; song harsh notes singly or in series: *chaa chaa chaa*.

NESTING Open cup of vegetation, placed in thorny tree; 5 eggs; 1 brood; March–June.

FEEDING Kills large insects and small vertebrates—rodents, birds, reptiles—with powerful bill.

GEARED FOR HUNTING
The Loggerhead Shrike perches upright on tall shrubs or small trees, where it scans for prey.

SIMILAR SPECIES

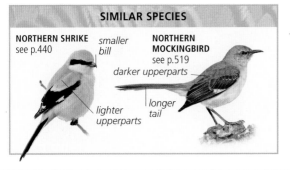

NORTHERN SHRIKE
see p.440

smaller bill

NORTHERN MOCKINGBIRD
see p.519

darker upperparts

lighter upperparts

longer tail

OCCURRENCE
Found in semi-open country with scattered perches, but its distribution is erratic, occurring in relatively high densities in certain areas, but absent from seemingly suitable habitat. Occurs in congested residential areas in some regions (south Florida), but generally favors fairly remote habitats.

| Length **9in (23cm)** | Wingspan **12in (31cm)** | Weight **1¼–2⅛oz (35–60g)** |
| Social **Solitary** | Lifespan **Unknown** | Status **Declining** |

| Order **Passeriformes** | Family **Laniidae** | Species *Lanius excubitor* |

Northern Shrike

ADULT

conspicuous white wing bar

pale gray upperparts

IN FLIGHT

strongly hooked bill

delicately barred breast

brownish underparts

long tail

IMMATURE

large head

narrow black mask

pale gray upperparts

black wings

ADULT

gray-white underparts

black tail, with white outer tail feathers

FLIGHT: short flights between hunting perches; pounces on prey.

This northern version of the familiar Loggerhead Shrike is an uncommon winter visitor to the northern US and southern Canada. In some winters, this species is widespread across the mid-latitudes of North America, in other winters it is nearly absent. The Northern Shrike is paler, larger bodied, and larger billed than the Loggerhead Shrike, which enables it to attack and subdue larger prey than the Loggerhead. Many Northern Shrike populations worldwide are in decline, but to date there is no sign of a similar decline in North America.

VOICE Variety of short warbles, trills, and harsh notes; generally silent on wintering grounds.

NESTING Open, bulky cup in low tree or large shrub, lined with feathers and hair; 4–6 eggs; 1 brood; May–June.

FEEDING Swoops down on prey, such as rodents, small birds, and insects, which it impales on thorns or pointed branches.

BLACK-AND-WHITE DISPLAY
The Northern Shrike flashes its distinctive black-and-white markings while in flight.

SIMILAR SPECIES

LOGGERHEAD SHRIKE
see p.439

shorter bill

darker, smaller overall

NORTHERN MOCKINGBIRD
see p.519

straight, white-edged tail

thin bill

less black in wings

OCCURRENCE
Breeds in sub-Arctic coniferous forests, across Canada and Alaska. Winters in more southerly open country with sufficient perches. Avoids built-up and residential districts, but spends much time perching on fence posts and roadside signs.

| Length **10in (25cm)** | Wingspan **14in (35cm)** | Weight **1¾–2⅝oz (50–75g)** |
| Social **Solitary** | Lifespan **Unknown** | Status **Vulnerable** |

Order **Passeriformes**	Family **Vireonidae**	Species *Vireo griseus*

White-eyed Vireo

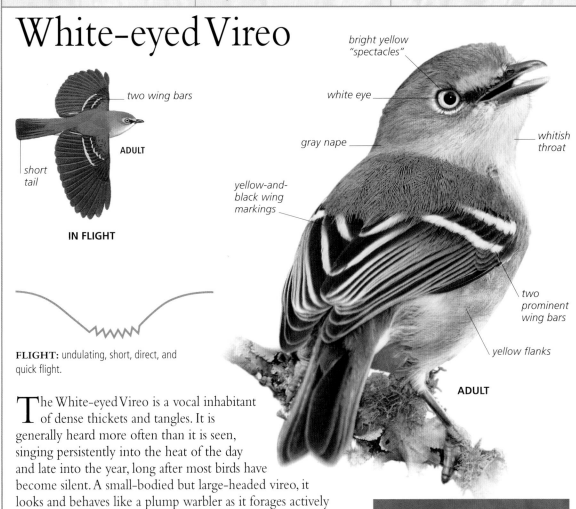

two wing bars

ADULT

short tail

IN FLIGHT

bright yellow "spectacles"

white eye

gray nape

yellow-and-black wing markings

whitish throat

two prominent wing bars

yellow flanks

ADULT

FLIGHT: undulating, short, direct, and quick flight.

The White-eyed Vireo is a vocal inhabitant of dense thickets and tangles. It is generally heard more often than it is seen, singing persistently into the heat of the day and late into the year, long after most birds have become silent. A small-bodied but large-headed vireo, it looks and behaves like a plump warbler as it forages actively in shrubbery. It is heavily parasitized by the Brown-headed Cowbird, and as many as half of the White-eyed Vireo's offsprings do not survive.

VOICE Call a raspy, angry scold; male's song a highly variable and complex repertoire of over a dozen distinct songs.

NESTING Deep cup in dense vegetation, outer layer composed of coarse material, lined with finer fibers, often near water, suspended from twigs by the rim; 3–5 eggs; 2 broods; March–July.

FEEDING Hops from branch to branch pursuing bees, flies, beetles, and bugs, plucking them from leaves or sallying out to snatch them in the air; feeds primarily on fruit in winter.

WHITE EYE, WHITE WING BARS
The White-eyed Vireo's distinctive markings ensure that it is highly conspicuous.

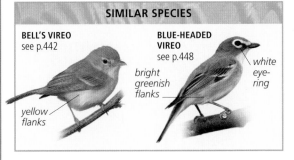

SIMILAR SPECIES

BELL'S VIREO
see p.442

yellow flanks

BLUE-HEADED VIREO
see p.448

bright greenish flanks

white eye-ring

OCCURRENCE
A common breeder in dense brush and scrub across the eastern US, from Texas to the Great Lakes region and southern New England. Retreats to southern states of the US, the Atlantic slope of Mexico, Cuba, and the Bahamas in winter.

Length **5in (13cm)**	Wingspan **7½in (19cm)**	Weight **⅜oz (10g)**
Social **Solitary**	Lifespan **Up to 7 years**	Status **Secure**

Order **Passeriformes**	Family **Vireonidae**	Species **Vireo bellii**

Bell's Vireo

single bright wing bar

gray head

ADULT

greenish back and rump

IN FLIGHT

long tail

yellowish lower sides

bright bluish legs

faint "spectacles"

thin, dark eye-line

short bill

ADULT

This pale, grayish, and nondescript vireo is hard to see as it moves through dense brushy vegetation searching for food. Its most distinctive feature is a long tail which it flicks as it moves. In the arid western parts of its range, in northern Mexico and Arizona, Bell's Vireo is usually found close to rivers or streams. The Eastern subspecies (*V. b. belli*) is distinctly brighter in plumage than the three western subspecies, one of which, the Least Bell's Vireo (*V. b. pusillus*) of southern California, is endangered.

VOICE Call high, raspy, and nasal; males highly vocal and sing all day long during the breeding season; song quite fast for a vireo.

NESTING Deep, rounded cup constructed of coarse materials, lined with fine grasses and hair, and bound with spider webs, in dense shrubbery woven to twigs by the rim; 3–5 eggs; 2 broods; April–May.

FEEDING Actively gleans its insect and spider prey from leaves and twigs, hopping from branch to branch in brushy vegetation.

FLIGHT: slightly undulating flight with rapid wing beats followed by short glides.

TAIL FLICKING
Unlike other vireos, Bell's Vireo is known for flicking its long tail as it sings.

OCCURRENCE
Fairly common breeder in the bushy habitats of the central US, and the riverside thickets of the southwestern US, southward into northern Mexico. Winters along the Pacific slopes of Mexico.

SIMILAR SPECIES

WARBLING VIREO see p.450

white eyebrow

no wing bar

PHILADELPHIA VIREO see p.451

greenish upperparts

Length **4¾in (12cm)**	Wingspan **7in (18cm)**	Weight **⁵⁄₁₆oz (9g)**
Social **Solitary**	Lifespan **Up to 8 years**	Status **Vulnerable**

Order **Passeriformes**	Family **Vireonidae**	Species *Vireo atricapilla*

Black-capped Vireo

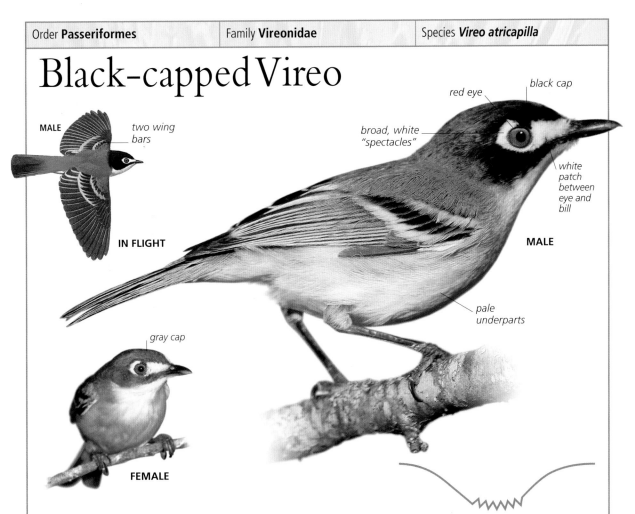

MALE

two wing bars

IN FLIGHT

red eye

black cap

broad, white "spectacles"

white patch between eye and bill

MALE

pale underparts

gray cap

FEMALE

Unique amongst vireos in showing a sexually dimorphic (different) plumage, the Black-capped Vireo is restricted to central southern US and Mexico. Although it has broad, white "spectacles" and a red eye, it is not easy to spot as it forages in dense shrubby vegetation. It sings persistently from near the top of bushes, often long into the day. Habitat changes and Brown-headed Cowbird parasitism have caused declines in the bird's population.
VOICE Calls are variable scolds; song an extensive repertoire of trills, whistles, chips, and squeaks, with individual variations.
NESTING Rounded, thick-walled cup of plant and animal fibers, often lined with finer fibers, hung from forked twigs in a shrub; 2–5 eggs; 1–2 broods; April–August.
FEEDING Hops and flutters through dense vegetation, gleaning grasshoppers, flies, beetles, and caterpillars from leaves.

FLIGHT: straight and undulating; series of quick wing beats followed by closed winged glides.

SUSPENDED NEST
Like other species, the Black-capped Vireo suspends its nest from twigs using spider webs.

OCCURRENCE
Breeds only in the hill country of central southern Texas, and adjacent Mexico, and a few sites in Oklahoma; breeding habitat includes oaks and shrubs of various species Winters on the foothill country of western Mexico.

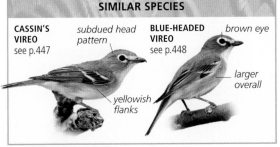

SIMILAR SPECIES

CASSIN'S VIREO see p.447

subdued head pattern

BLUE-HEADED VIREO see p.448

brown eye

larger overall

yellowish flanks

Length **4½in (11.5cm)**	Wingspan **7½in (19cm)**	Weight **⁵⁄₁₆oz (9g)**
Social **Solitary**	Lifespan **Up to 7 years**	Status **Vulnerable**

Order **Passeriformes**	Family **Vireonidae**	Species **_Vireo vicinior_**

Gray Vireo

gray rump

ADULT

faint wing bars

IN FLIGHT

rounded head

pale eye-ring

lead-gray body

paler gray patch between eye and bill

hooked bill

ADULT

pale gray underparts

FLIGHT: flies rapidly and directly between shrubs; hovers, sallies, and swoops when foraging.

A drab, inconspicuous vireo of the hot and arid southwestern US, the Gray Vireo is reminiscent of a miniature shrike in terms of posture and shape. Found mainly in dense, shrubby vegetation such as pinyon and juniper, it is most often detected by its distinctive voice. In its restricted habitat, it can be confused with other small, gray birds such as gnatcatchers, titmice, and the Bushtit.

VOICE Varied calls, include trills and chatters; song given by male, harsh three- to four-note phrase.

NESTING Cup of dry plant materials and spider webs, suspended from twigs by rim, fairly low in shrub or tree, lined with fine fibers; 3–4 eggs; 1 brood; April–May.

FEEDING Gleans insects and spiders from leaves, twigs, and branches; also catches flies in flight; in winter, primarily eats fruit.

PERCHED SINGER
From the top of a shrub, a male sings to declare his ownership of the surrounding territory.

UNCOMMON BIRD
The Gray Vireo is an uncommon little bird but can be difficult to spot in its scrubby habitat.

OCCURRENCE
Breeds in the hot and arid, shrubby scrublands of the southwestern US, in parts of Nevada, Colorado, Utah, Arizona, New Mexico, and Texas; short-distance migrant. Winters largely in Mexico, in similarly arid areas.

SIMILAR SPECIES

GRAY FLYCATCHER
see p.419

JUNIPER TITMOUSE
see p.482

crested head

pale lower bill with dark tip

white-edged tail

no eye-ring

Length **5½in (14cm)**	Wingspan **8in (20cm)**	Weight **7/16oz (13g)**
Social **Solitary/Pairs**	Lifespan **Up to 5 years**	Status **Localized**

| Order **Passeriformes** | Family **Vireonidae** | Species *Vireo flavifrons* |

Yellow-throated Vireo

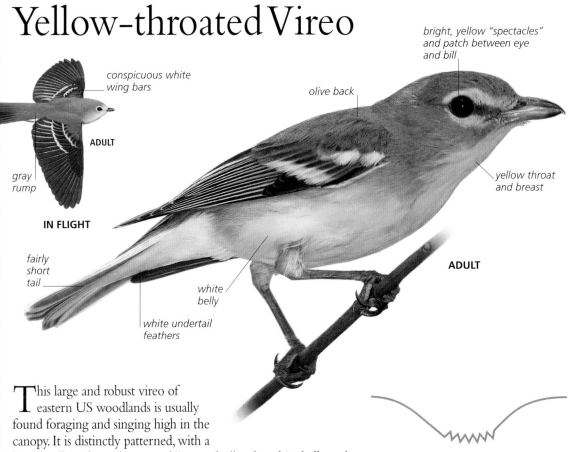

bright, yellow "spectacles" and patch between eye and bill

olive back

conspicuous white wing bars

ADULT

gray rump

IN FLIGHT

yellow throat and breast

fairly short tail

white belly

white undertail feathers

ADULT

This large and robust vireo of eastern US woodlands is usually found foraging and singing high in the canopy. It is distinctly patterned, with a bright yellow throat, breast, and "spectacles," and a white belly and flanks. The fragmentation of forests, spraying of insecticides, and cowbird parasitism have led to regional declines in Yellow-throated Vireo populations, but the bird's range, as a whole, has actually expanded.

VOICE Scolding, hoarse, rapid calls; male song a slow, repetitive, two- or three-note phrase, separated by long pauses.

NESTING Rounded cup of plant and animal fibers bound with spider webs, usually located towards the top of a large tree and hung by the rim; 3–5 eggs; 1 brood; April–July.

FEEDING Forages high in trees, picking spiders and insects from the branches; also eats fruit when available.

FLIGHT: direct, but jerky, alternating rapid wing beats with brief pauses.

CANOPY SINGER
The Yellow-throated Vireo sings from the very tops of tall trees.

HIGH FORAGER
This bird finds much of its food in the peeling bark of mature trees.

OCCURRENCE
Breeds in extensive, mature deciduous, and mixed woodlands in the eastern half of the US, and extreme southern Canada. Winters mainly from southern Mexico to northern South America, primarily in wooded areas.

SIMILAR SPECIES

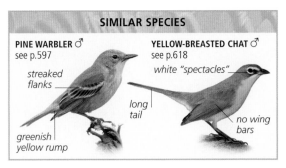

PINE WARBLER ♂ see p.597

streaked flanks

greenish yellow rump

YELLOW-BREASTED CHAT ♂ see p.618

white "spectacles"

long tail

no wing bars

| Length **5½in (14cm)** | Wingspan **9½in (24cm)** | Weight **⅝oz (18g)** |
| Social **Solitary/Pairs** | Lifespan **Up to 6 years** | Status **Secure** |

Order **Passeriformes**	Family **Vireonidae**	Species *Vireo plumbeus*

Plumbeous Vireo

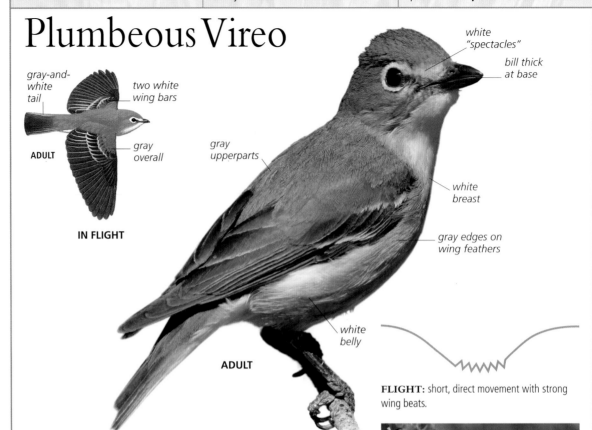

gray-and-white tail

two white wing bars

ADULT

IN FLIGHT

gray overall

gray upperparts

white "spectacles"

bill thick at base

white breast

gray edges on wing feathers

white belly

ADULT

FLIGHT: short, direct movement with strong wing beats.

This gray-and-white bird, with its conspicuous white "spectacles" and wing bars was recognized as a distinct species only in 1997. In that year, the bird formerly known as "Solitary Vireo" was split into three Vireo species—Cassin's, Blue-headed, and Plumbeous—based on genetic, plumage, and voice differences. The range of the Plumbeous Vireo has been expanding west since the 1940s and it can now be found alongside the greenish-toned Cassin's Vireo.

VOICE Call a harsh scold; male song a series of rough, slurred, two- or three-note phrases.

NESTING Loose, round cup of fibers, bound with spider webs, lined with fine material, suspended by rim from twigs; 3–5 eggs; 1 brood; April–June.

FEEDING Plucks insects from leaves or twigs, slowly hopping through foliage; often sallies to catch prey.

NEST COVER
This species tends to build its nest at the end of a branch and may cover it with lichens.

BIG VOICE
Like other vireos, the Male Plumbeous Vireo will often sing continuously.

OCCURRENCE
Breeds largely in coniferous or mountainous forests of the interior Southwest and down the Sierra Madre; found in Mexico through to Central America; also occurs close to rivers and streams in Arizona and New Mexico. Winters mostly on the Pacific Slope of Mexico.

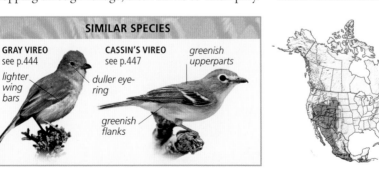

SIMILAR SPECIES

GRAY VIREO
see p.444

lighter wing bars

CASSIN'S VIREO
see p.447

duller eye-ring

greenish upperparts

greenish flanks

Length **5¾in (14.5cm)**	Wingspan **10in (25cm)**	Weight **⅝oz (18g)**
Social **Solitary**	Lifespan **Unknown**	Status **Secure**

Order **Passeriformes**	Family **Vireonidae**	Species *Vireo cassinii*

Cassin's Vireo

two whitish wing bars

ADULT

IN FLIGHT

dark patch between eye and bill

white "spectacles"

hooked bill

gray head

greenish gray back

ADULT

short tail

pale yellowish flanks

whitish belly

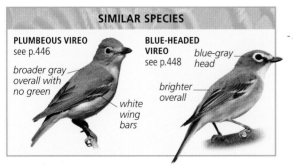

FLIGHT: short, direct movement with strong wing beats; can hover briefly.

Cassin's Vireo is similar to the closely related Plumbeous and Blue-headed Vireos in appearance and song. It is conspicuous and vocal throughout its breeding grounds in the far west of the US and north into southwest Canada. In winter, virtually the entire population migrates to Mexico. Cassin's Vireo was named in honor of John Cassin, who published the first comprehensive study of North American birds in 1865.

VOICE Call a harsh, scolding chatter; male's song a broken series of whistles, which ascend then descend; lower in tone than Blue-headed Vireo and higher than the Plumbeous.

NESTING Cup of fibers, lined with fine plant down; suspended from twigs; 2–5 eggs; 1–2 broods; April–July.

FEEDING Picks insects and spiders from leaves and twigs as it hops from branch to branch; occasionally sallies out or hovers.

TIRELESS SINGER
Cassin's Vireo is well known for its loud and incessant singing throughout the spring and into the summer.

SIMILAR SPECIES

PLUMBEOUS VIREO
see p.446

broader gray overall with no green

white wing bars

BLUE-HEADED VIREO
see p.448

blue-gray head

brighter overall

OCCURRENCE
Breeds in coniferous and mixed forests in the hills and mountains of British Columbia, Alberta, and, in the US, the Pacific Northwest through to southern California. Winters in western Mexico.

Length **5½in (14cm)**	Wingspan **9½in (24cm)**	Weight **9/16oz (16g)**
Social **Solitary/Pairs**	Lifespan **Unknown**	Status **Secure**

| Order **Passeriformes** | Family **Vireonidae** | Species *Vireo solitarius* |

Blue-headed Vireo

two wing bars

ADULT

greenish back

IN FLIGHT

gray head

looks "big-headed"

conspicuous white "spectacles"

contrasting white throat

ADULT

white belly

bright greenish flanks

relatively short tail

Closely related to the Cassin's Vireo and Plumbeous Vireo, the fairly common Blue-headed Vireo is the brightest and most colorful of the three. Its blue-gray, helmeted head, adorned with striking white "spectacles" around its dark eyes also helps to distinguish it from other vireos in its range. This stocky and slow moving bird is heard more often than it is seen in its forest breeding habitat. However, during migration it can be more conspicuous and, is the first vireo to return in spring.

VOICE Call a harsh, scolding chatter; male's song a series of rich, sweet, high phrases of two to six notes slurred together.

NESTING Shallow, rounded cup loosely constructed of animal and plant fibers, lined with finer material and suspended from twigs by the rim; 3–5 eggs; 2 broods; May–July.

FEEDING Gleans insects from branches and leaves, usually high in shrubs and trees; often makes short sallies after prey.

FLIGHT: slow, heavy, undulating flight with a series of deep wing beats followed by short pauses.

SPECTACLED VIREO
Its rather thick head with conspicuous "spectacles" and gray color are distinctive field marks.

SIMILAR SPECIES

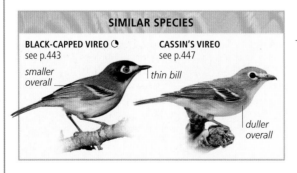

BLACK-CAPPED VIREO ☾
see p.443

smaller overall

CASSIN'S VIREO
see p.447

thin bill

duller overall

OCCURRENCE
Breeds in large tracts of undisturbed coniferous and mixed forests with a rich understory, largely across eastern North America. It winters in woodlands across the southeastern US from Virginia to Texas, as well as in Mexico and northern Central America to Costa Rica.

| Length **5½in (14in)** | Wingspan **9½in (24cm)** | Weight **⁹⁄₁₆oz (16g)** |
| Social **Solitary/Pairs** | Lifespan **Up to 7 years** | Status **Secure** |

| Order **Passeriformes** | Family **Vireonidae** | Species *Vireo huttoni* |

Hutton's Vireo

short, rounded wings

ADULT

IN FLIGHT

large, rounded head

pale patch

broken eye-ring

white wing bars

thick, hooked bill

ADULT

blue-gray legs

This unobtrusive bird is understood at present to be a geographically variable species with about a dozen subspecies. These subspecies can be grouped into two populations. The first is a coastal population occurring from British Columbia to Baja California; the second is an interior population found from the Southwest and south to Central America. These two isolated populations, widely separated by desert, may actually represent different species. Very similar in appearance to the Ruby-crowned Kinglet with which it flocks in winter, Hutton's Vireo is distinguishable by its larger size and thicker bill. Unlike other vireos, this bird is largely nonmigratory.

VOICE Varied calls include harsh mewing and nasal, raspy *spit*; male's song a repetition of a simple phrase.

NESTING Deep cup constructed from plant and animal fibers, lined with finer materials, often incorporating lichens, suspended from twigs by the rim; 3–5 eggs; 1–2 broods; February–May.

FEEDING Hops diligently from branch to branch searching for caterpillars, spiders, and flies; also eats berries; gleans from leaves usually while perched, but occasionally sallies or hovers.

FLIGHT: weak and bouncy with rapid wing beats.

FOLLOW THE SONG
This kinglet-sized vireo is easily overlooked and is often detected by its song.

SIMILAR SPECIES

PACIFIC SLOPE FLYCATCHER
see p.420

unbroken eye-ring

long tail

wide, flat bill

RUBY-CROWNED KINGLET ♂
see p.499

thin bill

smaller overall

OCCURRENCE
Year-round resident in mixed evergreen forests; particularly common in live oak woods. Breeds in mixed oak-pine woodlands along the Pacific coast from British Columbia southward to northern Baja California, and from southwest California and New Mexico to Mexico and Guatemala.

| Length **5in (13cm)** | Wingspan **8in (20cm)** | Weight **⅜oz (11g)** |
| Social **Solitary/Pairs** | Lifespan **Up to 13 years** | Status **Secure** |

Order **Passeriformes**	Family **Vireonidae**	Species *Vireo gilvus*

Warbling Vireo

pale brownish
crown contrasts
with darker back

grayish green
upperparts

blackish
bill

ADULT

white
eyebrow

grayish
behind eye

**ADULT
(FALL)**

IN FLIGHT

grayish
overall

pale
patch
between
eye
and bill

yellowish
flanks

ADULT

FLIGHT: fast and undulating; rapid wing beats followed by brief, closed-winged glides.

Widely distributed across North America, this rather drab vireo is better known for its cheerful warbling song than for its plumage, and coincidentally, its thin bill and longish tail give this rather active vireo a somewhat warbler-like appearance. The eastern subspecies (*V. g. gilvus*), which is heavier and has a larger bill, and the western subspecies (*V. g. swainsonii*) are quite different and may in fact be separate species. Out of all the vireos, the Warbling Vireo is most likely to breed in human developments, such as city parks, suburbs, and orchards.

VOICE Harsh, raspy scold call; male's persistent song a high, rapid, and highly variable warble.

NESTING Rough cup placed high in a deciduous tree, hung from the rim between forked twigs; 3–5 eggs; 2 broods; March–July.

FEEDING Gleans a variety of insects, including grasshoppers, aphids, and beetles from leaves; eats fruit in winter.

PLAIN-LOOKING SONGSTER
The Warbling Vireo makes up for its plain appearance by its colorful voice, full of rounded notes and melodious warbles.

SIMILAR SPECIES

BELL'S VIREO
see p.442

faint wing
bar

longer
tail

**PHILADELPHIA
VIREO**
see p.451

no wing
bar

dark line
extends
to bill

shorter
bill

yellow on
breast and
throat

OCCURRENCE
Extensive distribution across most of temperate North America, from Alaska, around the northern limit of the northerly zone, and through western, central, and eastern North America. Breeds in deciduous and mixed forests, particularly near water. Winters in southern Mexico and Central America.

Length **5½in (14cm)**	Wingspan **8½in (21cm)**	Weight **⁷⁄₁₆oz (12g)**
Social **Solitary/Pairs**	Lifespan **Up to 13 years**	Status **Secure**

Order **Passeriformes**	Family **Vireonidae**	Species *Vireo philadelphicus*

Philadelphia Vireo

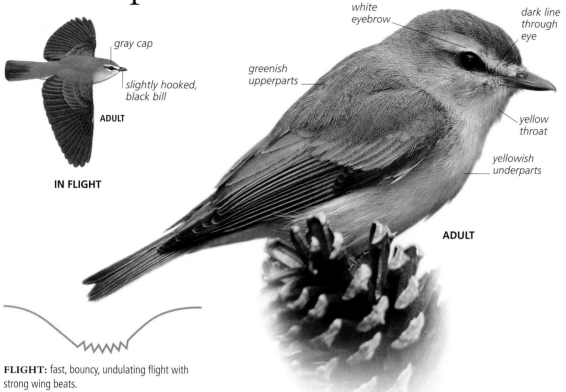

gray cap

slightly hooked, black bill

ADULT

IN FLIGHT

white eyebrow

dark line through eye

greenish upperparts

yellow throat

yellowish underparts

ADULT

FLIGHT: fast, bouncy, undulating flight with strong wing beats.

Despite being widespread, the Philadelphia Vireo remains rather poorly studied. It shares its breeding habitat with the similar looking, but larger and more numerous, Red-eyed Vireo, and, interestingly, it modifies its behavior to avoid competition. It is the most northerly breeding vireo, with its southernmost breeding range barely reaching the US. Its scientific and English names derive from the fact that the bird was first discovered near Philadelphia in the mid-19th century.

VOICE Song a series of two and four note phrases, remarkably similar to the song of the Red-eyed Vireo.

NESTING Rounded cup of plant fibers bound by spider webs, hanging between forked twigs that narrows at the rim; 3–5 eggs; 1–2 broods; June–August.

FEEDING Gleans caterpillars, bees, flies, and bugs from leaves; usually forages high in trees, moving with short hops and flights.

DISTINGUISHED APPEARANCE
The Philadelphia Vireo's gentle expression and pudgy appearance help separate it from its neighbor, the Red-eyed Vireo.

OCCURRENCE
Breeds in deciduous woodlands, mixed woodlands, and woodland edges, in a wide belt across Canada, reaching the Great Lakes and northern New England. The Philadelphia Vireo winters from Mexico to Panama and northern Colombia.

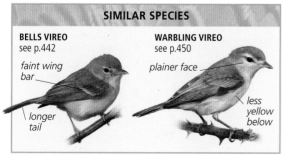

SIMILAR SPECIES

BELLS VIREO
see p.442

faint wing bar

longer tail

WARBLING VIREO
see p.450

plainer face

less yellow below

Length **5¼in (13.5cm)**	Wingspan **8in (20cm)**	Weight **⁷⁄₁₆oz (12g)**
Social **Solitary/Pairs**	Lifespan **Up to 8 years**	Status **Secure**

| Order **Passeriformes** | Family **Vireonidae** | Species *Vireo olivaceus* |

Red-eyed Vireo

gray crown

heavy eye-line

white eyestripe with black upper border

long bill

deep red eye

ADULT

whitish underparts

bluish legs and toes

generally olive above

head held at downward angle

ADULT

bird appears long and slender

IN FLIGHT

Probably the most common songbird of northern and eastern North America, the Red-eyed Vireo is perhaps the quintessential North American vireo, although it is heard far more often than it is seen. It sings persistently and monotonously all day long and late into the season, long after other species have stopped singing. It generally stays high in the canopy of the deciduous and mixed woodlands where it breeds. The entire population migrates to central South America in winter. To reach their Amazonian winter habitats, Red-eyed Vireos migrate in fall (August–October) through Central America, Caribbean Islands, and northern South America to Educador, Peru, and Brazil.

VOICE Nasal mewing call; male song consists of slurred three-note phrases.

NESTING Open cup nest hanging on horizontal fork of tree branch; built with plant fibers bound with spider's web; exterior is sometimes decorated with lichen; 3–5 eggs; 1 brood; May–July.

FEEDING Gleans insects from leaves, hopping methodically in the canopy and sub-canopy of deciduous trees; during fall and winter, primarily feeds on fruit.

FLIGHT: fast, strong, and undulating with the body angled upwards.

HOPPING BIRD
The Red-eyed Vireo's primary form of locomotion is hopping; at ground level and in trees.

OCCURRENCE
Breeds across North America from the Yukon and British Columbia east to the Canadian maritimes, southward from Washington to south central Texas, and west to Canada in central and northern states. Inhabits the canopy of deciduous forests and pine hardwood forests.

SIMILAR SPECIES

BLACK-WHISKERED VIREO
see p.453

faint black "mustache"

duller green upperparts

BROWN EYES
Immature Red-eyed Vireos have brown eyes, but those of the adult birds are red.

| Length **6in (15cm)** | Wingspan **10in (25cm)** | Weight **⅝oz (17g)** |
| Social **Solitary/Pairs** | Lifespan **Up to 10 years** | Status **Secure** |

Order **Passeriformes**	Family **Vireonidae**	Species *Vireo altiloquus*

Black-whiskered Vireo

brownish green above

ADULT

IN FLIGHT

brownish back with green tinge

no wing bars

black "whiskers"

red eye

long bill

creamy-colored flanks

ADULT

FLIGHT: direct flight with rapid wing beats; short flights between perches.

The Black-whiskered Vireo is a Caribbean breeder that is restricted to mangrove and hardwood forests on both coasts of southern Florida. During migration (October–November), it can also be found along the Gulf and Atlantic coasts. Its restricted range and habitat and secretive habits make this bird difficult to spot. Its song, however, is distinctive, with phrases ending on alternate ascending and descending notes.

VOICE Nasal mewing call; male song a series of loud, clear one to four note phrases with distinct pauses between them.

NESTING Cup suspended by rim from forked twigs; woven of grass, lichens, and spider webs; 2–4 eggs; 1 brood; May–July.

FEEDING Hops slowly among upper branches gleaning insects and fruit; rarely takes prey from air.

THE BIRD WITH "WHISKERS"
Its long bill and usually conspicuous black "whiskers" help distinguish this species from the similar Red-eyed Vireo.

MANGROVES AND MORE
Found in mangroves and hardwood hammocks, it can also be seen in other habitats during migration.

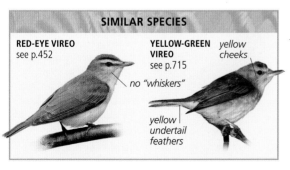

SIMILAR SPECIES

RED-EYE VIREO see p.452

YELLOW-GREEN VIREO see p.715

yellow cheeks

no "whiskers"

yellow undertail feathers

OCCURRENCE
In the US, found only in mangrove and hardwood forests of coastal Florida, from the Atlantic coast, along the Gulf of Mexico, to the Florida Keys. Also breeds on a number of Caribbean Islands. Winters in Hispaniola (rare) and South America from Colombia and Venezuela to Amazonian Brazil.

Length **6½in (16cm)**	Wingspan **10in (26cm)**	Weight **⅝oz (18g)**
Social **Solitary/Pairs**	Lifespan **Unknown**	Status **Localized**

| Order **Passeriformes** | Family **Corvidae** | Species *Perisoreus canadensis* |

Gray Jay

ADULT

brownish back with white streaks

P. c. obscurus **(NORTHWESTERN)**

dark gray upperparts

long, tail with white corners

IN FLIGHT

gray overall, darker upperparts

white collar

dark crown

white forehead

short bill

whitish "mustache"

uniform medium to dark gray

JUVENILE

dark, smoky gray tail and wings

black legs and toes

P. c. canadensis **(NORTHERN)**

Fearless and cunning, the Gray Jay can often be a nuisance to campers due to its inquisitive behavior. It is particularly adept at stealing food and shiny metal objects, which has earned it the colloquial name of "Camp Robber." One of the interesting aspects of its behavior is the way it stores food for later use, by sticking it to trees with its viscous saliva. This is thought to be one of the reasons that enable it to survive the long northern winters. Gray Jays can often collect in noisy groups of three to six birds in order to investigate intruders encroaching upon their territory.

VOICE Mostly silent, but also produces variety of odd clucks and screeches; sometimes Blue Jay-like *jay!* and eerie whistles, including bisyllabic *whee-oo* or *ew*.

NESTING Bulky platform of sticks with cocoons on south side of coniferous tree; 2–5 eggs; 1 brood; February–May.

FEEDING Forages for insects and berries; also raids birds' nests.

FLIGHT: hollow-sounding wing beats followed by slow, seemingly awkward, rocking glides.

BUILT FOR COLD
The Gray Jay's short extremities and dense, fluffy plumage are perfect for long, harsh winters.

SIMILAR SPECIES

CLARK'S NUTCRAKER see p.464

white wing patch

NORTHERN MOCKINGBIRD see p.519

no dark crown

longer bill

longer tail

white wing patch

OCCURRENCE
Northerly forests, especially lichen-festooned areas with firs and spruces. Found in coniferous forests across northern North America from Alaska to Newfoundland, the Maritimes, and north New York and New England; south to the western mountains; an isolated population in the Black Hills.

| Length **10–11½in (25–29cm)** | Wingspan **18in (46cm)** | Weight **2⅛–2⅞oz (60–80g)** |
| Social **Family groups** | Lifespan **Up to 10 years** | Status **Secure** |

| Order **Passeriformes** | Family **Corvidae** | Species ***Cyanocorax yncas*** |

Green Jay

conspicuous yellow outer tail feathers

ADULT

IN FLIGHT

long, bluish green tail with yellow outer tail feathers

green upperparts

complex, blue-and-black facial pattern

blue nape and crown

black bill

white band on forehead flanked by black tufts

green or yellow underparts

black bib

ADULT

ADULT

tail yellow undertail

This brightly colored jay is restricted to southern Texas, where it is known locally as the "Rio Grande Jay." It is a common and conspicuous species, and will readily take food from birdfeeders. Away from birdfeeders, the Green Jay remains secretive, but it is relatively easy to locate by its remarkably varied vocal repertoire. It is a nonmigratory bird, and does not often wander far from where it nests, but it is occasionally known to form foraging flocks and fly to open country after breeding. However, it can be fairly aggressive to other unrelated Green Jays in the breeding season, if they trespass on its territory. A white-naped, yellow-eyed, indigo-crested population in South America may constitute a separate species: the Inca Jay.

VOICE A noisy, harsh, scolding *yank*; also soft, mewing calls; both sexes make an odd, bass-pitched clicking buzz, during the breeding season.

NESTING Platform of thorny twigs and roots, in thickets, shrubs, or trees, lined with grass and leaves; 3–5 eggs; 1 brood; April–June.

FEEDING Forages on the ground and tree trunks and limbs for insects; also eats fruits, berries, and seeds.

FLIGHT: short periods of quick flapping followed by prolonged glides, like most jays.

COMING IN TO FEED
Green Jays are common at feeding stations in the Rio Grande Valley's many nature parks.

HANGING OUT
This Green Jay reveals the bright yellow under its tail as it hangs on to a branch.

OCCURRENCE
Lives in woodland and scrubby thickets along the Rio Grande, where it is abundant. From this northernmost pocket in its range, the Green Jay occurs southward through Mexico, Central America, and South America to Bolivia.

| Length **10–11½in (25–29cm)** | Wingspan **13½in (34cm)** | Weight **2⅛–3¼oz (62–92g)** |
| Social **Flocks** | Lifespan **Up to 10 years** | Status **Localized** |

| Order **Passeriformes** | Family **Corvidae** | Species *Cyanocitta cristata* |

Blue Jay

long tail with white corners

white streak in blue wings

ADULT

white trailing edge feathers

IN FLIGHT

blue crest

black patch between eye and bill

black collar

plain blue mantle

blue wings and tail

long, black bill

whitish throat

ADULT

grayish underparts

black legs and feet

black bars on tail

The Blue Jay is one of the best known birds in North America; it is loud, flashy, and common in rural and suburban backyards across the eastern US. Beautiful as it is, the Blue Jay has a darker side. It often raids the nests of smaller birds for eggs and nestlings. Although usually thought of as a nonmigratory species, some Blue Jays undergo impressive migrations, with loose flocks sometimes numbering in the hundreds visible overhead in spring and fall.

VOICE Harsh, screaming *jay! jay!;* other common call an odd ethereal, chortling *queedle-ee-dee;* soft clucks when feeding.

NESTING Cup of strong twigs at variable height in trees or shrubs; 3–6 eggs; 1 brood; March–July.

FEEDING Eats insects, acorns, small vertebrates, such as lizards, rodents, bird eggs, birds, tree frogs; fruits and seeds.

FLIGHT: bursts of flapping followed by long glides on flat wings.

UNIQUE FEATURES
The Blue Jay is unique among Americans jays, in having white patches on its wings and tail.

VERSATILE BIRD
Blue Jays are true omnivores, eating almost anything they can find. They are also excellent imitators of other bird calls.

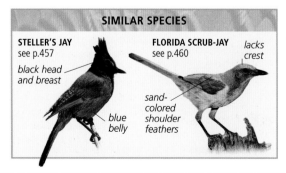

SIMILAR SPECIES

STELLER'S JAY
see p.457

black head and breast

blue belly

FLORIDA SCRUB-JAY
see p.460

lacks crest

sand-colored shoulder feathers

OCCURRENCE
Native to eastern deciduous, coniferous, and mixed woodlands, but also at home in suburban vegetation; found extensively in backyards. A generally nonmigratory bird, the Blue Jay is especially fond of oak trees and their acorns.

| Length **9½–12in (24–30cm)** | Wingspan **16in (41cm)** | Weight **2¼–3½oz (65–100g)** |
| Social **Small flocks** | Lifespan **Up to 7 years** | Status **Secure** |

| Order **Passeriformes** | Family **Corvidae** | Species *Cyanocitta stelleri* |

Steller's Jay

long, blue tail

black head and shoulder

ADULT (INTERIOR)

IN FLIGHT

white markings on face

slightly darker back

long, straight bill

deep blue belly

C. s. macrolopha **(INTERIOR)**

blue wings barred with black

long, black crest

bluish markings on face

dark back and shoulder

blue belly and breast

C. s. stelleri **(PACIFIC)**

black feet and legs

―――――〜〜〜―――――

FLIGHT: bursts of flapping interspersed with glides on flat wings.

The "Blue Jay of the West," Steller's Jay has a blackish breast and mantle, conspicuously crested head, and deep blue body, but plumage varies among local populations. Contrasting head markings are blue in coastal populations, white in the interior, and absent in the Queen Charlotte Islands. This species is often found scavenging at campsites and roadsides.

VOICE Series of harsh, short, rasping notes, *shek, shek, shek;* single longer pitch-changing *shuhrrrr.*

NESTING Bulky twig and mud nest, lined with finer plant fibers, close to trunk of tree; 2–6 eggs; 1 brood; March–June.

FEEDING Opportunistic feeder, eats acorns, pine nuts, fruit; also insects and spiders; small vertebrates such as lizards and rodents; also raids birds' nests.

ON THE LOOKOUT
Like most members of the corvid family, Steller's Jays appoint a lookout to keep watch while others in the flock feed nearby.

SIMILAR SPECIES

BLUE JAY see p.456
short blue crest
grayish white below

WESTERN SCRUB-JAY see p.459
white eyebrow
whitish below

OCCURRENCE
Found mainly in montane coniferous and mixed forests; but also in adjacent broad-leafed habitats; and occasionally, in winter, makes sudden migrations to lower elevations, east onto the Great Plains. Interbreeds locally with the Blue Jay where their ranges cross in the Rockies.

| Length **11–12½in (28–32cm)** | Wingspan **19in (48cm)** | Weight **3½–5oz (100–150g)** |
| Social **Small flocks** | Lifespan **Up to 15 years** | Status **Secure** |

| Order **Passeriformes** | Family **Corvidae** | Species *Aphelocoma ultramarina* |

Mexican Jay

long, pale blue tail

pale gray back

ADULT (A. u. couchii)

IN FLIGHT

blue wing feathers

long, blue tail

whitish undertail feathers

dark blue cheeks

black patch between eye and bill

pale gray back

robust, grayish black bill

pale gray underparts

ADULT (A. u. couchii)

black legs and feet

grayish back

ADULT (A. u. arizonae)

The bell-like calls from a flock of Mexican Jays is a familiar sound in the pine-oak canyons of Mexico and the adjacent US. Mexican Jays have a fascinating social breeding system. Instead of territorial pairs, they form territorial flocks, within which females mate with several males. Nestlings are not fed only by their parents, but also by other members of the flock, including other birds who have failed to breed. In winter, Northern Flickers can often be found near Mexican Jays; the Flickers use the Jays' warning calls to protect themselves from predators.
VOICE Rapid-fire, ringing *wink, wink*; harsher and less bell-like in Texas population, which also gives rattle call similar to scrub-jays.
NESTING Cup of dead, usually juniper twigs lined with fibers, in trees; 3–5 eggs; 1 brood; March–July.
FEEDING Feeds on arthropods, such as crickets; lizards in summer; acorns and pine nuts in winter.

FLIGHT: loud, hollow-sounding bouts of flapping followed by long glides on flat wings.

OCCURRENCE
Resident in mountain woodlands of pine-oak-juniper, especially in canyons. Birds from Arizona and New Mexico (usually subspecies *arizonae*) are duller-colored than those from Texas (subspecies *couchii*).

SIMILAR SPECIES

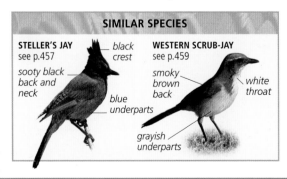

STELLER'S JAY see p.457
sooty black back and neck
black crest
blue underparts

WESTERN SCRUB-JAY see p.459
smoky brown back
white throat
grayish underparts

DULL COLORED
The latin name for this jay means "intense blue," ignoring its drab gray breast.

| Length **11–12½in (28–32cm)** | Wingspan **19½in (50cm)** | Weight **3½–5oz (100–150g)** |
| Social **Flocks** | Lifespan **Up to 20 years** | Status **Secure** |

| Order **Passeriformes** | Family **Corvidae** | Species *Aphelocoma californica* |

Western Scrub-Jay

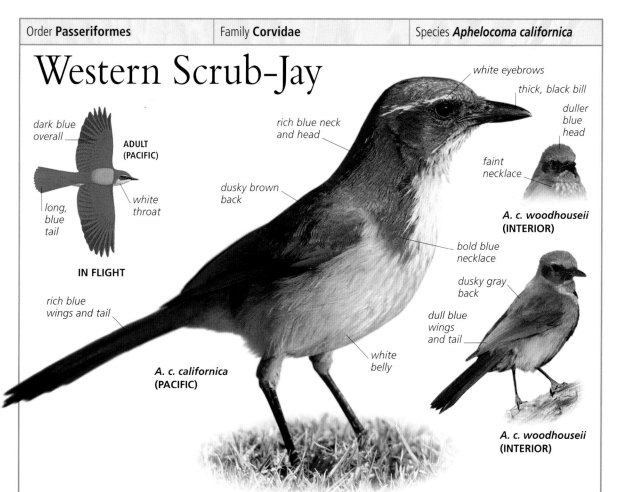

white eyebrows

thick, black bill

duller blue head

dark blue overall

ADULT (PACIFIC)

rich blue neck and head

faint necklace

A. c. woodhouseii (INTERIOR)

long, blue tail

white throat

dusky brown back

IN FLIGHT

bold blue necklace

dusky gray back

rich blue wings and tail

dull blue wings and tail

A. c. californica (PACIFIC)

white belly

A. c. woodhouseii (INTERIOR)

This species comprises three subspecies, two of which occur in the US, and the third, *A. c. sumichrasti*, in Mexico. The "Pacific" Scrub-Jay (*A. c. californica*) has bright-blue upperparts with a brownish shoulder, and whitish underparts with a bold blue breastband. The "Interior" Scrub-Jay (*A. c. woodhouseii*) has duller upperparts with a grayish shoulder, and dusky underparts with a very faint breastband; it also has a longer, straighter bill than the "Pacific." The "Interior" Scrub-Jay is shy and furtive, and is seen fleeing into bushes—if it is seen at all—whereas the "Pacific" subspecies is tame and bold, and is even found in backyards.
VOICE Varied, usually harsh, questioning, rising *rehnk*, vaguely robin-like *quill, quill*, and dry, hollow rattle.
NESTING Open cup of twigs lined with fibers and hair, concealed in shrub or tree; 2–6 eggs; 1 brood; March–July.
FEEDING Feeds on insects, fruits, acorns, and pine nuts.

FLIGHT: swift; slightly undulating; flurries of wing beats followed by weak glides.

HOME SWEET HOME
Western Scrub-Jays, especially the "Interior" subspecies, prefer to live in juniper scrubs.

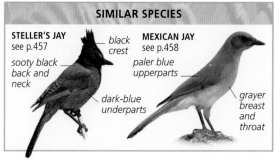

SIMILAR SPECIES

STELLER'S JAY see p.457

black crest

sooty black back and neck

dark-blue underparts

MEXICAN JAY see p.458

paler blue upperparts

grayer breast and throat

OCCURRENCE
The "Pacific" Scrub-Jay is found in suburbia and oak and riverside woodlands; the "Interior" subspecies is found in lower-elevation mountainous oak-pinyon-juniper scrub; the "Interior" occasionally makes sudden trips into the lowlands in winter, east into the Great Plains.

| Length **10–12in (26–31cm)** | Wingspan **15½in (40cm)** | Weight **2⅞–3½oz (80–100g)** |
| Social **Small flocks** | Lifespan **Up to 15 years** | Status **Secure** |

| Order **Passeriformes** | Family **Corvidae** | Species ***Aphelocoma coerulescens*** |

Florida Scrub-Jay

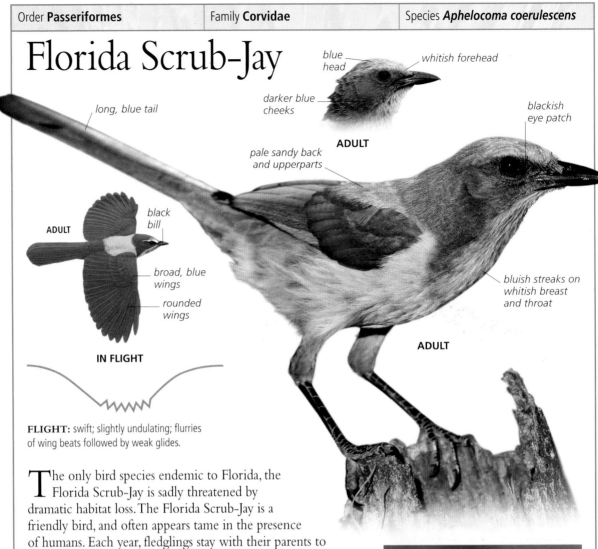

long, blue tail

blue head

whitish forehead

darker blue cheeks

ADULT

blackish eye patch

pale sandy back and upperparts

ADULT

black bill

broad, blue wings

rounded wings

IN FLIGHT

bluish streaks on whitish breast and throat

ADULT

FLIGHT: swift; slightly undulating; flurries of wing beats followed by weak glides.

The only bird species endemic to Florida, the Florida Scrub-Jay is sadly threatened by dramatic habitat loss. The Florida Scrub-Jay is a friendly bird, and often appears tame in the presence of humans. Each year, fledglings stay with their parents to help raise the next brood. Their feeding groups are often highly organized—while some birds hunt for food, others remain with the young, performing sentry duty to defend territory and keep predators away. The sentries give different warning calls to their group to distinguish between aerial and terrestrial predators. The Florida Scrub-Jay was once grouped with Western and Island Scrub-Jays as one species, the Scrub Jay.

VOICE Harsh, raspy notes, including a rolling *kreep*.
NESTING Open, bulky cup of oak twigs lined with palmetto fibers, concealed in low dense shrub; 2–5 eggs; 1 brood; March–July.
FEEDING Feeds on acorns; insects, spiders, and snails.

A LIVING RELIC
The Jays inhabit what is left of the extensive belt of dry oak scrub that used to stretch across the South.

OCCURRENCE
Restricted to short, fire-maintained evergreen oak scrub in Florida. Its specialized habitat is under threat from encroaching agricultural land and residential and industrial property development.

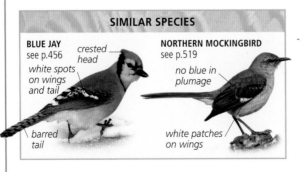

SIMILAR SPECIES

BLUE JAY
see p.456

crested head

white spots on wings and tail

barred tail

NORTHERN MOCKINGBIRD
see p.519

no blue in plumage

white patches on wings

| Length **10–11½in (25–29cm)** | Wingspan **13½in (34cm)** | Weight **2½–3oz (70–84g)** |
| Social **Family groups** | Lifespan **Up to 15 years** | Status **Vulnerable** |

Order **Passeriformes**	Family **Corvidae**	Species *Gymnorhinus cyanocephalus*

Pinyon Jay

short, square tail

ADULT

broad wings

IN FLIGHT

darker blue head

dull blue upperparts

strong, straight, nutcracker-like bill

duller and grayer upperparts

small, pink base of bill

JUVENILE

ADULT

black legs

FLIGHT: direct with constant, stiff flapping; often in tight, wheeling flocks.

Named after the pinyon pine, Pinyon Jays have coevolved along with the nuts of this pine called piñones. As a result of this, the species is restricted mostly to the western pinyon-juniper hills. Unlike most other members of the *Corvidae* family, the base of the Pinyon Jay's bill is featherless. This allows it to feed on the pith deep within pine cones, while keeping the feathers that cover its nostrils clean. Pinyons form long-term partnerships, yet nest in colonies that sometimes number into the hundreds.

VOICE Far-carrying, upslurred *howah, howah, howah* in flight.

NESTING Well-insulated, three layered cup on south side of tree or shrub; 3–5 eggs; 1–2 broods; February–May, sometimes also in fall if pine cones are plentiful.

FEEDING Feeds on piñones, other nuts, fruits, and insects; will also raid nests for eggs and hawk for insects.

PINE SPECIALIST
Pinyon Jays specialize in eating pine nuts from Ponderosas and their namesake pinyons.

OCCURRENCE
Nomadic, seeking out ripe piñones; restricted to foothills and plateaus covered by piñon-juniper scrub; less common in drier, open Ponderosa pine, especially if juniper understory present; flocks may descend into lower elevations in the fall and winter.

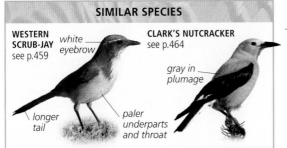

SIMILAR SPECIES

WESTERN SCRUB-JAY see p.459

white eyebrow

CLARK'S NUTCRACKER see p.464

gray in plumage

longer tail

paler underparts and throat

Length **10–11in (25–28cm)**	Wingspan **19in (48cm)**	Weight **3½oz (100g)**
Social **Colonies**	Lifespan **Up to 15 years**	Status **Vulnerable**

| Order **Passeriformes** | Family **Corvidae** | Species *Pica hudsonia* |

Black-billed Magpie

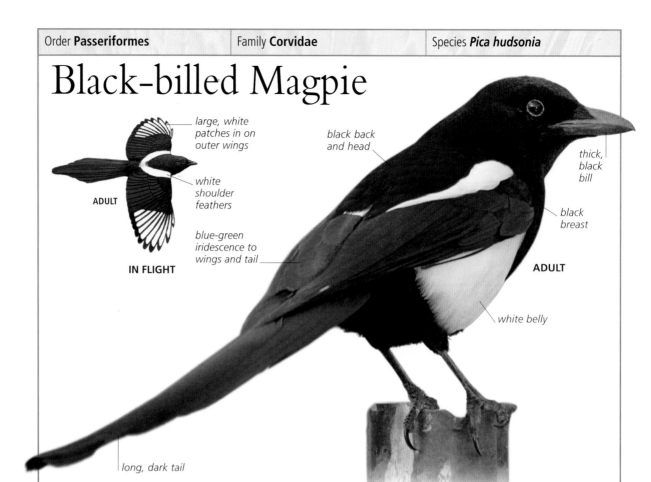

large, white patches in on outer wings

ADULT

white shoulder feathers

IN FLIGHT

blue-green iridescence to wings and tail

black back and head

thick, black bill

black breast

ADULT

white belly

long, dark tail

Loud, flashy, and conspicuous, the Black-billed Magpie is abundant in the northwestern quarter of the continent, from Alaska to the interior of the US. It has adapted to suburbia, confidently strutting across front lawns in some places. Until recently, it was considered the same species as the Eurasian Magpie (*P. pica*), and even though they look nearly identical, scientific evidence points instead to a close relationship with the other North American magpie, the Yellow-billed Magpie. Its long tail enables it to make rapid changes in direction in flight. The male will also use his tail to perform a variety of displays while courting a female. Black-billed Magpies are rarely found in large flocks; but they form sometimes in fall.

VOICE Common call a questioning, nasal *ehnk*; also raspy *shenk, shenk, shenk*, usually in series.

NESTING Large, domed, often made of thorny sticks; 5–8 eggs; 1 brood; March–June.

FEEDING Omnivorous; forages on ground, mainly for insects, worms, seeds and carrion; even picks ticks from mammals.

FLIGHT: direct, with slow, steady, and often shallow wing beats; occasional shallow glides.

IRIDESCENT SHEEN
In bright sunlight, beautiful iridescent blues, greens, golds, and purples appear on the wings and tail.

SIMILAR SPECIES

YELLOW-BILLED MAGPIE
see p.463

yellow bill

yellow patch around eye

OCCURRENCE
Found in open habitats, foothills, and plains of the western US and Canada; nests in streamside vegetation; persecution has made it wary and restricted to wilderness in some areas, but in others it has adapted to suburbs of towns and cities.

| Length **17–19½in (43–50cm)** | Wingspan **25in (63cm)** | Weight **6–7oz (175–200g)** |
| Social **Small flocks** | Lifespan **Up to 15 years** | Status **Secure** |

Order **Passeriformes**	Family **Corvidae**	Species *Pica nuttalli*

Yellow-billed Magpie

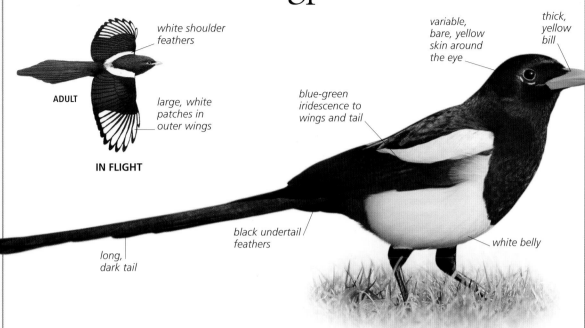

white shoulder feathers

ADULT

large, white patches in outer wings

IN FLIGHT

variable, bare, yellow skin around the eye

thick, yellow bill

blue-green iridescence to wings and tail

black undertail feathers

long, dark tail

white belly

ADULT

The striking Yellow-billed Magpie is endemic to California, but although it is a common species, it tends to be sporadically distributed within its range. Other than its yellow bill, small, bare, yellow patch beneath its eye, and smaller average size, there is little to distinguish the Yellow-billed from its close relative, the Black-billed Magpie. However, it is bolder and more social than the Black-billed, even nesting in loose colonies, but never with more than one pair to a tree. The Yellow-billed Magpie cannot tolerate extremes in temperature, which explains its localized distribution in sheltered valleys. Immature birds have less iridescent plumage than adults.

VOICE Whining *mag* call; also a series of *kwah-kwah-kwah*; similar to Black-billed Magpie, but higher-pitched and less harsh.

NESTING Dome of mud and sticks in outer branches of trees, commonly mistletoe, often oak; 5–7 eggs; 1 brood; March–June.

FEEDING Omnivorous; walks and hops along ground, foraging for insects, worms, seeds, acorns, carrion, and small mammals.

FLIGHT: direct, with slow, steady wing beats, and shallow glides.

BARE PATCH
The size and placement of the patch of bare yellow facial skin is variable.

LIMITED RANGE
It can only be found in an area roughly 500 miles (800km) long and 150 miles (240km) wide.

OCCURRENCE
Oak savannah, orchards, and other open habitats with widely spaced trees; also found in areas with close proximity to rivers and streams. The place of origin of strays far outside this area is difficult to determine.

SIMILAR SPECIES

BLACK-BILLED MAGPIE
different range; see p.462

black bill

slightly larger overall

Length **15–17½in (38–45cm)**	Wingspan **24in (61cm)**	Weight **5–6oz (150–175g)**
Social **Small flocks**	Lifespan **Up to 10 years**	Status **Secure**

| Order **Passeriformes** | Family **Corvidae** | Species **Nucifraga columbiana** |

Clark's Nutcracker

ADULT

white patches on black wings

IN FLIGHT

gray body

long, black wings

ADULT

strong, straight bill

paler face

ADULT

black central tail feathers

totally white tail from below

white undertail feathers

A bird of the mountainous western wilderness, Clark's Nutcracker is a highly intelligent species that frequents popular scenic overlooks, where it begs for food from visitors. This species gets its name from its dependence on pine nuts, which it forcefully extracts using its powerful feet and chisel-like bill. When food is abundant, nutcrackers hide it in caches—a special throat pouch enables them to carry up to 100 pine nuts per trip. The species was discovered by the explorers Lewis and Clark on their early 19th-century journey across the Louisiana Purchase.

VOICE Call a harsh, nasal, rolling rattle, often paired *kraaaa, kraaaa*; also mellower down-slurred *weee-uh*, and frog-like rattle.

NESTING Fine inner cup on stick platform on the side of tree away from trunk; 2–5 eggs; 1 brood; March–June.

FEEDING Hawks insects and raids nests; eats insects, spiders, and carrion.

FLIGHT: direct and even, with slow, deep wing beats.

CRACKING NUTS
Nutcrackers, such as Pinyon Jays, specialize in eating the seeds from pine cones.

SIMILAR SPECIES

GRAY JAY *white forehead*
see p.454

longer tail

shorter bill

PINYON JAY
see p.461

blue body

lacks black and white on tail

OCCURRENCE
Restricted to coniferous forests, especially those dominated by large-seeded pines in southwest Canda and US mountains; found higher up in summer; sudden journeys in massive flocks periodically into lower elevations and Great Plains when cone crops fail, otherwise resident.

| Length **12in (31cm)** | Wingspan **24in (62cm)** | Weight **4–5oz (125–150g)** |
| Social **Pairs/Flocks** | Lifespan **Up to 17 years** | Status **Secure** |

Order **Passeriformes**	Family **Corvidae**	Species **Corvus brachyrhynchos**

American Crow

black overall

ADULT

IN FLIGHT

black overall, with greenish sheen

long, black bill

dull black overall

shorter bill

ADULT

JUVENILE

strong legs and feet

One of the most widespread and familiar of North American birds, the American Crow is common in almost all habitats—from wilderness to urban centers. Like most birds with large ranges, there is substantial geographical variation in this species. Birds are black across the whole continent, but size and bill shape vary from region to region. The birds of the coastal Pacific Northwest (*C. b. hesperis*), are on average smaller and have a lower-pitched voice; Floridian birds (*C. b. pascuus*) are more solitary and warier than most.

VOICE Call a loud, familiar *caw!*; juveniles' call higher-pitched.
NESTING Stick base with finer inner cup; 3–7 eggs; 1 brood; April–June.
FEEDING Feeds omnivorously on fruit, carrion, garbage, insects, spiders; raids nests.

FLIGHT: direct and level with slow, steady flapping; does not soar.

LOOKING AROUND
Extremely inquisitive, American Crows are always on the look-out for food or something of interest.

SIMILAR SPECIES

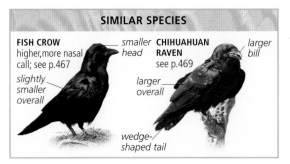

FISH CROW
higher, more nasal call; see p.467

smaller head

slightly smaller overall

CHIHUAHUAN RAVEN
see p.469

larger bill

larger overall

wedge-shaped tail

OCCURRENCE
Often seen converging on favored roosting areas; most numerous in relatively open areas with widely spaced, large trees; has become abundant in some cities; a partial migrant, some populations are more migratory than others.

Length **15½–19½in (39–49cm)**	Wingspan **3ft (1m)**	Weight **15–22oz (425–625g)**
Social **Social**	Lifespan **Up to 15 years**	Status **Secure**

| Order **Passeriformes** | Family **Corvidae** | Species *Corvus caurinus* |

Northwestern Crow

square tail

ADULT

long wings

IN FLIGHT

dark brown-black eyes

bluish black upperparts

relatively small, thick bill

folded wings shorter than tail

black underparts

ADULT

strong, black legs and feet

FLIGHT: direct and level with slow, steady flapping; does not soar.

Although smaller, with a lower-pitched voice than the American Crow, the Northwestern Crow is very similar to the American Crow subspecies, *C. b. hesperis*. In fact, ornithologists are still debating how closely related the Northwestern and American Crows actually are. Among its feeding habits, the Northwestern Crow is known to dig for clams, pry open barnacles, chase crabs, and catch small fish. It often feeds and roosts in large flocks.

VOICE Varied, but most common call a loud, familiar *caw!* lower, raspier, and more rapid than most American Crows.
NESTING Stick base with fine inner cup, placed on ground or in trees; 3–6 eggs; 1 brood; April–June.
FEEDING Raids nests; eats fruit, carrion, garbage, mollusks, and stranded sea life from areas between the high- and low-tide marks.

BEACHCOMBER
Like the Fish Crow of the northeast US, the Northwestern Crow searches for prey items along coastlines.

SIMILAR SPECIES

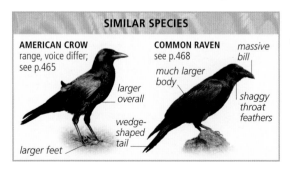

AMERICAN CROW
range, voice differ;
see p.465

larger overall

larger feet

COMMON RAVEN
see p.468

massive bill

much larger body

shaggy throat feathers

wedge-shaped tail

OCCURRENCE
Restricted to coastal areas from Alaska to Washington state, where it is found in tidal pools, refuse dumps, towns, and urban areas; avoids dense forest. It can be found along rivers at higher elevation inland.

| Length **13–16in (33–41cm)** | Wingspan **34in (86cm)** | Weight **11–16oz (325–450g)** |
| Social **Flocks** | Lifespan **Up to 15 years** | Status **Secure** |

Order **Passeriformes**	Family **Corvidae**	Species **Corvus ossifragus**

Fish Crow

dark brown-black eyes

long, square tail

ADULT

long wings

IN FLIGHT

slender neck and head

bluish black glossy sheen

thick, glossy black bill

slightly shaggy throat feathers

black overall

ADULT

strong, black legs and feet

The Fish Crow is, in many respects, the East Coast version of the Northwestern Crow. Like the Northwestern Crow, it is a highly social species, and not only forages in flocks but also breeds in small colonies. The Fish Crow is common along the eastern seaboard of the US, where it occurs alongside the nearly identical, but slightly larger, American Crow. The Fish Crow is also distinguishable as it has a higher-pitched and more nasal call. Its Latin species name *ossifragus* translates as "bone-breaker."
VOICE Call a paired *ehn uhn* with the second note lower.
NESTING Bulky stick platform with finer inner bowl in fork of tree, often high up; 3–5 eggs; 1 brood; April–August.
FEEDING Takes arthropods such as crabs and insects, small live fish and reptiles, nestling birds, bird and turtle eggs, fruit, carrion, and garbage; notorious for raiding nests in heron rookeries.

FLIGHT: rowing motion with quick, snappy wing beats; soars occasionally.

OMNIVORE
Fish Crows are numerous along coastlines and riverbanks where they eat virtually anything edible.

SIMILAR SPECIES

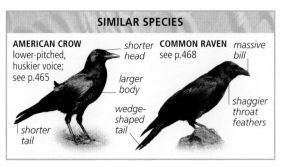

AMERICAN CROW
lower-pitched, huskier voice; see p.465

shorter head

larger body

shorter tail

wedge-shaped tail

COMMON RAVEN
see p.468

massive bill

shaggier throat feathers

OCCURRENCE
Found in lowland coastal and riverbank habitats such as beaches, estuaries, and marshes; also found inland and near human stuctures such as parking lots in suburban malls. Northern populations appear to be migratory.

Length **14–16in (36–41cm)**	Wingspan **36in (91cm)**	Weight **8–11oz (225–325g)**
Social **Flocks**	Lifespan **Up to 15 years**	Status **Secure**

| Order **Passeriformes** | Family **Corvidae** | Species **_Corvus corax_** |

Common Raven

ADULT

IN FLIGHT

long, black wings

flared outer wing feathers

large, protruding head

black upperparts, with purplish gloss

thick, long bill, with pronounced curvature

shaggy throat

dark gray neck and underparts

ADULT

long, black legs and feet

The Common Raven is twice the size of the American Crow, a bird of Viking legend, literature, and scientific wonder. Its Latin name, _Corvux corax_, means "crow of crows." Ravens are perhaps the most brilliant of all birds: they learn quickly, adapt to new circumstances with remarkable mental agility, and communicate with each other through an array of vocal and motional behaviors. They are master problem solvers and deceivers, tricking each other with ingenious methods.

VOICE Varied vocalizations, including hoarse, rolling _krruuk_, twangy peals, guttural clicks, and resonant _bonks_.
NESTING Platform of sticks with fine inner material on trees, cliffs, or man-made structure; 4–5 eggs; 1 brood; March–June.
FEEDING Feeds omnivorously on carrion, small crustaceans, fish, rodents, fruit, grain, and garbage; also raids nests.

FLIGHT: slow, steady, and direct; can also be quite acrobatic; commonly soars.

SHARING INFORMATION
Ravens in flocks can communicate information about food sources.

SIMILAR SPECIES

AMERICAN CROW lacks shaggy throat feathers; see p.465

CHIHUAHUAN RAVEN see p.469

smaller bill

much smaller overall

lacks wedge-shaped tail

slightly smaller overall

OCCURRENCE
Found in almost every kind of habitat, including tundra, mountainous areas, northern forest, woodlands, prairies, arid regions, coasts, and around human settlements; has recently recolonized areas on southern edge of range, from which it was once expelled by humans.

| Length **23½–27in (60–69cm)** | Wingspan **4½ft (1.4m)** | Weight **2½–3¼lb (1–1.5kg)** |
| Social **Solitary/Pairs/Small flocks** | Lifespan **Up to 15 years** | Status **Secure** |

| Order **Passeriformes** | Family **Corvidae** | Species ***Corvus cryptoleucus*** |

Chihuahuan Raven

tail rounded at tip

ADULT

IN FLIGHT

white base of neck feathers

black upperparts with glossy sheen

ADULT

nasal bristles

down-curved bill

shaggy throat feathers

black underparts

FLIGHT: slow, steady, and direct; can also be quite acrobatic; commonly soars.

The Chihuahua Raven is intermediate in size, between the larger Common Raven and the smaller American Crow. It was previously called the White-necked Raven, taken from its Latin name, *cryptoleucus*, which refers to the white feathers on its neck. These normally concealed white feather bases are often blown into view in the bird's windswept environment. A highly gregarious and vocal raven, it is often seen wheeling about in flocks that may number in the hundreds and even thousands.

VOICE High-pitched croak; little variety in vocal repertoire compared to the Common Raven.

NESTING Platform of sticks with finer material in cup, either in tree or man-made structure; 4–7 eggs; 1 brood; April–August.

FEEDING Omnivorous, eats small mammals, lizards, other birds and their eggs, carrion; also fruit, seeds and garbage.

EATS ANYTHING
A Chihuahua Raven is not a fussy eater, with a diet ranging from grain to carrion.

SIMILAR SPECIES

AMERICAN CROW
see p.465

smaller overall

lacks wedge-shaped tail

COMMON RAVEN
see p.468

smaller bill

larger overall

thicker bill

lacks white base to neck

OCCURRENCE
A North American species breeeding in the Southwest US and Mexico, this raven is common in lowland grassland and scrub habitat, ranging into deserts in Arizona, and avoiding mountains. Northern populations migrate south into Mexico in winter.

| Length **17½–20in (44–51cm)** | Wingspan **3½ft (1.1m)** | Weight **16–20oz (450–575g)** |
| Social **Large flocks** | Lifespan **Up to 12 years** | Status **Secure** |

Family **Paridae**

CHICKADEES & TITMICE

CHICKADEES AND TITMICE may be some of the most well-known and widespread birds in North America. Scientific studies have shown that more than one genus exists, despite the bird's plumage similarities.

CHICKADEES

Regardless of their genus, chickadees are frequent visitors to backyards and are readily distinguished from titmice by their smooth-looking, dark caps and black bibs. The name "chickadee" is derived from the common calls of several species. Highly social outside the breeding season and generally tolerant of people, these energetic little birds form flocks in winter. Some species, such as the Black-capped Chickadee, can lower their body temperature to survive the cold, but others, like the similar-looking Carolina Chickadee, have a high winter mortality rate. Most species eat a combination of insects and plant material.

TITMICE

Titmice are distinguished from chickadees by their crests; most, like the familiar Tufted Titmouse, also have plain throats. Like chickadees, titmice are highly territorial and insectivorous during the breeding season, then become gregarious seed-eaters afterwards. At that time they often form mixed-species flocks with other small birds, like Kinglets, as they move through woodlands searching for food. Titmice are nonmigratory.

TAME BIRDS
Black-capped Chickadees have distinctive black-and-white markings and are often very tame.

Family **Hirundinidae**

SWALLOWS

SWALLOWS ARE A COSMOPOLITAN family of birds with species found nearly everywhere, except in the polar regions and some of the largest deserts, although during migration the fly over the some of the world's harshest deserts, including the Sahara and Atacama. Ornithologists usually call the short-tailed species martins and the long-tailed ones swallows. For example, the bird known as a Bank Swallow North America is called Sand Martin in southern states such as Mississippi and Alabama, as well as in the UK. The Bank Swallow and the Barn Swallow, which is also found across Eurasia, are the most widespread. All North American swallows are migratory, and most of them winter in Central and South America, where they feed on flying insects that occur year-round. They are all superb fliers, and skilled at aerial pursuit and capture of flying insects. They are sometimes confused with swifts, which belong to a different group, and have a different style of flight. Swallows have relatively shorter, broader wings and less stiff wing beats.

SURFACE SKIMMER
This Tree Swallow flies low over fresh water to catch insects as they emerge into the air.

| Order **Passeriformes** | Family **Bombycillidae** | Species ***Bombycilla garrulus*** |

Bohemian Waxwing

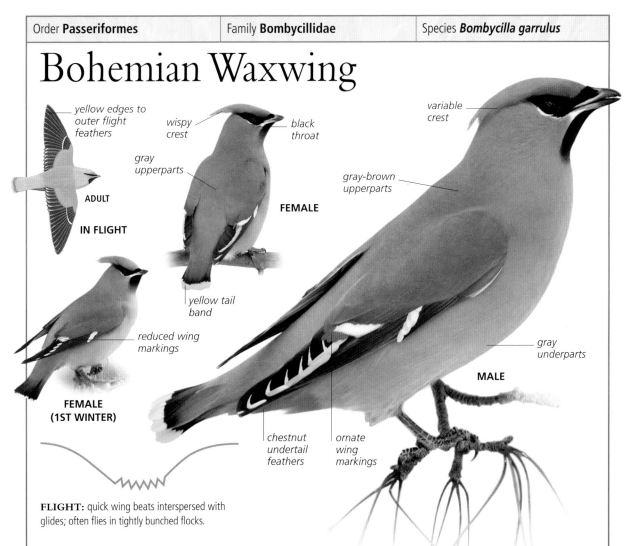

yellow edges to outer flight feathers

ADULT

IN FLIGHT

wispy crest

gray upperparts

black throat

FEMALE

variable crest

gray-brown upperparts

gray underparts

MALE

yellow tail band

reduced wing markings

FEMALE (1ST WINTER)

chestnut undertail feathers

ornate wing markings

FLIGHT: quick wing beats interspersed with glides; often flies in tightly bunched flocks.

The Bohemian Waxwing is the wilder and rarer of the two waxwing species in North America. It breeds mainly in Alaska and western Canada. The species is migratory, but the extent of its wintertime movement is notoriously variable, depending on the availability of wild fruits. In most winters, relatively few Bohemian Waxwings visit the lower 48 states, but in special "irruption" years, tens of thousands may reach as far south as Colorado.
VOICE Call actually a dull trill, but effect of hundreds of birds calling at the same time is remarkable; flocks vocalize constantly.
NESTING Dishevelled cup of sticks and grasses, placed in tree; 4–6 eggs; number of broods unknown; June–July.
FEEDING Catches insects on the wing in summer; flocks devour berries of native and exotic trees and shrubs throughout the year.

STRIKING TAIL
The Bohemian Waxwing's yellow tail band and chestnut undertail are evident here.

OCCURRENCE
Breeds in sub-Arctic coniferous forest, favoring disturbed areas such as beaver ponds and logging sites. Flocks gather at forest edges, hedges, and residential areas in winter. Hundreds or thousands of birds appear in an area, then disappear once food is depleted.

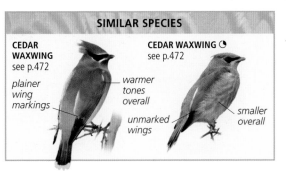

SIMILAR SPECIES

CEDAR WAXWING
see p.472

plainer wing markings

CEDAR WAXWING ☾
see p.472

warmer tones overall

unmarked wings

smaller overall

| Length **8½in (21cm)** | Wingspan **14½in (37cm)** | Weight **1⁹⁄₁₆–2½oz (45–70g)** |
| Social **Flocks** | Lifespan **Up to 12 years** | Status **Localized** |

| Order **Passeriformes** | Family **Bombycillidae** | Species *Bombycilla cedrorum* |

Cedar Waxwing

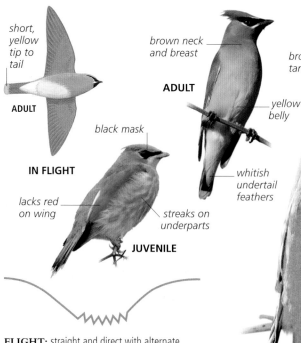

short, yellow tip to tail

ADULT

IN FLIGHT

black mask

lacks red on wing

streaks on underparts

JUVENILE

brown neck and breast

ADULT

yellow belly

whitish undertail feathers

wispy crest

white bars on face

brownish tan back

black "bandit" mask

ADULT

waxy, red tips on inner wing

FLIGHT: straight and direct with alternate glides; usually in small to medium flocks.

Flocks of Cedar Waxwings, a nomadic species, move around the US looking for berries, which are their main source of food. Common in a specific location one year, they may disappear the next and occur elsewhere. Northern breeders tend to be more migratory than southern ones. In winter, their nomadic tendencies send Cedar Waxwings as far south as South America. They can often be heard and identified by their calls, long before the flock settles to feed.

VOICE Basic vocalization a shrill trill: *shr-r-r-r-r-r* or *tre-e-e-e-e-e*, which appears to serve the function of both call note and song.

NESTING Open cup placed in fork of tree, often lined with grasses, plant fibers; 3–5 eggs; 1–2 broods; June–August.

FEEDING Eats in flocks at trees and shrubs with ripe berries throughout the year; also catches flying insects in summer.

BATHING ADULT
Cedar Waxwings love to take baths, and use birdbaths in suburban gardens.

SIMILAR SPECIES

BOHEMIAN WAXWING ♂
see p.471

larger overall

more ornate wing pattern

BOHEMIAN WAXWING ♀♂
see p.471

pale gray breast

rufous undertail

OCCURRENCE
Across northern US and southern Canada, in wooded areas. Breeds in woodlands, especially near streams and clearings. Winters anywhere where trees and shrubs have ripe fruits, especially in Mexico and South America. Spends a lot of time in treetops, but sometimes comes down to shrub level.

| Length **7½in (19cm)** | Wingspan **12in (30cm)** | Weight **1¹⁄₁₆–1¼oz (30–35g)** |
| Social **Flocks** | Lifespan **Up to 7 years** | Status **Secure** |

| Order **Passeriformes** | Family **Ptilogonatidae** | Species ***Phainopepla nitens*** |

Phainopepla

conspicuous
white wing
flashes

MALE

IN FLIGHT

variable crest

pale wing
bars

sooty gray
plumage

FEMALE

prominent
crest

red eye

silky smooth,
shiny black
plumage

long
black tail

slim body

black
underparts

MALE

FLIGHT: erratic flight; flies off perch to catch
prey; often somersaults mid-air before returning.

The Phainopepla's fascinating name is Greek for "shiny robe,"
in reference to the bird's glossy plumage. It is capable of
mimicking the calls of other species, which it often does when
being pursued by a predator. With regard to breeding, it is the
"Jekyll-and-Hyde" of North American birds. Between February
and April, it breeds in hot lowland deserts of the southwestern
US, where it is fiercely territorial. Later, between May and
August, it breeds again, in shady broadleaf canyons in mountains,
forming colonies of up to 15 pairs.

VOICE Call a mellow *wurp*, with upward inflection; song a
long series of short phrases, overall soft and halting delivery.
NESTING Small, compact nest made in tree, commonly in
mistletoe; 2–3 eggs; 2 broods; February–April, May–August.
FEEDING Eats mainly mistletoe berries from fall through
to early spring; also feeds on flying insects in the summer,
including flies and beetles.

FAVORITE HANGOUT
Phainopeplas love to perch high up in trees and
shrubs, where they can catch flying insects.

SIMILAR SPECIES

**TOWNSEND'S
SOLITAIRE**
see p.534

white
eye-ring

gray overall

PYRRHULOXIA ♀
see p.696

very
thick
bill

reddish
patch on
wings

OCCURRENCE
The only species in its genus,
the Phainopepla is a bird of
the southwestern US and
Mexico, where it lives in
lowland woodland and scrub
of oak, mesquite, and juniper
in winter and early spring.
Occurs later in the year at
slightly higher elevations
on slopes and in canyons.

| Length **7¾in (19.5cm)** | Wingspan **11in (28cm)** | Weight **⅝–1¹⁄₁₆oz (18–30g)** |
| Social **Flocks** | Lifespan **At least 3 years** | Status **Vulnerable** |

Order **Passeriformes**	Family **Paridae**	Species *Poecile carolinensis*

Carolina Chickadee

ADULT

plain gray
upperparts

IN FLIGHT

conspicuous
black-and-white
head

short, slightly
notched tail

buffy flanks

pale gray edges
on inner wing
feathers

white
cheeks

short,
black
bill

sharp-edged
bib margin

ADULT

FLIGHT: fast, undulating, with quick wing beats.

The Carolina Chickadee is the only chickadee found in the southeastern US, and was first described and named by John James Audubon in 1834, when he was in South Carolina. Its northern range limit locally overlaps the Black-capped Chickadee's southern limit in a narrow band from Kansas to New Jersey, where the two species interbreed regularly, creating hybrids with mixed plumage that are hard to identify. The Carolina Chickadee hides food in caches under branches or even within curled dead leaves, returning for it within a few days. It has a strong preference for sunflower seeds, and can be seen at birdfeeders along with the Black-capped Chickadee, where the Carolina's characteristic call is the easiest way to distinguish the two species.

VOICE Fast *dee-dee-dee* call; song clear, whistled, four-note sequence *wee-bee wee-bay*, second note lower in pitch.
NESTING Cavity lined with moss, fur, hair, plant down in soft, rotting tree; 5–8 eggs; 1–2 broods; April–May.
FEEDING Forages for insects and spiders; visits birdfeeders in winter.

DULL EXTREME
In worn plumage, and in its southwestern range, this bird has grayish white flanks.

BRIGHT EXTREME
In fresh plumage, some Carolina Chickadees have brighter, buffy flanks.

OCCURRENCE
Year-round dweller in deciduous, mixed and pine woodlands, urban parks, and suburbs. In the Appalachians, prefers lower elevations than Black-capped. Range is expanding northward, especially in Ohio and Pennsylvania, where it is gradually replacing Black-capped as the resident species.

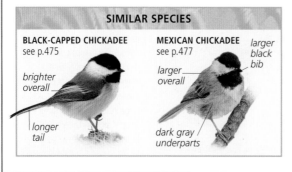

SIMILAR SPECIES

BLACK-CAPPED CHICKADEE
see p.475

brighter
overall

longer
tail

MEXICAN CHICKADEE
see p.477

larger
overall

larger
black
bib

dark gray
underparts

Length **4¾in (12cm)**	Wingspan **7½in (19cm)**	Weight **⅜oz (11g)**
Social **Mixed flocks**	Lifespan **Up to 10 years**	Status **Secure**

| Order **Passeriformes** | Family **Paridae** | Species *Poecile atricapillus* |

Black-capped Chickadee

white on wings and tail

black-and-white head

grayish brown upperparts

ADULT

IN FLIGHT

white edges on wing feathers

white edges on outer tail feathers

faded buff flanks

bright white cheeks

short black bill

black cap and bib

ADULT

The Black-capped Chickadee is the most widespread chickadee in North America, equally at home in the cold far north and in warm Appalachian valleys. To cope with the harsh winters in the northern parts of its range, this species can decrease its body temperature, entering a controlled hypothermia to conserve energy. There is some variation in appearance according to geographical location, with northern birds being slightly larger and possessing brighter white wing edgings than southern birds. Although it is a nonmigratory species, in winter flocks occasionally travel south of their traditional range in large numbers.

VOICE Raspy *tsick-a-dee-dee-dee* call; song loud, clear whistle *bee-bee* or *bee-bee-be*, first note higher in pitch.

NESTING Cavity in rotting tree stump, lined with hair, fur, feathers, plant fibers; 6–8 eggs; 1 brood; April–June.

FEEDING Forages for insects and their eggs, and spiders in trees and bushes; mainly seeds in winter; may take seeds from an outstretched hand.

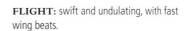

FLIGHT: swift and undulating, with fast wing beats.

ROUGH-EDGED BIB
The Black-capped Chickadee has a less well-defined lower bib margin than the Carolina Chickadee.

SIMILAR SPECIES

CAROLINA CHICKADEE
see p.474
lacks white wing edges

no white tail edges

MEXICAN CHICKADEE
see p.477

large bib extends to upper breast

OCCURRENCE
Variety of wooded habitats, from vast forests in the far north to small woodlands in urban parks and suburbs. In years of poor seed crops in northern parts of the range, large numbers migrate southward as far as the Carolina Chickadee's range.

| Length **5¼in (13.5cm)** | Wingspan **8½in (22cm)** | Weight **⅜oz (11g)** |
| Social **Mixed flocks** | Lifespan **Up to 12 years** | Status **Secure** |

Order **Passeriformes**	Family **Paridae**	Species **Poecile gambeli**

Mountain Chickadee

ADULT (EASTERN)

black crown

short, black bill

black bib

buff-tinged flanks

IN FLIGHT

ADULT (EASTERN)

white eyebrow

white cheeks

dull gray upperparts

gray flanks

pale gray underparts

ADULT (WESTERN)

FLIGHT: bouncy, with fast wing beats; interrupted by brief glides.

The Mountain Chickadee is aptly named as it is found at elevations—of up to 12,000ft (3,600m). Like other chickadees, it stores pine and spruce seeds for harsh mountain winters. Social groups defend their winter territories and food resources, migrating to lower elevations when seeds are scarce. Birds in the Rocky Mountains have a conspicuous white eyebrow and buff-tinged flanks; those in the California mountains have grayish flanks and a fainter eyebrow.

VOICE Call raspy *tsick-jee-jee-jee*; whistle song of descending notes *bee-bee-bay*.

NESTING Natural tree cavity or old woodpecker hole, lined with moss and fur; 7–9 eggs; 1–2 broods; May–June.

FEEDING Forages high in trees for insects and spiders; eats seeds and berries; stores seeds in fall in preparation for winter.

VARIABLE EYEBROW
The white eyebrow is evident, but it may become duller in worn spring and summer plumage.

TYPICAL PERCH
The species spends much time perched in conifer trees, where it feeds.

OCCURRENCE
High elevations, preferring coniferous forests. May even be seen higher than the limit of tree growth. Some birds, especially the young, move down to foothills and valleys in winter and may visit feeders. Some also wander away from the mountains and out onto the Great Plains.

SIMILAR SPECIES

BLACK-CAPPED CHICKADEE see p.475

no white eyebrow

MEXICAN CHICKADEE see p.477

no white eyebrow

larger black bib

Length **5¼in (13.5cm)**	Wingspan **8½in (22cm)**	Weight **⅜oz (11g)**
Social **Winter flocks**	Lifespan **Up to 10 years**	Status **Secure**

| Order **Passeriformes** | Family **Paridae** | Species *Poecile sclateri* |

Mexican Chickadee

plain gray upperparts

ADULT

IN FLIGHT

black cap

white cheeks

large bib extending to upper breast

dusky gray underparts

grayish black legs

ADULT

FLIGHT: bouncy, with fast wing beats and brief glides; typical chickadee style.

Although it is widespread in the mountains of Mexico, the Mexican Chickadee's range barely reaches the US; at the northern limit of its distribution it is restricted to mountaintops in southern Arizona and New Mexico. These distinctive high-elevation habitats forested by pine, spruce, and fir, are known as "sky islands," separated from one another by lower-elevation mountains and valleys. Each of the strictly limited areas of suitable habitat has its own tiny, isolated population. Diminishing habitat raises conservationists' concern about the Mexican Chickadee's prospects of survival at the northern most edge of its range.

VOICE Variety of rapid warbles, including *tse-tse tse-tse tse-tse*; also harsh *churr-churr* notes.

NESTING Natural cavity in tree, sometimes high above ground; lined with plant fibers, moss, hair; 5–9 eggs; 1–2 broods; April–May.

FEEDING Forages among conifers for insects and caterpillars.

DISTINCTIVE SONG
Unlike any of the other chickadees, the Mexican Chickadee has a fairly complex whistled song.

SIMILAR SPECIES

BLACK-CAPPED CHICKADEE
see p.475

white on upper wings

buffy flanks

MOUNTAIN CHICKADEE
see p.476

smaller bib

paler underparts

white eyebrow

smaller bib

OCCURRENCE
Restricted to high-elevation coniferous forests up to 9,000ft (2,750m)—Chiricahua Mountains of southeastern Arizona, Animas, and Peloncillo Mountains of southwestern New Mexico, and southward in mountains of Mexico; occurs as high as 12,800ft (3,900m). Some birds move lower in winter.

| Length **5in (13cm)** | Wingspan **8in (20cm)** | Weight **⅜oz (11g)** |
| Social **Large flocks** | Lifespan **Up to 10 years** | Status **Localized** |

Order **Passeriformes**	Family **Paridae**	Species *Poecile hudsonica*

Boreal Chickadee

ADULT

gray cheeks

gray tail

IN FLIGHT

grayish brown back

gray wings

brown cap

black bib

rich brown flanks and belly

ADULT

FLIGHT: bouncy, fast wing beats with brief glides.

The Boreal Chickadee was previously known by other names, including Hudsonian Chickadee, referring to its northern range, and the Brown-capped Chickadee, due to its appearance. In the past, this species made large, irregular journeys south of its usual range during winters of food shortage, but this pattern of invasions has not occurred in recent decades. Its back color is an interesting example of geographic variation—grayish in the West and brown in the central and eastern portions of its range.

VOICE Call a low-pitched, buzzy, lazy *tsee-day-day*; also a high-pitched trill, *didididididi*; no whistled song.

NESTING Cavity lined with fur, hair, plant down; in natural, excavated, or old woodpecker hole; 4–9 eggs; 1 brood; May–June.

FEEDING Gleans insects, conifer seeds; hoards larvae and seeds in bark crevices in fall in preparation for winter.

IDENTIFICATION TIP
A brown back or flank help distinguish a Boreal Chickadee from a Black-capped Chickadee.

SIMILAR SPECIES

CHESTNUT-BACKED CHICKADEE see p.479

narrow, white cheeks

chestnut sides

ACROBATIC FORAGER
This acrobatic feeder is able to cling on to conifer needles as it searches for insects and spiders.

OCCURRENCE
Found across the vast northern spruce-fir forests, from Alaska to Newfoundland, and from the treeline at the tundra south to the northeastern and northwestern states. The southern edge of the range appears to be retracting for unknown reasons.

Length **5½in (14cm)**	Wingspan **8½in (21cm)**	Weight **⅜oz (10g)**
Social **Flocks**	Lifespan **Up to 5 years**	Status **Secure**

| Order **Passeriformes** | Family **Paridae** | Species *Poecile rufescens* |

Chestnut-backed Chickadee

chestnut back and rump

ADULT

dark gray wings

IN FLIGHT

paler gray wings

gray sides and flanks

P. r. barlowi

white edges on outer wing feathers

chestnut sides

narrow white cheeks

dark brown cap

rich chestnut back

black bib extends to sides of neck and breast

ADULT

FLIGHT: bouncy, fast wing beats with brief glides.

The Chestnut-backed is the smallest of all chickadees and possesses the shortest tail. Northern populations have the most brightly colored sides and flanks of all North American chickadees—rich chestnut or rufous, matching the bright back and rump. Birds found southward into California have paler and less extensive rufous underparts. Further south still, in California, the sides and flanks are dull olive-brown or gray. The Chestnut-backed Chickadee may nest in loose colonies, unlike any other chickadee species.

VOICE A fast, high-pitched *sic-zee-zee*, *seet-seet-seet*, sharp *chek-chek*, crisp *twit-twit-twit*, and many variations; no whistled song.

NESTING Excavates hole, or uses natural cavity or old woodpecker hole; lined with moss, hair, fur; 5–8 eggs; 1 brood; April–June.

FEEDING Forages high in conifers for caterpillars and other insects; eats seeds and berries in winter.

A DASH OF WHITE
Bright white edges on the wing feathers are often a conspicuous field mark of this species.

SIMILAR SPECIES

BOREAL CHICKADEE
see p.478

grayish brown back

gray cheeks

rich brown flanks and belly

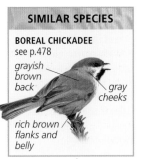

DARK CAP
In good light, this chickadee's brown cap is apparent; in poor light, the cap may look black.

OCCURRENCE
Year-round resident in humid coniferous forests of the Pacific Northwest; in drier mixed and deciduous woodlands, and even in urban and suburban habitats south of San Francisco, California. Northern coastal populations have one of the most specialized habitats of all chickadee species.

| Length **4¾in (12cm)** | Wingspan **7½in (19cm)** | Weight **⅜oz (10g)** |
| Social **Flocks** | Lifespan **Up to 9 years** | Status **Secure** |

| Order **Passeriformes** | Family **Paridae** | Species *Baeolophus wollweberi* |

Bridled Titmouse

ADULT

crest not evident in flight

gray tail

IN FLIGHT

black eyestripe

brightly patterned black-and-white face

gray upperparts

small, black bill

black throat

expansive tall dark crest covers crown

gray upperparts

ADULT

pale gray underparts

gray-black legs and feet

FLIGHT: bouncy, undulating, and with fast wing beats.

long tail

ADULT

The Bridled Titmouse is the smallest of the North American titmice. Its size and short tail make it an especially agile species, capable of maneuvering acrobatically and hanging upside down to catch insects. Its striking black-and-white facial marks and its tall, dark crest distinguish this species from the other titmice. The Bridled Titmouse differs from the other titmice in other ways, including its voice, which is softer and more chickadee-like. Uniquely, it forms large flocks in fall and winter that also include chickadees, nuthatches, and kinglets.

VOICE High-pitched *cheer cheer cheer* call; similar to chickadee; song a fast series of whistled *peet peet peet* notes.

NESTING Primarily in natural cavities in trees and abandoned woodpecker holes, lined with grass, hair, plant down; 5–7 eggs; 1–2 broods; April–May.

FEEDING Mostly gleans beetles, larvae, and pupae of various insect species from twigs or leaves; also feeds on seeds.

SILENT SPECTATOR
Unlike other titmice, the Bridled Titmouse is often silent for long periods of time.

OCCURRENCE
Primarily a Mexican species, the Bridled Titmouse reaches its northernmost range limit in the mountains of southeastern Arizona and southwestern New Mexico. It lives in mountainous oak and pine-oak forests up to 7,000ft (2,130m). Flocks winter at lower elevations.

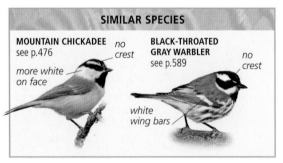

SIMILAR SPECIES

MOUNTAIN CHICKADEE see p.476 — no crest; more white on face

BLACK-THROATED GRAY WARBLER see p.589 — no crest; white wing bars

| Length **5¼in (13.5cm)** | Wingspan **8in (20cm)** | Weight **⅜oz (11g)** |
| Social **Large flocks** | Lifespan **At least 6 years** | Status **Secure** |

| Order **Passeriformes** | Family **Paridae** | Species *Baeolophus inornatus* |

Oak Titmouse

short crest

blackish bill

pale gray face
and underparts

ADULT

ADULT

crest may not be
evident in flight

pale gray
overall

IN FLIGHT

plain grayish
brown upperparts

long tail

gray-black
legs

FLIGHT: bouncy, with fast wing beats; short
dashes from branch to branch and tree to tree.

A long with the Juniper Titmouse, its look-
alike relative farther west in California and the western states
of the US, the Oak Titmouse is the least colorful species in its group.
The Oak and the Juniper forms were previously classified together as one species,
aptly named the Plain Titmouse. The habitat of the Oak Titmouse is threatened by
agricultural development and by a disease called Sudden Oak Death Syndrome,
however, work is being done to save the oak trees and the birds that live in them.

VOICE Rough *see-see-see-chrr* or *tsicka-tsicka jeer-jeer* call; song a series of clear,
whistled double notes, *peedle peedle peedle* or *pe-er pe-er pe-er.*

NESTING Natural tree cavities, abandoned woodpecker holes; base of cavity
lined with grass, moss, hair; 6–7 eggs; 1 brood; March–April.

FEEDING Methodically gleans insects, spiders, and insect larvae from oak
branches, foliage, and bark; also eats seeds.

EASY TO IDENTIFY
The Oak Titmouse is easily
identified as its range does not
overlap with other titmice.

OCCURRENCE
Year-round resident in oak or
oak-pine woodlands on dry
foothills of the Pacific slope.
Especially favors groves of
Coast Live Oak. Often visits
suburban yards containing oak
trees. Almost never wanders
away from its oak-covered
West Coast habitat.

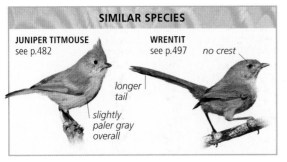

SIMILAR SPECIES

JUNIPER TITMOUSE
see p.482

WRENTIT
see p.497

no crest

*longer
tail*

*slightly
paler gray
overall*

| Length **5¾in (14.5cm)** | Wingspan **9in (23cm)** | Weight **⅝oz (17g)** |
| Social **Solitary/Pairs** | Lifespan **Up to 8 years** | Status **Declining** |

Order **Passeriformes**	Family **Paridae**	Species **Baeolophus griseus**

Juniper Titmouse

raised crest

ADULT

crest may not be evident

drab gray upperparts

straight bill

gray wings

IN FLIGHT

ADULT

plain gray tail

paler underparts

L ike its close relative, the Oak Titouse, the Juniper Titmouse is a plain bird; in fact, its drabness is a useful field mark. Although distributed over a much larger range, it is not as well known or studied as the Oak Titmouse, probably because the size of its population is only one-third that of the Oak Titmouse and it is less likely to be encountered in urban or suburban areas.

VOICE Call a rapidly repeated *shick-dee*; song a fast, rolling, or trilled series of short phrases such as *we-dee we-dee we-dee*; both calls and song have many variations.

NESTING Natural tree cavities or abandoned woodpecker holes, lined with shredded bark, moss, hair; 5–6 eggs; 1 brood; April–May.

FEEDING Forages acrobatically among branches, trunks, and among foliage for insects, spiders, and insect larvae; sometimes eats berries and seeds on the ground.

FLIGHT: swift and bounding; periods of fast wing beats alternating with short glides.

LIVING UP TO ITS NAME
A Juniper Titmouse can usually be found in juniper woodlands, perched on its namesake tree.

SIMILAR SPECIES

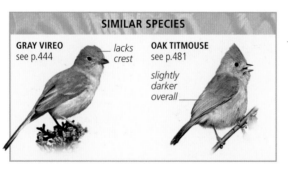

GRAY VIREO see p.444

lacks crest

OAK TITMOUSE see p.481

slightly darker overall

OCCURRENCE
Year-round resident of dry juniper and pinyon-juniper woodlands of the West. Inhabits moderate elevations, up to 8,000ft (2,400m) in the southern portions of the range. Its small population is irregularly and locally distributed, although it may be more common in its habitat than is generally known.

Length **5¾ in (14.5cm)**	Wingspan **9in (23cm)**	Weight **⅝oz (17g)**
Social **Family groups**	Lifespan **Up to 8 years**	Status **Secure**

Order **Passeriformes**	Family **Paridae**	Species **Baeolophus bicolor**

Tufted Titmouse

ADULT

crest may be flattened

gray wings

IN FLIGHT

tufted dark gray head

conspicuous black eye in whitish face

black fore-head

prominent orange flanks

gray tail

ADULT

gray underparts

gray-black legs and feet

FLIGHT: swift and undulating, with irregular wing beats; usually across short distances.

A familiar and friendly sight, the Tufted Titmouse is the most widespread of the North American titmice, and one of the two largest and most fearless; this lack of fear, particularly around people, has enabled it to adapt very well to human habitations. In the last century, its range has expanded significantly northward up to southern Canada, probably due to the increased numbers of birdfeeders, which allow the Tufted Titmouse to survive the cold northern winters.

VOICE Call a loud, harsh *pshurr, pshurr, pshurr*; song a ringing, far-carrying *peto peto peto*, sometimes shortened to *peer peer peer*.
NESTING Tree cavities, old woodpecker holes, and nest boxes, lined with damp leaves, moss, grass, hair; 5–6 eggs; 1 brood; March–May.
FEEDING Forages actively in trees and shrubs for insects, spiders, and their eggs; in winter, corn kernels, seeds, and small fruits, can split an acorn by hammering it with its bill.

COLOR VARIATION
The orange on the flanks varies between bright on freshly molted feathers and dull on worn adults.

SIMILAR SPECIES

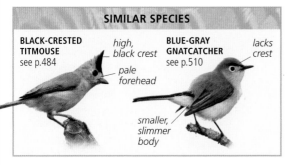

BLACK-CRESTED TITMOUSE
see p.484

high, black crest

pale forehead

BLUE-GRAY GNATCATCHER
see p.510

lacks crest

smaller, slimmer body

OCCURRENCE
Lives year-round in areas of large and small deciduous and coniferous woodlands in the eastern half of the US. It has flourished in parks and gardens and can often be found using nest boxes in suburban backyards.

Length **6½ in (16cm)**	Wingspan **10in (25cm)**	Weight **¹¹⁄₁₆ oz (20g)**
Social **Mixed flocks**	Lifespan **Up to 13 years**	Status **Secure**

Order **Passeriformes**	Family **Paridae**	Species *Baeolophus atricristatus*

Black-crested Titmouse

ADULT
black crest lowered

gray wings and tail

IN FLIGHT

plain gray upperparts

tall, black crest

short, black bill

white or whitish underparts

pale buffy orange flanks

ADULT

FLIGHT: rapid, undulating, with fast wing beats, and short dips.

Only found in Texas and southwest Oklahoma in the US, the Black-crested Titmouse resembles the Tufted Titmouse in virtually every way, except for its noticeably taller, black crest. Because of this striking difference, the two were traditionally considered separate species. However, as the two species interbreed freely along a wide strip of land that runs through Texas, ornithologists merged the two into a single species in 1983. Further studies distinguished them genetically and vocally, and the two species were seperated in 2002.

VOICE Call a rasping, scolding *jhree jhree jhree*; song a loud series of clear notes *pew, pew, pew*.

NESTING Hollows in trees, old woodpecker holes, bird boxes, lined with moss, uses grass, hair, and bark; 4–7 eggs; 1 brood; March–May.

FEEDING Searches trees for caterpillars, spiders, and insect eggs; also eats fruits, seeds, berries, and nuts, especially acorns; breaks open nuts with sharp bill.

NEST SITE
A Black-crested Titmouse flutters outside a typical nest site—a hole in a dead tree.

COLOR CONTRAST
The Black-crested Titmouse's buffy forehead contrasts with its prominent black crest.

OCCURRENCE
Year-round resident of scrubby oak woodlands; also towns and suburbs, where groups frequently visit feeders in winter. Sometimes found at higher elevations than its close relative, the Tufted Titmouse; reported to occur as high as 6,000ft (2,000m) in mountain forests of Mexico in the southern portion of its range.

SIMILAR SPECIES

JUNIPER TITMOUSE see p.482
smaller crest
grayish underparts

TUFTED TITMOUSE see p.483
gray crest
dark forehead

Length **6½in (16.5cm)**	Wingspan **10in (25cm)**	Weight **11/16 oz (20g)**
Social **Family groups**	Lifespan **Unknown**	Status **Secure**

Order **Passeriformes**	Family **Remizidae**	Species **Auriparus flaviceps**

Verdin

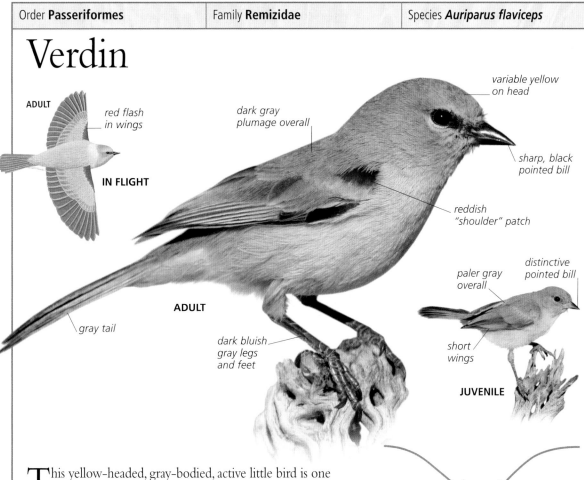

ADULT

red flash in wings

IN FLIGHT

dark gray plumage overall

variable yellow on head

sharp, black pointed bill

reddish "shoulder" patch

gray tail

ADULT

dark bluish gray legs and feet

paler gray overall

distinctive pointed bill

short wings

JUVENILE

This yellow-headed, gray-bodied, active little bird is one of the most characteristic species of the warm southwest deserts. The Verdin is constantly on the move, flitting from shrub to shrub, inspecting flowers and cobwebs, and flying short distances across clearings. In behavior and habitat preferences, Verdins resemble chickadees, bushtits, or perhaps even wrens. In fact, the evolutionary relationships of the Verdin is unclear, and the species is currently thought to be the only American representative of a bird family that is otherwise restricted to Eurasia, the Penduline Tits.

VOICE Call a bright, simple *beef*, made frequently as the bird forages, all day long and throughout the year.

NESTING Large-sized sphere with side entrance, made of twigs and leaves in thorny shrub; 4–5 eggs; 1–2 broods; April–July.

FEEDING Gleans small insects from leaves and flowers; also drinks nectar from flowers, and sometimes visits hummingbird feeders.

FLIGHT: weak, floppy, undulating; Verdins forage in shrubbery, sometimes fly across clearings.

NECTAR FEEDER
The Verdin will often drink nectar from tubular flowers, particularly in winter.

SIMILAR SPECIES

LUCY'S WARBLER ♀
see p.577

chestnut rump

longer, thinner bill

LUCY'S WARBLER ♂
see p.577

gray face

chestnut rump

OCCURRENCE
Permanent resident in thorny vegetation of southwestern deserts at low elevations, tamarisks in dry creek beds, and shrubs at the edge of desert oases. Many birds wander out into even sparser desert habitats. Ranges from the southwest US to Mexico.

Length **4½in (11.5cm)**	Wingspan **6½in (16cm)**	Weight **³⁄₁₆–¼oz (5–7g)**
Social **Solitary**	Lifespan **Up to 5 years**	Status **Secure**

Order **Passeriformes**	Family **Hirundinidae**	Species *Riparia riparia*

Bank Swallow

dark brown head

dark brown upperparts

whitish chin and throat

ADULT

dark breastband

white belly

IN FLIGHT

brownish cheeks

ADULT

wings dark underneath

forked tail

whitish underparts

ADULT

The Bank Swallow, known in the UK as the Sand Martin, is the slimmest and smallest of North American swallows. As its scientific name *riparia* (meaning "riverbanks") and common names suggest, the Bank Swallow nests in the banks and bluffs of rivers, streams, and lakes. It also favors sand and gravel quarries in the East. It is widely distributed across North America, breeding from south of the tundra–taiga line down to the central US. The nesting colonies can range from as few as 10 pairs to as many as 2,000, which are quite noisy when all the birds are calling or coming in to feed the young.

VOICE Call a soft *brrrrr* or *breee* often issued in pairs; song a harsh twittering or continuous chatter.

NESTING Burrow in soft, sandy bank containing a flat platform of grass, feathers, and twigs; 2–6 eggs; 1 brood; April–August.

FEEDING Catches insects, such as flies, moths, dragonflies, and bees in flight, but occasionally skims aquatic insects or their larvae off the water or terrestrial insects from the ground.

FLIGHT: fast, frantic, butterfly-like flight with glides, twists, and turns; shallow, rapid wing beats.

WAITING FOR MOM
Hungry youngsters still expect to be fed, even when they're ready to fledge.

SIMILAR SPECIES

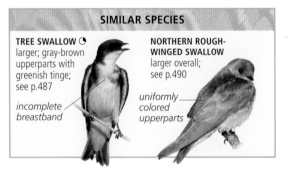

TREE SWALLOW ◑
larger; gray-brown upperparts with greenish tinge; see p.487

incomplete breastband

NORTHERN ROUGH-WINGED SWALLOW
larger overall; see p.490

uniformly colored upperparts

OCCURRENCE
Widespread in North America. Breeds in lowland habitats associated with rivers, streams, lakes, reservoirs, and coasts, as well as in sand and gravel quarries. Often prefers manmade sites; winters in grasslands, open farm habitat, and freshwater areas in South America.

Length **4¾–5½in (12–14cm)**	Wingspan **10–11in (25–28cm)**	Weight **⅜–¹¹⁄₁₆oz (10–19g)**
Social **Colonies**	Lifespan **Up to 9 years**	Status **Secure**

| Order **Passeriformes** | Family **Hirundinidae** | Species *Tachycineta bicolor* |

Tree Swallow

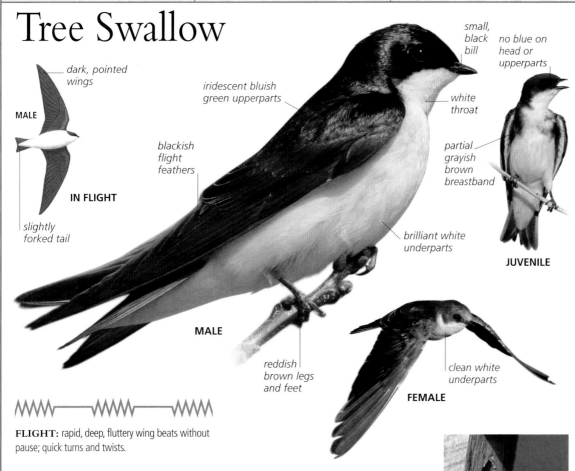

MALE

dark, pointed wings

IN FLIGHT

slightly forked tail

iridescent bluish green upperparts

blackish flight feathers

small, black bill

no blue on head or upperparts

white throat

partial grayish brown breastband

JUVENILE

brilliant white underparts

MALE

reddish brown legs and feet

clean white underparts

FEMALE

FLIGHT: rapid, deep, fluttery wing beats without pause; quick turns and twists.

One of the most common North American swallows, the Tree Swallow is found from coast to coast in the upper half of the continent all the way up to Alaska. As its Latin name *bicolor* suggests, it has iridescent bluish green upperparts and white underparts. Juveniles can be confused with the smaller Bank Swallow, which has a more complete breastband. The Tree Swallow lives in a variety of habitats, but its hole-nesting habit makes it completely dependent on abandoned woodpecker cavities in dead trees and on artificial "housing" such as nestboxes. The size of the population fluctuates according to the availability of the nesting sites.

VOICE Ranges from variable high, chirping notes to chatters and soft trills; also complex high and clear two-note whistle phrases.

NESTING Layer of fine plant matter in abandoned woodpecker hole or nest box, lined with feathers; 4–6 eggs; 1 brood; May–July.

FEEDING Swoops after flying insects from dawn to dusk; also takes bayberries.

KEEPING LOOKOUT
This species uses artificial nestboxes, which the males defend as soon as they arrive.

OCCURRENCE
Typically breeds close to water in open habitat such as fields, marshes, lakes, and swamps, especially those with standing dead wood for cavity-nesting. Winters in large roosts in hundreds of thousands of birds in tall marsh vegetation.

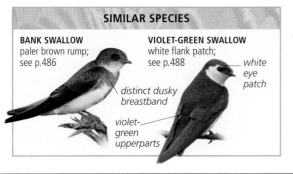

SIMILAR SPECIES

BANK SWALLOW
paler brown rump;
see p.486

distinct dusky breastband

VIOLET-GREEN SWALLOW
white flank patch;
see p.488

white eye patch

violet-green upperparts

| Length **5–6in (13–15cm)** | Wingspan **12–14in (30–35cm)** | Weight **⅝–⅞oz (17–25g)** |
| Social **Large flocks** | Lifespan **Up to 11 years** | Status **Secure** |

| Order **Passeriformes** | Family **Hirundinidae** | Species *Tachycineta thalassina* |

Violet-green Swallow

long wings

ADULT

white underparts

IN FLIGHT

brown on head and sides of face

FEMALE

green head

faint purplish neck patch

emerald green back

white, crescent-like patch on throat and face

purple rump and tail

MALE

wing tips extend beyond tail

FLIGHT: fluttering; close to the ground or circling at great heights with rapid wing beats; less soaring.

Although common in western North America from eastern Alaska south to Baja California, the Violet-green Swallow is poorly studied. Indeed, it is arguably the least well known of all North American swallows. It often occurs in mountainous conifer forests where it breeds in woodpecker holes in dead trees, or in cliff crevices, but it will also use birdhouses. A distinguishing feature of this swallow is the white patch that covers its throat and forms a line over its eyes. Its Latin name *thalassina* means "sea-green," while its common name refers to the same color, along with the violet of its rump. In its mountain habitat, the Violet-green Swallow can be encountered together with the White-throated Swift.

VOICE Primary call a twittering *chee-chee* of brief duration; alarm call a dry, brief *zwrack*.

NESTING Nest of grass, twigs, straw, and feathers in a natural or woodpecker cavity in a tree, also cliff or nesting box; 4–6 eggs; 2 broods; March–August.

FEEDING Catches flying insects, such as bees, wasps, moths, and flies; usually at higher levels than other species of swallows.

AT THE NEST HOLE
The female of this species can be distinguished from the male by her darker face.

OCCURRENCE
In US and Canada, breeds in open deciduous, coniferous, and mixed woodlands, especially Ponderosa and Monterey Pine and Quaking Aspen; also wooded canyons. Frequents waterways during migration; prefers higher elevations in general. Breeds south of the US, in Mexico.

SIMILAR SPECIES

WHITE-THROATED SWIFT
see p.359

white sides of rump

TREE SWALLOW ♂
see p.487

iridescent greenish blue upperparts

blackish brown crown

| Length **5in (13cm)** | Wingspan **11in (28cm)** | Weight **½oz (14g)** |
| Social **Solitary/Colonies** | Lifespan **Unknown** | Status **Secure** |

Order **Passeriformes**	Family **Hirundinidae**	Species **Progne subis**

Purple Martin

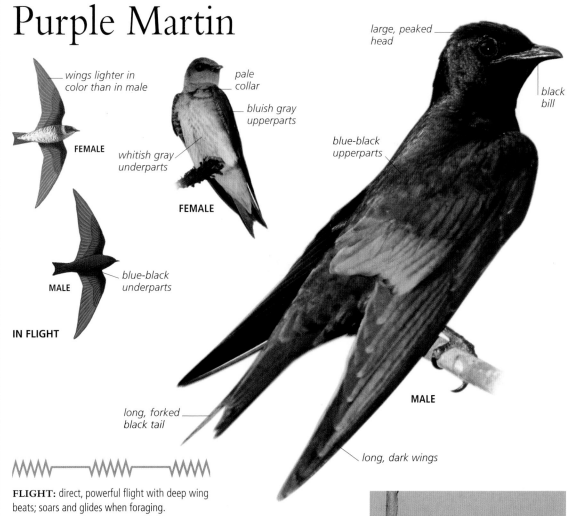

large, peaked head

wings lighter in color than in male

pale collar

bluish gray upperparts

black bill

blue-black upperparts

whitish gray underparts

FEMALE

FEMALE

blue-black underparts

MALE

IN FLIGHT

MALE

long, forked black tail

long, dark wings

FLIGHT: direct, powerful flight with deep wing beats; soars and glides when foraging.

The Purple Martin, the largest of all North American swallows, is one of the most popular of all backyard birds. Thousands of devoted Purple Martin-lovers belong to two national organizations that publish magazines and newsletters devoted to the species. Found mostly in the eastern half of the continent, with local populations scattered across the West, this glossy-blue swallow is common in some areas and yet quite scarce in others. In the West it nests in abandoned woodpecker holes, but in the East the Purple Martin now depends almost entirely on the provisioning of "apartment-type" birdhouses for breeding.

VOICE Alarm call a *zwrack* or *zweet*; other calls are a variety of rolling, bubbling sounds; song a series of gurgles, chortles, and croaking phrases.
NESTING Loose mat of vegetation and mud in birdhouse compartments, rarely in natural cavities; 4 eggs; 1 brood; April–August.
FEEDING Captures flying insects at 150–500ft (45–150m) in the air; sometimes gleans insects from foliage or the ground.

FLOCK TOGETHER
Purple Martins are social birds; they breed in colonies and roost in flocks, as shown.

OCCURRENCE
In North America, eastern birds found almost exclusively in towns and cities where nestboxes are provided; western populations occur in more rural areas such as mountain and coastal forests where woodpecker holes are abundant; also uses Saguaro cactus for nesting in the Southwest.

Length **7–8in (18–20cm)**	Wingspan **15–16in (38–41cm)**	Weight **1⁷⁄₁₆–2⅛oz (40–60g)**
Social **Large flocks/Colonies**	Lifespan **Up to 13 years**	Status **Secure**

Order **Passeriformes**	Family **Hirundinidae**	Species *Stelgidopteryx serripennis*

Northern Rough-winged Swallow

dark brown overall

ADULT

dark face

IN FLIGHT

black eye

JUVENILE

tan-buffy wing bars

pale underparts

light crescent from cheek to crown

brown head

pale brown breast

pale, grayish brown belly

ADULT

long, brown wings

square tail

Given the name *serripennis* "saw-like", by Audubon in 1888, and characterized by the serrations on its outer wing feathers, this species is otherwise somewhat drab in color and aspect. The Northern Rough-winged Swallow has a broad distribution in North America, being found across southern Canada and throughout the US. Often overlooked by birdwatchers, this brown-backed, dusky-throated swallow can be spotted hunting insects over water. In size and habit, the Northern Rough-winged Swallow shares many similarities with the Bank Swallow, including breeding habits and color, but the latter's notched tail and smaller size makes it easy to tell them apart.

VOICE Steady repetition of short, rapid *brrrt* notes inflected upward; sometimes a buzzy *jee-jee-jee* or high-pitched *brzzzzzt*.

NESTING Loose cup of twigs and straw in a cavity or burrow in a bank, such as road cuts; 4–7 eggs; 1 brood; May–July.

FEEDING Captures flying insects, including flies, wasps, bees, damselflies, and beetles in the air; more likely to feed over water and at lower altitudes than other swallows.

FLIGHT: slow, deliberate wing beats; short to long glides; long, straight flight, ends in steep climb.

BROWN BIRD
This swallow is brownish above and pale grayish below, with just a brown smudge on its neck.

SIMILAR SPECIES

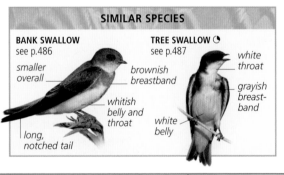

BANK SWALLOW
see p.486

smaller overall

brownish breastband

whitish belly and throat

long, notched tail

TREE SWALLOW ☾
see p.487

white throat

grayish breast-band

white belly

OCCURRENCE
In North America, widespread from coast to coast. Nests at a wide variety of altitudes, prefers exposed banks of clay, sand, or gravel such as gorges, shale banks, and gravel pits. Forages along watercourses where aerial insects are plentiful. Breeds south to Cost Rica. Winters in Central America.

Length 4¾–6in (12–15cm)	Wingspan **11–12in (28–30cm)**	Weight ⅜–⅝oz (10–18g)
Social **Solitary**	Lifespan **Unknown**	Status **Secure**

| Order **Passeriformes** | Family **Hirundinidae** | Species *Hirundo rustica* |

Barn Swallow

long, pointed wings

duller plumage than adult

JUVENILE

shiny blue head and uppperparts

chestnut forehead

ADULT

IN FLIGHT

reddish orange underparts

deep, chestnut -brown throat

slender wings

reddish orange belly

deeply forked tail

long tail "streamers"

ADULT

The most widely distributed and abundant swallow in the world, the Barn Swallow is found just about everywhere in North America south of the Arctic timberline. Originally a cave-nester before Europeans settlers came to the New World, the Barn Swallow readily adapted to nesting under the eaves of houses, under bridges, and inside buildings such as barns. It is now rare to find this elegant swallow breeding in a natural site. Steely blue upperparts, reddish underparts, and a deeply forked tail identify the Barn Swallow. North American breeders have deep, reddish orange underparts, but birds from Eurasia are white-bellied.
VOICE High-pitched, squeaky *chee-chee* call; song a long series of chatty, pleasant churrs, squeaks, chitterings, and buzzes.
NESTING Deep cup of mud and grass-stems attached to vertical surfaces or on ledges; 4–6 eggs; 1–2 broods; May–September.
FEEDING Snatches flying insects, such as flies, mosquitoes, wasps, and beetles in the air at lower altitudes than other swallows; sometimes eats wild berries and seeds.

FLIGHT: bursts of straight flight; close to the ground; weaves left and right, with sharp turns.

WELL PROTECTED
Whether in a barn or other structure, a Barn Swallow nest is protected from wind and rain.

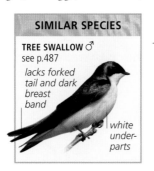

SIMILAR SPECIES

TREE SWALLOW ♂
see p.487
lacks forked tail and dark breast band

white underparts

OCCURRENCE
Breeds across North America, except in the tundra zone; south as far as central Mexico. Found in most habitats, but prefers agricultural regions, towns, and highway overpasses; migrates over coastal marshes; winters near sugarcane fields, grain fields, and marshes.

| Length **6–7½in (15–19cm)** | Wingspan **11½–13in (29–33cm)** | Weight **⅝–¹¹⁄₁₆oz (17–20g)** |
| Social **Small colonies/flocks** | Lifespan **Up to 8 years** | Status **Secure** |

| Order **Passeriformes** | Family **Hirundinidae** | Species *Petrochelidon pyrrhonata* |

Cliff Swallow

long, roundish wings

ADULT

IN FLIGHT

brown-tinged, black back

rusty cheek patch

mottled throat

JUVENILE

bluish black back

rusty-brown cheeks

bluish black cap

pale hind neck collar

whitish forehead

dark throat

ADULT

pale underparts

slight notch in squared tail

pale reddish rump

The Cliff Swallow is one of North America's most social land birds, sometimes nesting in colonies of over 3,500 pairs, especially in the western US. It is more locally distributed across the east. It can be distinguished from other North American swallows by its square tail and orange rump, but it resembles its close relative, the Cave Swallow, in color, pattern, and in affixing its mud nests to the sides of highway culverts, bridges, and buildings. The considerable increase in such structures has allowed the species to expand its range from the west to breed almost everywhere on the continent, south of the tundra forest.
VOICE Gives *purr* and *churr* calls when alarmed; song a low, squeaky, 6-second twitter given in flight and near nests.
NESTING Domed nests of mud pellets on cave walls, buildings, culverts, bridges, and dams; 3–5 eggs; 1–2 broods; April–August.
FEEDING Catches flying insects (often swarming varieties) while on the wing; sometimes forages on the ground; ingests grit to aid digestion.

FLIGHT: strong, fast wing beats; glides more often but less acrobatically than other swallows.

GATHERING MUD
The Cliff Swallow gathers wet mud from puddles, pond edges, and streamsides to build its nests.

SIMILAR SPECIES

CAVE SWALLOW see p.493

brighter orange cheek

paler overall

INDIVIDUAL HOMES
In a Cliff Swallow colony, each nest has a single opening.

OCCURRENCE
Breeds almost anywhere in North America from Alaska to Mexico, except deserts, tundra, and unbroken forest; prefers concrete or cliff walls, culverts, buildings, cliffs, and undersides of piers on which to affix mud nests; feeds over grasslands, marshes, lakes, and reservoirs. Migrates to South America.

| Length **5in (13cm)** | Wingspan **11–12in (28–30cm)** | Weight **¹¹⁄₁₆–1¼oz (20–35g)** |
| Social **Colonies** | Lifespan **Up to 11 years** | Status **Secure** |

| Order **Passeriformes** | Family **Hirundinidae** | Species ***Petrochelidon fulva*** |

Cave Swallow

dark cap

tawny to rufous forehead

tawny collar

light lines on back

brown-tinged wings

pale orange chin and orange cheeks

ADULT

blue-black upperparts

IN FLIGHT

pale underparts

ADULT

bright rump and sides of rear flanks

Distinguished from its close relative, the Cliff Swallow, by a pale rather than black throat and rufous rather than white forehead, the buffy-rumped Cave Swallow is limited in its breeding range to parts of New Mexico, Arizona, Texas, and southern Florida. As its name suggests, the Cave Swallow cements its cup nest to the walls of caves, which it often shares with bats; it also builds nests on bridges, water culverts, and buildings. The Cave Swallow was once rare in North America, but in recent years, it has been expanding both geographically and numerically because it has adapted to nesting on manmade structures. The three North American forms are similar in color and size, and somewhat difficult to tell apart. In winter the US Cave Swallow population moves south to Mexico.

VOICE Call a low *wheet*; song a series of bubbly sounds blending into warbling trill, ending in series of double-toned notes.

NESTING Open flat cup with tall, broad rim, made of mud and guano, glued to concrete structure or cave wall; 3–5 eggs; 1–2 broods; April–July.

FEEDING Captures a variety of flying insects while on the wing, including beetles, flies, and bees; sometimes flushes its prey out into the air by flying into vegetation.

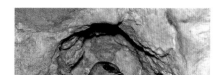

FLIGHT: uses rapid wing beats to swoop and dive, but also likes to glide.

MUD BOWL NEST
Cave Swallow nests are cup-like, and not domed like those of the Cliff Swallow.

SIMILAR SPECIES

CLIFF SWALLOW see p.492

light forehead

dark throat

OCCURRENCE
In US, breeds in the arid central west (Arizona, east to Texas) and southwest Florida, wherever nests can be attached to walls of caves, sinkholes, bridges, buildings, and culverts; preferably near open water for feeding on flying insects. Outside US, breeds in Mexico and the Greater Antilles.

| Length **5½in (14cm)** | Wingspan **13in (33cm)** | Weight ⅝– ⅞oz (17–25g) |
| Social **Colonies** | Lifespan **Up to 9 years** | Status **Localized** |

Order **Passeriformes**	Family **Aegithalidae**	Species ***Psaltriparus minimus***

Bushtit

FEMALE (PACIFIC; BREEDING)
brownish cap
yellow eye

FEMALE (INTERIOR; BREEDING)
pale ear patch

ADULT
gray upperparts

IN FLIGHT

mouse-gray upperparts

dark cap

black eye

tiny, black bill

pale underparts

MALE (PACIFIC; BREEDING)

long tail

black legs and feet

FLIGHT: short, fluttering flights from shrub, trailing its distinctive long tail.

For much of the year, the Bushtit roams the foothills and valleys of the western US, in flocks that usually number just a handful, but occasionally total many hundreds. This little bird is constantly on the move, foraging busily in the foliage of shrubs and small trees. One moment a flock is there; the next, it has moved on. Even during the breeding season, when most other perching birds become territorial, the Bushtit retains something of its social nature—raising the young is often a communal affair, with both siblings and single adults helping in the rearing of a pair's chicks.

VOICE Basic call a 2–3-part soft lisp, *ps psss pit*, interspersed with hard spit and spick notes, like little sparks.

NESTING Enormous pendant structure of cobwebs and leaves, hung from branch; 4–10 eggs; 2 broods; April–July.

FEEDING Gleans spiders and insects from vegetation; acrobatic while feeding, often hangs upside-down.

FORAGING
Constantly aflutter, the Bushtit flits through foliage, looking for insects and other small arthropods.

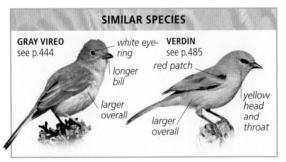

SIMILAR SPECIES

GRAY VIREO see p.444
white eye-ring
longer bill
larger overall

VERDIN see p.485
red patch
yellow head and throat
larger overall

OCCURRENCE
Away from the coast, common in open woodlands and areas of shrubs, mainly on hillsides in summer, some birds move down to low-elevation valleys in the fall. Coastal populations, commonly seen in cities and gardens as well as on hillsides, live in native and non-native plant communities.

Length **4½in (11.5cm)**	Wingspan **6in (15.5cm)**	Weight **³⁄₁₆–⁷⁄₃₂oz (4.5–6g)**
Social **Flocks**	Lifespan **Up to 8 years**	Status **Secure**

| Order **Passeriformes** | Family **Alaudidae** | Species **Eremophila alpestris** |

Horned Lark

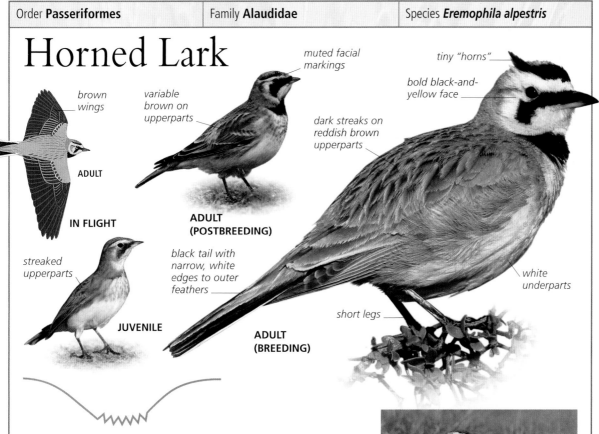

muted facial markings

tiny "horns"

bold black-and-yellow face

brown wings

variable brown on upperparts

dark streaks on reddish brown upperparts

ADULT

IN FLIGHT

ADULT (POSTBREEDING)

white underparts

streaked upperparts

black tail with narrow, white edges to outer feathers

short legs

JUVENILE

ADULT (BREEDING)

FLIGHT: undulating, with wings folded in after every few beats.

The Horned Lark is a bird of open country, especially places with extensive bare ground. The species is characteristic of arid, alpine, and Arctic regions; in these areas, it flourishes in the bleakest of habitats imaginable, from sun-scorched, arid lakes in the Great Basin, to windswept tundra above the timberline. In some places, the only breeding bird species are the Horned Lark and the equally resilient Common Raven. In Europe and Asia, this species is known as the Shore Lark.

VOICE Flight call a sharp *sweet* or *soo-weet*; song, either in flight or from the ground, pleasant, musical tinkling series, followed by *sweet… swit… sweet… s'sweea'weea'witta'swit.*

NESTING In depression in bare ground, somewhat sheltered by grass or low shrubs, lined with plant matter; 2–5 eggs; 1–3 broods; March–July.

FEEDING Survives exclusively on seeds of grasses and sedges in winter; eats mostly insects in summer.

GROUND FORAGER
With its short legs bent under its body, an adult looks for insects and seeds.

OCCURRENCE
Breeds widely, in any sort of open, even barren habitat with extensive bare ground, especially short-grass prairies and deserts. Winters wherever there are snow-free openings, including places along beaches and roads. Winters from southern Canada southward to Florida and Mexico.

VERY VOCAL
The Horned Lark is a highly vocal bird, singing from the air, the ground, or low shrubs.

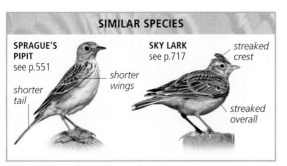

SIMILAR SPECIES

SPRAGUE'S PIPIT
see p.551

shorter tail

shorter wings

SKY LARK
see p.717

streaked crest

streaked overall

| Length **7in (18cm)** | Wingspan **12in (30cm)** | Weight **1¹⁄₁₆oz (30g)** |
| Social **Winter flocks** | Lifespan **Up to 8 years** | Status **Secure** |

| Order **Passeriformes** | Family **Sylviidae** | Species *Phylloscopus borealis* |

Arctic Warbler

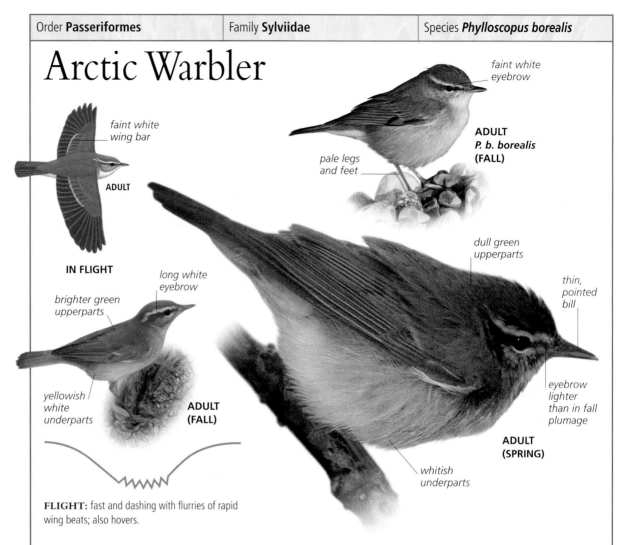

faint white
wing bar

ADULT

IN FLIGHT

faint white
eyebrow

ADULT
P. b. borealis
(FALL)

pale legs
and feet

long white
eyebrow

brighter green
upperparts

yellowish
white
underparts

**ADULT
(FALL)**

dull green
upperparts

thin,
pointed
bill

eyebrow
lighter
than in fall
plumage

**ADULT
(SPRING)**

whitish
underparts

FLIGHT: fast and dashing with flurries of rapid
wing beats; also hovers.

The Arctic Warbler is a small, slender, olive-colored bird with a prominent buffy yellow eyestripe and a faint, single wing bar. Predominantly a Eurasian species, in North America, it occurs mainly in willow thickets in Alaska. These birds move to southeast Asia for the winter. Little is known about the breeding biology of the Arctic Warbler in Alaska, while much more is known about its habits in Eurasia. The European subspecies, *P. b. borealis,* has occurred in the Aleutian Islands in the fall.
VOICE Alarm call a short hard metallic *dzik;* male's song a loud, vigorous, monotonous slow trill *chingingingingingng.*
NESTING Domed nest on ground with side entrance, composed of leaves, mosses, grasses, and moose hair, lined with fine grass; 5–6 eggs; 1 brood; June–July.
FEEDING Forages for insects such as flies, grasshoppers, and beetles on branches and leaves in upper regions of trees.

DIFFERENCES
This bird has relatively longer wings, a larger head, and shorter tail than the Tennessee Warbler.

OCCURRENCE
Breeds in stands of dwarf willow, often along streams or in shrubland. Winters in the tropics, in open rainforests, grasslands, gardens, and mangroves; Alaskan population winters in the Phillipines and in Indonesia.

FLICKING WINGS
Arctic Warblers constantly flick their wings when foraging for food.

| Length **4¼–5in (11–13cm)** | Wingspan **8in (20cm)** | Weight **⅜oz (10g)** |
| Social **Solitary/Pairs** | Lifespan **Up to 3 years** | Status **Localized (p)** |

Order **Passeriformes**	Family **Timaliidae**	Species **Chamaea fasciata**

Wrentit

tail cocked at an
upright angle

whitish
inner iris

gray-brown
plumage

small
bill

weak
streaking
on pinkish
breast

ADULT

short,
round
wings

long
tail

ADULT

brownish
legs and
feet

IN FLIGHT

This stealthy bird is difficult to glimpse but impossible not to hear, as it is *the* voice of the low-elevation country of the Pacific slope. The Wrentit is actually neither a wren nor a chickadee, but is the sole New World representative of the large and diverse Old World babbler family. Unlike many other small birds of shrubby habitats, the Wrentit is not especially sociable; pairs are rather aloof, jealously guarding their territories, and rarely join in mixed-species foraging flocks. Although Wrentits have suffered from the destruction of coastal brushwood, their numbers have increased where logging has opened up new habitats for them.

VOICE Calls varied, most sound agitated *jrrr, krrrrt;* sings a loud accelerating series all year long: *pip... pip... pip... pi'pi'pi'pi'pi'pi'pi.*
NESTING Cup of bark strips and cobwebs placed in lower regions of shrub; 3–4 eggs; 1–2 broods; April–July.
FEEDING Gleans insects, spiders from bark, also from foliage in dense thickets; also eats berries.

FLIGHT: flies short distances between shrubs, just above vegetation; long tail jerks as it flies.

RARE GLIMPSE
Wrentits mainly skulk in dense thickets, but may pop out briefly before disappearing again.

EXPRESSIVE TAIL
When seen out in the open, its long tail is often expressively flipped about.

OCCURRENCE
Found in Pacific Coast and dense foothill shrubs with Chamise, Manzanita, Sagebrush, and Poison oak. Ranges into inland forests with shrubby understory. Nonmigratory; pairs may wander a little through the year, but generally stay close to their breeding territories in Oregon and California.

SIMILAR SPECIES

BUSHTIT
see p.494
*stockier and
grayer
overall*

white
corners
on tail

BEWICK'S WREN
see p.506

longer
bill

smaller
bill

Length **6½in (16cm)**	Wingspan **7in (17.5cm)**	Weight **⁷⁄₁₆–⅝oz (12–18g)**
Social **Solitary**	Lifespan **At least 3 years**	Status **Localized**

| Order **Passeriformes** | Family **Muscicapidae** | Species **Regulus satrapa** |

Golden-crowned Kinglet

whitish wing bars

MALE

IN FLIGHT

yellow crown patch, with black border

FEMALE

orange-and-yellow patch on crown, with black border

broad whitish stripe above eye

olive-green upperparts

short, straight bill

MALE

white wing bar

notched tail

pale buff to whitish underparts

FLIGHT: quick and erratic, but not direct; high in the air; can hover while foraging.

This hardy little bird, barely more than a ball of feathers, breeds in northern and mountainous coniferous forests in the US, after a considerable hiatus in mountain forests of Mexico and Guatemala. Planting of spruce trees in parts of the US Midwest has allowed this species to increase its range in recent years to Ohio, Indiana, Illinois, and Pennsylvania.

VOICE Call a thin, high-pitched and thread-like *tsee* or *see see*; song a series of high-pitched ascending notes for 2 seconds; complex song *tsee-tsee-tsee-tsee-teet-leetle*, followed by brief trill.

NESTING Deep, cup-shaped nest with rims arching inward, made of moss, lichen, and bark, and lined with finer strips of the same; 8–9 eggs; 1–2 broods; May–August.

FEEDING Gleans flies, beetles, mites, spiders, and their eggs from tips of branches, under bark, tufts of conifer needles; eats seeds, and persimmon fruits.

EXPANDING RANGE
This bird has expanded its range southward following spruce forestation.

SIMILAR SPECIES

RUBY-CROWNED KINGLET
see p.499

white eye-ring

no eye-stripe

olive underparts

HIGHER VOICE
The Golden-crowned has a higher-pitched and less musical song than the Ruby-crowned.

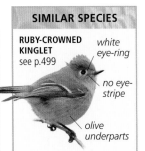

OCCURRENCE
Breeds in remote northern and subalpine spruce or fir forests, mixed coniferous–deciduous forests, single-species stands, and pine plantations; winters in a wide variety of habitats—coniferous and deciduous forests, pine groves, low-lying hardwood forests, swamps, and urban and suburban habitats.

| Length **3¼–4¼in (8–11cm)** | Wingspan **5½–7in (14–18cm)** | Weight **5/32–9/32oz (4–8g)** |
| Social **Solitary/Pairs** | Lifespan **Up to 5 years** | Status **Secure** |

Order **Passeriformes**	Family **Muscicapidae**	Species **Regulus calendula**

Ruby-crowned Kinglet

red patch
on crown

white wing
bars

ADULT

patch on crown
often concealed

incomplete
white eye-ring

olive-green
upperparts

notched
tail

IN FLIGHT

no red
patch on
crown

FEMALE

MALE

olive
underparts

MALE

small,
upturned bill

brown legs with
paler brown feet

The Ruby-crowned Kinglet is perhaps one of the most easily recognizable songbirds in North America because of its very small size, white eye-ring, two white wing bars, and habit of incessantly flicking its wings while foraging. This bird is renowned for its loud, complex song and for laying up to 12 eggs in a clutch—probably the highest of any North American songbird. Despite local declines resulting from logging and forest fires, the Ruby-crowned Kinglet is common across the continent. It will sometimes join mixed-species flocks in winter with nuthatches and titmice.

VOICE Call a low, husky *jidit*; song, remarkably loud for such a small bird, begins with 2–3 high, clear notes *tee* or *zee* followed by 5–6 lower *tu* or *turr* notes, and ends with ringing galloping notes *tee-da-leet, tee-da-leet, tee-da-leet*.

NESTING Globular or elongated nest hanging from or on large branch with an enclosed or open cup, made of mosses, feathers, lichens, spider's silk, bark, hair, and fur; 5–12 eggs; 1 brood; May–October.

FEEDING Gleans a wide variety of insects, spiders, and their eggs among the leaves on the outer tips of higher, smaller branches; eats fruit and seeds; often hovers to catch prey.

FLIGHT: short bursts of rapid wing beats, but overall quick and direct flight.

CONCEALED COLOR
This bird's red patch is often concealed unless the bird is agitated or excited.

OCCURRENCE
Within the northerly forest zone, breeds near water in Black Spruce and tamarack forests, muskegs, forests with mixed conifers and northern hardwoods; in the mountainous West, spruce-fir, Lodgepole Pine, and Douglas Fir forests. Winters in a broad range of forests, thickets, and borders.

SIMILAR SPECIES

HUTTON'S VIREO
see p.449

larger
head

stouter
bill

heavier
overall

ALWAYS FLICKING
Ruby-crowned Kinglets are easily identified by their habit of constantly flicking their wings.

Length **3½–4¼in (9–11cm)**	Wingspan **6–7in (15–18cm)**	Weight **³⁄₁₆–³⁄₈oz (5–10g)**
Social **Winter flocks**	Lifespan **Up to 5 years**	Status **Secure**

Family **Troglodytidae**

WRENS

WITH ONE EXCEPTION, the Eurasian Winter Wren, wrens are all small American songbirds. Generally dull-colored, most species are shades of brown with light and dark streaking. The scientific family name, which derives from a Greek word for "cave-dweller," seems apt in light of the furtive habits of some wren species. Wrens are also renowned in the avian world for their remarkable songs, and, in some species, for singing precisely synchronized duets.

COCKED TAIL
As they sing, Winter Wrens often hold their tails upward in a near-vertical position.

Family **Sittidae**

NUTHATCHES

EASILY RECOGNIZED BY their distinctive shape and characteristic feeding technique, nuthatches are common woodland birds. They are plump-bodied, short-tailed birds with blue-gray backs and often a contrasting darker crown. Nuthatches use their straight, pointed bills to probe for insects and spiders in crevices in tree trunks and branches. Strong feet and long claws allow these birds to move downwards, upwards, upside-down along the underside of branches in search of food. This contrasts with many other similar birds, which only move upward on a tree trunk.

ACROBATIC POSE
Downward-facing nuthatches such as this one often lift their heads in a characteristic pose.

Family **Mimidae**

THRASHERS

THE FAMILY NAME for thrashers is derived from the Latin for "to imitate," and perhaps no other word better represents the dozen or so species or subspecies found in North America. They are well known for their ability to mimic the songs of other species in their own song sequences. Members of this group are characterized by their long, curved bill and somewhat reclusive habits, though some, like the Northern Mockingbird, are as brash and conspicuous as any other species on the continent, and sport a short, straight bill.

DISTINCTIVE BILL
This Long-billed Thrasher is characterized by its slender, curved bill, long, thin legs, and long, rounded tail.

| Order **Passeriformes** | Family **Troglodytidae** | Species ***Campylorhynchus brunneicapillus*** |

Cactus Wren

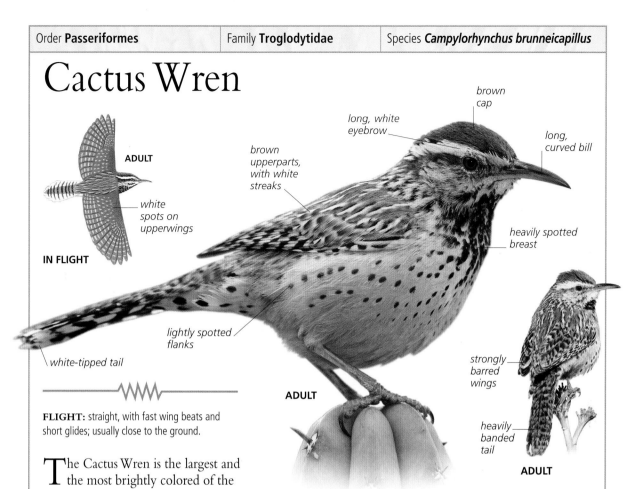

ADULT

IN FLIGHT

white spots on upperwings

brown upperparts, with white streaks

long, white eyebrow

brown cap

long, curved bill

heavily spotted breast

lightly spotted flanks

white-tipped tail

ADULT

strongly barred wings

heavily banded tail

ADULT

FLIGHT: straight, with fast wing beats and short glides; usually close to the ground.

The Cactus Wren is the largest and the most brightly colored of the North American wrens. Unfortunately, its population has been declining as its habitat is being destroyed as a result of agricultural development and wildfires. Its distinctively pale and weakly spotted subspecies, the "San Diego," is especially susceptible to loss of habitat. The Cactus Wren is known for building large, ball-shaped nests, often in cacti, which act as superbly effective deterrents to predators.

VOICE Call a loud *chack*; song a grating *kchar kchar kchar kchar*, with a harsh cluck-like quality; sings repeatedly from top of cactus or shrub, especially in the morning.

NESTING Bulky globular mass of woven grasses and stems with entrance hole on side; 3–5 eggs; 1–2 broods; March–August.

FEEDING Plucks insects and spiders from ground or shrubs.

SAFE HOUSE
The large globular nests that Cactus Wrens construct contain a small passage, which leads to the nest chamber.

NEST CONSTRUCTION
Woven with strong pieces of plant matter, the nest protects the young from the hot sun.

OCCURRENCE
Occupies deserts and arid hillsides dominated by cacti (especially cholla), and thorny shrubs throughout the Southwest of the continent. Also occurs in suburban areas where artificial plantings provide suitable nest sites. The "San Diego" subspecies is found in sagebrush along the coast of southern California.

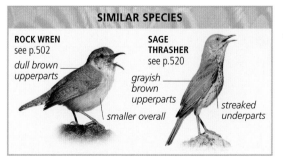

SIMILAR SPECIES

ROCK WREN
see p.502
dull brown upperparts

SAGE THRASHER
see p.520
grayish brown upperparts

smaller overall

streaked underparts

| Length **8½in (22cm)** | Wingspan **11in (28cm)** | Weight **1¼oz (35g)** |
| Social **Family groups** | Lifespan **Up to 7 years** | Status **Declining** |

Order **Passeriformes**	Family **Troglodytidae**	Species *Salpinctes obsoletus*

Rock Wren

faint eyestripe

rusty rump

ADULT

bright buff feather tips

IN FLIGHT

grayish brown upperparts

thin, brown streaks

pale lemon-yellow belly

ADULT

black-and-white barring on undertail

pale buff lower flanks

FLIGHT: straight, with fast wing beats; sometimes glides from high perch.

An inhabitant of various rocky landscapes—it often sings from the edge of a high precipice—the Rock Wren's voice, while not particularly loud, carries surprisingly far through the dry air of the West. It is perpetually busy running, fluttering, and darting in and out of crevices in search of food. A well-known behavioral quirk of the Rock Wren is to bob and sway conspicuously when a human approaches. However, its oddest habit is to "pave" the area in front of its nest entrance with a walkway of pebbles—the purpose of this is unknown.

VOICE Call a sharp *ch'keer*; varied series of warbles, trills, chatters, and repeated musical phrases such as *chuwee chuwee, teedee teedee*, reminiscent of a mockingbird or a thrasher; sings at all elevations.

NESTING Cup of various grasses lined with soft materials, in rock crevice or under overhang; 4–8 eggs; 1–2 broods; April–August.

FEEDING Probes in rock crevices on ground and in dirt banks for a variety of insects and spiders.

A CHANGE OF SCENERY
Rock Wrens occasionally venture out into open grasslands and perch on manmade structures, well away from their usual surroundings.

SIMILAR SPECIES

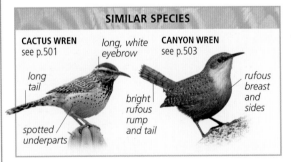

CACTUS WREN
see p.501

long, white eyebrow

CANYON WREN
see p.503

long tail

spotted underparts

bright rufous rump and tail

rufous breast and sides

OCCURRENCE
Inhabits arid country with rocky cliffs and canyons, as well as manmade quarries and gravel piles; a wide variety of elevations from hot, low deserts to windswept mountain tops as high as 10,000ft (3,000m). Northern birds migrate to southern states for winter.

Length **6in (15cm)**	Wingspan **9in (23cm)**	Weight ⅝**oz (17g)**
Social **Solitary/Pairs**	Lifespan **Unknown**	Status **Secure**

Order **Passeriformes**	Family **Troglodytidae**	Species *Catherpes mexicanus*

Canyon Wren

grayish cap
and cheeks

long
bill

thinly barred
rufous tail

small black-and-
white spots on
back and wings

white
throat

ADULT

bright
rufous
rump

long, curved
bill

ADULT

round
wings

rufous underparts
barred with black
and brown

IN FLIGHT

The Canyon Wren's loud, clear whistles echo across canyons
in the West, but the singer usually stays out of sight,
remaining high among the crevices of its cliffside home. When
it can be observed, the most striking aspect of its behavior is its
extraordinary ability to walk up, down, and sideways on vertical
rock walls. This remarkable agility is achieved through its strong
toes and long claws; these features enable Canyon Wrens to find
a grip in the tiniest of depressions and fissures in the rock.

VOICE Series of 10–15 loud, ringing
whistles, descending in pitch,
gradually slowing, and ending with
several thin buzzes.

NESTING Cup of sticks lined with
soft material like plant down, in
crevice or hole; 4–6 eggs; 1–2 broods;
April–August.

FEEDING Uses extremely long bill to
probe crevices for insects and spiders;
can flatten itself by spreading legs to
enter low overhangs.

FLIGHT: steady, straight, and fluttery; broad,
rounded wings let it glide to a lower perch.

BLENDING IN
Except for the white throat,
the Canyon Wren's plumage
matches its rocky habitat.

CLIFF-HOPPER
This bird can half-fly and half-hop up steep cliffs
by flapping its broad wings for extra lift.

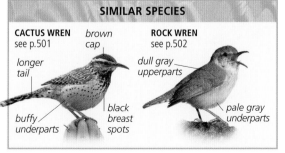

SIMILAR SPECIES

CACTUS WREN
see p.501

brown
cap

ROCK WREN
see p.502

longer
tail

dull gray
upperparts

buffy
underparts

black
breast
spots

pale gray
underparts

OCCURRENCE
Maintains year-round territory
on rocky hillsides, outcroppings,
and vertical rock-walled canyons
through much of the west
of the continent and southward
to Mexico. Sometimes nests
in holes in stone buildings,
old sheds, and other structures,
apparently unconcerned by
nearby human activity.

Length **5¾in (14.5cm)**	Wingspan **7½in (19cm)**	Weight **⅜oz (11g)**
Social **Solitary/Pairs**	Lifespan **Unknown**	Status **Secure**

Order **Passeriformes**	Family **Troglodytidae**	Species **Cistothorus platensis**

Sedge Wren

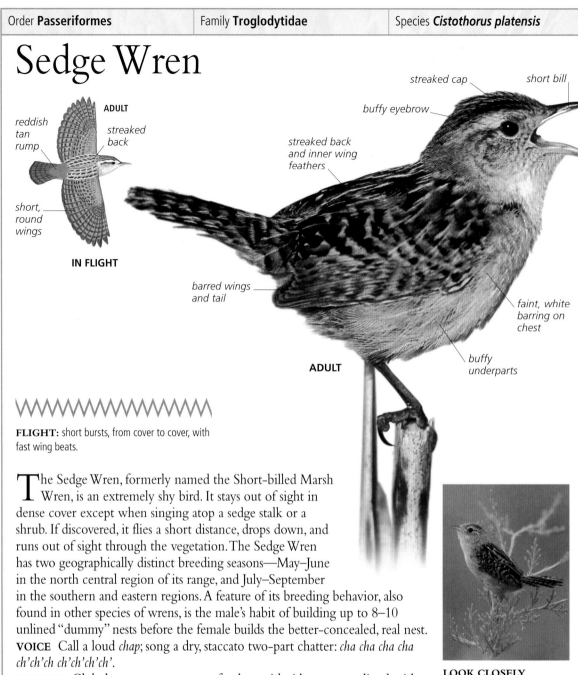

ADULT

reddish tan rump

streaked back

short, round wings

IN FLIGHT

streaked cap

short bill

buffy eyebrow

streaked back and inner wing feathers

barred wings and tail

faint, white barring on chest

buffy underparts

ADULT

FLIGHT: short bursts, from cover to cover, with fast wing beats.

The Sedge Wren, formerly named the Short-billed Marsh Wren, is an extremely shy bird. It stays out of sight in dense cover except when singing atop a sedge stalk or a shrub. If discovered, it flies a short distance, drops down, and runs out of sight through the vegetation. The Sedge Wren has two geographically distinct breeding seasons—May–June in the north central region of its range, and July–September in the southern and eastern regions. A feature of its breeding behavior, also found in other species of wrens, is the male's habit of building up to 8–10 unlined "dummy" nests before the female builds the better-concealed, real nest.

VOICE Call a loud *chap*; song a dry, staccato two-part chatter: *cha cha cha cha ch'ch'ch ch'ch'ch'ch'*.

NESTING Globular, woven structure of sedges with side entrance; lined with plant matter, down, and hair; 4–8 eggs; 1–2 broods; May–August.

FEEDING Forages for spiders and insects, such as grasshoppers, flies, mosquitoes, and bugs, close to or on ground in cover of sedges and grass.

LOOK CLOSELY
Close study is necessary to appreciate the Sedge Wren's subtle patterning, which is plainer than the Marsh Wren's.

OCCURRENCE
In North America, breeds in wet meadows and sedge marshes with low water levels. Widely distributed in the Americas from the Canadian prairies, east to Quebec and from northern US, to the south central states. Winters from Texas to Florida in drier habitats including grassy fields and coastal-plain prairies.

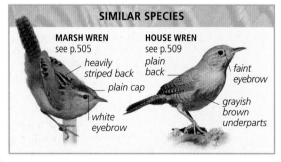

SIMILAR SPECIES

MARSH WREN
see p.505

heavily striped back

plain cap

white eyebrow

HOUSE WREN
see p.509

plain back

faint eyebrow

grayish brown underparts

Length **4½in (11.5cm)**	Wingspan **5½–6in (14–15.5cm)**	Weight **⁵⁄₁₆oz (9g)**
Social **Loose colonies**	Lifespan **Unknown**	Status **Secure**

Order **Passeriformes**	Family **Troglodytidae**	Species *Cistothorus palustris*

Marsh Wren

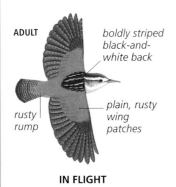

ADULT

boldly striped black-and-white back

rusty rump

plain, rusty wing patches

IN FLIGHT

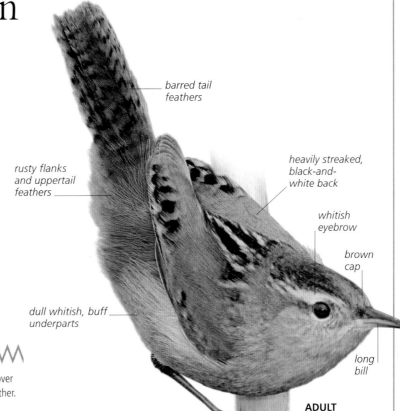

barred tail feathers

rusty flanks and uppertail feathers

heavily streaked, black-and-white back

whitish eyebrow

brown cap

dull whitish, buff underparts

long bill

ADULT

FLIGHT: straight, with rapid wing beats over short distances, from one reed patch to another.

The Marsh Wren, a common resident of saltwater and freshwater marshes, is known for singing loudly through both day and night. The males perform fluttery, aerial courtship flights while singing, and are polygamous, mating with two or more females. Like the Sedge Wren, the male builds several dummy nests before his mate constructs one herself. The Marsh Wren nests in taller vegetation than the Sedge Wren and over deeper water. Eastern (*C. p. palustris*) and Western (*C. p. paludicola*) Marsh Wrens differ in voice and behavior, and some ornithologists classify them as separate species.

VOICE Calls a low *chek* and a raspy *churr*; song a loud *chuk chuk chuk*, then fast *tih-tih-tih-rih-tih-tih*, an enthusiastic singer.

NESTING Oblong structure with side entrance, woven of reeds and lined with soft materials; 4–5 eggs; 2 broods; March–July.

FEEDING Forages acrobatically for insects, such as mosquitoes, dragonflies, and beetles, within dense clusters of cattails and reeds.

DELICATELY PERCHED
This wren perches on vertical reeds and often holds itself up by spreading its legs across two stalks.

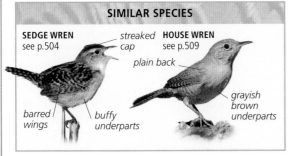

SIMILAR SPECIES

SEDGE WREN see p.504 — streaked cap

HOUSE WREN see p.509 — plain back

barred wings

buffy underparts

grayish brown underparts

OCCURRENCE
Breeds across North America from Canada to the mountains of the western and central northern states. Inhabits freshwater and saltwater marshes with tall vegetation, above water, sometimes more than 3ft (1m) deep. It is irregularly distributed in its range. Winters in grassy marshes and wetlands.

Length **5in (13cm)**	Wingspan **6in (15cm)**	Weight ⅜oz (11g)
Social **Loose colonies**	Lifespan **Unknown**	Status **Localized**

| Order **Passeriformes** | Family **Troglodytidae** | Species *Thryomanes bewickii* |

Bewick's Wren

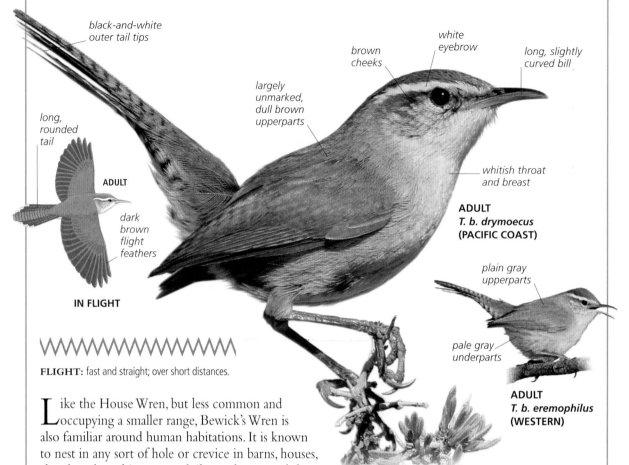

black-and-white outer tail tips

brown cheeks

white eyebrow

long, slightly curved bill

largely unmarked, dull brown upperparts

long, rounded tail

ADULT

dark brown flight feathers

IN FLIGHT

whitish throat and breast

ADULT
T. b. drymoecus
(PACIFIC COAST)

plain gray upperparts

pale gray underparts

ADULT
T. b. eremophilus
(WESTERN)

FLIGHT: fast and straight; over short distances.

Like the House Wren, but less common and occupying a smaller range, Bewick's Wren is also familiar around human habitations. It is known to nest in any sort of hole or crevice in barns, houses, abandoned machinery, woodpiles, and even trash heaps in farms and towns. Bewick's Wren has undergone large-scale changes in geographic distribution: in the 19th century its range expanded northward to the eastern and midwestern US, but it gradually disappeared from those regions in the 20th century. It has been suggested that the more aggressive House Wren slowly replaced Bewick's Wren in these areas.

VOICE Loud, complex, and varied mixture of cheeps, buzzes, and clear notes; vocalizations differ according to geographic location; also mimics other birds.
NESTING Cup of sticks lined with leaves, and other soft materials, in natural or human-made cavity, including nest boxes; 5–10 eggs; 2 broods; March–June.
FEEDING Forages for insects in brush, shrubs, crannies of buildings, and leaf litter on ground.

TALENTED MIMIC
Bewick's is sometimes known as the "Mocking Wren," due to its imitations of other species' songs.

OCCURRENCE
Year-round resident in brushy areas, open woodlands, and around human structures; from southern British Columbia southward to Baja California, east to Arkansas, and as far south as Oaxaca in Mexico. May withdraw slightly southward from northernmost portions of range in winter.

SIMILAR SPECIES

CAROLINA WREN
see p.507

rufous upperparts

buffy underparts

TYPICAL POSTURE
Bewick's Wren may often be spotted with its distinctive tail cocked vertically.

| Length **5in (13cm)** | Wingspan **7in (18cm)** | Weight **⅜oz (11g)** |
| Social **Solitary/Pairs** | Lifespan **At least 8 years** | Status **Secure** |

| Order **Passeriformes** | Family **Troglodytidae** | Species *Thryothorus ludovicianus* |

Carolina Wren

white eyebrow bordered by black above

huge head

tiny tail

ADULT

rufous upperparts

duller overall

FLEDGLING

thin, black barring on tail

white wing spots

IN FLIGHT

powerful-looking, bluish bill

white spots on wing

ADULT

buffy underparts

pinkish legs and toes

The Carolina Wren is a popular and common backyard bird in most of its range. It is rarely still, often flicking its tail and looking around nervously. Extremely harsh winters at the northernmost fringe of the Carolina Wren's range in New England can cause a sudden decline in numbers, as food resources are covered for long periods by ice and heavy snow. At such times, survival may depend on human help for food and shelter.

VOICE Calls variable; often a sharp *chlip* or long, harsh chatter; song a loud, long, fast *whee'dle-dee whee'dle-dee whee'dle-dee*.

NESTING Cup of weeds, twigs, leaves in natural or human-made cavity; 4–8 eggs; 2–3 broods; April–July.

FEEDING Forages for insects in shrubs and on ground; in winter, favorite foods are peanut butter or suet at a feeder.

FLIGHT: fast and straight over short distances, with rapid wing beats.

DISTINCTIVE BORDER
A unique feature of this wren, not always noticed but visible here, is the black border on the eyebrow.

SIMILAR SPECIES

BEWICK'S WREN see p.506

dull brown or gray upperparts

longer tail

TIRELESS SINGER
Unlike many birds, the male Carolina Wren sings all year long, even on cold winter days.

OCCURRENCE
Breeds in a variety of bushy woodland habitats, such as thickets, parks with shrubby undergrowth, suburban yards with dense, low trees or bushes, and gardens; from northeastern Mexico to the Great Lakes and northeastward to New England. A separate population can be found from Mexico to Nicaragua.

| Length **5¼in (13.5cm)** | Wingspan **7½in (19cm)** | Weight **¹¹⁄₁₆oz (19g)** |
| Social **Pairs/Family groups** | Lifespan **At least 9 years** | Status **Secure** |

| Order **Passeriformes** | Family **Troglodytidae** | Species *Troglodytes troglodytes* |

Winter Wren

distinct, tan eyebrow

stubby tail, usually cocked straight up

dark brown, barred back

small, thin bill

ADULT

short, barred tail

ADULT

barred, rounded wings

flanks strongly barred

IN FLIGHT

The Winter Wren has one of the loudest songs of any North American bird of a similar size: the male's song carries far through its forest haunts. It is a widespread breeder, found from the Aleutians and Alaska eastward to Newfoundland, and as far south as California in the West and the Appalachians in the East, where the subspecies *T. t. pullus* resides. Its winter range is also western (to California) and eastern (to Texas), with a wide hiatus in between. This species spends its time foraging in tangles of fallen trees and shrubs, appearing mouse-like as it creeps amid the shadows. In Europe, as its family's sole species, it is simply called "the Wren."
VOICE Call a double *chek-chek* or *chimp-chimp*; song a loud, extremely long, complex series of warbles, trills, and single notes.
NESTING Well-hidden in a cavity near ground with dead wood and crevices; nest a messy mound lined with feathers; 4–7 eggs; 1–2 broods; April–July.
FEEDING Forages for insects in low, dense undergrowth, often in wet areas along streams; sometimes thrusts its head into water to capture prey.

FLIGHT: fast and direct, with rapid beats of its short, broad wings.

VOCAL VIRTUOSO
The Winter Wren is a skulker, but in the breeding season singing males show up on lower perches.

SIMILAR SPECIES

HOUSE WREN
see p.509
pale brown back

long tail

plain, unbarred flanks

NERVOUS REACTION
When alarmed, this wren cocks its tail almost vertically, before escaping into a mossy thicket.

OCCURRENCE
Breeds in northerly and mountain forests dominated by evergreen trees with a dense understory, fallen trees, and banks of streams. In the Appalachians, breeds in treeless areas with grass near cliffs. Northernmost birds migrate south to winter in woodlands, brush piles, tangles, and secluded spots.

| Length **4in (10cm)** | Wingspan **5½in (14cm)** | Weight **⁵⁄₁₆oz (9g)** |
| Social **Solitary/Family groups** | Lifespan **At least 4 years** | Status **Secure** |

| Order **Passeriformes** | Family **Troglodytidae** | Species *Troglodytes aedon* |

House Wren

faintly barred wings

ADULT (EASTERN)

IN FLIGHT

plain brown crown

browner upperparts

pale buffy throat

ADULT T. a. aedon (EASTERN)

thin, indistinct eyebrow

narrow, pale eye-ring

thin, slightly curved bill

grayish brown back

narrow, black barring on tail

ADULT T. a. parkmanii (WESTERN)

pale gray-brown underparts

FLIGHT: straight, with fast wing beats; typically over short distances.

Of all the North American wrens, the House Wren is the plainest, yet one of the most familiar and endearing, especially when making its home in a backyard nest box. However, it can be a fairly aggressive species, driving away nearby nesting birds of its own species and others by destroying nests, puncturing eggs, and even killing young. In the 1920s, distraught bird lovers mounted a campaign calling for the eradication of House Wrens, though the campaign did not last long as most were in favor of letting nature take its course.

VOICE Call a sharp *chep* or *cherr*; song opens with several short notes, followed by bubbly explosion of spluttering notes.

NESTING Cup lined with soft material on stick platform in natural, manmade cavities, such as nest boxes; 5–8 eggs; 2–3 broods; April–July.

FEEDING Forages for insects and spiders in trees and shrubs, gardens, and yards.

SIMILAR SPECIES

WINTER WREN see p.508

dark brown overall

shorter tail

heavily barred flanks

NESTING MATERIAL
This small bird has brought an unusually large twig to its nest inside an old woodpecker hole.

OCCURRENCE
Breeds in cities, towns, parks, farms, yards, gardens, and woodland edges. Rarely seen during migration period (late July to early October). Winters south of its breeding range, from southern US to Mexico, in woodlands, shrubby areas, and weedy fields. Nests, or is resident as far south as Tierra del Fuego.

| Length **4½in (11.5cm)** | Wingspan **6in (15cm)** | Weight **⅜oz (11g)** |
| Social **Solitary** | Lifespan **Up to 9 years** | Status **Secure** |

| Order **Passeriformes** | Family **Sylviidae** | Species **Polioptila caerulea** |

Blue-gray Gnatcatcher

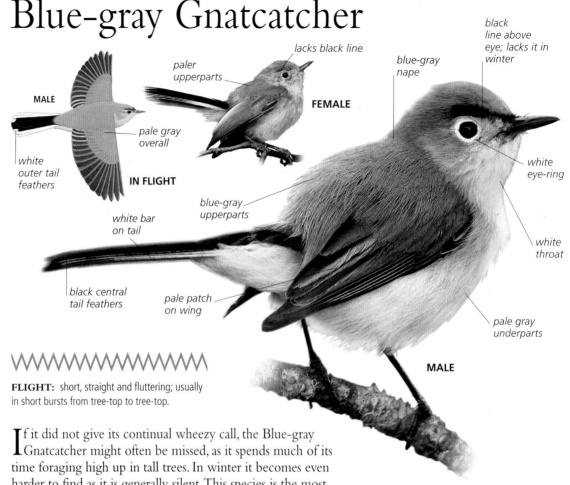

MALE

pale gray overall

white outer tail feathers

IN FLIGHT

paler upperparts

lacks black line

FEMALE

black line above eye; lacks it in winter

blue-gray nape

white eye-ring

white throat

blue-gray upperparts

white bar on tail

black central tail feathers

pale patch on wing

pale gray underparts

MALE

WWWWWWWWWWWWW

FLIGHT: short, straight and fluttering; usually in short bursts from tree-top to tree-top.

If it did not give its continual wheezy call, the Blue-gray Gnatcatcher might often be missed, as it spends much of its time foraging high up in tall trees. In winter it becomes even harder to find as it is generally silent. This species is the most northerly of the North American gnatcatchers and is also the only one to migrate. It can exhibit aggressive behavior and is capable of driving off considerably larger birds than itself. The range of the Blue-gray Gnatcatcher appears to be expanding and populations are increasing.

VOICE Call soft, irregular *zhee, zhee,* uttered constantly while foraging; song soft combination of short notes and nasal wheezes.
NESTING Cup of plant fibers, spider webs, mosses; usually high on branch; lined with soft plant material; 4–5 eggs; 1–2 broods; April–June.
FEEDING Forages for small insects and spiders by acrobatically flitting from twig to twig, while twitching long tail.

LISTEN CLOSELY
The complex song is rather faint; it is heard best when the bird is singing on a low perch.

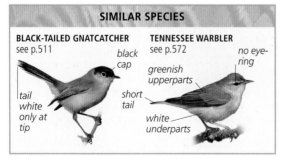

SIMILAR SPECIES

BLACK-TAILED GNATCATCHER
see p.511

black cap

tail white only at tip

TENNESSEE WARBLER
see p.572

no eye-ring

greenish upperparts

short tail

white underparts

OCCURRENCE
In eastern North America, breeds in deciduous or pine woodlands; in the West, in scrubby habitats, often near water. Winters in brushy habitats in southern US, Mexico, and Central America. Also breeds in Mexico, Belize, and the Bahamas.

| Length **4¼in (11cm)** | Wingspan **6in (15cm)** | Weight **⁷⁄₃₂oz (6g)** |
| Social **Solitary/Flocks** | Lifespan **At least 4 years** | Status **Secure** |

| Order **Passeriformes** | Family **Sylviidae** | Species ***Polioptila melanura*** |

Black-tailed Gnatcatcher

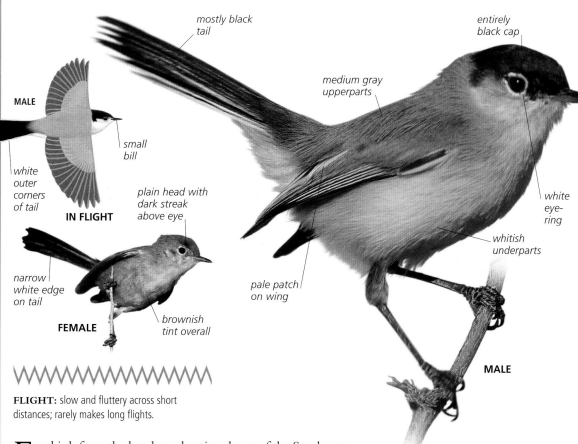

mostly black tail

entirely black cap

medium gray upperparts

MALE

small bill

white outer corners of tail

IN FLIGHT

plain head with dark streak above eye

narrow white edge on tail

FEMALE

brownish tint overall

pale patch on wing

white eye-ring

whitish underparts

MALE

FLIGHT: slow and fluttery across short distances; rarely makes long flights.

Few birds favor the hot, low-elevation desert of the Southwest as much as the Black-tailed Gnatcatcher. It is a tiny species that spends most of its time flitting about among shrubs and foliage, perpetually flicking its tail from side to side. It is a monogamous bird, and when pairs establish a nesting territory, they defend it aggressively throughout the year.

VOICE Various scolding notes *zhee-zhee-zhee*, *chih-chih-chih*, and *chee-chee-chee*; song, rarely heard, soft *tse-dee-dee-dee*.

NESTING Cup of plant fibers and spider webs, placed in shrub usually close to the ground; often lined with fine fibers; 3–4 eggs; 2 broods; April–July.

FEEDING Forages for insects, such as beetles and moths, among branches and leaves of shrubs; occasionally eats fruits and seeds.

DISTINGUISHING FEATURE
The male Black-tailed Gnatcatcher's black cap distinguishes it from the other gnatcatchers.

SIMILAR SPECIES

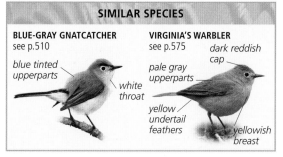

BLUE-GRAY GNATCATCHER
see p.510

blue tinted upperparts

white throat

VIRGINIA'S WARBLER
see p.575

pale gray upperparts

dark reddish cap

yellow undertail feathers

yellowish breast

OCCURRENCE
Resident in hot, low-elevation southwestern deserts in thorny scrub, acacia, Mesquite, Saguaro, creosote bush, saltbush, and other shrubs. Mostly found in dry riverbeds, but also in brushy groves along waterways. Range extends south into Mexico.

Length **4½in (11.5cm)**	Wingspan **5½in (14cm)**	Weight **⁷/₃₂oz (6g)**
Social **Solitary/Pairs**	Lifespan **Unknown**	Status **Localized**

Order **Passeriformes**	Family **Sylviidae**	Species *Polioptila californica*

California Gnatcatcher

IN FLIGHT

long, black tail

gray overall

MALE (BREEDING)

pale edge on outer wing feathers

black cap on head

inconspicuous eye-ring

dark gray upperparts

medium gray underparts

dark wingtips

MALE (BREEDING)

brownish-tinged overall

no black cap on head

white eye-ring

pale edges to feathers

FEMALE

black tail with small white tips on outer feathers

Scarce and threatened in its very patchy, localized habitat in southern California, the California Gnatcatcher is highly sought-after by birders. To spot this bird in one of its scattered localities along the coast, listen first for an odd "mewing" call, then watch very carefully for it to fly between patches of sage scrub. The California Gnatcatcher was formerly classified as a member of the more widespread Black-tailed Gnatcatcher but, the American Ornithologists' Union separated the two in 1989, on the basis of plumage, vocal, and genetic differences.

VOICE Characteristic call an odd "mewing" sound *wee-eeew*; *ch-ch-ch* when disturbed.

NESTING Cup of grasses, plant fibers, and spider's silk, low in dense shrub; 3–5 eggs; 1–3 broods; March–June.

FEEDING Hops and darts through shrubs, snatching insects including beetles, moths, flies, wasps, and bugs from branches and leaves; sometimes captures prey midair.

FLIGHT: slow and fluttery motion across short distances from shrub to shrub.

SEASONAL DIFFERENCE
In the nonbreeding season, the male's black cap is replaced by an inconspicuous black patch.

SIMILAR SPECIES

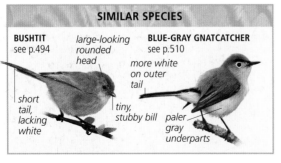

BUSHTIT see p.494

large-looking rounded head

short tail, lacking white

BLUE-GRAY GNATCATCHER see p.510

more white on outer tail

tiny, stubby bill

paler gray underparts

OCCURRENCE
Year-round resident in Baja California, Mexico, and scattered breeding localities in coastal sage scrub in Los Angeles, Orange, San Bernardino, Riverside, and San Diego counties of southern California. In Baja California, breeds in desert scrub and thorn thickets.

Length **4¼in (11cm)**	Wingspan **5½in (14cm)**	Weight **⁷⁄₃₂oz (6g)**
Social **Pairs**	Lifespan **At least 5 years**	Status **Vulnerable**

| Order **Passeriformes** | Family **Sittidae** | Species *Sitta pygmaea* |

Pygmy Nuthatch

rounded wings

ADULT

IN FLIGHT

grayish brown cap

pointed, chisel-like bill

blue-gray upperparts

black eyestripe

dusky underparts

very short tail

grayish flanks

ADULT

sharp claws

Pygmy Nuthatches are found in noisy and busy flocks throughout the year in their pine forest home of the American West. They are cooperative breeders, with young birds from the previous year's brood often helping adult birds raise the next year's young. They have a particular preference for Ponderosa and Jeffery Pines and are often absent from mountain ranges that lack their favourite trees. Pygmy Nuthatches are heard more often than they are seen, probably because they like to stick to the treetops.

VOICE Highly vocal species; calls piercing *peep* and *pip* notes, given singly or in frenzied series; in series, call resembles vocalizations of some Red Crossbills; calls of birds in flocks are somewhat bell-like.

NESTING Excavates cavity in pine tree; nest is a mass of plant material and feathers; 5–9 eggs; 1–2 broods; April–July.

FEEDING Forages on pine trees; mainly eats insects, caterpillars, moths, and grubs.

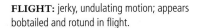

FLIGHT: jerky, undulating motion; appears bobtailed and rotund in flight.

SQUEEZING OUT OF A NEST
All nuthatches nest in tree cavities, which they wholly or partially excavate themselves.

SIMILAR SPECIES

BROWN-HEADED NUTHATCH
see p.514

richer brown crown

paler overall

PINE FORAGER
A Pygmy Nuthatch hangs upside down, carrying a tiny piece of food.

OCCURRENCE
Patchily distributed in pine forests of western North America, from British Columbia south to California, Arizona, New Mexico, and Texas; also in Mexico. Most numerous in dry mountain forests up to 650ft (2,000m), but in California ranges down to sea level. Generally patch distribution.

| Length **4¼in (11cm)** | Wingspan **8in (20cm)** | Weight **⅜oz (11g)** |
| Social **Small flocks** | Lifespan **Up to 2 years** | Status **Secure** |

Order **Passeriformes**	Family **Sittidae**	Species *Sitta pusilla*

Brown-headed Nuthatch

IN FLIGHT

- white spot on nape
- **ADULT**
- gray overall
- rounded wings

- **ADULT**
- warm brown nape and crown
- blue-gray upperparts
- pointed, chisel-like, dark bill
- pale lower bill
- white cheek and throat with pale yellow wash
- pale gray underparts
- sturdy legs and toes
- long claws
- short tail with white on uppertail feathers

FLIGHT: fairly weak and slow, with deeply undulating motion; appears tiny in flight.

This pine-loving species is the southeastern counterpart of the western Pygmy Nuthatch, but separated from it by the Great Plains. In most aspects of their history, these two nuthatch species are very similar and play the same ecological roles in their respective ecosystems. Like the Pygmy, the Brown-headed is a busy bird that travels in noisy packs. In each species, the young are raised by both parents and one or more nonparental relatives, or "helpers."

VOICE Call a short *bek*; foraging flocks *bwee! tutututu*, emphatic first note followed by soft series; chorus of sounds when calling in flocks.

NESTING Excavates cavity in pine tree; nest of plant material lined with fur and feathers; 4–6 eggs; 1–2 broods; March–May.

FEEDING Forages high in pine trees; in summer, gleans beetles, bugs, other insects, and also spiders; in winter, supplements diet with pine seeds.

INTREPID FORAGING
The Brown-headed Nuthatch forages upside down along branches, and head-first down tree trunks.

SIMILAR SPECIES

PYGMY NUTHATCH see p.513
- grayish crown
- pale yellowish wash

PERCHED ADULT
This bird depends upon forest tracts with standing dead wood and snags for nesting.

OCCURRENCE
Breeds in pine forests and oak-pine woods in southeastern US: Delaware, Virginia, and Maryland southward to Florida, westward to Oklahoma and Texas; also in the Bahamas. Prefers old and extensive forest stands with dead trunks for nesting. Resident; small groups wander in fall, but not far from breeding areas.

Length **4¼in (11cm)**	Wingspan **8in (20cm)**	Weight **⅜oz (10g)**
Social **Small flocks**	Lifespan **Up to 2 years**	Status **Declining**

Order **Passeriformes**	Family **Sittidae**	Species *Sitta canadensis*

Red-breasted Nuthatch

rounded wings

slightly muted head pattern

dark blue-gray crown and eyestripe

bold black-and-white head pattern

pointed, chisel-like bill

black eyestripe

MALE

pale orange underparts

FEMALE

white bands on tail

IN FLIGHT

blue-gray upperparts

white cheeks

blue-gray, short tail, with black side feathers

rusty underparts

compact body shape

MALE

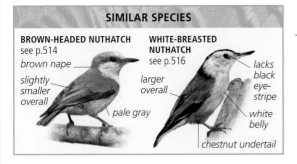

FLIGHT: short, swift dashes across forest clearings; irregular, undulating motion.

This aggressive, inquisitive nuthatch, with its distinctive black eyestripe, breeds in conifer forests across North America. The bird inhabits mountains in the West; in the East, it is found in lowlands and hills. However, sometimes it breeds in conifer groves away from its core range. Each fall, birds move from their main breeding grounds, but the extent of this exodus varies from year to year, depending on population cycles and food availability.

VOICE Call a one-note tooting sound, often repeated, with strong nasal yet musical quality: *aaank*, *enk*, *ink*, rather like a horn.

NESTING Excavates cavity in pine tree; nest of grass lined with feathers, with sticky pine resin applied to entrance; 5–7 eggs, 1 brood; May–July.

FEEDING Probes bark for beetle grubs; also eats insect larvae found on conifer needles; seeds in winter.

TASTY GRUB
This nuthatch has just extracted its dinner from the bark of a tree, a favorite foraging habitat.

SIMILAR SPECIES

BROWN-HEADED NUTHATCH
see p.514

brown nape

slightly smaller overall

pale gray

WHITE-BREASTED NUTHATCH
see p.516

larger overall

lacks black eye-stripe

white belly

chestnut undertail

OCCURRENCE
Found year-round in coniferous and mixed hardwood forests. During breeding season, absent from southeastern pine forests, except in the Appalachians. In the west, shares its habitat with Pygmy Nuthatch, but ranges to higher elevations.

Length **4¼in (11cm)**	Wingspan **8½in (22cm)**	Weight **⅜–⁷⁄₁₆oz (10–13g)**
Social **Solitary/Pairs**	Lifespan **Up to 7 years**	Status **Secure**

| Order **Passeriformes** | Family **Sittidae** | Species *Sitta carolinensis* |

White-breasted Nuthatch

white flashes on tail

MALE

IN FLIGHT

rounded wings

black crown and nape

conspicuous black eye

white face

long, pointed, chisel-like bill

white throat

blue-gray upperparts

short tail

chestnut undertail and lower belly

MALE

whitish gray underparts

long, strong claws

narrower, black band on nape

gray crown

dull gray upperparts

whitish underparts

FEMALE

FLIGHT: weak, with quick wing beats followed by glide; often short, from tree to tree.

UNUSUAL DESCENT
Nuthatches are unusual in that they routinely descend branches and trunks head-first.

The amiable White-breasted Nuthatch inhabits residential neighborhoods across the US and southern Canada, and often visits birdfeeders in winter. The largest of our nuthatches, it spends more time probing furrows and crevices on trunks and boughs than other nuthatches do. It walks irregularly on trees: forward, backward, upside-down, or horizontally. Of the eleven subspecies in its Canada-to-Mexico range, five occur in Canada and in the US. They differ in call notes and, to a lesser extent, in plumage.
VOICE Calls vary geographically: eastern birds nasal *yank yank*; interior birds stuttering *st't't't'*; Pacific slope birds tremulous *yiiiirk*; song of all populations a mellow *tu tu tu tu*, like a flicker, but softer.
NESTING Tree cavity, once used by woodpeckers, lined with grass and hair, adds mud to cavity opening; 5–9 eggs, 1 brood; April–June.
FEEDING Scours bark methodically for insects such as beetle larvae.

SIMILAR SPECIES

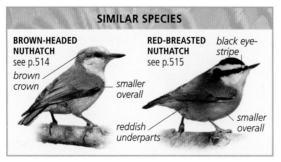

BROWN-HEADED NUTHATCH
see p.514
brown crown

RED-BREASTED NUTHATCH
see p.515

black eye-stripe

smaller overall

reddish underparts

smaller overall

OCCURRENCE
More liberal than other nuthatches in use of forest types; overlaps with the smaller species in coniferous forest ranges, but also common in broadleaf deciduous or mixed forests; weakly migratory: little movement in most falls, but moderate departures from breeding grounds in some years.

| Length **5¾in (14.5cm)** | Wingspan **11in (28cm)** | Weight **¹¹⁄₁₆–⅞oz (19–25g)** |
| Social **Solitary/Pairs** | Lifespan **Up to 9 years** | Status **Secure** |

Order **Passeriformes**	Family **Certhiidae**	Species **Certhia americana**

Brown Creeper

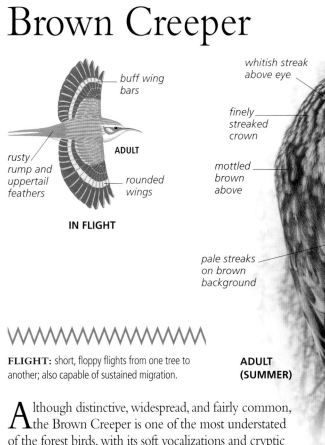

buff wing bars

ADULT

rusty rump and uppertail feathers

rounded wings

IN FLIGHT

thin, downward-curving bill

whitish streak above eye

white chin, throat, and breast

finely streaked crown

mottled brown above

pale streaks on brown background

FLIGHT: short, floppy flights from one tree to another; also capable of sustained migration.

ADULT (SUMMER)

rusty tint to belly and undertail

long, forked tail

Although distinctive, widespread, and fairly common, the Brown Creeper is one of the most understated of the forest birds, with its soft vocalizations and cryptic plumage. As it forages, it hops up a tree trunk, then flies down to another tree, starts again from near the ground, hops up, and so on. These birds have adapted to habitat changes in the northeast and their numbers have increased in regenerating forests. Mid- and southwestern populations, by contrast, have declined because forest cutting has reduced their breeding habitat. The Brown Creeper is a partial migrant—some individuals move south in the fall, and head north in the spring; others remain close to their breeding grounds.

VOICE High-pitched and easily overlooked call a buzzy *zwisss*, flight call an abrupt *tswit*; song a wheezy jumble of thin whistles and short buzzes.

NESTING Unique hammock-shaped nest, behind piece of peeling bark; 5–6 eggs, 1 brood; May–July.

FEEDING Probes bark for insects, especially larvae, eggs, pupae, and aphids.

SIMILAR SPECIES

PYGMY NUTHATCH see p.513
blue-gray upperparts

smaller overall

BROWN-HEADED NUTHATCH see p.514
straight bill

smaller overall

shorter tail

blue-gray upperparts

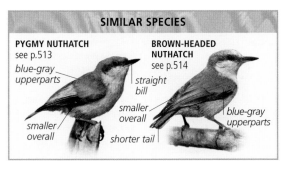

STRONG TAIL
The Brown Creeper uses its strong forked tail to prop it against the trunk of this tree.

OCCURRENCE
The only North American creeper, it breeds in a variety of forests, particularly fairly moist coniferous or mixed hardwood forests, also large stands with snags and standing dead trees. In winter, seen in small groves without coniferous trees; also in residential districts or suburbs.

Length **5¼in (13.5cm)**	Wingspan **8in (20cm)**	Weight **¼–⅜oz (7–10g)**
Social **Solitary**	Lifespan **Up to 4 years**	Status **Secure**

| Order **Passeriformes** | Family **Mimidae** | Species *Dumetella carolinensis* |

Gray Catbird

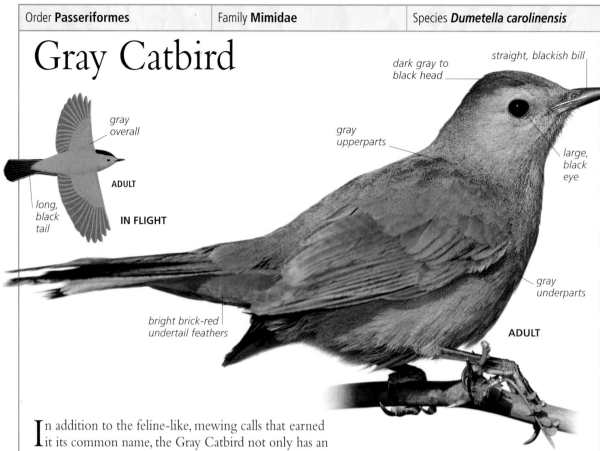

gray overall

ADULT

IN FLIGHT

long, black tail

dark gray to black head

straight, blackish bill

gray upperparts

large, black eye

gray underparts

ADULT

bright brick-red undertail feathers

In addition to the feline-like, mewing calls that earned it its common name, the Gray Catbird not only has an extraordinarily varied vocal repertoire, but it can also sing two notes simultaneously. It has been reported to imitate the vocalizations of over 40 bird species, at least one frog species, and several sounds produced by machines and electronic devices. Despite their shy, retiring nature, Gray Catbirds tolerate human presence and will rest in shrubs in suburban and urban lots. Another fascinating skill is the Gray Catbird's ability to recognize and remove eggs of the brood parasite, the Brown-headed Cowbird.

VOICE *Mew* call, like a young kitten; song a long, complex series of unhurried, often grouped notes, sometimes interspersed with whistles and squeaks.

NESTING Large, untidy cup of woven twigs, grass, and hair lined with finer material; 3–4 eggs; 1–2 broods; May–August.

FEEDING Feeds on a wide variety of berries and insects, usually whatever is most abundant in season.

FLIGHT: short flights between habitat patches with constant, medium-speed wing beats.

ANGLED ATTITUDE
Between bouts of feeding, a Gray Catbird often rests with its body and tail at a 50 degree angle.

LARGE BLACK EYES
Peering from the foliage, a Gray Catbird investigates its surroundings.

OCCURRENCE
Breeds in mixed young to mid-aged forests with abundant undergrowth, from British Columbia east to Maritimes and Newfoundland, and in the US diagonally west-east from Washington State to New Mexico, east to the Gulf Coast, north to New England. Northern population migratory.

SIMILAR SPECIES

NORTHERN MOCKINGBIRD see p.519

white wing patch

longer tail edged in white

lighter gray

CRISSAL THRASHER see p.526

longer, curved bill

brown-gray overall

| Length **8–9½in (20–24cm)** | Wingspan **10–12in (25–30cm)** | Weight **1¼–2⅛oz (35–60g)** |
| Social **Solitary/Pairs** | Lifespan **Up to 11 years** | Status **Secure** |

| Order **Passeriformes** | Family **Mimidae** | Species *Mimus polyglottos* |

Northern Mockingbird

ADULT

white patches on wing

IN FLIGHT

shorter tail

speckled breast and belly

JUVENILE

gray head

pointed, curved bill

yellow eye

long tail with white outer tail feathers

white undertail feathers

ADULT

white patch on wing feathers

FLIGHT: usually direct and level on constant, somewhat fluttering, quick wing beats.

The ability of the Northern Mockingbird to imitate sounds is truly impressive: some individuals can incorporate over 100 different phrases of as many different birds in their songs. Phrases are usually repeated, often quite a few times, and somewhat modified at each repetition. This species, once thought to be headed for extinction due to the caged-bird trade in the 1700s and 1800s, has largely recovered since then. In fact, the Northern Mockingbird's range has expanded in the last few decades, due partly to its high tolerance for humans and their habitats. A diagnostic field characteristic of the Northern Mockingbird is its tendency to "wing flash," showing its white outer wing feather patches when holding its wings overhead.

VOICE Long, complex repertoire often imitating other birds, non-bird noises, and the sounds of mechanical devices.

NESTING Bulky cup of twigs, lined, in shrub or tree; 3–5 eggs; 1–3 broods; March–August.

FEEDING Eats a wide variety of fruit, berries, and insects, including ants, beetles, and grasshoppers.

BERRY PICKER
Northern Mockingbirds love berries, and make good use of them during the fall.

OCCURRENCE
Widespread in the US from coast to coast south of the timberline, primarily along edges of disturbed habitats, including young forests and especially suburban and urban areas with shrubs or hedges.

SIMILAR SPECIES

LOGGERHEAD SHRIKE ◐
see p.439

brown mask

black wings

CLARK'S NUTCRACKER
see p.464
white patch low on wing

darker gray belly

whiter sides to tail

| Length **8½–10in (22–25cm)** | Wingspan **13–15in (33–38cm)** | Weight **1⁹⁄₁₆–2oz (45–55g)** |
| Social **Pairs** | Lifespan **Up to 20 years** | Status **Secure** |

| Order **Passeriformes** | Family **Mimidae** | Species *Oreoscoptes montanus* |

Sage Thrasher

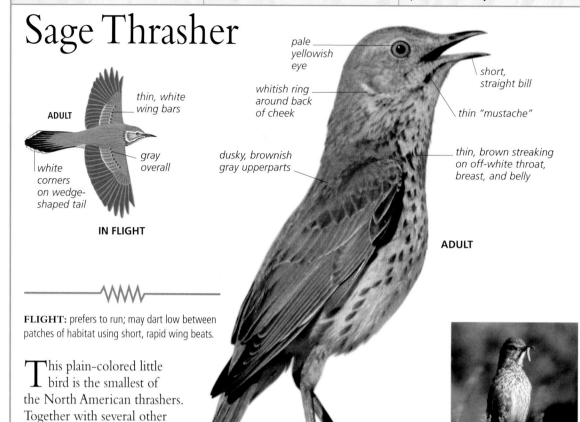

ADULT

IN FLIGHT

thin, white wing bars

gray overall

white corners on wedge-shaped tail

pale yellowish eye

whitish ring around back of cheek

dusky, brownish gray upperparts

short, straight bill

thin "mustache"

thin, brown streaking on off-white throat, breast, and belly

ADULT

FLIGHT: prefers to run; may dart low between patches of habitat using short, rapid wing beats.

This plain-colored little bird is the smallest of the North American thrashers. Together with several other members of this group, the Sage Thrasher recognizes and removes the eggs of brood parasites, especially those of the Brown-headed Cowbird. Unfortunately, it may also be the least studied of the thrasher group, perhaps because the dense nature of its habitat makes study difficult. The English name, "Sage Thrasher," truly describes this bird's western habitat.

VOICE Song varies in duration: low, repeated, very musical notes or phrases that may blend together in a melodious song.

NESTING Large cup with stick frame lined with grass, horse hair, sheep's wool, and fur; 3–6 eggs; 1–2 broods; April–July.

FEEDING Eats insects, especially ants and beetles, on the ground; will also consume berries when seasonally available.

JUICY MEAL
This thrasher forages mostly on or near the ground; it feeds on insects and berries.

SHOW-OFF TENDENCIES
Males attract mates and defend their territory with raised wings, in a fluttering display.

OCCURRENCE
Very closely associated with sagebrush habitat in low-elevation, semi-arid valleys of the western US. Winters from southwestern US to Baja California and continental Mexico, southwards to Sonora and Coquila.

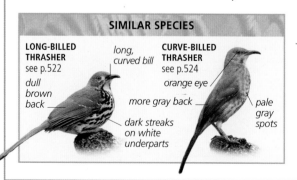

SIMILAR SPECIES

LONG-BILLED THRASHER see p.522

dull brown back

long, curved bill

dark streaks on white underparts

CURVE-BILLED THRASHER see p.524

orange eye

more gray back

pale gray spots

| Length **8–9in (20–23cm)** | Wingspan **10–13in (25–33cm)** | Weight **1⁷⁄₁₆–1¾oz (40–50g)** |
| Social **Solitary/Pairs** | Lifespan **Unknown** | Status **Localized** |

Order **Passeriformes**	Family **Mimidae**	Species *Toxostoma rufum*

Brown Thrasher

bright yellow eye

grayish cheeks

reddish brown upperparts

fairly straight, dark bill

indistinct "mustache"

dark streaking on pale underparts

two pale wing bars

rufous wings and upperparts

ADULT

long tail with pale outer tips

IN FLIGHT

long tail, paler than back

ADULT

The Brown Thrasher is usually difficult to view clearly because it keeps to dense underbrush. Like most other thrashers, this species prefers running or hopping to flying. When nesting, it can recognize and remove the eggs of brood parasites like the Brown-headed Cowbird. The current population decline is most likely the result of fragmentation of large, wooded habitats into patches, which lack the forest interior habitat this species needs.

VOICE Calls varied, including rasping sounds; song a long series of musical notes, sometimes imitating other species; repeats phrase twice before moving onto the next one.

NESTING Bulky cup of twigs, close to ground, lined with leaves, grass, bark; 3–5 eggs; 1 brood; April–July.

FEEDING Mainly insects (especially beetles) and worms gathered from leaf litter on the forest floor; will peck at cultivated grains, nuts, berries, and fruit.

FLIGHT: slow and heavy with deep wing beats; below treetops, especially in and around ground.

STREAKED BREAST
Displaying its heavily streaked underparts, this Brown Thrasher is perched and ready to sing.

OCCURRENCE
Widespread across central and eastern North America, from Canada to Texas and Florida, in a variety of densely wooded habitats, particularly those with thick undergrowth, but will use woodland edges, hedges, and riverside trees. A partial migrant, it winters in the southern part of its range.

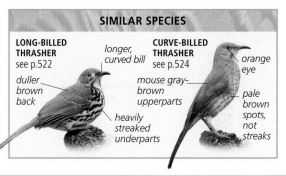

SIMILAR SPECIES

LONG-BILLED THRASHER
see p.522

longer, curved bill

duller brown back

heavily streaked underparts

CURVE-BILLED THRASHER
see p.524

mouse gray-brown upperparts

orange eye

pale brown spots, not streaks

Length **10–12in (25–30cm)**	Wingspan **11–14in (28–36cm)**	Weight **2⅛–2⅞oz (60–80g)**
Social **Solitary/Flocks**	Lifespan **Up to 13 years**	Status **Declining**

Order **Passeriformes**	Family **Mimidae**	Species *Toxostoma longirostre*

Long-billed Thrasher

ADULT

curved, black bill

two white wing bars

IN FLIGHT

orange eye

gray cheek

dark "mustache"

two conspicuous wing bars

brownish gray upperparts

white throat

white underparts with thick, black streaks

undertail feathers with black streaks

ADULT

long, reddish brown tail

In the US, this Mexican species is found only in southern Texas, where its habitat of semi-arid thickets and riverside woodlands has been much altered or destroyed by mechanized land-clearing practices. This habitat loss may be offset by the increase in area of invasive scrubby vegetation in other parts of its range. Should the distribution of the Long-billed Thrasher advance northward to meet the range of the Brown Thrasher, an interesting biological problem will arise—will they interbreed or overlap?
VOICE Call a harsh *tchek*; song a loud, harsh series of notes, usually repeated 2–4 times in succession.
NESTING Bulky cup of thorn-covered twigs, lined with moss and grass, in dense shrubs or low trees; 3–5 eggs; 1–2 broods; March–June.
FEEDING Forages for insects in summer; eats berries when available.

FLIGHT: rather slow, mostly brief and low flights; with erratic and rapid wing beats.

DISTINCTIVE STREAKING
Here, the black mustache, white thoat, and heavy black streaking of the underparts are in full display of this adult thrasher.

THE EYES HAVE IT
This species has darker eyes and duller brown plumage than the similar Brown Thrasher.

OCCURRENCE
Occurs only in southern Texas and eastern Mexico, southward to Puebla and Veracuz; lives in thick, scrubby vegetation on mountain slopes up to around 3,300ft (1,100m), and in lowlands along the Gulf of Mexico, commonly found in woodland by streams. Sedentary.

SIMILAR SPECIES

BROWN THRASHER see p.521
more rufous upperparts
less heavy streaking

CURVE-BILLED THRASHER see p.524
shorter bill
dull grayish brown
longer, deeply curved bill
pale gray spots on creamy breast

Length **10–11in (25–28cm)**	Wingspan **12–13in (30–33cm)**	Weight **2½oz (70g)**
Social **Solitary/Pairs**	Lifespan **Up to 8 years**	Status **Localized**

Order **Passeriformes**	Family **Mimidae**	Species *Toxostoma bendirei*

Bendire's Thrasher

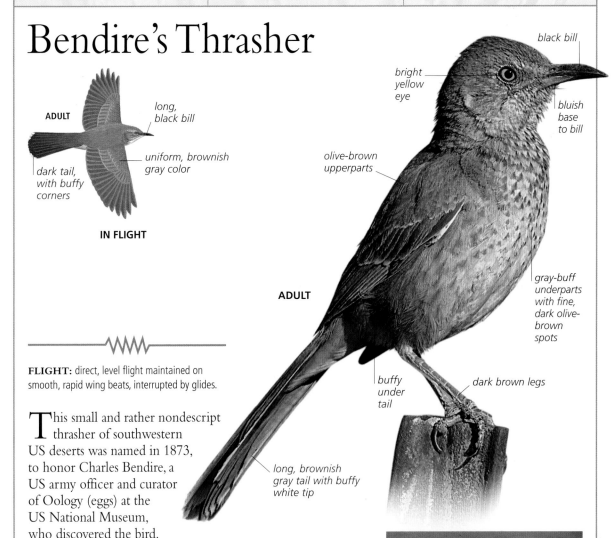

ADULT

long, black bill

uniform, brownish gray color

dark tail, with buffy corners

IN FLIGHT

black bill

bright yellow eye

bluish base to bill

olive-brown upperparts

ADULT

gray-buff underparts with fine, dark olive-brown spots

buffy under tail

dark brown legs

long, brownish gray tail with buffy white tip

FLIGHT: direct, level flight maintained on smooth, rapid wing beats, interrupted by glides.

This small and rather nondescript thrasher of southwestern US deserts was named in 1873, to honor Charles Bendire, a US army officer and curator of Oology (eggs) at the US National Museum, who discovered the bird. Bendire's Thrasher's life history is less well known than that of other thrashers. For example, it is still debated whether the same pair can raise up to three broods in one season, and what the bird's wintering range is in Baja California.

VOICE Call a hoarse *krrh*; song a clear, continuous series of notes, repeated 2–4 times, but not broken into distinct phrases.
NESTING Medium-sized cup of twigs lined with soft plant and animal matter; 3–4 eggs; 2 broods; March–July.
FEEDING Forages for insects, both adult and larvae, on the ground; also eats fruit and, occasionally, seeds.

GROUND DWELLER
Searching for food, Bendire's Thasher runs on the ground in open areas with sparse shrubbery.

SIMILAR SPECIES

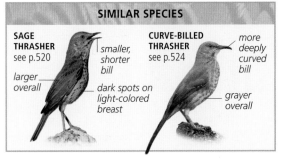

SAGE THRASHER
see p.520

larger overall

smaller, shorter bill

dark spots on light-colored breast

CURVE-BILLED THRASHER
see p.524

more deeply curved bill

grayer overall

OCCURRENCE
In the US, this species breeds in the deserts of southeast California, Nevada, Arizona, and New Mexico, in areas with much bare ground and sparse cover of cactus, thorn-scrub, and Joshua trees. Populations move south to Mexico in winter, Mexican populations resident.

Length **8–10in (20–25cm)**	Wingspan **11–13in (28–33cm)**	Weight **1¾–2½oz (50–70g)**
Social **Pairs/Family groups**	Lifespan **Up to 6 years**	Status **Localized**

| Order **Passeriformes** | Family **Mimidae** | Species ***Toxostoma curvirostre*** |

Curve-billed Thrasher

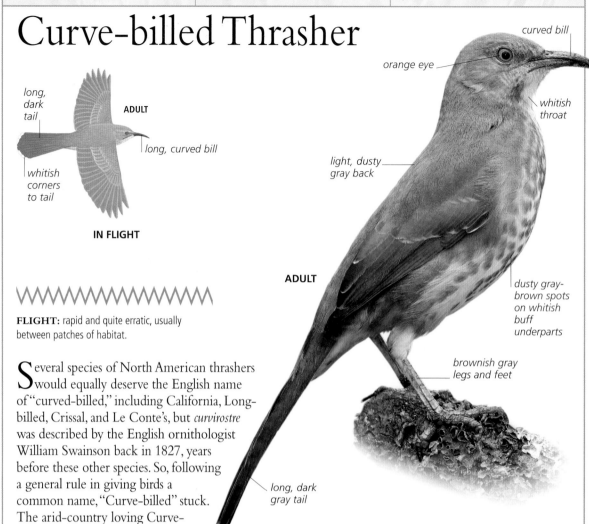

curved bill

orange eye

whitish throat

light, dusty gray back

ADULT

dusty gray-brown spots on whitish buff underparts

brownish gray legs and feet

long, dark tail

ADULT

long, curved bill

whitish corners to tail

IN FLIGHT

FLIGHT: rapid and quite erratic, usually between patches of habitat.

long, dark gray tail

Several species of North American thrashers would equally deserve the English name of "curved-billed," including California, Long-billed, Crissal, and Le Conte's, but *curvirostre* was described by the English ornithologist William Swainson back in 1827, years before these other species. So, following a general rule in giving birds a common name, "Curve-billed" stuck. The arid-country loving Curve-billed is somewhat unkempt looking, with a thick bill and powerful legs. Less of a mimic than other thrashers, it is nevertheless quite vocal, and its two-note *twit-twit* call is a characteristic sound of the southwestern semi-deserts.

VOICE Two-note *qwit-qweet*; song a series of clear, warbled whistles broken into distinct phrases; some mimicry of other species' calls.

NESTING Bulky, rather messy-looking cup of thorny sticks, in cactus or shrub, lined with grass, feathers, and hair; 3–5 eggs; 2 broods; February–July.

FEEDING Forages on ground and in leaf litter for insects and snails; eats fruit and berries in the fall.

DISTINCTIVE JUVENILE
Juvenile birds show less spotting on their underparts and paler eyes than the adults.

OCCURRENCE
In the US, the Curve-billed Thrasher inhabits open, scrubby, arid to semi-arid areas, where it is often found along edges between brush and clearings. Its Mexican range extends south to Veracuz and Oaxaca. It is largely resident throughout its US and Mexican range.

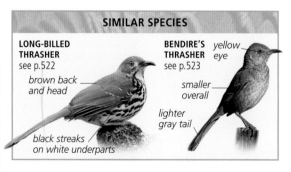

SIMILAR SPECIES

LONG-BILLED THRASHER
see p.522

brown back and head

black streaks on white underparts

BENDIRE'S THRASHER
see p.523

yellow eye

smaller overall

lighter gray tail

| Length **10–13in (25–33cm)** | Wingspan **12–15in (30–38cm)** | Weight **2⅛–2⅞oz (60–80g)** |
| Social **Pairs** | Lifespan **Up to 11 years** | Status **Localized** |

| Order **Passeriformes** | Family **Mimidae** | Species *Toxostoma redivivum* |

California Thrasher

dark eye

buffy eyestripe

dark grayish brown upperparts

very dark brown tail

long, curved bill

ADULT

IN FLIGHT

ADULT

long, deeply curved, black bill

dark gray cheeks with pale lines across

pale throat

grayish buff underparts

dark gray to black tail

rich buffy undertail

blackish legs and feet

FLIGHT: heavy, awkward flight, and not particularly quick; usually between stands of cover.

The largest of the North American thrashers, this species was first illustrated and described, though not named, in the 16th century. It was formally named *redivivum*, "resurrected" (actually rediscovered) in 1845. Ironically, this term could also apply to its ability to re-establish itself in the years following a fire that burned through its habitat. Like several other members of its genus, this species prefers to run and usually only flies when absolutely necessary. This makes it more susceptible to predation by domestic cats, which is one of the key threats to this species' continued survival, along with human development encroaching into areas of previously suitable habitat.

VOICE Call a dry *tchek*; song a loud, clear series of twice-repeated phrases, delivered in succession; often includes bits of song from other species.

NESTING Bulky shallow cup of branches in shrub, lined with bark, small sticks, and roots; 3–4 eggs; 1–3 broods; January–July.

FEEDING Eats variety of insects; also fruit and berries when available.

FIELD MARKS
A uniformly dark body, pale throat patch, and light eyestripe distinguish this thrasher.

OCCURRENCE
This true Californian prefers arid to semi-arid, brushy canyons, especially those with dense, scrubby undergrowth; also uses areas in and around human development, including various suburban parks and gardens; needs adequate undergrowth vegetation.

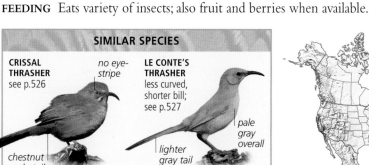

SIMILAR SPECIES

CRISSAL THRASHER see p.526

no eye-stripe

chestnut undertail

LE CONTE'S THRASHER less curved, shorter bill; see p.527

pale gray overall

lighter gray tail

| Length **11–13in (28–33cm)** | Wingspan **15–17in (38–43cm)** | Weight **2½–3⅛oz (70–90g)** |
| Social **Solitary/Pairs** | Lifespan **Up to 12 years** | Status **Localized** |

| Order **Passeriformes** | Family **Mimidae** | Species *Toxostoma crissale* |

Crissal Thrasher

dusky gray overall

ADULT

double black-and-white "mustache"

yellow eyes

long, curved bill

dark tail corners with buffy outward edges

IN FLIGHT

dark chestnut undertail coverts

long, dark tail

ADULT

Although it is locally common, little is known about the life history of this secretive bird, which lives in dense mesquite thickets and shrubland. It is easily confused with other, similar-looking southwestern thrashers of arid habitats, but the melodious quality of its song is distinctive. Its Latin name *crissale*, from which its English name is derived, refers to the color of its undertail feathers, or "crissum," which are a bright spot in an otherwise pretty uniformly gray plumage. Although loss of habitat in lower elevations may restrict the numbers of this species, its preference for high-elevation habitats insulate it somewhat from human encroachment.

VOICE Call a rather soft-sounding *Krrrt;* song a strong numerical note, or group of notes, with double repetitions, delivered softly.

NESTING Substantial cup of sticks in shrub, lined with soft grass, roots, and hair; 2–4 eggs; 1–3 broods; January–July.

FEEDING Forages on the ground for insects, which make up almost all of its diet; will eat some seeds and fruits in season.

FLIGHT: not a skilled flier; constant, rapid flaps to maintain height; "heavy" flight appearance.

MAKING ITSELF HEARD
Usually reclusive, males are conspicuous in the breeding season, often singing from high perches.

SIMILAR SPECIES

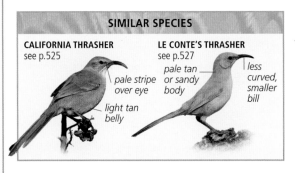

CALIFORNIA THRASHER
see p.525

pale stripe over eye

light tan belly

LE CONTE'S THRASHER
see p.527

pale tan or sandy body

less curved, smaller bill

OCCURRENCE
Breeds in the arid southwestern US (California, Utah, Nevada, Arizona, New Mexico, Texas) and adjacent Mexico, especially in dense shrubbery at mid-elevations, but can occur up to about 6,500ft (2,000m), usually in canyons or along dry watercourses, often with scattered trees or shrubs.

| Length **10–13in (25–33cm)** | Wingspan **13–16in (33–41cm)** | Weight **2⅛–2½oz (60–70g)** |
| Social **Solitary/Pairs** | Lifespan **Up to 13 years** | Status **Localized** |

Order **Passeriformes**	Family **Mimidae**	Species ***Toxostoma lecontei***

Le Conte's Thrasher

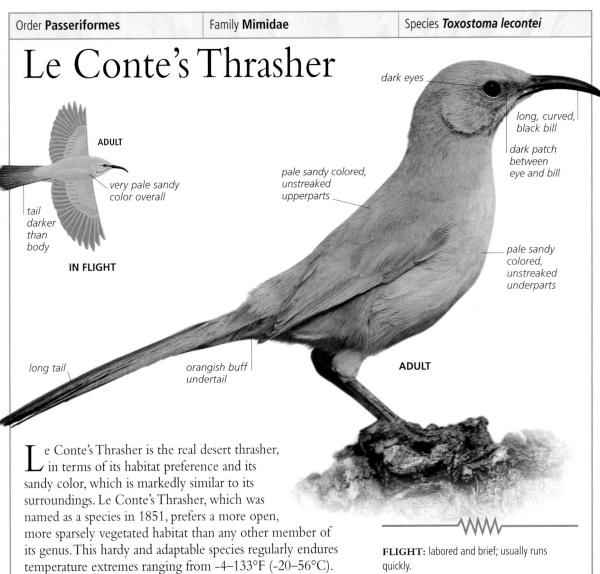

dark eyes

long, curved, black bill

dark patch between eye and bill

pale sandy colored, unstreaked upperparts

pale sandy colored, unstreaked underparts

ADULT

IN FLIGHT

very pale sandy color overall

tail darker than body

long tail

orangish buff undertail

ADULT

L e Conte's Thrasher is the real desert thrasher, in terms of its habitat preference and its sandy color, which is markedly similar to its surroundings. Le Conte's Thrasher, which was named as a species in 1851, prefers a more open, more sparsely vegetated habitat than any other member of its genus. This hardy and adaptable species regularly endures temperature extremes ranging from -4–133°F (-20–56°C). Habitat loss in the Southwest due to increased irrigation and the transformation of areas of desert into agricultural land may be an important factor in the continued decline of Le Conte's Thrasher in the US.

VOICE Call *ti-WHIP*; song a long, squeaky musical series of varied notes or phrases, often repeated twice or thrice.
NESTING Large cup of twigs in scrub, with finer and softer material as lining; 3–5 eggs; 2 broods; February–June.
FEEDING Catches prey on or in the soil; eats mostly insects and spiders; also takes bird eggs, small reptiles, berries, and seeds.

FLIGHT: labored and brief; usually runs quickly.

SURVIVAL INSTINCTS
Le Conte's Thrasher is a hardy bird, surviving in some of the harshest habitats in North America.

OCCURRENCE
Resident in southwestern US (south California, Arizona, south Utah, south Nevada, New Mexico) and in Mexico (Baja California, Sonora) in very open sandy desert, with sparse vegetation of creosote and saltbush, also in more sheltered areas along desert washes, and clumps of grass.

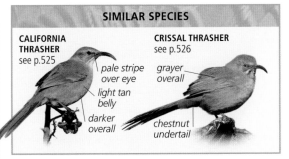

SIMILAR SPECIES

CALIFORNIA THRASHER
see p.525

pale stripe over eye

light tan belly

darker overall

CRISSAL THRASHER
see p.526

grayer overall

chestnut undertail

Length **10–12in (25–30cm)**	Wingspan **12–14in (30–36cm)**	Weight **1¾–2⅞oz (50–80g)**
Social **Pairs/Family groups**	Lifespan **Up to 6 years**	Status **Localized**

| Order **Passeriformes** | Family **Sturnidae** | Species *Sturnus vulgaris* |

European Starling

short, square tail

pointed, triangular wings

ADULT (BREEDING)

IN FLIGHT

body feathers tipped whitish or buff

wing feathers edged bright orange-buff

large spots on undertail

ADULT (NONBREEDING)

black face with hints of shiny, glossy purple

glossy black body with mostly green sheen

blue-based, sharp, yellow bill; pink-based on female

dark, glossy, blue-black belly

MALE (BREEDING)

long, pinkish brown legs and strong toes

dull brownish head

plain brown body

dark bill

IMMATURE (FALL)

JUVENILE

This distinctive non-native species is perhaps the most successful bird in North America—and probably the most maligned. In the 1890s, 100 European Starlings were released in New York City's Central Park; these were the ancestors of the many millions of birds that now live all across the US. This adaptable and aggressive bird competes with native species for nest sites, and the starling usually wins—even against larger species such as the Northern Flicker.
VOICE Highly varied; gives whooshing *ssssheer*, often in flight; also whistled *wheeeooo*; song an elaborate pulsing series with slurred whistles and clicking notes; imitates other species' vocalizations.
NESTING Natural or artificial cavity of any sort; 4–6 eggs; 1–2 broods; March–July.
FEEDING Omnivorous; picks at anything that might be edible; insects and berries are common food items; also visits birdfeeders and trashcans; often feeds on grubs in lawns.

FLIGHT: individuals fly in direct, buzzy manner; flocks bunch up tightly in flight.

INSECT EATER
Despite its parents' omnivorous diet, the nestlings are fed almost exclusively on insects and larvae.

SIMILAR SPECIES

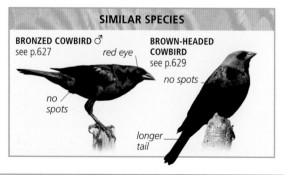

BRONZED COWBIRD ♂
see p.627

red eye

no spots

BROWN-HEADED COWBIRD
see p.629

no spots

longer tail

OCCURRENCE
In North America from southern Canada to the US–Mexico border; also Puerto Rico and other Caribbean islands. Common to abundant in cities, towns, and farmlands; also occurs in relatively "wild" settings far from human habitation. Forms flocks at all times, huge in winter.

| Length **8½in (21cm)** | Wingspan **16in (41cm)** | Weight **2⅝– 3⅜oz (75–95g)** |
| Social **Colonies** | Lifespan **Up to 17 years** | Status **Secure** |

Family **Turdidae**

THRUSHES

MOST THRUSHES ARE medium-sized brown- or olive-brown-backed birds with varying amounts of spotting or speckling underneath. Although undistinguished in color, they more than make up for their drab plumage with beautiful flutelike songs. By contrast, the Varied Thrush, which is the sole member of the *Ixoreus* genus, differs dramatically from many other thrushes with its bold black-and-rust pattern, and is one of the most distinctive birds in the US. Similarly, the brightly colored bluebirds, which have been the target of many successful conservation efforts, and the duller Townsend's Solitaire, are both striking enough to stand out from other thrushes, although juvenile birds have markings that are similar to other species.

ORCHARD DWELLER
Bluebirds, for example this Mountain Bluebird, favor orchards far more than other thrushes.

GROUND BIRDS
Though they perch to sing, thrushes, including this Varied Thrush, spend a lot of their time on or near the ground.

Family **Motacillidae**

WAGTAILS AND PIPITS

THESE TWO GROUPS OF ground-dwelling songbirds are represented by more than 50 species worldwide. Only four of these, however, are found regularly in North America.

WAGTAILS

Named for their habit of constantly bobbing their long, slender tails up and down, wagtails' plumage contrasts bright colors with black. Although primarily a European genus, two species are considered regular North American breeders, and two others are routinely sighted along the Bering Sea coast and Aleutian Islands.

PIPITS

Unlike wagtails, the two species of pipit that breed in North America also winter there. Very much birds of open, treeless country, both pipit species are likely to be seen on their widespread wintering grounds more often than in their breeding range.

COUNTRY-LOVERS
Pipits, such as this female American Pipit, like to live in open countryside.

| Order **Passeriformes** | Family **Turdidae** | Species *Ixoreus naevius* |

Varied Thrush

white double underwing bar

brownish gray upperparts

orange breast and throat with distinct spotting

MALE

FEMALE

black breastband

IN FLIGHT

rusty orange patches

white undertail feathers

orange eyebrow

black cheeks

bluish gray upperparts

MALE

rusty orange breast, faintly spotted

The voice of the old-growth forests of southern Alaska and British Columbia, the Varied Thrush is also the most beautiful of the thrushes. Its song is so haunting and ethereal that to hear it can give the listener goosebumps. To see the bird is another matter, as it is often rather shy, except when bringing food to its nestlings. The Varied Thrush's orange and black head, deep bluish black back, and its two rusty wing bars are an unmistakable combination of markings.

VOICE Song is a single note that rises or falls in tone; repeats its song after about 10 seconds; sings for long periods of time from one perch, then moves to another to start anew.

NESTING Bulky cup of twigs, dead leaves, pieces of bark, stems of grass and weeds, lined with fine grass stems, mainly in conifer trees, against trunk; 3–4 eggs; 1–2 broods; April–August.

FEEDING Feeds on insects and caterpillars while breeding; fruit and berries in winter.

FLIGHT: rapid wing beats; fast and direct.

SUMMER DIET
During its breeding season, this thrush forages for insects, often outside the forest interior.

SIMILAR SPECIES

AMERICAN ROBIN see p.541

dark back

yellow bill

brick-red breast

FOREST DWELLER
The Varied Thrush is often difficult to find, because it inhabits dark forests.

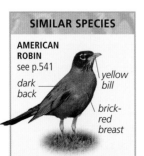

OCCURRENCE
Breeds from Alaska south to Montana; prefers moist coniferous forests throughout breeding range; likely to be found in mature forests. Winters south of its breeding range; habitat varies between ravines and thickets to suburban lawns. Habitat in migration much like winter choices.

| Length **7–10in (18–25cm)** | Wingspan **13–15in (33–38cm)** | Weight **2¼–3½ oz (65–100g)** |
| Social **Solitary/Flocks** | Lifespan **At least 5 years** | Status **Declining** |

| Order **Passeriformes** | Family **Turdidae** | Species *Sialia sialis* |

Eastern Bluebird

MALE

IN FLIGHT

bluish gray underwings

bright blue upperparts

white belly

rufous breast and throat

spotted throat and breast

gray-brown upperparts

JUVENILE

chestnut brown chin, throat, breast, and flanks

MALE

white belly

white undertail

pale chestnut throat

gray upperparts

blue wings, rump, and tail

FEMALE

The Eastern Bluebird's vibrant blue and chestnut body is a beloved sight in eastern North America, especially after the remarkable comeback of the species in the past 30 years. After much of the bird's habitat was eliminated by agriculture in the mid-1900s, volunteers offered the bluebirds nest boxes as alternatives to their tree cavities, and they took to these like ducks to water. The Eastern Bluebird's mating system involves males seeking (or not minding) multiple partners.

VOICE Main song a melodious series of soft, whistled notes; *churr-wi* or *churr-li*; songs for mating and asserting territoriality.
NESTING Cavity nester, in trees or man-made boxes; nest of grass lined with grass, weeds, and twigs; uses old nests of other species; 3–7 eggs; 2 broods; February–September.
FEEDING Feeds on insects, like grasshoppers, and caterpillars in breeding season; in winter, also takes fruits and plants.

FLIGHT: shallow wing beats; slow and easy.

HOME DELIVERY
A female bluebird delivers food to a nest box.

SIMILAR SPECIES

WESTERN BLUEBIRD ♀
see p.532

brownish back

grayish throat

MOUNTAIN BLUEBIRD ♀
see p.533

gray-brown head and body

OCCURRENCE
Found in eastern Canada and the eastern US, where it lives in clearings and woodland edges; occupies multiple open habitats in rural, urban, and suburban areas: woodlands, plains, orchards, parks, and spacious lawns. Breeds and winters across the eastern half of the US.

| Length **6–8in (15–20cm)** | Wingspan **10–13in (25–33cm)** | Weight **1¹⁄₁₆oz (30g)** |
| Social **Flocks** | Lifespan **8–10 years** | Status **Vulnerable** |

| Order **Passeriformes** | Family **Turdidae** | Species *Sialia mexicana* |

Western Bluebird

blue hood

short wings and tail

MALE

brownish back

grayish throat

rust patch on back

blue shoulder and wing

pale blue belly

IN FLIGHT

FEMALE

chestnut breast and flanks

blue wings and tail

blue wings

spotted underparts

pale blue belly

rusty undertail

MALE

JUVENILE

Very similar to its close relative, the Eastern Bluebird, but with a distribution restricted to the western part of the continent, the male Western Bluebird is endowed with a spectacular plumage—brilliant blue upperparts and deep chestnut-orange underparts. Unlike the Eastern Bluebird, the Western Bluebird has a brown back and a complete blue hood. Females and juveniles are harder to distinguish, but their ranges are quite different.

VOICE Vocalizations similar to those of the Eastern Bluebird; calls soft *few, few* or *fewrr-fewrr*; song a pleasant, soft series of churring notes, all strung together, often given at dawn.

NESTING Shallow cup of dry grass and feathers in natural tree cavity or old woodpecker cavity; 4–6 eggs; 1–2 broods; March–July.

FEEDING Feeds mainly on insects in breeding season; eats berries, such as juniper, in winter.

FLIGHT: slow and easy-looking, with shallow wing beats.

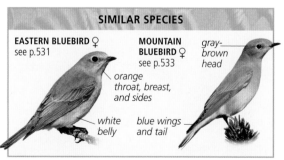

SIMILAR SPECIES

EASTERN BLUEBIRD ♀
see p.531

MOUNTAIN BLUEBIRD ♀
see p.533

gray-brown head

orange throat, breast, and sides

white belly

blue wings and tail

PERCHED MALE
The Western Bluebird hunts from low perches, from which it takes insects from the ground or air.

OCCURRENCE
During breeding season, open woodlands (coniferous and deciduous) and forest edges. In winter, moves to lower elevations and occupies open and semi-open areas such as pinyon-juniper forests and deserts. Partial migrant; northern birds move south where southern breeders reside.

| Length **6–7in (15–18cm)** | Wingspan **11½–13in (29–33cm)** | Weight **⅞–1¹⁄₁₆ oz (25–30g)** |
| Social **Winter flocks** | Lifespan **Up to 7 years** | Status **Secure** |

Order **Passeriformes**	Family **Turdidae**	Species *Sialia currucoides*

Mountain Bluebird

long wings
and tail

blue overall

vibrant blue
upperparts

MALE

IN FLIGHT

light
blue
flanks

whitish
underparts

MALE

lightly
spotted
back

blue wings
and tail

JUVENILE

gray-brown head
and body

gray-brown
flanks and
breast

bright
blue wings

FEMALE

A bird of the American West, especially sub-alpine meadows, the Mountain Bluebird is as striking as the other two *Sialia* species, but, unlike them, lacks any reddish chestnut in its plumage. It is also more slender-looking, and flies in an almost lazy manner. More often than its two relatives, it feeds by hovering, kestrel-like, over meadows, before pouncing on insects. Males guard their mates from pair-bond time to egg-hatching time.

VOICE Calls rolled, soft churring; one song, loud but infrequent, similar to the American Robin's song—*sing-song cheerily cheer-up cheerio*; the other, soft and repetitive whistle.
NESTING Cavity nest of grass, weeds, and bark; 5–6 eggs; 2 broods; May–July.
FEEDING Insects, including crickets, grasshoppers, bees, and caterpillars, dominate its diet year round; also berries.

FLIGHT: slow unhurried, almost leisurely, with shallow wing beats.

BERRY LOVER
Berries are an important part of the bird's diet along with insects and caterpillars.

OCCURRENCE
Breeds in western North America, in grassland or open canyons with scattered trees, or alpine parklands. In winter, prefers open habitats and avoids dry areas. Winter habitat includes juniper forest and Ponderosa Pine in the south of its territory.

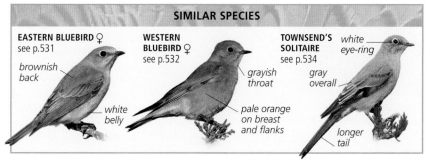

SIMILAR SPECIES

EASTERN BLUEBIRD ♀
see p.531

brownish
back

white
belly

WESTERN
BLUEBIRD ♀
see p.532

grayish
throat

pale orange
on breast
and flanks

TOWNSEND'S
SOLITAIRE
see p.534

white
eye-ring

gray
overall

longer
tail

Length **6–8in (15–20cm)**	Wingspan **11–12½in (28–32cm)**	Weight **1¹/₁₆oz (30g)**
Social **Flocks**	Lifespan **At least 5 years**	Status **Secure**

| Order **Passeriformes** | Family **Muscicapidae** | Species *Myadestes townsendi* |

Townsend's Solitaire

ADULT

dark gray outer flight feathers

wide, buff bands on flight feathers

long tail

short head

IN FLIGHT

plain gray

upright posture

ADULT

black legs and feet

large, black eye

white eye-ring

gray upperparts and head

short, black bill

paler underparts

ADULT

spotted back

heavily spotted breast

JUVENILE

long tail

pale chestnut-tan patches

long, dark tail with white outer feathers

The rather shy Townsend's Solitaire inhabits most of western North America, especially high-elevation coniferous forests of the Sierras and Rockies. Its drab gray plumage, with a chestnut-tan wing pattern, remains the same throughout the year, and the sexes look alike. From a perch high on a branch, Townsend's Solitaire darts after flying insects and snaps its bill shut after catching its prey, unlike other thrush-like birds.

VOICE Calls are single-note, high-pitched whistles; sings all year, but especially when establishing territories; main song robin-like, full of rolled or trilled sounds, interspersed with squeaky notes.

NESTING Cup of pine needles, dry grass, weed stems, and bark on ground or under overhang; 4 eggs; 1–2 broods; May–August.

FEEDING Forages for a wide variety of insects and spiders during breeding season; feeds on fruits and berries after breeding, particularly junipers.

FLIGHT: unhurried motion, usually over short distances, with slow, steady wing beats.

JUNIPER LOVER
Solitaires love the berry-like cones of junipers, which they eat to supplement their winter diet.

OCCURRENCE
During breeding season, found in open conifer forests along steep slopes or areas with landslides; during winter, at lower elevations, in open woodlands where junipers are abundant. Partial-migrant northern populations move south in winter, as far as central Mexico.

SIMILAR SPECIES

MOUNTAIN BLUEBIRD ♀
see p.533

dull bluish back

blue in wings and tail

short tail

GRAY PLUMAGE
Townsend's Solitaire is a drab gray overall, but a conspicuous white eye-ring.

| Length **8–8½in (20–22cm)** | Wingspan **13–14½in (33–37cm)** | Weight **1¹⁄₁₆–1¼oz (30–35g)** |
| Social **Solitary** | Lifespan **Up to 5 years** | Status **Secure** |

Order **Passeriformes**	Family **Turdidae**	Species **Catharus fuscescens**

Veery

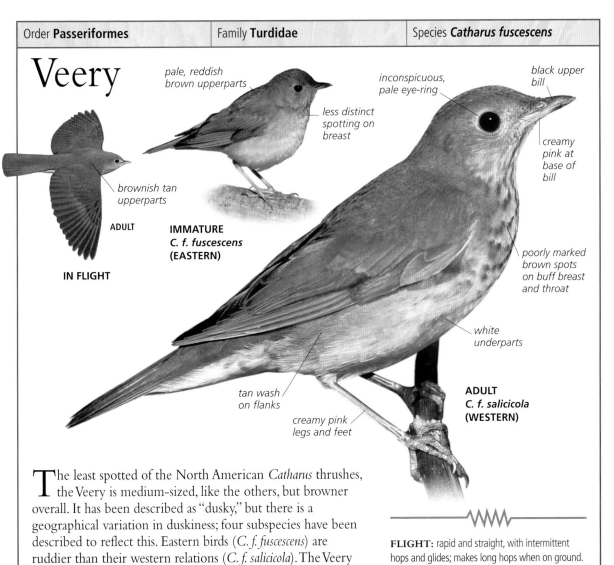

pale, reddish brown upperparts

less distinct spotting on breast

brownish tan upperparts

ADULT

IN FLIGHT

IMMATURE
C. f. fuscescens
(EASTERN)

inconspicuous, pale eye-ring

black upper bill

creamy pink at base of bill

poorly marked brown spots on buff breast and throat

white underparts

ADULT
C. f. salicicola
(WESTERN)

tan wash on flanks

creamy pink legs and feet

The least spotted of the North American *Catharus* thrushes, the Veery is medium-sized, like the others, but browner overall. It has been described as "dusky," but there is a geographical variation in duskiness; four subspecies have been described to reflect this. Eastern birds (*C. f. fuscescens*) are ruddier than their western relations (*C. f. salicicola*). The Veery is a long-distance migrant, spending the northern winter months in central Brazil, in a variety of tropical habitats.

VOICE A series of descending *da-vee-ur, vee-ur, veer, veer*, somewhat bi-tonal, sounding like the name Veery; call a rather soft *veer*.

NESTING Cup of dead leaves, bark, weed stems, and moss on or near ground; 4 eggs; 1–2 broods; May–July.

FEEDING Forages on the ground for insects, spiders, snails; eats fruit and berries after breeding.

FLIGHT: rapid and straight, with intermittent hops and glides; makes long hops when on ground.

DAMP DWELLINGS
The Veery breeds in damp habitats such as moist wooded areas or in trees near or in swamps.

OCCURRENCE
In summer, mainly found in damp deciduous forests, but in some places habitat near rivers preferred. In winter, choice of habitat flexible; found in tropical broadleaf evergreen forest, on forest edges, in open woodlands, and in second-growth areas regenerating after fires or clearing.

SIMILAR SPECIES

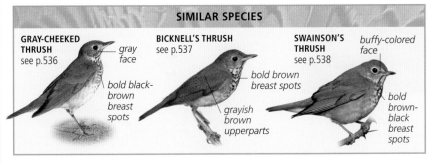

GRAY-CHEEKED THRUSH see p.536

gray face

bold black-brown breast spots

BICKNELL'S THRUSH see p.537

bold brown breast spots

grayish brown upperparts

SWAINSON'S THRUSH see p.538

buffy-colored face

bold brown-black breast spots

Length **7in (18cm)**	Wingspan **11–11½in (28–29cm)**	Weight **1¹⁄₁₆–2oz (28–54g)**
Social **Pairs**	Lifespan **Up to 10 years**	Status **Declining**

| Order **Passeriformes** | Family **Turdidae** | Species **Catharus minimus** |

Gray-cheeked Thrush

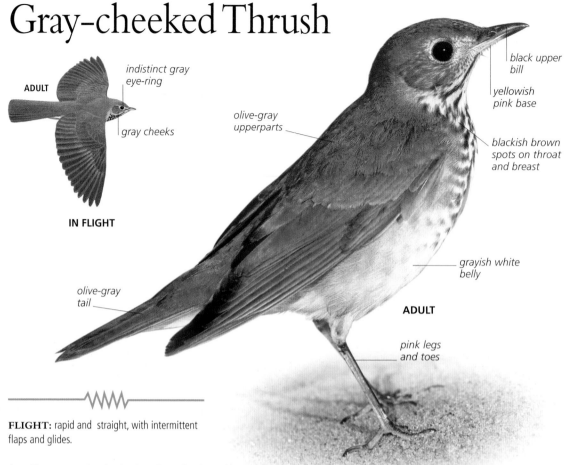

ADULT

IN FLIGHT

indistinct gray eye-ring

gray cheeks

olive-gray upperparts

black upper bill

yellowish pink base

blackish brown spots on throat and breast

grayish white belly

ADULT

olive-gray tail

pink legs and toes

FLIGHT: rapid and straight, with intermittent flaps and glides.

The Gray-cheeked Thrush is the least known of the four *Catharus* thrushes, largely because it breeds in remote areas of northern Canada. In fact, most of the existing information on this species is a result of research on the Bicknell's Thrush, which was considered to be a subspecies of the Gray-cheeked Thrush until 1993. During migration, the Gray-cheeked Thrush is more likely to be heard in flight at night than seen on the ground by birdwatchers.

VOICE Call a thin *kweer*, sometimes two notes; song flute-like, somewhat nasal, several notes ending on a lower pitch.

NESTING Cup of grass, twigs, moss, dead leaves, and mud, placed near ground in shrubbery; 4 eggs; 1 brood; May–July.

FEEDING Forages insects, including beetles, ants, spiders, earthworms, and fruits.

FEEDING HABITAT
A Gray-cheeked Thrush hops across the forest floor looking for prey.

SIMILAR SPECIES

BICKNELL'S THRUSH see p.537

olive-brown upperparts

brownish spots

MIGRATION PATTERN
During migration, this bird can be seen near a variety of sites with trees or shrubs.

OCCURRENCE
On breeding grounds, occupies densely vegetated areas with small shrubs; preference for spruce forests in northern Canada and Alaska. During migration, favors wooded areas with dense understory. In winter, prefers forested areas and secondary succession woodlands.

| Length **6½–7in (16–18cm)** | Wingspan **11½–13½in (29–34cm)** | Weight **⅞–1¹⁄₁₆oz (26–30g)** |
| Social **Mixed flocks** | Lifespan **Up to 7 years** | Status **Secure** |

| Order **Passeriformes** | Family **Turdidae** | Species *Catharus bicknelli* |

Bicknell's Thrush

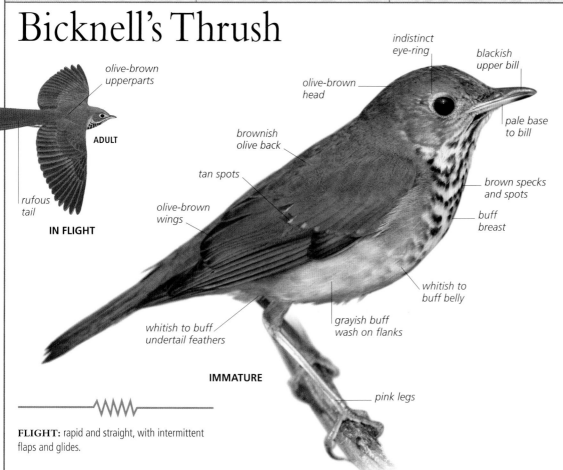

olive-brown
upperparts

ADULT

rufous
tail

IN FLIGHT

indistinct
eye-ring

blackish
upper bill

olive-brown
head

pale base
to bill

brownish
olive back

tan spots

olive-brown
wings

brown specks
and spots

buff
breast

whitish to
buff belly

grayish buff
wash on flanks

whitish to buff
undertail feathers

IMMATURE

pink legs

FLIGHT: rapid and straight, with intermittent
flaps and glides.

Bicknell's Thrush was long considered a subspecies of the
Gray-cheeked Thrush, until 1993 when it was shown to
be a distinct species with a slight difference in color, song, habitat,
and migration. In the field, it is best distinguished from the Gray-
cheeked Thrush by its song, which is less full and lower in pitch.
Bicknell's Thrush breeds only in dwarf conifer forests on
mountain tops in the northeastern US and adjacent Canada,
usually above 3,000ft (1,000m). Habitat loss threatens this species
on its wintering grounds in Cuba, Hispaniola, and Puerto Rico.
Males and females mate with multiple partners in a single season;
because of this, males may care for young in multiple nests.
VOICE Call *pheeuw*, one or two notes; complicated flute-like
song of about four parts, ending with rising pitch; males sing,
especially during flight; females rarely sing; song varies
among populations.

NESTING Cup of moss
and evergreen twigs,
near ground; 3–4 eggs;
1 brood; June–August.
FEEDING Feeds mainly
on caterpillars and
insects; in addition, fruit
during migration and
possibly in winter.

MOUNTAIN-TOP BREEDING
This species breeds in high-elevation woodland
areas, especially in conifers.

SIMILAR SPECIES

GRAY-CHEEKED THRUSH
see p.536
olive-gray
brown
grayish
face

OCCURRENCE
Restricted to dense spruce or fir
forest at or near the treeline, at
3,000ft (1,000m), often in
disturbed areas undergoing
successional changes. During
migration, found in a variety
of habitats, such as woodlots
and beaches. In winter, strong
preference for wet mountainous
Caribbean forests.

| Length **6½–7in (16–18cm)** | Wingspan **12in (30cm)** | Weight **⅞–1¹⁄₁₆ oz (26–30g)** |
| Social **Solitary/Small flocks** | Lifespan **Up to 8 years** | Status **Vulnerable** |

| Order **Passeriformes** | Family **Turdidae** | Species *Catharus ustulatus* |

Swainson's Thrush

ADULT

IN FLIGHT

olive-brown rump and tail

more rufous in upperparts

russet back

smaller, less distinct, sparser spotting

ADULT
C. c. ustulatus
(WESTERN)

olive-brown upperparts

buffy eye-ring

buff breast

distinct blackish spots

ADULT
C. c. swainsoni
(EASTERN)

Swainson's Thrush can be distinguished from other spotted thrushes by its buffy face and the rising pitch of its flute-like, melodious song. This species is also distinctive as it feeds higher up in the understory than most of its close relatives. The western subspecies of Swainson's Thrush is russet-backed and migrates to Central America for the winter, while the other populations are olive-backed and winter in South America.

VOICE Single-note call *whit* or *whooit*; main song delivered by males, several phrases, each one spiraling upward; flute-like song is given during breeding and migration.

NESTING Open cup of twigs, moss, dead leaves, bark, and mud, on branches near trunks of small trees or in shrubs; 3–4 eggs; 1–2 broods; April–July.

FEEDING Forages in the air, using fly-catching methods to capture a wide range of insects during breeding season; berries during migration and in winter.

FLIGHT: rapid and straight, with intermittent flaps and glides.

DISTINCTIVE SONG
This bird's song distinguishes it from other thrushes.

TREE DWELLER
Shy and retiring, Swainson's Thrush feeds in trees more than other *Catharus* thrushes.

SIMILAR SPECIES

VEERY
see p.535

tawny brown back

lightly spotted breast

HERMIT THRUSH
see p.539

grayish cheeks

streaks on sides of breast

rust-colored tail

OCCURRENCE
Breeds mainly in coniferous forests, especially spruce and fir, except in California, where it prefers deciduous riverside woodlands and damp meadows with shrubbery. During spring and fall migrations, dense understory is preferred. Winter habitat is mainly old growth forest.

| Length **6½–7½in (16–19cm)** | Wingspan **11½–12in (29–31cm)** | Weight **⅞–1⁹⁄₁₆ oz (25–45g)** |
| Social **Pairs/Flocks** | Lifespan **Up to 11 years** | Status **Declining** |

Order **Passeriformes**	Family **Turdidae**	Species *Catharus guttatus*

Hermit Thrush

gray-brown upperparts

ADULT
C. g. faxoni
(EASTERN)

IN FLIGHT

darker brown upperparts

dark spots on whitish breast

paler gray flanks

ADULT
C. g. guttatus
(NORTHWESTERN)

gray-brown upperparts

more extensive breast spotting

ADULT
C. g. audoboni
(ROCKIES)

reddish tail

ADULT
C. g. faxoni
(EASTERN)

thin, white eye-ring

brownish back

dark spots on buff breast

tawny buff flanks

The Hermit Thrush's song is the signature sound of northerly and mountain forests in the West—fluted, almost bi-tonal, far-carrying, and ending up with almost a question mark. The Hermit Thrush is so named because of its solitary lifestyle, especially in winter, when birds maintain inter-individual territories. Geographical variation within the vast range of the species has led to the recognition of nine subspecies (three are illustrated here). It generally winters south of the US, in Mexico, Guatemala, and El Salvador.

VOICE Calls *tchek*, soft, dry; song flute-like, ethereal, falling, repetitive, and varied; several phrases delivered on a different pitch.
NESTING Cup of grasses, mosses, twigs, leaves, mud, hair, on ground or in low tree branches; 4 eggs; 1–2 broods; May–July.
FEEDING Mainly forages on ground for insects, larvae, earthworms, and snails; in winter, also eats fruit.

FLIGHT: rapid and straight, with intermittent flaps and glides.

URBAN VISITOR
This thrush is frequently seen in wooded areas in urban and suburban parks.

OCCURRENCE
Occurs in coniferous forests and mixed conifer–deciduous woodlands; prefers to nest along the edges of a forest interior, like a bog location. Found in forest and other open woodlands during winter. During migration, found in many wooded habitats.

SIMILAR SPECIES

VEERY
see p.535
tawny brown back
lightly spotted breast

BICKNELL'S TRUSH
see p.537
olive-brown back
yellow base of bill

SWAINSON'S THRUSH
see p.538
olive-brown upperparts

Length **6–7in (15–18cm)**	Wingspan **10–11in (25–28cm)**	Weight **⅞–1¹⁄₁₆ oz (25–30g)**
Social **Solitary**	Lifespan **Up to 9 years**	Status **Secure**

Order **Passeriformes**	Family **Turdidae**	Species *Hylocichla mustelina*

Wood Thrush

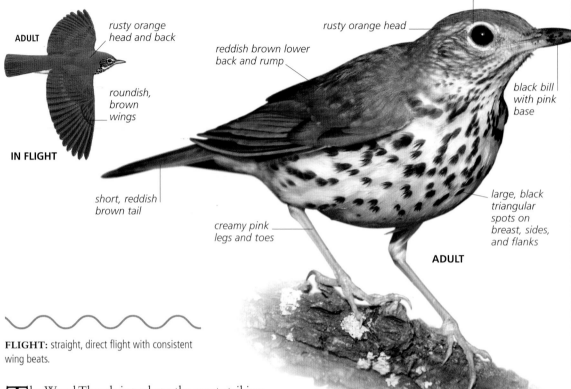

ADULT

rusty orange head and back

roundish, brown wings

IN FLIGHT

short, reddish brown tail

white eye-ring

rusty orange head

reddish brown lower back and rump

black bill with pink base

large, black triangular spots on breast, sides, and flanks

creamy pink legs and toes

ADULT

FLIGHT: straight, direct flight with consistent wing beats.

The Wood Thrush is perhaps the most striking of the small North American thrushes, due to the black spots that cover its underparts, and its rufous head and back. In the breeding season, its flute-like song echoes through the Northeastern hardwood forests and suburban forested areas. Wood Thrush populations have fallen over the past 30 years, largely due to forest destruction and fragmentation. Sadly, this decline has been exacerbated by the Wood Thrush's susceptibility to parasitism by the Brown-headed Cowbird.

VOICE Rapid *pip-pippipip* or *rhuu-rhuu*; a three-part flute-like song—first part indistinct, second part loudest, third part trilled; males have variations of all three parts; mainly before sunrise.

NESTING Cup-shaped nest made with dried grass and weeds in trees or shrubs; 3–4 eggs; 1–2 broods; May–July.

FEEDING Forages in leaf litter, mainly for worms, beetles, moths, caterpillars; eats fruits after breeding season.

STUNNING SOLOIST
The Wood Thrush can often be seen singing its melodious songs from a conspicuous perch.

SIMILAR SPECIES

VEERY see p.535

smaller overall

longer tail

HERMIT THRUSH see p.539

fainter spotting

reddish tail

spotting only on throat and upper breast

OCCURRENCE
Hardwood forests in the East, from Texas and Florida to Minnesota and the Canadian Maritimes. Breeds in interior and at edges of deciduous and mixed forests; needs dense understory, shrubbery, and moist soil. Winters in Texas, Louisiana, Florida, and south through Central America to Panama.

Length **7½–8½in (19–21cm)**	Wingspan **12–13½in (30–34cm)**	Weight **1⁷⁄₁₆–1¾oz (40–50g)**
Social **Pairs/Flocks**	Lifespan **Up to 9 years**	Status **Declining**

Order **Passeriformes**	Family **Turdidae**	Species *Turdus migratorius*

American Robin

MALE

dark head

IN FLIGHT

more complete white eye-ring

gray back

orangish red breast

white rump

FEMALE

broken white eye-ring

yellow bill

dark streaks on chin

dark gray back

mottled gray back

spotted breast

JUVENILE

fairly long, dark tail

brick-red underparts

MALE

FLIGHT: strong, swift flights with intermittent flaps and glides.

The American Robin, the largest and most abundant of the North American thrushes, is probably the most familiar bird on the continent, and its presence on suburban lawns is an early sign of spring. Unlike other species, it has adapted and prospered in human-altered habitats. It breeds across the entire US and Canada and also winters across the US, migrating out of most of Canada in fall. The decision to migrate is largely governed by changes in the availablity of food. As the breeding season approaches, it is the males that sing first, either late in winter or early spring. The bird's brick-red breast—more vivid in males than in females—is its most distinguishing feature.

VOICE Calls a high pitch *tjip* and a multi-note, throaty *tjuj-tjuk*; primary song a melodious *cheer-up, cheer-up, cheer-wee*, one of the first birds to be heard during dawn chorus, and one of the last to cease singing in the evening.

NESTING Substantial cup of grass, weeds, twigs, occasional garbage in tree or shrub, in fork of tree, or on branch on tree; 4 eggs; 2–3 broods; April–July.

FEEDING Forages in leaf litter, mainly for earthworms and small insects; mostly consumes fruit in the winter season.

SEASONAL DIET
Robins are particularly dependent on the availability of fruit during the winter months.

OCCURRENCE
Breeding habitat a mix of forest, woodland, suburban gardens, lawns, municipal parks, and farms. A partial migrant, these robins tend to be found in woodlands where berry-bearing trees are present. Nonmigrating populations' winter habitat is similar to breeding habitat.

SIMILAR SPECIES

VARIED THRUSH see p.530
orange eyebrow
bluish gray upperparts
wide black necklace

Length **8–11in (20–28cm)**	Wingspan **12–16in (30–41cm)**	Weight **2⅝oz (75g)**
Social **Flocks**	Lifespan **Up to 13 years**	Status **Secure**

Order **Passeriformes**	Family **Turdidae**	Species *Luscinia svecica*

Bluethroat

grayish brown upperparts

blue throat

MALE

IN FLIGHT

mouse-gray upperparts

white throat with black bib

grayish tan underparts

FEMALE (BREEDING)

large, black eye

white eyebrow

black border

whitish breast

reddish base to tail

tan wing bar

similar to female, but duller

JUVENILE

black tail with reddish sides

thin, black legs

MALE (BREEDING)

FLIGHT: swift and direct with rapid wing beats.

Ten subspecies of Bluethroat have been identified across the world, but the only one found in North America is *L. s. svecica*, distinguishable from the others as it has a distinctive reddish spot on its blue throat. It is limited to the far northern reaches of Alaska and the Yukon. Although the bird's stunning, iridescent-blue throat is unmistakable, it is rarely seen because it spends most of its time in thick vegetation. It is perhaps better known for its vocal genius as a mimic—in Lapland, its indigenous name means "a hundred tongues," and it can be heard imitating many of the species that share its far northern breeding range.
VOICE Call a sharp, dry *krak* and a softer, whistled *whooit*; also lengthy songs that may combine the songs of many other species.
NESTING Cup-shaped nest of woven sedges, on or near grassy tussocks; 4–7 eggs; 1 brood; June–August.
FEEDING Gleans a variety of insects from trees and shrubs including mosquitoes, bees, and wasps.

A BEAKFUL
A male Bluethroat brings a beak-full of insects to its hungry nestlings in willow shrubbery.

BIRD OF "A HUNDRED TONGUES"
This Bluethroat exercises its vocal chords while showing its characteristic blue and reddish colors.

OCCURRENCE
Breeds on the far northern tundra of northern and western Alaska and the northern Yukon, in areas of tundra dominated by thickets of trees or shrubs, especially willows. Winter habitat is similar, but generally close to water. Migrants from Alaska fly across Asia to winter in tropical Africa.

Length **6in (15cm)**	Wingspan **9in (23cm)**	Weight **½–¾oz (15–22g)**
Social **Solitary**	Lifespan **Up to 8 years**	Status **Secure**

| Order **Passeriformes** | Family **Muscicapidae** | Species *Oenanthe oenanthe* |

Northern Wheatear

MALE (BREEDING)

tail has a black "T"

black mask

IN FLIGHT

long, black wings

FEMALE (BREEDING)

mouse-brown back

tan eyebrow

tan throat and breast

FEMALE (BREEDING)

white forehead and eyebrow

black bill

gray back

white underparts

similar to female, but duller

JUVENILE

MALE (BREEDING)

long, thin, black legs

Although widely distributed in Europe, the Middle East and Africa, the Northern Wheatear is present in North America only during its brief breeding season, where it is confined to Alaska and northeastern Canada. The two subspecies that breed in North America, the larger *O. o. leucorhoa* in the Northeast and *O. o. oenanthe* in the Northwest, migrate to wintering grounds in sub-Saharan Africa. The Northern Wheatear can be distinguished by its black-and-white tail, which bobs when the bird walks.
VOICE Multiple calls, a sharp *tuc* or *tek* common; three types of songs—territorial, conversational, and perched—consisting of mixtures of sweet and harsh notes; imitates other species.
NESTING Under rocks or in abandoned burrows; nests have coarse outer foundation, with cradle and cup within of finer material; 5–6 eggs; 1 brood; June–July.
FEEDING Eats insects, but also takes berries; diet in North America not well known.

KEEP YOUR DISTANCE
Northern Wheatears are highly territorial, so neighbors get yelled at if they come too close.

FLIGHT: undulating when flying long distances; fluttering from perch to perch.

OCCURRENCE
Breeds in rocky tundra of Alaska and northern Canada, including the Yukon (*O. o. oenanthe*) and the Arctic archipelago (*O. o. leucorhoa*). Both subspecies winter in Africa, *O. o. oenanthe* by flying across Asia, *O. o. leucorhoa* by flying across the Atlantic.

| Length **5½–6in (14–15cm)** | Wingspan **10¾in (27cm)** | Weight **½oz (14g)** |
| Social **Solitary/Flocks** | Lifespan **Up to 7 years** | Status **Secure** |

Order **Passeriformes**	Family **Cinclidae**	Species *Cinclus mexicanus*

American Dipper

white eyelid

broad, rounded wings

short tail

short wings

straight, black bill

ADULT

IN FLIGHT

dark gray overall

ADULT

frosty scalloping on wings

pinkish bill

sturdy, pink legs

paler than adult

JUVENILE

The most aquatic North American songbird, the American Dipper is at home in the cold, rushing streams of the American West. It is known for its feeding technique of plunging into streams for insect larvae under stones or in the streambed. When it is not foraging, it watches from a rock or log, bobbing up and down, constantly flashing its nictating membrane (the transparent third eyelid that protects the eye when the bird is underwater). Susceptible to changes in water chemistry and turbulence, which alters the abundance of its main food, caddisfly larvae, this bird has been proposed as an indicator for stream quality.
VOICE Call a harsh *bzzt*, given singly or in rapid series; song a loud, disorganized series of pleasing warbles, whistles, and trills.
NESTING Domed nest with side entrance, placed underneath bridge or behind waterfall; 4–5 eggs; 1–2 broods; March–August.
FEEDING Forages for insects and insect larvae, especially caddisflies; sometimes eats small fish and fish eggs.

FLIGHT: low over water, twisting and turning with the stream with rapid, buzzy wing beats.

BOBBING MOTION
The American Dipper often pauses on rocks in streams, where it bobs up and down.

OCCURRENCE
Found from Alaska, the Yukon, and British Columbia, south to California, Arizona, New Mexico, Mexico, and Panama. On Pacific slope, breeds down to sea level; in Interior West, breeds mainly in mountains and foothills; retreats to lower elevations in winter.

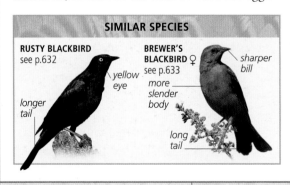

SIMILAR SPECIES

RUSTY BLACKBIRD
see p.632

yellow eye

longer tail

BREWER'S BLACKBIRD ♀
see p.633

sharper bill

more slender body

long tail

Length **7½in (19cm)**	Wingspan **11in (28cm)**	Weight **1¾–2¼oz (50–65g)**
Social **Solitary**	Lifespan **Up to 7 years**	Status **Secure**

| Order **Passeriformes** | Family **Passeridae** | Species *Passer domesticus* |

House Sparrow

white wing bar

pale rump

MALE (SUMMER)

IN FLIGHT

buff eyestripe

yellowish bill

drab brown underparts

FEMALE

gray crown

brown nape

black-and-brown streaks on upperparts

black throat

gray breast

white wing bar

MALE (SUMMER)

This is the familiar "sparrow" of towns, cities, suburbs, and farms. The House Sparrow is not actually a sparrow as understood in North America, but rather a member of a Eurasian family called the weaver-finches. It was first introduced in Brooklyn, New York, in 1850. From this modest beginning, and with the help of several other introductions up until the late 1860s, this hardy, and aggressive bird eventually spread right through the North American continent. In a little more than 150 years, the House Sparrow has evolved and shows the same sort of geographic variation as some widespread native birds. It is pale in the arid southwest US, and darker in wetter regions.
VOICE Variety of calls, including a *cheery chirp*, a dull *jurv* and a rough *jigga*; song consists of *chirp* notes repeated endlessly.
NESTING Untidy mass of dried vegetable material in either natural or artificial cavities; 3–5 eggs; 2–3 broods; April–August.
FEEDING Mostly seeds; sometimes gleans insects and fruits.

FLIGHT: fast and bouncing, with rapid wing beats; short wings and tail give it a portly profile.

APTLY NAMED
This sparrow is seen near human structures—roofs, outbuildings, loading docks, curbs, and streetlights.

SIMILAR SPECIES

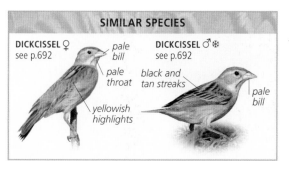

DICKCISSEL ♀
see p.692

pale bill

pale throat

yellowish highlights

DICKCISSEL ♂ ❄
see p.692

black and tan streaks

pale bill

OCCURRENCE
Flourishes in the downtown sections of cities and anywhere near human habitations, including agricultural outbuildings in remote areas of the continent. Found also in Mexico, Central and South America, and the West Indies.

| Length **6in (15.5cm)** | Wingspan **9½in (24cm)** | Weight **⅝–1¹⁄₁₆oz (18–30g)** |
| Social **Flocks** | Lifespan **Up to 7 years** | Status **Declining** |

Order **Passeriformes**	Family **Passeridae**	Species *Passer montanus*

Eurasian Tree Sparrow

tan rump and upper tail

IN FLIGHT

rounded wings

tan streaks on upperparts

two wing bars

white "necklace"

brown cap

black "mask" and chin

black spot on white cheek

pale "necklace"

grayish underparts

JUVENILE

ADULT

Like its successful cousin the House (or English) Sparrow, the Eurasian Tree Sparrow was introduced to the US in 1870. However, it has not spread as widely. Although not rare, it is not common either, and one has to work to spot it in parts of Illinois and Missouri; generally in parks, agricultural areas, and woodland edges, and also occasionally near human dwellings. The North American population is limited to western Illinois, Iowa, and Missouri, where this bird is said to compete with House Sparrows for nest sites, though it is more shy, and avoids city centers and heavily developed regions. In Eurasia, it also nests in rural and semi-rural areas, and is thus, not in competition with the House Sparrow.

VOICE Call notes tend to be dry and metallic: *chirp, chep*; song consists of series of dry notes interspersed with few more liquid ones.

NESTING Nest placed in tree hole, cavity in wall; 4–7 eggs, 2–3 broods; May–August.

FEEDING Forages on lawns and weedy patches for seeds, berries, insects, and spiders.

FLIGHT: fast with rapid wing beats; appears a little lighter than Eurasian Tree Sparrow.

MATING IN THE OPEN
Populations of the Eurasian Tree Sparrow are localized but not declining.

OCCURRENCE
In North America, the Eurasian Tree Sparrow is only found locally, in Missouri, Iowa, and Illinois. Here, it favors parks, farmyards, and residential neighborhoods; but avoids towns and cities, unlike the House Sparrow. It is a resident within this North American range.

SIMILAR SPECIES

HOUSE SPARROW ♀
see p.545

bold buff eyebrow

no "necklace"

lacks black spot

HOUSE SPARROW ♂
see p.545

white cheek

white wing bar

Length **6in (15cm)**	Wingspan **9in (23cm)**	Weight ⅝–1¹⁄₁₆**oz (18–30g)**
Social **Flocks**	Lifespan **Up to 7 years**	Status **Localized**

Order **Passeriformes**	Family **Peucedramidae**	Species **_Peucedramus taeniatus_**

Olive Warbler

green edges to wings

ADULT

IN FLIGHT

orange head with black "mask"

gray uppparts

orange head with black mask

thin, black bill

two conspicuous white wing patches

ADULT

gray underparts

green edges to wing feathers

white outer tail feathers

gray uppparts

brownish "mask"

FEMALE

yellow head and breast

FLIGHT: weak, bouncy flight; white flashes in wings and tail visible.

Although it looks and behaves like a warbler of the family Parulidae, this gorgeous, orange-headed, and black-masked "warbler" is actually so different in its song, breeding behavior, and genetic make-up that it is placed in its own family, the Peucedramidae. The Olive Warbler is one of a number of species whose US ranges are associated with the mountains of New Mexico and Arizona. This pine-loving bird lives at high elevations in pine and fir forests, and can be found from the border of the US with Mexico, south to Nicaragua.
VOICE Calls include smacking *bit*; soft, bluebird-like *view*; songs varied, but all are simple and repetitive.
NESTING Open-cup of lichens and pine needles, placed high in pine tree, far from trunk; 3–4 eggs; 1 brood; May–July.
FEEDING Forages around branches and pine needle for insects.

PINEWOODS SPECIALIST
The Olive Warbler feeds high in pine trees, where it plucks at insects like flies and beetles.

SIMILAR SPECIES

YELLOW WARBLER ♂♀
see p.580

olive green body

plain face

WESTERN TANAGER ♀
see p.691

plain face

OCCURRENCE
In North America, occurs in pine and pine-oak forests. Prefers Ponderosa Pine, but also found in Douglas Fir. Some range downslope into mixed forest, especially that with an oak component. Partial migrants, US birds winter in Mexico, and Central American birds are resident.

Length **5¼in (13.5cm)**	Wingspan **9in (23cm)**	Weight **⅜oz (11g)**
Social **Solitary/Small flocks**	Lifespan **At least 3 years**	Status **Secure**

| Order **Passeriformes** | Family **Motacillidae** | Species ***Motacilla flava*** |

Yellow Wagtail

MALE

long black tail with white outer tail feathers

IN FLIGHT

light gray-blue head

light grayish back

white undertail feathers

FEMALE

pale yellow underparts

dark greenish gray back

ashy blue-gray head

dark cheeks

bold, white eyebrow

bright yellow throat

inconspicuous wing bar

bright yellow belly

long, thin, dark legs

MALE

grayish brown head, with white eyebrow

dark brown markings on breast

yellow undertail feathers

whitish underparts

JUVENILE

FLIGHT: direct, alternating strong wing beats on upswing and glide on the downswing.

The Yellow Wagtail, like the White Wagtail and several other songbird species, is a widely distributed Eurasian breeder with a nesting foothold in Alaska and the Yukon. An extroadinarily variable species, the Yellow Wagtail has about 17 subspecies. The Alaskan-Canadian population belongs to the subspecies *tschutschensis*, which was described as long ago as 1789. It likes to perch on exposed low shrubs and mossy mounds in the tundra, persistently wagging its tail and calling its insistent *tzeep*. Other than the North American tundra, its breeding grounds include the Kamchatka Peninsula in eastern Russia.

VOICE Call is a short, "outgoing" *tzeep!*; song a thin, musical, *tzee-ouee-sir.*

NESTING Small cup of woven plant matter including grass, moss, and bark, lined with hair and feathers; often positioned near clump of grass; 4–5 eggs; 1 brood; June–July.

FEEDING Forages, mainly for land- and water-based insects, especially mosquitoes on or near the ground, especially along the water's edge; sometimes makes short flights to catch insects in flight.

EYE-CATCHING
This conspicuous bird with bright yellow underparts perches in the open and constantly wags its tail.

OCCURRENCE
Its North American range is restricted to western Alaska and extreme western Yukon, where it is found in tundra with scattered shrub, especially along watercourses. It winters in eastern Asia, south to Indonesia.

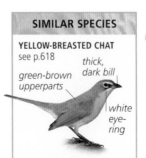

SIMILAR SPECIES

YELLOW-BREASTED CHAT see p.618

green-brown upperparts

thick, dark bill

white eye-ring

| Length **5–7in (13–18cm)** | Wingspan **7–9in (18–23cm)** | Weight **½–¹¹⁄₁₆oz (15–20g)** |
| Social **Flocks** | Lifespan **Up to 9 years** | Status **Localized** |

Order **Passeriformes**	Family **Motacillidae**	Species *Motacilla alba*

White Wagtail

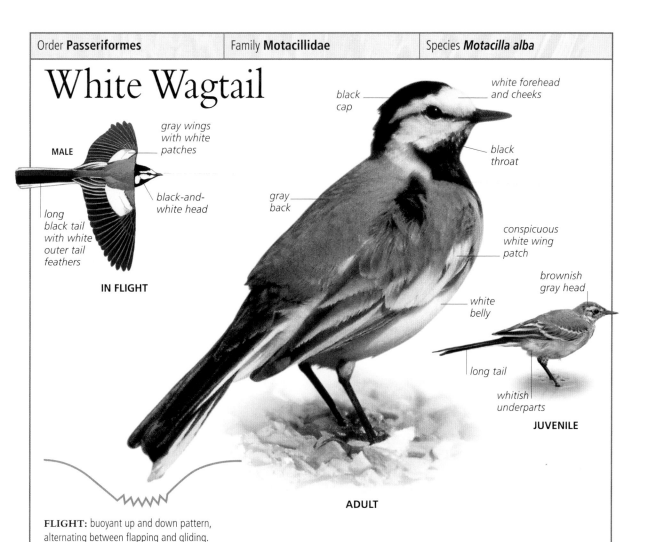

MALE

gray wings with white patches

black-and-white head

long black tail with white outer tail feathers

IN FLIGHT

black cap

white forehead and cheeks

black throat

gray back

gray back

conspicuous white wing patch

white belly

brownish gray head

long tail

whitish underparts

JUVENILE

ADULT

FLIGHT: buoyant up and down pattern, alternating between flapping and gliding.

Only one (*M. a. ocularis*) of the 11 subspecies of the wide-ranging Eurasian White Wagtail (from the British Isles to the Russian Far East) breeds in North America, in a very small geographical area of northwest Alaska and on St. Lawrence Island. It arrives in Alaska in late May or early June, breeds in a hurry, and leaves after slightly over two months, in August, moving on to wintering areas in tropical southeast Asia. On its Alaskan breeding grounds, the White Wagtail has adapted to human surroundings, and often builds its nests in abandoned buildings or decaying oil drums.

VOICE Call a single, sharp *tzzip* or double *tzzitip*; song is an extension of its call, blending into a sweet warble.

NESTING Cup of sticks and small branches lined with hair, feathers, and roots, in rock crevice; 4–6 eggs; 1 brood; June–July.

FEEDING Gathers insects from the ground, close to shallow water. Often runs to catch an insect, with a quick flight up if necessary. Eats mainly flying insects, such as midges, dragonflies, and mosquitoes.

LIMITED RANGE
In North America, this wagtail is found only along a small part of the northwestern coast of Alaska.

OCCURRENCE
An Eurasian species with an Alaskan toehold, the White Wagtail is found near water, either coastal areas or along rivers; also commonly associated with human development.

SIMILAR SPECIES

NORTHERN WHEATEAR
see p.543

gray cap

shorter dark tail

delicate salmon hue

dark wings

Length **6–8in (15–20cm)**	Wingspan **9–10in (23–25cm)**	Weight **⅞–1¹⁄₁₆oz (25–30g)**
Social **Small flocks**	Lifespan **Up to 10 years**	Status **Localized**

Order **Passeriformes**	Family **Motacillidae**	Species ***Anthus rubescens***

American Pipit

ADULT

IN FLIGHT
- gray cheek with buffy eyestripes
- white outer tail feathers

ADULT (NONBREEDING)
- faint streaking on gray upperparts
- pale eyebrow
- "mustache"
- whitish with heavier streaking on chest and flanks

- buffy eyestripe
- thin, dark bill
- dark "mustache"
- no streaking on grayish back
- wing bars
- light reddish buffy chest and flanks
- dark legs and toes
- long hind claw

ADULT (BREEDING)
- pale edges to wing feathers
- long tail with white outer tail feathers

FLIGHT: typically strong with a distinct, undulating, rise and fall pattern.

The American Pipit is divided into four subspecies, three of which breed in North America, and the fourth in Siberia. In nonbreeding plumage, the American Pipit is a drab-looking, brownish gray bird that forages for insects along water and shores, or in cultivated fields with short stems. In the breeding season, molting transforms it into a beauty—with gray upperparts and reddish underparts. American Pipits are known for pumping their tails up and down. When breeding, males display by rising into the air, then flying down with wings open and singing. Its migration takes the American Pipit as far south as Guatemala.
VOICE Alarm call a *tzeeep*; song repeated *tzwee-tzooo* from the air.
NESTING Cup in shallow depression on ground, outer frame of grass, lined with fine grass and hair; 4–6 eggs; 1 brood; June–July.
FEEDING Picks insects; also eats seeds during migration.

WINTER DRAB
Foraging in short vegetation, this bird is almost the same color as its surroundings.

SIMILAR SPECIES

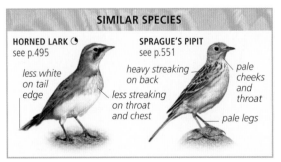

HORNED LARK see p.495
- less white on tail edge

SPRAGUE'S PIPIT see p.551
- heavy streaking on back
- less streaking on throat and chest
- pale cheeks and throat
- pale legs

OCCURRENCE
Breeds in Arctic tundra in the north, and alpine tundra in the Rockies; also breeds on treeless mountain tops in Maine and New Hampshire. Winters in open coastal areas and harvested agricultural fields across the US. Some North American migrants fly to Asia for the winter.

Length **6–8in (15–20cm)**	Wingspan **10–11in (25–28cm)**	Weight **$^{11}/_{16}$oz (20g)**
Social **Flocks**	Lifespan **Up to 6 years**	Status **Secure**

Order **Passeriformes**	Family **Motacillidae**	Species *Anthus spragueii*

Sprague's Pipit

eyes appear large

pale cheeks

thin "mustache"

thick, two-tone bill

heavily streaked back

two pale wing bars

buffy wash on flanks

pale whitish belly

ADULT

long, pale pink legs and toes

white outer tail feathers

long, dark hind claw

ADULT

broken "collar"

white outer tail feathers

IN FLIGHT

FLIGHT: strong with distinct up and down bobbing; prefers running to escape predators.

Sprague's is the only wholly North American pipit. Males perform a very extraordinary fluttering display flight, circling high above the earth while singing an unending series of high-pitched calls, for periods up to an hour. The current decline in the population of the Sprague's Pipit is quite likely the result of the conversion of tall-grass native prairie to extensive farmland. Interestingly, the Chaco Pipit of Argentina now breeds almost exclusively in wheat fields, offering some hope for this species.

VOICE Call a high *squeeek*; song a high, repetitive series of *szee- szee-szee*, usually given during lengthy aerial displays.

NESTING Small cup of loose woven grass on the ground and level with it, often attached to standing vegetation to form a sort of dome; 4–5 eggs; 1–2 broods; May–August.

FEEDING Feeds almost exclusively on insects when breeding, especially crickets and grasshoppers; eats seeds occasionally.

SONG PERCH
This Sprague's Pipit sings from a perch in its vanishing tall-grass prairie habitat.

SIMILAR SPECIES

HORNED LARK ☾
see p.495

shorter tail, less white

less-streaked on throat and chest

AMERICAN PIPIT
see p.550

unstreaked gray back

thin, dark bill

streaked chest, belly and flanks

dark legs

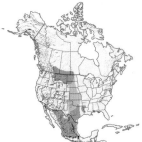

OCCURRENCE
Sprague's Pipit is truly North American, it breeds along the border of Canada with the US, in dry, open, tall-grass upland habitat, especially native prairie systems in the northern part of the Great Plains; most migrate to Mexico in winter, where habitat is similar to breeding grounds.

Length **4–6in (10–15cm)**	Wingspan **6–8in (15–20cm)**	Weight **¹¹⁄₁₆–⁷⁄₈oz (20–25g)**
Social **Solitary**	Lifespan **Unknown**	Status **Vulnerable**

Family **Fringillidae**

FINCHES

THE NAME "FINCHES" applies to the Fringillidae, a family of seed-eating songbirds that includes sixteen species in North America. They vary in size and shape from the small and fragile-looking redpolls to the robust and chunky Evening Grosbeak. Finch colors range from whitish with some pink (redpolls) to gold (American Goldfinch), bright red (crossbills), and yellow, white, and black (Evening grosbeak). However, irrespective of body shape, size, and color, all have conical bills with razor-sharp edges. Finches do not crush seeds. Instead, they cut open the hard hull, then seize the seed inside with their tongue and swallow it. The bills of conifer loving crossbills are crossed at the tip, a unique arrangement that permits them to open tough-hulled pine cones. Roughly 50 percent of crossbills are "left-billed" and 50 percent "right-billed"—lefties are right-footed, and vice versa. Most finches are social. Although they breed in pairs, after nesting finches form flocks, some of which are huge. Most finch populations fluctuate in size, synchronized with seed production and abundance. All finches are vocal, calling constantly while flying, and singing in the spring. Calls are usually sharp, somewhat metallic sounds, although the American Goldfinch's tinkling calls are sweeter. Songs can be quite musical, clear-sounding melodies, like that of the Cassin's Finch. Finches make open cup-shaped nests of grasses and lichens, in trees or shrubs, and are remarkably adept at hiding them.

CROSSBILL
Perched on a pine tree branch, a female Red Crossbill grinds a seed in her bill to break open the hull and reach the fat-rich kernel inside.

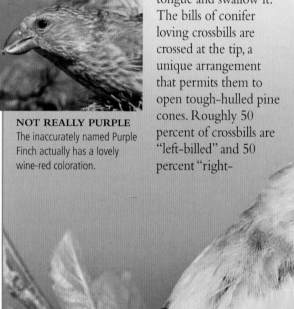

NOT REALLY PURPLE
The inaccurately named Purple Finch actually has a lovely wine-red coloration.

GARDEN GLOW
Even pink flower buds cannot compete with the yellow of a male American Goldfinch.

| Order **Passeriformes** | Family **Fringillidae** | Species *Carduelis pinus* |

Pine Siskin

notched tail

conspicuous yellow wing bar

MALE

IN FLIGHT

yellow in outer wing feathers

yellow base of tail

ADULT

pale eyebrow

brownish cheek

heavily streaked back

slender, pointed bill

heavily streaked underparts

FLIGHT: undulating, with quick series of wing beats and closed-winged glides.

This unpredictable little bird of the conifer belt runs in gangs and hordes, zipping over the trees with incessant twittering. An expert at disguise, the Pine Siskin can resemble a clusters of pine needles or cones, and even disappear when a Sharp-shinned Hawk appears. Often abundant wherever there are pines, spruces, and other conifers, Pine Siskins may still disappoint birdwatchers by making a mass exodus from a region if the food supply is not to their liking. A vicious fighter at feeding tables, nomadic by nature, with high energy and fearlessness, the Pine Siskin is a fascinating species.

VOICE Rising *toooeeo*, mostly when perched; also raspy *chit-chit-chit* in flight.

NESTING Shallow cup of grass and lichens near the end of a conifer branch; 3–4 eggs; 1–2 broods; February–August.

FEEDING Eats conifer seeds; gleans insects and spiders; also seen feeding on roadsides, lawns, and weed fields.

FOREST DWELLER
The streaked Pine Siskin inhabits northern and western coniferous forests.

QUARRELSOME
A bird warns off a neighbor at a food source, displaying its yellow wing stripe.

OCCURRENCE
Widespread across North America; occurs in coniferous and mixed coniferous forests, but also seen in parkland and suburbs. In some winters may appear south of regular breeding range to Missouri and Tennessee, also Mexico. Prefers open areas to continuous forest.

SIMILAR SPECIES

COMMON REDPOLL
see p.557

tiny, pale bill

heavier streaking

YELLOW-RUMPED WARBLER ♀
see p.588

yellow rump

yellow patches

| Length **4¼–5½in (11–14cm)** | Wingspan **7–9in (18–23cm)** | Weight **⁷⁄₁₆–⅝oz (12–18g)** |
| Social **Flocks** | Lifespan **Up to 10 years** | Status **Secure** |

| Order **Passeriformes** | Family **Fringillidae** | Species ***Carduelis tristis*** |

American Goldfinch

MALE (NONBREEDING)

bright yellow back

IN FLIGHT

tan back

brownish bill

yellow throat and collar

pale tan underparts

MALE (NONBREEDING)

brownish olive back

pinkish bill

FEMALE (BREEDING)

black forehead and crown

short conical pinkish bill

black tail

white rump

white wing bar

bright yellow underparts

pinkish legs and feet

MALE (BREEDING)

brownish overall

dull yellow throat

FEMALE (NONBREEDING)

O ften described as a giant yellow-and-black bumblebee, a male American Goldfinch in full breeding plumage is a common summer sight. Even when not seen, the presence of goldfinches in an area is quickly given away by the sound of the birds calling in flight. If there are weed seeds around, goldfinches will find them, whether they are out in the fields or on the feeding table. When a male performs his courtship songs, often singing them while circling his female, he does justice to the nickname "American canary."
VOICE Loud, rising *pter-yee* by males; 3–5-note *tit-tse-tew-tew* by both sexes, usually in flight; song complex warbling.
NESTING Open cup nest of grass, usually shaded from above; 4–5 eggs; 1–2 broods; July–September.
FEEDING Feeds mainly on seeds from annual plants, birch, and alder; some insects; prefers sunflower and thistle seed at feeders.

FLIGHT: deeply undulating; wing beats alternating with closed-wing dips.

OCCURRENCE
In low shrubs, deciduous woodlands, farmlands, orchards, suburbs, and gardens across much of North America, from southern Canada to California and Georgia; in winter south to Northern Mexico and Florida; winter habitats similar to those used at other times.

SIMILAR SPECIES

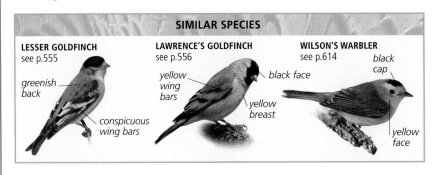

LESSER GOLDFINCH
see p.555

greenish back

conspicuous wing bars

LAWRENCE'S GOLDFINCH
see p.556

yellow wing bars

black face

yellow breast

WILSON'S WARBLER
see p.614

black cap

yellow face

| Length **4¼–5in (11–13cm)** | Wingspan **7–9in (18–23cm)** | Weight **⅜–¹¹⁄₁₆oz (11–20g)** |
| Social **Small flocks** | Lifespan **Up to 11 years** | Status **Secure** |

Order **Passeriformes**	Family **Fringillidae**	Species *Carduelis psaltria*

Lesser Goldfinch

black "T"

white patches on wings

MALE

IN FLIGHT

greenish olive back

dark conical bill

FEMALE

black cap

greenish back and rump

bright yellow throat

white wing bar

bright yellow underparts

less distinct cap

brownish green back

yellowish underparts

IMMATURE MALE

MALE (PACIFIC COAST)

black tail

The Lesser Goldfinch is a highly vocal bird, commonly found in gardens, suburbs, and farmlands, in addition to its natural habitats of open fields and scrub. Single birds and small flocks are often seen zooming around and flying overhead, calling noisily or singing in flight. The male has a brighter yellow breast and belly than the female. It also has a black cap, unlike the female, and its nape and back color varies from black in Texas and Mexico, to green along the Pacific coast.

VOICE Call descending *peeyee* and 2-note *tee-eee*, with second note higher; also rapid *dididit*; song warbles and trills.
NESTING Well-concealed cup, 10–30ft (3–9m) up in densely foliaged trees; 4 eggs; 1 brood; April–September.
FEEDING Eats a range of weed seeds; also eats insects, especially aphids, when available.

FLIGHT: undulating with dips; similar to other goldfinches.

GREENISH BACK
A western version of the American Goldfinch, the male Lesser Goldfinch is also greenish above.

SIMILAR SPECIES

AMERICAN GOLDFINCH
see p.554
all yellow
black forehead
white rump

LAWRENCE'S GOLDFINCH
see p.556
gray back
yellow breast
yellow wing bars

OCCURRENCE
This western species is not picky in its choice of habitat, which includes deciduous and coniferous woodlands, thickets, desert oases, parks and gardens; occurs from California to Texas in the breeding season and south to Mexico in winter.

Length **3½–4¼in (9–11cm)**	Wingspan **6–6¾in (15–17cm)**	Weight **⅜oz (10g)**
Social **Flocks**	Lifespan **Up to 6 years**	Status **Secure**

| Order **Passeriformes** | Family **Fringillidae** | Species *Carduelis lawrencei* |

Lawrence's Goldfinch

MALE

bright yellow patch

small pale bill

forked tail

IN FLIGHT

gray head

grayish green back

black forehead and crown

all-gray head

FEMALE

large, conspicuous wing patches

yellow breast

forked tail

MALE

An erratic winter wanderer, Lawrence's Goldfinch is an exciting addition to any birdwatcher's list. It prefers drier chaparral, grassy slopes, and generally hotter climates than the other goldfinches, and it may nest in an area one year but be absent the next. With abundant yellow in its wings, this bird can easily be distinguished from the two other species, both of which may occur in the same habitats and even flock together. The best way to identify each is by their species-specific calls.

VOICE Single, bell-like call notes and harsh *kee-urr*; song canary-like; may imitate other species.

NESTING Open cup of grass and plant down in tree or shrub; 4–5 eggs; 1-2 broods; April–August.

FEEDING Eats seeds of many species of weeds, also buds; some insects.

FLIGHT: active and agile, with undulating flight pattern.

DRAB FEMALE
The female has large yellow wing patches but no black face.

STRIKING MALE
Black face, gray cheeks, and yellow breast mark a male.

OCCURRENCE
Breeds in open foothills and valleys of California at elevations up to 9,000ft (2,750m). Northern populations migratory; southern populations may wander in winter north to Arizona and irregularly to far west Texas. Most migration is east and west rather than north and south.

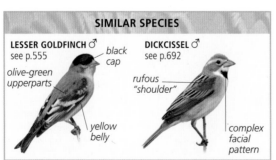

SIMILAR SPECIES

LESSER GOLDFINCH ♂
see p.555

black cap

olive-green uppparts

yellow belly

DICKCISSEL ♂
see p.692

rufous "shoulder"

complex facial pattern

| Length **4–4¾in (10–12cm)** | Wingspan **6–6½in (15–16cm)** | Weight **5⁄16–½oz (9–14g)** |
| Social **Flocks** | Lifespan **Unknown** | Status **Localized** |

Order **Passeriformes**	Family **Fringillidae**	Species *Carduelis flammea*

Common Redpoll

ruby-red cap

small, pointed yellow bill

MALE

red cap

wing bars

IN FLIGHT

MALE (BREEDING)

rosy-red breast

reddish cap

streaked underparts

FEMALE

pale wing bars

notched tail

JUVENILE

pale wing bar

black streaks on rosy-red breast

MALE (NONBREEDING)

E very other year, spruce, birch, and other trees in the northern forest zone fail to produce a good crop of seeds, forcing the Common Redpoll to look for food farther south than usual— as far south as the northern US states. The common Redpoll is oddly tame around people and is easily attracted to winter feeders. The degree of whiteness in its plumage varies greatly among individuals, due to sex and age. The taxonomy of the Common Redpoll includes four subspecies around the world, and there are suggestions that some may be distinct species.

VOICE Flight call dry *zit-zit-zit-zit* and rattling *chirr*; also high *too-ee* call while perched; song series of rapid trills.

NESTING Cup of small twigs in spruces, larches, willows, alders; 4–6 eggs; 1–2 broods; May–June.

FEEDING Feeds on small seeds from conifers, sedge, birch, willow, alder; also insects and spiders.

FLIGHT: deeply undulating, with dips between bouts of wing beats.

SIMILAR SPECIES

PINE SISKIN see p.553

HOARY REDPOLL see p.558

red cap

brownish upperparts

yellow on tail

two wing bars

pale overall

whitish underparts

FRIENDLY FLOCK
Common Redpolls are only weakly territorial, sometimes even nesting close together.

OCCURRENCE
Mainly in extreme northern North America from Alaska to Quebec and Labrador, in low forest, subarctic, and shrubby tundra habitats. More southerly winter appearances typically occur every other year, rarely south of northern US states, from Dakota east to New York City and New England.

Length 4¾–5½in (12–14cm)	Wingspan 6½–6¾in (16–17cm)	Weight ⅜–¹¹⁄₁₆oz (11–19g)
Social **Flocks**	Lifespan **Up to 10 years**	Status **Secure**

| Order **Passeriformes** | Family **Fringillidae** | Species ***Carpodacus mexicanus*** |

House Finch

brown cap

red face

brown upperparts

MALE (BREEDING)

IN FLIGHT

pale brown streaking

streaked belly

usually brick-red bib and head

grayish streaks all over

FEMALE

pinkish head

MALE (NON-BREEDING)

brown streaked undertail feathers

long tail feathers

MALE (BREEDING)

FLIGHT: bouncy, undulating flight typical of finches; usually flies above treetop level.

Historically, the House Finch was a western bird, and was first reported in the eastern side of the US on Long Island, New York City in 1941. These birds are said to have originated from the illegal bird trade. The population of the eastern birds started expanding in the 1960s, by the late 1990s, their population had expanded westward to link up with the original western population. The male House Finch is distinguished from the Purple and Cassin's finches by its brown streaked underparts, while the females have plainer faces and generally blurrier streaking.

VOICE Call note *queet*; varied jumble of notes, often starting with husky notes to whistled and burry notes, and ending with a long *wheeerr*.

NESTING Females build nests from grass stems, thin twigs, and thin weeds in trees and on man-made structures; 1–6 eggs; 2–3 broods; March–August.

FEEDING Eats, almost exclusively, vegetable matter, such as buds, fruits, and seeds; readily comes to feeders.

RED IN THE FACE
The breeding male House-Finch can be identified by its stunning brick-red plumage.

OCCURRENCE
Found in urban, suburban, and settled areas; in the West also in wilder areas such as savannas, desert grasslands, and chaparral, particularly near people; in the East almost exclusively in settled areas, including the centers of large cities. Resident, some birds move after breeding.

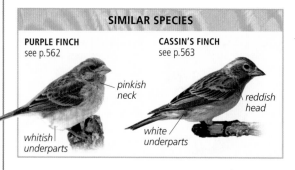

SIMILAR SPECIES

PURPLE FINCH see p.562

pinkish neck

whitish underparts

CASSIN'S FINCH see p.563

reddish head

white underparts

| Length **5–6in (12.5–15cm)** | Wingspan **8–10in (20–25cm)** | Weight **9⁄16–1oz (16–27g)** |
| Social **Flocks** | Lifespan **Up to 12 years** | Status **Secure** |

| Order **Passeriformes** | Family **Fringillidae** | Species ***Pinicola enucleator*** |

Pine Grosbeak

two white wing bars

greenish head

greenish rump

pale patch under eye

MALE

gray belly

FEMALE

IN FLIGHT

stubby, curved, blackish bill

pinkish-red head

short neck

pinkish rump

IMMATURE MALE

long, blackish tail

pinkish red underparts (but regionally variable)

MALE

FLIGHT: undulating, buoyant, calm wing beats interrupted by glides.

The largest member of the family Fringillidae in North America, and easily distinguished by the male's unmistakable thick, stubby bill, the Pine Grosbeak is a resident of high elevations in the Rocky Mountains in the West. The bird is also found across northern Eurasia, where nine subspecies have been identified, four of which are found in North America. Due to extensive color variation of individual plumages, the age and sex of the bird are not always easily determined.

VOICE Contact calls of eastern birds *tee-tew*, or *tee-tee-tew*; western forms give more complex *tweedle*; warbling song.

NESTING Well-hidden, open cup nest usually in spruce or larch trees; 2–5 eggs, 1 brood; June–July.

FEEDING Eats spruce buds, maple seeds, and mountain ash berries throughout the year; consumes insects in summer.

FRUIT LOVER
This species can often be seen hanging from branches, gorging on ripe fruit.

SIMILAR SPECIES

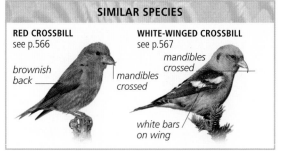

RED CROSSBILL
see p.566

brownish back

mandibles crossed

WHITE-WINGED CROSSBILL
see p.567

mandibles crossed

white bars on wing

OCCURRENCE
Found in the boreal zone from Alaska to Quebec and Newfoundland, in open, northerly coniferous forests of North America in summer, usually near fresh water. Winters throughout its breeding range, but may move southward to southern Canada and the northeastern US.

| Length **8–10in (20–25cm)** | Wingspan **13in (33cm)** | Weight **2–2½oz (55–70g)** |
| Social **Flocks** | Lifespan **Up to 10 years** | Status **Secure** |

| Order **Passeriformes** | Family **Fringillidae** | Species *Loxia curvirostra* |

Red Crossbill

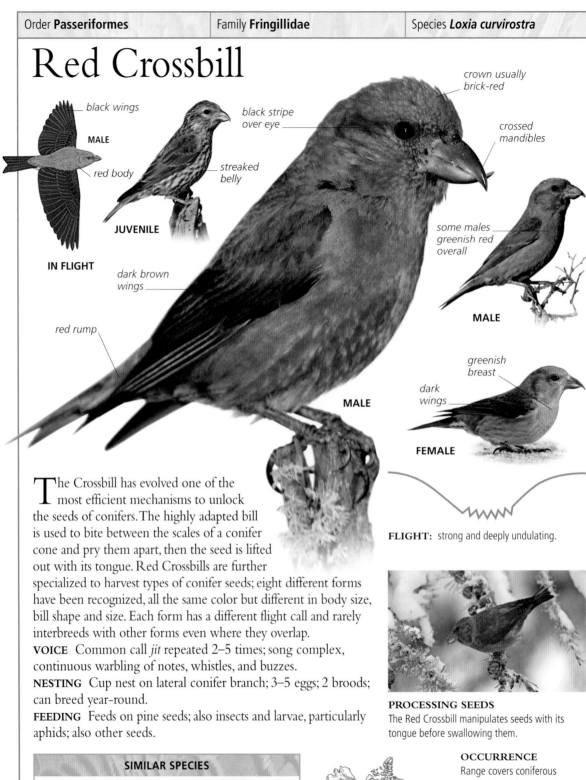

MALE
black wings
red body

JUVENILE
black stripe over eye
streaked belly

IN FLIGHT
dark brown wings

red rump

crown usually brick-red

crossed mandibles

some males greenish red overall

MALE

MALE

greenish breast
dark wings

FEMALE

FLIGHT: strong and deeply undulating.

The Crossbill has evolved one of the most efficient mechanisms to unlock the seeds of conifers. The highly adapted bill is used to bite between the scales of a conifer cone and pry them apart, then the seed is lifted out with its tongue. Red Crossbills are further specialized to harvest types of conifer seeds; eight different forms have been recognized, all the same color but different in body size, bill shape and size. Each form has a different flight call and rarely interbreeds with other forms even where they overlap.

VOICE Common call *jit* repeated 2–5 times; song complex, continuous warbling of notes, whistles, and buzzes.

NESTING Cup nest on lateral conifer branch; 3–5 eggs; 2 broods; can breed year-round.

FEEDING Feeds on pine seeds; also insects and larvae, particularly aphids; also other seeds.

PROCESSING SEEDS
The Red Crossbill manipulates seeds with its tongue before swallowing them.

OCCURRENCE
Range covers coniferous or mixed-coniferous, and deciduous forests from Newfoundland to British Columbia and southern Alaska; also mountain forests in the Rockies, south to Mexico; irregular movements, depending on the availability of pine cones.

SIMILAR SPECIES

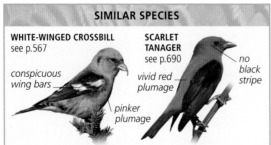

WHITE-WINGED CROSSBILL
see p.567

conspicuous wing bars

pinker plumage

SCARLET TANAGER
see p.690

vivid red plumage

no black stripe

| Length **5–6¾in (13–17cm)** | Wingspan **10–10½in (25–27cm)** | Weight **⅞–1¼oz (25–35g)** |
| Social **Flocks** | Lifespan **Up to 10 years** | Status **Secure** |

Order **Passeriformes**	Family **Fringillidae**	Species *Loxia leucoptera*

White-winged Crossbill

two conspicuous white wing bars

dark brown wings

red body

MALE

IN FLIGHT

brownish green head

greenish streaked underparts

FEMALE

crossed mandibles

variable dark patch on cheek

MALE

pinkish red underparts

blackish wings

notched tail

FLIGHT: strong and undulating with quick wing beats alternating with glides.

Cone debris, needles, and whole cones clatter down from a spruce in the otherwise silent winter forest. Some twittering is heard, and then a chorus of metallic, yanking notes reveals that a flock of a dozen White-winged Crossbills has been causing all the commotion. In an instant, the entire flock erupts into the air, calling loudly in flight, only to disappear completely in the distance. Few other creatures of the northerly forest go about their business with such determined energy, and no others accent a winter woodland with hot pink and magenta—the colors of the White-winged Crossbill's head and breast.

VOICE Calls are sharp, chattering *plik*, or deeper *tyoop*, repeated in series of 3–7 notes; song melodious trilling.

NESTING Open cup nest, usually high on end of a spruce branch; eggs 3–5; 2 broods; July, January–February.

FEEDING Eats seeds from small-coned conifers; spruces, firs, larches; feeds on insects when available.

EATING SNOW
The White-winged Crossbill frequently eats snow to provide essential moisture.

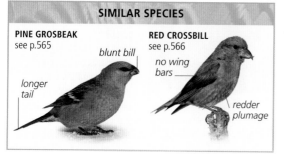

SIMILAR SPECIES

PINE GROSBEAK
see p.565

blunt bill

longer tail

RED CROSSBILL
see p.566

no wing bars

redder plumage

OCCURRENCE
Nomadic; most common in the spruce zone of Alaska and Canada but has bred as far south as Colorado in the West; in the East, from Quebec and Newfoundland southward to New York City and New England.

Length **5½–6in (14–15cm)**	Wingspan **10–10½in (26–27cm)**	Weight **¹¹⁄₁₆–1¹⁄₁₆oz (20–30g)**
Social **Flocks**	Lifespan **Up to 10 years**	Status **Secure**

| Order **Passeriformes** | Family **Parulidae** | Species *Vermivora peregrina* |

Tennessee Warbler

gray head

white eyestripe

MALE (BREEDING)

IN FLIGHT

olive-green upperparts

olive-gray head

FEMALE

whitish belly

blue-gray crown

spiky bill

olive back and wings

grayish white underparts

olive-gray back

white undertail feathers

yellowish throat and breast

MALE (FALL)

MALE (BREEDING)

The Tennessee Warbler was named after its place of discovery, but this bird would have been on migration, as it breeds almost entirely in Canada and winters in Central America. These warblers inhabit fairly remote areas, and their nests are difficult to find. It is one of a number of species that takes advantage of outbreaks of spruce budworm; the population of Tennessee Warblers tends to increase in years when budworms are abundant.

VOICE Call a sharp *tzit*; flight call a thin slightly rolling *seet*; song usually three-part staccato series, *chip-chip-chip*, each series increasing in pitch and usually in tempo.

NESTING Nest woven of fine plant matter, in ground depression, concealed from above by shrubbery; 4–7 eggs; 1 brood; June.

FEEDING Searches outer branches of trees for caterpillars, bees, wasps, beetles, and spiders; also eats fruits in winter and drinks nectar by piercing base of flowers.

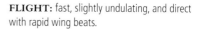

FLIGHT: fast, slightly undulating, and direct with rapid wing beats.

UNIQUE UNDERPARTS
The breeding male is the only North American warbler with unmarked grayish white underparts.

SIMILAR SPECIES

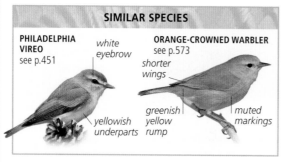

PHILADELPHIA VIREO
see p.451

white eyebrow

yellowish underparts

ORANGE-CROWNED WARBLER
see p.573

shorter wings

greenish yellow rump

muted markings

OCCURRENCE
Breeds in a variety of habitats, especially woodlands with dense understory and thickets of willows and alders. Very common in suburban parks and gardens during migration, particularly in the Midwest. Winters from southern Mexico to northern Ecuador and northern Venezuela.

| Length **4¾in (12cm)** | Wingspan **7¾in (19.5cm)** | Weight **⁹⁄₃₂–⁵⁄₈oz (8–17g)** |
| Social **Flocks** | Lifespan **Up to 6 years** | Status **Secure** |

Order **Passeriformes**	Family **Parulidae**	Species *Vermivora celata*

Orange-crowned Warbler

dull olive overall

MALE

IN FLIGHT

crown shows orange when bird alarmed

pale yellow eyebrow

olive-green upperparts

short wings

greenish yellow rump

muted breast markings

ADULT (WEST)

gray head

drabber plumage overall

yellow undertail feathers

IMMATURE (EAST; 1ST WINTER)

Common and relatively brightly colored in the West but uncommon and duller in the East, the Orange-crowned Warbler has a large breeding range. The 19th-century American naturalist Thomas Say described this species on the basis of specimens collected in Nebraska. He was struck by the tiny orange cap, but because it was so concealed in the plumage of the crown, he named it *celata*, which is Latin for "hidden." The orange cap is not usually visible in the field.

VOICE Call a clean, sharp *tsik*; flight call a high, short *seet*; song a loose, lazy trill; eastern birds lazier, western birds more emphatic.
NESTING Cup of grasses, fibers, and down, usually on ground under bush; 4–5 eggs; 1 brood; March–July.
FEEDING Gleans mostly arthropods such as beetles, ants, spiders, and their larvae; also eats fruits; collects nectar by piercing base of flower.

FLIGHT: fast, slightly undulating, and direct with rapid wing beats.

FACE MARKINGS
In eastern populations of this warbler, the birds have whitish facial markings during their first winter.

SIMILAR SPECIES

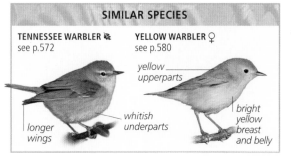

TENNESSEE WARBLER 🦉
see p.572

longer wings

whitish underparts

YELLOW WARBLER ♀
see p.580

yellow upperparts

bright yellow breast and belly

OCCURRENCE
Breeds in varied habitats across North America from Alaska eastward to Newfoundland, and in the West from British Columbia southward to California, New Mexico, and western Texas. Prefers streamside thickets. Some winter in the West, while others go to Mexico and Guatemala.

Length **5in (13cm)**	Wingspan **7¼in (18.5cm)**	Weight **¼–⅜oz (7–11g)**
Social **Winter flocks**	Lifespan **Up to 6 years**	Status **Secure**

Order **Passeriformes**	Family **Parulidae**	Species *Vermivora ruficapilla*

Nashville Warbler

MALE
V. r. ruficapilla
(EASTERN)

olive-green
upperparts

IN FLIGHT

rounded
wings

rufous
crown patch

conspicuous
white eye-ring

blue-gray
helmet

grayish
green back

olive
wings

yellow undertail
feathers

duller olive
back

less contrast
between gray
and yellow

white
patch on
belly

MALE
V. r. ridgwayi
(WESTERN)

FEMALE
V. r. ruficapilla
(EASTERN)

Although often confused with the ground-walking, chunky Connecticut Warbler, the Nashville Warbler is much smaller, hops about up in trees, and has a yellow throat. Nashville has two subspecies: *V. r. ruficapilla* in the East and *V. r. ridgwayi* in the West. Differences in voice, habitat, behavior, and plumage hint that they may in fact be separate species. *V. r. ridgwayi* can be distinguished as it has more extensive white on its belly and a grayish green back.

VOICE Call sharp *tik*, sharper in West; flight call high, thin *siit*; eastern song two parts: first part lazy, second faster trill *tee-tsee tee-tsee tee-tsee tititititi*; western song slightly lower and fuller with lazier second part, a seldom trilled *tee-tsee tee-tsee tee-tsee weesay weesay way*.

NESTING Cup hidden on ground in dense cover; 3–6 eggs; 1 brood; May–July.

FEEDING Gleans insects and spiders from trees.

FLIGHT: fast, slightly undulating, and direct, with rapid wing beats.

SIMILAR SPECIES

VIRGINIA'S WARBLER
see p.575

lacks
yellow
belly

CONNECTICUT WARBLER ♂
walks on ground;
see p.609

chunky
pink bill

lacks
olive
wings

shorter
tail

FIELD MARKS
The white eye-ring and belly are evident on this singing male.

OCCURRENCE
Ruficapilla breeds in wet habitats of Saskatchewan east to Newfoundland and south to West Virginia; *ridgwayi* in brushy montane areas in Sierras and northern Rockies; *ridgwayi* winters in coastal California and south Texas to Guatemala; *ruficapilla* migrates to winter mainly in Mexico.

Length **4¾in (12cm)**	Wingspan **7½in (19cm)**	Weight **¼–⁷⁄₁₆oz (7–13g)**
Social **Migrant/Winter flocks**	Lifespan **Up to 7 years**	Status **Secure**

Order **Passeriformes**	Family **Parulidae**	Species *Vermivora virginiae*

Virginia's Warbler

conspicuous yellow rump

plain gray overall

MALE
IN FLIGHT

yellow rump

dark gray wings

MALE

rufous on crown

complete white eye-ring

yellow breast

yellow undertail feathers

pale gray underparts

FLIGHT: fast, slightly undulating, and direct, with rapid wing beats.

This western warbler can be quite shy, and its preference for dense brushy habitat and unforgiving terrain make it all the more difficult to see. Virginia's Warbler shares the habit of constantly bobbing its tail about with Nashville's Warbler. Although Virginia's Warblers nest on the ground, singing males frequent the tops of junipers and pines. In the Davis Mountains of west Texas, a small population of Virginia's Warblers has recently interbred with the rare Colima Warbler.

VOICE Call hard, sharp, yet hollow *ssink*; song lazy, sweet warble: *sweet sweet sweet sweet teedle-eedle-eedle-eedle tyew tyew.*

NESTING Cup of grassy material on steep slope, hidden in hole or vegetation; 3–5 eggs; 1 brood; May–July.

FEEDING Gleans a variety of insects, especially caterpillars, from branches and leaves.

CONSPICUOUS BREAST PATCH
The yellow breast patch on a singing male stands out against its overall gray plumage.

SIMILAR SPECIES

NASHVILLE WARBLER (WESTERN) ♀ see p.574

blue-gray helmet

olive wings

more extensive yellow

COLIMA WARBLER see p.576

orange upper- and undertail feathers

brownish back

brownish flanks

OCCURRENCE
Breeds in dense dry shrub on steep slopes, often with open pine canopy in southern Rockies, Great Basin, and the Black Hills; occupies similar habitats in migration and winter. WIntering range extends to Oaxaca in Mexico.

Length **4¾in (12cm)**	Wingspan **7½in (19cm)**	Weight **¼–⅜oz (7–10g)**
Social **Flocks**	Lifespan **Up to 4 years**	Status **Secure**

| Order **Passeriformes** | Family **Parulidae** | Species *Vermivora crissalis* |

Colima Warbler

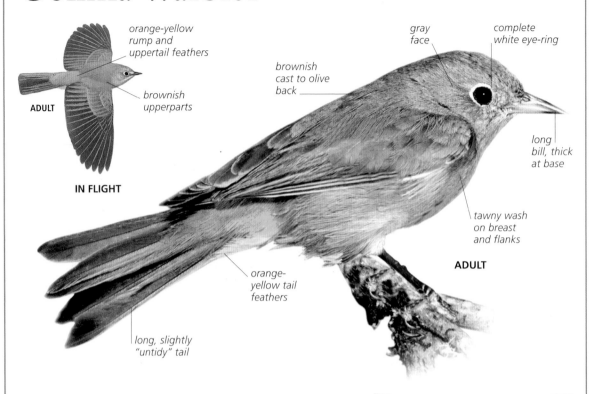

ADULT

orange-yellow rump and uppertail feathers

brownish upperparts

IN FLIGHT

brownish cast to olive back

gray face

complete white eye-ring

long bill, thick at base

tawny wash on breast and flanks

ADULT

orange-yellow tail feathers

long, slightly "untidy" tail

Big Bend National Park in Texas is home to the only breeding population of Colima Warblers in the US—it is thought that up to 300 pairs occur there. One of the most enigmatic of North American wood-warblers, this species was given its scientific name *crissalis* from the Latin *crissum*, referring to the bird's bright orange rump. Its common name, Colima, refers to the area of Mexico in which this warbler spends the winter. The species has occasionally been spotted in Texas's Davis Mountains, although identification outside its normal range is tricky, as hybrids with Virginia's Warbler have also been spotted.
VOICE Song a rapid trill, descending in pitch and ending with one or two emphatic motives *titititititi-tututu eet-choo eet-choo*.
NESTING Cup of grass, sometimes domed, hidden in hole or vegetation on steep slope; 3–4 eggs; 1 brood; May–July.
FEEDING Gleans insects and spiders, especially caterpillars, wasps, flies, and spiders.

FLIGHT: fast, slightly undulating, and direct with rapid wing beats.

BIG BEND BIRD
Delicately perched, this is the bird to look out for at Big Bend National Park, Texas.

SIMILAR SPECIES

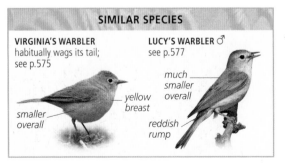

VIRGINIA'S WARBLER
habitually wags its tail;
see p.575

smaller overall

yellow breast

LUCY'S WARBLER ♂
see p.577

much smaller overall

reddish rump

OCCURRENCE
Breeds in the Chisos Mountains and Mexico, in canyons with pine-oak woodland with brushy understory, normally above about 4,900ft (1,500m). Almost never detected on migration. Winters in similar but more humid habitats in southwest Mexico, from southern Sinaloa to Guerrero and northern Oaxaca.

| Length **6in (15cm)** | Wingspan **8in (20cm)** | Weight **⁹⁄₃₂–⁷⁄₁₆oz (8–12g)** |
| Social **Flocks** | Lifespan **Unknown** | Status **Localized** |

| Order **Passeriformes** | Family **Parulidae** | Species ***Vermivora luciae*** |

Lucy's Warbler

reddish rump

mostly gray upperparts

MALE

black tail with gray outer feathers

IN FLIGHT

no reddish crown

plain face

reddish rump

dark, spiky bill

gray overall

pale edges to wings

IMMATURE FEMALE

tiny reddish crown patch

whitish eye-ring

dark gray upperparts

pale gray underparts

MALE

reddish chestnut rump

whitish undertail feathers

FLIGHT: fast, slightly undulating, and direct with rapid wing beats.

This small, unassuming species is one of two North American warbler species to nest in tree cavities—the other is the Prothonotary Warbler. As it lacks any yellow coloration, it is perhaps more likely to be mistaken for a gnatcatcher, an immature Verdin, or a Bell's Vireo than another warbler. Lucy's Warbler breeds in dense woodlands close to rivers, although its habitat is threatened by the spread of tamarisk (also known as salt cedar), an invasive, non-native shrub.

VOICE Call a sharp, metallic *vink*; flight call a soft *tsit*; song a loose trill, modulated in pitch and with variably emphatic ending.

NESTING Natural crevice under loose bark, woodpecker cavity, or old Verdin nest; rarely hole in riverbank; 4–5 eggs; often 2 broods; April–July.

FEEDING Gleans insects, such as flies and bees from foliage and flower clusters.

GRAY DESERT DWELLER
Lucy's Warbler thrives in hot, lowland deserts, where it is attracted to mesquite woodland.

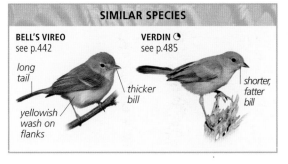

SIMILAR SPECIES

BELL'S VIREO
see p.442

long tail

yellowish wash on flanks

VERDIN ◐
see p.485

thicker bill

shorter, fatter bill

OCCURRENCE
Breeds in southeast California, Arizona, and north Baja California east to western Texas and northern Chihuahua. Within this range it is found in riverside woodlands with cottonwoods, sycamores, and oaks. Migrates along western seaboard of Mexico, winters from Sonora to Oaxaca.

| Length **4¼in (11cm)** | Wingspan **7in (18cm)** | Weight **³⁄₁₆–¼oz (5–7g)** |
| Social **Flocks** | Lifespan **Up to 5 years** | Status **Vulnerable** |

| Order **Passeriformes** | Family **Parulidae** | Species *Parula Americana* |

Northern Parula

MALE

two white wing bars

IN FLIGHT

dark patch between eye and bill

interrupted white eye-ring

blue-gray neck and head

yellow throat

chestnut streaks on chest

olive back

yellow chest, lacks chestnut streaks

FEMALE

gray rump and uppertail

delicate, pale gray belly

MALE

dark legs

pinkish yellow feet

FLIGHT: fast, slightly undulating, and direct with rapid wing beats.

white patches on outer tail feathers

The Northern Parula is a small wood-warbler, that somewhat resembles a chickadee in its active foraging behavior. This bird depends on very specific nesting materials—*Ushea* lichens, or "Old Man's Beard," in the north, and *Tillandsia*, or Spanish Moss, in the South. The presence of these parasitic plants on trees greatly limits the geographical range of this species. The Northern Parula interbreeds with the Tropical Parula in southern Texas where their ranges cross, producing hybrid birds.

VOICE Call a very sharp *tsip*; flight call a thin, weak, descending *tsiif*; song a variable, most common buzzy upslurred trill, variably continuous or in steps, ending very high, but then dropping off in an emphatic *zip*.

NESTING Hanging pouch in clump of lichens; 4–5 eggs; 1 brood; May–July (south) or April–August (north).

FEEDING Gleans for caterpillars, flies, moths, beetles, wasps, ants, spiders; also eats berries, nectar, some seeds.

THE AMERICAN TIT
This small yellow-and chestnut-breasted bird was named by Carl Linneus in 1758.

SIMILAR SPECIES

TROPICAL PARULA see p.718

dark face

more yellow

OCCURRENCE
Nests in almost any kind of wooded area with its preferred nesting material; migrants (some of which cross the Gulf of Mexico) occur in almost any habitat; winters in varied habitats from southern Texas and Florida across Caribbean and Mexico south to Panama.

| Length **4¼in (11cm)** | Wingspan **7in (18cm)** | Weight **¼–⅜oz (7–10g)** |
| Social **Winter flocks** | Lifespan **Up to 7 years** | Status **Secure** |

Order **Passeriformes**	Family **Parulidae**	Species *Dendroica pensylvanica*

Chestnut-sided Warbler

MALE (BREEDING)
two yellow wing bars

IN FLIGHT

white outer tail feathers

yellow cap

black "mustache"

chestnut band along flanks

FEMALE (BREEDING)

white tail spots

yellow-and-black streaks on upperparts

conspicuous white cheeks

yellow crown

white throat

two wing bars

rich chestnut flanks

MALE (BREEDING)

olive crown

bright lime-green above

plain face with white eye-ring

FEMALE (1ST FALL)

plain gray underside

The Chestnut-sided Warbler is one of the few wood-warbler species that has benefited from deforestation, because it depends on deciduous second-growth and forest edges for breeding. Once a rare bird, it is more common now than it was in the early 19th century. These birds vary in appearance, immature females looking quite unlike adult males in breeding. In all plumages, yellowish wing bars and whitish belly are the most distinguishing characteristics. Its pleasant song has long been transcribed as *pleased pleased pleased to MEET'cha*.

VOICE Call a sweet *chip*; flight call a low, burry *brrrt*; song a series of fast, sweet notes, usually ending with emphatic *WEET-chew*.

NESTING Open, easy-to-find cup just off ground in small deciduous tree or shrub; 3–5 eggs; 1 brood; May–August.

FEEDING Eats insects, especially larvae; also berries and seeds.

FLIGHT: fast, slightly undulating, and direct with rapid wing beats.

MALE TERRITORY
This singing, territorial male prefers second-growth thickets as its habitat.

OCCURRENCE
Breeds in successive stages of regrowth in deciduous forests, from Alberta to the Great Lakes, New England, and the Appalachians; isolated populations in the Midwest. Winters in the West Indies, Mexico, and Central America, south to Venezuela and northern Colombia.

SIMILAR SPECIES

BLACKPOLL WARBLER see p.581
white wing bars
pale stripe on face
fine streaks on breast

BAY-BREASTED WARBLER see p.582
white wing bars
olive upperparts
buffy undertail
greenish underside

Length **5in (13cm)**	Wingspan **8in (20cm)**	Weight **⁹⁄₃₂–⁷⁄₁₆oz (8–13g)**
Social **Winter flocks**	Lifespan **Up to 7 years**	Status **Secure**

Order **Passeriformes**	Family **Parulidae**	Species ***Dendroica petechia***

Yellow Warbler

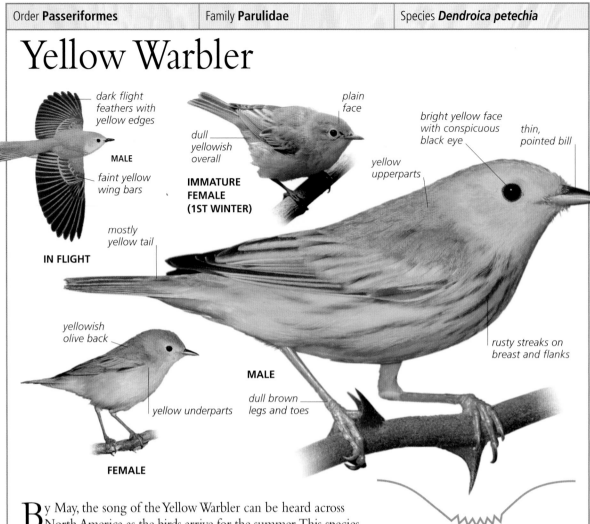

dark flight feathers with yellow edges

MALE

faint yellow wing bars

IN FLIGHT

mostly yellow tail

plain face

dull yellowish overall

IMMATURE FEMALE (1ST WINTER)

bright yellow face with conspicuous black eye

thin, pointed bill

yellow upperparts

rusty streaks on breast and flanks

MALE

yellowish olive back

yellow underparts

dull brown legs and toes

FEMALE

By May, the song of the Yellow Warbler can be heard across North America as the birds arrive for the summer. This species is extremely variable geographically, with about 40 subspecies, especially on its tropical range (West Indies and Central and South America). The Yellow Warbler is known to build another nest on top of an old one when cowbird eggs appear in it, which can result in up to six different tiers. The Yellow Warbler does not walk, but rather hops from branch to branch.

VOICE Call a variable *chip*, sometimes given in series; flight call buzzy *zeep*; song variable series of fast, sweet notes; western birds often add an emphatic ending.

NESTING Deep cup of plant material, grasses in vertical fork of deciduous tree or shrub; 4–5 eggs; 1 brood; May–July.

FEEDING Eats mostly insects and insect larvae, plus some fruit.

FLIGHT: fast, slightly undulating, and direct, with rapid wing beats.

ONE OF A KIND
This species has more yellow in its plumage than any other North American wood-warbler.

OCCURRENCE
Widespread in most shrubby and second-growth habitats of North America. Migrates to southern US and southward to Mexico, Central America, and South America. Resident populations live in Florida and the West Indies.

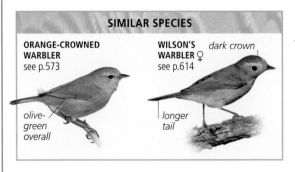

SIMILAR SPECIES

ORANGE-CROWNED WARBLER
see p.573

olive-green overall

WILSON'S WARBLER ♀
see p.614

dark crown

longer tail

Length **5in (13cm)**	Wingspan **8in (20cm)**	Weight **⁹⁄₃₂–½oz (8–14g)**
Social **Flocks**	Lifespan **Up to 9 years**	Status **Secure**

| Order **Passeriformes** | Family **Parulidae** | Species *Dendroica striata* |

Blackpoll Warbler

white tail spots

MALE

greenish upperparts with fine black streaks

FEMALE (BREEDING)

faint, fine streaking on underparts

black cap

white cheek

two white wing bars

IN FLIGHT

greenish overall

MALE (FALL)

streaking on breast

bold black streaks on gray back

streaked underparts

pale feet contrasting with darker legs

white undertail feathers

MALE (BREEDING)

orange legs

FLIGHT: fast, slightly undulating, and direct, with rapid wing beats.

The Blackpoll Warbler is well known for undergoing an epic fall migration that takes it over the Atlantic Ocean from the northeastern US to northern Brazil. Before departing, it almost doubles its body weight to cope with the physical demands of the nonstop journey. With the return of spring, most of these birds travel the less dangerous Caribbean route back north.

VOICE Call piercing *chip*; flight call high, buzzy yet sharp *tzzzt*; common song crescendo of fast, extremely high-pitched ticks, ending with a decrescendo *tsst tsst TSST TSST TSST tsst tsst*; less commonly, ticks run into even faster trill.

NESTING Well-hidden cup placed low against conifer trunk; 3–5 eggs; 1–2 broods; May–July.

FEEDING Gleans arthropods, such as worms and beetles, but will take small fruit in fall and winter.

REACHING THE HIGH NOTES
The song of the male Blackpoll is so high-pitched that it is inaudible to many people.

SIMILAR SPECIES

BAY-BREASTED WARBLER see p.582

greenish sides to neck

warm wash to flanks

BLACK-AND-WHITE WARBLER ♂ see p.600

black cheek

distinct black-and-white stripes

OCCURRENCE
Breeds in spruce-fir forests across the northern boreal forest zone from Alaska eastward to Newfoundland, southward to coastal coniferous forests in the Maritimes and northern New England. Migrants gather in the Atlantic Ocean to landfall in the Caribbean and northern South America.

| Length **5½in (14cm)** | Wingspan **9in (23cm)** | Weight ⅜–⅝oz (10–18g) |
| Social **Flocks** | Lifespan **Up to 8 years** | Status **Secure** |

581

Order **Passeriformes**	Family **Parulidae**	Species *Dendroica castanea*

Bay-breasted Warbler

MALE (BREEDING)

two white wing bars

bold buffy neck patch

IN FLIGHT

white tips on outer tail feathers

FEMALE (BREEDING)

chestnut crown, streaked black

buffy wash on flanks and under tail

dusky ear patch

two white wing bars

buff undertail

yellowish buff belly

olive crown and back

two wing bars

greenish cheeks

IMMATURE FEMALE (FALL)

unstreaked breast

gray upperparts with black streaks

chestnut brown crown

black face

chestnut brown chin and flanks

MALE (BREEDING)

FLIGHT: fast, slightly undulating, and direct, with rapid wing beats.

Splashed with deep chestnut, crisp white, warm buff, and jet black, a male Bay-breasted Warbler in breeding plumage is a particularly striking bird, but fall females are very different with their dull, greenish plumage. Like the Tennessee Warbler, this species depends largely on outbreaks of spruce budworms (a major food source), so its numbers rise and fall according to those outbreaks. Overall, the Bay-breasted Warbler population has decreased because of the increased use of pesticide sprays.

VOICE Call a somewhat upslurred *tsip*; flight call a high, buzzy, short, and sharp *tzzzt*; song of very high, thin notes, often ending on lower pitch: *wee-si wee-si wee-si wee*.

NESTING Fragile-looking cup of grass and lichens on horizontal branch at mid-level in forest; 4–5 eggs; 1 brood; May–July.

FEEDING Mostly eats moths, smaller insects, worms, spiders, and caterpillars during migration and on breeding grounds; eats mainly fruit in winter.

SINGING IN THE FOREST
A brilliantly colored breeding male sings its high-pitched song on a spruce branch.

SIMILAR SPECIES

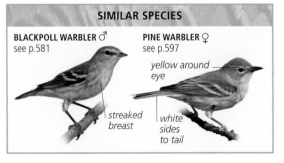

BLACKPOLL WARBLER ♂
see p.581

streaked breast

PINE WARBLER ♀
see p.597

yellow around eye

white sides to tail

OCCURRENCE
Breeds in mature spruce-fir-balsam forest across the forest belt from Yukon to the Maritimes, and south to the Great Lakes area and northern New England. Migrants occur in varied habitat, but especially woodland edges. Winters in wet forest in central America.

Length **5½in (14cm)**	Wingspan **9in (23cm)**	Weight **⅜–½oz (11–15g)**
Social **Migratory/Winter flocks**	Lifespan **Up to 4 years**	Status **Vulnerable**

| Order **Passeriformes** | Family **Parulidae** | Species **Dendroica fusca** |

Blackburnian Warbler

white edges to outer tail feathers

bold white wing patches

MALE

IN FLIGHT

pale orange line in center of crown

complex black-and-orange face pattern

white streaks on black back

white patch on wing

white belly

MALE

brilliant orange throat

black streaks on breast and belly

more subdued facial pattern

white wing bars

orange throat and breast

black streaks on flanks

FEMALE

This fiery beacon of the treetops is considered one of the most beautiful members of its family; its orange throat is unique among the North American warblers. The Blackburnian Warbler co-exists with many other *Dendroica* warblers in the coniferous and mixed woods of the north and east, but is able to do so by exploiting a slightly different niche for foraging—in this case the treetops. It also seeks the highest trees for nesting.

VOICE Call a slightly husky *chik*; flight-call a high, thin *zzee*; song variable, but always high-pitched; swirling series of lisps, spiraling upward to end in an almost inaudible *trill*.

NESTING Fine cup in conifer on horizontal branch away from trunk, usually high in tree; 4–5 eggs; 1 brood; May–July.

FEEDING Gleans arthropods, such as spiders, worms, and beetles; also fruit.

FLIGHT: fast, slightly undulating, and direct with rapid wing beats.

DISTINGUISHING FEATURES
The female is like a dull adult male, but with two wing bars and no black on the face.

AVIAN FIREFLY
This male in breeding plumage glows when seen against a dark forest background.

OCCURRENCE
Breeds in coniferous and mixed forests from Alberta east through the North Great Lakes to Newfoundland and south into the Appalachians of Georgia; migrants found in wooded, shrubby, or forest edge habitats. Winters in wet forests in Costa Rica and Panama, and southward as far as Peru.

SIMILAR SPECIES

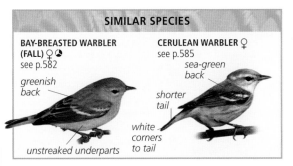

BAY-BREASTED WARBLER (FALL) ♀ ♂
see p.582

greenish back

unstreaked underparts

CERULEAN WARBLER ♀
see p.585

sea-green back

shorter tail

white corners to tail

| Length **5in (13cm)** | Wingspan **8½in (21cm)** | Weight **⁵⁄₁₆–⁷⁄₁₆oz (9–12g)** |
| Social **Winter flocks** | Lifespan **Up to 8 years** | Status **Secure** |

| Order **Passeriformes** | Family **Parulidae** | Species **_Dendroica magnolia_** |

Magnolia Warbler

yellow rump

gray crown

MALE (BREEDING)

broken white tail band

IN FLIGHT

greenish back

white undertail feathers

IMMATURE (FALL)

plain face with pale eye-ring

black face

white eyebrow

incomplete eye-ring

large white patch on wing

yellow underparts with black streaks

greenish back with black stripes

black streaking on breast and flanks not as heavy

FEMALE (BREEDING)

MALE (BREEDING)

FLIGHT: fast, slightly undulating, and direct with rapid wing beats.

The bold, flashy, and common Magnolia Warbler is hard to miss as it flits around at eye level, fanning its uniquely marked tail. This species nests in young forests and winters in almost any habitat, so its numbers have not suffered in recent decades, unlike some of its relatives. Although it really has no preference for its namesake plant, the 19th century ornithologist Alexander Wilson discovered a Magnolia Warbler feeding in a magnolia tree during migration, which is how it got its name.

VOICE Call a tinny _jeinf_, not particularly warbler-like; also short, simple whistled series _wee'-sa wee'-sa WEET-a-chew_; short, distinctive, flight call a high, trilled _zeep_.

NESTING Flimsy cup of black rootlets placed low in dense conifer against trunk; 3–5 eggs; 1 brood; June–August.

FEEDING Gleans mostly caterpillars, beetles, and spiders.

SPRUCE WARBLER
The conspicuous male Magnolia Warbler can be found singing its distinctive, loud song throughout the day often in a spruce tree.

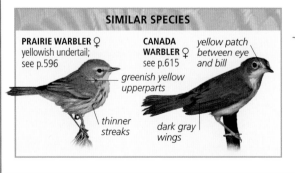

SIMILAR SPECIES

PRAIRIE WARBLER ♀
yellowish undertail; see p.596

thinner streaks

CANADA WARBLER ♀
see p.615

greenish yellow upperparts

yellow patch between eye and bill

dark gray wings

OCCURRENCE
Breeds in dense, young mixed and coniferous forests from Yukon east to Newfoundland and south into Appalachians of Tennessee; migrates across the Gulf and Caribbean; winters in varied habitats in Caribbean and from southeast Mexico to Panama; rare vagrant in the West.

| Length **5in (13cm)** | Wingspan **7½in (19cm)** | Weight **7/32–7/16oz (6–12g)** |
| Social **Migrant/Winter flocks** | Lifespan **Up to 6 years** | Status **Secure** |

Order **Passeriformes**	Family **Parulidae**	Species *Dendroica cerulea*

Cerulean Warbler

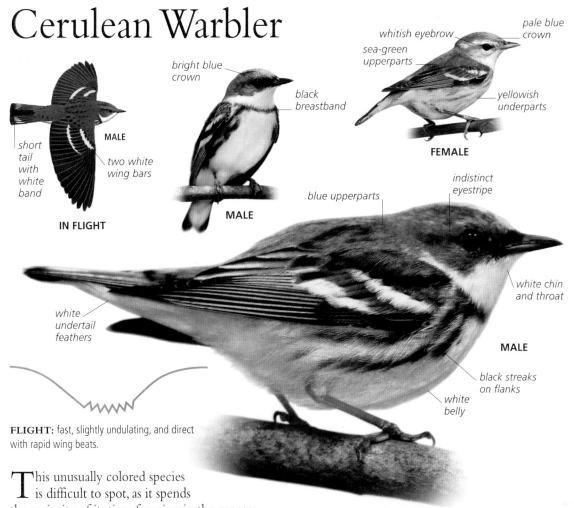

IN FLIGHT
short tail with white band
MALE
two white wing bars

MALE
bright blue crown
black breastband

whitish eyebrow
sea-green upperparts
pale blue crown
yellowish underparts
FEMALE

blue upperparts
indistinct eyestripe
white chin and throat
MALE
black streaks on flanks
white belly
white undertail feathers

FLIGHT: fast, slightly undulating, and direct with rapid wing beats.

This unusually colored species is difficult to spot, as it spends the majority of its time foraging in the canopy of deciduous forests. It was once common across the Midwest and the Ohio River Valley, but its habitat is being cleared for agriculture and fragmented by development. In winter, this bird lives high in the canopy of the Andean foothills, but sadly this habitat is threatened by coffee cultivation.

VOICE Call a slurred *chip*; flight call a buzzy *zeet*; three-part, buzzy song consisting of a short series of low paired notes followed by a mid-range trill and upslurred high-pitched *zhree*.

NESTING Compact cup high on fork in deciduous tree, far from trunk; 2–5 eggs; 1 brood; May–July.

FEEDING Gleans insects high in canopy, especially from leaf bases.

UNIQUE COLOR
Female Cerulean Warblers have a unique blue color on their head and upperparts.

OCCURRENCE
Mainly breeds in mature deciduous forests across the northeastern US; tends to prefer dense woodlands during migration. Winters in evergreen forests in the Andes, principally from Columbia to Peru.

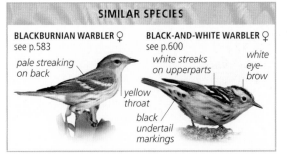

SIMILAR SPECIES

BLACKBURNIAN WARBLER ♀ see p.583
pale streaking on back

BLACK-AND-WHITE WARBLER ♀ see p.600
white streaks on upperparts
white eyebrow
yellow throat
black undertail markings

Length **4¾in (12cm)**	Wingspan **7¾in (19.5cm)**	Weight **⁹⁄₃₂–³⁄₈oz (8–10g)**
Social **Migrant/Winter flocks**	Lifespan **Up to 6 years**	Status **Vulnerable**

| Order **Passeriformes** | Family **Parulidae** | Species **Dendroica tigrina** |

Cape May Warbler

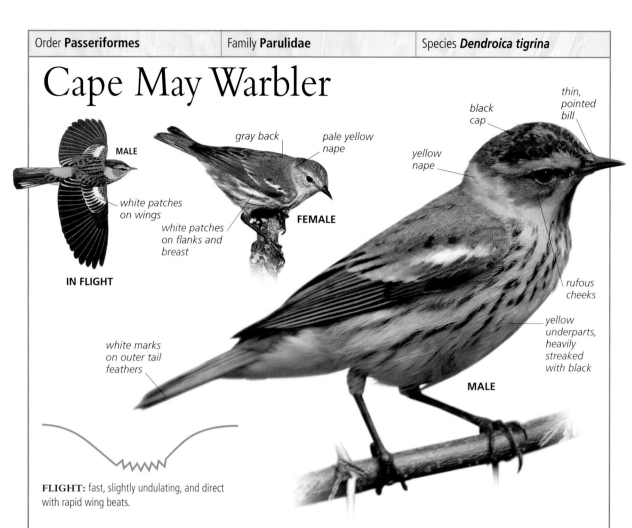

MALE

white patches on wings

IN FLIGHT

gray back

pale yellow nape

white patches on flanks and breast

FEMALE

thin, pointed bill

black cap

yellow nape

rufous cheeks

yellow underparts, heavily streaked with black

MALE

white marks on outer tail feathers

FLIGHT: fast, slightly undulating, and direct with rapid wing beats.

The Cape May Warbler is a spruce budworm specialist, and so the populations of this bird increase during outbreaks of that insect. These birds often chase other birds aggressively from flowering trees, where they use their especially thin and pointed bills and semitubular tongues to suck the nectar from blossoms. In its summer forest habitat, the Cape May Warbler uses its bill to feed on insects by plucking them from clumps of conifer needles.

VOICE Song a high, even-pitched series of whistles *see see see see*.
NESTING Cup placed near trunk, high in spruce or fir near top; 4–9 eggs; 1 brood; June–July.
FEEDING Gleans arthropods, especially spruce budworms, but also flies, moths, and beetles from mid-high levels in canopy; also fruit and nectar during the nonbreeding season.

SPRING FLASH
Magnificently colored, a male warbler displays its chestnut cheek, yellow necklace, and yellow rump.

SIMILAR SPECIES

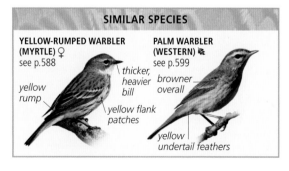

YELLOW-RUMPED WARBLER (MYRTLE) ♀
see p.588

yellow rump

thicker, heavier bill

yellow flank patches

PALM WARBLER (WESTERN)
see p.599

browner overall

yellow undertail feathers

OCCURRENCE
Breeds from the Yukon and British Columbia to the Great Lakes, the Maritimes, and New England in mature spruce–fir forests. Migrants found in varied habitats. Winters in varied habitats, especially backyard gardens, in Central America, as far south as Honduras.

| Length **5in (13cm)** | Wingspan **8in (20cm)** | Weight $^{5}/_{16}$–$^{7}/_{16}$**oz (9–13g)** |
| Social **Migrant flocks** | Lifespan **Up to 4 years** | Status **Secure** |

| Order **Passeriformes** | Family **Parulidae** | Species *Dendroica caerulescens* |

Black-throated Blue Warbler

MALE

dark blue overall

black face

white wing patches

white patches on outer tail feathers

IN FLIGHT

olive upperparts

pale eyebrow

white patch

FEMALE

incomplete eye-ring, only below eye

dark blue upperparts

dark blue crown

black "mask" and throat

white breast ("kerchief")

black flanks

white belly

MALE

FLIGHT: fast, slightly undulating, and direct with rapid wing beats; typical warbler flight.

Male and female Black-throated Blue Warblers look so dissimilar that early ornithologists thought they were different species. Many of the females have a blue wash to their wings and tail, and almost all have a subdued version of the male's white "kerchief," so identification is not difficult. This beautiful eastern North American species migrates northward in spring, along the eastern flank of the Appalachians, but a small number of birds fly, along an imaginary line, northwestward to the Great Lakes. This "line" is so clearly defined that this bird is common in Chicago but extremely rare in St. Louis.

VOICE Call a husky junco-like *tchunk*; flight call a distinctive, drawn-out, metallic *ssiiink*, reminiscent of some Northern Cardinal calls; song a relatively low-pitched series of upslurred buzzes *zu zu zo zhray zhree*, or slower *zhray zhray zhreee*.

NESTING Bulky cup of plant material a meter off ground in dense forest; 3–5 eggs; 1–2 broods; May–August.

FEEDING Gleans arthropods, mainly caterpillars, from mid-low level in forest; takes small fruit and nectar.

BLACK, WHITE, AND BLUE
Males are gorgeous year-round, especially when viewed against contrasting, fall foliage.

SIMILAR SPECIES

YELLOW-RUMPED WARBLER (MYRTLE) ♀
see p.588

yellow rump

two wing bars

OCCURRENCE
Breeds in relatively undisturbed deciduous and mixed hardwood forests from southern Ontario and northern Minnesota to Nova Scotia and into the Appalachians of Georgia. Fall migration through wooded habitats; a Caribbean migrant. Winters in Central and South America.

| Length **5in (13cm)** | Wingspan **7½in (19cm)** | Weight **9/32–7/16oz (8–12g)** |
| Social **Migrant flocks** | Lifespan **Up to 10 years** | Status **Secure** |

| Order **Passeriformes** | Family **Parulidae** | Species *Dendroica coronata* |

Yellow-rumped Warbler

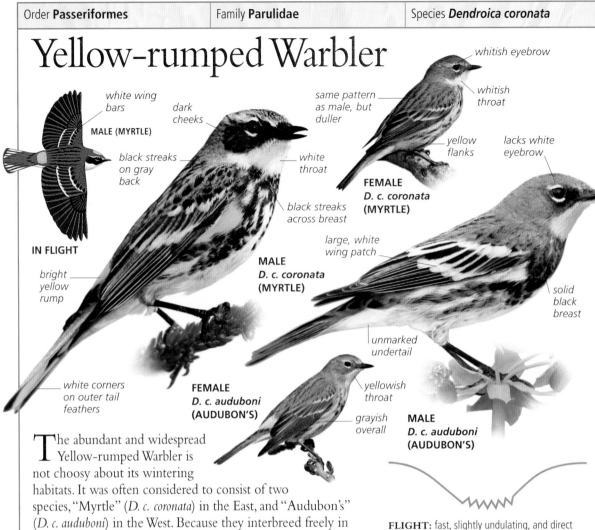

white wing bars

MALE (MYRTLE)

dark cheeks

IN FLIGHT

black streaks on gray back

bright yellow rump

white corners on outer tail feathers

whitish eyebrow

whitish throat

same pattern as male, but duller

yellow flanks

FEMALE
D. c. coronata
(MYRTLE)

white throat

black streaks across breast

MALE
D. c. coronata
(MYRTLE)

lacks white eyebrow

large, white wing patch

solid black breast

unmarked undertail

FEMALE
D. c. auduboni
(AUDUBON'S)

yellowish throat

grayish overall

MALE
D. c. auduboni
(AUDUBON'S)

The abundant and widespread Yellow-rumped Warbler is not choosy about its wintering habitats. It was often considered to consist of two species, "Myrtle" (*D. c. coronata*) in the East, and "Audubon's" (*D. c. auduboni*) in the West. Because they interbreed freely in a narrow zone of contact in British Columbia and Alberta, the American Ornithologists Union merged them. The two forms differ in plumage and voice, and their hybrid zone appears stable.
VOICE Myrtle's call a flat, husky *tchik*; Audubon's a higher-pitched, relatively musical, rising *jip*; flight call of both a clear, upslurred *sviiit*; song loose, warbled trill with an inflected ending; Myrtle's song higher and faster, Audubon's lower and slower.
NESTING Bulky cup of plant matter in conifer; 4–5 eggs; 1 brood; March–August.
FEEDING Feeds mostly on flies, beetles, wasps, and spiders during breeding; takes fruit and berries at other times of the year, often sallies to catch prey.

FLIGHT: fast, slightly undulating, and direct with rapid wing beats.

WIDESPREAD WARBLER
Yellow-rumped Warblers are widespread and are likely to be spotted often.

SIMILAR SPECIES

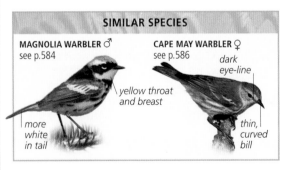

MAGNOLIA WARBLER ♂
see p.584

more white in tail

CAPE MAY WARBLER ♀
see p.586

dark eye-line

yellow throat and breast

thin, curved bill

OCCURRENCE
Both eastern and western populations are widespread across the continent from Alaska eastward to Quebec and Labrador, and westward in the mountains south to Arizona, New Mexico, and Northern Mexico. Prefers coniferous and mixed hardwood coniferous forests.

| Length **5in (13cm)** | Wingspan **9in (23cm)** | Weight **⅜–⅝oz (10–17g)** |
| Social **Flocks** | Lifespan **Up to 7 years** | Status **Secure** |

| Order **Passeriformes** | Family **Parulidae** | Species **Dendroica nigrescens** |

Black-throated Gray Warbler

MALE
white wing bars
gray overall
IN FLIGHT

pattern more subdued than male
white throat
black band across breast
FEMALE

bold white cheeks
no eye-ring
yellow spot between eye and bill
plain gray back

white outer tail feathers
MALE

white undertail feathers

one or two white wing bars
heavy, black streaks on underparts

FLIGHT: fast, slightly undulating, and direct with rapid wing beats.

The Black-throated Gray Warbler, a somewhat chickadee-like bird, inhabits the understory of forests and woodlands of oak and mixed woodlands in dry to arid western North America. Remarkably, considering that it is fairly common, not much is known about its life history, except that it has a rather leisurely foraging style, that its nest is built by both males and females, placed only a feet few away from the ground, and that it lingers in its range until late fall, sometimes even wintering in California and Arizona.

VOICE Call a hard, flat *chep*; flight call a rising *siiit*; song a series of mid-range, paired, buzzy notes, slightly rising then dropping in pitch with the last note, *buzz-zu buzz-zu buzz-zu buzz-zo buzz-zo buzz-zee BEE-chu!*

NESTING Deep and compact cup of grass, lined with feathers, in brush; 3–5 eggs; 2 broods; May–July.

FEEDING A rather deliberate forager, gleans insects, especially caterpillars, from foliage at mid-levels.

LIVELY SONG
The buzzy song of this species is typical of the "black-throated" warbler group.

SIMILAR SPECIES

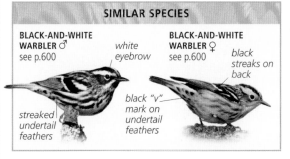

BLACK-AND-WHITE WARBLER ♂
see p.600
streaked undertail feathers
white eyebrow

BLACK-AND-WHITE WARBLER ♀
see p.600
black streaks on back
black "v" mark on undertail feathers

OCCURRENCE
Ranges from British Columbia south to California. Breeds in open coniferous and mixed woodlands with dense scrubby understory of pinyon, juniper, and/or oak; migrants use a greater variety of habitats; winters in dry scrub and woodlands southward away from its breeding range.

| Length **5in (13cm)** | Wingspan **7½in (19cm)** | Weight **¼–⅜oz (7–10g)** |
| Social **Flocks** | Lifespan **Unknown** | Status **Secure** |

| Order **Passeriformes** | Family **Parulidae** | Species ***Dendroica chrysoparia*** |

Golden-cheeked Warbler

two white wing bars

MALE

IN FLIGHT

olive-green back

yellow chin

black side of chest

streaked flanks

FEMALE

thin, black eye-line

broad, yellow eyebrow

black back

black chin and throat

white outer tail feathers

white undertail feathers

dark brownish legs and toes

MALE

FLIGHT: fast, slightly undulating, and direct with rapid wing beats.

The strikingly beautiful Golden-cheeked Warbler breeds in a very small area of Texas, near, and on, the Edwards Plateau, where the male can be found singing throughout the day from conspicuous perches. Its habitat is similarly restricted; it is found in fairly specific types of woodland, with junipers being its preferred tree or shrub. Continuing destruction of its habitat by urban development and agriculture has made this species even scarcer, and it has been on the Endangered Species list since 1990.

VOICE Dry *tsk* call; song a variable series of relatively low, buzzy notes, often ending on a high, clear note *zo zu zu zo zu zhray ZHEE*; another version ends at a lower pitch *ZOH zu ZO-ZOH zhray*.

NESTING Cup of juniper strips in fork of juniper, often in canyon bottom; 3–5 eggs; 1 brood; April–June.

FEEDING Gleans a variety of different insects, sucg as moths, flies, wasps, bees from high up in trees.

TEXAS BEAUTY
Singing in the open, this warbler shows off its golden head, black bib, and streaked flanks.

OCCURRENCE
Found exclusively in Texas, where it breeds in extensive oak-juniper woodlands mixed with hardwood species like maple and ash. Winters in high-elevation pine-oak woodlands, sometimes also cloud forests from southern Mexico to Nicaragua.

SIMILAR SPECIES

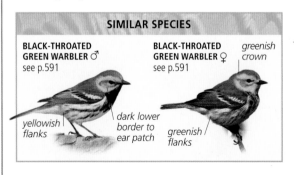

BLACK-THROATED GREEN WARBLER ♂
see p.591

yellowish flanks

dark lower border to ear patch

BLACK-THROATED GREEN WARBLER ♀
see p.591

greenish crown

greenish flanks

| Length **5in (13cm)** | Wingspan **8in (20cm)** | Weight **⁹⁄₃₂–⁷⁄₁₆oz (8–12g)** |
| Social **Migrant/Winter flocks** | Lifespan **Up to 8 years** | Status **Endangered** |

| Order **Passeriformes** | Family **Parulidae** | Species *Dendroica virens* |

Black-throated Green Warbler

olive-green back

same as male, but duller

greenish cap

yellow face

MALE

two white wing bars

greenish flanks

FEMALE

black bib and chin

IN FLIGHT

white outer tail feathers

heavily streaked underparts

yellowish flanks

MALE

FLIGHT: fast, slightly undulating, and direct with rapid wing beats; typical warbler flight.

This species is easy to distinguish as its bright yellow face is unique among birds inhabiting northeastern North America. It is a member of the *virens* "superspecies," a group of non-overlapping species that are similar in plumage and vocalizations—the Black-throated Green, Golden-cheeked, Townsend's, and Hermit Warblers. Sadly, this species is vulnerable to habitat loss in parts of its wintering range.
VOICE Flat *tchip* call; flight call a rising *siii*; two high-pitched, buzzy songs, fast *zee zee zee zee zoo zee*; and lower, slower *zu zee zu-zu zee*.
NESTING Cup of twigs and grasses around 10–65ft (3–20m) on horizontal branch near trunk in the North, away from trunk in the South; 3–5 eggs; 1 brood; May–July.
FEEDING Gleans arthropods, especially caterpillars; also takes small fruit, including poison ivy berries, in nonbreeding season.

YELLOW-AND-BLACK GEM
From a high perch on a spruce tree, a male bird advertises his territory with a song.

OCCURRENCE
Breeds in many forest types, especially a mix of conifers and hardwood, from British Columbia east to Newfoundland and into southeast US along the Appalachians. Migrants and wintering birds use a variety of habitats. Winters from southern Texas into Venezuela; small numbers in Caribbean.

SIMILAR SPECIES

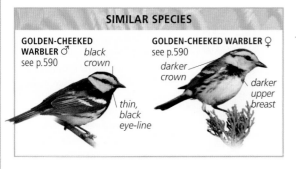

GOLDEN-CHEEKED WARBLER ♂
see p.590

black crown

thin, black eye-line

GOLDEN-CHEEKED WARBLER ♀
see p.590

darker crown

darker upper breast

| Length **5in (13cm)** | Wingspan **8in (20cm)** | Weight ⁹⁄₃₂–³⁄₈oz (8–11g) |
| Social **Migrant/Winter flocks** | Lifespan **Up to 6 years** | Status **Secure** |

| Order **Passeriformes** | Family **Parulidae** | Species ***Dendroica dominica*** |

Yellow-throated Warbler

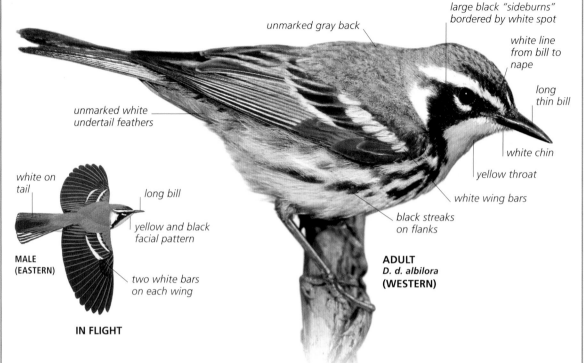

unmarked gray back

large black "sideburns" bordered by white spot

white line from bill to nape

long thin bill

white chin

yellow throat

white wing bars

black streaks on flanks

unmarked white undertail feathers

ADULT
D. d. albilora
(WESTERN)

white on tail

long bill

yellow and black facial pattern

MALE (EASTERN)

two white bars on each wing

IN FLIGHT

This is one of the earliest warblers to return from its southerly wintering grounds to its breeding grounds in the forests of the eastern US in the spring; in fact, some birds arrive by late March. The Yellow-throated Warbler is perhaps best known for its habit of creeping along branches, much like its cousin, the Black-and-white Warbler. Four subspecies have been described; the western subspecies, *D. d. albilora*, has a penchant for sycamore trees. The species occasionally interbreeds with the Northern Parula, creating the so-called "Sutton's Warbler."
VOICE Flight call high, thin *siit*; song long, descending cascade of clear whistles, often with jumbled or slightly emphatic ending *Tseu'-ee tseu'-ee tseu'-oh tseu'-oh tseu'-uh tseu'-uh teedle-ee-EEdle*.
NESTING Cup of fine grasses on branch tip, usually in tree canopy; 3–5 eggs; 1–2 broods; April–July.
FEEDING Gleans spiders, insects, and insect larvae, especially caterpillars, from foliage and bark.

FLIGHT: fast, slightly undulating, and direct, with rapid wing beats.

SOUTHERNER
The Yellow-throated Warbler is a species of southern woodlands, such as cypress swamps.

SIMILAR SPECIES

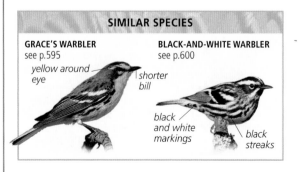

GRACE'S WARBLER
see p.595

yellow around eye

BLACK-AND-WHITE WARBLER
see p.600

shorter bill

black and white markings

black streaks

OCCURRENCE
Breeds in the eastern half of North America, but not in southern Florida, in woods with cypress, sycamore, or live oak; wintering birds may prefer tall palms and parklike settings. Range has extended northwards in recent years. Southern US population is non-migratory.

| Length **5in (13cm)** | Wingspan **8in (20cm)** | Weight **9/32–3/8oz (8–11g)** |
| Social **Winter flocks** | Lifespan **Up to 5 years** | Status **Secure** |

| Order **Passeriformes** | Family **Parulidae** | Species *Dendroica graciae* |

Grace's Warbler

two white
wing bars

yellow
face

less black
on head

duller pattern
than male

FEMALE

large yellow streak
between bill and eye

yellow streak
below eye

gray
upperparts

yellow
throat
and
breast

white wing
bars

black streaks
on flanks

white
sides
to tail
feathers

MALE

IN FLIGHT

white undertail
feathers

MALE

This little-studied warbler is the western counterpart of the longer-billed Yellow-throated Warbler. The two look similar, but their separate distribution, distinct habitats, and remarkably differerent songs make confusion very unlikely. Grace's Warbler lives almost exclusively in the tops of tall pines, and tends to have large territories, making it very hard to spot—and even harder for scientists to study. As with its eastern counterpart, this bird's range has been expanding northward in recent years, possibly due to climate change. A subspecies, *D. g. decoria*, lives in Central America.

VOICE Call soft *chip*; flight call very high, thin *ssss*; song loose trill, louder toward the end and sometimes ending with a change in pitch: *chew chew chew chew chew CHEW CHEW CHEE-DEED-DEED-DEED*.

NESTING Needle-concealed cup high up in tree, well out on horizontal branch; 3–4 eggs; 1 brood; May–July.

FEEDING Gleans insects from pine needles; sometimes snatches flying insects from the air.

FLIGHT: fast, slightly undulating, and direct, with rapid wing beats.

SIMILAR SPECIES

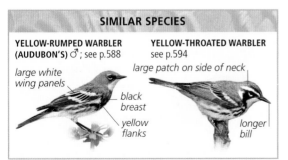

YELLOW-RUMPED WARBLER (AUDUBON'S) ♂; see p.588

large white
wing panels

black
breast

yellow
flanks

YELLOW-THROATED WARBLER see p.594

large patch on side of neck

longer
bill

SOUTHWESTERNER Grace's Warbler breeds in forests and woodlands at high elevations.

OCCURRENCE Breeds in mature, open pine and pine-oak forests in mountains of southwestern US and Mexico, south to the lowland pine savanna of the Caribbean coast in northern Nicaragua, Belize, Honduras; migratory in US portion of range, but resident year-round elsewhere.

| Length **5in (13cm)** | Wingspan **8in (20cm)** | Weight **¼–⁵⁄₁₆oz (7–9g)** |
| Social **Winter flocks** | Lifespan **Up to 5 years** | Status **Secure** |

Order **Passeriformes**	Family **Parulidae**	Species ***Dendroica kirtlandii***

Kirtland's Warbler

MALE

IN FLIGHT

white-edged tail

thin, wing bars

black patch between eye and bill

interrupted, white eye-ring

bluish gray cheeks

streaked, blue-gray upperparts

thick bill

blackish "mustache" between cheeks and yellow throat

pale, lemon-yellow underparts with marked streaks on flanks

MALE

dark cheeks

interrupted, white eye-ring

yellow throat

duller breast streaks

FEMALE

Kirtland's Warbler is one of the rarest songbirds of North America. The suppression of fires and the spread of the Brown-headed Cowbird, a brood parasite, had decreased this warbler's population to a low of 167 singing males by 1987. Controlled burning and cowbird eradication programs have allowed the population to climb back to perhaps as many as 5,000 birds by 2007.

VOICE Call a strong *chip*; flight call a high *zit*; song a loud, low-pitched series of staccato *chips*, rising in pitch and intensity and ending with bubbly, whistled phrase: *tup-CHUP-chup tup-CHEEP-cheep chew-EEP*.

NESTING Cup of plant fibers concealed by grasses in sandy depression; 4 eggs; 1 brood; May–June.

FEEDING Gleans a variety of insects, including grasshoppers and moths from near the ground; also eats blueberries in summer.

FLIGHT: fast, slightly undulating, and direct with rapid wing beats.

HAPPY SINGER
Head held high and bill wide open, a Kirtland's Warbler sings from the top of a Jack Pine.

OCCURRENCE
Rare and local breeder in northern Michigan, in dense, low (not higher than 30ft (9m)), 6- to 20-year-old Jack Pine stands regrowing after forest fires, with sandy soil on level or gently rolling terrain. Found in scrubby vegetation during migration, and tropical thickets on its Bahamas winter grounds.

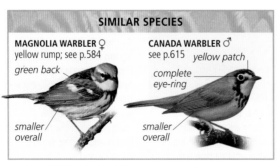

SIMILAR SPECIES

MAGNOLIA WARBLER ♀
yellow rump; see p.584
green back
smaller overall

CANADA WARBLER ♂
see p.615
yellow patch
complete eye-ring
smaller overall

Length **6in (15cm)**	Wingspan **9in (23cm)**	Weight **7⁄16–9⁄16oz (12–16g)**
Social **Solitary**	Lifespan **Up to 9 years**	Status **Vulnerable**

| Order **Passeriformes** | Family **Parulidae** | Species **Dendroica palmarum** |

Palm Warbler

ADULT (EASTERN)

chestnut crown

yellow undertail feathers

dark upperparts

white-edged tail

IN FLIGHT

dull gray upperparts

ADULT *D. p. hypochrysea* (EASTERN; BREEDING)

chestnut streaks on breast

rich yellow underparts

yellow eyestripe

grayish green "mustache"

ring below eye

yellow throat

dark gray upperparts

dusky streaks on breast and belly

dull grayish brown overall

whitish below with brown streaks

yellowish rump

yellow under tail

ADULT *D. p. palmarum* (WESTERN; NONBREEDING)

ADULT *D. p. palmarum* (WESTERN MALE; BREEDING)

The Palm Warbler is one of North America's most abundant warblers. Its tail-pumping habits make it easy to identify in any plumage. It was named *palmarum* (meaning "palm") in 1789 because it was first recorded among palm thickets on the Caribbean island of Hispaniola. The western subspecies (*D. p. palmarum*) is found in Western and Central Canada. It is grayish brown above and lacks the chestnut streaks of the eastern subspecies (*D. p. hypochrysea*), which has a yellower face, and breeds in southeastern Canada and northeastern US.

VOICE Call a husky *chik* or *tsip*; flight call a light *ziint*; slow, loose, buzzy trill: *zwi zwi zwi zwi zwi zwi zwi zwi*.

NESTING Cup of grasses on or near ground in open area of conifers at forest edge of a bog; 4–5 eggs; 1 brood; May–July.

FLIGHT: fast, slightly undulating, and direct with rapid wing beats.

SIMILAR SPECIES

CAPE MAY WARBLER ♀
see p.586

olive gray back

thin patch of yellow on throat and neck

YELLOW-RUMPED WARBLER (MYRTLE) ♀
see p.588

streaking on back

white throat

FAR FROM THE PALMS
This male Palm Warbler is far north of the coastal palms where its kin spend the winter.

OCCURRENCE
In North America, breeds in spruce bogs within the northerly forest zone, across Canada from Yukon to the Maritimes and Labrador, and in the US from Minnesota to Maine. Often migrates through central portions of eastern US; winters in southeastern US, Florida, and Central America.

| Length **5½in (14cm)** | Wingspan **8in (20cm)** | Weight **¼–⁷⁄₁₆oz (7–13g)** |
| Social **Flocks** | Lifespan **Up to 6 years** | Status **Secure** |

| Order **Passeriformes** | Family **Parulidae** | Species *Mniotilta varia* |

Black-and-white Warbler

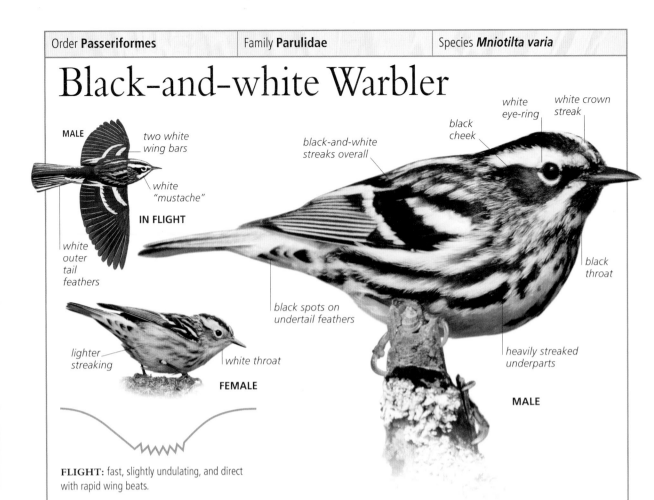

MALE
two white wing bars
white "mustache"
IN FLIGHT

white outer tail feathers

white eye-ring
white crown streak
black cheek
black-and-white streaks overall

black throat

black spots on undertail feathers

heavily streaked underparts

MALE

lighter streaking
white throat
FEMALE

FLIGHT: fast, slightly undulating, and direct with rapid wing beats.

The Black-and-white Warbler is best known for its creeper-like habit of feeding in vertical and upside-down positions as it pries into bark crevices, where its relatively long, curved bill allows it to reach tiny nooks and crannies. These habits, combined with streaked plumage, make this bird one of the most distinctive warblers in North America. It is a long-distance migrant, with some birds wintering in parts of northern South America.

VOICE Sharp *stik* call; flight call a very high, thin *ssiit*, often doubled; song a thin, high-pitched, wheezy series *wheesy wheesy wheesy wheesy wheesy wheesy*.
NESTING Cup on ground against stump, fallen logs, or roots; 4–6 eggs; 1 brood; April–August.
FEEDING Creeps along branches and trunks, probing into bark for insects and insect larvae.

SQUEAKY WHEEL
The high-pitched, wheezy song of this warbler is said to be reminiscent of a squeaky wheel.

UPSIDE-DOWN
Black-and-white Warblers often creep head-first along trunks and branches of trees.

OCCURRENCE
Breeds in deciduous and mixed mature and second-growth woodlands; migrants occur on a greater variety of habitats; winters in a wide range of wooded habitats in southern US, Mexico and into Central and South America.

SIMILAR SPECIES

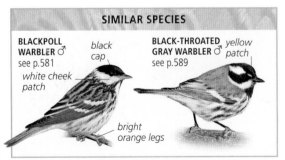

BLACKPOLL WARBLER ♂ see p.581
black cap
white cheek patch

BLACK-THROATED GRAY WARBLER ♂ see p.589
yellow patch
bright orange legs

| Length **5in (13cm)** | Wingspan **8in (20cm)** | Weight **5/16–1/2oz (9–14g)** |
| Social **Migrant/Winter flocks** | Lifespan **Up to 11 years** | Status **Secure** |

| Order **Passeriformes** | Family **Parulidae** | Species ***Setophaga ruticilla*** |

American Redstart

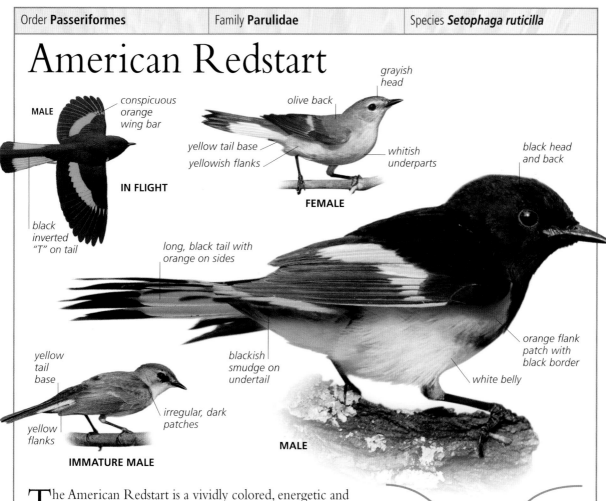

MALE

conspicuous orange wing bar

IN FLIGHT

black inverted "T" on tail

grayish head

olive back

yellow tail base

yellowish flanks

whitish underparts

FEMALE

black head and back

long, black tail with orange on sides

orange flank patch with black border

white belly

blackish smudge on undertail

MALE

yellow tail base

yellow flanks

irregular, dark patches

IMMATURE MALE

The American Redstart is a vividly colored, energetic and acrobatic warbler with a reasonably broad range across North America. One of its behavioral quirks is to fan its tail and wings while foraging, supposedly using the flashes of bold color to scare insects into moving, making them easy prey. It possesses well-developed rictal bristles, hair-like feathers extending from the corners of the mouth, which help it to detect insects.

VOICE Harsh *tsiip* call; flight call a high, thin *sweep*; song a confusingly variable, high, thin, yet penetrating series of notes; one version burry, emphatic, and downslurred *see-a see-a see-a see-a ZEE-urrrr*.

NESTING Cup of grasses and rootlets, lined with feathers; placed low in deciduous tree; 2–5 eggs; 1–2 broods; May–July.

FEEDING Gleans insects and spiders from leaves at mid-levels in trees; also catches moths, flies in flight; will also eat fruit.

FLIGHT: fast, slightly undulating, and direct with rapid wing beats.

COMMON SONG
This bird's short, ringing song is a common sound in the moist deciduous woods of the East and North.

MALE CARER
As with most warblers, male Redstarts help raise the young, though they may be polygamous.

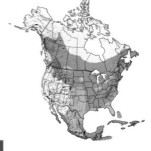

OCCURRENCE
Breeds in moist deciduous and mixed woodlands across North America; migrants and wintering birds use a wide range of habitats. Winters from Baja California and south Florida through Middle America and the Caribbean to northern South America.

| Length **5in (13cm)** | Wingspan **8in (20cm)** | Weight **⁷⁄₃₂–³⁄₈oz (6–11g)** |
| Social **Flocks** | Lifespan **Up to 10 years** | Status **Secure** |

Order **Passeriformes**	Family **Parulidae**	Species **Protonotaria citrea**

Prothonotary Warbler

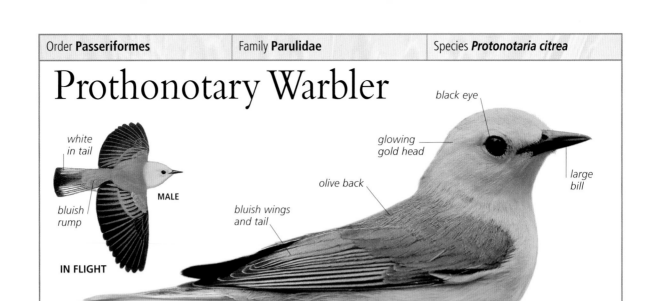

black eye

glowing
gold head

olive back

large
bill

white
in tail

MALE

bluish
rump

IN FLIGHT

bluish wings
and tail

bright yellow
underparts

duller
colored
head

blue wings
and tail

large bill

yellowish breast
and head

MALE

FEMALE

The ringing song of the Prothonotary Warbler—
once known as the Golden Swamp Warbler—echoes
through the swamps of the southeastern US every summer.
This is one of the few cavity-nesting warbler species; it will use
manmade bird houses if they are placed close enough to still
water. Prothonotary Warblers also tend to stay fairly low over the
water, making them easy to spot. This warbler's yellow head and breast
reminded an early naturalist of the bright yellow robes worn by Prothonotaries
(high ranking papal clerks), and he passed the name to this colorful bird.
VOICE Flight call a loud, high *sviit*; call note a loud *chip*; song a loud series of
penetrating and internally rising notes *tsveet tsveet tsveet tsveet tsveet tsveet tsveet*.
NESTING Over or near still water; woodpecker
holes often used; 3–8 eggs; 1–2 broods; April–July.
FEEDING Mostly eats insects and small mollusks;
also seeds, fruit, and nectar.

FLIGHT: fast, with slight undulations, and
direct with rapid wing beats.

OCCURRENCE
Breeds in wooded areas
over or near still water,
especially in cypress swamps
and bottomlands across the
southeastern US. Winters
in mangroves and dry forests
in Southern Mexico.

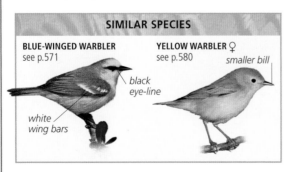

SIMILAR SPECIES

BLUE-WINGED WARBLER
see p.571

YELLOW WARBLER ♀
see p.580

smaller bill

black
eye-line

white
wing bars

GOLDEN SONGBIRD
Visible in the darkness of a
southern swamp, a Prothonotary
Warbler sings its ringing song.

Length **5½in (14cm)**	Wingspan **9in (23cm)**	Weight **½–⅝oz (14–18g)**
Social **Winter flocks**	Lifespan **Up to 8 years**	Status **Endangered**

| Order **Passeriformes** | Family **Parulidae** | Species *Helmitheros vermivorum* |

Worm-eating Warbler

short tail

ADULT

IN FLIGHT

dull olive overall

boldy striped buff-and-black crown

blurry pattern on undertail feathers

large, pinkish bill

ADULT

tawny wash on breast

FLIGHT: fast, slightly undulating, and direct with rapid wing beats.

Contrary to its name, the Worm-eating Warbler does not eat real worms such as earthworms. Rather, it consumes inchworms and other caterpillars. It can often be found hanging upside down, quietly prying into a mass of suspended dead leaves in search of unsuspecting prey. It specializes in probing the curled leaves that have been adopted by caterpillars as safe havens for feeding or resting, examining them carefully for potential occupants and then levering the curl open with its bill to claim its prize. Although this bird nests on the ground and tends to forage fairly low, singing males may perch quite high in trees. It is the only member of the *Helmitheros* genus and is unlike any other North American warbler, except perhaps the elusive Swainson's Warbler.

VOICE Thick *chip* call; flight call an upslurred, thin, rolling *ziiit*, often given in series of two to three notes; song a thin, dry trill.

NESTING Well-concealed cup of leaf litter at base of sapling or shrub on an often steep hillside; 3–6 eggs; 1 brood; May–July.

FEEDING Forages in low shrubs, mainly for caterpillars, but also insects and spiders.

CAMOUFLAGED WARBLER
Worm-eaters are patterned to blend in with the leaf litter of rich deciduous forests.

SIMILAR SPECIES

SWAINSON'S WARBLER
see p.604

paler head

paler underparts

OCCURRENCE
Breeds locally in large expanses of hilly, rich, mature, deciduous forests with abundant leaf litter and dense undergrowth; migrants prefer similar forested habitats. Winters in Central America and the Caribbean, in varied forested habitats, but prefers dense undergrowth.

| Length **5in (13cm)** | Wingspan **8½in (21cm)** | Weight **⁷⁄₁₆–⅝oz (12–17g)** |
| Social **Solitary/Flocks** | Lifespan **Up to 7 years** | Status **Secure** |

Order **Passeriformes**	Family **Parulidae**	Species *Limnothlypis swainsonii*

Swainson's Warbler

short tail

IN FLIGHT

ADULT

plain brown uperparts

rusty brown crown

pale eyebrow

long bill

dusky wash on underparts

ADULT

FLIGHT: fast, slightly undulating, and direct with rapid wing beats.

Few people ever get to see Swainson's Warbler—not even those enthusiasts who regularly go looking for it. The bird's impressive song makes it relatively easy to track, but its reclusive nature, drab plumage, and liking for dense thickets make it one of the most difficult birds in North America to actually spot. The species is also quite unusual in that it has two seemingly identical populations that breed in distinct habitats—one in dense, giant canebreaks in swampy lowlands, and the other in Appalachian rhododendron or mountain laurel thickets.

VOICE Flight call high *siiii*, often doubled; song loud series of downslurred whistles ending emphatically and purposefully *su see-a see-oh WEE-chuh WEE-oh.*

NESTING Bulky mass of vegetation placed low in dense understory thicket; 2–5 eggs; 1 brood; May–July.

FEEDING Forages slowly and methodically on the forest floor for insects, insect larvae, and spiders.

PROUD PROTECTOR
A male Swainson's Warbler guards his breeding territory from the vantage of a perch.

SIMILAR SPECIES

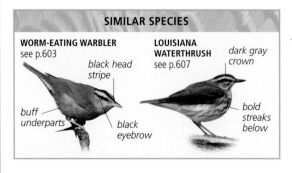

WORM-EATING WARBLER
see p.603

black head stripe

buff underparts

black eyebrow

LOUISIANA WATERTHRUSH
see p.607

dark gray crown

bold streaks below

OCCURRENCE
Breeds in floodplains, often in areas of dense undergrowth, and in mountain forests with suitable undergrowth; during migration and in winter found in forests with suitable understory and leaf litter.

Length **5½in (14cm)**	Wingspan **9in (23cm)**	Weight **⁷⁄₁₆–¹¹⁄₁₆oz (12–20g)**
Social **Solitary/Winter flocks**	Lifespan **Up to 7 years**	Status **Declining**

| Order **Passeriformes** | Family **Parulidae** | Species *Seiurus aurocapillus* |

Ovenbird

plain olive overall

ADULT

IN FLIGHT

orange-and-black striped crown

bold white eye-ring

olive upperparts

white throat

black streaked underparts

ADULT

FLIGHT: fast, slightly undulating, and direct with rapid wing beats.

Like members of the unrelated, tropical ovenbird family (Furnariidae), this little bird is so-called for the domed, oven-like nests it builds on the ground; unique structures for a North American bird. The Ovenbird is also noted for its singing. Males flit about boisterously, often at night, incorporating portions of their main song into a jumble of spluttering notes. In the forest, one male singing loudly to declare his territory can set off a whole chain of responses from his neighbors, until the whole forest rings.

VOICE Call variably pitched, sharp *chik* in series; flight call high, rising *siiii*; song loud, ringing crescendo of paired notes *chur-tee' chur-tee' chur-tee' chur-tee' chur-TEE chur-TEE chur-TEE.*

NESTING Domed structure of leaves and grass on ground with side entrance; 3–6 eggs; 1 brood; May–July.

FEEDING Forages mainly on the forest floor for insects and other invertebrates.

STRUTTING ITS STUFF
The Ovenbird is noted for the way it struts across the forest floor like a tiny chicken.

SIMILAR SPECIES

NORTHERN WATERTHRUSH much slimmer; see p.606
dark brown upperparts
no eye-ring

LOUISIANA WATERTHRUSH see p.607
white eyebrow
dark brown upperparts

OCCURRENCE
Breeds in closed-canopy mixed and deciduous forests with suitable amount of fallen plant material for nest building and foraging; migrants and wintering birds use similar habitats.

| Length **6in (15cm)** | Wingspan **9½in (24cm)** | Weight **⁹⁄₁₆–⁷⁄₈oz (16–25g)** |
| Social **Solitary/Flocks** | Lifespan **Up to 7 years** | Status **Declining** |

| Order **Passeriformes** | Family **Parulidae** | Species *Seiurus noveboracensis* |

Northern Waterthrush

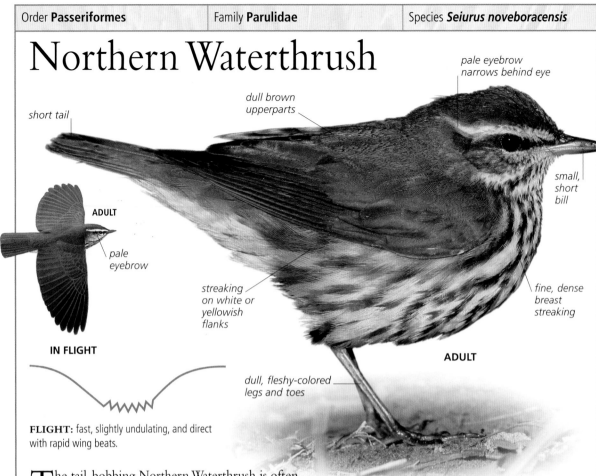

short tail

dull brown upperparts

pale eyebrow narrows behind eye

small, short bill

ADULT

pale eyebrow

streaking on white or yellowish flanks

fine, dense breast streaking

IN FLIGHT

ADULT

dull, fleshy-colored legs and toes

FLIGHT: fast, slightly undulating, and direct with rapid wing beats.

The tail-bobbing Northern Waterthrush is often heard giving a *spink!* call as it swiftly flees from observers. Although this species may be mistaken for the closely related Louisiana Waterthrush, there are clues that are helpful in its identification. While the Northern Waterthrush prefers still water, its relative greatly prefers running water; in addition, its song is quite unlike that of the Louisiana Waterthrush.

VOICE Call a sharp, rising, ringing *spink!*; flight call a rising, buzzy *ziiiit*; song a loud series of rich, accelerating, staccato notes, usually decreasing in pitch *teet, teet, toh-toh toh-toh tyew-tyew!*.

NESTING Hair-lined, mossy cup placed on or near ground, hidden in roots of fallen or standing tree or in riverbank; 4–5 eggs; 1 brood; May–August.

FEEDING Mostly eats insects such as ants, mosquitoes, moths, and beetles, both larvae and adult, plus slugs, and snails; when migrating, also eats small crustaceans, and even tiny fish.

YELLOW FORM
Many Northern Waterthrushes have yellow underparts, like this one, while others have white.

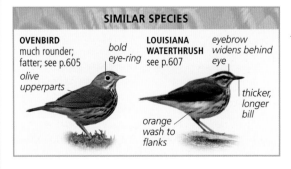

SIMILAR SPECIES

OVENBIRD
much rounder; fatter; see p.605

bold eye-ring

olive upperparts

LOUISIANA WATERTHRUSH
see p.607

eyebrow widens behind eye

thicker, longer bill

orange wash to flanks

OCCURRENCE
Breeds right across northern North America in dark, still-water swamps and bogs; also in the still edges of rivers and lakes; migrant birds use wet habitats; winters in shrubby marshes, mangroves, and occasionally in crops, such as rice fields and citrus groves.

| Length **6in (15cm)** | Wingspan **9½in (24cm)** | Weight **½–⅞oz (14–23g)** |
| Social **Solitary** | Lifespan **Up to 9 years** | Status **Secure** |

| Order **Passeriformes** | Family **Parulidae** | Species *Seiurus motacilla* |

Louisiana Waterthrush

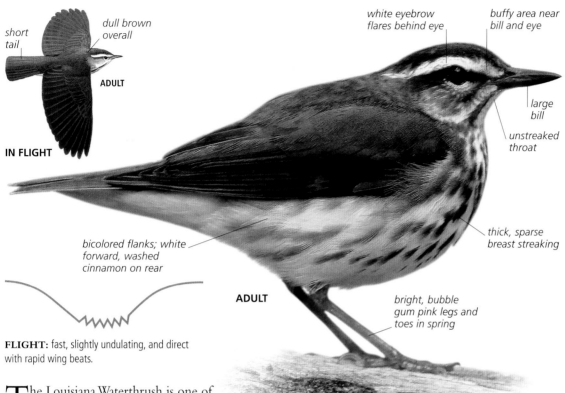

short tail

dull brown overall

ADULT

IN FLIGHT

white eyebrow flares behind eye

buffy area near bill and eye

large bill

unstreaked throat

thick, sparse breast streaking

bicolored flanks; white forward, washed cinnamon on rear

ADULT

bright, bubble gum pink legs and toes in spring

FLIGHT: fast, slightly undulating, and direct with rapid wing beats.

The Louisiana Waterthrush is one of the earliest warblers to return north in the spring; as early as March, eastern ravines are filled with cascades of its song. Both the stream-loving Louisiana Waterthrush and its still-water cousin, the Northern Waterthrush, bob their tails as they walk (the genus name, *Seiurus*, means "tail-bobber"), but the Louisiana Waterthrush arcs its entire body at the same time. In spring, this species shows brighter pink legs than the Northern Waterthrush.
VOICE Call a round *spink*; flight call a rising, buzzy *ziiiit*; song a loud, descending, ringing, whistled cascade, ending with sputtering *see'-oh see'-oh see'-uh see'-uh tip-uh-tik-uh-tip-whee'ur-tik*.
NESTING Bulky mass of leaves, moss, and twigs, under steep stream bank over water; 4–6 eggs; 1 brood; May–August.
FEEDING Forages in streams for insect larvae, snails, and small fish; also catches flying insects such as dragonflies and stoneflies.

TAKING A LITTLE DIP
In many ways, this species is the "dipper of the East," picking invertebrates from shallow streams.

SIMILAR SPECIES

OVENBIRD
much rounder; fatter; see p.605
olive upperparts

bold eye-ring

NORTHERN WATERTHRUSH
see p.606
thinner, shorter bill

fine breast streaks

OCCURRENCE
Breeds along fast-moving streams in deciduous forests in the eastern US; migrants stop over anywhere near running water, including gardens; winters along wooded streams and rivers in mountains and hills in the Caribbean, Mexico, Central America, and northern parts of South America.

| Length **6in (15cm)** | Wingspan **10in (25cm)** | Weight ⅝–⅞oz (18–25g) |
| Social **Solitary** | Lifespan **Up to 8 years** | Status **Secure** |

| Order **Passeriformes** | Family **Parulidae** | Species *Oporornis formosus* |

Kentucky Warbler

black crown with gray spots

yellow streak above eyes

black cheek

dark olive upperparts

black-and-yellow facial pattern

ADULT

short tail

IN FLIGHT

yellow chin and throat

ADULT

bright yellow underparts

pale pinkish legs and feet

pale olive upperparts

less black on face

FEMALE

FLIGHT: fast, slightly undulating, and direct with rapid wing beats.

The loud and cheery song of the Kentucky Warbler is one of the characteristic sounds of dense, moist eastern US forests. Unlike the Connecticut Warbler, it is appropriately named, because it actually breeds in its namesake state, Kentucky. This species is a rather secretive inhabitant of dense US hardwood forests, where it forages close to or on the ground, looking for insects that live on the forest floor.

VOICE Call a low, hollow *chup*, flight call a buzzy *dziiip*; song a loud rolling series of paired notes *chur-ee' chur-ee' chur-ee' chur-ee' chur-ee'*, with little variation.

NESTING Concealed bulky cup of leaves and grass on or just above ground in shrub; 4–5 eggs; 1–2 broods; May–August.

FEEDING Gleans beetles, spiders, and other arthropods, mainly in low vegetation.

LUCKY SHOT
This bird is mostly seen in the underbrush of moist forests, not out in the open like this migrant.

OCCURRENCE
Breeds in eastern US moist, deciduous forests with dense deciduous understory. Migrants prefer dense woodlands and thickets. Winters from Mexico to Panama and northern South America, in dense, wet lowland thickets and forests.

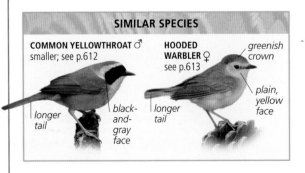

SIMILAR SPECIES

COMMON YELLOWTHROAT ♂
smaller; see p.612

HOODED WARBLER ♀
see p.613

greenish crown

longer tail

black-and-gray face

longer tail

plain, yellow face

| Length **5in (13cm)** | Wingspan **8½in (21cm)** | Weight **⁷⁄₁₆–¹¹⁄₁₆ oz (12–19g)** |
| Social **Solitary/Flocks** | Lifespan **Up to 7 years** | Status **Secure (p)** |

| Order **Passeriformes** | Family **Parulidae** | Species *Oporornis agilis* |

Connecticut Warbler

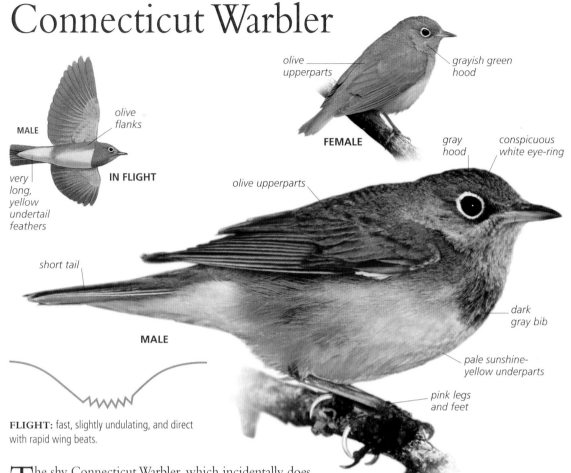

MALE

olive flanks

IN FLIGHT

very long, yellow undertail feathers

olive upperparts

grayish green hood

FEMALE

gray hood

conspicuous white eye-ring

olive upperparts

short tail

MALE

dark gray bib

pale sunshine-yellow underparts

pink legs and feet

FLIGHT: fast, slightly undulating, and direct with rapid wing beats.

The shy Connecticut Warbler, which incidentally does not breed in this state, breeds in remote, boggy habitats in Canada and is hard to spot during its spring and fall migrations. It arrives in the US in late May and leaves its breeding grounds in August. It is the only warbler that walks along the ground in a bouncy manner, with its tail bobbing up and down.

VOICE Seldom-heard call a nasal *champ*, flight call a buzzy *ziiiit*; song a loud "whippy," accelerating series, often ending with upward inflection *tweet, chuh WHIP-uh chee-uh-WHIP-uh chee-uh-WAY*.

NESTING Concealed cup of grass or leaves, lined with fine plant matter and hair; placed near or on ground in damp moss or grass clump; 3–5 eggs; 1 brood; June–July.

FEEDING Gleans a variety of adult insects, insect larvae, and spiders from under leaves; also eats small fruits.

EXCEPTIONAL UNDERTAIL
The yellow undertail feathers nearly reach the tip of the Connecticut Warbler's tail.

OCCURRENCE
Breeds across Canada from British Columbia to Quebec and in the US in Minnesota and the Great Lakes region, in bogs and pine forests. Winters in forest habitats of Amazonian Peru and Brazil.

SIMILAR SPECIES

NASHVILLE WARBLER ♀
see p.574

MOURNING WARBLER ☿
see p.610

darker breast patch

yellowish throat

pale gray back

| Length **6in (15cm)** | Wingspan **9in (23cm)** | Weight ⁷⁄₁₆–¹¹⁄₁₆oz (13–20g) |
| Social **Solitary** | Lifespan **Up to 4 years** | Status **Secure (p)** |

Order **Passeriformes**	Family **Parulidae**	Species *Oporornis philadelphia*

Mourning Warbler

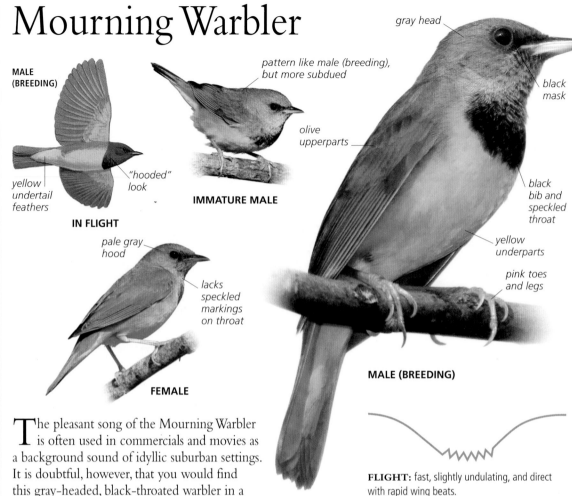

MALE (BREEDING)

yellow undertail feathers

"hooded" look

IN FLIGHT

pattern like male (breeding), but more subdued

olive upperparts

IMMATURE MALE

pale gray hood

lacks speckled markings on throat

FEMALE

gray head

black mask

black bib and speckled throat

yellow underparts

pink toes and legs

MALE (BREEDING)

The pleasant song of the Mourning Warbler is often used in commercials and movies as a background sound of idyllic suburban settings. It is doubtful, however, that you would find this gray-headed, black-throated warbler in a backyard, as it prefers dense, herbaceous tangles—both for breeding and during migration. These birds are late spring migrants and the leaves are fully out when they arrive in the eastern US, making it difficult to see them. The easiest way to see a Mourning Warbler is to track a male by its song.

VOICE Call a flat *tchik*; flight call a high, thin, clear *svit*; song a very burry series of paired notes with low-pitched ending: *churrr-ee churrr-ee churrr-ee churr-ee churrr-ee-oh*.

NESTING Well-concealed cup of leaves, lined with grass, on or near ground in dense tangle; 2–5 eggs; 1 brood; June–August.

FEEDING Mainly gleans insects and spiders in low foliage; eats some plant material in winter.

FLIGHT: fast, slightly undulating, and direct with rapid wing beats.

FOLLOW THAT BIRD
Tracking down a singing male is the easiest way to find this skulking species.

SIMILAR SPECIES

MACGILLIVRAY'S WARBLER ♀
see p.611

incomplete eye-ring

longer tail

COMMON YELLOWTHROAT ♀
see p.612

smaller, black bill

longer tail

OCCURRENCE
Breeds in dense thickets of disturbed woodlands from the Yukon and British Columbia, east to Quebec and Newfoundland, south to the Great Lakes, New England, New York, and the Appalachians. Winters in dense thickets in Central and South America.

Length **5in (13cm)**	Wingspan **7.5in (19cm)**	Weight **⅜–⁷⁄₁₆oz (10–13g)**
Social **Solitary**	Lifespan **Up to 8 years**	Status **Secure**

| Order **Passeriformes** | Family **Parulidae** | Species *Oporornis tolmiei* |

MacGillivray's Warbler

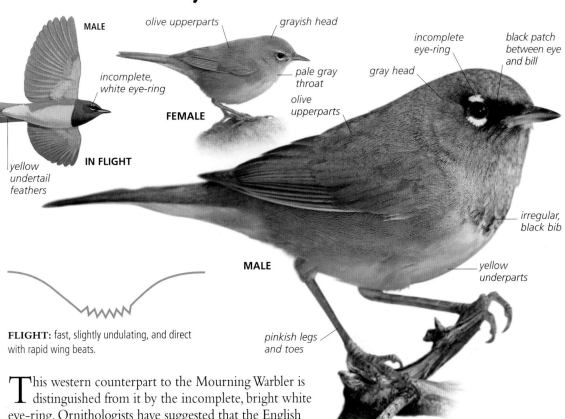

MALE

olive upperparts

grayish head

incomplete, white eye-ring

FEMALE

pale gray throat

olive upperparts

IN FLIGHT

yellow undertail feathers

incomplete eye-ring

gray head

black patch between eye and bill

irregular, black bib

MALE

yellow underparts

pinkish legs and toes

FLIGHT: fast, slightly undulating, and direct with rapid wing beats.

This western counterpart to the Mourning Warbler is distinguished from it by the incomplete, bright white eye-ring. Ornithologists have suggested that the English name of this species should be "Tolmie's Warbler," as this species was described and given its Latin species name, *tolmiei*, in April 1839, to honor the Scottish-born physician W. F. Tolmie. But a month later, John James Audubon, apparently unaware of the name *tolmiei*, named the same species *macgillivrayi*, to honor the naturalist, William MacGillivray. This problem was easily solved, as the rule of priority establishes the first scientific name as the valid one, so the name *tolmiei* was retained. However, the English name, MacGillivray, has also stuck.

VOICE Call a sharp *tssik*; flight call a high, thin, clear *svit*; song a loud, staccato, rolling series; ends lower or higher than rest of song.

NESTING Cup of plant material just off the ground in deciduous shrubs and thickets; 3–5 eggs; 1 brood; May–August.

FEEDING Gleans beetles, flies, bees, caterpillars from low foliage.

FAIRLY EASY TO FIND
This species is easy to spot, often popping up onto a branch in response to some disturbance.

SIMILAR SPECIES

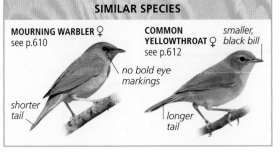

MOURNING WARBLER ♀
see p.610

shorter tail

COMMON YELLOWTHROAT ♀
see p.612

smaller, black bill

no bold eye markings

longer tail

OCCURRENCE
Breeds in thickets within mixed and coniferous forests, often along streams from southeast Alaska and British Columbia south to southern and Baja California, and across the western states. Winters in varied habitats with sufficient thickets in Mexico and in Central America.

| Length **5in (13cm)** | Wingspan **7.5in (19cm)** | Weight **⁵⁄₁₆–⁷⁄₁₆oz (9–12g)** |
| Social **Solitary** | Lifespan **Up to 4 years** | Status **Secure** |

| Order **Passeriformes** | Family **Parulidae** | Species *Geothlypis trichas* |

Common Yellowthroat

plain, olive-green overall

black mask

MALE

IN FLIGHT

olive upperparts

pale eye-ring

yellow throat

FEMALE

pale stripe over "mask," varies from gray to white or yellowish

black "mask" including forehead

olive-green upperparts

yellow throat

greenish gray underparts

olive-green tail

MALE

FLIGHT: fast, slightly undulating, and direct with rapid wing beats.

This common and easy-to-see warbler is noticeable partly because of its loud, simple song. This species varies in voice and plumage across its range and 14 subspecies have been described. In the western US, the birds have yellower underparts, brighter white head stripes, and louder, simpler songs than the eastern birds. The male often flies upwards rapidly, delivering a more complex version of its song.

VOICE Call a harsh, buzzy *tchak*, repeated into chatter when agitated; flight call a low, flat, buzzy *dzzzit*; song a variable but distinctive series of rich (often three-note) phrases: *WITCH-uh-tee WITCH-uh-tee WITCH-uh-tee WHICH*; more complex flight song.

NESTING Concealed, bulky cup of grasses just above ground or water; 3–5 eggs; 1 brood; May–August.

FEEDING Eats insects and spiders in low vegetation; also seeds.

UNFORGETABLE CALL
The song of the male Common Yellowthroat is an extremely helpful aid in its identification.

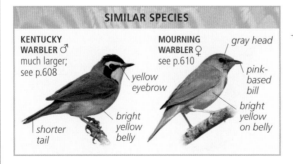

SIMILAR SPECIES

KENTUCKY WARBLER ♂
much larger;
see p.608

yellow eyebrow

shorter tail

bright yellow belly

MOURNING WARBLER ♀
see p.610

gray head

pink-based bill

bright yellow on belly

OCCURRENCE
Found south of the tundra, from Alaska and the Yukon to Quebec and Newfoundland, and south to California, Texas, and to southeastern US. Habitats dense herbaceous understory, from marshes and grasslands to pine forest and hedgerows. Winters from Mexico to Panama and the Antilles.

| Length **5in (13cm)** | Wingspan **6¾in (17cm)** | Weight **29oz (825g)** |
| Social **Migrant/Winter flocks** | Lifespan **Up to 11 years** | Status **Secure** |

| Order **Passeriformes** | Family **Parulidae** | Species ***Wilsonia citrina*** |

Hooded Warbler

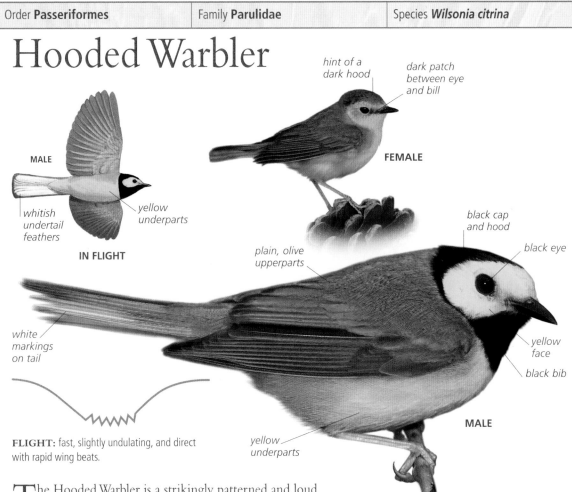

hint of a dark hood

dark patch between eye and bill

FEMALE

MALE

whitish undertail feathers

yellow underparts

IN FLIGHT

plain, olive upperparts

black cap and hood

black eye

white markings on tail

yellow face

black bib

MALE

FLIGHT: fast, slightly undulating, and direct with rapid wing beats.

yellow underparts

The Hooded Warbler is a strikingly patterned and loud warbler, and is often particularly conspicuous over its eastern US breeding range. Both male and females frequently flash the white markings hidden on the inner webs of their tails. The extent of the black hood varies in female Hooded Warblers; it ranges from none in first fall birds to almost as extensive as males in some adult females. Genetic (DNA) and vocal information point to a close relationship with *Dendroica* warblers.

VOICE Call a metallic *tsink*; flight call a high, thin *sweep*; song a rich, whistled series, ending loudly and emphatically: *tu-wee' tu-wee' tu-wee-TEE-tee-yu*.

NESTING Bulky cup of leaves lined with hair, in shrub near eye level; 3–5 eggs; 1–2 broods; May–July.

FEEDING Eats many different kinds of insects found low in vegetation.

STRIKING MASK
The black and yellow face of the Hooded Warbler makes the male an unmistakable bird.

SIMILAR SPECIES

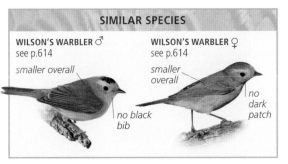

WILSON'S WARBLER ♂
see p.614

smaller overall

no black bib

WILSON'S WARBLER ♀
see p.614

smaller overall

no dark patch

OCCURRENCE
Breeds in moist deciduous forests with dense understory in eastern US; has bred in some moist mountain canyons. Migrants like similar habitat. Winters in moist woodlands with good understory, especially lowland rainforest, from eastern Mexico to Panama and the West Indies.

| Length **5¼in (13.5cm)** | Wingspan **7in (17.5cm)** | Weight **⁵⁄₁₆oz – ⁷⁄₁₆oz (9–12g)** |
| Social **Migrant/Winter flocks** | Lifespan **Up to 8 years** | Status **Secure (p)** |

| Order **Passeriformes** | Family **Parulidae** | Species **Wilsonia pusilla** |

Wilson's Warbler

MALE

IN FLIGHT

long, narrow tail

olive or blackish crown

yellow eyebrow and chin

FEMALE

olive upperparts

black cap

large black eye

yellow brightest on face

MALE

FLIGHT: fast, slightly undulating, and direct with rapid wing beats.

The tiny Wilson's Warbler is perhaps the most common spring migrant of all the wood-warblers across many areas of the western US and Canada. In the East, however, it is much scarcer in spring. Wilson's Warblers have a wide range of habitats, yet their numbers are declining, especially in the West, as its riverside breeding habitats are gradually being destroyed by development. This species and the entire genus are named after the renowned early 19th-century ornithologist, Alexander Wilson.

VOICE Call a rich *chimp* or *champ;* flight call a sharp, liquid *tsik;* song a variable, chattering trill, often increases in speed *che che che che chi-chi-chi-chit.*

NESTING Cup of leaves and grass placed on or near ground in mosses or grass, higher along Pacific coast; 4–6 eggs; 1 brood; April–June.

FEEDING Captures insects in foliage, leaf litter, or during flight; also takes berries and honeydew.

BRIGHT WESTERN BIRD
In its western range, male Wilson's Warblers have a glowing yellow-orange face; eastern birds are duller.

EASY IDENTIFICATION
The black cap and yellow face of the otherwise olive-colored Wilson's Warbler are good field marks.

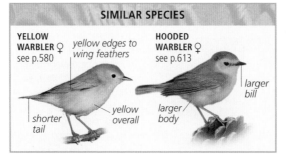

SIMILAR SPECIES

YELLOW WARBLER ♀ see p.580

yellow edges to wing feathers

shorter tail

yellow overall

HOODED WARBLER ♀ see p.613

larger body

larger bill

OCCURRENCE
Breeds in wet shrubby thickets with no canopy, often along streams and lakes; Pacific slope birds use more varied habitats, including moist forests. Widespread in forests south of tundra, from Newfoundland, the Great Lakes, and northern New England; British Columbia to California and New Mexico.

| Length **4¾in (12cm)** | Wingspan **7in (17.5cm)** | Weight **⁷⁄₃₂–⁵⁄₁₆oz (6–9g)** |
| Social **Flocks** | Lifespan **Up to 6 years** | Status **Declining** |

| Order **Passeriformes** | Family **Parulidae** | Species ***Wilsonia canadensis*** |

Canada Warbler

paler crown
bicolored eye-ring
faint necklace
FEMALE

plain gray tail
MALE
white undertail feathers
IN FLIGHT

yellow patch between eye and bill
dark crown
conspicuous yellow eye-ring
plain gray upperparts
yellow throat
black "necklace" across breast
yellow belly
MALE

One of the last species of wood-warblers to arrive in the US and Canada in the spring, and among the first to leave in the fall, the Canada Warbler is sometimes called the "Necklaced Warbler," for the conspicuous black markings on its chest. This uncommon bird is sadly declining, probably because of the maturation and draining of its preferred breeding habitat, consisting of old mixed hardwood forests with moist undergrowth.

VOICE Call a thick *tchip;* flight call a variable, clear *plip;* song a haphazard jumble of sweet notes, often beginning with or interspersed with *tchip,* followed by a pause.
NESTING Concealed cup of leaves, in moss or grass, on or near ground; 4–5 eggs; 1 brood; May–June.
FEEDING Gleans at mid-levels for many species of insects; also flycatches and forages on ground.

FLIGHT: fast, slightly undulating, and direct with rapid wing beats.

TAKING FLIGHT
This species often waits for prey to fly by, before launching into flight to pursue it.

FAMILIAR MEAL
Flying insects, including crane flies, make up the bulk of the Canada Warbler's diet.

SIMILAR SPECIES

MAGNOLIA WARBLER ♀ see p.584
white eyebrow
streaked flanks
KIRTLAND'S WARBLER ♂ see p.598
streaked mantle and flanks

OCCURRENCE
Breeds in moist deciduous, mixed, and coniferous forests with well-developed understory, especially swampy woods; migrants use well-vegetated habitats; winters in dense, wet thickets and a variety of tropical woodlands in South America.

| Length **5in (13cm)** | Wingspan **8in (20cm)** | Weight **⁹⁄₃₂–½oz (8–15g)** |
| Social **Flocks** | Lifespan **Up to 8 years** | Status **Declining** |

| Order **Passeriformes** | Family **Parulidae** | Species *Cardellina rubrifrons* |

Red-faced Warbler

mostly gray upperparts

white rump

MALE

IN FLIGHT

black helmet

white nape

red eye-ring

red face

gray upperparts

red throat

whitish underparts

ADULT

This dazzling bird, with its glowing red head, ornamented with a black helmet and a white nape, is a favorite with birdwatchers visiting the mountains of the southwestern US. Its closest relatives aren't clearly known and, at present, the Red-faced warbler, whose plumage is unlike any other species in its range, has its own genus, *Cardellina*. It may, however, be related to two very differently colored species of the genus *Wilsonia*, the Hooded and Wilson's Warblers.

VOICE Call a sharp *chik*; song a variable, sweet warble; often has emphatic ending: *swee-wee-wee tuh-wee-wee-wee WEE-chee-chew*.

NESTING Cup on ground hidden at base of rocks or logs; 3–4 eggs; 1 brood; May–June.

FEEDING Mostly gleans insects, such as caterpillars, usually from branches or from needles of conifer trees; also catches insects in flight.

FLIGHT: fast, slightly undulating, and direct with rapid wing beats.

FULL FRONTAL
The red face of this species is quite impressive head-on.

HIGH-ELEVATION SONGSTER
This warbler's song is a characteristic sound of the high mountains in Arizona and New Mexico.

SIMILAR SPECIES

MOUNTAIN CHICKADEE
see p.476

white cheek

white eye-line

black throat

MEXICAN CHICKADEE
see p.477

white cheek

black throat

OCCURRENCE
Breeds in Arizona, New Mexico, and Mexico, in high-elevation fir, pine, and pine-oak forests. Winters in mountain pine and pine-oak forests from Mexico, southward to Central America (Honduras).

| Length **5½in (14cm)** | Wingspan **8½in (21cm)** | Weight **⁹⁄₃₂–³⁄₈oz (8–11g)** |
| Social **Solitary/Winter flocks** | Lifespan **Unknown** | Status **Declining** |

Order **Passeriformes**	Family **Parulidae**	Species ***Myioborus pictus***

Painted Redstart

MALE

blackish underwings

conspicuous white crescent below eye

slight crest to black head

black bill

ADULT

white wing patch

geranium red belly

white side to tail

IN FLIGHT

black-edged undertail feathers

blackish legs and feet

The easily identified Painted Redstart is a fairly common sight in shaded pine-oak woodlands along canyons of Arizona, New Mexico, and western Texas. Its habit of constantly flicking open its wings and tail to show off its brilliant white patches has been interpreted as behavior meant to flush out its insect prey. There are 10 other species of the genus *Myioborus* living in Mexico, and Central and South America. All but one have yellow, not red, underparts and, for some reason, ornithologists have chosen to give these tropical species the English name "Whitestart," instead of the more obvious "Yellowstart." Juvenile Painted Redstarts have no red coloration but are, instead, a sooty gray color overall.

VOICE Call a distinctive, downslurred, bisyllabic *TSHEE-ew*; song a rich, whistled series of paired notes, at times with emphatic ending: *wee-dee wee-dee wee-dee chichi-chichi-tyew*.

NESTING Concealed cup on ground on steep hillside; 3–5 eggs; 1 brood; April–July.

FEEDING Gleans and flycatches insects such as beetles and moths.

SWEET SONG
This species emits a distinctive melodic song. Males and females sometimes perform duets.

FLIGHT: fast, slightly undulating, and direct with rapid wing beats.

TRICOLOR BIRD
When seen from below, the Painted Redstart shows three colors: white, red, and black.

OCCURRENCE
Found in mountain oak, pine-oak forest, and woodlands in canyons at high elevations in southwestern US; in similar habitats from Mexico to Nicaragua. A partial migrant, it winters south of its breeding range.

Length **5¾in (14.5cm)**	Wingspan **8½in (22cm)**	Weight **⁷⁄₃₂–⁵⁄₁₆oz (6–9g)**
Social **Solitary/Winter flocks**	Lifespan **Up to 7 years**	Status **Secure**

| Order **Passeriformes** | Family **Parulidae** | Species *Icteria virens* |

Yellow-breasted Chat

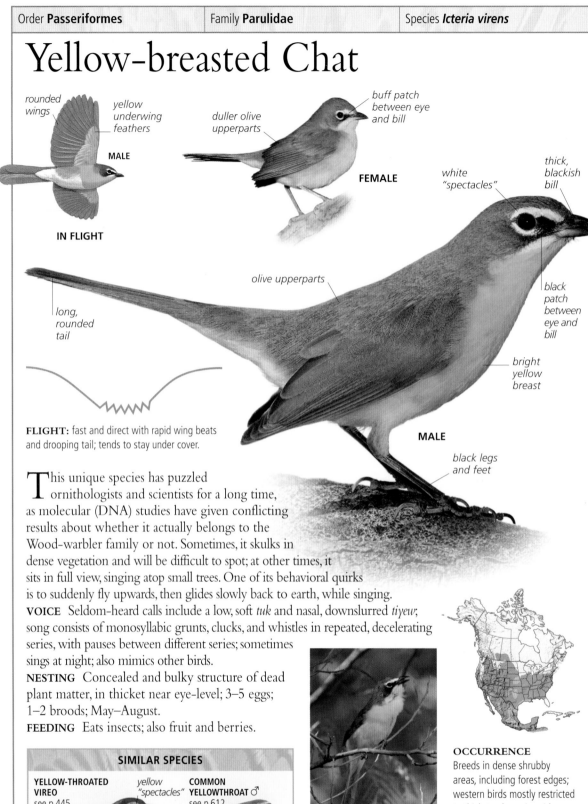

rounded wings

yellow underwing feathers

MALE

IN FLIGHT

duller olive upperparts

buff patch between eye and bill

FEMALE

white "spectacles"

thick, blackish bill

black patch between eye and bill

olive upperparts

long, rounded tail

bright yellow breast

MALE

black legs and feet

FLIGHT: fast and direct with rapid wing beats and drooping tail; tends to stay under cover.

This unique species has puzzled ornithologists and scientists for a long time, as molecular (DNA) studies have given conflicting results about whether it actually belongs to the Wood-warbler family or not. Sometimes, it skulks in dense vegetation and will be difficult to spot; at other times, it sits in full view, singing atop small trees. One of its behavioral quirks is to suddenly fly upwards, then glides slowly back to earth, while singing.

VOICE Seldom-heard calls include a low, soft *tuk* and nasal, downslurred *tiyew*; song consists of monosyllabic grunts, clucks, and whistles in repeated, decelerating series, with pauses between different series; sometimes sings at night; also mimics other birds.

NESTING Concealed and bulky structure of dead plant matter, in thicket near eye-level; 3–5 eggs; 1–2 broods; May–August.

FEEDING Eats insects; also fruit and berries.

SIMILAR SPECIES

YELLOW-THROATED VIREO
see p.445

yellow "spectacles"

COMMON YELLOWTHROAT ♂
see p.612

shorter tail

black mask

CLUCKS AND WHISTLES
This bird has a remarkably varied vocal repertoire, including loud clucks and whistles.

OCCURRENCE
Breeds in dense shrubby areas, including forest edges; western birds mostly restricted to thickets along riverside corridors; migrants found in varied habitats. Winters in scrubby habitats from Mexico to Panama.

| Length **7½ in (19cm)** | Wingspan **9½ in (24cm)** | Weight **¹¹⁄₁₆–1¹⁄₁₆ oz (20–30g)** |
| Social **Solitary** | Lifespan **Up to 9 years** | Status **Declining** |

Family **Icteridae**

ORIOLES & BLACKBIRDS

THE ICTERIDS exemplify the wonderful diversity that exists among birds. Its members are common and widespread, occurring from coast to coast in nearly every habitat in North America. The species reveal extremes of color, nesting, and social behavior—from the vibrant, solitary orioles to the vast nesting colonies of comparatively drab blackbirds.

ORIOLES

Generally recognized by their contrasting black and orange plumage, although some species tend more toward yellow or chestnut shades, Orioles are common tropical to subtropical seasonal migrants to North America. Their intricate hanging nests are an impressive combination of engineering and weaving. Most species boast a melodious song and tolerance for humans, a combination that makes them popular throughout their range.

COWBIRDS

These strictly parasitic birds have been known to lay eggs in the nests of close to 300 different species in North and South America. All three species found in North America are readily identified by their thick bill and dark, iridescent plumage.

NECTAR LOVER
The magnificently colored Baltimore Oriole inserts its bill into the base of a flower, taking the nectar, but playing no part in pollination.

BLACKBIRDS

As their name suggests, this group of birds is largely covered in dark feathers, and their long, pointed bills and tails add to their streamlined appearance. Not as brilliantly colored as some other Icterids, these are among the most numerous birds on the continent after the breeding season, and form an impressive sight during migration.

SUBTLE BRILLIANCE
Although its plumage is dark, the Common Grackle displays a beautiful iridescence.

MEADOWLARKS

There are just two species in this group, the Eastern and Western Meadowlark, but they are nevertheless distinctive (although difficult to tell apart). Birds of open country, both species have a characteristic bright-yellow chest with a black bib and a sweet singing voice.

BIG VOICE
A Meadowlark's melodious voice is a defining feature in many rural landscapes.

| Order **Passeriformes** | Family **Icteridae** | Species *Icterus spurius* |

Orchard Oriole

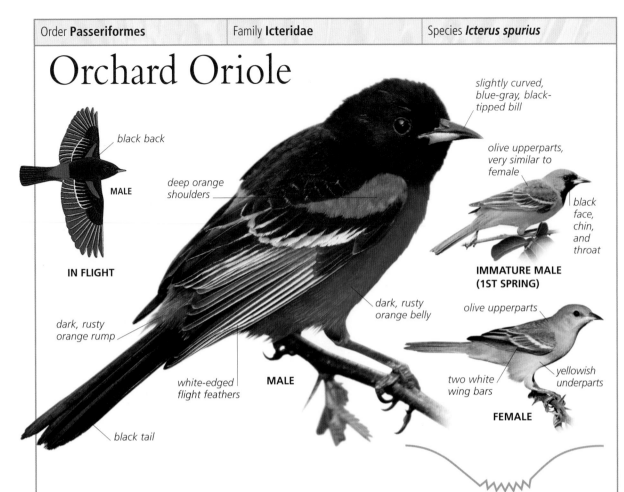

black back

MALE

IN FLIGHT

deep orange shoulders

dark, rusty orange rump

white-edged flight feathers

MALE

black tail

slightly curved, blue-gray, black-tipped bill

olive upperparts, very similar to female

black face, chin, and throat

IMMATURE MALE (1ST SPRING)

dark, rusty orange belly

olive upperparts

two white wing bars

yellowish underparts

FEMALE

A small bird, the Orchard Oriole resembles a large warbler in size, color, and the way it flits among leaves while foraging for insects. It flutters its tail, unlike other orioles. It spends less time on the breeding grounds than other migrant orioles, often arriving there as late as mid-May and leaving as early as late-July. The Orchard Oriole tolerates humans and can be found breeding in suburban parks and gardens. In recent years, its numbers have increased in the eastern part of its range.
VOICE Fast, not very melodious, series of high warbling notes mixed with occasional shorter notes ending in slurred *shheere*.
NESTING Woven nest of grass suspended in fork between branches; 4–5 eggs; 1 brood; April–July.
FEEDING Mainly eats insects during breeding season, but will also feed on seeds, fruit, and occasionally, nectar; in winter, mostly fruit and nectar, and some insects.

FLIGHT: quite bouncy flight due to shallow, quick wing beats; interrupted by glides.

RUSTY ORANGE SPLASH
The male Orchard Oriole has distinctive black upperparts and dark, rusty orange underparts.

SIMILAR SPECIES

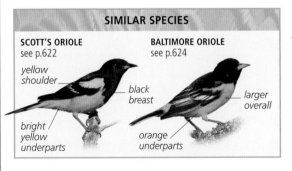

SCOTT'S ORIOLE see p.622
yellow shoulder
bright yellow underparts

BALTIMORE ORIOLE see p.624
black breast
larger overall
orange underparts

OCCURRENCE
Breeds in the eastern US, in open forest and woodland edges with a mixture of evergreen and deciduous trees, especially along river bottoms and in shelter belts surrounding agricultural land. Winters in Mexico, Central America, and South America.

| Length **7–8in (18–20cm)** | Wingspan **9in (23cm)** | Weight **11/16oz (20g)** |
| Social **Pairs** | Lifespan **Up to 9 years** | Status **Secure** |

| Order **Passeriformes** | Family **Icteridae** | Species *Icterus cucullatus* |

Hooded Oriole

two white wing bars

MALE (BREEDING)

greenish yellow head

brownish gray wings and back

IMMATURE MALE

IN FLIGHT

golden-orange head

black face and bib

white wing bar

long, slightly curved black bill

MALE (BREEDING)

long, black tail

golden-orange underparts

blackish back

MALE (NONBREEDING)

conspicuous white wing bars

pale yellow-green head

slightly curved, blue-gray bill

greenish gray upperparts

yellow-green underparts

FEMALE

FLIGHT: deep, strong wing beats enabling deceptively powerful flight.

The tall palm trees in suburban and urban landscapes, especially in California, have become popular nesting sites for the Hooded Oriole—called by some birders the "Palm-leaf Oriole." The increasing number of palm trees combined with the offerings of nectar intended for hummingbirds has led to the expansion of its range in California and the southwestern US. By contrast, its numbers in Texas have been shrinking, in part because of its susceptibility to brood parasitism by Brown-headed and Bronzed Cowbirds.

VOICE A harsh *weeek* call; song a weakly whined and rapid series of whistles where notes often run together; imitates other birds.

NESTING Hanging basket of coarse plant fibers, usually suspended from leaves or branches; 3–5 eggs; 1–2 broods; April–July.

FEEDING Feeds on insects; hangs upside down to reach them under leaves; also feeds on nectar from flowers and at feeders.

FULLY ALERT
On the alert, this male flashes its bright orange and black plumage.

SIMILAR SPECIES

BULLOCK'S ORIOLE see p.625

black eye-stripe

more white on wings

ALTAMIRA ORIOLE see p.626

thicker bill

OCCURRENCE
Breeds in Mexico, Belize, California and southwestern US, and also in southern Texas. Habitats are open forests along water courses, especially those containing palm trees; increasingly lives in suburban parks and backyards; in Texas in mesquite woodlands. Winters in Mexico.

| Length **7–8in (18–20cm)** | Wingspan **9–11in (23–28cm)** | Weight **⅞oz (25g)** |
| Social **Pairs** | Lifespan **Unknown** | Status **Secure** |

Order **Passeriformes**	Family **Icteridae**	Species *Icterus parisorum*

Scott's Oriole

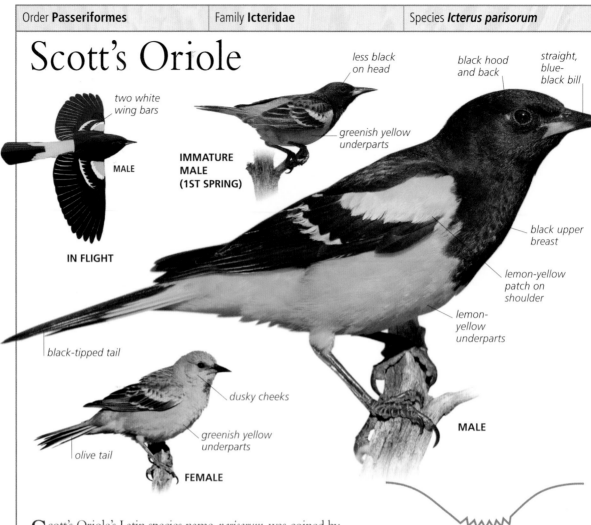

two white wing bars

MALE

IN FLIGHT

less black on head

greenish yellow underparts

IMMATURE MALE (1ST SPRING)

black hood and back

straight, blue-black bill

black upper breast

lemon-yellow patch on shoulder

lemon-yellow underparts

MALE

black-tipped tail

dusky cheeks

greenish yellow underparts

olive tail

FEMALE

Scott's Oriole's Latin species name, *parisorum*, was coined by Prince Charles Bonaparte in 1838 for the Paris brothers, two French natural history specimen dealers. The bird's English name honors General Winfield Scott, commander-in-chief of the American troops in the Mexican War. This Oriole's bright yellow plumage is unusual among North American orioles, most of which are varying degrees of orange. It lives in semiarid and rocky slopes, a fact that is largely responsible for its colloquial names of "Desert" or "Mountain" Oriole.

VOICE Call a sharp *chek*; song a musical series of whistles *tew-tew-treew*.
NESTING Shallow cup woven from thin plant strips, often yucca, hung from leaves or branches; 3–5 eggs; 1–2 broods; March–July.
FEEDING Eats insects, adults and larvae, such as flies, wasps, and beetles; feeds on nectar and fruit where available; visits feeders.

FLIGHT: quick wing beats; more bouncing between flapping than other orioles.

SIMILAR SPECIES

ORCHARD ORIOLE see p.620

smaller, darker head

chestnut-colored belly

AUDUBON'S ORIOLE see p.623

greenish yellow back

black hood

all-black tail

YUCCA LOVER
Found in all kinds of arid scrubland—yuccas are a favorite of Scott's Orioles.

OCCURRENCE
Breeds in mid-elevation, semiarid open scrub on level ground or slopes with oak scrub, pinion pine, and yucca. Winters in oak-pine scrub valleys of sub-tropical Mexico. Individuals wander widely and have been reported as far away from their usual habitat as New York City.

Length **8–9in (20–23cm)**	Wingspan **11–13in (28–33cm)**	Weight **1⁷⁄₁₆oz (40g)**
Social **Pairs/Family groups**	Lifespan **Up to 6 years**	Status **Secure**

| Order **Passeriformes** | Family **Icteridae** | Species *Icterus graduacauda* |

Audubon's Oriole

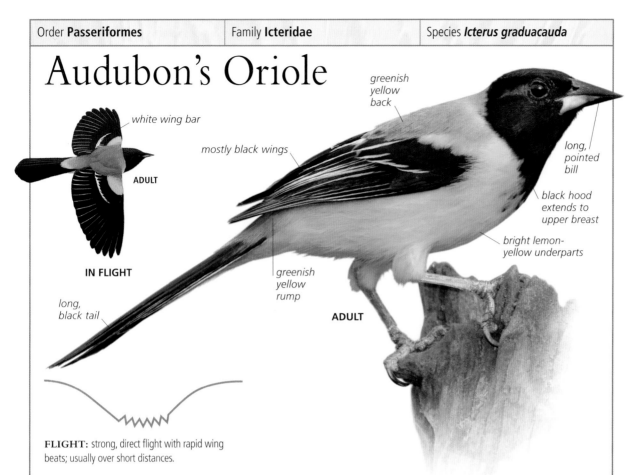

greenish yellow back

mostly black wings

long, pointed bill

black hood extends to upper breast

bright lemon-yellow underparts

greenish yellow rump

ADULT

white wing bar

ADULT

IN FLIGHT

long, black tail

FLIGHT: strong, direct flight with rapid wing beats; usually over short distances.

Because of its secretiveness and its occurrence in dense thickets, Audubon's Oriole remains a little-studied species, and accurate estimates of its population size in the US are few. It was thought to be declining, due to the expansion of agricultural land, which restricted its habitats along the Lower Rio Grande Valley in Texas. It has also suffered as a result of brood parasitism by the Bronzed Cowbird. However, in recent years, Audobon's Oriole has adapted to suburban parkland and is attracted to feeders, a development that may well stop any further declines in its population.

VOICE Low, slow whistle with slurred, broken notes, like a human learning how to whistle: *heoo-heeooo-heeeww*.
NESTING Small cup of woven grass and other plant matter, attached to branches; 3–5 eggs; 1 brood; April–July.
FEEDING Forages for insects, spiders, snails, and fruit; eats from birdfeeders.

BLACK HOOD
Audubon's Oriole is the only oriole with a black hood that does not extend to its back.

DULLER FEMALES
Both sexes share similar plumage, but females can be slightly duller.

OCCURRENCE
Confined to southeastern Texas in the US, but distributed more widely in Mexico, this oriole lives in woodlands, mesquite thickets, and pine-oak woodlands; also found in parks and gardens.

SIMILAR SPECIES

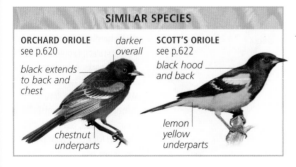

ORCHARD ORIOLE see p.620 · darker overall · black extends to back and chest · chestnut underparts

SCOTT'S ORIOLE see p.622 · black hood and back · lemon yellow underparts

| Length **9–10in (23–26cm)** | Wingspan **11–13in (28–33cm)** | Weight **1¹/₁₆–1³/₄oz (30–50g)** |
| Social **Solitary/Pairs** | Lifespan **Unknown** | Status **Declining** |

Order **Passeriformes**	Family **Icteridae**	Species **Molothrus bonariensis**

Shiny Cowbird

long, rounded wings

MALE (BREEDING)

IN FLIGHT

brown back, wings, and tail

light brown-gray eyebrow

glossy purplish black overall

pale brownish gray underparts

FEMALE (BREEDING)

dark eye

thin, pointed bill

MALE (BREEDING)

black toes and legs

black tail

Native to South America, the glossy purplish Shiny Cowbird has only recently expanded its range into Florida via the West Indies, where it was perhaps aided by introductions on some islands, such as Barbados. It is an active and aggressive brood parasite, laying it eggs in the nests of more than 200 different bird species, 80 of which raise the young as its own. The Shiny Cowbird nestlings grow quickly and leave the host's nest in less than two weeks. Its impact on native North American birds remains to be studied.

VOICE Low pitched rambling series of soft *purr-purr- purr*, interspersed with *tee-tsss-tseeee* running higher to slurred finish.

NESTING Brood parasite, lays eggs in the nests of other species; perhaps as many as 20–35 eggs per female; April–September.

FEEDING Omnivorous, eats seeds, snails, and many species of insects; catches insects flushed by livestock.

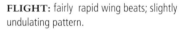

FLIGHT: fairly rapid wing beats; slightly undulating pattern.

EXPANDING RANGE
The range of the Shiny Cowbird is expanding and it can be found as far north as Canada.

OCCURRENCE
Found in open fields usually containing agricultural crops, in addition to scattered open forested areas; increasingly using rural and suburban developments such as parks, gardens, and backyards.

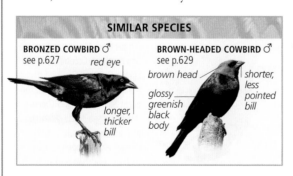

SIMILAR SPECIES

BRONZED COWBIRD ♂
see p.627

red eye

longer, thicker bill

BROWN-HEADED COWBIRD ♂
see p.629

brown head

shorter, less pointed bill

glossy greenish black body

Length **7in (18cm)**	Wingspan **10–12in (25–30cm)**	Weight **1¹⁄₁₆–1⁷⁄₁₆oz (30–40g)**
Social **Large flocks**	Lifespan **At least 5 years**	Status **Secure**

| Order **Passeriformes** | Family **Icteridae** | Species *Molothrus ater* |

Brown-headed Cowbird

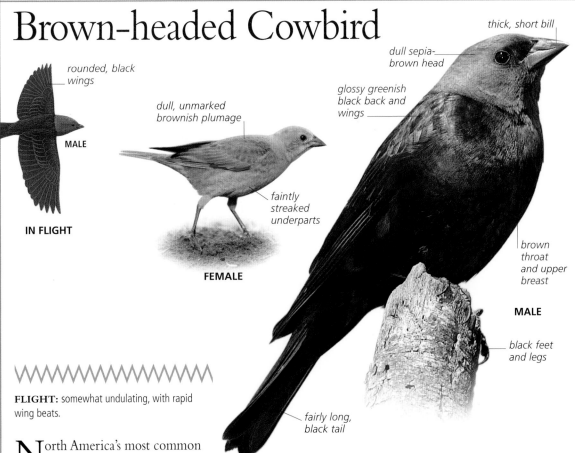

thick, short bill

dull sepia-brown head

glossy greenish black back and wings

rounded, black wings

MALE

IN FLIGHT

dull, unmarked brownish plumage

faintly streaked underparts

FEMALE

brown throat and upper breast

MALE

black feet and legs

fairly long, black tail

FLIGHT: somewhat undulating, with rapid wing beats.

North America's most common and best-known brood parasite, the Brown-headed Cowbird was once a bird of the Great Plains, following vast herds of bison to prey on insects kicked up by their hooves. Now, due to forest clearance and suburban development, it is found continent-wide. It has recently become a serious threat to North American songbirds, laying its eggs in the nests of more than 220 different species, and having its young raised to fledglings by more than 140 species, including the highly endangered Kirtland's Warbler.

VOICE High-pitched, squeaky whistles and bubbling notes, *dub-dub-come-tzeee*; also various clucks and *cheks*.

NESTING No nest, lays eggs in nests of other species; a single female may lay 25–55 (or more) eggs per season; April–August.

FEEDING Primarily eats grass seeds and cereal grains, but also insects when available, especially grasshoppers and beetles.

AT A FEEDER
A female Brown-headed Cowbird enjoys a snack of seeds at a suburban feeder.

OCCURRENCE
Favors habitats modified by human activity, such as open wooded patches, low grass fields, fruit orchards, agricultural pastures with livestock, and gardens and residential areas. Widespread across North America.

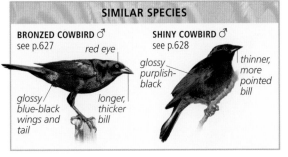

SIMILAR SPECIES

BRONZED COWBIRD ♂ see p.627
red eye
glossy blue-black wings and tail
longer, thicker bill

SHINY COWBIRD ♂ see p.628
glossy purplish-black
thinner, more pointed bill

| Length **6–8in (15–20cm)** | Wingspan **11–13in (28–33cm)** | Weight **1⁷⁄₁₆–1¾oz (40–50g)** |
| Social **Large flocks** | Lifespan **Up to 16 years** | Status **Secure** |

| Order **Passeriformes** | Family **Icteridae** | Species *Agelaius phoeniceus* |

Red-winged Blackbird

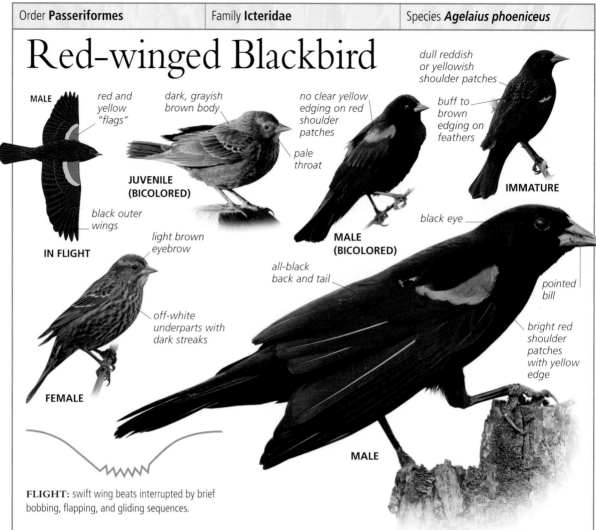

MALE
red and yellow "flags"

black outer wings

IN FLIGHT

dark, grayish brown body

JUVENILE (BICOLORED)

no clear yellow edging on red shoulder patches

pale throat

MALE (BICOLORED)

all-black back and tail

dull reddish or yellowish shoulder patches

buff to brown edging on feathers

IMMATURE

black eye

pointed bill

bright red shoulder patches with yellow edge

MALE

light brown eyebrow

off-white underparts with dark streaks

FEMALE

FLIGHT: swift wing beats interrupted by brief bobbing, flapping, and gliding sequences.

One of the most abundant native bird species in North America, the Red-winged Blackbird is also one of the most conspicuous in wetland habitats. The sight and sound of males singing from the tops of cattails is a sure sign that spring is near. This adaptable species migrates and roosts in flocks that may number in the millions. There are numerous subspecies, one of the most distinctive being the "Bicolored" Blackbird (*A. p. gubernator.*)

VOICE Various brusk *chek*, *chit*, or *chet* calls; male song a *kronk-a-rhee* with a characteristic nasal, rolling and metallic "undulating" ending.

NESTING Cup of grasses and mud woven into dense standing reeds or cattails; 3–4 eggs; 1–2 broods; March–June.

FEEDING Forages for seeds and grains; largely insects when breeding.

DENSE FLOCKS
The huge flocks of Red-winged Blackbirds seen in migration are quite an amazing sight.

SIMILAR SPECIES

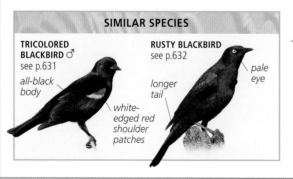

TRICOLORED BLACKBIRD ♂
see p.631

all-black body

white-edged red shoulder patches

RUSTY BLACKBIRD
see p.632

longer tail

pale eye

OCCURRENCE
Widespread across Canada and the US from Alaska to the Maritimes, and south to Mexico, Central America, and the Bahamas. Lives in wetlands, especially freshwater marshes but also saltwater; wet meadows with tall grass cover and open woodlands with reedy vegetation.

| Length **7–10in (18–25cm)** | Wingspan **11–14in (28–35cm)** | Weight **1⁹/₁₆–2½oz (45–70g)** |
| Social **Flocks** | Lifespan **At least 14 years** | Status **Secure** |

| Order **Passeriformes** | Family **Icteridae** | Species *Agelaius tricolor* |

Tricolored Blackbird

red and white "flags"

MALE

roundish wings

IN FLIGHT

black head

black pointed, bill

all-black body

dark red shoulders edged with white

dark underparts with whitish streaks

dark grayish brown back

MALE

FEMALE

square, black tail

black underparts

FLIGHT: swift, strong with up and down motion; alternate flapping and gliding.

Unlike its abundant and widespread close relative, the Red-winged Blackbird, the Tricolored Blackbird occurs primarily in California. It nests in large, densely packed colonies, sometimes numbering in excess of 100,000 pairs, which effectively protects them against predators and ensures that the young birds survive. However, this highly sociable breeding habit often causes problems when crops are harvested, as it deprives the birds of insects residing among the agricultural crops. The evolution of the Red-winged and Tricolored Blackbirds from a common ancestor is currently being studied through DNA analysis.

VOICE Both sexes call a *chip*, *chuk*, and *chu-aah* when alarmed; male song a grave, nasal *kera-oooow* or *kerrrraaaa*.

NESTING Small cup of plant strips and mud woven into dense standing vegetation; 3–4 eggs; 2 broods; March–July.

FEEDING Eats seasonally abundant insects, including grasshoppers, but also relies on cultivated grains in winter.

DISPLAYING MALE
Perched on a stick, a male advertises its small territory by singing and displaying his colors.

OCCURRENCE
Found in western California, northward to Washington State and southward to Baja California. In its restricted range, found in cattail marshes but exploits a variety of human altered upland and wetland habitats; after breeding moves outside nesting habitats, especially to agricultural land.

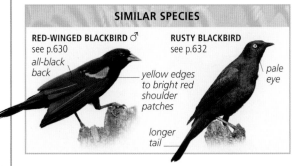

SIMILAR SPECIES

RED-WINGED BLACKBIRD ♂
see p.630
all-black back

yellow edges to bright red shoulder patches

RUSTY BLACKBIRD
see p.632
pale eye

longer tail

| Length **7–9½in (18–24cm)** | Wingspan **10–13in (26–33cm)** | Weight **1⁷⁄₁₆–2½oz (40–70g)** |
| Social **Flocks/Colonies** | Lifespan **At least 13 years** | Status **Secure** |

| Order **Passeriformes** | Family **Icteridae** | Species *Euphagus carolinus* |

Rusty Blackbird

MALE (BREEDING)

long tail

short, narrow bill

IN FLIGHT

pale eyebrow

rusty brown edging to feathers

MALE (FALL)

rusty brown crown

black "mask" between eye and bill

FEMALE (FALL)

gray-brown eyebrow

pale gray to rusty brown underparts

green sheen on head

pale whitish or yellow eye

black overall, with blue-green to greenish sheen

MALE (BREEDING)

FLIGHT: strong, direct, with slight undulations between flapping and brief gliding.

The Rusty Blackbird is perhaps the least studied of all North American blackbirds. This is mainly because it breeds in remote, inaccessible swampy areas, and is much less of a pest to agricultural operations than some of the other members of its family. Unlike most other blackbirds, the plumage on the male Rusty Blackbird changes to a dull, reddish brown during the fall—giving the species its common name. It is also during the fall migrations that this species is most easily observed, moving south in long, wide flocks that often take several minutes to pass overhead.

VOICE Both sexes use *chuk* call during migration flights; male song a musical *too-ta-lee*.

NESTING Small bowl of branches and sticks, lined with wet plants and dry grass, usually near water; 3–5 eggs; 1 brood; May–July.

FEEDING Eats seasonally available insects, spiders, grains, seeds of trees, and fleshy fruits or berries.

OPEN WIDE
Seldom seen, the male's courtship display includes gaping and tail-spreading.

OCCURRENCE
Breeds in moist to wet forests up to the timberline in the far north (farther north than any other species of North American blackbird); winters in eastern US, in various swampy forests.

SIMILAR SPECIES

BREWER'S BLACKBIRD
see p.633

purplish sheen on head

longer tail

COMMON GRACKLE
see p.634

bill thicker at base

large tail

bluish sheen on head

glossy bronze body

| Length **8–10in (20–25cm)** | Wingspan **12–15in (30–38cm)** | Weight **1⁹⁄₁₆–2⁷⁄₈oz (45–80g)** |
| Social **Pairs/Winter flocks** | Lifespan **At least 9 years** | Status **Secure** |

Order **Passeriformes**	Family **Icteridae**	Species *Euphagus cyanocephalus*

Brewer's Blackbird

purplish sheen on head

yellow eyes

black body with greenish blue sheen

brown eyes

gray brown overall

stout bill

MALE

FEMALE

long, dark tail

IN FLIGHT

MALE

black legs and feet

FLIGHT: several wing beats followed by short glides with shallow rise and fall pattern.

The Brewer's Blackbird, unlike the swamp-loving Rusty Blackbird, seems to prefer areas disturbed by humans to natural ones throughout much of its range. It is likely that the relatively recent eastward range expansion of Brewer's Blackbird has been aided by changes in land practices. Interestingly, when the Brewer's Blackbird range overlaps with that of the Common Grackle, it wins out in rural areas, but loses out in urban areas. This species can be found feasting on waste grains left behind after the harvest.

VOICE Buzzy *tshrrep* song ascending in tone.

NESTING Bulky cup of dry grass, stem and twig framework lined with soft grasses and animal hair; 3–6 eggs; 1–2 broods; April–July.

FEEDING Forages on the ground for many species of insects during breeding season, also snails; seeds, grain, and occasional fruit in fall and winter.

BROWN-EYED BIRD
Brown eyes distinguish the female Brewer's from the yellow-eyed, female Rusty Blackbird.

OCCURRENCE
Breeds and winters in open areas, readily adapting to, and preferring, disturbed areas and human developments such as parks, gardens, clear-felled forests, and fallow fields edged with dense trees or shrubs.

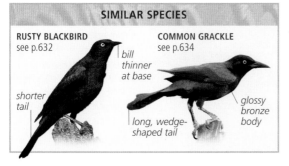

SIMILAR SPECIES

RUSTY BLACKBIRD
see p.632

shorter tail

bill thinner at base

COMMON GRACKLE
see p.634

glossy bronze body

long, wedge-shaped tail

Length **10–12in (25–30cm)**	Wingspan **13–16in (33–41cm)**	Weight **1¾–2½oz (50–70g)**
Social **Flocks/Colonies**	Lifespan **Up to 13 years**	Status **Secure**

Order **Passeriformes**	Family **Icteridae**	Species *Quiscalas quiscala*

Common Grackle

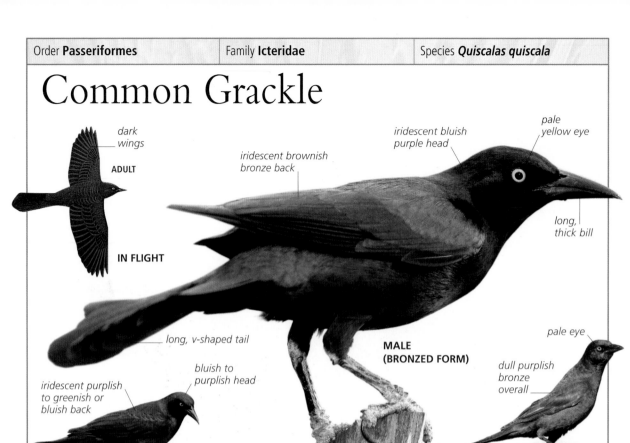

dark wings

ADULT

IN FLIGHT

iridescent bluish purple head

pale yellow eye

iridescent brownish bronze back

long, thick bill

long, v-shaped tail

MALE (BRONZED FORM)

bluish to purplish head

iridescent purplish to greenish or bluish back

MALE (PURPLE FORM)

pale eye

dull purplish bronze overall

FEMALE

This adaptable species has expanded its range rapidly in the recent past, thanks to human land clearing practices. The Common Grackle is so well suited to urban and suburban habitats that it successfully excludes other species from them. During migration and winter, Common Grackles form immense flocks, some of which may be made up of more than 1 million individuals. This tendency, combined with its preference for cultivated areas, has made this species an agricultural pest in some regions.

VOICE Call a low, harsh *chek*; loud song series of odd squeaks and whistles.

NESTING Small bowl in trees, with a frame of sticks filled with mud and grasses; 4–6 eggs; 1–2 broods; April–July.

FEEDING Eats beetles, flies, spiders, and worms, as well as small vertebrates; also seeds and grain, especially in nonbreeding season; an omnivore.

FLIGHT: straight, level, and direct without the up and down undulation of blackbird species.

SIMILAR SPECIES

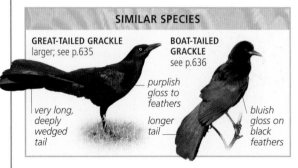

GREAT-TAILED GRACKLE
larger; see p.635

BOAT-TAILED GRACKLE
see p.636

very long, deeply wedged tail

purplish gloss to feathers

longer tail

bluish gloss on black feathers

HIGHLY ADAPTABLE
This grackle is comfortable near human developments, resulting in the expansion of its range.

OCCURRENCE
The Common Grackle lives in a wide variety of open woodlands, suburban woodlots, city parks, gardens, and hedgerows. It is absent west of the Great Plains. Wintering range extends south to the Gulf Coast.

Length **11–13½in (28–34cm)**	Wingspan **15–18in (38–46cm)**	Weight **3⅛–4oz (90–125g)**
Social **Flocks**	Lifespan **Up to 20 years**	Status **Secure**

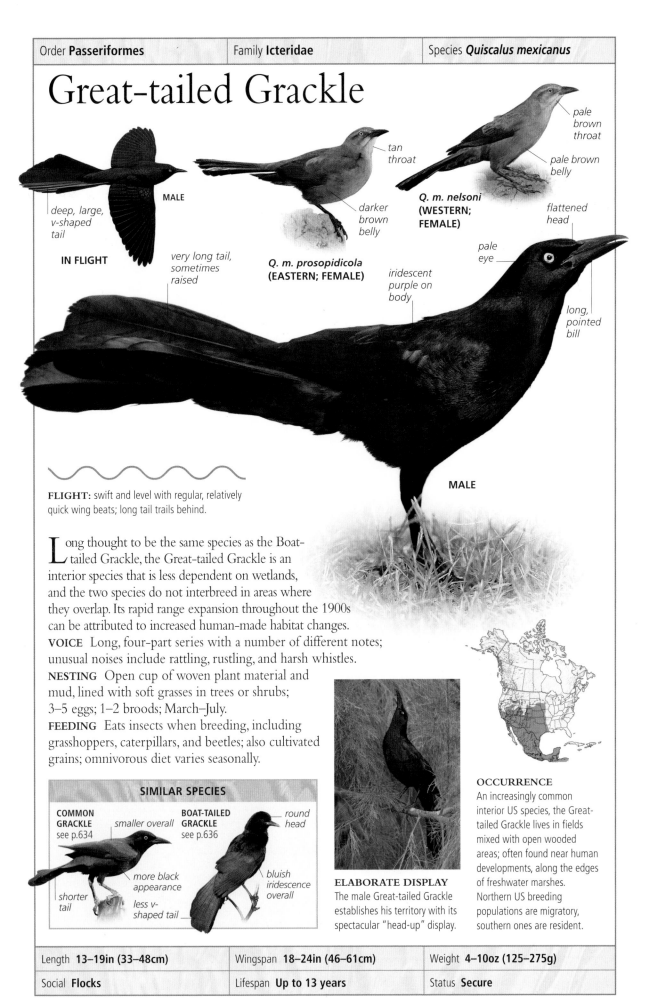

| Order **Passeriformes** | Family **Icteridae** | Species *Quiscalus mexicanus* |

Great-tailed Grackle

MALE

deep, large, v-shaped tail

IN FLIGHT

very long tail, sometimes raised

tan throat

darker brown belly

Q. m. prosopidicola (EASTERN; FEMALE)

pale brown throat

pale brown belly

Q. m. nelsoni (WESTERN; FEMALE)

flattened head

pale eye

iridescent purple on body

long, pointed bill

MALE

FLIGHT: swift and level with regular, relatively quick wing beats; long tail trails behind.

Long thought to be the same species as the Boat-tailed Grackle, the Great-tailed Grackle is an interior species that is less dependent on wetlands, and the two species do not interbreed in areas where they overlap. Its rapid range expansion throughout the 1900s can be attributed to increased human-made habitat changes.

VOICE Long, four-part series with a number of different notes; unusual noises include rattling, rustling, and harsh whistles.

NESTING Open cup of woven plant material and mud, lined with soft grasses in trees or shrubs; 3–5 eggs; 1–2 broods; March–July.

FEEDING Eats insects when breeding, including grasshoppers, caterpillars, and beetles; also cultivated grains; omnivorous diet varies seasonally.

SIMILAR SPECIES

COMMON GRACKLE see p.634 — smaller overall — more black appearance — shorter tail — less v-shaped tail

BOAT-TAILED GRACKLE see p.636 — round head — bluish iridescence overall

ELABORATE DISPLAY The male Great-tailed Grackle establishes his territory with its spectacular "head-up" display.

OCCURRENCE An increasingly common interior US species, the Great-tailed Grackle lives in fields mixed with open wooded areas; often found near human developments, along the edges of freshwater marshes. Northern US breeding populations are migratory, southern ones are resident.

| Length **13–19in (33–48cm)** | Wingspan **18–24in (46–61cm)** | Weight **4–10oz (125–275g)** |
| Social **Flocks** | Lifespan **Up to 13 years** | Status **Secure** |

| Order **Passeriformes** | Family **Icteridae** | Species *Quiscalus major* |

Boat-tailed Grackle

ADULT

long, black bill

long, spread out, wedge-shaped tail

IN FLIGHT

tawny cinnamon eyebrow

dark brown upperparts

much smaller overall

FEMALE

black wings

round head

brown or yellow eyes

glossy blue-black overall

MALE

black legs and feet

very long tail, often spread out

FLIGHT: swift wing beats with occasional glides, maintaining same level; no undulating pattern.

So similar is the Boat-tailed Grackle to the Great-tailed Grackle that the two birds were once thought to be the same species. The Boat-tailed Grackle is a bird of coastal marshes, but it readily scavenges in nearby human settlements. In spring, females form large nesting colonies. These attract many males, but only the most dominant males succeed in mating.

VOICE Long, loud, three-part series of high pitched notes, *chreeet chreeet*, followed by low growl, and finally by *shreet shreet*.

NESTING Rough cups of grass and mud, woven into standing marsh vegetation like cattails or branches of shubs or trees; 2–5 eggs; 1–2 broods; March–June.

FEEDING Highly varied diet includes insects, crayfish, clams, seeds, fruit, fish, frogs, lizards, nestling birds; also human refuse.

PLAIN BROWN
Unlike the glossy blue-black males, females are brown, with darker wings and tail.

OCCURRENCE
Breeds along the Gulf and Atlantic coasts of the US, and Florida; resident in tidal areas of coastal marshes and their neighboring upland components; also urban and suburban, human-altered habitats. Roosts colonially in same areas in winter.

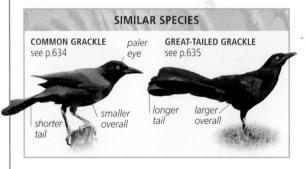

SIMILAR SPECIES

COMMON GRACKLE see p.634

paler eye

shorter tail

smaller overall

GREAT-TAILED GRACKLE see p.635

longer tail

larger overall

| Length **13–18in (33–46cm)** | Wingspan **16–24in (41–61cm)** | Weight **3½–8½oz (100–240g)** |
| Social **Loose colonies/Winter flocks** | Lifespan **Up to 12 years** | Status **Localized** |

| Order **Passeriformes** | Family **Icteridae** | Species **Sturnella magna** |

Eastern Meadowlark

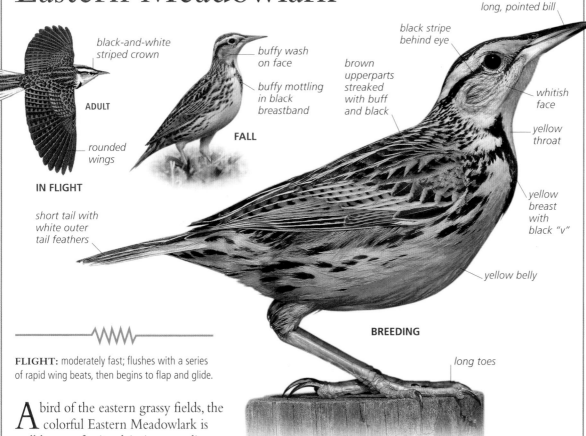

IN FLIGHT

black-and-white striped crown

ADULT

rounded wings

short tail with white outer tail feathers

buffy wash on face

buffy mottling in black breastband

FALL

long, pointed bill

black stripe behind eye

brown upperparts streaked with buff and black

whitish face

yellow throat

yellow breast with black "v"

yellow belly

BREEDING

long toes

FLIGHT: moderately fast; flushes with a series of rapid wing beats, then begins to flap and glide.

A bird of the eastern grassy fields, the colorful Eastern Meadowlark is well known for its plaintive sounding song. During courtship, the male sings enthusiastically from the highest available perch. This species overlaps with the very similar looking Western Meadowlark in the western Great Plains, but is the only meadowlark further west. Where they overlap, these birds are most easily distinguished by their different calls and songs. Throughout its range, numbers of the Eastern Meadowlark have fallen due to human encroachment on its habitat, although in the last decade or so, the species has made a slow (and local) comeback.

VOICE Call a sharp *dzzeer*; song a series of clear, descending whistles consisting of 3–8 notes, *tseeeooou tseeeeou*.

NESTING Loosely woven, usually domed, cup of grasses and other plants, located on the ground in tall grass fields; 3–8 eggs; 1 brood; March–May.

FEEDING Forages on ground, mainly for insects, especially grasshoppers, but also caterpillars and grubs; seeds and grain in winter.

FAVORITE PERCH
Eastern Meadowlarks are partial to fenceposts as a favorite perch for singing.

OCCURRENCE
Breeds in native tallgrass openings, pastures, and overgrown roadsides. Widespread in eastern North America, from Quebec to New Mexico and Arizona; also in Mexico and Cuba, and locally in South America. Partial migrant in the US, resident in Mexico and South America.

SIMILAR SPECIES

AMERICAN PIPIT
see p.550

more slender, shorter bill

no yellow on chest

WESTERN MEADOWLARK
see p.638

slightly paler

more yellow at corner of bill

| Length **7–10in (18–25cm)** | Wingspan **13–15in (33–38cm)** | Weight **2⅛–4oz (60–125g)** |
| Social **Pairs/Winter flocks** | Lifespan **Up to 9 years** | Status **Declining** |

| Order **Passeriformes** | Family **Icteridae** | Species *Sturnella neglecta* |

Western Meadowlark

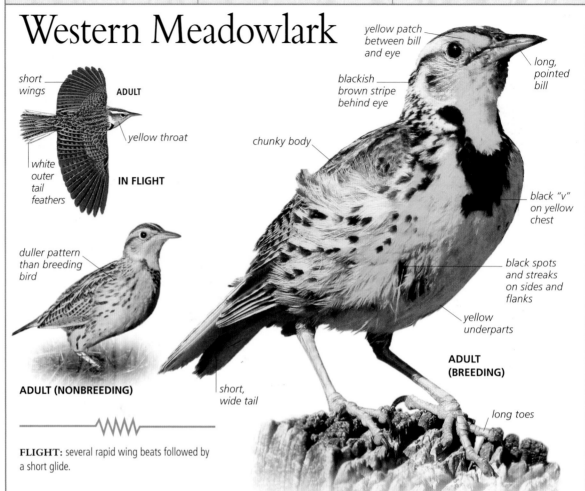

short wings

ADULT

yellow throat

white outer tail feathers

IN FLIGHT

yellow patch between bill and eye

blackish brown stripe behind eye

long, pointed bill

chunky body

black "v" on yellow chest

black spots and streaks on sides and flanks

yellow underparts

ADULT (BREEDING)

long toes

duller pattern than breeding bird

ADULT (NONBREEDING)

short, wide tail

FLIGHT: several rapid wing beats followed by a short glide.

A lthough the range of the Western Meadowlark overlaps widely with that of its Eastern counterpart, hybrids between the two species are very rare and usually sterile. The large numbers of Western Meadowlarks in the western Great Plains, the Great Basin, and the Central Valley of California, combined with the male's tendency to sing conspicuously from the tops of shrubs, when fence posts are not available, make this species attractive to birdwatchers. Where the two meadowlarks overlap they are best identified by their song.

VOICE Series of complex, bubbling, whistled notes descending in pitch.

NESTING Domed grass cup, well hidden in tall grasses; 3–7 eggs; 1 brood; March–August.

FEEDING Feeds mostly on insects, including beetles, grubs, and grasshoppers; also grains and grass seeds.

SIMILAR SPECIES

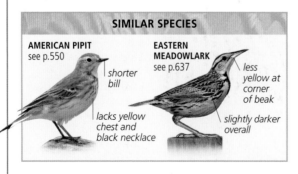

AMERICAN PIPIT see p.550

shorter bill

lacks yellow chest and black necklace

EASTERN MEADOWLARK see p.637

less yellow at corner of beak

slightly darker overall

A SHRUB WILL DO
With few fenceposts in the Western Meadowlark's habitat, it perches on a shrub to sing.

OCCURRENCE
Common in western North America, across much of southern Canada and the western US, south to Mexico. Breeds primarily in open grassy plains, but also uses agricultural fields with overgrown edges and hayfields. Partial migrant in US, winters south to Mexico.

| Length **7–10in (18–26cm)** | Wingspan **13–15in (33–38cm)** | Weight **2⅞–4oz (80–125g)** |
| Social **Pairs/Winter flocks** | Lifespan **Up to 10 years** | Status **Secure** |

| Order **Passeriformes** | Family **Icteridae** | Species *Xanthocephalus xanthocephalus* |

Yellow-headed Blackbird

MALE
yellow head

IN FLIGHT

conspicuous white wing patches

black, conical bill

black mask and crown on yellow head

JUVENILE MALE

bright yellow head and chest

black overall

white wing patch

MALE

long tail

FEMALE

brownish overall

yellowish throat and facial patch

FLIGHT: direct with shallow rise and fall pattern; flaps and glides.

The male Yellow-headed Blackbird is unmistakable, with its conspicuous bright yellow head. Females, however, are more drab. Populations of this species fluctuate widely, but locally, according to available rainfall, which controls the availability, and quality, of its breeding marshland habitat. In some wetlands, the Yellow-headed Blackbird can be extremely abundant, and is easily noticeable due to its amazing song.

VOICE Call a nasal *whaah*; song a series of harsh, cackling noises, followed by a brief pause, and a high, long, wailing trill.

NESTING Cup of plant strips woven into standing aquatic vegetation; 3–4 eggs; 1 brood; May–June.

FEEDING Eats insects while breeding; agricultural grains and grass seeds in winter.

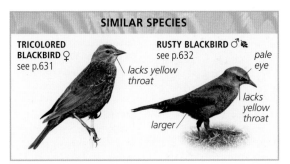

SIMILAR SPECIES

TRICOLORED BLACKBIRD ♀
see p.631
lacks yellow throat

RUSTY BLACKBIRD ♂
see p.632
pale eye
lacks yellow throat
larger

YELLOW GARLAND
Five evenly spaced yellow-headed males watch over their wetland habitat from a twig.

OCCURRENCE
Widely distributed in western Canada and the central and western US, this species breeds in marshes with cattail and bullrush vegetation, and also, locally, in wetlands within wooded areas. Winters in Mexico; resident in Baja California.

| Length **8½–10½in (21–27cm)** | Wingspan **15in (38cm)** | Weight **2⅛–3½oz (60–100g)** |
| Social **Flocks/Colonies** | Lifespan **Up to 9 years** | Status **Localized** |

| Order **Passeriformes** | Family **Icteridae** | Species *Dolichonyx oryzivorus* |

Bobolink

black wings

buff-colored hindneck

MALE (BREEDING)

IN FLIGHT

blackish brown crown

gold-buff overall

pinkish bill

central crown stripe

FEMALE (BREEDING)

sparrow-like markings

buffy throat

pointed tail feathers

ADULT (FALL)

white shoulder feathers

black face and crown

black underparts

white rump

black tail with pointed feathers

MALE (BREEDING)

FLIGHT: typically direct flight; series of rapid wing beats; glides of varying length.

The Bobolink is a common summer resident of open fallow fields through much of the northern US and southern Canada. In spring, the males perform a conspicuous circling or "helicoptering" display, which includes singing, to establish territory and to attract females. Bobolink populations have declined on its breeding grounds and in wintering areas because of habitat loss and changing agricultural practices.

VOICE Calls like the end of its name *link*; song a long, complex babbling series of musical notes varying in length and pitch.

NESTING Woven cup of grass close to or on the ground, well hidden in tall grass; 3–7 eggs; 1 brood; May–July.

FEEDING Feeds mostly on insects, spiders, grubs in breeding season, but seasonally variable; also cereal grains and grass seeds.

TAKING A BREAK
This male has fled the sun of the open fields to seek shelter in the shade of a tree.

SIMILAR SPECIES

RED-WINGED BLACKBIRD
see p.630

lacks buff-colored hindneck

red shoulder patches

larger overall

LARK BUNTING
see p.647

lacks buff-colored hindneck

larger

white wing patches

OCCURRENCE
Breeds in open fields with a mixture of tall grasses and other herbaceous vegetation, especially old hayfields. In Canada from British Columbia to the East Coast; in the US from Idaho to New England. Migrates through the southern US and the Caribbean; winters in northern South America.

| Length **6–8in (15–20cm)** | Wingspan **10–12in (25–30cm)** | Weight **1¹⁄₁₆–2oz (30–55g)** |
| Social **Winter flocks** | Lifespan **Up to 10 years** | Status **Declining** |

Family **Emberizidae**

AMERICAN SPARROWS

T HE EMBERIZIDS ARE A DIVERSE group, with an almost worldwide distribution; only Australasia and Antarctica are without them. In Europe, emberizids are called buntings. North American emberizids tend to be duller than their Eurasian relatives, with most in shades of brown. Early settlers in North America thought they resembled European sparrows, so most North American emberizids are

TYPICAL SPARROW
A White-crowned Sparrow shows the typical stout emberizid beak.

named as sparrows, despite having no close relationship with European sparrows, which are really weavers. Species of emberizids not called sparrows are the longspurs and the Snow Bunting, which are shared with Eurasia. All members of the family Emberizidae tend to forage on or near the ground. Their stout, conical bills are used for eating seeds. Most species of American sparrows show little difference between the sexes. While identifying sparrows can be daunting, clues such as habitat, behavior, voice, and body shape make the task easier.

BEST VIEW
Singing males, like this Chestnut-collared Longspur, are easily seen in summer.

Family **Thraupidae**

TANAGERS

T HE TANAGERS COMPRISE a large and diverse family of songbirds found only in the Western Hemisphere. Some are dull and feed on insects from the forest floor, others are rainbow-colored, fruit-eating, and dart through the high canopy. North American species of tanagers of the genus *Piranga*, have brightly colored males and dull, olive-colored females. They are relatively sluggish birds that feed mostly on insects such as bees, wasps, and fruit. While their songs are very similar, each species has a distinctive call.

MALE COLORS
Male Western Tanagers are some of North America's most colorful birds.

Family **Cardinalidae**

CARDINALS

V ISUALLY STUNNING AND VOCALLY conspicuous, male cardinalids are among best known birds in North America. The smaller members of the family are called buntings, but they are unrelated to the Eurasian buntings, members of the family Emberizidae. Cardinalidae range in color from the red and gray of the Pyrrhuloxia to the electric-blue Indigo Bunting and the multicolored Painted Bunting.

STRONG BILLS
Male Pyrrhuloxias have impressive bills, perfect for cutting open seeds hulls and nuts, and opening large fruits.

Order **Passeriformes**	Family **Emberizidae**	Species *Calcarius mccownii*

McCown's Longspur

MALE (BREEDING)
black "T" on white tail

IN FLIGHT

pale broad eyebrow

duller face markings

thick, pinkish bill

grayish brown breast

FEMALE (BREEDING)

pale gray head

large, pointed bill

conspicuous black breast patch

bright rufous shoulder

grayish, lightly barred underparts

MALE (BREEDING)

short tail

FLIGHT: deeply undulating, with birds often calling in troughs as they flap.

Confederate Major-General John Porter McCown discovered this bird while shooting at a flock of Horned Larks in Texas. It is a characteristic inhabitant of native, shortgrass prairies, and males can often be found performing their spectacular flight displays over this barren, windswept habitat. Flying high, these birds sing as they hover and float downward on wings held in a V position, similar to that of a Monarch butterfly. With their black chest patches and gray underparts, males look surprisingly dark against the pale sky. A dull female could be potentially confused with a female House Sparrow, but the former can be distinguished by the white patches on its tail. Recent genetic (DNA) evidence suggests that McCown's Longspur may actually be more closely related to the Snow Bunting than to the other species of longspurs.

VOICE Flight call a short, liquid *rit-up*; also an abrupt *poink* and metallic *tink*; song melodious; high-pitched tinklings in flight.

NESTING Cup of dried grass placed in depression on the ground, often against a clump of grass; 3–4 eggs; 1–2 broods; April–July.

FEEDING Eats insects while breeding; seeds in winter.

IN THE OPEN
This species favors open habitats such as heavily grazed fields and other areas with very short grass.

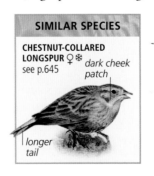

SIMILAR SPECIES

CHESTNUT-COLLARED LONGSPUR ♀ ❄
see p.645

dark cheek patch

longer tail

OCCURRENCE
Breeds in the shortgrass prairie of the the High Plains, from Alberta and Saskatchewan, southward to northwest Nebraska and northeast Colorado. Winters in grasslands and barren ground from southeast Colorado southward into Texas and westward into southeast Arizona.

Length **6in (15cm)**	Wingspan **10–11in (25–28cm)**	Weight **⅞–1¹⁄₁₆oz (25–30g)**
Social **Large flocks**	Lifespan **Unknown**	Status **Declining**

| Order **Passeriformes** | Family **Emberizidae** | Species *Calcarius lapponicus* |

Lapland Longspur

thin, white edge to tail

MALE (BREEDING)

black face

IN FLIGHT

streaked crown

white eye-line

black streak on throat

FEMALE (BREEDING)

thick, yellowish bill

bright rufous nape

rich buffy hood

rusty wing panel

thick streaking on flanks

ADULT (NONBREEDING)

black flanks

white underparts

MALE (BREEDING)

FLIGHT: deeply undulating, with birds often calling in troughs as they flap.

One of the most numerous breeding birds of the Arctic tundra, the Lapland Longspur is found in huge flocks over open habitats of the US in the winter. They can be seen on gravel roads and in barren countryside immediately following heavy snowfalls. Genetic (DNA) evidence suggests that the four longspur species and the two *Plectrophenax* buntings do not belong to the Emberizidae family, but rather form a distinct group of their own. This species is known as the Lapland Bunting in Great Britain and Ireland.

VOICE Flight call a dry rattle, *tyew*, unlike other longspurs; song a series of thin tinklings and whistles, often in flight.

NESTING Cup of grass and sedges placed in depression on ground next to a clump of vegetation; 4–6 eggs; 1 brood; May–July.

FEEDING Eats insects during breeding season; seeds in winter.

CONSPICUOUS SPECIES
This longspur is one of the most conspicuous breeding birds on the Arctic tundra.

OCCURRENCE
Breeds in tundra right across Arctic North America and Eurasia. Winters in open grasslands and barren fields, and on beaches across the northern and central US and parts of southern Canada.

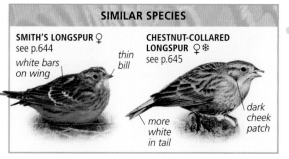

SIMILAR SPECIES

SMITH'S LONGSPUR ♀
see p.644

white bars on wing

thin bill

CHESTNUT-COLLARED LONGSPUR ♀ ✳
see p.645

dark cheek patch

more white in tail

| Length **6½in (16cm)** | Wingspan **10½–11½in (27–29cm)** | Weight **⅞–1¹⁄₁₆oz (25–30g)** |
| Social **Large flocks** | Lifespan **Up to 5 years** | Status **Secure** |

| Order **Passeriformes** | Family **Emberizidae** | Species *Calcarius pictus* |

Smith's Longspur

MALE (BREEDING)
white cheek patch
white outer tail feathers
relatively long wings
IN FLIGHT

rich, buffy overall
wings extend past tail
FEMALE (FALL)
fine breast streaks
white shoulder

black-and-white "helmet"
thin bill
orange collar
rich pumpkin colored underparts

MALE (BREEDING)
white undertail feathers

With its pumpkin colored breast and black-and-white "helmet," Smith's Longspur in its breeding colors contrasts strongly with its drab winter plumage. On both its remote breeding grounds in the Arctic, and its restricted shortgrass range in winter, this bird hides on the ground at all times, making it very hard to spot. Smith's Longspur migrates through the Great Plains to reach its wintering grounds, but on the return journey it swings east, giving it an elliptical migration path. This species breeds communally: males mate with several females who, in turn, mate with other males.

VOICE Flight call a mechanical, dry, sharp rattle; also a nasal *nief* when squabbling; song a series of thin, sweet whistles.

NESTING Concealed cup of sedges, lined with feathers, placed in hummock on ground; 3–5 eggs; 1 brood; June–July.

FEEDING Eats mainly seeds and insects; migrants may rely heavily upon introduced foxtail grass.

FLIGHT: deeply undulating, with birds often calling in troughs as they flap.

LINEBACK LONGSPUR
On his breeding or spring staging grounds, the male sports a striking black-and-white "helmet."

SIMILAR SPECIES

LAPLAND LONGSPUR
♀❄ see p.643
thicker bill
broad, reddish edges to wings

CHESTNUT-COLLARED LONGSPUR ♀❄
see p.645
lacks rich buff color and streaks
more white in tail

OCCURRENCE
Breeds along the tundra-taiga timberline from northern Alaska southeast to northern Ontario; also mountainous southeastern Alaska and southwestern Yukon. Migrant birds are found in shortgrass prairie. Winters in various open areas with shortgrass in Kansas, Texas, and Arkansas.

| Length **6–6½in (15–16cm)** | Wingspan **10–11½in (25–29cm)** | Weight **⅞–1¹⁄₁₆oz (25–30g)** |
| Social **Large flocks** | Lifespan **Up to 5 years** | Status **Secure** |

| Order **Passeriformes** | Family **Emberizidae** | Species **Calcarius ornatus** |

Chestnut-collared Longspur

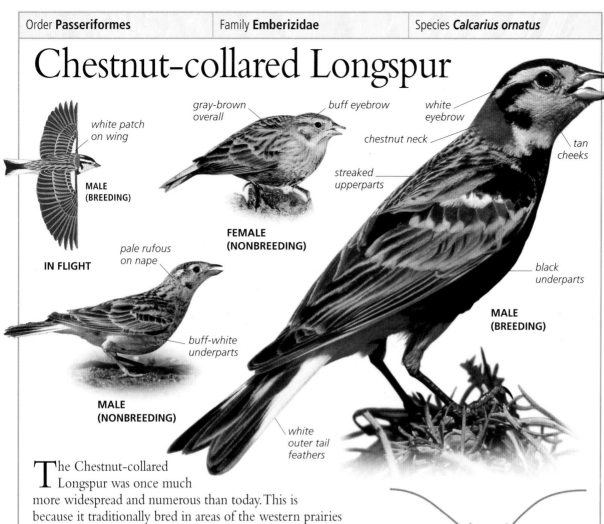

MALE (BREEDING)
white patch on wing

IN FLIGHT

gray-brown overall

buff eyebrow

FEMALE (NONBREEDING)

streaked upperparts

white eyebrow

chestnut neck

tan cheeks

black underparts

MALE (BREEDING)

pale rufous on nape

buff-white underparts

MALE (NONBREEDING)

white outer tail feathers

The Chestnut-collared Longspur was once much more widespread and numerous than today. This is because it traditionally bred in areas of the western prairies that had been recently disturbed by huge, roaming herds of bison, or by wild fires. After the elimination of the bison, however, and the "taming" of the plains, such areas were hard to find, and so the bird declined. One of the Chestnut-collared Longspur's distinguishing features is the triangular black patch on its tail. The breeding male's black belly is also unique among the North American longspurs.

VOICE Flight call a chortling *KTI-uhl-uh*, often in series; also a soft rattle and short buzz; song a sweet, rich, whistled series, in fluttering, circular flights over the prairies.

NESTING Grassy cup on ground, in grass clump or next to rock; 3–5 eggs; 1–2 broods; May–August.

FEEDING Eats seeds year-round; also feeds on insects when breeding.

FLIGHT: deeply undulating, with birds often calling in troughs as they flap.

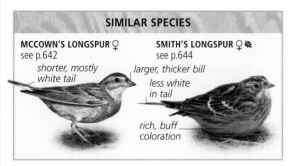

SIMILAR SPECIES

MCCOWN'S LONGSPUR ♀
see p.642
shorter, mostly white tail

SMITH'S LONGSPUR ♀ ⚥
see p.644
larger, thicker bill
less white in tail
rich, buff coloration

NOW AND THEN
The male bird usually sings from the air, but occasionally from a prominent perch.

OCCURRENCE
Breeds in shortgrass prairie from Alberta east to Minnesota, south to northeastern Colorado and northwestern Nebraska; on migration, grasslands and cultivated fields. Winters in grasslands and other barren areas in the southern Great Plains west to southeastern Arizona and south to Mexico.

| Length **5½–6in (14–15cm)** | Wingspan **10–10½in (25–27cm)** | Weight **⅜–11⁄16oz (11–20g)** |
| Social **Large flocks** | Lifespan **Up to 4 years** | Status **Declining** |

Order **Passeriformes**	Family **Emberizidae**	Species ***Plectrophenax nivalis***

Snow Bunting

less white in wings

white outer tail feathers

MALE (NONBREEDING)

white head and underparts

black back

yellow bill

black bill

pale rufous crown

white underparts

FEMALE (BREEDING)

dark brown eyes

rusty orange cheek patch

black peeks through buffy feather edgings

IN FLIGHT

large white patches on black wings

MALE (BREEDING)

FEMALE (NONBREEDING)

rusty orange breast patch

gray body

white eye-ring

white underparts

MALE (NONBREEDING)

JUVENILE

The bold white wing patches of the Snow Bunting make it immediately recognizable in a whirling winter flock of dark-winged longspurs and larks. In winter, heavy snowfall forces flocks onto roadsides, where they can be seen more easily. To secure and defend the best territories, some of the males of this remarkably hardy species arrive as early as April in their barren high-Arctic breeding grounds. The Snow Bunting is very similar in appearance to the rare and localized McKay's Bunting. Although McKay's Bunting generally has less black on the back, in the wings, and on the tail, the two species cannot always be conclusively identified. This is especially true since Snow and McKay's Buntings sometimes interbreed, producing hybrids.

VOICE Flight a call musical, liquid rattle, also *tyew* notes and short buzz; song a pleasant series of squeaky and whistled notes.

NESTING Bulky cup of grass and moss, lined with feathers, and placed in sheltered rock crevice; 3–6 eggs; 1 brood; June–August.

FEEDING Eats seeds (sedge in Arctic), flies and other insects, and buds on migration.

FLIGHT: deeply undulating; flocks "roll" along as birds at back overtake those in front.

ROCKY GROUND
About the only perches in the Snow Bunting's barren breeding grounds are large boulders.

OCCURRENCE
Breeds in rocky areas, usually near sparsely vegetated tundra, right across the Arctic. North American birds winters in open country and on shores across the whole of southern Canada and the northern US, and in southern and western coastal areas of Alaska.

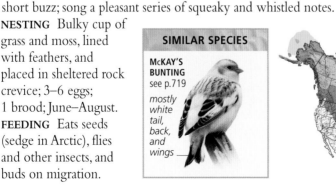

SIMILAR SPECIES

McKAY'S BUNTING see p.719

mostly white tail, back, and wings

Length **6½–7in (16–18cm)**	Wingspan **12½–14in (32–35cm)**	Weight **1¼–2oz (35–55g)**
Social **Large flocks**	Lifespan **Unknown**	Status **Secure**

| Order **Passeriformes** | Family **Emberizidae** | Species *Calamospiza melanocorys* |

Lark Bunting

white tail tips

MALE (BREEDING)

black upperparts

thick, silvery gray bill

variable black marks

white wing patch

blunt-tipped wings

large, white wing patches

IN FLIGHT

white wing patch

black spots on undertail feathers

MALE (NONBREEDING)

black underparts

MALE (BREEDING)

brown-and-white streaks

blue-gray bill

short, slightly rounded tail

brown legs and toes

FEMALE (NONBREEDING)

Perhaps the most frequently seen bird on the North American High Plains, the stocky Lark Bunting—unlike the Chestnut-collared Longspur, which lives alongside it—has been able to cope with the changes wrought on its habitat by humans, and occurs in extraordinary density throughout its range. Nomadic flocks of thousands scour the high deserts, open grasslands, and sage bush for seeds. Breeding-plumaged males are unmistakable: black with large white wing patches. Females and immature birds are duller, with more subdued wing patches.
VOICE Call a low, soft, whistled *hwoik*; song a partly melodious, partly "scratchy," with repetitions of phrases, then whistles.
NESTING Open cup of grass, lined with fine plant material, in depression in ground; 4–5 eggs; 1 brood; May–August.
FEEDING Mainly seeds in winter, insects in summer.

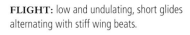

FLIGHT: low and undulating, short glides alternating with stiff wing beats.

CAUGHT BY ANY MEANS
The Lark Bunting hawks, gleans, and forages insect prey throughout the breeding season.

SIMILAR SPECIES

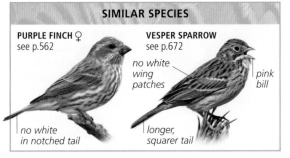

PURPLE FINCH ♀
see p.562

VESPER SPARROW
see p.672

no white wing patches

pink bill

no white in notched tail

longer, squarer tail

OCCURRENCE
Breeds in grasslands and sage flats on High Plains from Alberta south to the Texas panhandle. Winters in similar habitats—and also in desert, cultivated plains, and open shrub–steppe—across interior southwestern US and northern Mexico. Migrants use similar open-country habitats.

| Length **7in (18cm)** | Wingspan **10½–11in (27–28cm)** | Weight **1¹⁄₁₆–1¾oz (30–50g)** |
| Social **Large flocks** | Lifespan **Unknown** | Status **Secure** |

| Order **Passeriformes** | Family **Emberizidae** | Species *Zonotrichia albicollis* |

White-throated Sparrow

two white wing bars

ADULT

IN FLIGHT

tan stripe

browner face

bold white stripe

bright rufous back and tail

ADULT (TAN-STRIPED)

yellow patch

white throat

gray bill

streaking on breast

IMMATURE (TAN-STRIPED)

fairly long tail

gray underparts

ADULT (WHITE-STRIPED)

Common almost everywhere in eastern North America, White-throated Sparrows sing all year round. This distinctive, whistled, rhythmic song can be remembered with the popular mnemonics *Oh sweet Canada Canada Canada*, or the less accurate *Old Sam Peabody*. This species has two different color forms, one with a white stripe above its eye, and one with a tan stripe. In the nonbreeding season, large flocks roam the leaf litter of woodlands in search of food. Often the only indication of their presence is the occasional moving leaf or thin, lisping flight call.

VOICE Call loud, sharp *jink*; flight call lisping *tssssst!*; song clear whistle comprising 1–2 higher notes, then three triplets.

NESTING Cup placed on or near ground in dense shrubbery; 2–6 eggs; 1 brood; May–August.

FEEDING Mainly forages on the ground for seeds, fruit, insects, buds, and various grasses.

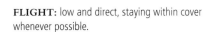

FLIGHT: low and direct, staying within cover whenever possible.

DIFFERENT COLOR FORMS
The presence of white or tan stripes on White-throated Sparrows is not related to their sex.

OCCURRENCE
Breeds in forests from eastern Yukon to Newfoundland, south into Great Lakes and northern Appalachians. Nonbreeders prefer wooded thickets and hedges. Winters across the eastern US and extreme south of the Southwest. Rare but regular along the Pacific Coast.

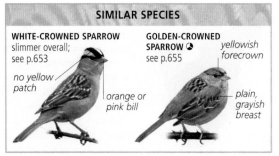

SIMILAR SPECIES

WHITE-CROWNED SPARROW
slimmer overall;
see p.653

no yellow patch

orange or pink bill

GOLDEN-CROWNED SPARROW ♀
see p.655

yellowish forecrown

plain, grayish breast

| Length **6½–7½in (16–17.5cm)** | Wingspan **9–10in (23–26cm)** | Weight **¹¹⁄₁₆–1¼oz (20–35g)** |
| Social **Flocks** | Lifespan **Up to 10 years** | Status **Secure** |

Order **Passeriformes**	Family **Emberizidae**	Species *Zonotrichia atricapilla*

Golden-crowned Sparrow

bright yellow crown

thick black eyebrow

streaks on head

dull yellow crown

white wing bars

ADULT (BREEDING)

IMMATURE

IN FLIGHT

duller yellow on crown

much less black on face

light grayish brown underparts

long tail

ADULT (NONBREEDING)

ADULT (BREEDING)

The Golden-crowned Sparrow is in many respects the western counterpart of the White-throated Sparrow. It sings in a minor key and, as a result, has a reputation for sounding melancholy. Many late 19th-century Klondike gold prospectors called this bird "Weary Willie"—to them, its song sounded remarkably like *I'm so tired* or *No gold here*. It has been regarded as a pest in the past because of its habit of consuming crops in agricultural fields and gardens. Nonbreeding adults retain their distinctive golden crown in the winter, but it appears duller.

VOICE Call loud *tsik*; flight call soft, short *seeep*; song variable series of melancholy whistles, sometimes slurred or trilled.

NESTING Concealed bulky cup placed on ground at base of bush; 3–5 eggs; 1–2 broods; June–August.

FEEDING Predominantly forages on the ground for seeds, insects, fruit, flowers, and buds.

FLIGHT: low and direct, staying within cover whenever possible.

GROUND FORAGER
This sparrow can be found by listening for the noise it makes as it roots around in the leaf litter.

OCCURRENCE
Breeds in shrubby habitat along the tree line and open, boggy forests from Alaska east to southwest Northwest Territories, south to British Columbia and southwest Alberta. Winters in dense thickets from south coastal British Columbia to north Baja California.

SIMILAR SPECIES

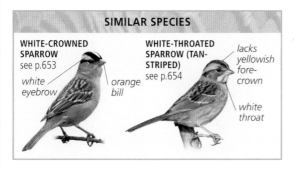

WHITE-CROWNED SPARROW
see p.653

white eyebrow

orange bill

WHITE-THROATED SPARROW (TAN-STRIPED)
see p.654

lacks yellowish fore-crown

white throat

Length **7in (18cm)**	Wingspan **9–10in (23–25cm)**	Weight **¹¹⁄₁₆–1¼oz (20–35g)**
Social **Flocks**	Lifespan **Up to 10 years**	Status **Secure**

| Order **Passeriformes** | Family **Emberizidae** | Species *Junco hyemalis* |

Dark-eyed Junco

MALE
(SLATE-COLORED)

dark area between
eye and bill

dark gray
head

bluish gray
hood

dull, brownish
back

gray body
with brown
wash to back

white
outer tail
feathers

pinkish flanks

IN FLIGHT

FEMALE
(PINK-SIDED)

white
belly

reddish
brown back

black mask

gray
rump

pale gray
underparts

MALE
(SLATE-COLORED)

MALE
(GRAY-HEADED)

blackish
hood

rust
back

reddish flanks

MALE
(OREGON)

The Dark-eyed Junco's appearance at birdfeeders during snowstorms has earned it the colloquial name of "snowbird." The name "Dark-eyed Junco" is actually used to describe a group of birds that vary geographically in an incredibly diverse way. Sixteen subspecies have been described. "Slate-colored" populations are widespread across Canada and the northeastern US, the "White-winged" nests in the Black Hills, "Pink-sided" birds breed in Idaho, Montana, and Wyoming, and "Oregon" birds breed in the Pacific West, from Alaska to British Columbia and the mountainous western US in the Sierras south to Mexico. "Red-backed" populations reside in the mountains of Arizona and New Mexico, while "Gray-headed" birds range between the "Red-backed" and "Pink-sided" populations.
VOICE Loud, smacking *tick* and soft *dyew* calls; flight call a rapid, twittering, and buzzy *zzeet*; song a simple, liquid, 1-pitch trill.
NESTING Cup placed on ground hidden under vegetation or next to rocks; 3–5 eggs; 1–2 broods; May–August.
FEEDING Eats insects and seeds; also berries.

FLIGHT: low and direct, staying within cover whenever possible.

PINK-SIDED MALE
Like most juncos, this male is brighter with greater contrasts, darker eye areas, and more vivid colors.

SIMILAR SPECIES

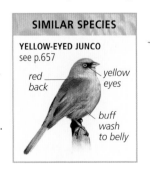

YELLOW-EYED JUNCO
see p.657

red
back

yellow
eyes

buff
wash
to belly

OCCURRENCE
Breeds in coniferous and mixed forests across Canada and the southern US, south in the east Appalachians to Georgia, and in the west, in mountains from Alaska and British Columbia to New Mexico and northern Baja California. Winters from southern Canada to northern Mexico.

| Length **6–6¾in (15–17cm)** | Wingspan **8–10in (20–26cm)** | Weight **⅝–1¹⁄₁₆oz (18–30g)** |
| Social **Flocks** | Lifespan **Up to 11 years** | Status **Secure** |

Order **Passeriformes**	Family **Emberizidae**	Species *Junco phaeonotus*

Yellow-eyed Junco

gray rump

white outer tail feathers

ADULT

IN FLIGHT

gray head

rusty wings

pale red on wing feathers

bicolored bill; black above, yellow below

black patch between eye and bill

"staring of" yellow eyes

pale gray underparts

ADULT

white outer tail feathers

The Yellow-eyed Junco is the Mexican representative of the Dark-eyed Junco, replacing it south of the border at high elevations in pine and pine-oak forests. The combination of its "glaring" yellow eyes set off by a black mask, a reddish brown back, and pale-gray underparts distinguish it from all the Dark-eyed Juncos. Like its dark-eyed relative, the Yellow-eyed Junco is geographically variable; five subspecies have been described. All forage on the ground by hopping and walking, and are common, confident birds. Small flocks often scavenge under picnic tables.
VOICE Loud *dip*, soft *dyew* calls; flight call a twittering, buzzy *zzeet*; song 2–3 whistles followed by various trills and buzzes.
NESTING Cup constructed on ground, often within grass, sometimes placed low in tree; 3–4 eggs; 1–2 broods; April–June.
FEEDING Eats mostly insects in summer, seeds in winter.

FLIGHT: low and direct, staying within cover whenever possible.

LOOKING UP
A Yellow-eyed Junco shows its distinguishing red-backed and yellow-eyed aspect.

SIMILAR SPECIES

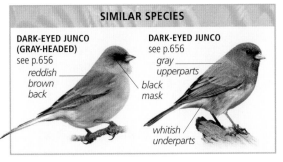

DARK-EYED JUNCO (GRAY-HEADED)
see p.656
reddish brown back

DARK-EYED JUNCO
see p.656
gray upperparts

black mask

whitish underparts

OCCURRENCE
Breeds in open pine-oak and conifer forests at 5,900–8,200ft (1,800–2,500m) elevation in southeast Arizona and southwest New Mexico, and more widely in Mexico; also in Guatemala. Resident geographically but altitudinal migrant, moving to lower elevations in winter.

Length **6½in (16cm)**	Wingspan **9½–10in (24–25cm)**	Weight **⁹⁄₁₆–⁷⁄₈oz (16–25g)**
Social **Solitary/Flocks**	Lifespan **Up to 7 years**	Status **Secure**

| Order **Passeriformes** | Family **Emberizidae** | Species *Passerculus sandwichensis* |

Savannah Sparrow

brown overall

ADULT

IN FLIGHT

short, notched tail

yellow patch between eye and bill

small bill

crisp black streaking on underparts

ADULT (EASTERN)

pale sandy overall

reddish streaks on underparts

ADULT
P. s. princeps
(IPSWICH SPARROW)

white belly

ADULT (WESTERN)

FLIGHT: square-tailed with an often undulating or "stair-step" flight pattern.

whitish tail edgings

The Savannah Sparrow shows tremendous variation—21 subspecies—across its vast range, but it is always brown, with dark streaks above and white with dark streaks below. The pale "Ipswich Sparrow" (*P. s. princeps*), originally described as a species, breeds on Sable Island, Nova Scotia, and winters along the East Coast. The "Large-billed Sparrow" (*P. s. rostratus* and *P. s. atratus*) breeds in Baja, California, and Sonora, Mexico. The most distinct of all populations, these birds occur as nonbreeders, near California's Salton Sea. Their distinct song consists of three buzzy trills, and their flight calls are lower and more metallic than other populations.

VOICE Call a sharp, but full *stip*; flight call a thin, weak, down-slurred *tseew*; song a *sit sit sit sit suh-EEEEE say*, from perch or in display flight with legs dangling.

NESTING Concealed cup of grass placed in depression on ground, protected by overhanging grass or sedges; 2–6 eggs; 1–2 broods; June–August.

FEEDING Forages on the ground, mostly for insects; in summer also eats seeds; in winter berries and fruit when available; also small snails and crustaceans.

BELDING'S SPARROW
This darker, more heavily streaked subspecies inhabits coastal marshes in southern California.

OCCURRENCE
Breeds in meadows, grasslands, pastures, bushy tundra, and some cultivated land across northern North America. Also along Pacific Coast and in Mexican interior. Nonbreeders use varied open habitats. Winters across southern US to Honduras, also Cuba, the Bahamas, and Cayman Islands.

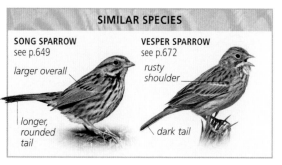

SIMILAR SPECIES

SONG SPARROW
see p.649

larger overall

longer, rounded tail

VESPER SPARROW
see p.672

rusty shoulder

dark tail

| Length **5½–6in (14–15cm)** | Wingspan **6¾in (17cm)** | Weight **½–1¹⁄₁₆oz (15–30g)** |
| Social **Solitary/Loose flocks** | Lifespan **Unknown** | Status **Secure** |

| Order **Passeriformes** | Family **Emberizidae** | Species **Ammodramus maritimus** |

Seaside Sparrow

ADULT — dark overall — round tail

IN FLIGHT

olive-toned upperparts and head

blackish streaking on underparts

ADULT
A. m. mirabilis
(CAPE SABLE)

gray cheek bordered by dusky brown line

rusty wing panel

yellow patch between eye and bill

long bill

white throat

ADULT

blurry, dusky streaks on underparts

FLIGHT: low and weak, with tail pointed down; much flapping.

The song of the Seaside Sparrow is a characteristic summer sound of East Coast US saltmarshes with *Spartina* grass. Seaside Sparrows vary geographically. East Coast subspecies are the dullest, with smudgy markings and dusky gray coloration. Gulf Coast birds are more boldly marked, with brighter plumage, and orangish color to the head and breast. Sadly, marsh drainage caused the extinction of the blackish, boldly marked "Dusky" Seaside Sparrow (*A.m. nigresceus*) in 1987, which was endemic to eastern Florida. The crisply marked "Cape Sable" Seaside Sparrow of southwest Florida (*A.m. mirabilis*) is now endangered.
VOICE Call a husky *tchup*, sometimes in series; also a descending *tchee-tchee choh, choh, CHOO*; song *drrr'-tiz'-uh-ZHAAAAY*.
NESTING Cup of grasses, occasionally domed, placed near ground; 2–5 eggs; 1–3 broods; May–August.
FEEDING Eats seeds of grasses, and sedge; also insects in the breeding season.

FAMILIAR PHRASING
The song of the Seaside Sparrow resembles that of a distant Red-winged Blackbird.

OCCURRENCE
Breeds in coastal salt and brackish marshes from the Rio Grande in southeast Texas east and north to New Hampshire. Absent from many parts of Florida. Mostly resident, but retreats from areas north of Boston in the winter.

SIMILAR SPECIES

SAVANNAH SPARROW
see p.658

paler, square tail

much smaller bill

SALTMARSH SHARP-TAILED SPARROW
see p.661

shorter, spikier tail

small, pale bill

| Length **5¼–6in (13.5–15cm)** | Wingspan **7–8in (17.5–20cm)** | Weight **¹¹⁄₁₆–⅞oz (20–25g)** |
| Social **Solitary** | Lifespan **Up to 8 years** | Status **Vulnerable** |

| Order **Passeriformes** | Family **Emberizidae** | Species *Ammodramus nelsoni* |

Nelson's Sharp-tailed Sparrow

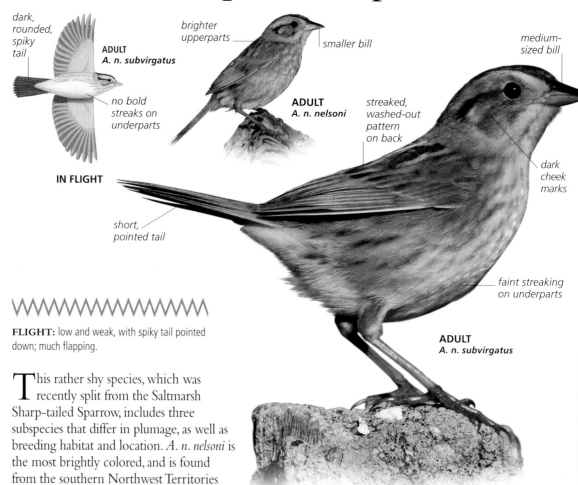

dark, rounded, spiky tail

ADULT
A. n. subvirgatus

no bold streaks on underparts

IN FLIGHT

brighter upperparts

smaller bill

ADULT
A. n. nelsoni

streaked, washed-out pattern on back

medium-sized bill

dark cheek marks

short, pointed tail

faint streaking on underparts

ADULT
A. n. subvirgatus

FLIGHT: low and weak, with spiky tail pointed down; much flapping.

This rather shy species, which was recently split from the Saltmarsh Sharp-tailed Sparrow, includes three subspecies that differ in plumage, as well as breeding habitat and location. *A. n. nelsoni* is the most brightly colored, and is found from the southern Northwest Territories south to northwest Wisconsin. *A. n. subvirgatus* breeds in coastal Maine and the Maritimes, and along the St. Lawrence River. It is visually duller than *A. n. nelsoni*, with a longer bill and flatter head. The intermediate-looking *A. n. alterus* breeds along the southern and western coasts of Hudson Bay.

VOICE Sharp *tik* call; song a husky *t-SHHHHEE-uhrr*.
NESTING Cup of grass placed on or just above ground; 4–5 eggs; 1 brood; May–July.
FEEDING Forages on the ground mainly for insects, spiders, and seeds.

SIMILAR SPECIES

SALTMARSH SHARP-TAILED SPARROW
see p.661

longer bill

darker streaks

LE CONTE'S SPARROW
see p.662

white crown stripe

white stripes on back

darker streaking

IDENTIFYING MARKS
The orange-and-gray facial pattern and streaks on the breast are clearly visible.

OCCURRENCE
Breeds in a variety of marsh habitats across Canada and extreme north central North America. Nonbreeders found in marshes and wet, weedy fields. *A. n. nelsoni* and *A. n. alterus* winter on coast from Texas northeast to New Jersey; *A. n. subvirgatus* from eastern Florida to New Jersey.

| Length **4¾in (12cm)** | Wingspan **7in (17.5cm)** | Weight **⁷⁄₁₆–¹¹⁄₁₆oz (13–20g)** |
| Social **Solitary/Flocks** | Lifespan **Unknown** | Status **Secure** |

| Order **Passeriformes** | Family **Emberizidae** | Species *Ammodramus caudacutus* |

Saltmarsh Sharp-tailed Sparrow

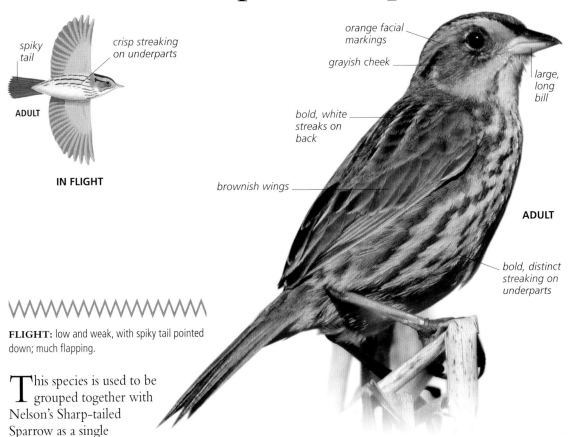

spiky tail

crisp streaking on underparts

ADULT

IN FLIGHT

orange facial markings

grayish cheek

large, long bill

bold, white streaks on back

brownish wings

ADULT

bold, distinct streaking on underparts

FLIGHT: low and weak, with spiky tail pointed down; much flapping.

This species is used to be grouped together with Nelson's Sharp-tailed Sparrow as a single species—the Sharp-tailed Sparrow. When the two were split, they each simply acquired an additional name, which was added to the beginning of the original species name. Birdwatchers refer to them simply as "Saltmarsh Sparrows" and "Nelson's Sparrows" respectively. They can be distinguished as the Saltmarsh Sparrow has more defined facial markings, darker streaks on its breast, and a longer bill. Additionally, the Saltmarsh Sparrow is only found along the East Coast of the US, whereas Nelson's Sparrow is quite widespread.

VOICE Call a sharp *tik*; complex flight song given just above the grass; song a series of muted, thin, airy notes, often without pausing.

NESTING Cup, occasionally domed, placed on or near ground; 3–5 eggs; 1 brood; May–August.

FEEDING Forages on ground for insects, spiders, and seeds.

STREAKY BREAST
Its distinct breast streaks distinguish the Saltmarsh Sparrow from Nelson's Sparrow.

OCCURRENCE
Breeds in saltmarshes, especially those with salt-meadow cordgrass, from Virginia to southern Maine. Nonbreeders use same habitat. Winters from eastern Florida to New Jersey.

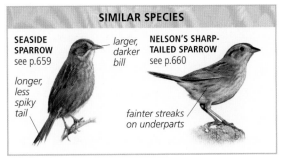

SIMILAR SPECIES

SEASIDE SPARROW see p.659

larger, darker bill

NELSON'S SHARP-TAILED SPARROW see p.660

longer, less spiky tail

fainter streaks on underparts

| Length **5in (13cm)** | Wingspan **7–7½in (17.5–19cm)** | Weight **⅝–¹¹⁄₁₆oz (17–20g)** |
| Social **Solitary/Loose flocks** | Lifespan **Up to 10 years** | Status **Declining** |

Order **Passeriformes**	Family **Emberizidae**	Species *Ammodramus leconteii*

Le Conte's Sparrow

spiky tail

ADULT

boldly striped back

pale, tawny rump

IN FLIGHT

orange eyebrow

small bill

white median crown stripe

purplish and gray streaks on nape

orange throat

gray ear patch

white-edged wing feathers

fine streaks on buffy breast

ADULT

FLIGHT: low and weak, with spiky tail pointed down; much fast flapping.

Although intricately patterned in glowing colors, Le Conte's Sparrow is usually very difficult to see. Not only is it tiny—one of the smallest of all sparrows—but in the grasslands and marshes of interior North America where it lives it prefers to dart for cover under grasses instead of flushing when disturbed. Meanwhile the flight call and song of this elusive little bird are remarkably insect-like. Many people who hear it often then pass off the unseen bird as a grasshopper. Its nest is even harder to find, making this bird a real challenge to study as well as observe.

VOICE Call long, down-slurred *zheeep*; flight call similar to grasshopper; song insect-like, buzzy *tik'-uht-tizz-ZHEEEEEE-k*.

NESTING Concealed little cup placed on or near ground; 3–5 eggs; 1 brood; June–August.

FEEDING Forages on the ground and in grasses for insects, insect larvae, spiders, and seeds.

HIDEAWAY BIRD
Le Conte's Sparrow is usually found skulking in medium-to-tall grass in all seasons.

OCCURRENCE
Breeds in marshes, wet meadows, and bogs from southwest Yukon to Lake Superior and west Quebec. Migrants or wintering birds found in tall grass and marshes in southwest Kansas to south Indiana, and central Texas to coastal Carolinas.

SIMILAR SPECIES

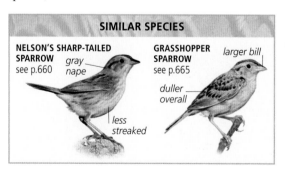

NELSON'S SHARP-TAILED SPARROW
see p.660

gray nape

less streaked

GRASSHOPPER SPARROW
see p.665

larger bill

duller overall

Length **4½–5in (11.5–13cm)**	Wingspan **6½–7in (16–18cm)**	Weight **⁷⁄₁₆–⁹⁄₁₆oz (12–16g)**
Social **Solitary/Loose flocks**	Lifespan **Unknown**	Status **Secure**

Order **Passeriformes**	Family **Emberizidae**	Species ***Ammodramus bairdii***

Baird's Sparrow

ADULT

streaked upperparts

IN FLIGHT

square tail with pale edges

small "necklace" of breast streaks

rufous streaks on flanks

ADULT

ocher head

large bill

fine streaks on nape

streaked brown upperparts

whitish belly

ADULT

The sweet, tinkling song of Baird's Sparrow is a sure sign of high-quality mixed-grass prairie on the Northern Plains. This sparrow's musical song is quite different to the buzzy songs of the other *Ammodramus* sparrows. Its square, pale-edged tail is also unique within its genus. Baird's Sparrow is usually seen only on its breeding grounds, for it is very difficult to find elsewhere, scurrying out of sight if disturbed. Like other birds that depend on native grasslands, it has not coped well with the intensive agriculture that has swept across the Northern Plains in the last century or so.

VOICE Call soft, metallic *tsink*; flight call insect-like *tisk*; song *tsk tsk tsuck tsooweeeeee*.

NESTING Well-concealed grass cup placed on ground in depression or in grass clump or shrub; 4–5 eggs; 1–2 broods; May–August.

FEEDING Forages for seeds and insects.

FLIGHT: low and weak, short in duration, much flapping.

HABITAT SPECIALIST
Baird's Sparrow needs the previous year's dead grass as suitable breeding habitat.

OCCURRENCE
Breeds in light mixed-grass prairie, from south Alberta southeast to northern South Dakota and northern Wyoming. Migrates through the High Plains. Winters in diverse, patchy grasslands, in Chihuahua, northern Sonora in Mexico, and in adjacent US.

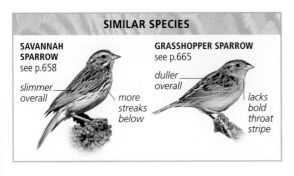

SIMILAR SPECIES

SAVANNAH SPARROW
see p.658

slimmer overall

more streaks below

GRASSHOPPER SPARROW
see p.665

duller overall

lacks bold throat stripe

Length **5½in (14cm)**	Wingspan **8½–8¾in (21–22.5cm)**	Weight **½–¹¹⁄₁₆oz (15–20g)**
Social **Solitary/Loose flocks**	Lifespan **Unknown**	Status **Declining**

| Order **Passeriformes** | Family **Emberizidae** | Species *Ammodramus henslowii* |

Henslow's Sparrow

round, spiky tail

dark reddish overall

ADULT

IN FLIGHT

flat, greenish head with black stripes

whitish scaling on purplish back

rufous-edged wing feathers

heavy bill

black streaks on buffy breast

ADULT

The combination of a large, flat, greenish head, and purplish back are unique to Henslow's Sparrow. A bird of the tallgrass prairies and wet grasslands, the breeding range of this sparrow closely mirrors the extent of its habitat. While it has suffered greatly from the drainage, cultivation, and urbanization of much of its preferred breeding grounds, the Henslow's Sparrow has also recently started to use reclaimed strip mines in northwest Missouri and Iowa for breeding.

VOICE Call a sharp *tsik*, flight call a long, high, shrill *tseeeeee*; song a hiccupping sputter with second note higher *tsih-LIK!*

NESTING Cup of grass placed on or near ground; 2–5 eggs; 1–2 broods; May–August.

FEEDING Eats seed that forages for insects, insect larvae, and spiders in the summer.

FLIGHT: low and weak, with spiky tail pointed down; much flapping.

INTO THE AIR
The male puts considerable effort into his short, but surprisingly far-carrying song.

OCCURRENCE
Breeds predominantly in tallgrass prairie and wet grasslands from Oklahoma eastward to New York, and southward to North Carolina. Winters in weedy, brushy fields, grassy pine woods, and undergrowth along Gulf Coastal Plain from Texas to North Carolina.

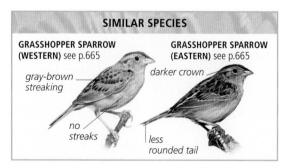

SIMILAR SPECIES

GRASSHOPPER SPARROW (WESTERN) see p.665

gray-brown streaking

no streaks

GRASSHOPPER SPARROW (EASTERN) see p.665

darker crown

less rounded tail

| Length **4¾–5in (12–13cm)** | Wingspan **6½in (16cm)** | Weight **⅜–½oz (11–15g)** |
| Social **Solitary/Loose flocks** | Lifespan **Unknown** | Status **Declining** |

| Order **Passeriformes** | Family **Emberizidae** | Species ***Ammodramus savannarum*** |

Grasshopper Sparrow

short, spiky tail

buff overall

ADULT

IN FLIGHT

large head

fairly long bill

pale eyebrow

reddish and dark spots on upperparts

white eye-ring

buff breast, sides, and flanks

yellow at bend of wing

ADULT
A. s. perpallidus
(WESTERN)

darker crown

darker overall

shorter tail

ADULT
A. s. pratensis
(EASTERN)

FLIGHT: low and weak, with spiky tail pointed down; much flapping.

A Grasshopper Sparrow singing briefly atop a weed is usually the first glimpse people get of a member of the secretive *Ammodramus* genus. Although its large head and spiky tail are typical of its genus, the Grasshopper Sparrow is the only *Ammodramus* sparrow to have a plain breast and two completely different songs. While it does eat grasshoppers, its common name derives from its song, which resembles the sounds grasshoppers make. It varies geographically, with about 12 subspecies.

VOICE Sharp *tik* call; flight call a long, high *tseeee*; song an insect-like trill *tik'-tok-TREEEE*, or series of quick buzzes.

NESTING Cup of grass placed in clump of grass; 3–6 eggs; 1–2 broods; April–August.

FEEDING Forages on ground for seeds and insects.

YELLOW PATCH
The pale crown stripe and small yellow patch at the bend of its wings are visible here.

OCCURRENCE
Breeds in short grassland, pastures, and even mown areas across much of the US and southern Canada. Locally distributed in the Southwest, also patchily through central US. Winters in similar habitats from southern US to Colombia; also found in the West Indies.

SIMILAR SPECIES

LE CONTE'S SPARROW
see p.662

brighter overall

orange eyebrow

gray cheek patch

BAIRD'S SPARROW
see p.663

ocher crown

dark, lateral throat stripe

| Length **5in (13cm)** | Wingspan **8in (20cm)** | Weight **½–¹¹⁄₁₆oz (15–20g)** |
| Social **Solitary/Flocks** | Lifespan **Up to 7 years** | Status **Declining** |

Order **Passeriformes**	Family **Emberizidae**	Species *Spizella arborea*

American Tree Sparrow

rufous crown

black-and-yellow bill

gray head and nape

rusty stripe behind eye

rust patch on shoulder

dark, central spot

rusty tones on shoulder and wings

streaked underparts

JUVENILE

ADULT (BREEDING)

IN FLIGHT

black and rust streaking on back

striped back

cleft tail

ADULT (NONBREEDING)

long, squarish tail

ADULT (BREEDING)

The first heavy snowfalls of the winter often bring large flocks of American Tree Sparrows to birdfeeders. This bird is commonly mistaken for the smaller Chipping Sparrow, but the two species look quite dissimilar in the winter. The American Tree Sparrow's central breast spot, bicolored bill, and large size are unique among the *Spizella*. A highly social, vocal, and misnamed species, noisy winter flocks numbering in the hundreds can be found feeding in weedy fields and along the roadsides of the northern US.

VOICE Call a bell-like *teedle-ee*; flight call a thin, slightly descending *tsiiiu*; song *seee seee di-di-di di-di-di dyew dyew*.

NESTING Neat cup on ground concealed within thicket; 4–6 eggs; 1 brood; June–July.

FEEDING Feeds on seeds, berries, and a variety of insects.

FLIGHT: lightly undulating, often flies to open perch when flushed.

WINTER HABITATS
In winter, this species frequents barren habitats, like old fields and roadsides, as well as feeders.

OCCURRENCE
Breeds in scrubby thickets of birch and willows in the area between taiga and tundra across Alaska and north Canada. Nonbreeders choose open, grassy, brushy habitats. Winters across south Canada and the northern US. Casual to Pacific coast and southern US.

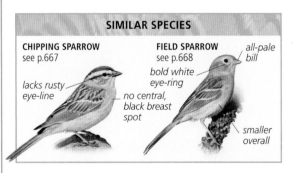

SIMILAR SPECIES

CHIPPING SPARROW
see p.667

lacks rusty eye-line

FIELD SPARROW
see p.668

all-pale bill

bold white eye-ring

no central, black breast spot

smaller overall

Length **6¼in (16cm)**	Wingspan **9½in (24cm)**	Weight **⁷⁄₁₆–⁷⁄₈oz (13–25g)**
Social **Flocks**	Lifespan **Up to 11 years**	Status **Secure**

| Order **Passeriformes** | Family **Emberizidae** | Species *Spizella passerina* |

Chipping Sparrow

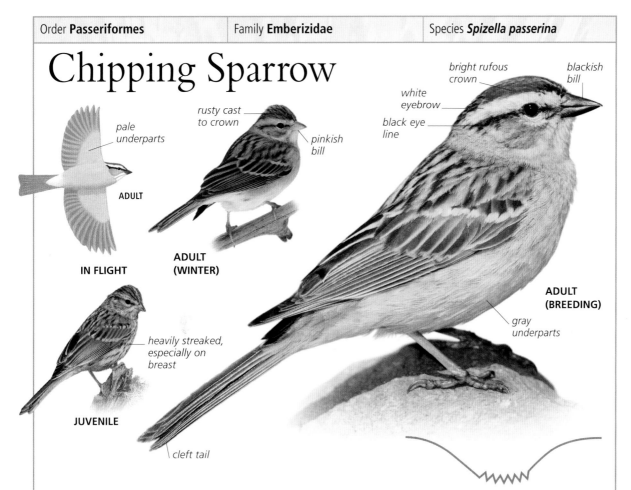

pale underparts

ADULT

IN FLIGHT

rusty cast to crown

pinkish bill

ADULT (WINTER)

bright rufous crown

blackish bill

white eyebrow

black eye line

ADULT (BREEDING)

gray underparts

heavily streaked, especially on breast

JUVENILE

cleft tail

The Chipping Sparrow is a common, trusting bird, which breeds in backyards across most of North America. While they are easily identifiable in the summer, "Chippers" molt into a drab, nonbreeding plumage during fall, at which point they are easily confused with the Clay-colored and Brewer's Sparrows they flock with. Most reports of this species across the north in winter are actually of the larger American Tree Sparrow. In the winter, Chipping Sparrows can be easily recognized as they lack their bright, rusty crown and are restricted to the south.

VOICE Call a sharp *tsip*; flight call a sharp, thin *tsiiit*; song an insect-like trill of *chip* notes, variable in duration and quality.

NESTING Neat cup usually placed well off the ground in tree or shrub; 3–5 eggs; 1–2 broods; April–August.

FEEDING Eats seeds of grasses and annuals, plus some fruits; when breeding, also eats insects and other invertebrates.

FLIGHT: lightly undulating, often to open perch when flushed.

BACKYARD BIRD
Chipping Sparrows are a very common sight in gardens and backyards all across the continent.

SIMILAR SPECIES

CLAY-COLORED SPARROW see p.670

heavy streaks

BREWER'S SPARROW see p.671

partial "necklace"

streaked crown

pale underparts

OCCURRENCE
Found in a wide variety of habitats: open forest, woodlands, grassy, park-like areas, shorelines, and backyards. Breeds in North America south of the Arctic timberline and in Mexico, and in Central America, as far south as Nicaragua. Winters from southern states to Nicaragua.

| Length **5½in (14cm)** | Wingspan **8½in (21cm)** | Weight **⅜–½oz (10–15g)** |
| Social **Large flocks** | Lifespan **Up to 9 years** | Status **Secure** |

| Order **Passeriformes** | Family **Emberizidae** | Species *Spizella pusilla* |

Field Sparrow

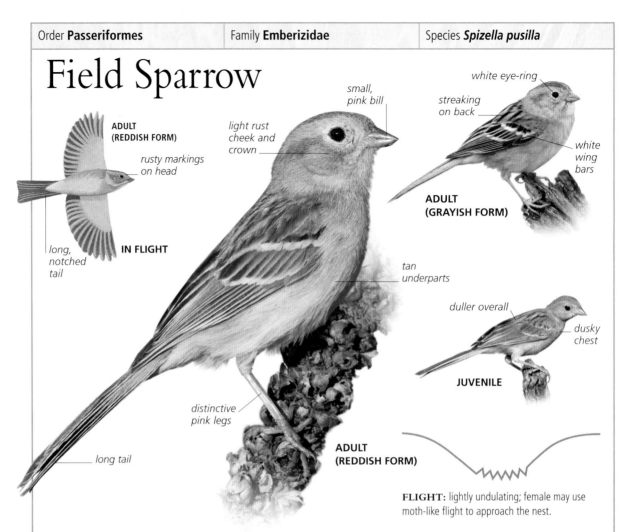

ADULT (REDDISH FORM)
rusty markings on head

long, notched tail

IN FLIGHT

light rust cheek and crown

small, pink bill

white eye-ring

streaking on back

white wing bars

ADULT (GRAYISH FORM)

tan underparts

duller overall

dusky chest

JUVENILE

distinctive pink legs

long tail

ADULT (REDDISH FORM)

FLIGHT: lightly undulating; female may use moth-like flight to approach the nest.

The distinctive accelerating trill song of the Field Sparrow is a characteristic sound of shrubby fields and scrubby areas in the eastern US. The bird's bright-pink bill, plain "baby face," and white eye-ring make this sparrow one of the easiest to identify. The Field Sparrow has brighter plumage in the East, and drabber plumage in the interior part of its range, a pattern followed by many other sparrows, such as the Vesper Sparrow. Although quite dissimilar at first glance, the Black-chinned Sparrow may in fact be the Field Sparrow's closest relative, sharing its pink bill, relatively unpatterned plumage, and its song.

VOICE Call a sharp *tsik*; flight call a strongly descending *tsiiiu*; song a series of sweet, down-slurred whistles accelerating to a rapid trill.

NESTING Grass cup placed on or just above ground in grass or bush; 3–5 eggs; 1–3 broods; March–August.

FEEDING Eats seeds; also insects, insect larvae, and spiders in the summer.

FAMILIAR SONG
Male Field Sparrows sing their familiar and distinctive song throughout the summer.

OCCURRENCE
Breeds in overgrown fields, woodland edges, roadsides, and other shrubby, overgrown areas; occasionally in orchards and parks in the eastern US, west to Dakota, east to New England. Winters in similar habitats in the southern US. Casual in Atlantic Canada and on the Pacific Coast.

SIMILAR SPECIES

WHITE-CROWNED SPARROW ♀
see p.653
larger body

pale crown stripe

AMERICAN TREE SPARROW
see p.666

lacks bold, white eye-ring

central, black breast spot

| Length **5½in (14cm)** | Wingspan **8in (20cm)** | Weight **⅜–½oz (11–15g)** |
| Social **Solitary/Flocks** | Lifespan **Up to 6 years** | Status **Declining** |

Order **Passeriformes**	Family **Emberizidae**	Species **Spizella atrogularis**

Black-chinned Sparrow

MALE (BREEDING)

gray underparts

long tail

IN FLIGHT

plain gray head

streaked, brown back

FEMALE (BREEDING)

black chin

rusty back with black streaks

brownish black wings

black "mask"

pointed, pink bill

MALE (BREEDING)

gray underparts

brownish legs and toes

paler gray overall

lacks dark facial pattern

JUVENILE

This elegant bird is a common but secretive inhabitant of dense brush and shrub on steep hillsides in the southwest US. In the nonbreeding season its plumage is quite drab, making it difficult to spot. However, it is much easier to find a loudly-singing, brightly plumaged male atop a bush in the breeding season. Although its dark grayish breeding plumage and bright pink bill are suggestive of juncos, the Black-chinned Sparrow always has a streaked back and never has white in its tail.

VOICE Call a high *tsip*; song an accelerating, bouncy trill climaxing in a rapid, metallic, ascending echo.
NESTING Loose cup placed just off the ground; 3–4 eggs; 1–2 broods; May–August.
FEEDING Eats seeds; also insects in the summer.

FLIGHT: lightly undulating; with short bursts of rapid wing beats.

MEMORABLE SONG
The hollow, echoing quality of this bird's song is unforgettable once heard.

OCCURRENCE
Occurs on arid, steep slopes covered by dense brush. Breeds in northern California, southwestern Utah, and northeast New Mexico to central Mexico. Winters in southern Arizona, western Texas to southwest Mexico, and south of Baja California.

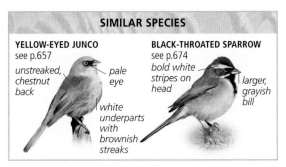

SIMILAR SPECIES

YELLOW-EYED JUNCO
see p.657

unstreaked, chestnut back

pale eye

white underparts with brownish streaks

BLACK-THROATED SPARROW
see p.674

bold white stripes on head

larger, grayish bill

Length **5¾in (14.5cm)**	Wingspan **7¾in (19.5cm)**	Weight **⅜–½oz (11–15g)**
Social **Solitary/Small flocks**	Lifespan **Unknown**	Status **Secure**

Order **Passeriformes**	Family **Emberizidae**	Species *Spizella pallida*

Clay-colored Sparrow

bold, dark cheek stripes

white crown stripe

unstreaked, gray nape

bold, dark brown streaks on upperparts

very pale buffy wash across breast

whitish gray underparts

ADULT

long tail

white wing bars

thick, white eyebrow

brown rump

ADULT

IN FLIGHT

notched tail

FLIGHT: lightly undulating, often flies to open perch when flushed.

The little Clay-colored Sparrow is best known for its mechanical, buzzy song. This bird spends much of its foraging time away from the breeding habitat; consequently, males' territories are quite small, allowing for dense breeding populations. Clay-colored Sparrows have shifted their breeding range eastward and northward over the last century, most likely because of changes in land practices. During the nonbreeding season, they form large flocks in open country, associating with other *Spizella* sparrows, especially Chippings and Brewer's.
VOICE Call a sharp *tsip*; flight a call short, rising *sip*; song a series of 2–7 mechanical buzzes on one pitch.
NESTING Cup of grass placed just off the ground in shrub or small tree; 3–5 eggs; 1–2 broods; May–August.
FEEDING Forages on or low to the ground for seeds and insects.

CHRISTMAS PRESENT
The Clay-colored Sparrow is fond of short conifers for breeding, so Christmas tree farms form a perfect habitat.

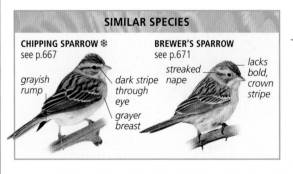

SIMILAR SPECIES

CHIPPING SPARROW ❄
see p.667

grayish rump

dark stripe through eye

grayer breast

BREWER'S SPARROW
see p.671

streaked nape

lacks bold, crown stripe

OCCURRENCE
Breeds in open habitats: prairies, shrubland, forest edges, and Christmas tree farms along the US/Canadian border and northward to the southern Northwest Territory. Winters in a large variety of brushy, weedy areas from south Texas to Mexico. Migration takes it to the Great Plains.

Length **5½in (14cm)**	Wingspan **7½in (19cm)**	Weight **⅜–½oz (10–15g)**
Social **Large flocks**	Lifespan **Up to 5 years**	Status **Secure**

| Order **Passeriformes** | Family **Emberizidae** | Species *Spizella breweri* |

Brewer's Sparrow

dark streaks on crown

streaked nape

conspicuous white eye-ring

small, conical bill

brown facial markings

pale grayish rump

buff wing bars

ADULT

notched tail

IN FLIGHT

pale grayish brown upperparts with marked dark streaks

grayish white underparts

long, notched tail

ADULT

Brewer's Sparrow is a small, fairly drab-looking bird, but its conspicuous eye-ring and streaked nape are good identification features. In addition, its varied, loud, trilling and chattering song is a memorable sound of the West. Most Brewer's Sparrows nest on arid sagebrush in the western US, but there is an isolated population, subspecies "Timberline," which breeds in the Canadian Rockies and into Alaska. It is usually darker, more boldly marked, and longer-billed with a lower, slower, more musical song than its relative.

VOICE Call a sharp *tsip*; flight call a short, rising *sip*; song a series of descending trills, rattles, and buzzes on different pitches.

NESTING Compact cup on or near ground in small bush; 3–4 eggs; 1–2 broods; May–August.

FEEDING Forages on ground for insects and seeds.

FLIGHT: lightly undulating; alternates rapidly between glides and active flight.

CONTINUOUS CHORUS
Across its range in spring, the male Brewer's Sparrow sings continuously to attract a mate.

HIGH AND DRY
These sparrows are fond of the arid brushland and deserts of the High Plains and Great Basin.

OCCURRENCE
Timberline subspecies breeds in valleys in eastern Alaska through Yukon to northwestern British Columbia. Brewer's subspecies breed in brushland, shrubland, thickets, and mountain basins of the western US. Winters in desert scrub and weedy fields in the Southwest and northwestern Mexico.

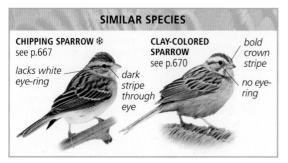

SIMILAR SPECIES

CHIPPING SPARROW ❀
see p.667

lacks white eye-ring

dark stripe through eye

CLAY-COLORED SPARROW
see p.670

bold crown stripe

no eye-ring

| Length **5½in (14cm)** | Wingspan **7½in (19cm)** | Weight **⁵⁄₁₆–½oz (9–14g)** |
| Social **Solitary/Flocks** | Lifespan **Unknown** | Status **Declining** |

| Order **Passeriformes** | Family **Emberizidae** | Species *Pooecetes gramineus* |

Vesper Sparrow

rusty shoulders

ADULT

IN FLIGHT

dark-bordered ear patches

bold white eye-ring

pale brown upperparts

streaked breast

ADULT

uniformly colored and streaked overall

white outer tail feathers

ADULT

bold white-edged long, dark, square tail

The Vesper Sparrow got its common name because its pleasant song was considered to sound sweetest in the evening, when prayers known as "vespers" are sung in the Catholic and Eastern Orthodox churches. When Henry David Thoreau wrote of this species, he called it the "Bay-winged Bunting," because of its (sometimes concealed) rusty shoulder patches and its relation to the Old World *Emberizidae* buntings. The Vesper Sparrow needs areas with bare ground to breed, so it is one of the few species that can successfully nest in areas of intense agriculture; the bird's numbers seem to be declining in spite of this.

VOICE Full *tchup* call, flight call thin *tseent*; song consists of 2 whistles of same pitch, followed by 2 higher-pitched ones, then trills, ends lazily.

NESTING Cup placed on patch of bare ground, against grass, bush, or rock; 3–5 eggs; 1 brood; April–August.

FEEDING Eats insects and seeds.

FLIGHT: strong, often perches when flushed; often moves on ground.

GIFTED SONGSTER
The sweet song of the Vesper Sparrow is a characteristic sound of more northerly open areas.

OCCURRENCE
Breeds in sparse grassland, cultivated fields, recently burned areas, and mountain parks across south Canada and the northern US. Winters in sparsely vegetated, open habitats from southern US to southwest Mexico. Found in patches of bare earth in all seasons.

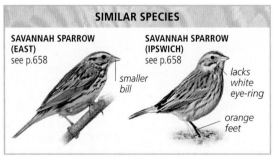

SIMILAR SPECIES

SAVANNAH SPARROW (EAST)
see p.658

smaller bill

SAVANNAH SPARROW (IPSWICH)
see p.658

lacks white eye-ring

orange feet

| Length **6¼in (16cm)** | Wingspan **10in (25cm)** | Weight **¹¹⁄₁₆–1¹⁄₁₆oz (20–30g)** |
| Social **Flocks** | Lifespan **Up to 7 years** | Status **Declining** |

Order **Passeriformes**	Family **Emberizidae**	Species **Chondestes grammacus**

Lark Sparrow

rounded tail with white corners

ADULT

IN FLIGHT

large gray bill

pale patch at base of outer wings

central breast spot

JUVENILE

unique bold facial pattern

brown upperparts

pale plain rump

ADULT

FLIGHT: strong flight, in straight lines; often perches when flushed.

The bold harlequin face pattern, single central breast spot, and long, rounded, black tail with white corners make the Lark Sparrow one of the most easily identifiable of all sparrows. It is commonly found singing from the top of a fencepost or small tree in the western US. Conversely, Lark Sparrow numbers have declined precipitously in the East, where the species is mostly associated with western-like sandy soils. It is likely, however, that its presence in the East was only possible because of the clearing of forests, so the species may in fact simply be retreating to its natural range. Male birds are strongly territorial of their nesting sites, though this does not extend as a wider area to other species.

VOICE Thin, up-slurred *tseep* call, flight call sharp *tink*; song series of trills, whistles, and rattles on varying pitches.

NESTING Cup usually placed on ground at base of plant, or off-ground in tree or bush; 3–5 eggs; 1–2 broods; April–August.

FEEDING Eats seeds and insects.

ON THE FENCE
The Lark Sparrow is a common roadside bird, often found perching on barbed wire fences.

OCCURRENCE
Breeds in varied open habitats such as sage flats and grassland from British Columbia and Saskatchewan to Baja California and central Mexico, east to Ohio; localized breeder in East, associated with well-drained, poor soils. Winters from southern US to southwest Mexico.

Length **6–6¾in (15–17cm)**	Wingspan **11in (28cm)**	Weight **¹¹⁄₁₆–1¹⁄₁₆oz (20–30g)**
Social **Large flocks**	Lifespan **Up to 8 years**	Status **Secure**

Order **Passeriformes**	Family **Emberizidae**	Species *Amphispiza bilineata*

Black-throated Sparrow

white-edged black tail

ADULT

white stripe on side of neck

bold white eyebrow

brownish gray upperparts

grayish overall

black throat

IN FLIGHT

ADULT

faint streaking on breast

JUVENILE

Due to perceived similarities in their songs, the Black-throated Sparrow has been called "the Song Sparrow of the desert." This bird is easily distinguished as it possesses a bold white "eyebrow" in all plumages. The unique plumage prevents it from being easily confused with other species; it is possible, however, for first-time observers to mistake juvenile Black-throated Sparrows for Sage Sparrows. Sometimes it is also confused with the Black-chinned Sparrow, but this is perhaps due to the similar name, as the two are quite dissimilar in all plumages.

VOICE Weak *tink* call; song consists of few short, clear notes, followed by higher trill: *tink tink-tink treeeeee*, also *ti-ti-tink churrrrrrrrrrr*.

NESTING Loose cup placed on or near ground in bush or grass; 3–4 eggs; 1–2 broods; March–September.

FEEDING Eats seeds, insects, and cactus fruit.

FLIGHT: direct with rapid wing beats, flies low between shrubs and trees.

CLEAR PLUMAGE
No other sparrow comes close to equaling this species' bold head and throat patterning.

OCCURRENCE
Found in desert scrub, Great Basin east to Texas, south to Baja California and central Mexico. Breeds sporadically in east Washington state. Withdraws from Great Basin in winter. Casual to the Pacific coast and the East.

SIMILAR SPECIES

SAGE SPARROW
see p.675

lacks bold eyebrow

central breast spot

SPRING SINGER
In spring the male declares his territory by singing from the top of a yucca or other high perch.

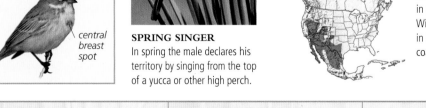

Length 5½in (14cm)	Wingspan 7¾in (19.5cm)	Weight ⅜–⁹⁄₁₆oz (10–16g)
Social **Solitary**	Lifespan **Up to 6 years**	Status **Secure**

| Order **Passeriformes** | Family **Emberizidae** | Species **Amphispiza belli** |

Sage Sparrow

white eye-ring

white-edged square tail

ADULT

gray head contrasts with brownish body

IN FLIGHT

streaking on back

white stripe on the side of the neck

central breast spot

lacks bold, white eyebrow

complete eye-ring

pale overall

ADULT
(*A. b. nevadensis*)

JUVENILE

FLIGHT: weak; undulating over short distances; drops quickly to the ground.

With its tail cocked and held high above the ground, the Sage Sparrow can be found darting from bush to bush in sage flats and dense shrub growth. There are two main subspecies populations, which vary in habitat, plumage, migratory habits, and song, and were once considered separate species. Bell's Sparrow (*A. b. belli*) has much darker upperparts with an unstreaked upper shoulder, a thick, lateral throat stripe, and a plain, dark tail. The True Sage Sparrow (*A. b. nevadensis*) has pale upperparts with dark upper-shoulder streaking, a thin, lateral throat stripe, and a white-edged tail. There are three other recognized subspecies. All five are declining, due mainly to habitat loss, and one—*A. b. clementeae*, found only on San Clemente Island, off California—is listed as threatened.

VOICE Call sharp, short *tink*; Bell's song consists of jumbled squeaky notes; True Sage's song low-pitched *free FROOH dudu*, *free FROOH dudu*.

NESTING Cup placed just off ground in shrub or on the ground (never in case of Bell's Sparrow); 1–5 eggs; 1–3 broods; March–July.

FEEDING Eats seeds, insects, and fruit.

SAGE FLAT SPECIALIST
The Sage Sparrow requires a habitat with extensive expanses of sagebrush.

OCCURRENCE
Bell's Sparrow is a resident of steep hillsides with dense shrub growth, in northern California south to central Baja California. The True Sage Sparrow breeds on Great Basin sage flats, and winters in southwest interior. Casual on Great Plains, accidental in the East.

SIMILAR SPECIES

BLACK-THROATED SPARROW ☾
see p.674

bold white eyebrow

larger bill

BELL'S SPARROW
Bell's Sparrow is much darker than the True Sage Sparrow, and has a completely black tail.

| Length **6–6½in (15-16cm)** | Wingspan **8½in (21cm)** | Weight **⁷⁄₁₆–¹¹⁄₁₆oz (13–19g)** |
| Social **Solitary** | Lifespan **Up to 7 years** | Status **Declining** |

Order **Passeriformes**	Family **Emberizidae**	Species *Aimophila carpalis*

Rufous-winged Sparrow

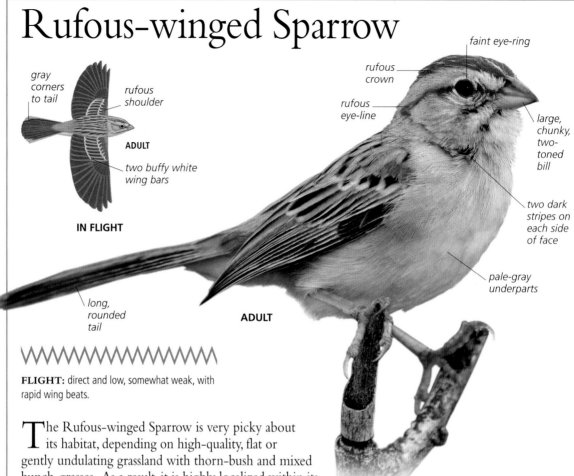

gray corners to tail

rufous shoulder

ADULT

two buffy white wing bars

IN FLIGHT

faint eye-ring

rufous crown

rufous eye-line

large, chunky, two-toned bill

two dark stripes on each side of face

pale-gray underparts

long, rounded tail

ADULT

FLIGHT: direct and low, somewhat weak, with rapid wing beats.

The Rufous-winged Sparrow is very picky about its habitat, depending on high-quality, flat or gently undulating grassland with thorn-bush and mixed bunch-grasses. As a result, it is highly localized within its small US range. It also depends on the late summer rains to green up the grasslands before it begins breeding. Since the rains can come at almost any time, if at all, the male Rufous-winged Sparrow stays ready by keeping a territory all year. This, together with the bird's habit of siting its nest conspicuously, makes this sparrow easier to find than most others in the genus. It tends to run for cover rather than fly if disturbed.

VOICE Call high, strident *tseeep!*; song consists of couple of chips or whistles followed by long, loose trill, or accelerating series of *chips*.

NESTING Cup placed in edge of bush, near or below eye-level; 4–5 eggs; 1–3 broods; April–September.

FEEDING Forages on ground for seeds, insects, and insect larvae.

KEEPS ON SINGING
The male Rufous-winged Sparrow sings his distinctive song all year round.

SIMILAR SPECIES	
CHIPPING SPARROW see p.667	**RUFOUS-CROWNED SPARROW** see p.680

black eye-line

lacks black face stripe

bolder eye-ring

smaller, gray bill

notched tail

OCCURRENCE
Almost a northwest Mexican endemic. Resident in fairly flat Sonoran Desert scrub bunch-grass—much of which habitat has been lost to grazing—from south-central Arizona to central Sinaloa, Mexico.

Length **5¾in (14.5cm)**	Wingspan **7½in (19cm)**	Weight **⁷⁄₁₆–⁵⁄₈oz (12–17g)**
Social **Solitary/Pairs**	Lifespan **Unknown**	Status **Localized**

| Order **Passeriformes** | Family **Emberizidae** | Species *Aimophila cassinii* |

Cassin's Sparrow

pale corners to tail

IN FLIGHT

ADULT

small bill

streaked crown

pale eye-ring

scalloped upperparts

fine patterning on breast

ADULT

more buffy overall

brown streaked underparts

JUVENILE

long, rounded, barred tail

Cassin's Sparrow is a rather drab little brown bird, but more than makes up for its modest appearance with its impressive song, which it often delivers during a bout of skylarking. The end of the song (all of which seems to be in a minor key) is usually a whistled quadruplet that ends on a discordant, questioning note. The bird's occurrence outside its core range—the arid grasslands of central-southern US—depends on rainfall, so it may be rare in some locations one summer, but abundant in the same places the next.

VOICE Calls high *seeps* and *chips*, often in series; song *see-eee sii-ii-i-i-i-i-i-i-i zee-zooo' zee-ZWAAAY*, ending on questioning note.
NESTING Cup placed in grass on or near ground, often in prickly-pear cactus; 2–5 eggs; 1–2 broods; May–September.
FEEDING Scratches around on ground for seeds, flowers, buds, insects, insect larvae, and spiders.

FLIGHT: direct and low, somewhat weak, with fast wing beats in bursts.

COMMON TUNE
This sparrow's song is well-known in the South, and is the easiest way to identify this bird.

OCCURRENCE
Breeds in arid grasslands with scattered shrubs, yuccas, and low trees, from western Nebraska to central Mexico. Winters from US–Mexican border to central Mexico.

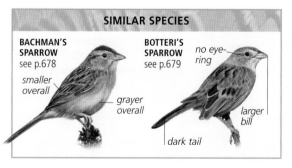

SIMILAR SPECIES

BACHMAN'S SPARROW see p.678
smaller overall
grayer overall

BOTTERI'S SPARROW see p.679
no eye-ring
larger bill
dark tail

| Length **6in (15cm)** | Wingspan **9in (23cm)** | Weight **⅝–¹¹⁄₁₆oz (18–20g)** |
| Social **Solitary** | Lifespan **Unknown** | Status **Declining** |

677

| Order **Passeriformes** | Family **Emberizidae** | Species *Aimophila ruficeps* |

Rufous-crowned Sparrow

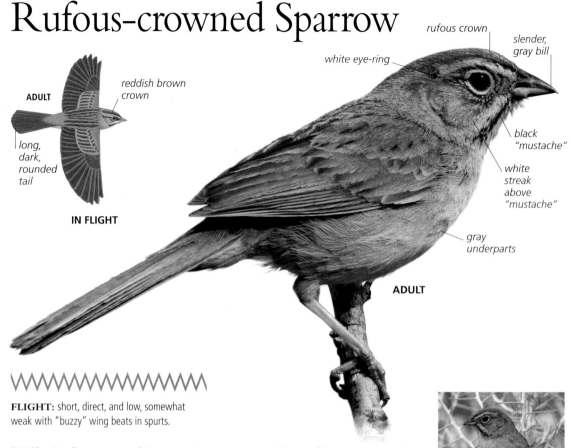

ADULT

reddish brown crown

IN FLIGHT

long, dark, rounded tail

rufous crown

white eye-ring

slender, gray bill

black "mustache"

white streak above "mustache"

gray underparts

ADULT

FLIGHT: short, direct, and low, somewhat weak with "buzzy" wing beats in spurts.

The Rufous-crowned Sparrow is a common resident of dry canyons and sparsely wooded hillsides across the Southwest US, locally up to 5,000ft (1,500m). Its range is very similar to that of the Greater Roadrunner. It is a real skulker, running and hiding at the first sign of danger. For this reason, it is often first detected by its unique *deeer* call note, which it sometimes gives in a laughter-like series. The Rufous-crowned Sparrow is visually quite similar to the rarer Rufous-winged Sparrow, but they have very different calls, and live in quite separate habitats.

VOICE Call a low, nasal *deeer*; song a jumble of chattering notes.

NESTING Cup of twigs and grass placed in bush or rocks on or near ground; 2–5 eggs; 1–3 broods; March–September.

FEEDING Forages on ground and in shrubs for seeds, insects, and insect larvae.

BOLD MARKINGS
This bird's bold white eye-ring and black lateral throat stripes are good field marks.

CATCHING A GLIMPSE
It is possible to tempt this bird into the open by making squeaking noises.

OCCURRENCE
Breeds in arid scrub and low trees on hillsides and in canyons in California, Colorado, Utah, Arizona, New Mexico, Oklahoma, Texas, and Arkansas; also in Mexico (Baja California, on mainland to Isthmus of Tehuantepec). In Mexico found in oak-pine woodlands.

SIMILAR SPECIES

CHIPPING SPARROW see p.667

black eye-line

notched tail

RUFOUS-WINGED SPARROW see p.676

two-toned bill

rufous shoulder patch

| Length **6in (15cm)** | Wingspan **7½in (19cm)** | Weight **½–⅞oz (15–25g)** |
| Social **Solitary** | Lifespan **Unknown** | Status **Secure** |

| Order **Passeriformes** | Family **Emberizidae** | Species *Pipilo chlorurus* |

Green-tailed Towhee

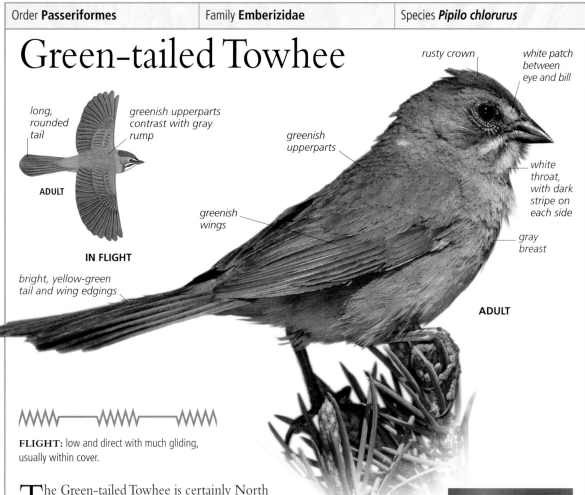

rusty crown

white patch between eye and bill

long, rounded tail

greenish upperparts contrast with gray rump

greenish upperparts

greenish wings

white throat, with dark stripe on each side

gray breast

ADULT

IN FLIGHT

bright, yellow-green tail and wing edgings

ADULT

FLIGHT: low and direct with much gliding, usually within cover.

The Green-tailed Towhee is certainly North America's most distinctive towhee, being the only one with a rusty crown and green plumage. However, it is seldom seen, because it tends to stay hidden on the ground in dense cover, both in the breeding season and on its wintering grounds. Sometimes, in winter, the Green-tailed Towhee comes out to feed on seeds on deserted, dusty roads, but generally you are more likely to hear this bird scratching about in the undergrowth than see it. Although the Olive Sparrow is superficially similar, the two seldom overlap in range or habitat.

VOICE Call a nasal mewing, rapid chips in excitement; flight call a high *tzhreeee*; song a slurred whistle followed by 1–2 trills.

NESTING Bulky cup of twigs and grasses placed on or near ground at base of sagebrush; 3–4 eggs; 1–2 broods; May–July.

FEEDING Forages under cover, often by "double-scratching" with both feet at the same time, for insects, insect larvae, seeds, and some fruit.

WHERE TO SEE IT
Finding a single male atop a bush or tree is the easiest way to see this bird.

OCCURRENCE
Breeds in varied habitats, including chaparral, shrubby hillsides, sage flats, and high-elevation creeks, in much of the western US and northern Baja California. Winters in desert thickets and shallow ravines from the US–Mexican border region to central Mexico.

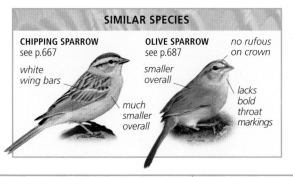

SIMILAR SPECIES

CHIPPING SPARROW
see p.667

white wing bars

much smaller overall

OLIVE SPARROW
see p.687

smaller overall

lacks bold throat markings

no rufous on crown

| Length **7¼in (18.5cm)** | Wingspan **9½in (24cm)** | Weight **¹¹⁄₁₆–1¼oz (20–35g)** |
| Social **Solitary/Small flocks** | Lifespan **Up to 8 years** | Status **Secure** |

Order **Passeriformes**	Family **Emberizidae**	Species *Pipilo maculatus*

Spotted Towhee

rounded tail

white wing bars

white tail tips

MALE

IN FLIGHT

brown tail

white spots on dark sepia-brown upperparts

blackish brown head

FEMALE

long tail, with white outer feathers

blackish head

red eye

broad white spots on black upperparts

rusty flanks

white underparts

MALE

FLIGHT: low and direct, with much gliding, usually within cover.

This large and colorful sparrow can often be heard rummaging through dry leaves in the undergrowth in search of food, when it may even produce roughly circular pits in the soil, using its feet like a garden rake. The Spotted Towhee is variable across its range, and has been seperated into 20 rather complex subspecies, but all are distinguished from the Eastern Towhee by the presence of white spots and bars on their upperwings.
VOICE Depending on geographical location, call *zhreee* or a buzzy, nasal, descending *reeeer*; song ends with a trill.
NESTING Large cup in depression on ground, under cover, also low in thicket; 3–5 eggs; 1–2 broods; April–June.
FEEDING Scratches for food, including insects, fruits, seeds, and acorns; sometimes eats small snakes and lizards.

RUFOUS SIDES
The Spotted Towhee was once grouped with the Eastern Towhee under the name "Rufous-sided Towhee."

DIVERGENT DIALECTS
The vocalizations of the Spotted Towhees vary according to geographical location.

OCCURRENCE
Breeds mainly in thickets, shrubby hillsides, and disturbed forests, from south British Columbia and Saskatchewan across the western US, southward to south Oaxaca, Mexico. Winters in the south-central US and western Midwest.

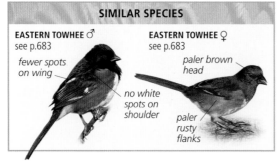

SIMILAR SPECIES

EASTERN TOWHEE ♂
see p.683

fewer spots on wing

no white spots on shoulder

EASTERN TOWHEE ♀
see p.683

paler brown head

paler rusty flanks

Length **8in (20cm)**	Wingspan **10½in (27cm)**	Weight **1¼–1⁹⁄₁₆oz (35–45g)**
Social **Solitary/Small flocks**	Lifespan **Up to 11 years**	Status **Secure**

Order **Passeriformes**	Family **Emberizidae**	Species *Pipilo erythrophthalmus*

Eastern Towhee

black hood and upperparts

red eye

white corners to tail

single white patch in each wing

ADULT

IN FLIGHT

MALE

white belly

white wing patches

long tail

brown hood and upperparts

small white markings on wings

rusty flanks

FEMALE

The Towhees get their name from the up-slurred *chew-eee* (or *to-whee*) call they make. The Eastern Towhee is famous for its vocalizations and has one of the best-known mnemonics for its song: "drink your tea." The Eastern Towhee was once lumped with Spotted Towhees under the name "Rufous-sided Towhee," because they interbreed in the Great Plains. In the southeastern US, Eastern Towhees have paler eyes the further south they are located; individuals with nearly white eyes are found in Florida. Like all towhees, the Eastern Towhee feeds noisily by jumping backwards with both feet at once to move leaves and reveal the insects and seeds that may be hidden underneath.

VOICE Call a nasal, up-slurred *chew-eee*; flight call *zeeeooooweeet*; song sounds like *dweee, dyooo di-i-i-i-i-i-i-i-i-i-i-i-i*.

NESTING Large cup in depression on ground under cover, also low in thicket; 3–5 eggs; 1–2 broods; May–August.

FEEDING Eats seeds, fruits, insects, and buds.

FLIGHT: low and direct with much gliding, usually within cover.

TERRESTRIAL LIFE
The bird stays close to the ground, and is usually found not more than a few yards off it.

OCCURRENCE
Found in dense thickets, woodland, dense shrubbery, forest edges and disturbed forests from southeast Saskatchewan, east Nebraska, west Louisiana, east to south Quebec, south Maine, and south Florida. Retreats from areas north of Chicago to winter in east Texas.

SIMILAR SPECIES

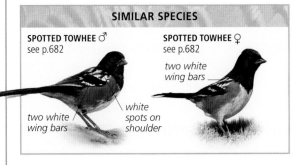

SPOTTED TOWHEE ♂
see p.682

two white wing bars

SPOTTED TOWHEE ♀
see p.682

two white wing bars

white spots on shoulder

Length **7½–8in (19–20cm)**	Wingspan **10½in (27cm)**	Weight **1¹⁄₁₆–1¾oz (30–50g)**
Social **Solitary/Small flocks**	Lifespan **Up to 12 years**	Status **Declining**

Order **Passeriformes**	Family **Emberizidae**	Species *Pipilo fuscus*

Canyon Towhee

faint crown patch

duller undertail feathers

ADULT

denser streaking on underparts

JUVENILE

rusty brown crown

tan patch between eye and bill

pale, buffy facial markings

blackish streaks across lower throat

dark spot on breast

whitish corners to dark tail

IN FLIGHT

long tail

rusty undertail feathers

ADULT

FLIGHT: low and direct with long glides, usually under cover of shrubs.

The Canyon Towhee (once merged with the California Towhee as a single species, the "Brown Towhee") is a bird of the arid Southwest, where it occurs in a wide variety of bushy habitats. Its pale, sandy coloration helps it to blend in with the dusty ground on which it forages. Other species of birds inhabiting the arid Southwest, such as Curve-Billed, LeConte's, Bendire's, and Crissal Thrashers also share this pale color scheme of sand-colored bodies and rusty undertail feathers. The Canyon Towhee, however, can be easily distinguished from the others by its stubby, conical bill.

VOICE Call a nasal *cheemp*; also various clicking and lisping notes, sometimes in series; song a variable slow trill.

NESTING Cup placed at about eye-level close to, or against trunk of tree or bush; 2–5 eggs; 1–2 broods; February–October.

FEEDING Forages on the ground for insects and seeds.

DESERT CAMOUFLAGE
Its sandy coloration helps this towhee to blend in with its desert habitat.

OCCURRENCE
Lives in a variety of habitats, including rocky hillside scrub, desert grasslands, and suburban areas from west Arizona, southeast Colorado, and central Texas to central Mexico. Largely resident, but some birds undertake local movements.

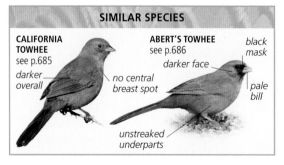

SIMILAR SPECIES

CALIFORNIA TOWHEE
see p.685

darker overall

no central breast spot

ABERT'S TOWHEE
see p.686

darker face

black mask

pale bill

unstreaked underparts

Length **8½in (21cm)**	Wingspan **11½in (29cm)**	Weight **1¼–1¾oz (35–50g)**
Social **Solitary/Small flocks**	Lifespan **Up to 7 years**	Status **Secure**

Order **Passeriformes**	Family **Emberizidae**	Species *Pipilo crissalis*

California Towhee

long, rounded tail

ADULT

IN FLIGHT

rich tan facial markings

grayish or dusky overall

faint throat streaks

plain grayish brown breast, sometimes with faint streaks

ADULT

all-dark tail

rusty undertail feathers

The California Towhee is a fairly large, grayish sparrow, which is common around human settlements. Ornithologists have wondered for a long time whether the Pacific Coast populations of the "Brown Towhee" belonged to the same species as the interior Southwest ones, which are paler and have a brownish cap. In the 1990s, they were split into California and Canyon Towhees, due to differences in DNA, vocalizations, plumage, and geographically distinct ranges.
VOICE Call a ringing, metallic *tink*; song an accelerating trill of ringing *chips*, occasionally ending with squeaky chatter.
NESTING Bulky cup in bush or tree, usually fairly close to the ground; 2–5 eggs; 1–3 broods; February–August.
FEEDING Forages on the ground for various seeds and grass shoots; also consumes insects, including beetles.

FLIGHT: low and direct with much gliding, usually within cover.

LAWN JOCKEY
These towhees are a common sight in California's city parks and suburban gardens.

SIMILAR SPECIES

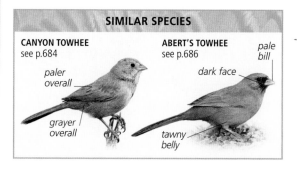

CANYON TOWHEE
see p.684

paler overall

grayer overall

ABERT'S TOWHEE
see p.686

pale bill

dark face

tawny belly

OCCURRENCE
Resident along the Pacific Coast of California in a variety of bushy habitats including dense shrubs and thickets, woodlands close to rivers and streams, gardens, suburban lots, and parks, with open areas for foraging and bush for cover.

Length **9in (23cm)**	Wingspan **11½in (29cm)**	Weight **1⁷⁄₁₆–2⅛oz (40–60g)**
Social **Solitary/Small flocks**	Lifespan **Up to 13 years**	Status **Secure**

| Order **Passeriformes** | Family **Emberizidae** | Species *Pipilo aberti* |

Abert's Towhee

dark tail

black "mask"

ADULT

IN FLIGHT

brownish upperparts

tan head

pale grayish blue bill

grayish tan underparts

pale reddish undertail feathers

ADULT

Restricted to the southwestern US, from Utah and southwest Nevada to southern California, Arizona, and adjacent Baja California, Abert's Towhee was originally a specialist of the dense undergrowth of cottonwood-willow stands along the seasonally flooded Colorado River and its low-lying tributaries. It has declined markedly since its discovery, due to habitat destruction, overgrazing, and invasive plant species such as salt cedar. The species is named after Major James W. Abert, who discovered the first specimen.

VOICE Sharp *peek* call; song a short, accelerating *peek* notes followed by harsh, squeaky chatter; pairs often duet.

NESTING Open cup of dry vegetation placed in shrub; 2–3 eggs; 1 brood; March–September.

FLIGHT: low and direct with much gliding, usually within cover.

LEAF SCRATCHER
Abert's Towee frequently scratches leaf litters to uncover insects hidden underneath.

MASKED TOWHEE
This perched bird displays its characteristic facial mask in addition to its reddish brown undertail.

SIMILAR SPECIES

CANYON TOWHEE
see p.684

lacks dark face

lacks pale bill

pale tail to tips

grayer, streaked underparts

CALIFORNIA TOWHEE
see p.685

lacks dark face

less pale bill

gray-brown belly

OCCURRENCE
Resident in dense brush, remnant patches of mesquite, woodland close to river and streams, and desert scrub; also suburban areas. Prefers the proximity of water, even small streams. Occurs up to about 3,280ft (1,000m).

| Length **9½in (24cm)** | Wingspan **11in (28cm)** | Weight **1⁷⁄₁₆–2oz (40–55g)** |
| Social **Solitary/Small flocks** | Lifespan **Up to 9 years** | Status **Declining** |

| Order **Passeriformes** | Family **Emberizidae** | Species **_Arremonops rufivirgatus_** |

Olive Sparrow

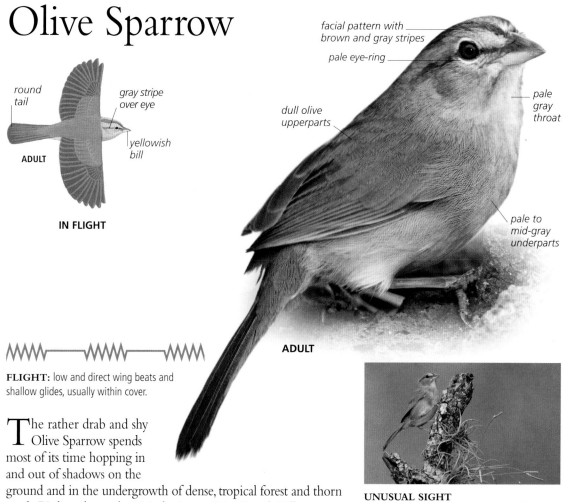

facial pattern with brown and gray stripes

pale eye-ring

dull olive upperparts

pale gray throat

pale to mid-gray underparts

round tail

gray stripe over eye

yellowish bill

ADULT

IN FLIGHT

ADULT

FLIGHT: low and direct wing beats and shallow glides, usually within cover.

The rather drab and shy Olive Sparrow spends most of its time hopping in and out of shadows on the ground and in the undergrowth of dense, tropical forest and thorn scrub. Birdwatchers who visit the Lower Rio Grande Valley in winter look eagerly for this difficult-to-find species. Olive Sparrows do not sing at this time of year, but their lisping calls will often lead to a birdfeeder, where tamer individuals may be observed at length. Their greenish upperparts, larger size, and lack of wing bars make them readily distinct from all plumages of the Chipping Sparrow.

VOICE Dry _chip_ call, also a drawn-out _sreeeeee_; song a series of _chips_ accelerating to a level or down-slurred trill.
NESTING Bulky cup with a dome just above ground in low bush; 2–5 eggs; 1–2 broods; March–September.
FEEDING Eats seeds and insects.

UNUSUAL SIGHT
Olive Sparrows will occasionally fly up to an exposed perch to check their surroundings.

GROUND FORAGER
Under the cover of shrubs, this olive-green bird methodically forages for seed.

OCCURRENCE
Resident in thorn scrub, old fields, "brush country," and tropical forests and forest edges from southern Texas and northwest Mexico south locally to northwest Costa Rica. Often found at backyard feeders in southern Texas.

SIMILAR SPECIES

CHIPPING SPARROW
see p.667

lacks greenish back and wings

lacks round, green tail

GREEN-TAILED TOWHEE
see p.681

white wing bars

reddish crown

white throat

| Length **6½ in (16cm)** | Wingspan **8in (20cm)** | Weight **1¹⁄₁₆–1¹⁄₁₆ oz (19–30g)** |
| Social **Solitary/Small flocks** | Lifespan **Up to 6 years** | Status **Localized** |

| Order **Passeriformes** | Family **Thraupidae** | Species *Piranga flava* |

Hepatic Tanager

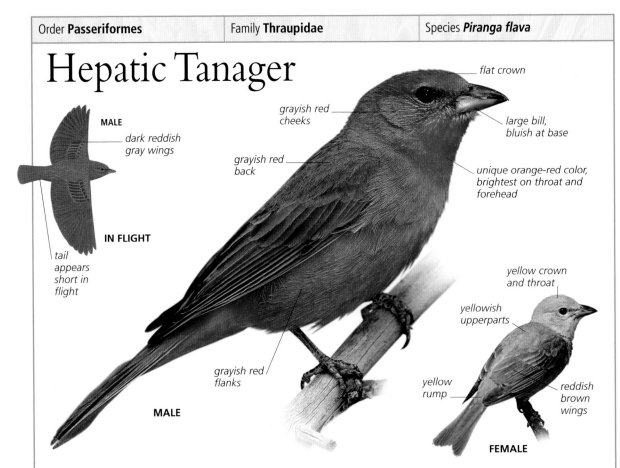

MALE
— dark reddish gray wings

IN FLIGHT

tail appears short in flight

flat crown

grayish red cheeks

grayish red back

large bill, bluish at base

unique orange-red color, brightest on throat and forehead

grayish red flanks

MALE

yellow crown and throat

yellowish upperparts

yellow rump

reddish brown wings

FEMALE

In the US, this species is the Summer Tanager's larger, higher elevation counterpart in the Southwest. Hepatic Tanagers visually differ from Summer Tanagers in having darker gray bills, darker orange plumage, and a flat-headed profile. This species ranges from the southwestern US to Mexico, Central America, and South America, all the way to Argentina. In total, there are 15 subspecies of Hepatic Tanager, but only two of these occur in North America, *P. f. hepatica*, in the far southwestern US, and *P. f. dextia* farther east.

VOICE Flat, single-noted *chuk* or *chup* call; flight call an upslurred, slightly burry *veet;* song less burry than other tanager and fairly similar to American Robin and Black-headed Grosbeak.

NESTING Loosely constructed cup of grasses placed high in tree; 3–5 eggs; 1 brood; May–August.

FEEDING Eats a variety of insects, such as flies, beetles, and caterpillars; also consumes fruit and nectar.

FLIGHT: strong, purposeful, and direct with quick wing beats.

PLAINER PLUMAGE
The orange-red plumage, and a pine forest habitat distinguish this bird from the Summer Tanager.

OCCURRENCE
Found in southwestern US in open, mountain woodlands of pine and pine-oak from southeast California and Colorado to Texas. Winters away from US, except in extreme southeast Arizona. Also found from Mexico to Panama, and Columbia to Argentina.

SIMILAR SPECIES

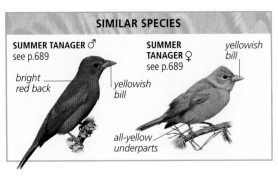

SUMMER TANAGER ♂ see p.689
bright red back
yellowish bill

SUMMER TANAGER ♀ see p.689
yellowish bill
all-yellow underparts

| Length **8in (20cm)** | Wingspan **12½in (32cm)** | Weight **⅞–1⁹⁄₁₆oz (25–45g)** |
| Social **Solitary** | Lifespan **Unknown** | Status **Secure** |

Order **Passeriformes**	Family **Thraupidae**	Species *Piranga rubra*

Summer Tanager

tail appears short in flight

MALE (BREEDING)

IN FLIGHT

dark eye

thick, long, yellowish bill

variable red-and-yellow patchwork

bright red upperparts

red head and breast

IMMATURE (1ST SPRING)

lacks grayish cheek patches

red wash overall

**FEMALE
P. r. rubra
(EASTERN)**

brownish legs and toes

**MALE
(BREEDING)**

crested head

olive-yellow upperparts

**FEMALE
P. r. cooperi (SOUTHWESTERN)**

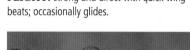

FLIGHT: strong and direct with quick wing beats; occasionally glides.

The stunning male Summer Tanager is the only North American bird that is entirely bright red. Immature males in their first spring plumage are almost equally as striking, with their patchwork of bright yellow-and-red plumage. There are two subspecies of the Summer Tanager that are visually quite similar—*P. r. rubra* breeds in the East while *P. r. cooperi* breeds in the West. The latter is, on an average, paler, larger, and longer-billed.

VOICE Call an explosive *PIT-tuck!* or *PIT-a TUK*; flight call a muffled, airy *vreee*; song similar to American Robin, but more muffled and with longer pauses.

NESTING Loosely built cup of grasses usually placed high up in tree; 3–4 eggs; 1 brood; May–August.

FEEDING Eats bees, wasps, and other insects; also consumes fruit.

MAD FOR MULBERRIES
All *Piranga* tanagers are frugivores in season, with mulberries, one of their favorites.

SIMILAR SPECIES

HEPATIC TANAGER ♀
see p.688
yellowish upperparts

reddish brown wings

SCARLET TANAGER ♀
see p.690
greenish overall

smaller, grayish bill

darker, wings and tail

OCCURRENCE
P. r. rubra breeds in deciduous and mixed woodlands from New Jersey and Nebraska south to Texas; *P. r. cooperi* in cottonwood-willow habitats near streams and rivers from California and Utah to Texas and Mexico. Both winter from southern Texas and Mexico to Bolivia and Brazil, and the Bahamas.

Length **8in (20cm)**	Wingspan **12in (31cm)**	Weight **⅞–1⁷⁄₁₆oz (25–40g)**
Social **Solitary**	Lifespan **Unknown**	Status **Secure**

| Order **Passeriformes** | Family **Thraupidae** | Species *Piranga olivacea* |

Scarlet Tanager

black wings

red body

vibrant scarlet head and body

dark brown eyes

grayish yellow bill

yellow patches in red plumage

MALE (MOLTING)

tail appears short in flight

MALE (BREEDING)

IN FLIGHT

greenish rump and upper tail

overall greenish upperparts

FEMALE

black wings

dark gray feet and legs

yellow-green body, head, and rump

black tail

MALE (BREEDING)

MALE (NONBREEDING)

Although the male Scarlet Tanager, in its breeding plumage, is one of the brightest and most easily identified North American birds, its secretive nature and preference for the canopies of well-shaded oak woodlands makes it difficult to spot. The male is most easily located by its distinctive and easily recognizable song. Male Scarlet Tanagers can vary in appearance—some are orange, not scarlet, and others have a faint reddish wing bar.

VOICE Call a hoarse, drawn out *CHIK-breeer*, often shortened to *CHIK*; flight call an upslurred, whistled *pwee*; song a burry, slurred *querit-queer-query-querit-queer*.

NESTING Loosely woven cup of grass, lined with fine material, high up in tree; 3–5 eggs; 1 brood; May–July.

FEEDING Gleans insects, larvae, fruit, buds, and berries.

FLIGHT: strong and direct; rapid wing beats.

STUNNING MALE
Taking a bath away from the treetops, a male Scarlet Tanager can be seen in all its glory.

SIMILAR SPECIES

VERMILION FLYCATCHER ♂
see p.423

brown wings and tail

SUMMER TANAGER ♀
see p.689

olive-yellow upperparts

thinner bill

larger bill

yellowish underparts

OCCURRENCE
Breeds in mature deciduous and mixed forests (especially with large oaks) from southern Manitoba and eastern Oklahoma east to the Maritime Provinces and the Carolinas. Trans-Gulf migrant. Winters in varied habitats along the eastern slope of the Andes from eastern Panama to Bolivia.

| Length **7in (18cm)** | Wingspan **11½in (29cm)** | Weight **¹¹⁄₁₆–1¼oz (20–35g)** |
| Social **Solitary/Small flocks** | Lifespan **At least 10 years** | Status **Secure** |

Order **Passeriformes**	Family **Thraupidae**	Species *Piranga ludoviciana*

Western Tanager

two wing bars

orange head

MALE (BREEDING)

IN FLIGHT

more olive and grayish overall

FEMALE (NONBREEDING)

orange head and hood, blending into yellow

yellow collar

yellow upperwing bar

jet-black back

white lower wing bar

black tail

bright yellow rump

MALE (BREEDING)

bright yellow underparts

bluish gray feet and legs

red wash on face

MALE (NONBREEDING)

olive-green upperparts

FEMALE (BREEDING)

FLIGHT: strong and direct; deliberate.

The hoarse song of the exquisitely plumaged male Western Tanager is a characteristic sound of coniferous forests in western North America. All *Piranga* tanagers have songs and whistled flight calls that closely resemble those of the *Pheucticus* grosbeaks. Recent studies hint that this is not a coincidence and that *Piranga* tanagers are actually part of the family Cardinalidae, not Thraupidae (tanagers).

VOICE Distinctive call, a rolled *pruh-DHIT!* or *pur-duh-RIT!*; flight call a *hweee*; song similar to Scarlet Tanager, but less burry.

NESTING Loosely woven cup of grasses, lined with rootlets, high in tree; 3–5 eggs; 1 brood; May–August.

FEEDING Forages for insects such as termites, flies, moths, and bees in breeding season; eats berries in nonbreeding season.

ORANGE AND YELLOW
Two Western Tanagers proudly display their bright fall-colored plumage.

SIMILAR SPECIES

SCARLET TANAGER ♀
see p.690

greener overall

lacks bold wing bars

BRIGHT BLEND
This colorful bird blends into its surroundings surprisingly well.

OCCURRENCE
Breeds farther north than any other tanager, in open coniferous and mixed forests of the West, from southeastern Alaska and southwestern Northwest Territories to north Baja California and western Texas. Winters from southern California and northeastern Mexico.

Length **7½in (19cm)**	Wingspan **11½in (29cm)**	Weight **⅞–1¼ oz (25–35g)**
Social **Solitary**	Lifespan **Up to 8 years**	Status **Secure**

Order **Passeriformes**	Family **Cardinalidae**	Species *Spiza americana*

Dickcissel

streaked back

MALE (BREEDING)

IN FLIGHT

yellow eyebrow

gray nape

rufous shoulder

large, pointed bill

yellow-tinged, long eye-line

bold braces on back

black "v" on yellow breast

FEMALE

finely streaked underparts

MALE (BREEDING)

paler gray on face

no rufous shoulder

MALE (NONBREEDING)

The Dickcissel is a tallgrass prairie specialist and seldom breeds outside this core range. Known for its dramatic seasonal movements, the Dickcissel winters in Venezuela, with flocks in tens of thousands ravaging rice fields and damaging seed crops, making it a notorious pest. Immature birds, without yellow and rusty plumage, are very similar to female House Sparrows—vagrant and wintering Dickcissels in North America are often mistaken as such.

VOICE Call a flat *chik*; flight call a distinctive, low, electric buzz *frrrrrrt*; song a short series of sharp, insect-like stutters followed by few longer chirps or trill *dick-dick-dick-SISS-SISS-suhl*.

NESTING Bulky cup placed near ground in dense vegetation; 3–6 eggs; 1–2 broods; May–August.

FEEDING Forages on ground for insects, spiders, and seeds.

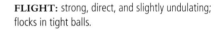

FLIGHT: strong, direct, and slightly undulating; flocks in tight balls.

UNIQUE SONG
The Dickcissel's onomatopoeic song is the classic sound of a healthy tallgrass prairie.

SIMILAR SPECIES

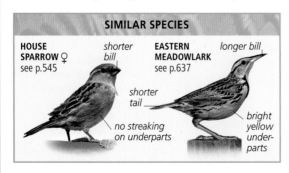

HOUSE SPARROW ♀ see p.545

shorter bill

shorter tail

no streaking on underparts

EASTERN MEADOWLARK see p.637

longer bill

bright yellow underparts

OCCURRENCE
Breeds in tallgrass prairie, grassland, hayfields, unmown roadsides, and untilled cropfields across eastern central US. Barely reaches southernmost Canada and northeast Mexico. Winters in huge flocks in Venezuela, in open areas with tall grass-like vegetation, including rice fields.

Length **6½in (16cm)**	Wingspan **9½in (24cm)**	Weight **⅞–1¼oz (25–35g)**
Social **Large flocks**	Lifespan **Up to 5 years**	Status **Declining**

Order **Passeriformes**	Family **Cardinalidae**	Species *Pheucticus ludovicianus*

Rose-breasted Grosbeak

black head and back

white rump

MALE (BREEDING)

IN FLIGHT

short tail with white corners

IMMATURE MALE (1ST FALL)

rosy or orange breast

white marks on head

large, pinkish bill

white wing bars

thick streaks on underparts

FEMALE

bold, white wing patches

rose-red breast

white belly

brown patches on back

streaked underparts

MALE (NONBREEDING)

MALE (BREEDING)

For many birdwatchers in the East, the appearance of a flock of dazzling male Rose-breasted Grosbeaks in early May signals the peak of spring songbird migration. Adult males in their tuxedo attire, with rose-red ties, are unmistakable, but females and immature males are more somber. In the fall, immature male Rose-breasted Grosbeaks often have orange breasts, and are commonly mistaken for female Black-headed Grosbeaks. The difference is in the pink wing lining usually visible on perched birds, pink bill, and streaking across the center of the breast.

VOICE Call a high, sharp, explosive *sink* or *eeuk*, reminiscent of the squeak of sneakers on floor tiles, flight call an airy *vreee*; song a liquid, flute-like warble, rather slow in delivery, almost relaxed.

NESTING Loose, open cup or platform, usually in deciduous saplings, mid to high level; 2–5 eggs; 1–2 broods; May–July.

FEEDING Eats arthropods, fruit, seeds, and buds.

FLIGHT: undulating but powerful flight with bursts of wing beats.

SIMILAR SPECIES

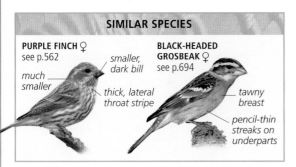

PURPLE FINCH ♀
see p.562

much smaller

smaller, dark bill

thick, lateral throat stripe

BLACK-HEADED GROSBEAK ♀
see p.694

tawny breast

pencil-thin streaks on underparts

STUNNING MALE
A striking male Rose-breasted Grosbeak in springtime is quite unmistakable on a tree.

OCCURRENCE
Breeds in deciduous and mixed woods, parks, and orchards across the northeastern quarter of the US, and across Canada westward from Newfoundland through Ontario to southeast Yukon. Winters from Mexico and the Caribbean, south to Guyana and Peru. Rare in the West.

Length **8in (20cm)**	Wingspan **12½in (32cm)**	Weight **1¼–2oz (35–55g)**
Social **Solitary/Small flocks**	Lifespan **Up to 13 years**	Status **Secure**

| Order **Passeriformes** | Family **Cardinalidae** | Species *Pheucticus melanocephalus* |

Black-headed Grosbeak

MALE (BREEDING)
large, white wing patch

IN FLIGHT
brown head and upperparts
white eyebrow

FEMALE
tawny breast
fine brown streaks on underparts

blackish brown cheek patch
white tip to feathers
MALE (1ST FALL)
pencil-thin streaks on breast
black upperparts
two white wing bars
orange rump

black head
thick, gray-and-black bill
orange hind collar
orange breast
MALE
short tail, with white corners

FLIGHT: undulating but powerful, with few rapid wing beats followed by glides.

Well-known and widespread across the West, this orange-breasted grosbeak is the western counterpart of the Rose-breasted Grosbeak. The two species are closely related, despite their color differences, and interbreed where their ranges meet in the Great Plains. The Black-headed Grosbeak is aggressive on its breeding grounds, with both sexes fighting off intruders.

VOICE Call a *hwik*, similar to Rose-breasted Grosbeak, but flatter, "hollow," and less squeaky; song generally higher, faster, less fluid, and harsher.

NESTING Loose, open cup or platform, usually in deciduous sapling, not far above eye level; 3–5 eggs; 1–2 broods; May–September.

FEEDING Gleans insects and spiders; also eats seeds and fruit.

STREAMSIDE SONGSTER
Through much of its range, this species is common along riverside corridors containing a variety of trees.

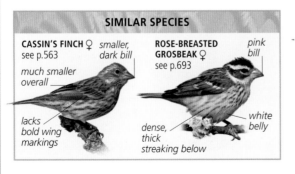

SIMILAR SPECIES

CASSIN'S FINCH ♀ see p.563
smaller, dark bill
much smaller overall
lacks bold wing markings

ROSE-BREASTED GROSBEAK ♀ see p.693
pink bill
dense, thick streaking below
white belly

OCCURRENCE
Breeds in dense deciduous growth—old fields, hedgerows, next to waterways, disturbed forests, and hillside thickets—from British Columbia and Saskatchewan, south to Baja California, and central Mexico. Winters in interior, highlands, and Pacific slope of Mexico.

| Length **8½in (21cm)** | Wingspan **12½in (32cm)** | Weight **1⁷⁄₁₆–2oz (40–55g)** |
| Social **Solitary/Small flocks** | Lifespan **Up to 9 years** | Status **Secure** |

| Order **Passeriformes** | Family **Cardinalidae** | Species *Cardinalis cardinalis* |

Northern Cardinal

MALE

warm red overall

IN FLIGHT

smaller, duller crest

brownish wings

darker bill

JUVENILE

prominent crest

thick, orange-red bill

bright red back and wings

black patch on face, extends onto throat

MALE

reddish crest

buff-olive upperparts

dark patch not as extensive as male

red on outer tail feathers

grayish brown underparts

FEMALE

brownish toes and legs

long, red tail

The Northern Cardinal, or "redbird," is a familiar sight across the eastern US. Its range was expanding in the early- to mid-20th century, when state birds were being chosen, and was considered a novelty at the time; as a result, it is the state bird of seven different states. The male aggressively repels intruders and will occasionally attack his reflection in windows and various shiny surfaces.

VOICE Sharp, metallic *tik* call, also bubbly chatters; song a loud, variable, sweet, slurred whistle, *tsee-ew-tsee-ew-whoit-whoit-whoit-whoit-whoit*.

NESTING Loose, flimsy cup of grass, bark, and leaves, in deciduous thicket; 2–4 eggs; 1–3 broods; April–September.

FEEDING Eats seeds and insects, such as beetles and caterpillars; also buds and fruit.

FLIGHT: weak, flapping with downward-angled tail; interrupted by short glides; low within cover.

CONSPICUOUS COLOR
This Northern Cardinal's vivid plumage means that it is often easy to spot on snowy winter days.

OCCURRENCE
Resident in thickets of various relatively moist habitats, such as deciduous woodland, scrub, desert washes, and backyards. Range spans across the eastern US, southernmost Canada, the extreme Southwest, and south into Mexico, northern Guatemala, and northern Belize.

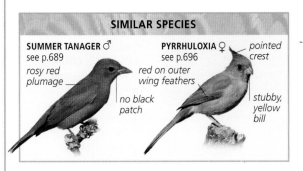

SIMILAR SPECIES

SUMMER TANAGER ♂
see p.689
rosy red plumage
no black patch

PYRRHULOXIA ♀
see p.696
pointed crest
red on outer wing feathers
stubby, yellow bill

| Length **8½in (22cm)** | Wingspan **12in (30cm)** | Weight **1⁷⁄₁₆–1¾oz (40–50g)** |
| Social **Solitary** | Lifespan **Up to 16 years** | Status **Secure** |

Order **Passeriformes**	Family **Cardinalidae**	Species ***Cardinalis sinuatus***

Pyrrhuloxia

red flight feathers

red restricted to wings and tail

thin, wispy, pointed crest

mostly pale buffy gray

duller bill

tall, pointed crest

gray neck and back

stubby, parrot-like, yellow bill

MALE

IN FLIGHT

FEMALE

long, rounded, red tail

red outer wing feathers

red tail

rosy red breast and face

MALE

The "Pyro" is considered to be the Southwest's equivalent of the Northern Cardinal and was once known as the "Arizona Cardinal." Their ranges do overlap, and, although the two birds share very similar habits and vocalizations, they seem to tolerate each other's presence well. The Pyrrhuloxia's odd common name was once its genus name, when it was considered less closely related to the Northern Cardinal; it is formed by the combination of two genera, *Pyrrhula*, taken from the Greek *pyrros*, meaning flame-colored, and *loxia*, from the Greek *loxos*, meaning crooked (in reference to its bill).

VOICE Call a distinctive dry, flat, low *chik*, often accelerating into chatter; song generally higher, thinner, and less musical than the Northern Cardinal's.

NESTING Compact cup of fine material near or above eye level; 2–5 eggs; 1–2 broods; April–August.

FEEDING Eats seeds, insects, fruit, and nectar.

FLIGHT: weak with much flapping with downward-angled tail; interrupted by brief glides.

PRETTY PYRO
The male Pyrrhuloxia is one of the Southwest's most striking birds.

OCCURRENCE
Desert scrub of southeastern Arizona, southern New Mexico, southern Texas, and Mexico. Where they occur together, Pyrrhuloxia often prefers drier, more upland habitats than the Northern Cardinal, at elevations up to 6,500ft (2000m), but there is much overlap.

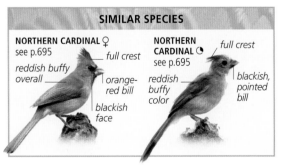

SIMILAR SPECIES

NORTHERN CARDINAL ♀
see p.695

reddish buffy overall

full crest

orange-red bill

blackish face

NORTHERN CARDINAL ♂
see p.695

full crest

reddish buffy color

blackish, pointed bill

Length **8½in (22cm)**	Wingspan **12in (30cm)**	Weight **⅞–1⁹⁄₁₆oz (25–45g)**
Social **Solitary**	Lifespan **Up to 10 years**	Status **Secure**

Order **Passeriformes**	Family **Cardinalidae**	Species *Passerina caerulea*

Blue Grosbeak

rufous wing bars

blue upperparts

MALE

IN FLIGHT

upperparts like adult male, but with brown patches

IMMATURE MALE (1ST SUMMER)

uniform dark indigo head

black patch between eye and bill

black streaks on shoulder feathers

rufous shoulder

MALE

tawny wing bars

huge bill

pale tan overall

FEMALE

T̲he massive bill of this species earned it the name "grosbeak." Blue Grosbeaks, previously seen only in the South, have expanded their range northward in recent years, especially in the Great Plains. Nevertheless, they are not abundant in any area and spotting one is fairly rare. In the East, dull-plumaged, male Indigo Buntings with brown wing bars can be misidentified as Blue Grosbeaks in the spring. Features that help identification are the Grosbeak's huge bill, uniformly dark plumage, black face, and reddish shoulder, which the buntings lack.

VOICE Call a loud, sharp, metallic *tchink*; similar to Indigo Bunting, but lower-pitched, louder, and burrier; song rambling, husky.

NESTING Compact cup placed low in deciduous tangle; 3–5 eggs; 1–2 broods; April–July.

FEEDING Eats seeds in winter, insects such as beetles, caterpillars, and grasshoppers in summer, and fruit.

FLIGHT: lightly undulating, fast, and direct.

SIMILAR SPECIES

INDIGO BUNTING ♂ 1ST ☙ see p.698	LAZULI BUNTING ♀ see p.699
pale blue markings overall	pale brown upperparts	much smaller bill

TRUE INDIGO
The Blue Grosbeak is truly indigo in color, with beautiful rufous shoulders.

OCCURRENCE
Breeds in dense undergrowth of disturbed habitats: old fields, hedgerows, and desert scrub across southern US from California to New Jersey, and southward to northwestern Costa Rica; breeders are trans-Gulf migrants; winters from Mexico to Panama and West Indies.

Length **6¾in (17cm)**	Wingspan **11in (28cm)**	Weight **⅞–1¹⁄₁₆oz (25–30g)**
Social **Large flocks**	Lifespan **Up to 6 years**	Status **Declining**

Order **Passeriformes**	Family **Cardinalidae**	Species *Passerina cyanea*

Indigo Bunting

blue overall; often appears black in flight

MALE (BREEDING)

IN FLIGHT

intermediate between male and female plumage

IMMATURE MALE (1ST SPRING)

darker head

indigo face

bright, cyan-blue body

MALE (BREEDING)

dull brown overall

small bill

whitish throat

blurry streaks on breast

bluish cast to wings and tail

FEMALE

Few North American birds are more brilliantly colored than the Indigo Bunting. However, it is not particularly well named, because the bird is really not indigo but rather a vibrant, almost cyan-blue. The color only turns to indigo on the male's head before finally becoming a rich violet on the face. Indigo Buntings are specialists of disturbed habitats, originally depending on tree-falls within forests and the grassland-forest edge. Human activity, however, has radically increased suitable breeding habitats. As a result, Indigo Buntings are much more common and widespread than they were a hundred years ago. This adaptable species has even learned to nest in cornfields.

VOICE Call a sharp, dry, rattling *pik!*; flight a call long buzz; song series of simple, high-pitched, paired whistles, often described as "*fire!-fire!, where?-where?, there!-there!, put-it-out!, put-it-out!*"

NESTING Open cup above ground in dense tangle or shrub; 3–4 eggs; 1–3 broods; May–September.

FEEDING Eats seeds, insects, fruits, and buds.

FLIGHT: lightly undulating, fast, and direct; gliding and fluttering in territorial encounters.

SOUND OF SUMMER
This is one of the most common and cheerful songbirds found in eastern North America.

OCCURRENCE
Breeds in moist disturbed habitats—weedy fields, forest edges, and areas of heavy cultivation across the eastern US, southeastern Canada, and also locally in the Southwest. Winters from Mexico and the Caribbean south to Panama, and in small numbers along the Gulf Coast and in Florida.

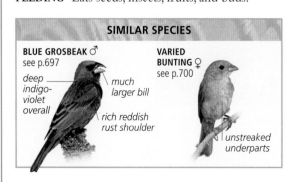

SIMILAR SPECIES

BLUE GROSBEAK ♂
see p.697

deep indigo-violet overall

much larger bill

rich reddish rust shoulder

VARIED BUNTING ♀
see p.700

unstreaked underparts

Length **5½in (14cm)**	Wingspan **8in (20cm)**	Weight **⁷⁄₁₆ –¹¹⁄₁₆oz (12–19g)**
Social **Large flocks**	Lifespan **Up to 11 years**	Status **Secure**

Order **Passeriformes**	Family **Cardinalidae**	Species *Passerina amoena*

Lazuli Bunting

MALE (BREEDING)

bold, white wing bars

blue tinge to wings and tail

IN FLIGHT

tawny breast

unstreaked underparts

FEMALE

sky-blue head

mantle tinged with brown

dull orange breast

conspicuous white shoulder

white belly

MALE

white shoulder

bluish rump

whitish belly

IMMATURE MALE (1ST SPRING)

sky-blue rump

Resembling a small bluebird, the dazzling Lazuli Bunting is the Indigo Bunting's western counterpart. The two species are closely related and hybrids are locally common where the two species meet on the Great Plains. Male hybrids are of two main types—the first resembles an Indigo Bunting with a white belly and wing bars, and the second resembles a dull Indigo Bunting with a brownish smudged back. Females may be impossible to identify. The Lazuli Bunting's common name is taken from the blue, semiprecious gemstone, lapis lazuli.

VOICE Call a sharp, dry, rattling *pik!* similar to Indigo Bunting; song a higher, faster, thinner, and with less repetition than Indigo Bunting.

NESTING Open cup above ground in dense tangle or shrub; 3–4 eggs; 1–2 broods; April–August.

FEEDING Eats seeds and fruits; insects if breeding.

FLIGHT: lightly undulating, fast, and direct; erratic flights during territorial encounters.

SIMILAR SPECIES

BLUE GROSBEAK ♀
see p.697

reddish rust on shoulder

larger overall

bigger bill

INDIGO BUNTING ♀
see p.698

lacks bold wing bars

streaking on breast

DAPPLED AND DAPPER
Brightly colored males blend into their surroundings surprisingly well in dappled sunlight.

OCCURRENCE
Breeds in various open, disturbed habitats, especially alongside waterways and in thickets from southern British Columbia and southern Saskatchewan to northern Baja California and northern New Mexico. Winters from southern Arizona to southwestern Mexico. Casual in the East.

Length **5½in (14cm)**	Wingspan **8½in (22cm)**	Weight **⁷⁄₁₆–⁵⁄₈oz (13–18g)**
Social **Large flocks**	Lifespan **Up to 10 years**	Status **Secure**

| Order **Passeriformes** | Family **Cardinalidae** | Species *Passerina versicolor* |

Varied Bunting

BREEDING MALE

blue rump appears black

black face

lacks streaking and bold wing bars

IN FLIGHT

gray bill

plain brown overall

FEMALE

red nape

red eye-ring

blackish back and wings

purple breast

brown scaling on feather edges

MALE

glowing blue rump

FLIGHT: lightly undulating, fast, and direct; fluttering in territorial encounters.

The Varied Bunting is distinctive as it is the only purple-and-red songbird in North America. When seen in good light, males are a rich, deep, plum color with ruby-red napes and sparkling, sapphire-blue foreheads and rumps. However, in poor light, they appear black. The female, by contrast, is the dullest member of the Cardinalidae group, but the lack of patterning or distinct coloring is a good field mark. This bunting is a Mexican species with a small US range, where it is localized and hard to find. In Texas, its vocal similarity to the Painted Bunting makes finding one challenging.

VOICE Call a sharp, dry, rattling *pik!* similar to Indigo Bunting; song a pleasant, rambling, burry warble, jerkier than Blue Grosbeak and Painted Bunting.

NESTING Open cup placed high in thorny scrub; 2–5 eggs; brooding unknown; May–September.

FEEDING Eats seeds, arthropods, and fruit.

PLUM PURPLE
No other US songbird shares the male Varied Bunting's dazzling color combination.

OCCURRENCE
Breeds in dense desert scrub, particularly in canyons and washes, and in thorn forests from southern Arizona, southeastern New Mexico, and southern Texas to Guatemala. In winter, most US birds migrate south to the coastal slopes of Mexico.

SIMILAR SPECIES

INDIGO BUNTING ♀
see p.698
pale edges to wing feathers

straight bill

streaked underparts

LAZULI BUNTING ♀
see p.699
whitish or buffy wing bars

bright blue on tail extends to rump

tawny wash across breast

| Length **5½in (14cm)** | Wingspan **7½–8in (19–20cm)** | Weight **⅜–½oz (10–15g)** |
| Social **Large flocks** | Lifespan **Unknown** | Status **Secure** |

| Order **Passeriformes** | Family **Cardinalidae** | Species *Passerina ciris* |

Painted Bunting

blue head

**MALE
(BREEDING)**

IN FLIGHT

irregular bluish patches on head

irregular reddish patches on wings and underparts

**MALE
(1ST SPRING)**

lime-green color above

yellowish underparts

FEMALE

glowing chartreuse back

red-and-green wings

red rump

violet-blue hood

red underparts

MALE

FLIGHT: lightly undulating, fast, and direct hovering "butterfly flight" when males meet.

With its violet-blue head, red underparts, and vibrant lime-green back, the adult male Painted Bunting is the most brightly colored bunting in North America. Although dull, the female is still quite distinctive as one of the few truly green songbirds of the region. Young male Painted Buntings take on a variety of appearances and can resemble an adult male, a female, or something between. There are two populations that differ in molt pattern. Western birds molt after leaving the breeding grounds, while eastern birds molt before they depart for the winter.
VOICE Call a soft, ringing, upward slurred *pwip!;* flight call a slurred, softer, and flatter than Indigo Bunting; song a sweet, rambling, relatively clear warble.
NESTING Deep cup in dense tangle or shrub, just above ground; 3–4 eggs; 1–3 broods; May–August.
FEEDING Eats seeds, fruit, and insects.

SIMILAR SPECIES

INDIGO BUNTING ♀
see p.698

lacks green upperparts

bluish wash to tail

VARIED BUNTING ♀
see p.700

streaked breast

tan overall

lacks green upperparts

stubbier bill

tan overall

"NONPAREIL"
In Louisiana, the French word for "unparalleled" is fittingly used to describe this gorgeous species.

OCCURRENCE
Breeds in dense thickets, tangles, and disturbed areas, across south central US and northern Mexico and along the East Coast from Florida to North Carolina. Nonbreeders use similar habitats. Western birds winter from tropical Mexico to western Panama; eastern birds winter in southern Florida and Cuba.

| Length **5½in (14cm)** | Wingspan **8½in (22cm)** | Weight **⁷⁄₁₆–¹¹⁄₁₆oz (12–21g)** |
| Social **Solitary/Flocks** | Lifespan **Up to 12 years** | Status **Secure** |

RARE SPECIES

Family **Phasianidae**	Species *Tetraogallus himalayensis*

Himalayan Snowcock

Introduced in the 1960s to overcome Nevada's lack of upland gamebirds, the Himalayan Snowcock took nearly 20 years to become successfully established. This large, wary species with its white head and brown body usually appears gray when viewed at a distance.

OCCURRENCE High elevations; local in Ruby Mountains of northwestern Nevada.

VOICE Variety of low and high whistles; clucks, cackles, and chuckles to signal food, alarm, mating, and to communicate.

gray background with mottled brown-and gray-streaks

dark brown stripes on each side of neck

ADULT

Length 23½–29in (60–74cm)	Wingspan 28–31in (71–79cm)

Family **Anatidae**	Species *Cygnus cygnus*

Whooper Swan

The Whooper Swan is the Eurasian counterpart of the Trumpeter Swan, differing in having a conspicuous yellow patch at the base of the bill, which extends along the sides of the bill to form a point.

OCCURRENCE Rare vagrant to western North America; breeds across northern Eurasia and is generally found in freshwater wetlands.

VOICE Loud, deep, resonant call *whoop-whoop*, given in flight.

yellow base of bill

long neck

white overall

ADULT

Length 4½–5¼ft (1.4–1.6m)	Wingspan 7–7¾ft (2.1–2.4m)

Family **Anatidae**	Species *Cairina moschata*

Muscovy Duck

The Muscovy Duck is a neotropical species whose range barely reaches the US. Wild ducks are all-black with bold white wing patches. There are many feral Muscovy Ducks, particularly from Texas to Florida, but these usually have more white in their plumage. Muscovy Ducks interbreed with other ducks, creating odd-looking hybrids.

OCCURRENCE From Mexico to South America; wild Muscovy Ducks only found along the Rio Grande River in southern Texas.

VOICE Males give a high-pitched hiss; female a soft quack; normally silent.

pale bands on black bill

ragged crest

black overall

ADULT

Length 26–34in (66–86cm)	Wingspan 4¼–5ft (1.3–1.5m)

Family **Anatidae**	Species *Anas penelope*

Eurasian Wigeon

The adult male Eurasian Wigeon is distinctive with its bright chestnut head and broad, creamy yellow forehead. Its bold white forewing, with a green patch bordered in black, is conspicuous in flight. In recent decades, the number of Eurasian Wigeons recorded has increased, particularly in the Pacific Northwest.

OCCURRENCE Winters regularly on both Atlantic and Pacific coasts, with small numbers found inland.

VOICE Males a high-pitched, whistled *wheeeo*; females a low, growling *krrr* or *karr*.

ADULT

pinkish breast

gray body

Length 17½–20in (45–51cm)	Wingspan 30–34in (75–86cm)

Family **Anatidae**	Species *Anas querquedula*

Garganey

The Garganey is a small dabbling duck, the same size and shape as the Blue-winged Teal. A male in breeding plumage is unmistakable, its bold white eyebrow contrasting sharply with its dark brown head. In flight, it has a silver-gray forewing with a broad, white trailing edge.

OCCURRENCE Native to Eurasia, records span North America; prefers wetland habitats with emergent vegetation.

VOICE Male a low, dry rattling *knerek* or *kerrek* call; female a high-pitched quack.

gray sides contrast with brown breast

bold white eyebrow extends to nape

MALE

Length **14½–16in (37–41cm)**	Wingspan **23½–25in (60–64cm)**

Family **Anatidae**	Species *Aythya fuligula*

Tufted Duck

This medium-sized diving duck is a close relative of the scaups and the Ring-necked Duck. Males are quite distinctive with their all-black head, breast, and back, brilliant white sides, and long, drooping crest. The females are brown with a smaller crest and white undertail feathers.

OCCURRENCE Regular migrant in western Aleutians; casual winter visitor to West Coast; rare Great Lakes to East Coast; accidental midcontinent.

VOICE Mostly silent; males a vibrant whistled *wheep-wee-whew* during courtship; females a low, repeated growling *err*.

long, drooping crest

black back and white sides

ADULT (BREEDING)

Length **15½–18½in (40–47cm)**	Wingspan **26–29in (67–73cm)**

Family **Anatidae**	Species *Mergellus albellus*

Smew

The Smew, a small member of the merganser tribe of ducks, is a rare vagrant on the West Coast. Males are unmistakable in breeding plumage—white with a black mask and other black markings. In flight, the wings are black with a white forewing patch. It is rarely seen with other species. Females are gray with a reddish cap and white chin and cheek.

OCCURRENCE Native of Eurasia from Scandinavia to Siberia; rare but regular in west Alaska; casual south to California; accidental elsewhere in North America.

VOICE Mostly silent; during courtship, males give various grunts and whistles; occasional low growl by female.

black, white, and gray upperparts

black mask

ADULT (BREEDING)

Length **15–17½in (38–44cm)**	Wingspan **21½–27in (55–69cm)**

Family **Anatidae**	Species *Nomonyx dominicus*

Masked Duck

A small, widespread, neotropical species, the Masked Duck is rarely seen due to its secretive behavior. Like grebes, it sinks below the surface to avoid detection, and drags its tail under the water. In flight, its white wing patch is characteristic. Females have two dark bars across their face, and a mottled brown body.

OCCURRENCE Resident of south Texas, with scattered records elsewhere in the US; in heavily vegetated freshwater marshes and ponds; resident from Mexico to Argentina, and the Caribbean.

VOICE Male a throaty *coo-coo-coo*, or *kir-roo-kirroo-kiroo* during courtship; females a short, repeated hiss.

blue bill with black tip

deep chestnut with black mottling

MALE

Length **13–15in (33–38cm)**	Wingspan **17in (43cm)**

Family **Diomedeidae**	Species *Phoebastria albatrus*

Short-tailed Albatross

The Short-tailed Albatross is one of the world's rarest seabirds. Its population has drastically declined from many thousands to only several hundred; this is attributed to hunting. Today, this species is unfortunately threatened by fishing nets in the North Pacific Ocean, in which it is caught and drowns. A more extensive white plumage and a completely pink bill set the Short-tailed Albatross apart from the much more abundant Laysan Albatross.

OCCURRENCE Breeds on very few islands off Japan; rare visitor to open waters off California to Alaska.

VOICE Usually silent at sea.

huge, bright pink bill

golden nape and crown

black-and-white plumage

ADULT

Length **35in (90cm)**	Wingspan **7¾ft (2.4m)**

Family **Diomedeidae**	Species *Thalassarche melanophrys*

Black-browed Albatross

One of a group of dark-backed albatross species known as the mollymawks, the Black-browed Albatross is best identified by its dark eye patch, black-and-white underwing pattern, and thick, orange bill. It effortlessly soars over the waves and travels on the wind over vast distances, rarely drifting into North American waters. Due to the pressures of longline and trawler fishing, this species is now considered to be threatened.

OCCURRENCE Breeds at a dozen sites in the Southern Ocean; extremely rare vagrant to Atlantic Ocean off North America throughout the year.

VOICE Usually silent at sea.

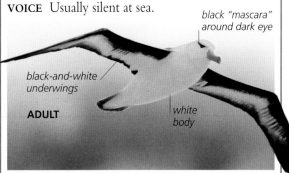

black "mascara" around dark eye

black-and-white underwings

ADULT

white body

Length **31–37in (80–95cm)**	Wingspan **6½–7½ft (2–2.3m)**

Family **Procellariidae**	Species *Pterodroma feae/madeira*

Fea's-Zino's Petrel

Although the taxonomy of the Fea's-Zino's group of *Pterodroma* petrels is unresolved, individuals of this group do occur regularly in North American Gulf Stream waters. Found annually on ocean birding trips, this petrel shows up in the same areas of the North Atlantic as Black-capped and Herald Petrels. Its soft gray upperpart coloring is helpful in separating it from other similar petrels.

OCCURRENCE Breeds on a few islands in the eastern North Atlantic Ocean; rare summertime visitor to deep Gulf Stream waters off the southeastern US.

VOICE Silent at sea.

ADULT

mottled dark underwing

gray nape

white body

Length **13–14in (33–36cm)**	Wingspan **34–37in (86–94cm)**

Family **Procellariidae**	Species *Pterodroma inexpectata*

Mottled Petrel

The Mottled Petrel is a rare South Pacific seabird species found in North American waters. It migrates north after breeding in New Zealand, with some even reaching the Bering Sea and Gulf of Alaska. Key identification marks include a black-barred, white underwing and dark smudging on the chest and belly.

ADULT

OCCURRENCE Breeds in New Zealand; migrates to open ocean off the Pacific coast of North America, especially Alaska in summer.

VOICE Silent at sea.

pale gray panel on upperwing

mostly dark gray and white

Length **13–14in (33–35cm)**	Wingspan **29–32in (74–82cm)**

Family **Procellariidae**	Species ***Pterodroma cookii***

Cook's Petrel

Cook's Petrel is one of the potential treasures of offshore birdwatching off the US West Coast in the summer months. This New Zealand species is known as *Titi* by the Maori because of its *ti-ti-ti* calls. It breeds in burrows on steep, forested slopes and ridges. The gray-and-black Cook's Petrel occurs regularly off California.

OCCURRENCE Breeds on two or three islands near New Zealand; rare visitor to deep waters far off the Pacific Coast of North America.

VOICE Silent at sea.

blackish outer wing feathers

pale dove-gray body

dark patch below eye

ADULT

Length **10–12in (25–30cm)**	Wingspan **26in (66cm)**

Family **Procellariidae**	Species ***Puffinus bulleri***

Buller's Shearwater

Like other species of tubenoses that occur occasionally off the west coast of North America, this migrant breeds on islands off New Zealand. Abundant, yet threatened by long-line fishing operations, Buller's Shearwater is the only silvery gray *Puffinus* species to show a black zigzag wing pattern that is found in North American waters.

OCCURRENCE Breeds at Poor Knights Island, New Zealand. Uncommon in open ocean off California and north to Alaska during the late summer and fall.

VOICE Silent at sea; strange wailing calls at colonies.

dark zigzag pattern

dark-gray cap

long, dark, wedge-shaped tail

ADULT

Length **18–18½in (46–47cm)**	Wingspan **38–39in (97–99cm)**

Family **Procellariidae**	Species ***Puffinus carneipes***

Flesh-footed Shearwater

The Flesh-footed Shearwater, an uncommon visitor to the nutrient-rich marine waters off the Pacific coast of North America, can be found in large numbers with other tubenoses. It is distinguished from the Sooty and Short-tailed shearwaters by its dark color and pink bill and legs.

OCCURRENCE Two breeding populations: one in the southwest Pacific Ocean, the other in the Indian Ocean; summer visitor to open ocean off California northward to Alaska.

VOICE Silent at sea; mewing calls at the breeding sites at night.

ADULT

dark body and wings

pale feet

pink bill with dusky tip

Length **18in (46cm)**	Wingspan **4½ft (1.4m)**

Family **Phoenopteridae**	Species ***Phoencopterus ruber***

Greater Flamingo

The only one of the world's five flamingo species to occur in North America, the Greater Flamingo is easily distinguished from all other large wading birds by its odd-looking bent bill and very long neck, usually held in an S-shape. The only similar species in its range is the Roseate Spoonbill.

OCCURRENCE Nonbreeders in Florida; strays in eastern North America as far north as Canada; localized in the West Indies and Central and South America.

VOICE Goose-like honking in flight; feeding flocks give low, guttural calls.

bill bent at end

long, pink legs

pink body

long neck

ADULT

Length **4–4½ft (1.2–1.4m)**	Wingspan **4½–5¼ft (1.4–1.6m)**

Family **Phaethontidae**	Species *Phaethon lepturus*

White-tailed Tropicbird

The smallest and most common of the three species of tropicbirds, the White-tailed's range overlaps that of the Red-billed in the Atlantic Ocean and Gulf of Mexico. At a distance, the wings of the White-tailed Tropicbird appear entirely white, but up close the black wingtips and diagonal are striking.

OCCURRENCE Solitary vagrants off Atlantic coast and in the Gulf of Mexico.

VOICE Silent at sea; harsh, squeaky calls and shrill whistles while breeding.

black diagonal

ADULT

long, white tail streamers

Length **15in (38cm)**	Wingspan **3ft 1in (94cm)**

Family **Sulidae**	Species *Sula dactylatra*

Masked Booby

The largest of the boobies occurring in North America, the Masked Booby is easily identified by its distinctive black outer wing and tail feathers and its yellow bill.

OCCURRENCE Roosts and breeds on coral sand beaches and lava flows, under shrubs and trees, in the south Florida Keys, also in the Hawaiian and other tropical islands.

VOICE Generally silent but honks and brays loudly at the breeding colony.

yellow eyes

black chin

yellow bill

black outer wing feathers

black tail

ADULT

Length **32in (82cm)**	Wingspan **5¼ft (1.6m)**

Family **Sulidae**	Species *Sula leucogaster*

Brown Booby

The Brown Booby, which is actually a sooty brown and white, overlaps with the Masked and Red-footed boobies and often nests in mixed colonies with them. Unlike juvenile Brown Boobies, the juvenile Masked Booby has a whitish ring around the neck and a pale rump.

OCCURRENCE Breeds on tropical islands of Atlantic, Pacific, and Indian oceans, and on Caribbean islands. Rare on Atlantic and Pacific coasts. Found closer to shore than Masked Booby.

VOICE Silent, but can make loud or subdued quacking, honking or braying.

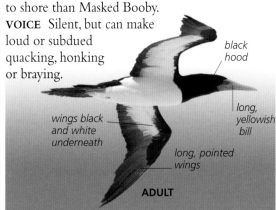

black hood

long, yellowish bill

wings black and white underneath

long, pointed wings

ADULT

Length **30in (76cm)**	Wingspan **4½ft (1.4m)**

Family **Cathartidae**	Species *Gymnogyps californianus*

California Condor

Nearly 20,000 years ago, this vulture was widespread across the southern US. In the 20th century, shooting, low birthrate, and other factors, such as death from poisoned baits, all contributed to this bird almost becoming extinct. However, recent breed-and-release programs in California and Arizona have succeeded and these magnificent birds can be seen flying again.

OCCURRENCE Released birds are seen in south California and Arizona.

VOICE Hisses and grunts.

shaggy black plumage

ADULT

Length **3½–4¼ft (1.1–1.3m)**	Wingspan **8¼ft (2.5m)**

Family **Accipitridae**	Species *Chondrohierax uncinatus*

Hook-billed Kite

This kite occurs in the tropical Americas from Mexico all the way south to Argentina, but in the US it is found only in southeast Texas, where fewer than 60 pairs have nested since the late 1960s. The Hooked-billed Kite is long-tailed, and broad at its wingtips.

OCCURRENCE Only in the Rio Grande Valley of southern Texas; breeds in riverside scrub and woodlands.

VOICE Rapid rattle; *kekekekekekekeke* highest in the middle.

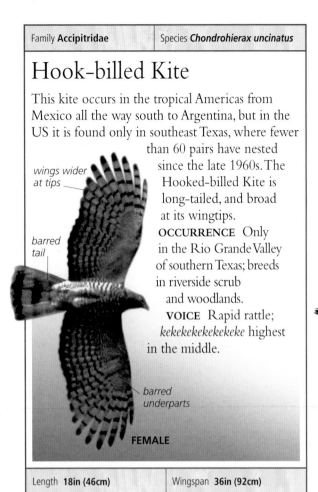

wings wider at tips

barred tail

barred underparts

FEMALE

Length **18in (46cm)**	Wingspan **36in (92cm)**

Family **Charadridae**	Species *Charadrius hiaticula*

Ringed Plover

The Ringed Plover is widespread in Eurasia. It also breeds in North America, where it only overlaps with the closely related Semipalmated Plover locally on Baffin Island. This species does not have toe webbing, and usually has a wider black breastband than its Semipalmated cousin.

OCCURRENCE Breeds on St. Lawrence and St. Matthew Islands in Alaska, and in the Canadian Arctic Archipelago (Baffin, Bylot, Ellesmere).

VOICE Soft, mellow two-note *poo-eep* from the ground or in flight.

brown upperparts

MALE (BREEDING)

clean, white underparts

wide, black breastband

Length **7–8in (18–20cm)**	Wingspan **19–22½in (48–57cm)**

Family **Charadridae**	Species *Charadrius mongolus*

Lesser Sand Plover

The Lesser Sand Plover, also called the Mongolian Plover, breeds in Eurasia from the Russian Far East south to Tibet. It differs from the Semipalmated and Ringed plovers in nonbreeding plumage, with longer, black legs, a large-looking head, huge eyes, and a black bill. It is smaller overall, and has a darker facial pattern than the Mountain Plover.

OCCURRENCE Regular, uncommon migrant to Alaska; has bred in western Alaska.

VOICE Flight call low, rolled, hard *kurrip!*

brownish gray upperparts

white underparts

fading wide rust breastband

ADULT (NONBREEDING)

Length **7½–8½in (19–21cm)**	Wingspan **17½–23in (44–58cm)**

Family **Scolopacidae**	Species *Gallinago gallinago*

Eurasian Snipe

The Eurasian Snipe is known as the "Common Snipe" in Europe. It is the counterpart of North America's Wilson's Snipe, and occurs in the western Aleutian Islands in North America, and very occasionally elsewhere.

OCCURRENCE Regular on Near Islands (western Alaska); may breed there.

VOICE Tearing *kretsch* flight call given by flushed and flying birds.

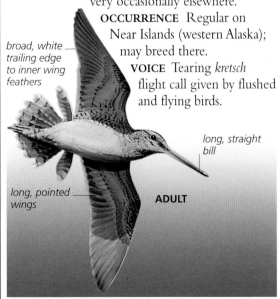

broad, white trailing edge to inner wing feathers

long, straight bill

long, pointed wings

ADULT

Length **10–10½in (25–27cm)**	Wingspan **17½–18½in (44–47cm)**

Family **Scolopacidae**	Species *Limosa limosa*

Black-tailed Godwit

This large Eurasian shorebird is stockier and bigger than the Hudsonian Godwit. Both species have long legs and bills, and a black tail band. Breeding adults have unstreaked necks; juveniles are more richly colored.
OCCURRENCE Regular migrant to western Alaska, mainly in spring.
VOICE Sharp, dry, loud *kwika-kwicka-kwicka*.

long, orange bill with black tip

orange-russet upper breast, neck, and head

heavily barred belly and breast

ADULT (BREEDING)

Length **15½–17½in (40–44cm)**	Wingspan **28–32in (70–82cm)**

Family **Scolopacidae**	Species *Tringa glareola*

Wood Sandpiper

This species breeds across northern Eurasia but also in western Alaska. It is a medium-sized sandpiper, longer-legged and shorter-billed than the Solitary Sandpiper, with larger spots above, a bolder "eyebrow," and a white rump. It is smaller than the Lesser Yellowlegs, with duller legs, bolder "eyebrows," and a shorter, stockier bill, and can be identified by its loud, high-pitched calls.
OCCURRENCE Western Alaskan islands, regular in the spring but rare in the fall.
VOICE Sharp *twhit-twhit-twhit*.

spotted brownish black upperparts

MALE

whitish underparts

yellowish legs

streaked upper breast

Length **7½–8½in (19–21cm)**	Wingspan **22–22½in (56–57cm)**

Family **Scolopacidae**	Species *Actitis hypoleucos*

Common Sandpiper

The Common Sandpiper is the Eurasian counterpart to North America's Spotted Sandpiper, though without spots. Its tail projects farther past its wingtips than the Spotted's, and it has a longer, broader, white upper-wing stripe. In fall, or when not breeding, the Spotted Sandpiper is also spotless.
OCCURRENCE Regular migrant in the Aleutians, Pribilof, and St. Lawrence islands; rare elsewhere.
VOICE Sweet, clear, almost bell-like *twee-twee-weeet-wheeet*.

pale, buff fringes to upperpart feathers

long, barred tail

JUVENILE (FALL)

white underparts

dark sides of breast

Length **7½–8½in (19–21cm)**	Wingspan **15–16in (38–41cm)**

Family **Scolopacidae**	Species *Heteroscelus brevipes*

Gray-tailed Tattler

This Asian counterpart to the Wandering Tattler is poorly studied, though it is known as a regular migrant on islands off western Alaska. In breeding plumage, the Gray-tailed Tattler is more finely barred below, with a whiter belly. In all plumage it has a broader eyestripe, longer neck, and paler coloring than the Wandering Tattler.
OCCURRENCE Regular on the Aleutians and Pribilofs, also St. Lawrence Islands.
VOICE Flight call a double-note, fluid *tjuu-wheet*.

gray upperparts and crown

strong, dark facial stripe

MALE

clean, white underparts

gray barring on upper breast and flanks

Length **10–11in (25–28cm)**	Wingspan **17½–21½in (44–54cm)**

Family **Scolopacidae**	Species *Calidris ruficolis*

Red-necked Stint

This small Siberian stint or peep is very similar to nonbreeding and juvenile Semipalmated Sandpipers. However, it has a more slim and tapered body; slimmer, finer-tipped bill; and unwebbed toes. Breeding birds have a rich, rufous-orange face, throat, and upper breast, with spotted breast sides.

OCCURRENCE Uncommon migrant and rare breeder in western Alaska; rare, but annual migrant elsewhere in North America.

VOICE Flight call rough *kiirp*, similar to Semipalmated Sandpiper but usually higher pitched.

white underparts

short, dark legs

MALE

Length **5–6½in (13–16cm)**	Wingspan **14–15in (35–38cm)**

Family **Scolopacidae**	Species *Calidris temminckii*

Temminck's Stint

With its long wings and tail, this small, chunky Eurasian stint resembles Baird's Sandpiper. When foraging, it creeps along on bent legs like a Least Sandpiper. In nonbreeding plumage, its unstreaked, gray head and upper breast separate it from Baird's and White-rumped Sandpipers.

OCCURRENCE Rare migrant on west Alaska islands; accidental in British Columbia; no records in the lower 48 states. Seen singly or in small flocks feeding on upper margins of mudflats or in marsh vegetation.

VOICE Flight call a rolled, dry *trrrriitt*.

dark upperparts

rusty tint to head

ADULT (SPRING)

Length **5–6in (13–15cm)**	Wingspan **13½–14½in (34–37cm)**

Family **Scolopacidae**	Species *Calidris subminuta*

Long-toed Stint

The Long-toed Stint is the Asian counterpart of the Least Sandpiper. This stint has a longer neck, legs, and toes, and a shorter, finer-tipped bill than the Least Sandpiper. The longer legs cause it to appear more tilted over when feeding, but more upright when alert. Unlike the Least Sandpiper, its toes extend past its tail in flight.

OCCURRENCE Fairly common spring migrant on outer Aleutian Islands, Alaska; accidental elsewhere in Alaska, and in Oregon and California.

VOICE *Chrrip*; flight call more musical and lower-pitched than that of Least Sandpiper.

small head

yellowish legs

JUVENILE

Length **5–5½in (13–14cm)**	Wingspan **13–14in (33–35cm)**

Family **Scolopacidae**	Species *Calidris acuminata*

Sharp-tailed Sandpiper

This intermediate-sized sandpiper is similar to the Pectoral Sandpiper, but breeds only in Siberia. It is slightly rounder in body shape than the Pectoral Sandpiper with longer legs and a shorter, slimmer bill. Breeding birds have rufous caps, a buff wash on the face and breast, and V-shaped breast markings.

OCCURRENCE Accidental in spring but common in fall in western Alaska; rare fall migrant along Pacific Coast; accidental in fall elsewhere in North America.

VOICE Call a rolled, soft *prrrt*.

small head

JUVENILE

Length **6¾–8in (17–20cm)**	Wingspan **16½–19in (42–48cm)**

Family **Scolopacidae**	Species *Calidris ferruginea*

Curlew Sandpiper

The Curlew Sandpiper is a medium-sized sandpiper that breeds in northern Siberia. It resembles the Dunlin and Stilt Sandpiper in nonbreeding plumage. It is slimmer than the Dunlin, with longer wings, neck, legs, and bill, and differs from the nonbreeding Stilt Sandpiper by its shorter legs and faint white eyebrow.

OCCURRENCE Rare, but regular migrant on Atlantic Coast; accidental elsewhere.

VOICE Flight call musical, trilled, or rolled *chrreep*, dropping in the middle.

JUVENILE

black legs

long decurved bill

Length 7–7½in (18–19cm)	Wingspan 16½–18in (42–46cm)

Family **Scolopacidae**	Species *Philomachus pugnax*

Ruff

The Ruff is well known for the elaborately colored head ruffs and tufts of breeding male birds. Males are 20 percent larger than the females (known as Reeves), which are more muted in appearance.

OCCURRENCE Rare, but regular migrant along Atlantic and Pacific coasts, in the Upper Midwest, and western Alaska; rare in winter in California.

VOICE Mostly silent; occasionally gives a soft *krruk*.

short, slightly drooped bill

JUVENILE (FALL)

Length 8–12in (20–30cm)	Wingspan 19–23in (48–58cm)

Family **Laridae**	Species *Larus schistisagus*

Slaty-backed Gull

This rare visitor from eastern Russia and Japan is most likely to be confused with the Western Gull. Adults have a series of white spots on the outer wing feather tips, referred to as "a string of pearls." Winter adults have heavily streaked heads with white linings to their underwings that contrast with the gray outer and inner wing feathers.

OCCURRENCE Occurs regularly in coastal western Alaska; accidental in winter across Canada and US.

VOICE Slow *aah-aah-aah*.

ADULT (BREEDING)

Length 24–26in (61–66cm)	Wingspan 4½–5ft (1.4–1.5m)

Family **Laridae**	Species *Rhodostethia rosea*

Ross's Gull

In adult breeding plumage, this small, delicate gull is unmistakable. Dove-gray upperparts, pale-pink underparts, red legs, and a black collar, make it an elegant and beautiful-looking bird.

OCCURRENCE Siberian breeder found only along Alaskan north coast in fall; expanded as a breeding bird into Arctic Canada; winter strays found across Canada and to northeast and northwest US.

VOICE Rarely heard in winter; tern-like *kik-kik-kik*.

black "necklace"

wedge-shaped tail

ADULT (BREEDING)

Length 11½–12in (29–31cm)	Wingspan 35–39in (90–100cm)

| Family **Laridae** | Species *Pagophila eburnea* |

Ivory Gull

The Ivory Gull, all white with black legs, is unlikely to be confused with any other gull. Adults are pure white in summer and winter. Juveniles are patterned to varying degrees with black spots on the tips of their flight feathers, and tail and wing outer feathers, and they have a smudgy black face.

OCCURRENCE High Arctic breeder; rarely strays far south of the pack ice, even in winter; casual in winter to British Columbia and Maritime Provinces; accidental elsewhere.

VOICE Tern-like, harsh *keeuur*; rarely heard away from breeding grounds.

pure white plumage

yellow-tipped slate-blue bill

ADULT

black legs

| Length **15½–17in (40–43cm)** | Wingspan **3½–4ft (1.1–1.2m)** |

| Family **Laridae** | Species *Anous minutus* |

Black Noddy

Since 1962, small numbers of nonbreeding Black Noddies have been seen nearly annually in the Brown Noddy colony of the Dry Tortugas off the Florida Keys. Slightly smaller than the Brown Noddy, it can be distinguished from that species by its longer and thinner bill, a blacker body, and generally whiter forehead.

OCCURRENCE Subtropical and tropical tern, breeds south of North America; pelagic away from breeding colonies; regular at Dry Tortugas, but does not breed; accidental on Texas coast.

VOICE High-pitched *caw* or *kark* calls; not vocal away from breeding colonies.

white cap

ADULT

black body

| Length **14–15½in (35–40cm)** | Wingspan **26–28in (65–72cm)** |

| Family **Stercorariidae** | Species *Stercorarius skua* |

Great Skua

Similar to the South Polar Skua, this large and aggressive predator and scavenger can be differentiated by its heavier streaking and more reddish tones to its brown body. Known in Scotland as the "bonxie," a name with nordic origins, the Great Skua is closely related to several species of southern skuas including the Falkland Skua.

OCCURRENCE Rare visitor, mostly in fall through spring, to pelagic waters off the Atlantic Coast of North America.

VOICE Rough, cackling *rah-rah-rah*.

dark nape

hooked, dark bill

mottled gray to warm brown plumage

ADULT

| Length **19½–23in (50–58cm)** | Wingspan **4–4½ft (1.2–1.4m)** |

| Family **Alcidae** | Species *Synthliboramphus craveri* |

Craveri's Murrelet

Craveri's Murrelet is one of the southernmost breeding murrelets. Unlike the other two species in its genus, its nestlings scramble down steep sea slopes and stumble down cliffs to follow their parents to the sea, just a day after hatching. They are fed and raised to independence by the adults.

OCCURRENCE Warm waters off the west coast of Mexico, and less regularly, Baja California. On nesting islands, two eggs laid in crevices on steep sea cliffs.

VOICE Adult at sea gives high rattling or trilling *streeeer*; other calls unknown.

blackish back and head

long, heavy bill

ADULT

| Length **9½in (24cm)** | Wingspan **15in (38cm)** |

Family **Columbidae**	Species *Columba flavirostris*

Red-billed Pigeon

This tropical, Central American and Mexican pigeon is found in North America only in southern Texas, where it breeds in dense riverside woodlands. Wine-red below, bluish-gray above, with yellow eyes and a red eye ring, it is unmistakable.

OCCURRENCE Often perches in tall trees above brushy understory in wooded bottomlands of Texas's Rio Grande Valley.

VOICE Long, high-pitched, hoarse *coooo* followed by 2–5 *up, cup-a-coos.*

bill red at base

wine-red below

ADULT

Length **14½in (37cm)**	Wingspan **24in (62cm)**

Family **Columbidae**	Species *Streptopelia chinensis*

Spotted Dove

Originally from southern Asia, the Spotted Dove was introduced into urban areas of California over a century ago. More chunky and with broader wings and tail than the Mourning Dove, this medium-sized dove has grayish brown upperparts and pinkish brown underparts. The Spotted Dove has a long, gray tail with black edges and white corners, a black bill, and pink legs and toes.

OCCURRENCE Found in urban habitats of southern California from Santa Barbara and Bakersfield south to Baja California.

VOICE Hoarse *coo-coo-croooo* call with emphasis on the middle and last notes.

black-and-white neck patch

ADULT

Length **12in (30cm)**	Wingspan **19½in (50cm)**

Family **Columbidae**	Species *Columbina talpacoti*

Ruddy Ground-Dove

Similar to the Common Ground-Dove, the Ruddy Ground Dove is usually very colorful, with an overall rusty-red color, and contrasting pale-grey head. Females are usually duller with less contrast between the head and body.

OCCURRENCE Occurs in localized areas of California, Arizona, New Mexico, and Texas; found in woodlands, gardens, cultivated fields, marshlands, and forest edges.

VOICE Monotonous, endlessly repeated 2-syllable *ca-whoop* given every second or so.

marked bars on wings

ADULT (FEMALE)

pale-gray head

Length **6¾in (17cm)**	Wingspan **11in (28cm)**

Family **Psittacidae**	Species *Nandayus nenday*

Black-hooded Parakeet

Native of Argentina, Bolivia, Brazil, and Paraguay, this green parakeet has a blackish cap and chin, black bill, bluish breast patch, and bright red "thighs." In flight, its dark outer wing feathers recall the Monk Parakeet. The Black-hooded Parakeet is often noticed by its loud screeches.

OCCURRENCE Urban and suburban habitats in parts of California and especially Florida, where they nest in cavities of palm snags or telephone poles.

VOICE Powerful screech: *kleeyarrk.*

bluish breast

red thighs

SUBADULT

Length **14in (36cm)**	Wingspan **18in (46cm)**

| Family **Psittacidae** | Species ***Brotogeris chiriri*** |

Yellow-chevroned Parakeet

This species belongs to a genus of small, tropical parakeets that occur from Mexico to Bolivia and Brazil. The Yellow-chevroned Parakeet is highly social and feeds on a variety of fruits, nuts, flowers, and seeds.

OCCURRENCE Populations, originally escapes, limited to urban and suburban areas in Los Angeles and San Francisco in California, and Fort Lauderdale and Miami in Florida.

VOICE Variety of high-pitched chirps and squawks; low-pitched mutterings.

yellow wing patch

ADULT

green overall

| Length **8½in (22cm)** | Wingspan **15in (38cm)** |

| Family **Cuculidae** | Species ***Cuculus canorus*** |

Common Cuckoo

The gray form of this unusual visitor from Eurasia resembles a small raptor in flight, with its long tail and pointed wings. The curve in the bill and lack of a hooked tip are the main differences. Its solid-gray back contrasts starkly with its white underparts.

OCCURRENCE Vagrant in Alaskan islands and very rarely to the East Coast of the US; in Europe and Asia uses wide variety of forests, fields, and parks.

VOICE *Kook-ooo* or *koo-ku-khoo*; females emit high, bubbling trill.

ADULT

white below

long, pointed wings

| Length **12–14in (30–35cm)** | Wingspan **14–16in (35–41cm)** |

| Family **Cuculidae** | Species ***Crotophaga ani*** |

Smooth-billed Ani

upper mandible lacks grooves

The Smooth-billed Ani is found in the US only in southern Florida. The bird colonized the state in the early 1930s, but steadily declined in the early 1980s, due to unknown causes. It is a communal breeder, with multiple females laying eggs in the same nest.

OCCURRENCE Occurs in shrubby areas, agricultural lands, and hedges in southern Florida, in Central and South America, and the West Indies.

VOICE Main call whiny, ascending *yaahnee*.

ADULT

| Length **14½in (37cm)** | Wingspan **18½in (47cm)** |

| Family **Strigidae** | Species ***Glaucidium brasilianum*** |

Ferruginous Pygmy-Owl

Quite widespread in the tropics, from Mexico to Argentina, this owl reaches the US only in Arizona and Texas, where it can be found close to rivers and in desert areas at lower elevations than the similar Northern Pygmy-Owl. The Ferruginous has a rufous tail, and its belly and crown are streaked.

OCCURRENCE Extreme southeast Arizona and southern tip of Texas; rare north of Mexico.

VOICE Quick series of repeated single rising notes.

brown bars on tail

ADULT

| Length **5½–7in (14–18cm)** | Wingspan **15in (38cm)** |

Family **Caprimulgidae**	Species *Chordeiles gundlachii*

Antillean Nighthawk

Only recently considered a species distinct from the Common Nighthawk, this West Indian native is seen fairly regularly in the Florida Keys. As with other members of the nightjar family, the Antillean Nighthawk often swoops around the evening sky capturing insects on the wing.

OCCURRENCE Regular visitor to Florida Keys; common in the Caribbean over low scrub and open areas such as agricultural fields and suburban parks.

VOICE Stuttered, buzzy, usually 2–5-syllable flight call that resembles *kitty-kattik-tik-tik*.

mottled gray, brown, and black back

ADULT

Length **8–10in (20–25cm)**	Wingspan **20–23in (51–58cm)**

Family **Trochilidae**	Species *Amazilia beryllina*

Berylline Hummingbird

Named after the glittering green gemstone, this hummingbird lives up to its name, adding extra colors with its rufous wing patch and buff belly.

OCCURRENCE Found in southeastern Arizona in summer; nests in high-elevation canyons and pine-oak woodlands; very rare in west Texas mountains.

VOICE Call rough, buzzy *tzrrr*; song series of high-pitched, squeaky *chips* and twitters.

ADULT

long bill

glittering green upperparts

Length **4in (10cm)**	Wingspan **5½in (14cm)**

Family **Tyrannidae**	Species *Pachyramphus aglaiae*

Rose-throated Becard

The Rose-throated Becard is a gray bird with a short crest. The male's pink throat and the female's charcoal cap and brown body are distinctive.

OCCURRENCE This Central American species reaches southeastern Arizona and the lower Rio Grande Valley in Texas.

VOICE Plaintive *tseeeuuuu*, and *pik* or *pidik* calls; song repeated *see-cheew, wee-chew*.

dark wings and back

pink throat patch

ADULT (MALE)

Length **7¼in (18.5cm)**	Wingspan **12in (30cm)**

Family **Vireonidae**	Species *Vireo flavoviridis*

Yellow-green Vireo

Closely related to the Red-eyed Vireo, the Yellow-green Vireo strongly resembles it in shape and size. However, its plumage has yellow-green upperparts and a bright yellow wash on the flanks and undertail feathers.

OCCURRENCE Rare summer visitor to the lower Rio Grande Valley of Texas, and rare vagrant in the fall in southern states; winters in Amazon region of South America.

VOICE Similar to Red-eyed Vireo, but faster and less musical.

large, pale bill

yellow cheeks and face

ADULT

Length **6½in (16cm)**	Wingspan **10in (26cm)**

VAGRANTS

The list that follows consists of species that occur only very rarely in North America (defined as Canada and the continental US). Vagrants to North America arrive from both the Northern and Southern Hemispheres—Europe, Russia and Siberia, and eastern Asia as well as South America, Africa, and Oceania. The US and Canada are well placed to receive birds that are blown off course from eastern Asia and Siberia, crossing the Pacific, and from Europe, crossing the Atlantic. Western Alaska has a particularly high concentration of vagrants because the western tip forms a series of islands, the

Aleutians, that reach almost all the way across the Bering Sea to Russia.

The occurrence of these species is classified by the American Birding Association as rare, casual, or accidental depending on how often they have been seen, and this terminology is used in the comment section on each species. Rare birds are seen every year, but in low numbers. Casual visitors have been seen in North America at least half a dozen times, including three sightings in the last 30 years. Accidental species have been recorded in Canada or the US no more than five times.

COMMON NAME	SCIENTIFIC NAME	FAMILY/SCIENTIFIC NAME	DESCRIPTION
Waterfowl			
Bean Goose	*Anser fabalis*	Waterfowl/Anatidae	Rare visitor from N Europe and Asia to SW Alaska
Pink-footed Goose	*Anser brachyrhynchus*	Waterfowl/Anatidae	Casual from Greenland, Iceland, and Europe to East coast
Lesser White-fronted Goose	*Anser erythropus*	Waterfowl/Anatidae	Accidental from Eurasia to Atlantic coast of Canada and US
Barnacle Goose	*Branta leucopsis*	Waterfowl/Anatidae	Accidental from Greenland and N Europe to the Maritime Provinces, Canada
Common Pochard	*Aythya ferina*	Waterfowl/Anatidae	Rare visitor from Europe and central Asia to W Alaska
Falcated Duck	*Anas falcata*	Waterfowl/Anatidae	Casual from Asia to W Alaska
Baikal Teal	*Anas formosa*	Waterfowl/Anatidae	Asian duck; casual in W Alaska and in western provinces and states
White-cheeked Pintail	*Anas bahamensis*	Waterfowl/Anatidae	Accidental from the Caribbean and N South America to Florida and the Gulf coast
Spot-billed Duck	*Anas poecilorhyncha*	Waterfowl/Anatidae	Accidental from Asia to SW Alaska
Albatrosses, Petrels, and Shearwaters			
Wandering Albatross	*Diomedea exulans*	Albatrosses/Diomedeidae	Accidental from oceans of Southern Hemisphere
Yellow-nosed Albatross	*Thalassarche chlororhynchos*	Albatrosses/Diomedeidae	Casual from Indian and S Atlantic oceans to Atlantic and Gulf coasts
Shy Albatross	*Thalassarche cauta*	Albatrosses/Diomedeidae	Casual to Pacific coast from South Pacific
Murphy's Petrel	*Pterodroma ultima*	Procellariidae/Petrels and Shearwaters	Rare visitor to Pacific coast; breeds on islands in the mid-Pacific

COMMON NAME	SCIENTIFIC NAME	FAMILY/SCIENTIFIC NAME	DESCRIPTION
Albatrosses, Petrels, and Shearwaters *continued*			
Bermuda Petrel	*Pterodroma cahow*	Procellariidae/Petrels and Shearwaters	Casual on Atlantic coast; breeds in Bahamas
Herald Petrel	*Pterodroma arminjoniana*	Procellariidae/Petrels and Shearwaters	Rare visitor off SE coast; breeds on islands off Brazil
Galapagos/Hawaiian Petrel	*Pterodroma phaeopygia/sandwichensis*	Procellariidae/Petrels and Shearwaters	Accidental on Pacific coast; breeds on Galapagos Islands and Hawaii
Stejneger's Petrel	*Pterodroma longirostris*	Procellariidae/Petrels and Shearwaters	Casual; breeds on Robinson Crusoe Island off Chilean coast
Parkinson's Petrel	*Procellaria parkinsoni*	Procellariidae/Petrels and Shearwaters	Accidental off California coast from New Zealand
Streaked Shearwater	*Calonectris leucomelas*	Procellariidae/Petrels and Shearwaters	Casual to Pacific coast from western Pacific
Cape Verde Shearwater	*Calonectris edwardsii*	Procellariidae/Petrels and Shearwaters	Accidental off North Carolina; breeds on Cape Verde islands
Wedge-tailed Shearwater	*Puffinus pacificus*	Procellariidae/Petrels and Shearwaters	Casual off California coast from tropical and subtropical Pacific
Little Shearwater	*Puffinus assimilis*	Procellariidae/Petrels and Shearwaters	Accidental off Atlantic coast, from tropical and subtropical oceans
Bulwer's Petrel	*Bulweria bulwerii*	Procellariidae/Petrels and Shearwaters	Accidental off California and North Carolina from tropical and subtropical oceans
White-faced Storm-Petrel	*Pelagodroma marina*	Hydrobatidae/Storm-Petrels	Casual to Atlantic coast from tropical and subtropical oceans
Black-bellied Storm-Petrel	*Fregetta tropica*	Hydrobatidae/Storm-Petrels	Accidental off North Carolina from tropical oceans
European Storm-Petrel	*Hydrobates pelagicus*	Hydrobatidae/Storm-Petrels	Accidental off North Carolina; breeds on islands in NE Atlantic and Mediterranean
Wedge-rumped Storm-Petrel	*Oceanodroma tethys*	Hydrobatidae/Storm-Petrels	Accidental to California coast; breeds on Galapagos and Peruvian coast
Ibises and Herons			
Jabiru	*Jabiru mycteria*	Ciconiidae/Storks	Accidental to S Texas from Central and South America
Scarlet Ibis	*Eudocimus ruber*	Threskiornithidae/Ibises and Spoonbills	Accidental to Florida from Central and South America
Pelicans and Relatives			
Red-billed Tropicbird	*Phaethon aethereus*	Phaethontidae/Tropicbirds	Rare off S California, Gulf of Mexico, and Atlantic coast to North Carolina, from the tropics
Red-tailed Tropicbird	*Phaethon rubricauda*	Phaethontidae/Tropicbirds	Casual off California coast from tropical Pacific and Indian oceans
White-tailed Tropicbird	*Phaethon lepturus*	Phaethontidae/Tropicbirds	Rare summer visitor off Atlantic coast up to North Carolina, from tropical oceans

COMMON NAME	SCIENTIFIC NAME	FAMILY/SCIENTIFIC NAME	DESCRIPTION
Pelicans and Relatives *continued*			
Blue-footed Booby	*Sula nebouxii*	Sulidae/Boobies and Gannets	Casual along the Pacific coast and in the Southwest; nests in the Gulf of California and south along the Pacific coast to Peru
Great Frigatebird	*Fregata minor*	Fregatidae/Frigatebirds	Casual to California coast from tropical Pacific and Indian oceans
Lesser Frigatebird	*Fregata ariel*	Fregatidae/Frigatebirds	Accidental to Maine from tropical oceans
Birds of Prey			
Collared Forest-Falcon	*Micrastur semitorquatus*	Falconidae/Birds of Prey	Accidental from Central and South America to S Texas
Eurasian Kestrel	*Falco tinnunculus*	Falconidae/Birds of Prey	Casual from Eurasia to W Alaska and Atlantic and Pacific coasts
Red-footed Falcon	*Falco vespertinus*	Falconidae/Birds of Prey	Accidental from Eurasia to Massachusetts
Aplomado Falcon	*Falco femoralis*	Falconidae/Birds of Prey	Casual from Central and South America to New Mexico and Texas
Eurasian Hobby	*Falco subbuteo*	Falconidae/Birds of Prey	Casual from Eurasia to W Alaska
White-tailed Eagle	*Haliaeetus albicilla*	Accipitridae/Birds of Prey	Casual from Eurasia to W Alaska
Steller's Sea-Eagle	*Haliaeetus pelagicus*	Accipitridae/Birds of Prey	Casual from NE Asia to W Alaska
Rails and Cranes			
Corn Crake	*Crex crex*	Rallidae/Rails	Accidental from Europe to Maritime Provinces, Canada
Spotted Rail	*Pardirallus maculatus*	Rallidae/Rails	Accidental from Cuba, Caribbean, and Galapagos to Pennsylvania and S Texas
Common Crane	*Grus grus*	Gruidae/Cranes	Casual from Eurasia to Great Plains
Shorebirds			
Double-striped Thick-knee	*Burhinus bistriatus*	Burhinidae/Thick-knees	Accidental from central and south Brazil to Texas
Northern Lapwing	*Vanellus vanellus*	Charadriidae/Plovers	Casual in late fall from Eurasia to NE states and Canada
European Golden-Plover	*Pluvialis apricaria*	Charadriidae/Plovers	Casual in spring from Eurasia to E Quebec and Nova Scotia
Collared Plover	*Charadrius collaris*	Charadriidae/Plovers	Accidental to Texas from Mexico, Central, and South America
Lesser Sand-Plover/Mongolian Plover	*Charadrius mongolus*	Charadriidae/Plovers	Rare visitor from Asia to W Alaska and Pacific coast
Greater Sand-Plover	*Charadrius leschenaultii*	Charadriidae/Plovers	Accidental from Asia to California
Eurasian Dotterel	*Charadrius morinellus*	Charadriidae/Plovers	Casual from Eurasia to Alaska and Pacific coast; rare breeder in NW Alaska

COMMON NAME	SCIENTIFIC NAME	FAMILY/SCIENTIFIC NAME	DESCRIPTION
Shorebirds *continued*			
Northern Jacana	*Jacana spinosa*	Jacanidae/Jacanas	Casual from Mexico and Central America to Texas; formerly bred in Texas
Eurasian Woodcock	*Scolopax rusticola*	Scolopacidae/Sandpipers	Accidental from Eurasia to NE North America
Jack Snipe	*Lymnocryptes minimus*	Scolopacidae/Sandpipers	Accidental from Eurasia to Alaska, California, and Labrador
Little Curlew	*Numenius minutus*	Scolopacidae/Sandpipers	Casual from Siberia to Alaska and Pacific coast
Eurasian Curlew	*Numenius arquata*	Scolopacidae/Sandpipers	Casual in fall and winter from Eurasia to Canada and NE states
Far Eastern Curlew	*Numenius madagascariensis*	Scolopacidae/Sandpipers	Casual from Asia to Aleutians
Spotted Redshank	*Tringa erythropus*	Scolopacidae/Sandpipers	Casual from Eurasia during migration
Common Redshank	*Tringa totanus*	Scolopacidae/Sandpipers	Accidental from Eurasia to Newfoundland
Common Greenshank	*Tringa nebularia*	Scolopacidae/Sandpipers	Rare visitor from Eurasia to Alaska, California, and E and W Canada
Green Sandpiper	*Tringa ochropus*	Scolopacidae/Sandpipers	Casual from Eurasia to Aleutians in spring
Terek Sandpiper	*Xenus cinereus*	Scolopacidae/Sandpipers	Rare visitor from Eurasia to Alaska and Pacific coast
Great Knot	*Calidris tenuirostris*	Scolopacidae/Sandpipers	Casual from Siberia to Alaska in spring
Red-necked Stint	*Calidris ruficollis*	Scolopacidae/Sandpipers	Rare visitor from Siberia to both coasts in summer and fall
Little Stint	*Calidris minuta*	Scolopacidae/Sandpipers	Casual from Eurasia to both coasts in summer and fall
Spoon-billed Sandpiper	*Eurynorhynchus pygmeus*	Scolopacidae/Sandpipers	Casual from Siberia to Alaska
Broad-billed Sandpiper	*Limicola falcinellus*	Scolopacidae/Sandpipers	Casual from Eurasia to Aleutians in fall; accidental in New York
Gulls and Terns			
Belcher's Gull	*Larus belcheri*	Laridae/Gulls	Accidental from South America to California and Florida
Kelp Gull	*Larus dominicanus*	Laridae/Gulls	Casual from Southern Hemisphere to E US
Yellow-legged Gull	*Larus cachinnans*	Laridae/Gulls	Casual from Europe to E North America
Gray-hooded Gull	*Larus cirrocephalus*	Laridae/Gulls	Accidental from South America and Africa to Florida
Whiskered Tern	*Chlidonias hybrida*	Laridae/Gulls	Acidental from Eurasia to mid-Atlantic states
White-winged Tern	*Chlidonias leucopterus*	Laridae/Gulls	Casual from Eurasia to E North America
Large-billed Tern	*Phaetusa simplex*	Laridae/Gulls	Accidental from South America to Great Lakes and E US

COMMON NAME	SCIENTIFIC NAME	FAMILY/SCIENTIFIC NAME	DESCRIPTION
Auks			
Long-billed Murrelet	*Brachyramphus perdix*	Alcidae/Auks	Casual from Asia to North America in fall and winter
Pigeons and Doves			
Scaly-naped Pigeon	*Columba squamosa*	Columbidae/Pigeons and Doves	Accidental from West Indies to Key West
Oriental Turtle-Dove	*Streptopelia orientalis*	Columbidae/Pigeons and Doves	Casual from Asia to Aleutians; accidental to British Columbia and California
Zenaida Dove	*Zenaida aurita*	Columbidae/Pigeons and Doves	Accidental from West Indies to Florida
Key West Quail-Dove	*Geotrygon chrysia*	Columbidae/Pigeons and Doves	Casual from Caribbean to S Florida
Ruddy Quail-Dove	*Geotrygon montana*	Columbidae/Pigeons and Doves	Accidental from Central and South America and West Indies to Florida and Texas
Parrots			
White-winged Parakeet	*Brotogeris versicolurus*	Psittacidae/Parrots	Uncommon in California and S Florida; introduced from South America
Cuckoos			
Himalayan Cuckoo	*Cuculus saturatus*	Cuculidae/Cuckoos	Casual from Eurasia to Aleutians
Owls			
Mottled Owl	*Ciccaba virgata*	Strigidae/Owls	Accidental from Central and South America to S Texas
Stygian Owl	*Asio stygius*	Strigidae/Owls	Accidental from Central and South America to S Texas
Goatsuckers			
Buff-collared Nightjar	*Caprimulgus ridgwayi*	Caprimulgidae/Nightjars	Casual from Mexico to California and New Mexico
Swifts			
White-collared Swift	*Streptoprocne zonaris*	Apodidae/Swifts	Casual from Central and South America to S Texas
Fork-tailed Swift	*Apus pacificus*	Apodidae/Swifts	Casual from Asia to Alaska
Hummingbirds			
Green Violet-ear	*Colibri thalassinus*	Trochilidae/Hummingbirds	Casual from Central and South America to S Texas
Green-breasted Mango	*Anthracothorax prevostii*	Trochilidae/Hummingbirds	Casual from Central and South America to S Texas
Xantus's Hummingbird	*Hylocharis xantusii*	Trochilidae/Hummingbirds	Accidental from Baja California to S California and British Columbia
Plain-capped Starthroat	*Heliomaster constantii*	Trochilidae/Hummingbirds	Casual from Mexico and Central America to S Arizona
Bahama Woodstar	*Calliphlox evelynae*	Trochilidae/Hummingbirds	Accidental from Bahamas to S Florida
Bumblebee Hummingbird	*Atthis heloisa*	Trochilidae/Hummingbirds	Accidental from Mexico to SE Arizona

COMMON NAME	SCIENTIFIC NAME	FAMILY/SCIENTIFIC NAME	DESCRIPTION
Trogons			
Eared Quetzal	*Euptilotis neoxenus*	Trogonidae/Trogons	Casual from Mexico to SE Arizona; may be resident
Tyrant Flycatchers			
Greenish Elaenia	*Myiopagis viridicata*	Tyrannidae/Tyrant Flycatchers	Accidental from Central and South America to S Texas
Caribbean Elaenia	*Elaenia martinica*	Tyrannidae/Tyrant Flycatchers	Accidental from Caribbean to Florida
Tufted Flycatcher	*Mitrephanes phaeocercus*	Tyrannidae/Tyrant Flycatchers	Accidental from Central and South America to Texas and Arizona
Piratic Flycatcher	*Legatus leucophaius*	Tyrannidae/Tyrant Flycatchers	Accidental from Central and South America to Florida, Texas, and New Mexico
Social Flycatcher	*Myiozetetes similis*	Tyrannidae/Tyrant Flycatchers	Accidental from Central and South America to S Texas
Variegated Flycatcher	*Empidonomus varius*	Tyrannidae/Tyrant Flycatchers	Accidental from South America to E North America
Fork-tailed Flycatcher	*Tyrannus savana*	Tyrannidae/Tyrant Flycatchers	Casual from Central and South America
La Sagra's Flycatcher	*Myiarchus sagrae*	Tyrannidae/Tyrant Flycatchers	Casual from Bahamas to Florida
Shrikes			
Brown Shrike	*Lanius cristatus*	Laniidae/Shrikes	Casual from Asia to Alaska, California, and Nova Scotia
Corvids			
Eurasian Jackdaw	*Corvus monedula*	Corvidae	Casual from Eurasia to E North America
Chickadees and Titmice			
Gray-headed Chickadee	*Poecile cincta*	Paridae/Chickadees and Titmice	Eurasian species resident in Brooks Range of Alaska to NW Yukon
Swallows			
Mangrove Swallow	*Tachycineta albilinea*	Hirundinidae/Swallows	Accidental from Mexico and Central America to Florida
Bahama Swallow	*Tachycineta cyaneoviridis*	Hirundinidae/Swallows	Casual from Bahamas to S Florida
Gray-breasted Martin	*Progne chalybea*	Hirundinidae/Swallows	Accidental from Central and South America to Texas
Brown-chested Martin	*Progne tapera*	Hirundinidae/Swallows	Accidental from South America to Massachusetts and New Jersey
Common House-Martin	*Delichon urbicum*	Hirundinidae/Swallows	Casual from Eurasia to Alaska
Old World Warblers			
Middendorff's Grasshopper-Warbler	*Locustella ochotensis*	Sylviidae/Old World Warblers	Casual from Asia to Alaska
Dusky Warbler	*Phylloscopus fuscatus*	Sylviidae/Old World Warblers	Casual from Asia to Alaska and California

COMMON NAME	SCIENTIFIC NAME	FAMILY/SCIENTIFIC NAME	DESCRIPTION
Mockingbirds and Thrashers			
Bahama Mockingbird	*Mimus gundlachii*	Mimidae/Mockingbirds and Thrashers	Casual from Bahamas and Jamaica to Florida
Thrushes			
Aztec Thrush	*Ridgwayia pinicola*	Turdidae/Thrushes	Casual from Mexico to SE Arizona and Texas
Orange-billed Nightingale-Thrush	*Catharus aurantiirostris*	Turdidae/Thrushes	Accidental from Central and South America to Texas
Eurasian Blackbird	*Turdus merula*	Turdidae/Thrushes	Accidental from Eurasia to E Canada
Eyebrowed Thrush	*Turdus obscurus*	Turdidae/Thrushes	Rare visitor from Asia to Alaska
Dusky Thrush	*Turdus naumanni*	Turdidae/Thrushes	Casual from Asia to Alaska and W Canada
Fieldfare	*Turdus pilaris*	Turdidae/Thrushes	Casual from Eurasia
Redwing	*Turdus iliacus*	Turdidae/Thrushes	Casual from Eurasia to NE North America in fall and winter
White-throated Robin	*Turdus assimilis*	Turdidae/Thrushes	Accidental from Central and South America to Texas in winter
Old World Flycatchers			
Siberian Rubythroat	*Luscinia calliope*	Muscicapidae/Old World Flycatchers	Rare visitor from Asia to Alaska
Red-flanked Bluetail	*Luscinia cyanura*	Muscicapidae/Old World Flycatchers	Casual from Eurasia to Alaska
Stonechat	*Saxicola torquatus*	Muscicapidae/Old World Flycatchers	Casual from Eurasia to Alaska
Gray-streaked Flycatcher	*Muscicapa griseisticta*	Muscicapidae/Old World Flycatchers	Casual from Siberia to Aleutians and Pribilof Islands
Dark-sided Flycatcher	*Muscicapa sibirica*	Muscicapidae/Old World Flycatchers	Casual from Asia to Aleutians and Pribilof Islands
Narcissus Flycatcher	*Ficedula narcissina*	Muscicapidae/Old World Flycatchers	Accidental from Asia to Aleutians
Mugimaki Flycatcher	*Ficedula mugimaki*	Muscicapidae/Old World Flycatchers	Accidental from Asia to Aleutians
Taiga Flycatcher	*Ficedula albicilla*	Muscicapidae/Old World Flycatchers	Casual from Asia to Aleutians and Pribilof Islands
Wagtails and Pipits			
Gray Wagtail	*Motacilla cinerea*	Motacillidae/Wagtails and Pipits	Casual from Eurasia to Aleutians and Pribilof Islands
Tree Pipit	*Anthus trivialis*	Motacillidae/Wagtails and Pipits	Accidental from Eurasia to W Alaska
Pechora Pipit	*Anthus gustavi*	Motacillidae/Wagtails and Pipits	Casual from Siberia to Aleutians and St. Lawrence Island
Cardueline Finches			
Oriental Greenfinch	*Carduelis sinica*	Fringillidae/Cardueline Finches	Casual from Asia to Aleutians and Pribilof Islands
Common Rosefinch	*Carpodacus erythrinus*	Fringillidae/Cardueline Finches	Casual from Eurasia to Aleutians and Pribilof Islands

COMMON NAME	SCIENTIFIC NAME	FAMILY/SCIENTIFIC NAME	DESCRIPTION
Cardueline Finches *continued*			
Eurasian Bullfinch	*Pyrrhula pyrrhula*	Fringillidae/Cardueline Finches	Casual from Eurasia to W Alaska
Hawfinch	*Coccothraustes coccothraustes*	Fringillidae/Cardueline Finches	Casual from Eurasia to W Alaska
Wood-warblers			
Gray-crowned Yellowthroat	*Geothlypis poliocephala*	Parulidae/Wood-warblers	Casual from Central America to S Texas; formerly resident
Slate-throated Redstart	*Myioborus miniatus*	Parulidae/Wood-warblers	Casual from Central America to SW US
Fan-tailed Warbler	*Euthlypis lachrymosa*	Parulidae/Wood-warblers	Casual from Central America to SE Arizona
Golden-crowned Warbler	*Basileuterus culicivorus*	Parulidae/Wood-warblers	Casual from Central and South America to S Texas and E New Mexico
Rufous-capped Warbler	*Basileuterus rufifrons*	Parulidae/Wood-warblers	Casual from Central and South America to Texas and Arizona
Blackbirds and Orioles			
Spot-breasted Oriole	*Icterus pectoralis*	Icteridae/Blackbirds and Orioles	Uncommon in S Florida; introduced from Central America
Bananaquit	*Coereba flaveola*	Coerebidae	Casual from Caribbean and South America to S Florida
Sparrows and Buntings			
Little Bunting	*Emberiza pusilla*	Emberizidae/Emberizids	Casual from Eurasia to W Alaska and California
Rustic Bunting	*Emberiza rustica*	Emberizidae/Emberizids	Rare visitor from Eurasia to Alaska and Pacific coast
Pallas's Bunting	*Emberiza pallasi*	Emberizidae/Emberizids	Accidental from Siberia to Alaska
Reed Bunting	*Emberiza schoeniclus*	Emberizidae/Emberizids	Casual from Eurasia to W Alaska
Worthen's Sparrow	*Spizella wortheni*	Emberizidae/Emberizids	Accidental from Mexico to New Mexico
Yellow-faced Grassquit	*Tiaris olivaceus*	Emberizidae/Emberizids	Casual from Caribbean, Central and South America to Florida and S Texas
Tanagers			
Flame-colored Tanager	*Piranga bidentata*	Thraupidae/Tanagers	Casual from Central America to Arizona and S Texas; has bred in Arizona
Western Spindalis	*Spindalis zena*	Thraupidae/Tanagers	Casual from Bahamas and West Indies to Florida
Cardinals and Grosbeaks			
Yellow Grosbeak	*Pheucticus chrysopeplus*	Cardinalidae/Cardinals and Grosbeaks	Casual from Mexico to SE Arizona
Crimson-collared Grosbeak	*Rhodothraupis celaeno*	Cardinalidae/Cardinals and Grosbeaks	Casual from Mexico to S Texas in fall and winter
Blue Bunting	*Cyanocompsa parellina*	Cardinalidae/Cardinals and Grosbeaks	Casual from Central and South America to S Texas

ACKNOWLEDGMENTS

Dorling Kindersley would like to thank the following people for their help in compiling this book: Lucy Baker, Rachel Booth, Kim Bryan, Arti Finn, Peter Frances, Lynn Hassett, Riccie Janus, Maxine Lea, Megan Jones, Ruth O'Rourke, Yen-Mai Tsang.

Producing such a comprehensive book would be impossible without the research and observations of hundreds of field and museum ornithologists and birdwatchers. The Editor-in-Chief would like to name four who have been especially inspirational and supportive over the years: the late Paul Géroudet, the late Ernst Mayr, Patricia Stryker Joseph, and Helen Hays. In addition, we acknowledge *Birds of North America Online*, edited by Alan Poole, a joint project of the American Ornithologists' Union and Cornell's Laboratory of Ornithology, and an invaluable source of information on the birds of North America.

The publisher would like to thank the following for their kind permission to reproduce their photographs:

Almost without exception, the birds featured in the profiles in this book were photographed in the wild.

(Key: a-above; b-below/bottom; c-centre; f-far; l-left; r-right; t-top)

Alamy Images: AfriPics.com 9cra; Derrick Alderman 16cl; All Canada Photos 299tr; blickwinkel 17cr; Rick & Nora Bowers 104crb, 358t, 575bc, 576ca, 688cra, 689fbl, 718br; Bruce Coleman Inc. 12tr, 17crb; Gay Bumgarner 16cb; Nancy Camel 17clb; Redmond Durrell 13cb; Elvele Images Ltd 16-17c; David Hosking 11fcrb; Juniors Bildachiv 11tr; Don Kates 14cla; Charles Melton 32fbl, 33ca, 33crb; Michele Molinari 628crb; Renee Morris 702; Rolf Nussbaumer 14clb; Peter Arnold, Inc. 14cl; Robert Shantz 173bc, 181ca, 511cla; Stock Connection Blue 11clb; © tbkmedia.de 14-15c.
Ardea: Auscape 705tl; Ian Beames 9cr; Peter Steyn 109ca, 111fbl; Ron Austing: 598cla.
Doug Backlund: 10-11ca, 30cb, 38cla, 38crb, 53crb, 160cra, 160tc, 170crb, 182cra, 192tr, 259crb, 477crb, 520cr, 534cla, 534cra, 534crb, 663bc.
Steve Baldwin: 319b.
The Barn Owl Centre, UK: 329cla.
Giff Beaton: 582tr.
Corbis: Tim Davis 2-3; Joe McDonald 12cla, 154cla.
Mike Danzenbaker: 28crb, 93tc, 103ca, 103crb, 103tc, 106ca, 108ca, 110ca, 110crb, 110tc, 111, 111cla, 111cra, 112cra, 113ca, 115crb, 197bc, 291cla, 296ca, 296crb, 296tc, 299crb, 305ca, 305crb, 305tc, 308tc, 320ca, 321bl, 326ca, 354ca, 354tl, 357ca, 357crb, 357tc, 359cra, 359crb, 359tc, 366cra, 408cb, 523crb, 576crb, 587tc, 616cb, 632tc, 644tc, 703bl, 706bl, 706tr, 708tl, 715tl, 719tr.
Greg & Yvonne Dean/WorldWildlifeImages.com: 351ca.
DK Images: Robin Chittenden 87tr, 496tr; Chris Gomersall Photography 40crb, 40tr, 62ca, 62crb, 62tr, 66crb, 84crb, 92crb, 102ca, 102tr, 137crb, 146crb, 159ca, 159crb, 163cra, 163tc, 230crb, 233crb, 241bc, 260cra, 262ca, 273cra, 275ca, 275crb, 277cb, 292cla, 292cra, 293cra, 294crb, 306crb, 306tc, 310cra, 468cla, 528tc, 545cla, 545tc, 704tr, 709bl; David Cottridge 542tc, 543cla; David Tipling Photo Library 64ca, 72cr, 72cra, 87tc, 89tc, 92tc, 119tc, 163crb, 205cla, 243cla, 253cl, 253cra, 260cla, 261cra, 266cla, 310cla, 495tc; Mark Hamblin 67ca, 72cla, 91c, 150cra, 330cra, 347cra, 543tc, 703tr, 714tr; Chris Knights 88crb; Mike Lane 40cla, 40cra, 44tc, 59ca, 72tr, 82cla, 89tr, 92ca, 120ca, 146cra, 234cla, 240tc, 241tr, 250tc, 262cra, 275tc, 276ca, 289cra, 289crb, 293crb, 294ca, 306cra, 468ca, 542cra, 709tl, 712bl, 718bl; Gordon Langsbury 135cla, 146tr, 207cra, 223tc, 227cla, 244tr; Tim Loseby 67crb, 248cra, 557cla; George McCarthy 41crb, 44tr, 132ca, 135cra, 230cla, 261bc, 277tc, 288ca; Natural History Museum, London 8cla, 10cl; Kim Taylor 306tr; Roger Tidman 55ca, 55tc, 58ca, 68tr, 78ca, 84ca, 89ca, 91tr, 127cra, 146cla, 218cl, 230tr, 235tc, 241tc, 247ca, 248ca, 248tr, 253tc, 270ca, 270crb, 273ca, 276crb, 287cra, 290ca, 294tc, 313cra, 528cla, 543cra, 646cla, 646tc, 704bl, 710tr, 711tr, 718tr; Ray Tipper 204tr; Steve Young 59tc, 68tc, 72crb, 72tc, 82cra, 82tr, 84tc, 84tr, 88ca, 88tc, 102tc, 112crb, 112tc, 150tc, 243tc, 250cla, 253crb, 261fcla, 262cla, 264cla, 266cra, 266crb, 266fcla, 276tc, 276tr, 287tc, 289cla, 508ca, 542cla, 646cra.
Dudley Edmondson: 21cra, 30tc, 36tr, 38cra, 41cla, 50b, 50cra, 50tl, 121ca, 121tc, 130cb, 138cla, 140cla, 144cla, 145cla, 145tr, 153tc, 161ca, 168ca, 168cb, 168cla, 168tc, 170cla, 170cra, 170tc, 172crb, 179cla, 179cra, 182crb, 192crb, 196crb, 199tc, 200crb, 202ca, 203crb, 211ca, 212cra, 218cla, 218crb, 221ca, 229crb, 232cra, 239tc, 249cr, 251tr, 255cla, 255cr, 265crb, 283crb, 339tl, 340cb, 344cla, 344cra, 350crb, 383br, 393bc, 423crb, 432crb, 456ca, 459ca, 504crb, 531crb, 532bc, 602bc, 630crb, 647ca, 648cra, 667cra.
Tom Ennis: 245ca, 710br.
Hanne & Jens Eriksen: 165crb, 204cla, 220crb, 271tc, 281ca, 281crb, 281tc, 284crb, 284tc, 286bc, 290crb, 290tc, 705tr, 707tr, 708bl, 710bl, 711bl, 718tl.

Neil Fletcher: 47cb, 48bc, 48cla, 49ca, 49cra, 49crb, 50cla, 52tc, 57ca, 57cra, 59tr, 67tr, 69tc, 70crb, 70tr, 75fcla, 313crb, 528cra, 545crb.
FLPA: Tui De Roy/Minden Pictures 15ca; Goetz Eichhorn / Foto Natura 94fbl, 95ca; John Hawkins 15cla; David Hosking 100bl, 101bl, 104tr; S Jonasson 96cra; Daphne Kinzler 15tr; S & D & K Maslowski 16clb; Geoff Moon 706tl; Roger Tidman 96tr; Winfried Wisniewski/ Foto Natura 15cr.
Joe Fuhrman: 149cra, 220ca, 351crb, 384bc, 420crb, 530bc, 578crb, 707br.
Getty Images: Marc Moritsch 12-13c; Brad Sharp 16c.
Bob Glover: 253fcra, 266fcra.
Melvin Grey: 63crb, 64crb, 124bc, 124cra, 126crb, 131ca, 131tr, 133ca, 133cra, 134crb, 135crb, 136cla, 139cra, 140crb, 160cla, 164cla, 164crb, 193cra, 193crb, 195cra, 206tr, 208cla, 208crb, 208tr, 211cra, 211crb, 211tr, 218crb, 218tc, 233cla, 234cra, 273tr, 274crb, 274tr, 285bl, 286tr, 330crb, 704tl; Tom Grey: 105cr, 123crb, 130cra, 155crb, 159cra, 165tc, 171crb, 182cla, 195crb, 250cl, 256crb, 256tl, 271crb, 295ca, 295crb, 314ca, 333bc, 387bc, 406tc, 428bc, 465cra, 472tc, 479tc, 502crb, 630fcla, 630fcra, 638cla, 638cra, 655crb.
Martin Hale: 115ca.
Josef Hlasek: 247crb.
Barry Hughes: 197, 282crb, 292crb.
justbirds.org: 173cra, 424crb.
Arto Juvonen: 43tc, 101ca, 101crb, 101tc, 150crb, 184cra, 546cla.
Kevin T. Karlson: 30cla, 31tc, 81ca, 81crb, 93ca, 138tc, 157cra, 157crb, 160crb, 166ca, 166tc, 177cla, 177tc, 178ca, 180tc, 201cla, 215cr, 215cra, 215crb, 215fcla, 217ca, 217cra, 245tc, 293cra, 431crb, 433crb, 453crb, 467crb, 596tc, 658cla, 706br; George Lin: 707tl.
Garth McElroy: 13cl, 23crb, 26tc, 54cla, 61crb, 76tr, 80tc, 81tc, 82ca, 83tc, 85cla, 86crb, 94tc, 120tc, 121cla, 127crb, 132tr, 134cla, 136tc, 137cra, 141cra, 141tc, 149crb, 149tc, 149tl, 151crb, 191cra, 191crb, 200ca, 201cra, 206cra, 207cla, 207crb, 209cra, 210cla, 210crb, 212cla, 213ca, 214cr, 214tc, 215ca, 216tr, 217crb, 217tc, 223cra, 224ca, 224cra, 224crb, 225cra, 226crb, 227cra, 229ca, 229cra, 231ca, 231crb, 232crb, 234crb, 234tr, 235cb, 237tc, 238crb, 238tc, 239ca, 248tc, 249crb, 251ca, 257crb, 257tc, 257tl, 258ca, 258cla, 258cra, 258crb, 263cra, 264crb, 279ca, 279crb, 279tc, 317ca, 323cra, 324crb, 338cr, 343crb, 345crb, 346cla, 347bc, 347tc, 367cla, 367tc, 374cra, 392bc, 398cb, 398cla, 398cra, 405crb, 405tc, 410crb, 416cla, 416crb, 419crb, 432ca, 450crb, 452bc, 454cla, 454cra, 454crb, 459crb, 471cla, 471cra, 471tc, 472cla, 475crb, 478bc, 478ca, 478crb, 483cla, 485cra, 487ca, 487crb, 490cra, 492bc, 492ca, 492crb, 495cr, 498crb, 500c, 500t, 503tr, 507crb, 508bc, 510tc, 513crb, 516cra, 516crb, 517bc, 517cra, 518cb, 518crb, 521bc, 527crb, 529b, 531ca, 531cra, 535cb, 535tc, 537ca, 537crb, 538cb, 538crb, 539cb, 539cra, 541crb, 541tc, 544crb, 550cra, 552tr, 553crb, 554cra, 554tc, 557bc, 558crb, 562cb, 562cra, 562tc, 565cra, 565crb, 566cr, 567cra, 567crb, 567tc, 568bc, 568ca, 574bc, 578cra, 579cra, 579crb, 579tc, 581cra, 581tc, 582crb, 583cla, 584cla, 584crb, 584tc, 587cra, 591cra, 596cra, 597bc, 600cb, 600cra, 601bl, 605ca, 605crb, 606crb, 607crb, 610cra, 612cra, 612crb, 615cb, 622cra, 624crb, 631ca, 631cra, 632crb, 632tr, 634bc, 635tr, 640crb, 640tc, 648crb, 649bc, 649tc, 650ca, 651tc, 654cla, 654crb, 654tc, 656cra, 659crb, 660bc, 660tc, 665cra, 666cra, 667crb, 667tc, 668crb, 669tc, 670ca, 672ca, 677cla, 680cb, 680crb, 682cb, 682tc, 683ca, 683crb, 685crb, 686cb, 686crb, 691cra, 693cra, 695crb, 698bc, 699tr.
Ian Montgomery/Birdway.com.au: 143tr.
Arthur Morris/Birds As Art: 275tr.
Bob Moul: 120cla, 157ca, 209crb, 441crb, 540crb, 612tc, 634cla.
Alan Murphy: 21cra, 24bc, 24tr, 118ca, 138crb, 142tr, 167ca, 167cra, 167crb, 180cra, 186tr, 189cla, 189crb, 201bl, 201crb, 309b, 323b, 323cl, 325crb, 327crb, 328crb, 348tr, 355b, 355cl, 375bl, 375br, 378cra, 379ca, 379cb, 380l, 387cla, 403tr, 413crb, 419cla, 424cb, 445cb, 445crb, 449crb, 453cb, 470ca, 475ca, 569b, 580cla, 590ca, 590crb, 619b, 623ca, 623cb, 623crb, 626crb, 668cra, 668tr, 690cra, 690crb, 704br, 716tl.
Tomi Muukonen: 59crb, 90cl, 119tr, 169tr, 184cla, 260fcla, 262crb, 268cla, 268crb, 277ca, 542crb, 543bc, 643crb, 646crb, 717tl.
naturepl.com: Barry Mansell 45c; Vincent Munier 8-9c; Nigel Marven 298fbl, 299ca; Rolf Nussbaumer 322crb; Tom Vezo 15crb, 181crb.
NHPA/Photoshot: ANT Photolibrary 705crb; Bill Coster 116bc, 199bc; Dhritiman Mukherjee 703tl; Mike Lane 316bc, 317bc, 713clb; Kevin Schafer 96cb.
Wayne Nicholas: 197c, 197tr.
Judd Patterson: 20, 35cra, 35tc, 140tc, 142bc, 143cb, 143cra, 143tl, 177bc, 177cra, 178fcra, 311crb, 331cla, 433ca, 438cra.
E. J. Peiker: 22bc, 26cla, 29cra, 46cra, 47ca, 47crb, 51cra, 55fcra, 55tr, 58tc, 60cb, 61ca, 64tc, 65ca, 65tr, 68cla, 68cra, 69ca, 69crb, 69tr, 70ca, 70cb, 70tc, 71cb, 71crb, 73ca, 73crb, 85crb, 86tc, 90tr, 93crb, 94crb, 122crb, 124cl, 127crb, 128cra, 136crb, 137cra, 145fcla, 149fcra, 152tc, 158ca, 158cla, 174cr, 174tl, 175bc, 176cra, 183cla, 183crb, 194tc, 199cr, 202crb, 203ca, 203cra, 205cra, 205crb, 210cra, 216tc, 222ca, 227crb, 228cla, 228crb, 230cr, 244cr, 249ca, 254crb, 268cra, 269cra, 274tc, 278tr, 285tc, 291cb, 301cla, 304bc, 308cra, 308crb, 314bc, 315crb, 330cla, 330tc, 336cra, 342cb, 367cra, 368tr, 369tr, 376cra, 380br, 383cra, 383tc, 384cra, 384crb, 388cb, 395cb, 395cla, 395cra, 403cl, 406cra, 421ca, 421crb, 427cra, 427tc, 430cb, 431bc, 431cra, 431tc,

435cra, 437crb, 441cra, 455bc, 455cra, 456cb, 457tc, 458ca, 458cra, 459ca, 459tr, 460tc, 462crb, 469cla, 469cra, 472cra, 476crb, 476tc, 479bc, 480cra, 480crb, 484cb, 484crb, 485crb, 488cla, 499c, 499crb, 500b, 501crb, 509bc, 522cb, 522crb, 524bc, 554tr, 555crb, 560bc, 560tc, 561cra, 561tc, 564crb, 564tr, 573cla, 580crb, 588tr, 618bc, 619tr, 620crb, 625bc, 627crb, 629tr, 635bc, 635tc, 637fcla, 639bc, 641br, 641cla, 671cra, 673ca, 674crb, 684crb, 684tc, 687cr, 687tr, 690tr, 693bc, 696ca, 696tc, 699cla, 701cla, 713tr.
Jari Peltomäki: 1c, 41tc, 43cra, 48ca, 76crb, 82crb, 90bc, 154bc, 185ca, 185cra, 185crb, 194cla, 194cra, 194crb, 277crb, 310crb, 329b, 339cb, 440crb, 486cra, 486crb, 552cla, 643cra, 708tr, 711tl.
David Plummer: 377ca, 378crb.
Eric Preston: 106crb.
Mike Read: 42bc, 99crb, 162crb.
George Reszeter: 712tl.
Robert Royse: 31cla, 34cla, 41cra, 52crb, 75ca, 75crb, 75tr, 80ca, 122ca, 189cra, 190ca, 190crb, 204cra, 220cra, 224cla, 225ca, 233tr, 238ca, 257cra, 271tr, 280ca, 324cra, 372ca, 396cra, 396tc, 416cra, 444cb, 444crb, 467ca, 474ca, 482crb, 506ca, 509tc, 511crb, 520crb, 523cra, 526crb, 529ca, 547ca, 547cra, 547crb, 577tr, 595cra, 595tc, 599cra, 609crb, 609tr, 610cla, 617bc, 642crb, 644cra, 644crb, 646tr, 647crb, 657ca, 657crb, 662ca, 662crb, 663cla, 663cra, 668ca, 670crb, 674cra, 676crb, 677cra, 690ca, 700crb, 700tc, 700tr, 711br.
Chris Schenk: 82fcla.
Bill Schmoker: 33cr, 34crb, 53ca, 54cra, 57tc, 95cla, 95tc, 97crb, 99cr, 105ca, 105crb, 105tr, 107ca, 107crb, 107tr, 108crb, 109crb, 109tc, 117crb, 121crb, 130ca, 161crb, 182tc, 183cr, 183cra, 245crb, 312crb, 356ca, 356crb, 361tc, 364cla, 364cra, 364crb, 376crb, 377crb, 425crb, 429crb, 439ca, 469crb.
Brian E. Small: 9fcra, 22tc, 23tr, 24tc, 25tc, 25tr, 27tc, 27tr, 28tc, 28tr, 29cr, 31cra, 34tr, 36crb, 37cla, 37cra, 38tr, 39cla, 39cra, 39crb, 46tc, 52ca, 56ca, 56tc, 60ca, 60tc, 63tc, 67tc, 71ca, 71tc, 73tc, 79tc, 80tr, 83ca, 86ca, 91ca, 93cla, 97ca, 97tr, 98cla, 98cra, 116tr, 117ca, 125ca, 125cra, 126cla, 126cra, 129cra, 131tc, 138cra, 139cla, 139tc, 140cra, 141cla, 144cra, 145cra, 147cla, 147crb, 148cla, 153ca, 153crb, 155ca, 155tc, 156cra, 156fcrb, 156tc, 165cra, 166cra, 168cra, 169ca, 171cra, 174ca, 175cra, 175crb, 176bc, 180cla, 181cra, 187ca, 187crb, 188ca, 188crb, 189cra, 193cra, 196c, 196cla, 198ca, 205tc, 206tc, 210tc, 212tc, 219ca, 219tc, 222cra, 225cla, 226ca, 227ca, 232ca, 232tr, 233tc, 235ca, 236ca, 236cra, 237tr, 242tc, 247fcla, 251cra, 252cra, 255ca, 255tr, 256ca, 256cra, 259ca, 259cla, 259cra, 264ca, 264cra, 265tr, 267ca, 272cra, 272crb, 272tc, 274ca, 274cra, 278ca, 283ca, 285ca, 311ca, 312ca, 314tc, 315ca, 318ca, 320crb, 321crb, 322ca, 325ca, 325cra, 326crb, 327tr, 328ca, 331cra, 331crb, 332cra, 333ca, 334ca, 334crb, 336cla, 338ca, 338cra, 339cra, 340cla, 340cra, 341cb, 342ca, 342cr, 342cra, 343cra, 348cl, 349ca, 349tr, 352ca, 354crb, 358crb, 360cra, 361cra, 361crb, 362ca, 363cra, 363crb, 363tc, 365cla, 365cra, 365crb, 368cla, 368crb, 369cra, 370ca, 370cra, 371cla, 371cra, 372bc, 373tr, 374cla, 375t, 376tc, 376tr, 377cra, 378tc, 379cra, 379tr, 380cra, 381cla, 382bc, 382cra, 385bc, 385cra, 385tc, 386bc, 386tc, 388cla, 388cra, 389cb, 389cla, 389cra, 390tc, 391cra, 391tc, 392cra, 394cb, 394cla, 394cra, 396crb, 399cb, 400ca, 400cb, 400cra, 400fcla, 401cra, 401tc, 402cla, 402cra, 404ca, 404cb, 405cb, 406crb, 407ca, 408ca, 409cla, 409cra, 410cra, 410tc, 411cb, 411cra, 413ca, 414cra, 415ca, 415crb, 417ca, 417crb, 418crb, 420cra, 422cb, 422crb, 423cra, 424ca, 425cra, 425tc, 426ca, 426crb, 429ca, 432cra, 434ca, 434crb, 435crb, 435tc, 436bc, 436ca, 437cra, 438cla, 439crb, 442crb, 443cla, 443crb, 443tr, 444ca, 445ca, 447cra, 448ca, 448crb, 449tr, 450cra, 451ca, 451crb, 452ca, 453ca, 454tc, 455ca, 457cra, 460ca, 460crb, 461ca, 461cra, 464ca, 464cra, 472crb, 474cb, 481ca, 481crb, 482ca, 483crb, 484ca, 486ca, 489cra, 490crb, 491ca, 494ca, 495tr, 497crb, 497tr, 498bc, 498cra, 499cla, 501ca, 504cra, 505crb, 506crb, 507bc, 507cra, 510ca, 511cra, 512cla, 512cra, 513bc, 513ca, 514bc, 514cra, 514crb, 515cra, 515tc, 516cla, 518ca, 519ca, 519crb, 519tc, 522cra, 524cra, 525ca, 527ca, 530cra, 530tc, 531tr, 532tc, 533ca, 533cra, 533tr, 535ca, 536bc, 536ca, 538cra, 538tc, 539cla, 539tc, 540cra, 548tc, 550tc, 551cra, 551crb, 553ca, 554cla, 556ca, 556cra, 557cra, 559tc, 560cra, 561crb, 563ca, 563crb, 565cla, 565tc, 566ca, 566cra, 566tl, 569tr, 570cla, 570cra, 570crb, 571bc, 571cla, 571cra, 572cra, 572tc, 573crb, 574tr, 575cra, 575crb, 578cla, 580cra, 581crb, 582ca, 582tc, 583tr, 584tr, 585ca, 585crb, 585tc, 585tr, 586cra, 586crb, 586tc, 587ca, 588cla, 589ca, 589crb, 589tc, 590tc, 591tc, 592cra, 592tc, 593cra, 593tc, 594ca, 594crb, 596crb, 597ca, 597cla, 597cra, 597tc, 599bc, 599cla, 599tc, 600cla, 601cra, 601tc, 602cla, 602cra, 603ca, 603crb, 604ca, 604crb, 606ca, 607ca, 608ca, 608cra, 609ca, 610tc, 610tr, 611cra, 611crb, 613ca, 614ca, 614tc, 615tc, 616ca, 616crb, 617crb, 618ca, 618tc, 620cla, 620cra, 620tr, 621cr, 621tr, 624cla, 624cra, 624tc, 626cra, 627ca, 627cla, 627cra, 628tc, 628tr, 629tc, 630cra, 633crb, 634ca, 634cra, 635ca, 636cra, 637ca, 637crb, 638bc, 639cra, 639tc, 640cla, 640cra, 641cra, 641tc, 642cra, 645bc, 645cla, 645cra, 647tr, 648cl, 649cra, 650crb, 651cra, 651crb, 652cra, 653cla, 653cra, 653crb, 653tc, 654cra, 655cla, 656cl, 656crb, 656fcla, 656tc, 658tr, 659tc, 659tr, 660cra, 661cra, 664bc, 664ca, 665ca, 667cla, 669cra, 672cra, 673tc, 674cla, 675bc, 675crb, 676ca, 678cra, 678crb, 679ca, 682ca, 683cra, 684ca, 685ca, 686ca, 687crb, 688tc, 689ca, 689cla, 689cra, 689crb, 689tr, 691cr, 691tc, 692cla, 692cr, 692crb, 692tr, 693cl, 693cla, 693tc, 694cla, 694cra, 694crb, 694tc, 695cla, 695cra, 695tc, 696bc, 697bc, 697cla, 697tr, 698cla, 698tc, 698tr, 699bc, 699tc, 701bc, 701cra, 701tr, 712tr, 713br, 714bl, 714br, 715bl,

715br, 716tr, 717bl, 717br, 719bl.
Michelle Lynn St.Sauveur: 213crb.
Bob Steele: 11cb, 23tc, 25cla, 25crb, 29tr, 30ca, 32ca, 32crb, 32tc, 35cla, 39tc, 42ca, 46crb, 46fbl, 48cra, 50tc, 51cla, 51crb, 53tc, 53tr, 54crb, 56crb, 57crb, 58tr, 60crb, 62tc, 63fcrb, 64tr, 65crb, 73tr, 79crb, 79tr, 83crb, 85tc, 86tr, 94tr, 98cb, 98tr, 99ca, 118crb, 118tc, 122tc, 123ca, 123cb, 125crb, 128cla, 128tr, 129bl, 129ca, 131cb, 132crb, 135tc, 139cla, 144tc, 145crb, 147cra, 151cra, 151tc, 152cla, 152crb, 152tr, 153cra, 158crb, 158tr, 169cra, 171ca, 173cla, 173crb, 175tc, 176cla, 176tc, 179bc, 179ca, 179tr, 183tr, 184crb, 186b, 186t, 191cla, 192ca, 192tc, 195cla, 196cra, 198cr, 198crb, 200cra, 202bl, 202cra, 202tc, 203cla, 204tc, 206ca, 207tc, 211cr, 212clb, 216ca, 216crb, 219crb, 221crb, 222crb, 223ca, 225crb, 226tc, 228ca, 229tc, 231crb, 236crb, 236tr, 237ca, 237crb, 239crb, 240bc, 240ca, 242cla, 242cra, 242crb, 242tr, 243cra, 244bc, 244ca, 246ca, 246crb, 246tc, 246tr, 247fcra, 249tr, 250cra, 250crb, 251cla, 251crb, 251tc, 252cla, 252cr, 252crb, 252tr, 254cla, 254cra, 254tc, 254tr, 255cra, 255crb, 256tr, 260crb, 260tc, 263cla, 263tc, 265ca, 267cla, 267crb, 270tc, 278crb, 278tc, 282ca, 282tc, 283tc, 284ca, 285crb, 286tc, 287bc, 287fcla, 289tc, 291cra, 295tc, 301cra, 301crb, 302cla, 302cra, 302crb, 304ca, 307bc, 307cra, 316ca, 316cb, 316crb, 317crb, 317tc, 328cb, 329tr, 335cra, 335tc, 336cb, 337cla, 337cra, 337crb, 341cra, 341tc, 343cla, 345ca, 345tc, 346crb, 348b, 349crb, 349tc, 350ca, 352crb, 353ca, 355tc, 360cla, 360crb, 362cla, 362crb, 365tc, 366cla, 366crb, 367cra, 368tc, 369ca, 369crb, 370crb, 370tr, 371cb, 371crb, 372cla, 372cr, 373cra, 373crb, 374cb, 374crb, 376cla, 381cra, 381fclb, 381fcrb, 383bl, 386cra, 387ca, 387cra, 390cla, 390cra, 390crb, 391bc, 392ca, 393tr, 397bc, 397ca, 397cla, 397cra, 399cla, 399cra, 401crb, 403b, 405cra, 407crb, 408crb, 409crb, 411cr, 412cra, 412crb, 412tc, 414crb, 418cla, 418cra, 419cra, 422cra, 423cla, 423tc, 428cra, 430ca, 430cra, 430crb, 438b, 439cra, 440tc, 442ca, 446ca, 446cb, 446crb, 450tc, 452crb, 455crb, 456crb, 457cb, 458bc, 461crb, 462ca, 463ca, 463cb, 463crb, 464crb, 465ca, 465crb, 466ca, 466crb, 468crb, 470b, 473cra, 473crb, 473tc, 474crb, 476cb, 476cra, 477ca, 479cra, 479crb, 480cla, 485cra, 487cra, 487tr, 488cra, 488crb, 489crb, 489tc, 490tc, 491crb, 491tc, 492tc, 494crb, 494tc, 494tr, 495bc, 495cla, 496bc, 496ca, 496cla, 496crb, 497cb, 498tc, 499bc, 499tr, 501cb, 501cra, 502ca, 503crb, 505cra, 506bc, 506ca, 507tc, 509cra, 510crb, 512crb, 515crb, 516ca, 520ca, 521ca, 525crb, 528fcla, 529cra, 530crb, 532cla, 532cra, 533cb, 534tc, 536crb, 541cla, 541cra, 544cla, 544tr, 548cla, 548cra, 548crb, 550crb, 552b, 553cb, 555cla, 555cra, 555tc, 556cb, 556crb, 557cl, 557tc, 559cla, 559cra, 559crb, 563tc, 564cla, 564cra, 568cra, 569cl, 572cla, 572crb, 573cra, 574cla, 575tc, 577crb, 577fcla, 579cla, 580tc, 581cla, 583cb, 583crb, 588c, 588cra, 588crb, 591cra, 592crb, 593crb, 595bc, 598bc, 598cra, 600crb, 601bc, 601cla, 608crb, 611tc, 613crb, 613tc, 614cb, 614crb, 615ca, 615crb, 617ca, 619cr, 621ca, 621crb, 621tc, 622bc, 622cl, 622tc, 625ca, 625cra, 625tr, 629crb, 630cla, 630tr, 631crb, 632cla, 633cra, 633tc, 636crb, 636tc, 639cla, 641bl, 645tc, 647cra, 648cla, 648tc, 649cl, 652cla, 652crb, 652tc, 655cra, 655tc, 658crb, 658tc, 661crb, 665crb, 666cla, 666crb, 666tc, 669bc, 669cla, 671ca, 671cb, 672bc, 673bc, 674bc, 675ca, 675cra, 677crb, 678cla, 679crb, 681ca, 681crb, 682crb, 688crb, 691bc, 691ca, 691crb, 697tc, 707bl, 709br, 709tr, 710tl, 715tr, 719tl.
Matthew Studebaker: 571tc.
Andy & Gill Swash: 37cra, 99tr, 128crb, 129crb, 133cb, 134cra, 144crb, 148cr, 148tc, 166crb, 503cb.
Glen Tepke: 114crb, 269crb, 297ca, 297cr, 297crb, 298cra, 298crb, 300tc, 303ca, 303crb.
Philippe Van Audenhove: 705bl.
Markus Varesvuo: 4–5, 10–11bc, 21cb, 40ca, 43crb, 44cra, 44fbr, 45cra, 48crb, 55crb, 66ca, 66cb, 66tr, 74cla, 74crb, 74tc, 74tr, 76ca, 76tc, 78cb, 78crb, 78tc, 80crb, 85ca, 87ca, 87crb, 91crb, 94ca, 94cb, 116cl, 119ca, 119crb, 120crb, 162cla, 169crb, 172cra, 172tr, 184ca, 184tr, 241ca, 243crb, 248cb, 288crb, 288tc, 292tc, 335crb, 346cra, 440cra, 471crb, 508crb, 528crb, 542bc, 546cb, 546cra, 549cra, 558cra, 558tc, 566crb, 643cla, 643tc, 703br, 708br, 716br; Vireo: Dr.Yuri Artukhin 280cr, 549crb; Christian Artuso 178crb; Rick and Nora Bowers 492fbl, 493ca, 493crb; Paula Cannon 178tr; Herbert Clarke 110bc, 113bc, 114ca, 115bc; Jim Culbertson 716bl; Martin Hale 280crb; Robert L. Pitman 102bc, 104ca, 300ca, 302bc; Don Roberson 298bc, 299bc, 712br; Ronald M. Saldino 113crb; Harold Stiver 100ca, 100crb, 100tr, 108fbl; Glen Tepke 298ca, 299fbl, 300crb; Doug Wechsler 549ca.
Cal Vornberger: 690cr.
Peter S Weber: 26crb, 27crb, 29crb, 35crb, 51tc, 63ca, 79ca, 117tc, 134tr, 136ca, 141crb, 145crb, 309cla, 312cr, 318crb, 332crb, 344crb, 350tr, 353crb, 382cla, 388fcla, 391cla, 393tc, 401clb, 402clb, 427crb.
David Welling: 713tl.
Ian Whetton: 102crb.
Roger Wilmshurst: 162cra.
Lee Zieger: 164tr, 319cla, 719br.
Jacket images: *Front*: Brian E. Small. *Back*: DK Images: Mike Lane fcl; George McCarthy cl; Dudley Edmondson: fbr; Garth McElroy: fclb; Tomi Muukonen: cb (Kittiwake); E. J. Peiker: bl, c, fbl, tl; Brian E. Small: ca, cb (Junco), cla, clb, cra, crb (Bluebird), crb (Painted Bunting), fcra, ftl, ftr; Bob Steele: tc; Markus Varesvuo: fcr. *Spine*: Alan Murphy. *Front and Back Endpapers*: Corbis: Stephen G. Maka/Photex.

All other images © Dorling Kindersley
For further information see: www.dkimages.com